Praise for *P*

"A lithely written, honest and perceptive account of a unique time."

—IAIN BANKS, author of *Stonemouth* & *The Wasp Factory*

"A superb memoir about coming of age in the bright haze of NYC's demimonde ... Belk writes with great candor and intelligence about his time and one cannot help but admire the searching young man who emerges in these pages."

—JUNOT DIAZ, Pulitzer Prize winning author of *The Brief Wondrous Life of Oscar Wao*

"Martin Belk is New York, losing and finding himself in the 'Mondo Trasho' epicentre of queer liberation. Belk reveals a Baudelarian sense of the city and a profound and burgeoning poetic power and sensibility. He may not know this — I'm telling him. *Pretty?* Perhaps. *Broken?* No more. *Poet?* Indeed. We will read much more from this writer."

—LORD GAWAIN DOUGLAS, great-nephew of Lord Alfred Douglas (Oscar Wilde's 'Bosie') & author of *Fortuna*

"I enjoyed your book a lot, Martin. Full of great memories, names, observations. It brought it all back. Don't change a word..."

—MICHAEL MUSTO, *The Village Voice*

PrettyBrokenPunks.com

Pretty Broken Punks
lipstick, leather jeans, a death of New York

Martin Belk

Pretty Broken Punks
lipstick, leather jeans, a death of New York

prettybrokenpunks.com

This paperback edition first published by
Polwarth Publishing LLP
25 Polwarth Crescent
Edinburgh EH11 1HR

PPLLP London
53 Beacon Road
London SE13 6ED

www.polwarthpublishing.com

PP

The moral right of Martin Belk to be identified as
the author of this work has been asserted by him in accordance
with the Copyright, Designs and Patents Act 1988

All rights reserved. ©2012 Martin Belk
With the exception of brief extracts for journalistic review no part of this
publication may be reproduced, stored or transmitted in any form, electronic or
otherwise, without prior written permission from the publisher.

This publication is a work of narrative non-fiction/memoir; a palimpsest of observation and
personal opinion; and with the exception of any inconsequential order of minor events,
the work is accurate, and in good faith, to the best of the author's recollection.

ISBN 978-0-9574356-9-8

British Library Cataloguing-in-Publication Data
A catalogue record for this book is available from the British Library

Printed and bound by Martin's the Printers, Berwick Upon Tweed
martins-the-printers.co.uk

10 9 8 7 6 5 4 3 2 1

CONTENTS

introduction i

I. Swimming

1. I Don't Go Anywhere Without My Calvins — 5
2. Gotta Get Out of this Place — 12
3. Does Jesus Know You're Waiting? — 19
4. Ignorance, Bliss and Drag — 25
5. Get Yr' Lawn Off My Car — 29
6. Goodbye to Burbia — 35
7. Lions and Tigers and Pervs ... Oh, hi — 39
8. Power of Goodbye — 53
9. Lead, Follow, or Leave — 58
10. Get Your Motor Runnin' — 61
11. Greener, No Grass — 70
12. Makin' It, Moses, Macy's — 74
13. Reality, Overrated — 82
14. Into the Groove — 89
15. There Goes the Neighborhood — 102
16. Less is More — 107
17. Everybody Wants You — 111
18. Together Apart — 121
19. The Only Fear-Thing We Have ... — 130
20. You Say Goodbye I Say Stop — 135
21. If You Like... As You Like... — 147
22. Oh-Oh Aunt Betty. Bam a Lam. — 153
23. B for Barney, Billy, Betty, Birthday — 157
24. Lost & Found — 162
25. Palaces, DC and Ritz — 165
26. Back on the Chain Gang — 175
27. Nothin' but Time — 184
28. Inventing the Reinvention — 191
29. Rock 'n' Roll Over — 194
30. Sometimes, I Feel — 203
31. Flesh and Fantasy — 211
32. Breakfast in Leather — 216
33. Who's Afraid of Debbie Harry? — 222

II. Art Likes Life

1. Queers in Your Kwoiffee — 228
2. Run On the Band — 233
3. More, More, More. How do you like it? — 239
4. Tossing Tea Leaves — 244
5. And You Are? — 255
6. Can You Repeat the Question? — 262
7. Such, Such Were the Toys — 265
8. Just, No — 271

III. Find the Frequency

1. Don't Look Back — 277
2. Goodbye to Billy — 282
3. Time for a Cool Change — 290
4. Look Back, Don't Stare — 298
5. Search and Destroy — 307
6. Living on the Ceiling — 312
7. The Men Who Sold the World — 325
8. Highway to Hell — 331
9. Road to Nowhere — 338
10. Time May Change, Me — 349
11. I'll Be Seeing You — 361
12. Missing — 368
13. Reprise — 371
14. Smiling Faces — 372
15. Another One Bites the Dust — 375
16. Save Me — 380
17. Mama Said There'd Be Days (Like That)… — 384
18. Dot Bomb — 387
19. Time Won't Give Me Time — 398
20. Chicken Little has Left the Building — 402
21. Just the Way It Is — 409
22. Wicked Little Town — 411
23. This is The End, Sort Of — 418
24. The New World to Come — 424
25. Back, in Black — 436
26. Sodacracker Redemption — 440
27. Just Gettin' Started — 449

epilogue — *461*

introduction

Don't get me wrong: at its grand finale, our club was just as big a spectacle as the day it opened. On the moist Friday night of April 15th 1994, my friend Blair and I threw our leather MC jackets on stage beneath Misstress Formika's six-inch heels as she belted a rousing 'You Gotta Fight, For Your Right, To Be Queer' to christen the joint. Just four months after Rudolf Giuliani raised his iron fist to be sworn in as Mayor of New York City, SqueezeBox! raised itself on Spring Street and would outlast Rudy's reign over Manhattan.

Every Friday night for a decade the crowds came, and came, and kept coming. They converged for a rock scene I took for granted as the only place in the world to be. Black outfits at midnight, guitars screeching til' dawn, glitter in your breakfast cereal. Torrid affairs before, during, and after. Those of us who worked there lived it, created it, and made love to it. Counter-culture became our career. This was good for me, most of the time — I was used to the back of the bus.

As a young twenty-something, if I'd not been running on the go–out–booze–get–laid–booze–recover hamster wheel, I could have turned Squeezebox! into a true empire – like Ian Shrager did with his loot from Studio 54. There was even talk of SqueezeBox! Records – we certainly had enough bands to sign. There were side gigs at colleges in New Jersey and Vermont. Private parties in LA and Tokyo.

Since the big Debbie Harry internet show in January '96, she and Chris got back onstage, reunited Blondie, and their new single Maria took over the international airwaves. John Cameron Mitchell blew the roof off with Hedwig. Patrick had Psychotica so sewn up, Marilyn Manson copied a lot of what he created. It was all a sparkling, delicious mess. I was a mess. But maybe, that's exactly how the twentieth century was supposed to end.

By mid-'97 Clinton's DNA was hardening on Monica's blue dress, and the Republicans would try for years to beat him from office. On the streets, America followed the vibe. We either blew or beat each other. Over time, the cocaine, drug vibe, infighting and troubles with other underground clubs began to wear me out. People seemed to be shifting from going out to be fabulous — like we did in the Big Apple to going out to get fucked-up — like they did in suburbia. As homogenization trickled down, a lot of folks forgot they were living in the center of the cultural universe.

Most of the so-called 'gay' community loathed SqueezeBox! from the start, most likely because we were only queers. Just queers. None of us went to a gym, owned lycra, or had any inclination to 'assimilate.' Local magazines wouldn't run our ads. Other so-called alternative clubs made it nearly impossible for us to promote. Nobody played fair — not since the old East-Village-Pyramid-Black-Lips-DeeLite-Blackbox-Channel-69-Boybar-Wigstock-at-Thompkins-Square-Park days. Not since the fame bugs began to bite.

Contributing to the atmosphere of beige, Giuliani's quality of life troops were hemorrhaging throughout the city. They'd harassed Coney Island High almost out of business. Some chick from Boston stood up at a community board meeting and whined because she couldn't sleep in her newly renovated apartment located just above the Coney dance floor - which had been there twenty years. A bunch of yuppies and bluehairs formed a group and named it 'Save Avenue A Association' – although Avenue A didn't need saving unless you were a real estate developer. A really fun night during the week popped up at a place called Cake on Avenue B, and, of course, the quality of lifers set their sights square on it. 'NO DANCING' signs popped up all over the city. Giuliani's cronies found a 79 year-old cabaret law concocted to discriminate against Harlem jazz clubs in the Twenties,' and were now using it to discriminate against Manhattan queers, trannies, hip-hoppers and ethnic parties in the boroughs. The city Fire Marshals were taken from protecting people against fires and put to harassing clubs with phony inspections at 2AM. Giuliani took the fireworks away from the Chinese New Year and sanitized Times Square so it would be just like home for all the squeaky tourists who apparently ached for more Disney in their lives.

To me it looked like every city agency was to be stacked with henchmen, and Giuliani's culture war didn't stop with nightlife or entertainment. He was forcing community libraries to close; museums to cut back hours. All over town, historic landmarks like the Palladium Theatre were falling to the wrecking ball. NYU was allowed to run rampant through the East Village - buying up every piece of property it could get its dirty purple hands on. Thousands upon thousands of arrogant, binge-drinking, yuppie adolescents were being herded over the rivers and into our woods to enroll for thirty-grand a year at NYU, a university originally founded to educate poor. Mr. & Ms. Fort Wayne and Nashville took out second mortgages and sent junior to New York City so he could pretend to be trendy and complain about things.

Winks, nods and blind oversight camouflaged the biggest case of housing fraud in city history. Rent regulations and housing department codes were ignored; inspectors paid off. Had to have been. How else could landlords turn seven-hundred-a-month tenement shitholes into fifteen-hundred-a-month 'Sunny Renovated Apartments' but with a cheap coat of paint and forged paperwork? My hunch was that Giuliani did it for spite first, profit second. To me, he acted like a spoiled, overgrown teenager who probably never got picked for the baseball team, probably grew up with Mommy as his only friend and probably never got laid until he was a sophomore in college, and even then probably had to pay for it. Now, the rest of us were paying for the mercy fuck he never received. Funny thing was, if he'd have calmed down for a minute or ten, he might have discovered real friendship in the very misfits he sought to destroy. For similar reasons, I resented other club 'rainbow' promoters who used the same kind of spin to crown themselves the new Kings and Queens of nightlife.

Too many folks like Haoui, who knew the real score, were gone. Because of AIDS, the credit for almost everything noteworthy on the downtown scene since Studio 54 was up for grabs — and the bottom-feeders began grabbing just like Rudy, who'd grabbed the credit for the drop in crime. 'He cleaned up New York...' said the news media and salesmen from Kansas City. Bullshit. Crime dropped everywhere because Clinton had balanced the budget and people had jobs to go to. My take on all this: Giuliani cleaned up for his pals, petty club promoters pocketed the proceeds of mediocre nightlife, and the whole fucking thing gave me a migraine.

So what's a boy to do? Go out, booze, get laid, recover. Repeat. Until he somehow fights a hole in the side of his paper bag. And aside from any criticism that the politically-correct naysayers could hurl, at least me and mine were at the pinnacle of our game. Collectively we were prettier, smarter, grotesque, hornier, and more glamorous than any other group in the whole tired, rotten city. We didn't need to lip synch – we could sing.

We didn't need to search for stars, they came to SqueezeBox! on their own — through the same door as everyone else. Simply by existing — boys in bikinis dancing next to the Steven Spielbergs of the world; trannies with new boob jobs dancing with the naked Drew Barrymores of the world; homeless kids chatting over martinis with the Sandra Bernhards of the world; East Village drag queens like Misstress Formika, Lily of the Valley and Sherry Vine were singing duets with the Deborah Harrys and Marc Almonds of the world; Michael Schmidt was creating fashion with the JFK Jrs of the world — for a brief moment on thescale of life, *we were the world* — and many would go on to put a chink in the bourgeoisie armor well into the 21st Century.

Me? I'd managed to climb from the foothills of North Carolina upstage to the hottest NYC scene since Max's Kansas City. In my teen-hood Debbie and folks like Freddie Mercury came through my hi-fi stereo console with stuff like 'dreamin' is free' and 'don't stop me now.' And I believed every word. I still do, but I've also learned beliefs come with a price.

For now, in the words of Sylvester,

let's party a little bit...

—MLB

For
Adrienne Belk
Alice Eisenberg, Alicia Trani, Amy Douglas, Andy Fair,
Andy Phelan, Andersen, Angi Lamb, Anthony Rully, B & Lou,
Barb Morrison, Barney Johnson, Betty Badum, Big Al from The
Bar, Billy Corcoran, Billy Erb, Bill Rice, Blair Schulman,
Blake Burba, Bob Gruen, Bobby B, Brandywine & Brenda-a-go-go,
Brenda O'Connor, Brian Butterick, Bruce Benderson,
Bruce LaBruce, Buzz, Candace Cayne, Carl our Bodyguard,
Carol Eicher, Carrie G. & Catherine H., Billy's friend Chris,
Cheryl Compton, Chezza Zoeller, Chip Duckett, Chris Stein,
CJ Kitsos-Holm, Clark Render, Crazy James, Dan Mathews,
Dan Renehan, Daniel Cartier, Daniel Nardicio, David Hurst,
David Ilku, David Russell, David Shepherd, David Silverberg,
Dean Johnson, Deborah Harry, Don Hill, Don Robinder,
Duard Klein, Duelling Bankheads, Ebony Jett, Eddie Scriba,
Edward Bottger, Ed Garrison, Ena Kostabi, Eric Otte,
Flotilla Debarge, Flloyd, Gant Johnson, Gawain Douglas,
Gaya Palmer, George McAvoy, Geraldine Sweeney, Gerri Britton,
Geylin Scherer, Giovanni DiMola, Glenn Belverio,
Grace Nemergut, Grace Teshima, Graeme Stone, Greg Gorman,
Greta Brinkman, Haoui Montaug, Iain Banks, Ian Luce, Ila,
Jack Steeb, James from The Bar, James J from Charlotte,
Jan Smith, Jarrod Cline, Jayne County, Jed Root, Jeffo & Peter,
Jim Haynes, Jim Morrison, Joe Best, Joe Landry, Joelle Pezely,
Joey Devito, Joey Ramone, John Badum, John Calder,
John Cameron Mitchell, John Toth, John Ngai, John Vinton,
John Waters, Jorge Soccarás, Josh Jordan, Josh Jackson,
JudgeCal™ Chamberlain, Junot Diaz, Justin Vivian Bond,
Kenny Mellman, Kevin 'lord protector and only man who can
hit notes as good as Robert Plant' Brennan, Kevin V. Smith,

Kurt B Reighley, The 'Lady' Bunny, Lady Miss Kier,
Lars Anderson, Laura Forbes, Lauren Pine, Lee Chappell,
Linda Simpson, Lindsey Anderson, Lisa Carbone,
Lorenzo Lopez, Louis Moran, Louis Surya Sierra, Lourds Lane,
Lucia, Marcus Leatherdale, Marilyn Saltzman, Mark Allen,
Mark Seamon, Marlene Stoffers, Martin Sheridan, Marty Lipton,
Mary Folliet, Matt Shields, Matt Vohr, Max Wixom,
Michael Cavadias, Michael Fernandez, Michael March,
Michael Matula, Michael Musto, Michael Schmidt, Michael T,
Mike Albo, Mike Daisey, Mike Ivie, Mike Potter, Mikey,
Miss Guy Furrow, Miss Ruby, Misstress Michael Formika Jones,
Mo Fischer, Monica Walsh, Myrna Brome, Natasha Soudek,
Nite Bob, Noel Alicea, Page Reynolds, Paul Likins, Pat Belk,
Patrick Briggs, Paul Donzella, Paul Likins, Perfidia,
Phoebe Fitch, Quentin Crisp, Raffaele, Ramón Woo, Randella,
Raymond Reid, Richard Brunson, Richard Green, Rikka B.,
Ronnie G, Rose Royale, Rudy Cardenas, Sammy Jo,
Sean Arcy Sparky Green, Scott Pyramid dancer,
Scotty from Seattle, Seth Lemay, Sherry Vine,
Shigeru McPherson, Sissy Fit, Sivani, Stephen Sprouse,
Steven Perfidia Kirkham, Steven Trask, Stevin Azo Michels,
Susan Coyne, Sweetie B, Tammy Parsons, Tanya Pacht,
Thomas Haywood, the illustrious Thomas Onorato,
Tim Richmond, Tim McClusky, Tim Smyre, Tim West,
Tommy Salmorin, Tommy Kenny, Tree Man,
Troy Lambert, Varda Ducovny, Wendy Wild

—plus anyone I've mistakenly not listed,
you're not forgotten

to

J. D. Pryce

Pretty Broken Punks
lipstick, leather jeans, a death of New York

Martin Belk

I. Swimming

'The anxiety is unbearable,
I hope it lasts forever.'
—Oscar Wilde

You wake from your disco nap. The noise outside your Lower East Side apartment window isn't your noise — it's their noise — the day people. They rustle their cheap plastic bags from the overpriced bodegas and stores, argue over parking spaces and scream at their children in tongues. They're scrambling to get inside — safely locked away — after a long day of the same thing they did the day before. You've been bored with them for years, and can't wait to reclaim the nocturnal avenues of Mannahatta.

The Manhattan morning penetrated all of me. I sat alone in Dad's Midtown hotel room and scribbled desperately in my new red notebook, 'I have to be here.' I was hooked. The early call of the maid's hoover ground its way down the corridor, but wasn't for me that day — an empathetic airline agent had given me three extra days before I had to return and face the gates of LaGuardia. You could do that kind of thing back then.

50th Street and Third Avenue — little did I know that Studio 54 and Danceteria were in walking distance, and Times Square raged just across town. Or that I was just three blocks away from one of the most notorious intersections in New York City for hustlers and other queer prizes, but was none the wiser. Downtown? No clue. Perhaps there's a reason Dad never gave me a full city map. If only I'd dared, I might've been swept away — although a bit young at 15, but hardly the first to disappear into the people-haze of Gotham. It didn't matter. The Big Apple was ripe in the spring of 1982 and I could taste it. The rest I gave over to instinct, although the place was overwhelming, exhilarating, and absurd — but I just kept repeating my new mantra: *I have to be here.*

Twenty-two years and eight lives later, I sat in George's office. 34th Street and Fifth Avenue. Psychotherapy. The familiar, comforting sounds of police sirens, car horns, people talking, screeching subways, street peddlers and amplified music penetrated the smoky, tinted glass windows. Even then, I still wasn't sure how the hell I made it to 2004, much less up from a backward-assed southern town with nothin' but four hundred bucks in my pocket and a dream on my mind. But I did. And although my fast young lifestyle — combined with an infamous September 11 surprise had taken a certain toll, I still had style, drive, and Rock 'n' Roll.

George waited as I gazed out at the steely grey stone Empire State building with its red trimming — no more real to me than the first time I'd seen it in photographs. Inside my jeans pocket were three grad school invitations. Two for Manhattan and one for Scotland. Not bad for 38, looking 28, feeling 18 again. My heart said stay. My intuition was to run like hell. My soul just plain ached. The New York I had loved was gone, sold off to real estate developers, women's fingernail salons and NYU — a city turned into a whore for the nostalgic masses, who will never appreciate the fine prostitute she once was.

'I could stay...' I reasoned to George — yeah, and spend the rest of my life lamenting the collusions of the sons of New Amsterdam. '...or, on the other hand...' I continued, stumbling over the words as I looked for my future hidden in the ceiling blemishes.

'You're allowed to feel better ya' know...' George interrupted, just before my gaze came down and hit the floor in a dangerous mix of friend and mental health professional.

'Who woulda' thunk?' I joked.

'You're surprised?' George inquired, catching me before I daydreamed off again.

'Yeah, well, sorta. I knew I'd always get into something, somehow, in spite of myself.'

'I'm not surprised in the least...'

'No?!' I said with a start, becoming agitated.

'No. Not in the least,' George quickly retorted in an earnest tone. 'All the broken people come to New York.'

'Huh? What... what do you mean?' I quipped with fake familiarity, pretending this wasn't about me.

'All the broken people come to New York, Martin — even the ones as pretty as you.'

'Pretty?' I said, digging for something.

Pretty-broken-people, huh?'

'Absolutely.'

Martin Belk

1. I Don't Go Anywhere Without My Calvins

1982. New York was still New *Fucking* York — and the state of mind fit the state of the place and I fell in love with the city. I spent my first night in my Dad's room at the Plaza 50 Hotel, 155 East Fiftieth Street. Midtown. I remember a distinct charge in the air. The smell of hot dogs and falafels on every other corner. Popcorn and the nauseating scent of roasted chestnuts mixed with car exhaust. The occasional steel-sifted breeze cleared it all out just so it could start over again. Big people, little people, sleazy people, spiffy people, white people, black people, pimps, businessmen and kids all on the same pavement. And queers. I was a skinny, goofy teenager from the south with big hair, brown penny loafers, a red sweater, brown checked scarf and gentleman's raincoat that was three sizes too big for me. And New York City didn't care and I loved her for it. People didn't stare at you. I'd never been in a place where you didn't have to worry about everyone around you. A place where freedom doesn't hang as a street sign, but climbs down and dances on the pole for you.

I was fifteen. Daddy'd started working for a clothing man named Calvin Klein, well Barry Schwartz to be exact — all a far cry from James River Knitwear back home in North Carolina. He flew me up to the Big Apple for the spring clothing market. Aside from the Brooke Shields ads, no one south of Wall Street knew much about the hot new Calvinism — and I got teased at school for wearing the mark of the denim beast. One day, as discreetly as she could, Kathy, the beautiful head cheerleader of Garinger High School, with long, feathered brunette hair, pulled me aside in front of a giggling class, and with all the diplomacy a popular teenaged girl could muster, told me in a hushed voice: 'Calvins aren't for guys...' as if she was mercifully delivering a decree of social damnation. However, within less than a year, boys' butts from the swamps of Fort Lauderdale to the heights of Harlem would go from covered to perky, with the help of Mr. Klein's tight-fitting jeans and back pocket stitching.

Soon after, I joined Daddy on the business trip. I was scared senseless — which was good because it forced me to reach and struggle. Other times it wasn't so good 'cause I just missed the mark completely — hard to walk in Daddy's big size thirteen shoes. To make matters more confusing, we even have the same name, except for my 'Jr' at the end. Talk about identity crisis. Like when I'd go to stay with him for a weekend and his girlfriends would come over to party. Or after he remarried, and we went to visit the new woman's family and they let me drink all the bourbon I wanted and then got mad 'cause I got drunk. Or another time when we went back to those same people's house and they were doing crystal meth and Daddy offered me some and I wouldn't take it because grandmother, his mother, had put the fear of God into me about drugs. And how that same night I was supposed to watch out for my 13-year-old sister, Adrienne, in the midst of people shouting and playing loud music and Daddy breaking the wooden front door 'cause he couldn't get the chain unlatched. And how I didn't know that you weren't supposed to close the door to my sister's room where she was sleeping because the fumes from the kerosene heater needed to get out. Daddy made up for it by taking us to the local theme park or on trips like this one to New York. One summer we travelled all through Virginia and where the Civil War was fought. Daddy had as much fun as me and Adrienne. As for the other stuff, nobody's perfect. Nobody's wrong all the time. Dad showed me life's horizon, and how to reach for it.

Mama dropped me off for my late-evening flight to LaGuardia Airport. Mama always looked worried when she let go of me for one of these little excursions. I'd been on planes before. Once. It would be an hour and a half flight — the same time it took for Mama to drive me and my sister Adrienne up to grandmother and Popey's house, a time anomaly which blew my mind. A lady sat in the row with me by the window seat. She didn't look like NC. Thin, sophisticated, middle-aged, wearing a plum-colored knit designer shawl. She must have been able to tell I was jumpy. She talked to me here and there. As we approached New York, the lady encouraged me to lean over and look past at the majestic city unfolding before us. She became attentive, like when you first go into a church or an ancient ruin or a graveyard. 'I just love to see the lights. Isn't it just wonderful?' I tried to memorize every detail of the crisp, twinkling lights and blur of dark indigos. A massive human-made sculpture of buildings and steel, topped by the World Trade Center, reached up to greet us as we banked a turn over downtown. We were transfixed.

I had my instructions upon arrival: 'Man with sign at gate. Go with him...' He drove a sleek, dark Lincoln Continental, my favorite kind of car. He was a black guy, mid-twenties. He didn't sound like folk from back home. He was sharp, articulate. Asked me about where I was from and if it was my first trip to the city, but he didn't try to make me feel out of place. 'There's nothin' like New York City man...' He was on the verge of giving me clues to all the hottest night spots and such, but either Daddy had warned him or he could tell I was just below the right age for all that.

Daddy took me out the first night with a group of co-workers from Calvin Klein. They were all talk about territories and sales and figures and buyers from the big retailers. We started at a Steak House, Christ Cella. I'll never forget the name because I had never been to a steakhouse that wasn't named steer-this or burnt-bull-that. I had to wear the nice clothes from the plane trip. They didn't quite fit. The place was run like a military establishment, but friendlier. Inside, a swarm of people zipped this way and that way, gracefully shuffling our group from door to table to seat to holding a menu and a glass of water in no time. I dropped my cloth napkin and before I could reach down to get it a new one was in my lap and the old one gone. I was liking me some Christ Cella. Except the grins I got when I asked for steak sauce. Daddy had to whisper to me that it was an insult to the chef. Well? I was winging it — which, as I'd later discover, when done well and with precise naivety, is one of the most valuable skills of both newcomer and native New Yorker.

As we left the restaurant, Daddy gave me tip money, and explained how to grasp it in the palm of my right hand. As I left, Mr. 'D' shook my hand and removed the bills with the art of Dickens' Dodger. I remain impressed.

Throughout the week, Daddy worked most of the time, and I wandered Midtown aimlessly. He'd drawn me a map. I wish it had included Greenwich Village. He'd been down plenty of times, but kept me out of there and especially that 'Uncle Charlie's,' a queer bar he and his co-workers sometimes frequented. I didn't even know where 'The Village' was. All I knew was where Daddy took me. We went to the Empire State Building and the Waldorf and Rockefeller Center and places like that. St. Patrick's Cathedral. Daddy called the great big altar a 'mosque' and I went along without a thought, both of us impressed at the scale of the altar. I was delighted in his enthusiasm. We didn't see things like that often. We rarely saw things like that together.

Over a few days, the people at Klein became a little more chatty with me, but seriously, what does a fifteen-year-old have to say to twenty-or-thirty-something salespeople? I didn't like being the 'kid-visitor.' I wanted to grow older, so bad it hurt. Daddy worked with a slick, good-looking blond guy. Smooth, pale skin. His body filled out his clothes like an athlete, solid. Young, a top seller in the office. Had the New York State territory. He noticed me noticing him when Dad wasn't looking. Little did he know. Little did I know.

One night Dad took me out to a dance club with the Klein people. The blond guy wasn't with us. I kinda' hoped he'd come. The club, called Heartbreak, was a cafeteria by day, dance hall by night. I had to keep my head down as Daddy and the others paid our way in past the bouncers. 'You know, if you weren't with us, you couldn't do this…' he'd say about the obvious gap in age. The booze started flowing. Daddy told me to order vodka tonics. Nice starter drink. OK. I probably guzzled a dozen of them in the first hour. Ended up dancing all night, even making friends with a big, black-haired Greek girl named Theresa. I was in New York City and hang out with somebody. Anybody. A local.

Theresa was a big girl, and wore a cream colored, tunic-style top. She had a heavy accent. I didn't know if she was from New York or Greece or Queens. Dad was partying 'til the break of dawn on the other side of the room. He'd given me fifty bucks. They were playing great music, a Grace Jones kind of jam. *Pull up to the bumper, bab-ay…* We drank a lot of drinks, which gave me an excuse to keep going back to the bar which I liked doing 'cause there was an Italian bartender wearing a purple tuxedo shirt, hair combed back, movie-star face. His shirt fell open when he leaned over to get ice or something. He reminded me of the good looking guys in Saturday Night Fever. Dark buh-lack hair. I'd never seen a guy with looks like that. In hindsight, I imagine his expression as if he'd liked to have said 'you know, there's a few places you might find more... appealing. Let me give you some directions... talk to Johnny at the door...'

Theresa's friend got tired and had to leave. She took down the name of the hotel. She told me to be ready in the morning, only a few hours away. She would call and pick me up and we would go to Bloomingdale's to buy her some bras. Only Bloomingdale's had the kind she liked. I agreed to go with her. I thought that it would be so cool to have my own friend in New York to run around with. The walk home was fuzzy, the scent of chestnuts made me ill.

The next morning I woke up early. I could still hear the music ringing in my ears. I felt real sick, but persisted in getting up. I didn't know how to make myself throw up back then, or that it could've helped the massive hangover. Daddy was snoring in the other bed. He raised his head to ask me what I was doing. With a ring in my voice I told him my new friend was coming to get me. He rolled over. I figured morning for Theresa meant anytime before noon, but generally thought she meant between ten and eleven. I dozed off again. Woke up when Daddy started shuffling around in the bathroom, electric shaver and all. Cologne. Knock at door — one of the men from 'Klein.' It was after noon. The man asked if we want to go down to the deli for some brunch. I started explaining that I was expecting this call. I could smell their patronage. Daddy started saying how I shouldn't get disappointed. I went to brunch. Dammit. I didn't want anything from her but to go to Bloomingdale's. I only wanted a local connection to the city.

I was supposed to leave on a flight the next day. I got on the phone and changed my ticket to the middle of the week. Dad went on to tell me not to expect a lot of partying, because he would be very busy. Good. I wanted to wander. I wrote in my diary how I had to be in this place, this city. How I had to come back here. I wandered the streets all day. Had no idea where I was going. It didn't dawn on me to buy a map. I just wandered and went into whatever I found interesting.

One morning, while walking in Midtown, I noticed a young blond guy, shorter than the man at the office. It was overcast. He had on a chocolate brown dress raincoat, but he didn't button it up the way Dad's friends did. His was open, slightly swinging behind him. He carried a package or something — leather case perhaps, in his left arm. It was early in the day, probably eleven or so. He took a look at me, kept walking. He was walking faster than me. I had on my red sweater, raincoat. I decided to follow him. I didn't know what I wanted from him. I didn't know what I'd say if he stopped. I just thought he looked different. Sophisticated even. After two blocks, I felt him notice me again but he made no gesture beyond a backward glance to confirm it. He varied his steps and sped up a little. I wasn't trying to intimidate, but I was, in fact, following the guy. He turned off of one of the side streets and into a private courtyard leading to a building entrance. His keys were out. Once the door was open he seemed to pause. I needed him to pause.

Then he disappeared inside.

2. I Gotta Get Out of this Place

1984. Charlotte, NC. The New York State of Mind, stuck in mine. Although I'd rationalize and listen to well-intended relatives who encouraged me to settle down, and waste a few years on 'what-if,' deep inside I knew where I was supposed to be. I just needed the confidence to get there. First, there were my last two years of education to suffer. Mama had the good fortune of being able to buy her own house — a major feat for a single mother at the time, which meant I had the bad fortune of having to change schools. The old one, Garinger, wasn't perfect, but was familiar, as were my classmates of over ten years. The new one was a 1967 brick warehouse for *nouveau riche* Republikids — the spawn of suburban, credit-chomping yuppies born with plastic sporks in their mouths. I begged and pleaded not to go. Tried to explain that I actually had friends for the first time in my life. All I had to do was find a way to get one mile up the road to the another bus stop.

No dice. Mama wasn't budging and Daddy showed up just in time to issue the final blow, 'no.' Not the first time, and certainly would not be the last. I would remain angry for a very long time. In the meantime, I'd survive the same way as I did when I was six and used to win swimming races against the older teenagers: inhale, close eyes, think of my Olympic Hero Mark Spitz, jump in stroking. No stop, no air until my head hit the other side of the pool. Self-destructive victory. Not the best strategy, but at least I had one, and not many people did. By then we had an actor in the White House, and America was in transition from being a great nation to being the 'greatest nation' — and the happy 70s party was over. Cozy places for queers to hide were undergoing a rabid, biting change. Homogenization for homos. At the turn of the 21st century in New York City, Rudolph Giuliani would be the culprit. Through the turning of my adolescence it would be my high school principal.

Independence High School, pronounced 'Innapenance,' was a prison. Mr. Principal, like most good head-men, was short, overweight, and his gut protruded over his belt and brown poly-blend slacks. He smelled like breakfast. His neck extended above his collar and clip-on tie like a glob of jelly. His face was round, his head balding. He kept a stubbly beard on his face, and large, bulky plastic glasses over his eyes. He wouldn't look at you when he spoke. From his office-bunker, the most original thing the man could muster was to get on the loudspeaker and read the 'Eight Behavior Guidelines,' followed by a litany of don'ts, better-nots and can'ts which contained phrases like 'food stuffs.' A distinctly negative vibe, tingling with anger and pine cleaner, filled the hallways. The atmosphere held an unnecessarily hostile, Columbine-esque texture. The band teacher stank of smoke and encouraged his favorites to abuse other kids. Bullying, physical, mental — all there. I think Mr. Principal was afraid of him and the football coach. Most other teachers were unable to keep control of their classes and conspired to rally behind the chosen few, while everyone else was left to face the languid 1950s revival in which we'd found ourselves unwillingly cast.

Swimming: life with my head down as America's mind closed. School days. Avoiding. Weekdays, up at 7:10. Speed to school in my 1974 Oldsmobile Cutlass Supreme at 7:20. First-period, 7:30, for Bill Hanna's orchestra class — the only class I liked. I played the violin and string bass by ear. We spent day after day rehearsing the theme to Star Wars or practicing Hungarian Rhapsody number 2 in E Minor by Franz Liszt. I discovered the Liszt piece in a Bugs Bunny cartoon and suggested we try it. Hanna, a man with tight curly graying hair and thick, brown plastic glasses who maintained a perpetually sour mood, agreed. Hanna didn't like me. I didn't like me and I didn't like him. Hanna didn't seem to like anybody. During class, he'd scream at the violinists for not attacking their strings with the bow, shouting 'you can't make chicken salad out of chicken shit.' He spoke his mind. We knew where we stood. I didn't have to think. I only had to feel, and listen, and play. Music came naturally. It was one of the few times in the school day we weren't bombarded by behavior guidelines and that most important piece of teenage Americana, popularity.

Safely back at home, I couldn't get enough of the music. Once, I put together a massive sound system — combining a rats' nest of wires and speakers I found in the neighborhood dumpster; I scraped the grooves thin on my Elton John, Queen, Blondie, B-52s and Pretenders record albums, and relied on late-night radio for everything in between. I knew every word to every song and made a dance move for every note deliberately, passionately, soulfully — for my venue: my Mom's basement. Freddie Mercury, Debbie Harry, Chrissie Hynde and Kate Pierson would've been proud. It could have been Madison Square Garden.

I liked to imagine what Freddie, Debbie and all of them felt and thought when they did a show. I studied their album covers and devoured live recordings for every hint of a word, breath and groan of a human being, being superhuman. I watched American Bandstand every week. Sometimes Debbie was good, with a bow and arrow and pretty dress. Other times, I didn't get it — like one appearance on Solid Gold when she dressed in green combat gear. Mom said she looked high as a loon. At that point I'd never gotten to see Freddie actually perform, other than on the Bohemian Rhapsody and a few videos, but I had a lot of concert photos and I could decipher how fast or slow he was moving from the vocals on the concert records. I knew these people could sing and dance and keep an audience for hours. At the time I thought they could fly — despite current misconceptions, there was plenty of life before cables, pundits and MTV.

As I choreographed my afternoons away, I could see the bright sky just up and out Mom's basement windows. I dreamed of launching myself up into the jet stream and being carried to where the people of the world gathered and grooved. I'd tried and tried to imagine finding a vital vibe in my hometown, but deep down I knew it was futile. Charlotte is a great place to be from — a place you make it out of, if you're born with my kind of genes — especially when the town fathers started following Reagan's style of rhetoric by naming Charlotte a 'World Class City.' A carefully worded title that means nothing. The Charlotte I knew had always been its own worst enemy — a milieu of misguided conservatism, politics; a new & improved God and poor planning; rich white folk on one side of the tracks, poor blacks, queers and undesirables on the other; halfwits who still believed the Civil War was winnable hung on the sidelines — the Jersey City of the South — but this wasn't always the case.

Charlotte had once been a nice little place, named for a benefactor, Queen Charlotte of Mecklenburg-Strelitz, mulatto wife of mad King George III. She was a patron of Johann Christian Bach as well as Mozart, and friend to Marie Antoinette, who, incidentally never uttered the infamous phrase that got her killed. High culture. Somewhere along the line, the Puritans and their 'Nascar' days set in and they wrecked most of the Uptown for a football stadium, where Mama and her friends liked to shop at specialty shops like Montaldo's and have lunch at Kofina's Deli.

Years before, Popey, my infant nickname for her father and my grandfather, used to tell me how every year or so he and some friends would drive down out of the mountains to Charlotte, and visit the local tailor. '...two each: a handmade suit of clothes, shirts, ties and one pair of shoes for twenty dollars' he'd say. On weekends, a lot of folks liked taking drives for entertainment, or spending time in parks. It was a lazy Southern town and that was alright. Queers and hippies and business people mixed for the fireworks on the 4th of July and no one much noticed. Being in the middle meant you had nowhere else to rush to, and nothing to prove and defend. Charlotte, after all, was no reconstruction town like Atlanta. And even in the town where a black girl named Dorothy Coates was stoned on her way to classes at East Mecklenburg High School during the start of the Black Civil Rights Movement, despite the best efforts of her white classmates to stand with her, a deal was later worked out between black activists and students at the local college which helped avoid a portion of the ugliness that prevailed in the segregated South.

Like how Fiorello LaGuardia and Robert Moses leveled almost a third of the middle class housing in New York City back in the 1930s and 40s to build super highways, carpet-bagging commissioners showed up in Charlotte sometime in the mid-70s. Ten years later, IBM arrived and brought half of backward Endicott NY with it. Endicott is not in any way part of the Big Apple but the NC banks acted like Wall Street had come to town, and started lending people all sorts of outrageous money they'd never pay back. Cheap strip shopping centers, sprawling subdivisions and fast-food joints popped up like mushrooms on cow shit — all in the name of 'progress,' and 'consumer choice.' Charlotte did not have a Bella Abzug like New York City to stand in the way of the wrecking balls. I watched as human beings became units and resources, just like the dead Jews at Bitburg were to the Nazis that Reagan visited, proclaiming himself a World-Class President. And Charlotte fell for it.

From my high school principal to the right-wing preachers choking the radio airwaves, my hometown fell under occupation, and I felt occupied. And cheated. And angry at the knowledge that an insidious political cancer was breeding in the belly of our nation. I hid in Mom's basement, the furthest I could get from the onslaught of 'family values,' and I made one key mistake that would follow me all the way to the end of this book: I took it all personally. Fire and brimstone devoured my self esteem. I believed that I was a bad person for not going along with their crowd. I also thought that my self-inflicted abuse against my creativity and God-given sex drive was justified.

And if it weren't for mistakes in judgement like this, I might have been a darn-good baseball player in school, or actually tried out for the team, or would have actually made a go of the Boy Scouts instead of dropping out. And would've been able to say 'f*ck off' to my high school principal when he wasted class time making us all feel like worthless, inferior human beings. Or better still, got up and walked out entirely. I'm not sorry, I still don't want to be a redneck. I'm not a cowboy. Neither were people in any parts of the South I came from. And what about cowboys? Let's see: men who want to go live in the middle of nowhere with hoards of sweaty men, no women, and wear chaps. Coincidence? The rest of the John Wayne type myths should be relegated to a book called 'brokeback bullshit.'

So, as a proper second-class citizen, I hid. Blondie, Freddie Mercury, Prince, Pretenders and B-52s kept me company. I yearned to know what they knew, to be like them. Little did I realize my path had already begun leading me to almost every one of them.

You touch yourself to make sure it's still there — the thing that must be obeyed — but not so much to stimulate, just a lateral scratch to facilitate the opening of your dry eyes. You rub off the crusty sleep crumbs from your eyelids. The flakey pus bounces over your comforter like tiny snowflakes. As you raise your head, your musty, fashionably-matted hair sticks to the stale bed sheets. Signs of an old romance cover them. To the right of your periphery, blue numbers on a clock radio blur into a partially legible 10:30PM.

3. Does Jesus Know You're Waiting?

1986. After high school I'd spent a couple of years flunking out of my first attempt at college by exploring hallucinogenics and their discontents. Dad had moved to Texas and had convinced me to try it too. Needless to say, Texas is not New York and Dallas is not cool, really, no matter how many Gallerias and Neiman Marcus's they build. And I didn't fit in at an agricultural college for jocks. So, like a homing pigeon in survival mode, I found my way to the most notorious scene of the time, called the Starck Club — a brief flash in the only pan of culture Dallas will probably ever see, brought on by the ready, legal availability of MDMA. Boys wearing pearls and brooches. Girls in 1920s furs with cigarette holders. Nina Hagen's 'New York New York' on the dance floor and Kid Creole and The Coconuts for New Year's Eve. Everybody loved everybody, or at least acted like they did when the drugs kicked in, until the state legislature caught up by outlawing 'Ex' in all its names and forms. Our game at the time was asking potential E-buyers 'are you a member of law enforcement?' and if they were, they were supposed to tell us. One night a young woman looked me straight in the face and said 'yes' without flinch or smirk. I decided to get out while the gettin' was good. My last little bag of stimulants ran out in the early morning of the 4th of July, about 13 hours into an 18 hour drive, in my brown-with-leather-interior uninsured 1977 Ford Thunderbird somewhere around Nashville, Tennessee. I'd first tried to stop in Knoxville, but a sneering woman with thick lipstick and a big blonde wig circa 1962 refused to rent me a room, so I went one town further and found one. As I lay in my temporary Tennessee bed, completely exhausted, a complete mess, unaware that I'd miss one of the biggest drug busts in club-kid history by less than two weeks, I became transfixed on the television coverage of the New York Harbor celebration for the Centennial of the Statue of Liberty. Something was once again calling me. In the South, 'calling' can take lots of forms.

Eventually, I ended up on the doorstep of my paternal grandmother in North Carolina, Ruby Frances Huntley Belk. She'd been my buddy since I was a little kid. Much more than a 'grandmother' in the greeting card sense of the word. She used to pick me up from school if it was raining, so I wouldn't have to walk, and we'd go back with my Grandaddy, who'd been suffering from a heart condition for years, to their house and eat ice cream. Years later, I'd stay over with them and help nurse my Grandaddy, who eventually succumbed to his fifth or sixth heart attack and a stroke. After his death, I stayed over with her so she wouldn't be by herself, and I'd catch a ride to Garinger High School with a teacher who lived a few doors down.

Almost all my Dad's family belonged to a non-denominational church congregation in what I'll call Podunk, North Carolina — a blip on the outskirts of Southeast Charlotte. Then the church was a pretty hardcore book-of-revelations, judgement-day-is-coming-repent-now affair. The children were micromanaged with the precision of a nuclear clock, and only one, that I knew of, listened to Rock 'n' Roll. I had my gripes, but on a larger scale I have to give them credit: as committed pacifists, they took 'thou shalt not kill' seriously, and the men risked prosecution for not fighting in wars. Some were imprisoned. And something else I like about them is that they thumbed their noses at the Federal Government and got away with it — not a small order in the decades of Ruby Ridge and David Koresh.

They had a preacher who reminded me of Richard Nixon's nickname: Tricky Dick. He was Grandma's sister's husband's brother. The leader of a congregation close to a thousand members who collectively held land, businesses and money worth multiples of multiples of millions. So, when the Feds moved in and tried to stop them from homeschoolin' their kids and sending them to work in the afternoons, apparently a violation of child labor laws, they stood up. David Brinkley even came down from New York City with the national ABC News to do a story, and man did they put on a show. Tricky Dick could do just as good a PR campaign as Ronnie Reagan, and the Feds backed down. Apparently, censoring people who were teaching their kids to do things besides buy a Walkman didn't make good political sense.

Grandma never once tried to force me to comply, which was good because I didn't get it — I was looking for wings, not roots. She knew it, although she always guaranteed me a place called home. My cousins would work and not attend public schools. The women and girls were not allowed to wear pants, or jewelry or makeup. They were to grow their hair long and become matronly. The boys could never wear short pants or go shirtless. No one was to curse. No smokin.' No drinkin.' Cover thy self and all you see. Beware the 'Wicked One.' To me, the wicked ones were the Tricky Dicks of the world. They tend to rule their roosts with iron fists and never let you forget judgement day has been at hand for a long, long time. And like all good unaffiliated congregations, they'd even gone through a split — half went with one reverend, the brother of the reverend of the half that stayed. Very Cain and Abel.

So, after my brush with becoming a rebellious teenage cliché in Texas, I moved in with Miss Ruby. I called Grandma 'Miss Ruby' because my Grandaddy used to affectionately call her that. Miss Ruby believed in stayin' out of other people's business, including mine. She didn't try to jump to conclusions about things she didn't understand. She didn't feel the need to understand everything. She didn't bother you unless you bothered her — sadly, a sign of a vanishing generation. I'd had boys come by the house — not a lot. She even got to know some of them, would even comment on liking this one, not liking that one. Advising me that I was 'judged by the company you keep' and hence to rid myself of certain hangers-on. Miss Ruby even went to stay at my youngest aunt's house so I could have a party once. My uncle, who was on the church council, would have worked himself into a lather if he'd known: the two biggest things that prompt the battle cry of the Bible-thumpers are homos and taxes. But I knew that much of the ultra-conservative world revolves around fear, which is usually enough to keep folks in their places. No one, but no one spoke up, except rogues like me, and fear-mongers were rarely prepared for such a confrontation — they depend on silence. It had only been a few years since Harvey Milk took Anita Bryant apart on national television.

One Sunday, out of respect for Miss Ruby, I drove her to church and sat with her through the service. I got stares as if to ask 'what are you doing here' from some, general curiosity from others — although I was related, somehow, to just about every one fo them. Maybe because I was a new face, or maybe because I was wearing the ugliest teal green designer cardigan money could buy, but either way Miss Ruby stood beside me in stone shoes. And as only the Lord would have it, that particular day, of all the Sundays for ten years comin' or goin,' was the very Sunday that had been chosen for a Congregational hearing and excommunication of a man who'd been stirring up bad blood among the brethren. We sat for an hour or two as men went, one by one, up to the pulpit to make statements. I had no clue what was to happen, or even what in hell they were all yammering on about, but began to expect a 'hootnanny.' The statements began in deep, quiet country tones, with the phrase 'If a man...' repeated over and over.

Everyone took the proceedings quite seriously, as if Jesus himself would take a break from whatever business might be at hand in starving Africa or war-torn South America, and join us. This congregation was no stranger to controversy — once splitting in two, one group going with Tricky Dick's rival, who just happened to be my great-uncle, the others, including my immediate family, remained. Soon after, proclamations of the separation were signed by a judge, and are nailed on the front doors of the temple to this day.

Usually on the Sabbath, I was most interested in lunch and the people that came with it. We'd left the house smelling like Sunday, with the rich aroma of fresh-baked biscuits wafting across Grandma's golden wool carpeting; roast beef dancing among the crystals of the brass chandelier; rice, mustard greens and vinegar; pound cake, green beans with salty pork, fried chicken or chicken diván, gravy, and vanilla egg custard all mingling before the party in the kitchen. But on this particular day, all that could wait for the curtain of the Theatre of the Almighty to fall. Suddenly, Tricky Dick got back to his place in the pulpit and called a vote. I figured, 'when in Mint Hill, do what Miss Ruby does.' So we all stood to seal the damnation. Thank God. Time had run way over and pot roasts across the county were burning in their ovens.

The condemned man shuffled up to Tricky Dick and tried to force him out of the pulpit with a walking cane as he closed the day with a prayer. We watched as a Gospel-driven shoving match ensued, reminding me that I need to say a special prayer of thanks for humanity, because you just can't make this stuff up. Finally, it was over, and we went home, thank God. Miss Ruby and her friends had survived the Great Depression on potatoes, peaches and faith — wasn't much going to spook her. My Daddy came to eat, as did quite a few others, and we rehashed the events over and over, and after a while, just when Daddy, who didn't go to church at the time, looked relieved that the subject had finally been changed, I'd chime in with '...but that man!' and start it all up again, just for 'pure meanness' as Miss Ruby would say.

I was an outsider on most of it, but if certain members of my family had actually known I'd spent much of my young adulthood at The Rocky Horror Picture Show, they might've tried an exorcism. The only regret I have in dealing with the tribe was once when a nosey aunt used her door-opening toddlers as a reason to go snoopin' through my room. She found what she was looking for, an incriminating Boy George makeup book. Truth was I'd only got it on a whim from a sale bin. Boy George only marginally impressed me. But when confronted by my uncle, seeking to preserve family values, I denied it as a gag gift. And that was the first time in this life I learned how it felt to give a piece of myself away for nothing, like a whore.

4. Ignorance, Bliss and Drag

I took a job as a salesperson at a local department store, Belk's to be precise, still one of, if not the largest privately owned retailers in the US. Miss Ruby and me used to have a good laugh when people would ask 'Are you 'a' Belk?,' actually referring to the family that owned the chain. 'Yes, I'm 'a' Belk,' she'd reply. Which was true, John and Susannah Belk were from Glasgow, well Cambeltown, Scotland and apparently emigrated just before the turn of the 19th century, to which we are related. But we got the name not the business.

I hustled for my Belk bosses in the men's department while taking advertising design courses at the local community college. I sold polo shirts to the fresh, strapping, preppie, elite young men of Charlotte. Earning commission on their superiority. Selling them shirts, pants, socks and anything Ralph or Tommy told them was hip that season. Measuring everything to size. At night I hung out with a bunch of other young queers, fag hags and the occasional closet case from the store. We'd go to the only fag disco in Charlotte, officially named The Scorpio Lounge — but known as 'Scorps' among the locals when making plans to drain away another Saturday night.

Marion owned Scorpio. She sat at the front, took the money and talked to us. 'How y'all doin t'ni-ite? Thray dahlerrs puh-leeze.' Marion was a big woman, like those Russian parodies on TV, — robust and round and wore polyester blouses and heavy plastic glasses which hid her face. Large, 70s-style plastic frames. Reddish-brown teased hair. Gold nugget jewelry with a rock-hard attitude to go with it. The entrance to the club was plate glass with wood panelling and scattered posters of clown-faced drag queens. Over-dressed queers in off-price couture shirts lined up every weekend night to get in, cruise each other mercilessly and watch cabaret-style lip synch shows by drag queens with names like Tiger Lil,' Hot Chocolate, Boom-Boom Latour, Fay Ways, Fonda Boys and Naomi Sims.

There are three types of drag queens in urban-suburbia: clowns, boogers and female impersonators. Drag clowns are spoofs of life. Parodies of themselves — the woman at the café who picks her teeth and wears a three-foot-high beehive hairdo, circa 1963; the big fat aunt you always had, but never asked for. Next come the boogers, the not-quite-crispy cornbread. They are men. In dresses. Dresses usually borrowed from a sister, or inherited from that dead aunt. Dresses that don't fit. Wigs that are never on straight. Toes protruding beyond the tips of their size 13 pumps. Moustaches, man hands, complete with hair on the knuckles. On the eyes, every color from a dimestore makeup pack — three bucks buys the rainbow, for the world to endure.

The female impersonators are a bit more serious. They want to be women, at least for the night. Draped in lamé, rhinestones or a slightly-used Chanel evening gown, they take the stage in all seriousness. They try to become the songs they mime. Whether Whitney Houston, Patti Labelle or Cher — they become supreme divas for the crowds, channelling the powerful for the powerless. Every weekend, all across America and in a ghetto near you, queers line up to worship and make an offering to the deities. They huddle around the stage-turned-altar as the songs begin in a wash of lights and blinking strobes for their turn to wander up to the diva with a one-dollar bill, folded in half — longways, held out between the first two fingers of an extended arm. If the timing is right, the diva takes the dollar, and gives a blessing in return. Drag church.

One night I made my way, again, to the Scorpio Lounge. Slow night. Boom-Boom was doing her usual schtick. My friends were having the same conversation we'd had the night before. Bored, I wandered up to the front to chat with Marion. Chat is an overstatement — Marion never had a lot to say. If you knew Marion, you were allowed to stand to her side while she took the money. Her .38 caliber pistol sat in the tray below the desk and held down the large bills. You could almost smell the tangy gun oil riding up on the heat of her green glass desk lamp. 'What's goin' on hun?' she'd ask as she changed the tens into fives and hand them back to the people in line. 'Nu-thin. Absolutely nuthin. Bored out of my skull.' She asked me if I was still moving to New York City, something I'd mentioned before.

Charlotte didn't import much in the way of culture. When it did, it usually got picketed by some extremist religious group. People didn't want people being human in Charlotte. Or at least the news media, local car dealers and a lot of churches didn't — there's only so much shopping, country crafts and local television one can stand. The park where a lot of gay men cruised was called, interestingly enough, 'Freedom Park.' It's probably still patrolled by undercover agents, entrapping queers on charges of 'Crimes Against Nature,' in many cases just for saying 'hello.'

Once, they dragged my painting teacher from the local community college, Rad, to jail for taking pictures of ducks in that very park. Apparently, an undercover cop approached him, interrupted his picture taking, and tried to get him to say anything remotely sexual so the cuffs could be justifiably slapped on to cart him away. Rad told me he'd avoided the man for a long time, moving his equipment and walking away. Finally, Rad just flat out asked him to leave, saying he wanted to continue with his pictures. The cop persisted in his badgering. After decades of entrapping jungle-bunnies they were well prepared to deal with butt-bandits: the new second class. Frustrated, and hip to what the guy was, Rad finally blurted 'WHAT? Are you going to just keep standing there 'til I say I wanna' suck yer cock?'

Click, click, cuffs.

He said his story, like all the other nothings that happen in that town, made the morning paper so choir ladies would have their day's supply of gossip and confirmation of the need to stay in the flock. Regardless, Rad refused to be embarrassed, which I respected. And he refused to cower and plead guilty like so many others had, to save face, families and jobs. He showed up for his day in court, and explained what happened. Rad was exonerated on all charges, a fact which most likely didn't appear in the morning paper. Even good queers, like the mythic 'good negro,' as championed by god-fearing racists, don't matter.

Even the Scorpio Lounge, private property, wasn't immune to what we called the 'Godsquad.' While people were inside cruising the dance floor, the brethren were outside cruising the parking lot. Sneaking around like ferry rats in the name of the Lord. Copying down license plate numbers to take to fellow believers on the police force who'd righteously furnish the names and addresses of the owners. From this, a weekly blacklist was formed and circulated around World-Class Charlotte, still affectionately known as the Queen City.

5. Get Yr' Lawn Off My Car

May, 1988. How do you survive in Reagan's America and capitalist concentration camps like Charlotte? We drank. We danced. We drove. Most Saturday nights I'd load up in my giant brown, 8-cylinder 1977 Ford Thunderbird, pick up my best buddy Tim Smyre and go out. I knew Smyre from working in the same mall as I did. He was tall, with cropped dark hair, and a couple of years older than me and known for selling a half million dollars worth of polo shirts a year.

The good thing about Charlotte in the mid-80s was that the brethren were home in bed by 9pm, missionary position — a blessing that the streets were pretty empty at night, otherwise it was but for the Grace of God we didn't kill anybody behind the wheel. 'Good people' weren't supposed to be 'out' in the Bible Belt, but we were. And for some reason it was allowed that we could drink all the alcohol we could buy. I drank to belong. I drank to numb-out the fears of the life I knew was before me. I drank to cover up that I was awkward — caught somewhere between clumsy and autistic, immature and insane, attractive but just not attractive enough to matter. I'd drink and pretend to be OK for the drive home. I can remember trips in freezing cold weather, window rolled down, air conditioning at full blast, cruise control set to exactly 34.5mph, radio blasting, one eye closed, both hands gripping the steering wheel, aimed precisely on the yellow line, police car just behind, waiting for me to swerve.

Other times, we begged to be caught, deciding in a stupor to clean out my car along the way: mounds of empty McFood bags, cups, ice cream tubs and wrappers filled the back seat of my car. 'No time like the present!' Smyre chirped as he tossed a fistful of sacks out his window with a deliberate flick of the wrist. I joined in as I drove away from the nightclub, located on the desolate end of a half-empty strip shopping center, stop-starting, punching the gas and brakes like a jalopy in a B-movie — music blasting and garbage flying out of every window leaving behind an obstacle course of grease-stained Americana. We laughed harder than I'd done in years and the cops paid no mind. Oh, they cared if you kissed openly in public, or if you asked the boy behind the McIdiot counter for a date, but apparently not if you got behind the wheel drunk enough to speak in tongues throwing garbage like confetti from a parade float.

Smyre and I were a little more tame at the occasional house party, usually given by our friends Tim and his lover Richard — we used 'lovers' because back then 'partners,' as a concept, hadn't yet materialized — who we all called 'Timanrichard.'

Tim of Timanrichard worked in the same store I did. Tim was a display person — otherwise known as a fashion merchandiser. He decorated the store. Tim was usually overdressed in couture or something fancy, a quality I've learned to appreciate. A tall, healthy black man, with long, pulled-back hair and a ponytail. I don't think I ever saw him in blue jeans. Woven, sewn shirts — never a t-shirt. Some sort of makeup. Hoity-toity accent. Perhaps a lot to take, but I admired him for trying to transcend: the one thing we had in common, in our own separate ways. He was always in the latest styles, always on top of trends and people. Fashion was Tim's way of dealing with Charlotte. He was very defensive, 'attitudinal' some might say. Bitchy, but couldn't help it. He, too, wanted something more out of life than cable TV, 10k 'Fun-Runs,' and Top 40 radio.

It's enough to grow up in Charlotte, the South, as a skinny white boy like me — but as an outspoken, tall, queer black? Tim got harassed by the goons who worked around the store — dressed-up rednecks for security and housewares people, rejects from the buying office left to rot on the sales floor, or jarhead jocks drawing an after-school paycheck until Daddy decided to take out a second mortgage for college. I admired his tenacity, but thanked God from a distance it was not me.

Timanrichard made seasonal trips to New York City and after one in particular announced they'd be moving there. Jealous, I chalked it up to typical after-trip longing, until they asked me if I wanted to be their third roommate. 'We can put up with some roaches, we want to just get there…' I agreed, and had been waiting for the signal, any signal. I was surprised they'd even asked me, I was generally too rough around the edges for their liking.

The map of North America had been hanging on my wall at Grandma's for a long time, and with every glance, my eyes travelled up the coast and became stuck in the little cranny that led to Manhattan. Throughout my younger years, I tried in vain to consider other places: *Atlanta?* — nah, just a bigger Charlotte. *Chicago?* — nah. *Philadelphia?* — might as well go to New York. *LA?* — just, no. *Back to Dallas?* — Hell no, warrant out for my arrest. *Vegas, New Orleans, Austin, Phoenix, San Francisco?* — nope. Temptation, each time, bit the Apple. And my ants-in-the-pants only got itchier from watching every New York film I could get my hands on, like 'Boys in the Band' or 'Parting Glances,' but 'Torch Song Trilogy' spoke to my young, inexperienced, not-yet-tainted heart. It was not such a great film production *per se*, but the powerful narrative was just what I needed to clinch my deal. I already knew all about the towns where, as Harvey Fierstein says: 'Queers don't matter, queers don't love, and those that do deserve what they get.'

I became desperate for the chance to be something other than a second-class citizen. I wanted to have a chance at love without the Godsquad waiting in the parking lot, or the glares from the brethren in the shopping mall. I was beginning to quote more Fierstein in my travels — 'If you want to be a part of my life I'm not editing out the things you don't like.' And the fuck of it was, I'd sat only a few years earlier, in mixed company, seething 'dirty fuckin' faggot' at the TV screen when Torch Song swept the Tony Awards, and Fierstein walked up to accept his prize. Nothing has ever been easy, or clear. We learn to hate ourselves first. But now, like any other young twentysomething, all I wanted, dreamed of, was someone — what I really needed was to connect. Until then, I was just like the rest of the queer Charlotte rabble: single and ready. Ready for something, anything. Someone to talk to and be friends with and break into the drive-in porno theatre with and stay out all night with at Athens Diner. Most crave it, few get it. Queer or otherwise. We were raised to be stoic, neutered, ice sculptures. I fantasized a warm tent in the middle of the desert. Late summer winds. Me, him, and a pianist playing 'Music Maestro Please.' Banquet on a table illuminated by a late sun giving way to the glow of golden candlelight. A dance…

After weeks and months of delay, it finally dawned on me that Timanrichard and the others were full of it. My disgust with myself, Charlotte and the people in it grew and grew. I was taking everything too seriously. I harbored an excruciatingly primal desire to break free, like needing to pee after riding in a car for hours, and the ache turns to mental abscess. What I hadn't yet realized was that the cosmic forces were just waiting for me to shut the hell up and open my eyes. Kinda like with my quiet, ex-military, welder grandfather Popey — how I'd told him all my teenage life that all I wanted to be was a rock star. And a few years later, he asked me when I'd be getting on with being a rock star. He took me seriously ... something I wasn't used to. I started to realize I need to take me seriously, and make a new plan to get myself to Gotham.

Timanrichard rarely went to Scorps, but during the late spring of 1988 I ran into them there one Sunday night. They'd become annoyed with my badgering, so I promised myself not to give them any more of my New York dreams to smirk at. I'd leave them stuck in their happy little ruts. I got the 'Oh no here he comes' looks, except from Timanrichard-Tim, who intercepted me. 'Hey you still wanting to move to New York?' Stunned at his suggestion, I reply 'Ye-ah...'

'Come here!' He grabbed my shirt and took me over to a solid-framed guy, about 5'10" tall, with very long curly hair. Gene Simmons from Kiss or Leo Sayer type of thick curly hair and heavy, brown eyebrows covering a Roman brow. Light auburn freckles cover his face. 'This is Seth, say hello.'

'Hello Seth.' I'm suspicious.

'This one's been driving us crazy about moving to New York.' I got irritated at the objectification.

'Oh really?' Seth said back to me with one of the friendliest smiles I'd seen in a while. Nothing promiscuous — just a smile.

'Seth-here is from New York, right Seth?' My interest increased. I thought to myself: What the hell is he doing in here if he's from New York?

'Yeah, Brooklyn' he says. It sounded like *bwrahwklin*. He led me over to the bar to order a beer. 'You can come visit, anytime. I have room...' he continued in a light, inviting tone. I started to notice my breathing. I felt light, and suddenly everything in that room, the clouds of cigarette smoke, the shards of hazy sparkle from the giant disco ball, the bright fluorescent light that betrays everyone on the dance floor each time someone entered for a pee — all became flickering images, like an outdoor projection of an old movie.

6. Goodbye to Burbia

Tim swished his hips away, swinging his Yves St Somebody trousers. Seth and I got chummy, and I became exhilarated — I hadn't felt that high since Daddy gave me my first taste of New York. After that, I hadn't been many places — Charleston, Atlanta, Wrightsville Beach. Seth told me all about 'his' New York, and a new concept: living in Brooklyn. I'd already seen a copy or two of the *Village Voice* and even though I had no clue, really, how Greenwich Village differed from Hell's Kitchen or Harlem, any corner of the grand human warehouse looked great to me and I was becoming dangerous: an excitable young almost twenty-three-year-old with his first credit card gradually losing his sense of restraint.

Within days, I booked a trip. This Big Apple trip would be different from before. Dad hadn't been back to New York in years. This was all me. I was older, and independent. At least I thought I was. Coincidentally, Timanrichard and another guy named Eddie had planned their 'seasonal trip' on the very same weekend and I ended up on the very same airplane, but with one key difference: I was going as a prospective resident; them, tourists. God delivered me from obsequious pandering.

Back then, people made up their own stories while they were acclimating to the congested metropolis. Seth said he'd been raised in New York but ironically his entire family was in Charlotte. I figured he was kinda like me — when your dreams are better than your reality, the dreams thankfully get the better of you. What did I care whether he was actually from Charlotte or not? He got out, and got to Brooklyn.

Mama took me to the airport, just like before. She had the same worried look on her face. New York was ready and waiting, or so I thought. She knew I wouldn't return, really. It was at times like that I could actually see my mother, a young fashionable career woman, who made it out of an even smaller town in the NC mountains to come to Charlotte, split up with Daddy, worked like a soldier at IBM, and managed to buy us a nice house. And the one thing I'll give her, even though she'd prefer otherwise, she's never once tried to hold me back.

I kissed her goodbye outside the terminal and set out for my gate. She didn't need to walk me to the door like on my first trip, I was becoming a real jet-setter. I strolled through security wearing a decent pair of jeans and a t-shirt, and my Converse high tops. Sporty at least. I slowed as I reached my gate area. Timanrichard and Eddie were already there, dressed like peacocks on a promenade. Eddie's blond hair was 'jacked up for Jesus.' Tim's ponytail flowed behind him. Designer sunglasses crowned every head. Flowing, draping outfits, traveling jackets, fancy Louis Vuitton kind of luggage. The stench of cologne wafting all the way down the terminal.

My feet barely touched the ground as I walked down the gangway to the airplane. It could have been the excitement. It could have been the cologne fumes emanating from the group of Southern Belles in front of me. I had a healthy fear of flying, but I figured if I didn't die what waited for me on the other end would be well worth the risk. We arrived just after lunchtime under a hot sun and clear blue sky. Seth had given me directions on where to go once I got in. I was going to Greenwich Village, the Greenwich Village, which I knew a little about thanks to Harvey Fierstein and *Interview Magazine*. I thought I was a bit more up on my game now, but first I'd share a ride in a taxi with the three Karl Lagerfeld wannabees.

Outside LaGuardia Airport, a gypsy cab driver approached us and asked if we'd prefer a 'luxury car.' The Belles said yes, and negotiated a fare. We got into a white Pontiac something or other. I'd have preferred a yellow taxi. Something city-like. When the driver was asked about the state of the day's road congestion, he nodded his head in a patronizing preparation to state the obvious for gullible tourists, dropped his tone and said 'bad, very bad.' Little did we know that commuting was always bad in New York. The group nodded with faux-familiar concern, as if digesting a critical piece of information from the altar of traffic church. 'M-mmm.'

Right off, I began to recognize buildings — Chrysler, Empire State, World Trade. We got up to their hotel in Midtown. Times Square, of course, where these 'ladies' started acting a bit ridiculous — phony accents and all. Fair enough, we all do it when traveling. I went up to the room just to take a pee and called Seth. They started dropping hints about plans and things... I knew they were worried about getting stuck with me. I was clear that I was merely a tolerated accessory to the cliqué, and that was just fine, albeit awkward. I was just as nervous — scared to death — as they were about being in that newest, biggest place, and was happy to leave them to their outfit changes. I wanted the fucking city to myself, was pretty sure the streets would have me, and ventured forth.

So you get your lazy butt out of the bed and begin your walk down the short East Village tenement hallway to the kitchen. You need your coffee. Ten years ago you'd have just done a couple of lines from whatever bag was left over from the night before, but you're a little wiser now — maybe. You notice your legs, like clockwork, are a little stiffer than the day before. Your hands carry themselves beside your body, waiting on a nice rush of oxygenated blood. The color in your hair must be redone. 'Something else to do!' you whisper under your breath as if your adoring fans could hear you. There are no adoring fans. Only people who have your answering machine ringing off the hook right now who want to suck your tits for comp admission and free drinks. Getting ready is an old, universal conspiracy between the conscious and subconscious mind to entertain oneself. You plug in the coffee pot. You turn around, your white knit gym pants barely cover the crack in your ass. The black, worn out Kmart tank top slouches to the side, revealing one of your perky nipples. You love cracks and nipples, especially your own. You carry your package of self to the bathroom, for a narcissistic dive. The mirror hovers from the opposite wall, waiting to be addressed.

7. Lions and Tigers and Pervs ... Oh, hi

The scene outside the hotel was deliciously chaotic: noise, people, chatter, horns, alarms. I was overwhelmed and anxious. I needed to get to Perry Street, to a basement hair salon called The Hair Place on Perry where Seth worked. The taxicab air was stuffy and hot — the air conditioning barely pulsed up and over the dark blue plastic seats. I was covered in sweat within minutes. Sweat, sweet sweat. The driver wound through side streets, up and down. I felt queasy. We did not speak. It took a little while to get downtown. All I knew was that I was lost in the middle of the city of eight million people. In the cavernous distances of the buildings I could hear a blend of car stereos. Flavors and aromas reminding me of everything from barbecues to freshly cut crass mixed with acidic steam billowing from the depths of hell through the subway grates. Colors flashed on and off — neon, bright afternoon sun, arid radiations from thick asphalt and people of all blacks, whites, browns and blues. This city was alive and I became more alive than ever before. Mine.

We wound this way and that way, through what was the West Village. The blocks started getting nicer — I noticed trees and antique buildings, shiny cars and manicured window boxes filled with flowers — pink and blue and yellow. Stone apartment buildings — brown, red brick, white brick — grand awnings supported by 19th-century iron structures. I became aware of many men, obviously queer, walking along amongst the rest of the 'peopleing.' A fresh, surreal sight for my North Carolina eyes, where the police were still busy entrapping people for lesser things.

I was glued to the side window, hands folded over each other, chin on my arm looking out. Transfixed and scared to death. Thoughts of my grandmother shot in between the sights and beats of the city. Soon enough, the car came to a halt. As my anxiety increased, the driver said something like 'Hey man. This you? This where you want right?'

I came-to. '77 Perry Street?' He nodded yes. I looked around, nervous, afraid to get out until certain. I couldn't see anything that resembled a salon until I glimpsed a sign just above street level, beside a black wrought-iron staircase leading below. I paid the fare, got my bag out of the back. Followed the wrought-iron rails. The door opened, Seth was in there doing a client's hair. He greeted me and introduced me to Nina, the owner, and Marty Lipton, another hairdresser. Then I felt so relieved. I felt so, new. Marty gave me a warm smile. Marty was cute. But then again, I thought just about everybody was cute at that point. Marty looked kinda' like a cross between a young Al Pacino and John Cryer, bright white teeth and a million dollar smile. Nice. I could feel Seth and Marty's sissy giggles as they grinned at each other about my bug-eyed newness.

Stepping into that salon on Perry Street was like stepping into another time, another era. If felt smoother, like one I would like to have been born in — the time before machines and systems had completely conquered people. A scene Woody Allen would have seized upon. Exposed bricks that'd been darkened by time, unevenly crushed by the weight of the building above. Red furnishings. Black seats and counter tops. Painted tin ceilings with ornately pressed contours — the yellowing of time and hair bleach revealing the corners and crannies. A black and white checkered floor was illuminated by little incandescent spotlights pointing from all directions. Damn. To me this was New York — right out of Fierstein's movie.

Seth still had a couple of hours to go, but they made room under one of the waiting seats for my bags. Seth and Nina gave me a few hints of places to shop — Eighth Street for shoes, Broadway for clothes. I didn't really want to go anywhere, fearful of the great unknown. I wanted to watch them be New Yorkers. Marty Lipton chimed in with some more ideas on where to go.

I liked Marty from the start: he was a creature from my wild imagination... a queer who was only part queer. Nice shoulder-length black hair, combed back. No poofy lookin' hairdos like all the hair people I knew back home. He had on nice broken-in Levi's, the real ones before they started making them in rural China. Short-heeled cowboy boots, a worn dark t-shirt that showed off his muscular chest. A thick leather armband and big watch on his left forearm. Marty was the kind of guy who I'd probably have avoided in North Carolina. Queers didn't dress like that in North Carolina. People who beat them up did. Although I'd temporarily forgotten how to walk, talk and function in groups of two or more, I was loving every second of the Perry Street salon.

I think Seth gave me some aspirins and Marty gave me one of his sodas from the tiny refrigerator underneath a bookshelf which held hundreds of tubes of hair color. It all helped my throbbing head. They knew the feeling — everyone was brand-new at one point or another. I was an introverted social retard, especially by New York standards, but everything started in New York back then. Anything worth knowing about. I decided I had to try to cut the mustard. I acted like I understood what everyone was saying as they shouted directions at me over the roar of hair dryers. They didn't know my head was still spinning from the trip alone, the winding cab ride, and just being there.

Outside, Perry Street. I stood at the top of the wrought iron staircase and took my first official Manhattan steps onto Perry pavement. I could go left. I could go right. Neither mattered. Free. I wasn't on a holiday. I was here to figure out how to stay, if Lady Luck would let me. I wandered. People brushed past, blew past, cruised past — unaware that I'd begun my life-altering summer afternoon. The day was incredibly hot, but becoming a nice evening. The streets were oozing with boys. Everywhere. On the prowl. I got a lot of looks. I'd tried my best to blend in — but I stuck way out. Perhaps it was my homely-looking white Converse double-high top sneakers and Southern Comfort hairstyle which made me stick out like a naked Ken doll on a wedding cake. New meat. I knew a few things about things. In the south, I dodged the evil eye of God-fearing fag haters. Now, a plane ride later, I was dodging the horny eyes of fearless fags. Thank God. I hit a few stores on 8th Street — Doc Martens and shiny patent leather shoes with silver-capped toes galore. I'd seen the red stitching on some, yellow stitching on other feet all over town. When in Rome... I saw that I needed to make a ton of changes soon — my high tops just didn't work, but I kept going, shopping, wandering, looking, lusting. Walking around the same block over and over until I got so frustrated I stopped at a pay phone to call for directions. The West Village is not known for ease of navigation.

Later, I met back up with Seth at the salon, and he asked me if I wanted to go out for a drink. Was he kidding? Seth was not big on the queer scene, or any scene for that matter. He didn't bother keeping up with the Janes or Joneses, but was game to try and show me around. He took me to one of the oldest queer bars in the city, The Monster on Sheridan Square. He said it would be good because they had a regular bar upstairs and a dance club beneath and it was free to get in the dance club at happy hour. 'Is that OK?' Is that OK indeed. I was from fucking North Carolina, where the only place to go was that dilapidated old Scorpio which was only open late at night on the weekend. A drink in a popular bar open to the public on a weekday at 6:30pm? Like normal people? No question.

There was a big man Seth addressed as 'Sacha' at the door. Big wrestler-biker type. Bandana around his head, combat boots. Seth chatted with Sacha, I could already see that Seth liked to show off his connections to the city. Sacha let us in right away and I was immediately overwhelmed by the incredibly happy atmosphere: laughter, a bunch of guys gathered around a piano and singing, a celebration of chatting, talking & cruising — all, surprisingly, in plain view of the passers-by on the street through the glass windows surrounding the entire ground floor.

The place was properly decorated — no wood panel to be found. Brass fixtures, wooden bar, freshly painted walls. Huge flower arrangements at both ends. The place was on the corner so there were views of Grove Street as well as onto Sheridan Square, and further across to Christopher Street and the old Stonewall building where the raids and riots broke out. The view through the windows of the Monster was new for me, I'd never in been in a room full of queers that wasn't hidden away like a dirty little secret in a dirty little hole. Some say the riots were the start of gay liberation but I'd heard it was a combination of liberation and the fact that Judy Garland died the day before and the drag queens and dykes were spoiling for a fight, and the NYPD found one. Either way, if I'd been sitting in a raid, I'd have fought back too.

A while later we checked my bags and went down to the dance club. Free entry before 9PM. Hell, who needed to wait for 9? It filled up as soon as the doors opened. The music was loud and alive. Pretty good stuff. A thousand times better than anything I'd heard before. Some very queer, like 'It's Raining Men,' other songs were more middle of the road — almost everyone was dancing, or at least groovin.' Seth didn't dance, but watched me from a row of peopled barstools which lined a mirrored wall beside the dance floor.

I'd been aching for such a moment and a thousand more like it all my life. The dance floor is the only place I'd ever felt comfortable in public. I was a social misfit who talked either too much or not enough. Didn't know whether I was ever saying the right thing or wrong thing — in reality I'm actually shy, but force talk in all directions to try to cover it up.

I couldn't flirt for shit. I'd either give a guy some cheesy come-on line I'd heard in the movies or blurt out exactly what was on my mind, like 'let's get naked.' The latter usually worked best. But on the dance floor, I had moves. My time spent alone in my Mom's basement paid off. I'd watched the videos, seen the TV shows. I'd watched people. No need for talk when you can move as good or better than Madonna, are new in town and radiate the glow of the young.

How it works is one, two, three... the music takes you. The guy beside you knows from your moves if you like him. No matter if he can dance, when you can. Outsiders know the moment they're allowed to toddle into your personal space. I'd met all my boyfriends to date on the dance floor. I spoke the language. Girls know when you find them sexy by the way you move around them. And you make plenty of dance-floor friends, especially to certain songs. Songs that tell the stories that you both feel inside and out. Songs you share. Songs with words and a purpose. From the depths of old soul to the lament of top ten. You understand each other, and never, ever speak off the floor.

To do so would be to risk ruining a perfect relationship. One minute I'd find a tall Latin type with blue jeans and a black t-shirt on one side of me, a hot blond, Billy Idol type on the other. Everyone dancing and revolving around each other, our own pristinely coordinated choreography. Hands meeting but not touching, sets of hips finding a parallel then spinning back out. Faces orbiting each other, coming close, lips exchanging a hint of their steam.

Seth waited patiently and chatted with friends as I became lost in a sea of people. Then, 'Into the Groove' must have come on, and if my going berserk on the dance floor didn't give away my out-of-town depravity, my thrift-shop 1950s shiny jacket did. *And you can dance, for inspiration... come on...* Yes, Madonna, music can 'be such a revelation.' I watched myself in the mirror and noted how I differed from the others on the floor and planned how to take care of some of that, right away.

The music vibrated my arms higher than ever, my hips around more than I thought possible. I whipped into a frenzy. Not like when big queens come onto the floor trying to put on a ballet. But, hipper, more with it, more connected, sexy. I don't think I'd ever felt truly sexy before that moment. I don't think I'd ever considered that others could find me sexy. The crowd made room for me. Crowds make room for you if they like you. Some offer a smile, others share a move. And in 1988, it took more than just designer labels and good looks. You have to be 'down.' Down means not being up. A bank account might buy you friends, but it ain't gonna' buy you cool. I was down because I was new, looked it, and carried on anyway. Everything about me screamed 'just got here' — nothing matched, nothing fit in — but back before the yuppie invasions of the late 90s, real New Yorkers liked it when new people showed up. All aboard!

They knew why we'd come.

The DJ played on and on. It was only early evening and everyone was covered in sweat. Sometimes things like this can lead to something else, but not now. This time it was about the music. After one song ended we all stood for a second, exchanged a slight smile from the sides, retreated back to our corresponding corners. Seth asked me if I was having a good time. My face said it all. 'And it's only 8:30, girl!' We both laughed. I was astounded. Imagine that, not having to wait until the wee hours to have a little fun. I fell in love with the town all over again, for the thousandth time that day.

'Wanna go somewhere else?' Seth caught me off guard. Somewhere else? Else?? Obviously I knew there were other bars and places around, but my internal clock was still in the process of its release from small-town shackles. When you went out in suburbia, you usually stayed at one place. Not here. No car to fuss with. No worries about drunk driving or the Godsquad. No waiting around for a 'good crowd' to have fun with — here, you make your own fun. 'Sure, where?'

In those days the West Village had an overwhelming number of places to choose from and within a few days I'd try to hit them all. We got my bag out of coat check. Through the huge, plate-glass windows you could see a line of guys winding down the block waiting to get in. I'll never forget those windows: all on view, in broad dusklight, street-level. Kissing, singing, drinking, touching, cruising, carousing, laughing for all the world to see. Seth said goodbye to Sacha at the door. We walked up Christopher Street to Seventh Avenue and up to Greenwich Avenue, which looked extra cool to me. Lots of personality, the buildings more ornate than most. On the north side in the middle of the block was Uncle Charlie's. Along the way I was overwhelmed that the streets were full of people going this way and that, standing, talking, cruising, buying, window shopping, stumbling, dog-walking, strolling, yelling, taxi-hailing, eating, carrying, dancing, drugging, running, bus-waiting, looking, seeing — life. I'd never experienced so much life, especially after 6PM — life that was doing something besides going to the store or rushing home from work.

Just before going in, Seth explained that Uncle Charlie's wasn't a dance club but a video bar. I didn't care. I was still reeling from the fact that it was not even nine o'clock at night on a weeknight and we had a the choice of a packed dance club and a video bar to go to. And we would get there by strolling through the general public, so-called normal people. This was my kind of normal.

To me, Uncle Charlie's was a 'classy' place. Along with what I'd seen at The Monster, these joints didn't apologize. Brick walls, floor-to-ceiling windows in front. Nice air conditioning. Smoke eradicators. Three large rooms. Huge video screens. Robust sound system, not too loud — didn't have to be because of the quality. Two-for-one drinks. Not some barn hidden behind a rail station. Heaven. The sweat from my Monster dance was drying, my clothes returning to normal. The place was filled with older guys chatting younger. Younger chatting even younger. Men in suits. Guys in jeans. Boys in late-80s trendy wear mixing with guys who looked exquisitely plain — polo shirt and jeans. People were going this way and that, crossing all lines of class and status. Some were dripping in money, others just workin' people. Others would drip for money.

I would have been quite intoxicated had it not been for the dancing and my adrenaline. I felt freer than I'd ever felt in my life, and ready to waltz along, anywhere, with just about anybody. I fantasized about going to someone's apartment in one of the Village tenements, and relaxing on a big comfy New York sofa. The city wasn't even getting started yet, but I'd seen more in one day than in the previous three years and was exhausted and scene-drunk with it all. Although I didn't want to miss a minute of the human parade before me, after a few more drinks it was a relief when Seth said he was hungry. We went to the Tiffany Diner, which turned out to be another great place to people watch. The inside wasn't what I'd call 'Downtown New York,' it was decorated like a suburban motel stuck in 1982: pine green carpeting speckled with tan and mauve, pleather seats and matching green walls with angle-cut mirrors. Odd, but strangely appropriate.

After downing some burgers and a few dozen more people, we paid the check and walked back outside. I was excited by even more activity on the streets, the lively mix of ethnicities, and little did I know that I was standing in the epicenter of queer Americana. We ventured into the maze of the West Fourth Street subway station. Bazillion degrees of hot down there. We went down this stair and that, winding under big, black, heavy signs with white letters and colored alphabet circles for each train. Downtown, uptown, IRT, BMT, local, express became a blur of words. All I know is that Seth finally got on the D train. 'This is your train' Seth told me. My train.

It took almost an hour to get home. We stopped at each and every station, and at each I began to notice the peculiar lines of demarcation that govern New York. Most of the Asian people got out at Grand Street. The car emptied of black folks at Church Avenue and Beverley Road. We got out at Kings Highway. 'You're three stops from Coney,' Seth tells me. C-o-n-e-y I-s-l-a-n-d seeped through my sticky, overloaded brain. We walked up three long blocks to Ocean Avenue. The people seemed different there. Harder. After we'd crossed over the bridge from Manhattan I was sure I wasn't going to be in the New York I'd seen in films, although I hadn't yet fully discovered Woody Allen's films either.

Kings Highway isn't on the tourist maps. The bricks that make up the buildings are darker, a dried blood color stained with soot, gathered by a white stone trim. The streets are larger than in Manhattan. A wide lawn of grass separates the coming and going sides down the entire length of nearby Ocean Parkway, with benches running along the sides. I've never encountered people just sitting in the middle of traffic. Exposed. Baby strollers. Kids tossing balls around. Chassidic men, dressed in black suits and brimmed hats, talking among themselves. Their wives, wrapped in long sleeves, standing nearby. A few Latin guys in brightly colored t-shirts sitting up on the back of the benches, watching the people in the passing cars. Old men playing chess.

We arrived at Seth's building, '2233 Ocean Avenue between Quentin and R, don't forget that. From the city a cab will cost ya twenty-five bucks,' he informed me studiously. We walked into a cream-toned foyer with white trim. Semi-ornate tile work on the floor, plaster floral patterns surround the light in the center of the ceiling. 'Nice,' I said. 'Oh they all look like this. Very middle class. It's clean at least,' he mumbled. 'Jay is a good landlord...' We climbed up flight after flight of stairs. I was wheezing and suddenly very aware I was a smoker. This wasn't the South, where you drive your car to visit the neighbor next door.

Seth opened the door onto a long hallway. The place was painted aqua green and smelled like paint, putty and the day's humid, leftover air. The scent mingled with a lemon-like aroma coming from the kitchen, toilet bowl blue from the bathroom, used candles from the living room, where he pointed for me to put my things. 'The couch is yours dear' he said as he continued back to his bedroom. He took a minute in there. I didn't mind. Touring is tiring. Touring people around is more tiring. The couch looked more appealing than Timanrichard's hotel room. He had the usual assortment of stuff — wooden coffee table, bookshelves, a three-year-old TV, video cassette player. The couch was dark camel-tan. A black halogen floor lamp stood in a corner. Pretty normal. The black and white tiles in the bathroom matched the ones my Grandma had back home. Familiar. I relax. 'I got seltzer… orange and lime I believe, want some?' 'Sure.' I'd never heard of flavored seltzer before. More new. More good.

We spent what was left of the evening in front of the television, and Seth entertaining a host of my curious questions about the city. I could feel the energy of the Boroughs pulsating around me, through me, with daydreams back to Perry Street, the Hair Place, and Sheridan Square. At some point, my mind calmed for sleep. I love to pay attention to the intricate noises a new place makes just before you drift off, mingled with the color of the lights from outside the window —sometimes cars passing and making a shape on the ceiling, sometimes the moon reaching over, projecting the indigo blur of night.

The next morning, I was awakened by what must be an increase in the hum of the traffic, and the eight million people reaching for their orange juice at tables throughout the city around me. The sound reminded me of going to the symphony, when the head violinist comes in and plays an 'A' for everyone to tune their instruments to. At first the sound is soft, but then the entire orchestra picks it up — strings, horns, flutes, everyone down to the tympani, in unison for a moment. Then, suddenly everyone breaks into other notes and phrases, and the entire place rises into a fluttering chaos.

I didn't want to miss a note. Seth wasn't awake yet. I was determined not to be one of those everybody-has-to-do-the-same-thing-all-the-time guests, so I left him alone. He'd said he had clients that afternoon. 'What a life! Clients!' I thought as I turned on the TV. Mostly typical morning stuff — cartoons, a news show with Ed Koch fighting for his political life. I'd noticed

Seth wore a 'DUMP KOCH' button. I'd always thought Koch was a cool mayor from the outside looking in, but Seth explained to me that he was a self-hating closet queen who kept an apartment on Fifth Avenue by Washington Square Park for screwing young guys.

When Seth woke up he asked me if I was hungry. The night before, he told me about a friend of his who lived upstairs who was looking for a roommate. Her name was Marilyn and he'd arranged for us to get together for brunch. Brunch! After a shower and a change of clothes, I followed Seth out into the bright, hot sunshine of Ocean Avenue. Neneh Cherry's 'Buffalo Stance' blasted through windows of passing cars. We backtracked toward the train station from the night before. I wasn't sure if we were going to have to take my D train to meet Marilyn or what. One good thing about being completely lost is being completely lost. I didn't have to think, just follow.

Seth stopped in front of a narrow building entrance and opened a door. A big sign hung above the door with fancy pink neon letters: Minerva's. Okay, this must be it. We walked in. The place had brick walls on either side, with a 1950s multi-colored stone floor. Tables in the middle, booths on the side divided by textured gold-yellow plastic extending up from the seatbacks on an aluminum frame. Seth passed the waitress who's about to try to seat us. He didn't give her a notice. She didn't care. I loved it.

He plopped into a booth just down the aisle, where a woman with freshly made red hair and red lipstick sat. A thin woman, shorter than most. Five-foot-three-ish. Mid-fifties or so. Her accent reminded me of Anne Bancroft in another scene from Fierstein's movie. 'Huh-eye, I'm Marilyn' she said, 'no-oice to meet-chou. Seth's told me a lot about-chou.' After exchanging pleasantries and checking each other out, the waitress came by and said, 'Kwoiffee?' Marilyn began to order her brunch like she would for the next ten years, and had for the twenty before that: 'two eggs over, toast and bacon... burn it.' I had something similar. Seth had kwoiffee and toast. Seth and Marilyn chattered like reminiscing school kids — stories about this person and that one, Marty and Nina and Jim at the hair salon, Jay the landlord, people. She asked me about where I was from, what I wanted to do in New York, and so on, speaking in a high-pitched, jovial staccato. After a while, in a clean non sequitur, Marilyn announced that she thought I was 'OK' and that I could stay with her. 'You can rent the middle room. Two-fifty a month. One up front. Plus gas, electric and phone. OK?' I hadn't the slightest clue what I was agreeing to. And I didn't care.

I spent the afternoon coasting the streets of Manhattan, and letting them adopt me.

8. Power of Goodbye

The next day I spoke to Timanrichard on the phone, and arranged to meet up with the old Charlotte crowd. They were planning a big night out after probably spending the past two days beating the ground thin under every department store in Manhattan. I was happy to miss the excitement. They were better than me at something back in Charlotte, but for the first time ever I had an edge on them: I was staying in a real house in New York City. Meeting locals. I didn't even realize I'd crossed an enormous spiritual bridge, putting miles between us. I went up to their hotel room. The place looked different now. Less impressive. My head was back on Kings Highway. Perry Street. Minervas, kwoiffee and burnt bacon. That was more New York to me than Times Square. The air hung hot from blow dryers and smelled of thick cologne.

Once outside, we hailed a cab and went to Soho to some fancy restaurant one of them picked on West Broadway. There wasn't but one other table of people when we got there around 9PM. Just like at Christ Cella all those years before with Dad, I studied the waiters. This time there was only a few. The looks on their faces told our little group's story. I remember black shiny walls and more pink and mauve decorations — apparently we'd come all the way to New York to sit and eat in a funeral parlor.

By 11 we'd finished and, after the rest of the group over-chatted the waitress and fretted about dividing up the bill, we went to a bar down the street for drinks. I couldn't help but feel our timing was off — like we were catching the remnants of an after-work party in a place otherwise filled with wide-eyed tourists. Around 1AM we got a taxi to a nightclub called Mars on the West Side Highway. Supposed to be the hot spot. We walked briskly up to the ropes and people standing underneath a display of red fluorescent lights that were hung in all directions on the face of the building up to the roof. The doorman gave our motley little over-dressed hair crew the once over. We're made to wait while he lets regulars in. Finally we're allowed in and once inside, I am again completely overwhelmed. People packed to the rafters. The only way around is to push and push hard. My group gets an attitude on. Strutting attitude. Probably because of their fancy new clothes or something. Somehow, big surprise, I got left behind. I didn't yet know the rhythm of preening through a crowd of fabulous. I fought my way to the bar and got a drink, broke away and tried to find a place to dance, look, and size the place up. I was good on a dance floor, but wasn't quite ready for this kind of intense, drugged-up crowd. Truth be told, it was probably what I'd soon learn was 'Bridge and Tunnel Trash.' The weekend warriors. People busy fronting New York.

I attempted to make room for myself in a corner of the main first-level dance floor. Some obnoxious looking queen with long black hair, big face and some ridiculous furry outfit didn't like this and proceeded to stomp all over me. I moved away some so as not to try to confront. The queen did it again. I'll never forget the nasty look on its face. All of a sudden the big oaf spun around and landed right on my foot. The next time he shoved my drink went everywhere. All over her-him I hoped. All over me for sure. I left before anything escalated. New in town: odd man out.

Thing was, I bet he was as 'B&T,' 'bridge-and-tunnel,' as I was. Probably Jersey.

Way in a back corner behind a sea of wildly gyrating dancers, I got caught up in a staircase leading up to a small attic sort of room absolutely crammed with more people. The music up there was better, and they all seemed drunker, so I was able to find myself a spot. Little did I know I'd wandered into the VIP room. There were black lights illuminating the room from above so everyone's skin looked grayish, teeth gleaming white except for spots of dental work. A few boys were dancing in their underwear, which glowed bright white to match their incisors. I guess I'm weird in these situations, but all I could think of was 'where did they put their clothes? Surely they didn't come like that…' I reached to one of the walls for support as the massive crowd swelled and leaned and bumped to and fro. The walls were dripping with sweat. After a few songs, I came to the realization that I wasn't ever going to get a handle on New York, it would have a handle on me. My brain began to swell with all the flashing sights, sounds, and the beautiful people — boys, everywhere. My eyes liberated me from a life of unmitigated conservatism, and I began to see the light. At one point the music paused between songs for no reason, and as matter-of-fact as factory workers on a shift break, everyone stopped, sighed and had a quick glance around the room before getting back at-it once the music fired up again. At that point I decided to plop like a blob of warm red jello back out the door and into the stairwell, satisfied that I'd just gotten more dance floor action in a half hour than in a whole string of Saturdays down South, and still had all night to go. Drenched from head to toe and somehow still carrying my empty drink cup for security, I explored the different levels of Mars until one of the hallways opened into a lounge area with a pool table where the Charlotte trio had set up shop. I remember

Timanrichard and Eddie trying to look more comfortable than the rest of the crowd — cooler, sitting back, being fabulous in their flowing outfits and all. I sauntered over, tipsy from the shots I'd done earlier. The mood was strange, like I didn't know how to act around them. In my mind I'd rejected everything they were and were from, and was already a native, although I couldn't find my own way home. 'What happened to you?' Tim said while cutting his eyes and laughing to the others. I decided not to answer. I wasn't in Charlotte anymore — desperate for friends and interaction. I had new friends in Brooklyn, and whoever upstairs had been groping me. I didn't answer Tim because what was happening to me was fantastic, even being stomped by the monster queen. And smashed in the attic room with a hundred other hot, sweaty bodies of all shapes and sizes. And meeting Marty Lipton and Marilyn. It was all unfolding as it should.

I knew when to leave, and not become a left-over. Time to go. What none of the Charlotte crowd knew was that I'd flunked out of my first attempt at college in Dallas on E at Stevie Nicks and Grace Jones' Starck Club. And although I knew a few things, Seth had me paranoid about getting mugged, and he'd gone on & on about how the trains were 'a horror' at night. Seth was peculiar and sometimes his accent varied, and if I'd known his real story — that he'd come to New York City only a few years before me, a fellow former-Southerner and graduate of West Charlotte High School — and that his New York native was as contrived as anyone else's, I might have relaxed a little.

Instead I took my D train to DeKalb Avenue in Brooklyn, then splurged for a cab to Ocean Avenue and took in some steely outer borough air.

Phweeee. The coffee kettle whistles from the kitchen. You drop your face for a moment to go pour a cup of instant energy, although it isn't as pleasant as it seems. You really should be asleep. You really should be doing a million other things. But as you sip the acidic black concoction and your heart begins to race, you remind yourself that 'should' has never fit well into your vocabulary. Nothing worth having ever came from 'should.' You found your way to New York in spite of family guilt and everyone else's personal relationship with our lord and savior. Now, you must satisfy the daemon, and immerse yourself in that which cannot be spoken, even found anyplace else. 'Mondo Trasho' as Mr. Waters calls it. 'Outcast among outcasts' according to Mr. Schmidt. 'Ambiguity 'according to Ms. Karen Finley. 'Should' — according to no one who's ever done anything with the chore we call life.

9. Lead, Follow, or Leave.

Late May, 1988. Charlotte was over for me. The long arm of the Right Wing was choking out whatever remnants of original Southern charm the place had left. Banks, strip malls and poorly planned housing developments, yuppies, jogging shoes. Progress. I quit the job at Belk's, just in time too: some new jackass had taken over as store manager and was sneaking around and threatening people. I said goodbye to family, friends. Seems like I tried to talk Smyre into making the move as well, and in return he'd tried to talk me into hanging tight at Grandma Ruby's 'You might just end up with something over there if you'd wait a while…' he said, referring to her house. No-could-do. I put everything I owned in a big yellow rental van that rattled when it hit potholes to drive north treating my return trip like one of my swimming races when I was a kid: jump in, head down, not a breath until I crashed into the other side.

My sister Adrienne cried when I said goodbye to her and Mom standing on their front porch, as our reflections bounced off the windows leading to the basement where I'd spent my teenage years. My last stop before the interstate was Grandma Ruby's. Chills shot up and down my spine as I entered that familiar house as a local for the very last time — the familiar aromas of baked bread and vegetables in the kitchen. My dog Henry jumping up on the back door to look in and watch me and Grandma talk. Even Grandma was acting more formally, holding the door as I came in and after I left. Right now I'd give just about anything for even a minute with Miss Ruby — I can still feel her delicate hug before I stepped down the red brick walkway to the van; one last wave and smile.

As I made the right turn off Medford Drive onto Central Avenue, my emotions overwhelmed me. All I'd prayed for was happening yet I felt like I would collapse at any second. But I couldn't — I knew it and everyone in my life knew it. I sat at the intersection of Central and Eastway Drive, waiting for the traffic light to turn. I'd cursed that light for being painfully slow a thousand times, but on that occasion was grateful for every extra second. To my left was Eastway Jr. High, where I'd spent two of the best years of my schooling; further across town was Scorpios. To my right was Garinger High, and Charades, the bar Smyre and I went to… my memories stepped on each other carelessly.

I drove for about seven hours and stopped for the night somewhere near Philadelphia. I loved the feeling that everything that was me was in that van, and I could easily put down anywhere, but would settle for nothing less than a city named after a fruit. In my room, I ate from a packed lunch box Grandma had made for me, with all my favorites — chicken diván, baked biscuits, some fresh yellow squash. As familiar continued to fade, I arrived the next day in the Big Apple. On a Sunday.

I came in through the Holland Tunnel, and somehow got completely caught up in Manhattan in the middle of the Puerto Rican Pride parade. The good thing about New York is that it's one big checkerboard and you can only go in one of four directions. After a long wait to cross Fifth Avenue somewhere along West Twelfth Street, all I knew instinctively was to head east. From there I found my way to the FDR Drive and onto the

Manhattan Bridge, straight into Brooklyn. Somehow I got turned around on the other side, and went round and round some deserted cobblestoned areas under the bridge, Red Hook they call it, but eventually twisted and maneuvered my way to Ocean Parkway. Eventually, I made it to 2233 Ocean Avenue, my new home — this time to Marilyn's apartment on the top floor. I spent the dusk and early evening of my first night on the roof, looking at the lights, switching from each direction — this way and back. Nothing's ever looked so promising, so silvery sweet, so unconquerable, tempting and exciting. I could taste freedom riding on the evening breeze, mingled with the scent of greasy Chinese food and car exhaust. Damned if I'd look back, but it was tempting. I'd run out of Grandma's food, and was on my own, with no obligations and nowhere to be but right there, doing nothing, held in place only by an unfamiliar night sky.

10. Get Your Motor Runnin'

So I began to sail into June in my new neighborhood, which Seth sometimes called Sheepshead Bay. Others called it Kings Highway, because of the main subway stop, 'two away from Brighton Beach, three from Coney.' All I knew was that it was now my place to live and connected by rails to Manhattan. While I still had the yellow rental van, Seth and a friend of his named Alisa talked me into a joyride. One evening we piled in and started toward the Brooklyn Promenade. I noticed some inconsistencies with Seth — directions, neighborhood names — but I went along. I was unnerved by traffic in New York, mainly because of the idea of it in my head. I'd never parallel parked in my life, so when attempting to back a large Chevy moving van into a space at the promenade, I punched the gas pedal once too hard, smashing into a parked car behind me, producing the unmistakable sound of breaking headlights and scraping metal. Seth had supposed to have been looking out, and telling me how far I was from the spot. He claimed he was checking out some guy walking down the street and forgot. Some guy on a front porch started yelling and I panicked. 'What do I do!?' I screamed.

'Go!' Seth shouted, 'Honey, you're in New York now! GO!' with Alisa joining in. So, with the Fine Young Cannibals' 'She Drives Me Crazy' blasting on the radio, I raced forward — my first hit-and-run. I was shaking, and thought of the poor person who owned the car I'd smashed, but thought more about getting beaten up by the guy on the porch, and that the NYPD would surely find me. The next day, I returned the rental van, which also had acquired a large parking ticket, to the Brooklyn dealer, and haven't heard a peep about it since. Everybody gets 'one.'

Marilyn's apartment was small, but OK. Same building as Seth's, top floor. She was a divorcée from Upstate New York. Middletown. I liked Marilyn, as far as she was likable. She was artsy, craftsy, somewhat motherly — at least sympathetic to someone who'd packed up everything and moved in the span of a few weeks. I didn't, however, like the fact that I hadn't been told Marilyn's boyfriend Johnny, a middle-aged hardcore alcoholic painter, came with the deal. For him, beer was breakfast, vodka was lunch. More vodka was dinner. He meant well. He tried to be friendly. But I didn't want his friendly. His friendly stuck to me and his breath smelled like rotting cantaloupes. Friendly meant 'setting upon you' as Grandma Ruby used to say, talking incessantly, stammering, and the drunker he got, the louder and slurrier and needier he became, and the hotter and stinkier his breath got. He'd play Pink Floyd and ramble on for hours about art and passion and feelings — working himself up into a bumbling excitement and working harder and harder to get consensus and agreement from me and Marilyn, or whoever was around.

In the evenings there was a lot of talk about shared property, and community time, and living arrangements, which basically meant I would get little or no privacy. Like a typical first-time tenant, I'd brought everything but the kitchen sink from down south, including an area carpet from Grandma Ruby's. I sectioned off the living room as best I could, and hung a large drape to create a barrier between my bed and the walkway, but nothing short of an electric fence and concrete would keep Johnny at bay. I didn't like Marilyn's cat either, which she called Zoomee. Johnny must have picked the thing up out of the gutter on a stagger home one night. Zoomee was a cat of the variety most Americans know as 'alley.' All it wanted was back outside. Hence, it destroyed everything it could get its sharp claws into. Including my arms and legs. Determined not to be fussed by Johnny or the felonious feline, I took to throwing it. I thought Zoomee would look great implanted on Johnny's face, like in the movies, 'Alien' style.

One particularly hot night I desperately needed something... to get out, get laid... party. Call of the wild. New York City was capitulating right under my nose and I was stuck in a sticky apartment with a cat and a belligerent drunk under a hot tar roof. There was another guy around in Manhattan I knew from North Carolina, named John. John and I had nothing in common back home except a boy named Tommy we'd both dated. Another good reason for leaving. Somehow I'd gotten John's number. So, with Johnny in full stammering tilt, Marilyn following him around arguing and Zoomee racing from her demons, I called John. He seemed happy to speak. He lived in the Village somewhere. He'd landed a little more centrally than me.

John was my age, early twenties, and tall. Like 6'3. Natural blonde. Hairless. Smooth. And a boy or guy. Not a man. Men are chiseled. Or burly. Or have too many features out of control. Boys are soft and pretty. Not to be confused with adolescent males. They are children in queer terms, not boys. Some can maintain a boyhood up to thirty and beyond. For others, hands of fate twist and turn around twenty-five or so. John was lucky in some ways, he'd stay a boy a long time.

'Hey, you made it!' he said through the pre-cordless telephone. 'How's everything with your place?'

'Well, it's OK. Marilyn…'

'Is she your roommate?'

'Yeah. She's nice but it's a little crowded. There's this…' I sailed into the story of Johnny. I hadn't yet realized that everyone in New York had their own tragic roommate story of some kind or another. Ask any New Yorker about their first living situation and you'll get a doozey of a tale.

'Uhm, sorry to cut you off but I'm getting ready to go out. Wanna come?'

'Where?'

'Out. Nevermind — you won't know it anyway. Meet me at…'

I put on my best clothes. I had no sense of NY style. I was nervous. I knew I was going to stick out, so I went for plain. Like jeans and a black t-shirt. I could play Joe Dean from Podunk. At least I had a fifty-fifty chance. I met John somewhere in the Village. Seth had kept putting the fear of God into me about the subways at night. And everything else for that matter. But I made the hour journey including the wait time. Seth'd been so busy telling me about all the muggings that he'd forgotten to tell me how to take the faster train. I stood, waiting on a D train, as three Q express trains whooshed by me.

'We've got to go, some friends are meeting us there.'

'Where?' Why I trusted him, I don't know. I would've trusted anybody at that moment. I figured the worst it could get was a tacky queer bar. Anything was better than that hot apartment on Ocean Avenue.

We got into a taxi. It flew up the avenues. I had no idea where I was and for the first time I just didn't try to notice. Instead, I watched the city unfold around me. The buildings, people, cars and noise. It truly never slept back then. Never stopped. Without warning we pulled over. John led me out of the cab and up the block, where a huge crowd was formed outside a club. Clubs in

New York were not like back home. They were part of the city. Part of the people. Not some shamefully hidden-away barn behind a burger shack. 'What's this place?' I asked. When you are new, strange, a stranger, you don't have the vocabulary. A lucid where-are-we becomes a rigid probe about 'place.' 'It's called M-K.' 'OK,' I think. That sure told me a lot. I was trying not to give off the lost-puppy vibe as best I could. I wished I'd have had enough confidence not to be skiddish. I'd seen other people be new quite successfully — allowing it to become charming. But that night, I couldn't.

12:30AM. As we approached the entrance of MK or whatever it was, John didn't boldly run up to the doorman, but he didn't get in a line either. This was my first experience with big New York City club doors. The people lined up around the ropes were just out for the night. They would get in eventually. They were customers. Apparently, we non-line people were somebody else. We had something to prove. Not waiting in lines meant something. I didn't want to stand with line people, but what I did realize in that split second was that they had the best vantage point. They got to watch some of the comings and goings during their wait. They could enjoy the clear, hot summer stars mingling with the city lights, or the people passing the whole affair, on their way home with a lover or midnight groceries. My mind danced around the people scene.

'How many?' The big doorman had made his way demurely over to John. He was a tall, thin black man, with dark sunglasses and headphones on. I think John called him by name, the kind of approach you give when you are the friend of someone important. 'Two,' John said, getting no endearing response while pointing back to me. 'OK.' The man opened the ropes. We went in. The place was jam-packed with people. Totally overwhelming. Like a real Hotel California. Music so loud my thoughts vanished. Boom, boom. The beats. The crowd. The loud. I only saw this size of a party mob once before back home, on an unusual, long holiday weekend. There wasn't more than a half-foot of personal space. The ceiling of the front room was vaulted up two stories, with a crowded balcony. Everyone looks sparkly. Shiny. Pretty girls and boys everywhere. Outfits of the highest calibre. Drag queens and characters and costumes everywhere. Not boogers. One had a blue Victorian dress and full makeup, with bird cage on its head, complete with live canaries. Others range from rock realness to baroque ballroom. There are queer boys and straight boys, and girls everywhere. John made our way to the bar and ordered drinks. For some unknown reason I asked for scotch. Homemade signs hung along the walls with 'Birthday BOY!' written all over them. 'What's the occasion?' I asked with my clumsy vernacular. 'Oh, didn't I tell you? It's Boy George's birthday party. Welcome to New York!' He handed me my drink and pulled me back, deep into a crowd, in a direction opposite the exit doors. A party promoter called Lee Chappell was throwing the party to celebrate the video release of 'Don't Take My Mind on a Trip.'

Damn. Boy f-ing George. My mind was on more than a trip. In my list of celebrities, he was certainly not on top, but this was here, now, and I played along. Where is he? I wondered. John took us back to a single spiral staircase that led to an overwhelmingly crowded basement. The dance floor. No room for big dancing, just sophisticated moving. Cocktail in hand. I turned my back to John a couple of times to watch a tall, thin guy dancing with the crowd. The moves were new to me — quick, but deliberate and interchangeable. A conversation. Moving mannequins. One would raise a hand and turn, while the other responded with a half twist, ending with a hand on a hip. It was aggressive, loud, but tempered with something colloquial.

Something in common. John, noticing my focus on the couple, pulls me close to him and says discretely in my ear 'Vogueing.'

'Vogey?' I shout back, too loudly.

'Vogue-ING.' John's free hand began to guide me, without commitment. New York was burning.

A few songs and quite a few drinks later, the music stopped. Showtime? Like I'm used to? No. Thank God. A queen dressed as Boy comes out, high on a big block. 'Do You Really Want to Hurt Me' playing. The queen lip synched and danced to only half the song, then the dance music started up again. 'Boy George must be coming out soon,' I awkwardly say in the pause between the loud. John gives me a scolding look, as if I've uttered my limit of awkward for the evening. But what's a birthday party with no birthday Boy? I overheard someone saying he'd been arrested for drugs in the UK, and wasn't allowed in the country. How strange it seemed: a birthday without its boy — the show must go on. Any excuse for a party. New York.

John and I danced a good while longer. I was happy with this. I didn't have to talk. I could tell he was a tad exasperated with dragging along a wide-eyed newbie. I watched my moves and learned new dances from people around me. Everyone was refreshingly different, each in their own groove. Later, we moved off to the side, where some of his girl friends met us. Talkative Long Island types as I recall — long brown hair, girly bright makeup, skirts and sandals — not unlike Theresa who I'd met at Heartbreak on my trip with Dad a few years earlier. They were busy discussing about where we'd go next. Next?— It was getting really late. It was a weeknight. Seth had me petrified of the trains. Not many choices for a barely not out of towner. Would John let me crash at his place? No money for cab fare — I followed their chatter.

Outside, the air felt great. It was as if we'd been kept working in a tenement sweatshop and just finished our shift, very in-and-out. The night had undergone a transition while we'd been inside, from a crisp suggestion of early evening to a dense curtain of pure night. The girls hailed a taxi, and gave the driver an address. This cab went twice as fast as the one before. Whisk this way, jerk and turn that way. My swimming drunk head went with it. I glanced at the speedometer. 40-50-60-something mph. We slammed to a stop on some block in some other neighborhood. I thought of Malcolm McLaren's phrase: 'deep in the city' — a romantic lyric I'd been saving for just such an occasion. I followed the group through an alley and up a metal staircase mounted on the side of a building.

Knock knock. Knock-knock-tap. A door opened. We were greeted by some guy with a thick accent.

Inside, there were a few other people sitting around in a cloud of smoke. All acted very high. No one from our group spoke directly to any of the others. Odd I thought. Our host disappeared into the bedroom with one of the two girls. No music was on, that I remember. I didn't like it there. 'Having fun?' John asked, trying to break the icy indifference in the room. I decided not to be revealed as the new guy at this little shindig, so I bitchily responded 'I was…' Nothing in New York like a little bit of honest attitude to ruin a perfectly good coke deal.

John actually looked relieved. One of the chatty girls struck up a conversation with one of the high-guys after emerging from the bedroom, more perky and alert. She displayed no intention of leaving without her friend, who was either fucking our host, or doing lines with him in the other room. Or fucking him for lines in the other room.

From my Dallas days, Starck Club to be precise, I was already well aware that cocaine is the nastiest of all drugs. It divides people upon arrival into haves and have-nots; wants and want-nots. At least with alcohol people seem to get belligerent together. People on ecstasy want sex. Heck, even junkies want to cuddle. Cokeheads don't want nothin' or nobody but more coke. They can't even dance good on it. Thankfully, John was a want-not. We sat there in silence. I started to go from pleasantly tipsy to tired and bored. I could have been back in North Carolina, or anywhere, sitting around a living room with a bunch of fucked-up losers chewing their upper lips. 'Can we go now?' I asked one more time. Just needing out of that stinking apartment. White walls, bright lighting and no decoration. Student housing. I couldn't breathe.

'Yeah sure.' Thank God. Relief. John reached over to the one girl who'd come back from the bedroom and tells her we're leaving. She put on a phony smile and manners. 'Bye, thanks!' I returned the half-hearted effort as I wasted no time in getting on the other side of the green metal door. The fresh air cleared my head. The lights were still glittering. We can continue.

'I know what we can do, come on,' John says, leading me down the stairs. Apparently he, too, is trying to shake off the stale air from the scene we'd just escaped. He looked this way, then that, trying to figure out where he was. The girls had given the directions to our next stop on the way down. It was at this point I realized that having moved here six months before me did not make John a full-fledged New Yorker. Like Seth, he too was winging it on a few fronts. I felt more confident. He hailed another cab and told the driver, '1st and First.'

11. Greener, No Grass.

We got to First Street and First Avenue in a hurry. The cab driver wanted his money in another hurry. Throngs of people were marauding up and down the avenue. It was probably 3:30AM on a Wednesday and to me the scene looked like midnight on a Saturday. Fantastic. John pulled me toward the door of another place, Cave Canem. It was the remains of what used to be a gay bathhouse, turned club. Not far from or unlike the St Mark's Baths, just a few blocks away, where Bette Midler started her career. We ducked through the front door. Inside, the scene was curiously erratic. About ten guys were hanging out at a long bar. Remnants from parties all over the city. Torn costumes, running makeup, drowsy heads. A few young cuties scampered around. One was wearing nothing but a pair of wet, white underwear. John sees me eyeing him. 'Be careful of that one,' he says. The boy caught my eye, gives me a wink, and without letting go makes a bee-line for me. 'Hi, want some Quaaludes?' Before I can answer, he shoves the tip of a bottle of Jägermeister to my lips and tips it up. I have no choice. I didn't care at that point. I was happy to have some new attention, albeit through Jaeger and Ludes on top of cheap scotch.

Little did I know I'd just been given club communion by the soon-to-be-notorious Michael Alig. John took me by the hand

and started us downstairs, somewhat protectively. We enter a basement room with only a few boys in it. There's some thankfully easy music playing from a small system in the corner. In the middle of the floor is a sunken concrete pool. Barely a hot-tub in reality. The water looked murky and dirty. Nearby was a cute young man, wet from head to toe. Cuter and wetter than anyone I'd met in North Carolina. His white underwear betrayed him as he smiled as if to say 'come on in' and started frolicking around to make it look more fun.

All of a sudden I was up on my beautiful balloon. Alig's Quaaludes packed a punch. John and I leaned on each other as we climbed the steps. I think. Outside, the scene had calmed to a dull roar. Daylight was about to threaten an appearance in the east. John got me into a cab and back to his place. Suddenly I was out of my clothes. Suddenly I was under the covers. Suddenly John was on top of me. Suddenly John pushed me away to the far side of the bed. About an hour later, I was awakened by John's alarm clock.

I tried to ignore the clock. Surely John had nowhere to be. Surely. I was feverishly ill, my head was on fire, my skinny young body trembled. 'Get up. You have to go. I have school.' Still I ignored him and the clock until he forced me up. He was acting very anxious. Could it be that he's just had no sleep? Or maybe he's still drunk. Maybe he took an indiscretion too many with me, and wanted to shirk the responsibility that came with it.

Dizzy, and with the room spinning, I sprang on my feet and fell towards the bathroom puking my guts out. With every surge my head pounded harder. I tried to be quiet. If I'd had a couple of hours to sleep a bit more of it off things probably wouldn't be so bad. But No, Mr. Asshole had to go to school. God forbid. As soon as my retching stopped for a second, John started hurrying me more. Somehow I got my clothes back on and somehow I was out on the street. John walked me, holding my arm like a kid, to the West Fourth Street train station. 'Here's your train, I gotta run, I'm late' he said. I hate you. I always hated you, I thought. He wouldn't look at me. He just left me there with nothing but a piece of advice ringing in my ears: 'You have to have a reason for coming to New York.'

As I stepped down into the stuffy, smelly train station, the stifling heat boiled up from below. It was summer, and already 85 degrees or so at 10AM. I was sweating profusely. I needed to vomit. I got all the way down to the bottom platform. The trains rattled through the station. Their brakes screeched through my head. Two or three Q express trains whooshed in and out, which could've gotten me back to Marilyn's faster. But I waited for my D, the local train, as instructed. The air conditioning was barely working. I tried to sit up and play like nothing was wrong. The loud signal bells penetrated my eardrums. Ding, dong. People stared at me. A woman across from me blanked an expression. I figured they all knew, so f-it I thought as I leaned my head forward into my lap and then onto the seat next to me until the train got into Brooklyn. The long trip of starts and stops out to Kings Highway made me almost pray for death.

DeKalb Ave. Atlantic Ave. Seventh Avenue. Prospect Park. Church Avenue. Beverly Road. Cortelyou Road. Avenue H. Avenue J. Avenue M. Kings Highway.

With each acceleration came the urge to scream. Each abrupt stop — the urge to puke. Start. Stop. In a car the trip took fifteen minutes. On the train — anywhere from thirty to an hour. Finally I arrived, and staggered up to 2233 Ocean Avenue, then dragging myself up the four flights of steps and fell on the couch — relieved just to lie still, before the surges came. I locked Zoomee the cat in Marilyn's bedroom, and proceeded to fill the toilet bowl with yellow. My entire body winced in pain. My head had never hurt so bad. But I didn't regret it too much. Deep inside I held the feeling of liberation. I could have it, apparently, whatever it was in that city, that New York. I imagined each cramp in my stomach and burning surge up my esophagus was some little due I was paying. Earning my badge of New Yorker.

I'd learn this lesson a few times before it sunk in. Another happy New York morning a homeless man caught me unaware that others could see me sulking. 'HOLD YOUR HEAD UP!' he shouted and winked at me. He'd probably given me everything he had.

12. Makin' It, Moses, Macy's

Take the 'N,' the 'e,' and the 'Y' out of 'New York' and what's left? 'w-o-r-k.' I'd left North Carolina with about seven hundred dollars. Marilyn got three hundred when I arrived. I'd spent one-fifty on the trip. The rest is just math.

I took a first job at Lord & Taylor, beside St Patrick's Cathedral. Miles from Kings Highway. I knew exactly the lines to say in the interview, and that they'd love an innocent looking kid with a Southern accent and with retail experience — they put me on in the men's dress shirt department. Old men to be precise, and their wives, and tourists: stupid tourists with no intention of buying anything; or stupid tourists simply aching to buy something. During the training classes I sat staring out the window at Saint Patrick's Cathedral while listening to the things I already knew: add-on selling, enter your salesperson number here, no returns without a receipt. They used those crappy IBM cash registers which were slow as Christmas and only aggravated clerk and customer alike. All things I'd come to New York City to get away from. In hindsight, I wish I'd gone and bussed some tables for money, or swept some floors. Or anything besides that, what I'd been doing back home.

The only redeeming thing about my sales job in North Carolina had been my commissions. If I worked hard, I got paid.

But hopes of a fair deal had long flitted away on the tip of Ronnie Reagan's tongue. Labor in America had begun its slow, downward spiral. Praise from your boss had become 'performance assessments.' Good sales totals were now 'performance realizations.' Sales people were now 'sales associates.' Personnel, 'Human Resources.' The newest trend in fashion was to offer a low hourly wage, with the promise of 'productivity increases' according to the 'associate's performance realization level.' Translation: we got screwed, they got rich. I was barely making my rent, and had no real chance of getting ahead no matter how hard I worked.

I sent my resume to a head hunter who got me a job at Sotheby's. Same little money but lots of art and nice people — eventually. At first I worked for this neurotic girl who I'll call Nancy. She was short. Probably twenty-seven years old. Acorn-shaped head that sat right on her shoulders — no neck to speak of. Big gold-rim glasses that covered the top third of her acorn face. Black hair, feathered like they used to do back in the 70s. Polyester pants, floral blousey tops. A real gem. She swung around like she owned the place, and everyone else in the department just let her believe it. Her job was to collect money from the people who weren't able to sell their art or antiques or general crap at auction. My job was to help Nancy. The customers hated Nancy. She was mean-spirited, territorial and bossy. I quickly came to hate Nancy. I was unable to make out whether she was saying 'can' or 'can't' when she spoke with her accent, which she'd thicken to suit her intent. She made both words sound like 'cah.' She used to smirk when people became confused at this, her only weapon against non-hostile co-workers. 'You cah do that…' I did it anyway. 'You cah take your lunch break…' I didn't feel like it. One day, after a screaming fight with Nancy, the division director Gail transferred me to Art Transport, where I stayed for almost a year. Nancy was green with envy as I moved from her center-building office — where you couldn't tell if it was night or day, and the air systems froze you in summer and baked the winter days — to my new desk on the main floor beside an enormous picture window. The money was still meager for a company owned by Mr. Alfred Taubman, who catered to the likes of Princess Gloria von Thurn und Taxis, Cher and Barbra Streisand, and constantly boasted of multi-million dollar sales in the press; run by characters like Robert Woolley, a filthy-rich old-school homo who surrounded himself with dashing young men. I was passed over for a spot in his club, as I hadn't yet learned to dash. My co-worker friends in the Art Transport department were a refreshing composite of regular folks from the reaches of the five boroughs. One guy even commuted from Philadelphia every day. Sotheby's became sexy. People loved being paid nothing to be sexy too. I got along well with the truckers and the packers and the shippers. They'd talk to you, as in really talk, as opposed to yuppie lip service. As would the young lady who sat opposite me, Cathy, who remains a friend to this day. Cathy and some others taught me a few things — the merciful kindness of strangers to a transplanted greenhorn. How to get a bank account to work, how to organize files, how to deal with co-workers, how to find a few extra minutes for your break time. A friend to have lunch with. Cathy was also a veteran of epic New York nightlife, from hotspots like the Paradise Garage, and we shared a love of good music. She also taught me how to walk. One day, I needed to cash a check at a bank a few blocks away for six hundred bucks, then walk the money to my own bank. When I told Cathy I was afraid to walk around with that much money, all I had in the world, she stood back and showed me a one-hand in pocket, leaned-slightly with shoulders relaxed type of posture and said "Baby you just go get your money and walk like y'ain't got a dime to your name. You'll be fine.'

Skills, NYC skills. You need them.

One of the best perks at Sotheby's was the art. Monet, Manet, Degas, Picasso, Warhol, Lichtenstein, Liebovitz, Stiegler, Adams. You name the artist and at some point their work had illuminated the dull, cream colored walls in the building at Seventy-second Street and York Avenue. I'd taken courses in art with my teacher Rad back in North Carolina. It was incredibly exciting to see paintings I'd only studied from books come alive on the dingy showroom walls. It took weeks for me not to become breathless in front of a Warhol screen print of Elvis, or the runny paint trails of Pollock. Sometimes they'd be out of proper storerooms for the work, and would cram canvases just about anywhere. One time, I took a long pee next to a stack of Warhols in the men's toilet, other times stuff would just line the hallways awaiting auction.

The second-best perk was when my co-worker, Thomas J. Sullivan, kept us fed and happy, ordering up meatball Parmesan heroes for everyone at lunch. Or when the boys from Macray Trucking sent presents for the holidays: crates of expensive liquor, chocolates and champagne, and checks for a hundred dollars a pop. I was really beginning to love New York. Not for the perks, but for these salt of the city types — real people, and what I didn't realize at the time were a dying breed.

My actual job was to insure the property while in transit. To do this, I simply had to fill out a half-sheet photocopied form with the name of the owner, artist and painting. A lot of times they'd forget to tell me about a painting, so million-dollar merchandise could technically travel uninsured. I just filled out the forms retroactively. Once a truck carrying millions of dollars worth of stuff ran off the road. There were rumors of something pricey like a Picasso on board, and I think one of the drivers was injured. My boss Laura cried over it. One sale in particular made big headlines, and caused a big stir — Vincent Van Gogh's Irises. The painting made a long journey, from Van Gogh's crazy house to the one I was working for. When the painting arrived, they unpacked it on the shipping dock, with lots of men with guns and security and internal fanfare around. I was allowed near 'cause I was the insurance dude. And because the foreman who ran the dock liked me. After the big uncrating, everyone cleared out, the union guys — packers, shippers, unpackers and gun carriers — and went to lunch. One guard stood just outside the garage door, but otherwise, Van Gogh's valuable painting and the momentous occasion stood still, all alone on the steel platform. I stood for a long time admiring the painting, appreciating the work. Nice brush motion, but I wasn't a big Van Gogh fan. Many years later, in Amsterdam, I'd discover his darker, more interesting, early side. This stuff, *Irises*, was too color-ey for me at the time. Too cheese-ball everyone-in-middle-America-will-like-it housewifey. But it was impressive. It just sat there, a piece of canvas worth more money than I could fathom. I imagined extending my right index finger and touching the third violet flower from the left. The moment was stunning — I cannot to this day remember if I actually did it.

I lasted at Sotheby's until my urge to commit to downtown living took over. In haste, I quit the job. Gail, Cathy and Laura threw me a cake party, and told me I'd 'come in an out-of-towner' but had learned how to be a New Yorker. The next gig was as an assistant manager at Kate's art supply store, which used to be on the southwest corner of Thirteenth Street and Fifth Avenue. I'd been told the job was permanent. I'd been told the gig was 'laid-back.' I would soon learn not to believe anything I was told about jobs in New York. 'Permanent' means until they don't need you anymore. No one invests long-term. 'Laid-back' means high stress in an environment run by incompetents, reacting to the bid and call of a neurotic owner, while dodging the antics of the staff of minimum-wage slaves. Employee morale was low, tension high, the store a shambles. I tried to bring some of my department-store knowhow to the scene, but they didn't care. After just a few weeks I was fired by my boss and the goon from the Paperie down the street. Apparently, a cashier had yelled at a customer and it was all my fault. Heads must roll. But not the cashier's head, who would stand and work for peanuts. Mine. All this on the very day my boss's girlfriend, the former assistant manager, returned from vacation. She was reinstated. How convenient. I was given unemployment money without a question. How nice.

I took another big step backward when I went to work at Macy's on the offer of more money. I had some fantasy that I could settle back into retailing just like in Charlotte. Not a chance. Although I explained I'd only ever worked in men's departments and knew the merchandise, the esteemed human resources coordinator placed me in the women's Donna Karan boutique. I'd never sold to women. Donna Karan was supposed to be New York 'hip' — but to me, only turned out to be fashion-world hype. Some of the clothes literally came apart, others fell off the hangers. Especially after the women tried them on. The entire DKNY department was a revolving door of overpriced sales and angry returns. I wasn't a sales professional — they didn't seem to want those anymore — I was a cash & carry stooge.

The girls I worked with were competitive and indifferent. Over nothing. No commission. Biding their time until their own wedding if one ever came along. One of the managers bullied me into ringing up some promotional fashion show merchandise as a cash sale. A Paula Abdul wannabee I'll call Sheila — light brown skin, jet black hair and faint freckles around her nose and eyes. She pronounced her name 'SHEE-lah' with a slack jaw and wore her black-plastic-framed glasses on the end of her nose, which hovered above a set of bright red polished lips that were constantly chomping on a wad of bubblegum which made clicking noises. She was just barely older than me and spoke with a slack jaw packed with the gum. She'd say things like 'Do you want to continya' yo' p'sition here at Macee Neoo Yawk He-aald Skweh?' which prompted me to go along with things like ringing up the bogus cash sale.

Sure enough, within a week store security people were following me everywhere. I thought, in Southern, that the whole place was just plain 'ate-up with the dumb-ass.' Very few people seemed to actually like working there. In the morning employees were herded like cattle through a dank hallway, and had to fight lines of other employees to get their cash register bags, then clip clop through a maze up onto the sales floor. I felt like one of Thomas Jefferson's servant slaves, who were kept hidden, below, and let out only when necessary. I could barely keep my stomach from turning sour the minute I hit the door.

My SHEE-lah-cash-sale security problem got worse and worse. Guilty until proven innocent. Rent-a-cops circulated in the department all day long. One in particular, an example of the lowest of the low, reminded me of my Innapenance High School band teacher. He was tall, lanky, aging, with dirty gray hair, yellowed nicotine fingers and the stench of stale smoke radiating from his stock-issue burgundy blazer. Things went from rumor to suspicion to a kangaroo court, with me being convicted right there on the sales floor by my fellow sales drones. They were probably planning to arrest me, but one day one of the only two girls I could stand in the department, Mandy, phoned in on her day off to explain the loss as SHEE-la's fault. She'd suddenly remembered the faulty cash transaction. Even SHEE-la's boss had told Sheila it was the wrong way to handle the transfer. One real class act who I'll call Lois made it her daily business to go from person to person gossiping about me. If I'd had an ounce of gumption, I would have gotten a lawyer and sued the cheap DKNY clothes off Macy's racks and the smirk off Lois's face. You don't learn this twice.

I'd hit a plateau with jobs I ended up hating, in a city I hadn't completely learned to groove with — not yet anyway — and a less than hospitable living situation. I needed me some change.

In North Carolina a job change happened every three years. New place to live, within two or so. There was always an impression that some big evil guilt monster was watching you. 'Don't job-jump, it doesn't look good on your resume!' In New York jobs could change every three days. Apartments, as often as you had to until you got your own. And no one gave a shit. A few more crap jobs, more unemployment, some fun in between. It's how things worked for me at the time. I heard SHEE-lah was later let go from Macee Neoo Yawk He-aald Skweh for a scam involving other employees' charge accounts.

13. Reality, Overrated

Before Rudy Giuliani and Antonio Pagan's onslaught of gentrification, the scene had a life of its own in the East Village, or rather, Lower East Side of Manhattan. It mingled and swarmed through what I found to be one of the most diverse communities in America. I wanted to be there, badly. Although we'd agreed to remain friends, things had worn thin at Marilyn's. The cat was a terror, Johnny too much to take — drunk all the time. He taught me a lot about painting, but I needed a door to close. His estranged son had come over once and Johnny was trying to get us to be friends. The kid thought Johnny was trying to get him to be queer with me — offering him up almost. I don't think that was exactly the case, but nonetheless he never spoke to Johnny again. Another sad product of alcoholism. The whole situation kept getting really fucked up. I found a place to share with Marilyn's daughter for a while. She called herself 'Bari-G,' a catchy name of a budding dance music record executive. We took an apartment in Park Slope, Brooklyn. It was halfway closer to Manhattan and I told myself lies about how close it actually was. It was also just a few blocks from where Seth had since moved in with Alisa.

Park Slope is named for the long, slow, inclined patch of land that extends up to Prospect Park, a literal slope. Little did I know at the time my 'Popey' Bill and grandmother Katie, had lived there while Bill, worked as a ship welder on the Brooklyn Navy yards during World War II. Bari and I took an apartment on Eleventh or Fifteenth Street, just next door to the fire station, which went in and out all night long with the ring of a bell followed by the roar of engines and the shrill shrieks of sirens. The whole apartment was less that ten feet wide in the living room. Upstairs, a woman kept kids during the day, who rarely saw the light of the sun: a massive public park two blocks up the street, with grass and swings and monkey bars, and she coddled them inside, to run up and down the length of the apartment all day long. Fun.

Bari-G was rarely at our apartment, opting for her boyfriend's house in Weehawken, New Jersey instead. She'd go on & on about 'big rooms' and a 'back yard' and a parking space for her car — everything I loathed at the time. A month or so later, Marilyn followed us to the neighborhood, on Seventh Avenue just down the Slope. I saw her at least once a week. We'd go to the flea market on Saturdays. She let me eat dinner with her when I ran out of money waiting on unemployment checks between jobs. Once, things got so bad I wrote to Governor Mario Cuomo's office, who intervened, and one day I came home and at least ten back-dated government checks fell out of my box worth around two grand. I called Grandma Ruby, who told me 'you better save that money!' and I tried, I really tried.

The Brooklyn place was serving its purpose, but I needed Manhattan — the history and character and the people of the nooks and crannies. Things to do. I agonized on many Brooklyn Saturday nights, sitting alone in that narrow apartment, aching for something to do and somebody to do it with. It's difficult to sit still when the endless stream of everything you want is just a bridge away, but things take time. In my early twenties time is all you got and I didn't have a clue what to do with it.

The actual train ride into the city was only about twenty-five minutes, once it came, but by the time you stood on a platform and waited, then push-pulled through every stop along the F line, the slowest line on NYC Transit at the time, any excitement or lust for life was diminished to a puddle of melancholy. Once out, everything you did was centered around getting home, somehow, and the decision whether to take the train and chance getting mugged or queerbashed, or to spend next week's lunch money on a taxi.

I needed to feel the vibes of the immigrants in the back alleys and to see the hidden spaces behind the buildings of the Lower East Side, incredibly decorated gardens where tenants threw parties, grew vegetables or just lounged their summers tucked neatly out of sight of tourists and television cameras. I yearned to experience the texture of the streets as part of my daily routine, the exciting young men, women and in-betweens who filled the sidewalks in the Village I'd first discovered with Seth; the sharp business people I'd encountered in midtown with Dad years earlier; and the rich ethnic flavors I'd yet to see, that tinted the air of Harlem, Spanish Harlem and Chinatown and all the other hidden corners on the island bought for beads. Before Giuliani arrived to finish the wrecking-job of Fiorello LaGuardia and Robert Moses, New York was not actually a city at all, it was a collection of delicate neighborhoods, held together by the stories and lives woven by her eight million living souls.

Over time, Bari-G migrated out to Jersey. She'd found success in a record company called Strictly Rhythm producing some big dance music acts, and the man she came in one night and announced he was 'the one.' I made some connections and found my way over the East River as well, but not as far as Jersey. That ride across the Brooklyn Bridge was my emancipation — I was joining Walt Whitman's 'Manhattanese' race. I remember the enormous cables and concrete support structures passing overhead, and the buildings of Chinatown in the distance, appearing larger and more formidable than ever. But I was, at long last, ready. For the first time, I had somewhere to be: M-a-n-h-a-t-t-a-n. My first stop for a few months was at 114 West Sixteenth Street. I rented a room from a man named Michael, an art director for a big fashion house. I'd arrived.

Michael lived in an enormous three-bedroom apartment in a quiet, solid brick building. It had polished wood floors and gray area carpeting. Trash chutes that went from the kitchen counter down to the basement and actually worked, electricity that didn't brown out and buzz, and windows all around that let bright sun in from all sides, illuminating the crisp white walls and, well, white everything. New Yorkers have their quirks. Michael was obsessed with white objects: pillows, beds, sheets, lamps, china, toasters, sofas and chairs — all white. And he informed me that he preferred to 'enjoy his home naked in the evening.' As a matter of course, I began to accept his nocturnal lack of anything below the waist but tennis shoes, and the place felt the closest to anything that felt like home since I'd left Grandma Ruby's.

I'd met Michael through a guy from Uncle Charlie's, where I'd been doing cheap after-work jaunts for my social outings — all I could afford on the low pay of Sotheby's and Kate's Art Store, then Macy's and finally unemployment money. Back then, the area was still old-school, which I found comfortable. Chelsea was nothing but a no-man's land between 14th Street and Midtown. The remnants of a pre-AIDS Christopher Street were still open, and a few lone haunts further west survived.

At Uncle Charlie's you got a two-for-one coupon with each drink. Me and a new friend I met there named Joey soon got hip to the fact that tourists weren't aware of what the coupons were after a bartender put them down on the bar. They'd fumble with the coins and change but leave everything else, tips and napkins as well. Joey and I would hang by, and wait for the guy to walk away before we'd snatch up the remains of the transaction from the lacquered countertops, and drink as long as we wanted for free. Most of the bartenders knew what we were doing, but since we kept the place young and left a dollar a pop, they didn't seem to give a shit.

My friend Joey was a tall, skinny-as-a-rake Italian guy with big jet-black hair, styled like Dave Gahan in Depeche Mode. He was training to be a school teacher back in Bay Ridge, Brooklyn. I met him at Uncle Charlie's before my Manhattan move. To keep life livable, we'd get together at least one night a week for some Greenwich Avenue Happy Hour fun. It wasn't long before Joey and I became thick as thieves, out on the prowl for a good story, good dance song or good lay. We'd tried for maybe a week to date, but it just wasn't in the cards. We were just as interested in watching the Golden Girls at 6pm on the giant screen at UC's as we were watching the parade of horny guys wandering in and out. We gave a lot of them names like 'Loud Man' or 'Banker Dude' or 'Teeth Boy.' He'd make me say lines like 'we shoulda' went bowlin' in my Southern accent, after a character on the 80s TV show 'The Facts of Life.'

Joey liked TV, al lot of TV. Madonna videos, Beavis and Butthead, and all things Tori Spelling. I never heard the end of it, but it was more of a schtick than I had at the time. To Joey, Disneyland was a dream vacation and Las Vegas was heaven. I figured someone had to go to these god-forsaken places, and it might as well be him. God bless America. He had a heavy Brooklyn-Italian accent. He said things like 'not-for-nuthin' and 'don't-touch-the-hair' and he meant it. All this intrigued me. I liked to make him angry by touching his hair anyway, or by making fun of the bad TV shows he was addicted to, or the fact that he lived at home and his mother did his laundry because he would fly off on me in an accent and teach me at least ten new Brooklyn slangs. Truth was I was bit jealous of his security and he knew it. In his attempts to halt my harassment, Joey tried to reason with me on numerous occasions with a phrase he'd learned in Brooklyn: 'Listen: never stand when you can sit, never sit when you can lie down, but, sometimes, (dramatic pause), it's just better to stand.' Joey became a symbol of my authentic New York — he was one of the few true natives in my new home, and family of choice.

Joey introduced me to other locals. One in particular was Randy, a tall blond guy from the Upper East Side who worked as a concierge at the Carlyle Hotel. Randy and I got along pretty well and over time I started getting an invitation or two to some uptown events for a nice change. At the Carlyle, Randy had become friends with a woman named Zelda Dupont, of the Dupont chemical empire, who kept a permanent room at the hotel. Ms. Dupont, or 'Zelda' as we were instructed to call her, was at least sixty years old, and kept a small enclave of young friends to play with. Apparently, her family had ostracized her for giving a pile of money to build a park for Israeli and Palestinian children in Israel. I didn't know much about all that, but I sure couldn't see anything wrong with the cheerful little lady who picked me and Randy up in either a black Lincoln, or a Rolls Royce for special occasions. Because of her, I got to see, taste and hear a lot of classic New York before it too disappeared — like a real jazz show with Lainie Kazan in the Rainbow & Stars Room at 30 Rockefeller Center, which had sparkling skyline views of the city in every direction from your table. Or an evening at La Côte Basque, where you dined on the best French cuisine to be found in North America, in the elegant ambience of a room once enjoyed by Truman Capote and blessed by Henri Soulé.

One night, Randy and I tried to take Zelda slumming by going out dancing at the Roxy. She felt overdressed in her handmade evening clothes and didn't stay long, but we had more fun than a peacock at high tea prancing out of her Bentley at the door and through the gathered party masses.

It was such a mind fuck — slaving at some hole like the art store or Macy's or some architect's office I pulled some time in, then rushing home to change into all black and glide uptown for an evening. And although I didn't necessarily know a lot about what I was hearing or ingesting, I'd mastered the art of sitting and feeling special — welcome was another matter. I had charm, manners and graceful moves, like when instinctively holding the door for Zelda and other people my senior, but I hadn't even begun to know my own sense of purpose — what I was doing in the world, what I might do with the world — which kept conversation on a light level. Nonetheless, whether being fussed over by French waiters or escorted through hallways filled with fine art, I watched, I learned. I ate.

14. Into the Groove

The little hole in the wall called Uncle Charlie's would be the *point de rendezvous* for an unusual number of people the gods intended me to crash into — some I'd know for the next fifteen years or more, others for the rest of their, or my, life. Not bad for a medium-priced video bar which I only even went to once or twice a week. I'd kinda' started going other places, late night places, like to Boy Bar with Joey on a Thursday on St Marks Place or Roxy on a Saturday, but they weren't as up-front and social as the cruise bars.

One night, just a few months before I moved from Brooklyn, I walked into a moderately filled UC's — the place was little more than a startoff point or nightcap stop after happy hour. I hung out in the back by the big built-in seats by the video wall for a while, until a blond-haired guy came over and stood next to me for a while, then started chatting. He was around 6' tall, healthy build, and smiled all the time. He had on a red or burgundy or maybe blue t-shirt, jeans and some kind of slip-on deck shoes — basic yet fashionable. His name was Barney Johnson. Little did I know at the time, but Barney had been sent to reel me in for a friend, who walked over, along with the rest of Barney's friends, to join us. Haoui and David. They all gave me a not-so-subtle impression that they were somehow not part of the Uncle

Charlie's rank and file. Suddenly, I found myself in the middle of a strange trio, who all chattered at the same time and shot grins and glances just ahead of my ability to catch them. I wasn't stupid. The one called Haoui made jokes in an offbeat NY accent which took me a while to follow. I knew he meant no harm from his big grin, which reached out on either side of his face toward his curly dark hair. Barney was clearly the class clown, and instigated quips and jabs as David laughed along taking sips from his long-neck beer. They were asking me where I was from, and mocking my Southern twang. Something about them made me stay and talk to them — they didn't seem to have the desperation of guys on the prowl, although they were prowling harder than anyone else in the place tenfold. But they didn't look like stereotypical fags.

David Russell, who turned out to be the manager of the Bandito's restaurant across the street where Joey and me would go sometimes, had put Barney up to fetching me. And I didn't know that Barney knew just about everyone on the entire downtown scene. And I certainly didn't know that Haoui Montaug used to run the doors at Studio 54, Danceteria and worked with Madonna, in fact they all knew her and a host of other famous faces. I didn't know anything except a deep feeling in my gut to respect the strange familiarity I felt with this group — perhaps the people I'd come all this way to find.

The night ended peacefully. I think they were headed off somewhere else, and I had work the next morning. I exchanged phone numbers with Barney, who was still bouncing and joking. He'd told me it was a fluke that they'd even come there, Uncle Charlie's apparently wasn't their usual kind of place.

Up to that point, St Marks Place was pretty much the furthest east I'd ventured. Seth had me scared shitless of the East Village, and I just hadn't made the jump. I'd learned early on that for whatever reason, Seth wanted to be a 'housey'-type, and seemed to want everyone else to be one too. Since our night at The Monster, I'd done most of my own venturing. Boy Bar was the only risk I took into the big bad East until the night I called Barney, who invited me to come on a romp with him. I met him at his place on East 6th Street between Avenue A and B. It was a small, ground-floor apartment that he'd redone completely himself. He'd crafted light wooden floors that rounded what was once the rough corners of the old building, put in new walls, sheetrock, and tiles in the kitchen. The back door led to a private courtyard, which he'd landscaped with big stones, green gardens of trees and shrubs, and finished with a small pond with live orange fish. Ever since I'd moved north the city had been confronting me with urban oxymorons, and Barney's home was no exception, an oasis in the middle of Sodom.

We had a drink as he toured me around the small, ornately decorated rooms. The place was a 'railroad,' which means four rooms back to back adjoined by a walkway on one side, boxcar style. The furnishings were robust fabrics — velvets and tapestries. I studied the large paintings and drawings by famous names I'd yet to discover that kept his walls company and the eclectic, colorful adornments to the windows and draped the love seats. The front room had a giant bay storefront window with frosted glass, and a door which led to the street which had been permanently bolted shut. I could hear conversations passing on the sidewalk and see the glow of headlights turning the corner of Avenue B as we sat and talked in the living room while listening to a Peggy Lee or something from his record collection. Tapes. Whichever. After a while we hit the streets. I remember still being a little shaky about wandering through the dark side. Even a guy from New York who worked at the store in Charlotte had told me to stay clear of 'Alphabet City.' Idiot. But if Prince had a song about it, I figured there must have been something to it.

I don't know what I expected, but what I found was everything... Avenue A and Avenue B peopled from wall to corner with rockers, mods, punks — lots of punks — Blacks, Whites, Puerto Ricans, straights, queers, business people, kids from a ball team, skateboarders, old people, and junkies. Delectable human chaos. Everyone humble-jumbling through and around each other, music blasting from cars and bars riding in on every fresh hot summer breeze. Dirty young white kids, most likely the children of rich Wall Streeters, hanging on street corners and asking for food. 'Can I get some money for a sandwich?' Sure, they maybe wanted food, or drug money, but Barney would smile and say 'sorry' and they'd smile back and I realized all they wanted was to be recognized. Other people sat in restaurants, everyday people, famous faces, rank and file, and all they wanted was to eat and not be noticed. Leather jackets on everywhere. Motorcycle black with shiny silver zips. Some had paintings on the back panels — James Dean or an original something or other heralding 'peace now' or the name of a hardcore punk band — 'Cycle Sluts from Hell,' with the outline of a cartoon face and spikey hair. I nearly choked the first time, in the course of walking a block, I watched two complete strangers from opposite sides of the street cruise and approach each other, exchange around three sentences, start making out then disappear together. The natives were restless. I was always restless.

Barney took me from place to place that night and many nights. The first time we'd gone to almost every joint in the neighborhood for a beer. I don't even think I had much money but Barney bought for me. All along the streets and into the clubs Barney was stopped and called by name — this person, that person. One asked me 'are you one of 'Barney's Boys?' I knew what that meant. No. Well, as far as I like meeting all of New York perhaps, it hadn't taken me long to realize my new friend Barney was a

Class-A operator, and his personality, classic Nordic looks and long blond hair let him get away with it. That, and the fact that he'd managed or worked in or been a fixture at a plethora of clubs on the notorious New York scene — Hurrah, Danceteria, Mudd Club, Studio 54, Palladium. Barney was older than me… he'd seen much more, 'been around.' As we got to know each other he talked of playing cards with Yul Brynner and how Madonna took an ex of his, also named Martin, off to California to care for him while he suffered AIDS. My head spun and spun and kept spinning. Thankfully I had Grandma Ruby's poker face.

We ended up at The Bar on the corner of 4th Street and 2nd Avenue. A rusty kind of place, with a gray metal door that squeaked long and deliberately to announce our arrival. Heavy wooden floors, railings, walls, benches lining the street-side window areas and a bar that looked like it had first been installed in a 19th-century pub around the corner on the Bowery. We got more beers, Rolling Rock — the choice of the neighborhood, and smoked more cigarettes — Camel Lights, the ones with the cartoon camels and coupons for free beach towels and other useless crap. As we sat, listening to the brilliant jukebox playing everything from Rock 'n' Roll to Soul II Soul, Barney started getting cozy. Hands down, he had moves. I watched him chatting his way up Avenue B, down A, and over to 4th Street. But for some reason, I just felt the incredibly strong sensation to do nothing. As he became understandably frustrated at my point-dodging, I couldn't think of what to say, until I blurted out: 'We could do a lot of things right now, but I want to know you in ten years. If we do anything, I know I won't.' Truth be told, I had no interest anyway, I had the misguided eyes of a romantic fool, looking for the youngest, sparkly pretty things — and in a city of eight million I couldn't barely see my own hand, much less anybody right in front of me. That night there was no crash.

Barney got it, he actually acted kinda' surprised at the logic, impressed almost, which struck me strange, and just said 'OK.'

Although I was not officially one of 'Barney's Boys,' I started hanging out with him a lot. He had parties in his back garden and Haoui and David would come and I quickly met a ton of other friends who would parade by. One in particular caught my attention. He was tall as me, thin, white, and had long rocker hair. Medium-tint sunglasses that you wouldn't be ashamed to wear indoors. Black leather jeans and sterling silver jewelry that would have been ostentatious on anyone else. We were hanging out, having a beer in the short hallway between Barney's apartment and the metal steps leading to the East Village garden oasis. When we first met, Michael Schmidt chatted me up as Barney looked on with a smirk and Schmidt followed by grabbing my chin with an open, backward hand for a kiss. I loved all the attention, I had no clue what to do with it.

Still more cool people, like Jorgé, asked me out here and there. Grace, who I thought was one of the most beautiful girls in New York, was always bouncing around and partying with the best of them. We went to parties up at Cal and Larry's apartment in Midtown, where Calvin took me in his bedroom and gave me the executive tour of his antique Barbie collection, after their friend Phoebe nearly killed me for flirting with her formerly available soon-to-be-husband Mark. Little did I know that this group was designing, working, producing, writing, painting, photographing and directing for the biggest names in the Big Apple business — and that's precisely why I think they accepted me: they had theirs. Some, like Schmidt, designed clothes for Tina Turner and Cher, others published major magazines like *Details* and *The Face* on three continents, some modeled and others owned property — none acted or looked it. There was a kind of hush about business and names and success — like an exotic pet, or a magnificent wild tropical bird that no one dared to scare from the picture window ledge when it visited. They were talented, energetic — and every single secret behind how they ticked inspired me. I wanted to know them, and in turn, I got a place at the table. First time for everything. And most took me seriously — which took me some gettin' used to.

I said I wanted to paint, and Barney wanted to see the paintings. I mentioned being a go-go boy was a fantasy, and the answer I got was 'when you starting?' All this do-it frightened me. One afternoon, while floating with Barney, David and Jorgé down East 5th Street, I said something stumbling and silly, trying my best to play in the conversation — I would always be the youngin' and subject to teasing, but this time no one said anything for a second until Jorgé looked at Barney and said 'He reminds me of a young Robert.' They remained silent. There was only one Robert I knew this crowd to know — dead, but certainly not gone. His photo of 'Smutty' had given me the shivers all the way down South. But Jorgé was also the person who told me that 'insanity was inevitable for painters,' so I'll never know if I'd been paid an incredible compliment or merely benchmarked on my way to the looney bin. Or both. I just watched the cracks in the sidewalk pass under my new combat boots and the black lapels of the motorcycle jacket Barney helped me pick out at a discount shop on Broadway, which I think I paid for with my rent money.

It was all very real, but with it came the reality. My new queer corps introduced me to people like their friend Keith Filbert, who wasn't doing very well. AIDS. Keith had little to say in general and nothing to say to me, obviously, so I kept back when Barney had him over to one of the garden parties. The others waited on him and gave him margaritas, which I found kind of strange in his condition. 'It can't hurt nothing now...' Barney said, and giggled, trying to cover his low barometer of emotion.

I felt honored to watch the group try their best to pretend everything was just like it'd always been... but it was clear it wouldn't be for long. I felt responsible to observe and keep all I could about Keith, a thin shell of a man who sipped his tequila as best he could through a straw while sitting in a reclined chaise longue. Like anyone in his position, I was sure, if times'd been different, he'd have a lot I'd want to hear. At the time I didn't really know what on earth these people wanted with me, if anything — really. But now I imagine that at the very least me and the few other early-twentysomethings had a job to do: keep going. Keep it going. Damn straight.

'It' was the times, time and memories which now all run together and overlap in my mind somewhere between '89 and '92. Barney, Haoui and Jorgé took me to my first Wigstock, where I spotted John from NC in the audience, who shifted his eyes away from mine when I shot him a smirk saved for just the right occasion. The day started off sanely enough, but after Jorgé gave me a little, tiny taste of what he said was E, things got faster. Deelight was the rancor *du jour*. And although in an expedited haze, I didn't miss the parades of liberated souls who 'donned-we-now' their gayest apparel for a celebration that was much more than any drag show. More than a party. Men dressed as flamboyant women. Girls decorated as nymphs, faeries and glamourpusses. All meticulously styled, groomed, manicured and presented. The point? Danger. Dare to become whatever is most feared, then enjoy it.

Thankfully, Wigstock was a threat to everything negative I'd known before, the people, places and things in our culture that'd pushed me to move to New York. If you watched Lady Bunny long enough, you saw beyond the drag, a producer, a genius at work. Her eyes gave her away, seeing to every detail, and I knew from the start she, and people like her, had a bigger plan in mind.

It was Dada, activism and pure human hutzpah rolled into one, congenially delivered from beneath a wig, something anyone can use to create change in as little as 30 seconds. As Misstress Formika would later put it on being a domanitrix in drag, 'I'm going to teach people to dominate their own lives, be independent and change the world.' And that day, in that park, I couldn't even begin to understand how to handle it. Nor the drugs. But I knew I was in exactly the right place.

We partied through the day in the hot, moist outside of Tompkins Square Park, and ended up on the floor of Jorgé's living room, where he revealed that the E turned out to be LSD, which was probably the reason me, him and some other boy from out of town had been busy for hours counting the speckle spots on his ceiling, while the boy — who had curly hair — kept saying 'Lady Bunny told us to go to the West Side Pier' over and over — determined to follow the deity. Groove was in the heart.

Other times were less overtly rambunctious, but just as Dee-groovy. Barney would lead me into the Pyramid, just up the block on Avenue A, for some dancing. At the time, Pyramid was an epicenter of downtown nightlife. Willi Ninja, the man who originated Vogueing on the silver screen with Malcom McLaren — long before Madonna — worked the door. We never paid to get in. Barney would just smile and say hey, and we'd pass into the milieu. Lady Miss Kier dancing on the bar, Wendy Wild checking our coats in between her own performances; intermingled shows with characters named Hattie Hathaway, Linda Simpson, Hapi Phace, Antony, Taboo, Lily of the Valley, The Black Lips Performance Cult started there — just to name a minute few from a scene that permeated downtown.

Sometimes Joey from Brooklyn would come along, especially on 80s music nights. There was my first Pride march when me and Jorgé chased a wet Lady Bunny in a red dress around the fountain at 13th and Hudson Streets. Another Pride we spent on Phoebe and Mark's rooftop, tripping our faces off on some magic mushrooms that kept going around in a huge Tupperware popcorn bowl. Some nights I got invited along to Bandito's across from Uncle Charlie's where David worked, and we'd eat burritos, drink tequila and be merry. Thursdays was always Boy Bar, on St Marks Place, where I met another thousand or so people and Joey Arias nearly sex-pested me out the door each week. No one would save me from the clutches of that mad drag queen — Barney did nothing but laugh hysterically, while others sheepishly ducked out of sight.

By the time Nirvana burst on the scene, my jaw dropped and hips started gyrating, as did every Rock 'n' Roll queer's trousers for this latest thing in American anthems. Plenty of us liked to get heavy, and somehow belonging to the underground second-class had relegated us to more Whitney Houston remixes than one should be forced to endure. Sure sometimes I wanted to dance with somebody; other times I wanted to jump and dive and writhe among sweaty bodies in a mosh pit. The sound of 'Smells Like Teen Spirit' made me horny — fucking hornier than I'd ever been — horny for something in between blood and guts — my spirit — and when it played I could feel the life singeing the insides of my nostrils as the vibrations rose from the speakers and into my head. Although I'd gotten close with Queen many times, edged with Blondie, tripped heavily with The Ramones and tried throughout the 80s to jump on the New Wave applecart, suddenly for the first time, possibly ever, I felt that I could be angry and sexy and hurt and queer all at once — and most of the world would never fucking get it. I was just a little too old to drink the Kool Aid, but I sure as hell knew how to take a swim in some.

My roommate Michael was friends with the stage manager up

at Saturday Night Live, so when Nirvana was booked as the musical act, I got an invitation to the rehearsal. The studio tickets were given out months in advance, so I got to hang out most of the afternoon in the studio. I didn't really know George, who was busy working anyway, so I got no formal introductions. At first I felt very anxious and strange going through the tight security then being left to wander around aimlessly. George stood me in a corridor across from some sort of meeting room, which had a table covered in fresh pizzas. New York pizza — thin, crispy and hot, with tangy fresh mozzarella cheese strung all over the top. A far cry from the mush they serve in faux Italian joints all over the rest of the country. People wandered back and forth. One of the main actors noticed me noticing him after making sure I noticed him for the first time. Over time, I'd perfect the art of calming my expressions, and take fame with the even bigger grain of salt it deserves. I'd certainly encountered some famous faces along the way with Haoui, Barney and the rest of the downtown crowd but my reaction was still a work in progress. Suddenly a door flung open and some skinny, awkward guys dressed in jeans and t-shirts started coming toward me. Cobain had on a tattered shirt and ratty green and brown striped sweater with vertical stripes. His blond hair was stringy and shoulder length. He passed by once and looked at me, unnaturally, out of the far reaches of the corners of his eye sockets. I averted my own eyes so as not to gawk, but honestly, I really didn't care. There wasn't much to gawk at, actually — he had a hit song but he wasn't that much different in age than me, so the fame-game was relative. This was long before they started giving lifetime achievement awards to teenagers, but I still didn't know what to do. The band was undeniably the hottest thing on the scene at the time, but had it not been for that very scene, I'd probably have said 'hi.' Scenes bother me because they are controlled and jackaled by people. I've always liked human beings, but can't stand people. Cobain looked like a freaky human being I might have actually liked in high school.

After a minute or ten, the group ducked back into the meeting room, and Cobain came back out alone, carrying a bent slice, giving me a mischievous, curious look out of the corner of his eye. Perhaps he'd figured out that in situations like that I was as socially retarded and as genuinely awkward as he seemed to be. He sort of motioned me to help myself to some pizza. After a pause to finally look back, I glanced down and noticed his shabby, worn sneakers and the strangest sensation came over me and I wondered: 'how come the biggest newest rock star in the world, with all the money he could spend, was wearin' ugly old sneakers?' Daddy taught me no matter who you were, no matter how poor or out of luck, you never wanted to get caught dead in shabby shoes. Even old shoes can be polished.

Once in the studio, George showed me a seat. There were a few others in the stands — most likely friends and children of NBC employees — to watch the Nirvana rehearsal. Everyone was acting tense, like they were in church or a library. The band went onstage and ran through their three songs without much of a hitch. After each one, I got another funny, awkward feeling: there we all were, watching a rehearsal, which might as well have been a performance. In reality, it was a performance. After each song, the vibe in the air was to clap, but nobody clapped. Why is it so awful for people to admit they've just enjoyed themselves? Little did I know at the time that Kurt had apparently overdosed the night before.

Cobain acted like he might smile or say something to the people in the studio, but he didn't. No one did anything. They left the stage. I sat still for a while, then carried myself out of Rockefeller Center and home to watch the live TV show, where

Cobain & Co wrecked the stage and French-kissed to reportedly piss off 'rednecks and homophobes.' The band looked so much bigger on the tube, sounded grander. The producers played an applause track after the songs. Whatever the reason, I was for the very first time in my life fitting in somehow. I was still a jumpy nervous wreck inside, but finally, after a long time of living in fear that somehow the secret hick police was going to drag me back down the river, I noticed that my world was opening — and I could actually feel my feet hitting the New York pavement.

15. There Goes the Neighborhood

Early spring, 1991. New move. I hired a guy to help, who turned out to be Jesse Malin, the lead singer of the popular band D-Generation. I can't remember if a friend gave me his number or if I found a 'Man-With-A-Van' ad on a laundromat pinup board. I paid him in cash. Rock 'n' Roll delivered me deeper into the guts of Gotham. 326 East 13th Street to be exact. A dilapidated pre-war, red-brick monstrosity with bending iron handrails leading up to a shakey aluminum door. A lot of the residents had been born there, others were waiting to die there. The smell of burning heroin could be caught in the air shafts. Water stains adorned the crooked walls. The apartment had one large living room, walk-through kitchen and smaller pantry room, with a hole cut in the floor surrounding a spiral staircase which led to the basement. I was to take the pantry room, Mikey and Eddie would split the basement.

The move would only be temporary. My whole life was temporary. I had little money and nowhere else to go. I'd been in and out of this job and that shift, and nothing particularly steady had come along. Back on West Sixteenth Street Michael had found a boyfriend, also named Martin, and had decided he wanted his whole place back. My friend Eddie had agreed to house me 'til I could do better. Eddie worked at The Bar — one of the popular local watering holes on 2nd Avenue. I was on unemployment. With nothing else to do with my days, I made friends with the Latino building superintendent, Raul, pronounced RAH-ool. Apparently he hadn't finished painting the apartment pre-move-in. Eddie had complained to the management company. One day Raul showed up at the door sweating, shaking, with a five-gallon bucket of paint and a brush in hand, wearing an old gray plaid shirt and matching dirty gray work pants. 'I'n da soopa. Raul. Joo gotta lemme ien to do tha' paintin.'

'OK. What's wrong with you?' I asked as I stood aside so the door could swing open.

'Flu. Been sick real bad, dat's why I'n not done.'

At first I didn't think the affair was my concern. The man groaned as he stirred the five gallons with our broomstick handle. Then moaned and coughed as he began painting. I was familiar with the feeling, that flu-ache. For some reason I thought of my grandfather, 'Popey'-Bill. He was about the same age and stature as Raul, although an inch or two taller. 'Popey' — which unbeknownst to me at the age of two in North Carolina, miles from any Latino person, was the same word for father in Spanish except spelled 'Papi' — had always taught me to help others. I'd been out with him in the wee hours of many a night to farms that had lost their water systems. Popey'd stay out all night until he'd repaired the well or submersible pumps that kept tens of thousands of animals — chickens, cows and the like — alive. This was certainly no farm, but Raul seemed a decent enough human being who operated by the old unspoken code, so I decided to assist. I had nothing else to do, and I wasn't about to sit in my room watching TV while the man suffered and moaned. Like Popey, it could have been the flu, or too many cigarettes on a rough night out. Nonetheless, when I asked if he wanted help, his face lightened and he handed me a roller. In one afternoon we knocked out the entire apartment, except for the trim 'cause no one could tell. It would have taken him two days to do it all alone otherwise. We chatted superficially about this and that as we worked. He learned I was decent enough and I learned he was a fixture on our block. Somehow, I think he sensed I wanted to be more than just another transient kid. As he made his way out he said 'If-ya eva need anythin' joo just come an' get me.' He smiled and left.

To celebrate, well, nothing in particular... me and the roommates decided to throw a party. Eddie, Mikey, Todd and me; and a few others from the neighborhood I'd gotten to know mainly from hanging out at The Bar on 2nd Avenue. My boyfriend John, another John, had just dumped me 'cause he needed his space and so I gave him space, which he got angry about. And then he really dumped me. Boys from Texas are not to be trusted. A party would take my mind off things, thankfully for the rest of the world, especially Barney and Jorgé, who'd survived their own first hundred broken hearts, and didn't want to hear any more about mine.

A cartoonist friend of ours made fliers with a big monster and a dick on them, and called the party 'MEAT.' For some reason, throwing a house party is a rite of passage when you're in your early twenties and move into a new place and don't know what else to do with yourself. You spend all your pensive teenage years trying to get away from everybody then when you finally do, you invite them to come to your sanctuary and trash the place.

Clue number one this wasn't going to be an ordinary party: the entire neighborhood got invited. Mike the cartoonist kept making invitations by the case, and we kept handing them out all over the neighborhood for the better part of a month. The apartment was a big place, listed as a duplex and all. Two floors.

The upstairs consisted of a huge living room, kitchen and my small bedroom. A spiral staircase led down to a two-bedroom basement with full bath and access to the alleyway.

When the night finally arrived, I played music upstairs, Mikey and Todd, another boy from the neighborhood, downstairs. No Mary Tyler Moore party here. The place filled to capacity right away, and the people kept coming and coming. Feather boas, smoke and laughter filled the air. Music, good music, boomed from both floors. Booze started to flow, we'd even bought a keg — not a very New York thing — too suburban — but it worked. In New York everyone has to bring a shopping bag full of bottled beer, or a fifth of liquor. Then, as the night progresses, you play the 'oops we're out' game. And then the token control freak takes over, demands money from everyone and calls for a delivery from the local bodega. The city never sleeps.

People smashed throughout our apartment until the back door naturally burst open and they spilled out into the unfinished alleyway behind the house. I think Haoui and some of the others from the old Danceteria crowd came, but the night became blurry as the pot started making rounds. And I remember looking out in the middle of the large living room to catch my first glimpse of James F. Murphy, a 6'7 tall performance artist, with long Jesus-like hair, beard stubble, lipstick and glamour glasses popping up and down on the living room, er, dance floor. Neighbors like Page Reynolds, one of the most exquisite trannies I'd ever met, strutted through the crowds. She was tall, had platinum bleached hair spiked up for a ceremony á la Grace Jones. Klaus Nomi could have styled her. And Linda Simpson, one of the most popular drag queens on the scene, graced us with her presence. Linda hosted the shows at Pyramid — her 'Channel 69' on Sundays was the best party around. Page and James performed for Linda a lot. I remember being astounded at how large the city was, and how close a community could be. Nothing to do with a small town, rather how people can be intimate if they choose to be. That night, although I was still brooding my arrested-development broken heart, I found a new kind of love in that crowd. One I'd been seeing over and over at all the parties and places in the faces of the people. A love that said 'fuck you America, we can make up our own rules.'

And it was lovely, until I remember going out back in the courtyard and having glass bottles pelted at us by the classy neighbors from the roofs behind us. One of them shouted 'It's Mother's Day' and I didn't give a shit — let them move to Weehawken. Later, I was propped at the door when the police came. 'If we have to come back you're going to jail.' Funny, how the cops'd come hunt queers at a party, but would barely even show up if you called them when someone was getting beaten up by a bunch of hateful teenagers with baseball bats: 'wilding,' the new urban pastime. That night I remember turning down the music, and waking up the following morning with a foul taste in my mouth. And man was it good.

16. Less is More

A few weeks later, although the party had been an East Village success, the roommate situation wasn't working out. Eddie was never around. Mikey had only wanted to live with Eddie and resented me being there, and was not happy that Eddie never showed up. Todd sat in his room smoking heroin all day. I asked Raul if he knew of somewhere else I could go, knowing full well that 'Supers' controlled New York. He let me take half of an unused basement apartment in the building next door. It hadn't been inhabited in quite some time, and was filled with garbage and debris — construction garbage, and he'd let Brandy, his big German Shepherd, have her run of it. I spent a week shoveling out dog shit, heaping mountains of black trash bags onto the street late at night, and lathering the place with paint.

Raul was probably the worst superintendent in the world, but a great person. Lonely Puerto Rican guy. Curly white and gray hair, and heavy, darker mustache. He looked like a cross between Colombo and The Man from 'Chico and The Man.' He usually drank himself to sleep in the evening. My basement quarters were connected by a labyrinth of narrow corridors underground to his side of the building. He'd taken to wandering over at night whilst I was busy cleaning out the mess. He'd talk to the point of tears about his wife who'd left him for another man. His own brother I think. He said that's why he drank. He claimed to be straight but kept up with all the eccentrics who lived on our street. He knew Linda and Page and James F. Murphy — all the characters from our block.

One late Friday night, just as I'd finished getting the basement within reach of being livable, Raul pounded on the front door. 'De 'potment upstairs… it's empty! That ole lady she died and then this other girl moved out. Four-fifty a month. If ya ain't at dee office eight-tirty in da mornin,' I'll give it to mah' brotha.'

I kicked into gear. I had twenty or so dollars. Needed nine hundred. Four-fifty for the first month. Four-fifty for the deposit. I started calling everyone I knew. Dad just happened to be in town on his first business trip in years. I borrowed ten here, fifty there and whined the rest out of Dad. Getting a place, especially your own, in New York is a feat, to be sure. Daddy also went with me the next morning to the rental office in the far reaches of Bay Ridge, Brooklyn. When Dad was good, he was real good.

We got there at 8AM just to be sure. Harry opened the door. Old-school Jewish man, about sixty years old. Yellow dress shirt. Tan pants. Brown belt & shoes. Large face with pinkish complexion. Gold rim glasses. Dark-wood-paneled office. Papers stacked everywhere. Smell of typewriter ribbons, Xerox fluid and carbon paper. Two women sat at gray metal desks at opposites sides. Harry's office is in the back. He sat us down at the woman's desk on the left. Permed hair, heavyset. Early sixties. Blue polyester dress. Large, plastic-framed glasses. I told her the apartment: '324 East Thirteenth, Apartment 17.' She started flipping through a book, then punched in her computer. I laid the pre-counted money in front of her. Two piles — four-fifty and four-fifty. The bills pressed out as good as I could manage. Ones, fives, tens, twenties. Payin' like a junky or a pimp, a jumble, but all there. She peered at the money, then me. Then Dad.

'Hold on, I have to check something.' My heart began its perilous journey down to the pit of my stomach. I knew that four-fifty a month was a little low rent-wise — even for the neighborhood where tourists were warned not to venture. The woman clicked something in her state-of-the-seventies telex computer, picked up a large register-style book she'd been referring to, and sauntered back to Harry's office. I looked at Dad in horror. He had a disappointed expression on his face. The woman came back and started talking without looking up. Must be bad news. 'This rent is wrong. It's not four-fifty...' Anxiety pulsed through me.

What hung in the air that very moment was the question of my own longevity in New York. Truth was, I'd grown tired of moving here and there, and was really, really ready to take a next step into being a native. Anyone could come and couch-surf around, even bounce from share to share, but if you were gonna' take root, as in become legitimate, you had to have your own place. I knew it. Dad knew it. Raul knew it. Everyone at our downtown misfit party knew it as well. 'Where do you live?' was a main topic of social conversation — where do you live how much do you pay do you like it?

Harry made himself scarce. Dad looked at me with that oh-well-try-again-next-time look. He had really been rooting for me. 'Fourteen minus one month by two...' The woman was muttering unintelligible figures as she punched more on her rattley computer buttons. I drifted into a daydream from long ago, preparing myself for familiar disappointment.

The scene was tense: 'No. Not four-fifty.' She whispered under her breath. I thought it odd she hadn't broken from her telex or registry book long enough to let me run away. I was obligated to stay for the outcome. She became quiet. Jotting things here, clicking keys there. 'Right, not four-fifty, got it.' She must've said that twenty times already. 'Three ninety-four. Recount your money. I need seven eighty-eight.' I sat stunned. Less!? Dad looked at me with that shut-up-and-pay-now look. I stopped any thought of questioning, not that there was much of one, and started counting. The worst thing about my Dad was you never really knew when he would show up. The best thing about my Dad was that he had a knack for showing up just at the right times, with the right moves. He knew the shuffle.

Seven eighty-eight. That leaves one sixty-two. Almost as much as my unemployment checks. I'd not realized that I was probably about to run out of food. That's how New York used to work: get a new place while jobless and starve in your new palace. You get by. Dad looked at me as if I was considering a loan refund. No chance. New York had not only decided I could stay, but that I could eat too. A six-month sabbatical courtesy of New York State — no more slaving at Macy's, no more schlepping to the Upper East Side or crappy art supply stores. Time. I had some. One of Boy George's best songs. The lyrics are something to the effect of 'time makin' you feel like you got something real, but it ain't nothin' but time.' I'd found the time, but I needed more of the 'something real.' I'd fallen into paradise and wanted to stay.

Within a week I put down roots that would last for the next decade and a half or so. My newest friends Dan, Kurt and Ramon helped me carry my few belongings and some recycled street furniture from the basement up to my new place on the top floor. Dad helped me hang a ceiling fan. A few days later Barney and a friend I knew from The Bar named Don Farata came over and helped me paint the whole place white.

324 East Thirteenth Street, Apartment 17. Home.

17. Everybody Wants You

The Bar on the corner of East Fourth Street and Second Avenue was a great place to start. I went there almost every night — even some during my Uncle Charlie's days. Barney introduced me to the place initially — a year or so earlier. You could go there every single night and not feel weird about it. We wanted beers, boys and music and The Bar did them well. A crowd of Hell's Angels kept the actual bar area to the right cozy, and us queers in the rest of the place guarded. Rumor had it they'd killed people in their big fortress tenement not too far away. We didn't bother them. They didn't bother anybody. Nobody bothered us. The whole neighborhood was rough enough.

On any given night the place would be littered with hot looking young guys dressed in anything and everything they could contrive to go with a leather motorcycle or 'MC' jacket. Our interpretation of the blossoming punk-meets-Madonna look. Madonna was already an urban legend at that point. Many folks, like Haoui, knew her as a former neighbor, and at Danceteria he'd hosted her first show. Albeit art with a lowercase 'a,' the 80s would have been pretty dull without the Material Girl. She held up a mirror and the world paid and worshipped her for it. And she was becoming active in the AIDS battle. People were dying left and right. Most evident in the West Village and with guys in their thirties. Not us — yet.

The Bar was a dump, which was its charm. Charming dump. The blueish gray metal front door which made the ominous squeaking noise over the music never got oiled, and would swing way open immediately propelling you front and center into the middle of the room. Whether twenty people on a Tuesday or a hundred on a Saturday, everyone turned around and saw you. You were there to be seen. You were to be looked at. You were to look. Everybody was to talk. 'Walking over and talking' was what you were supposed to do. Dancing in your spot was fine even if you kinda bumped into the guy next to you. A few girls were welcome. No one knew what kind of outfit they had on because everyone generally had on the same kind of outfit decorated to order... MC jacket, one of a zillion kinds of blue jeans, dark trousers, light pants, shorts in the summer, all manner of jewelry, more if you were boyish less if you were more glam. Hair, regular, this way that way the other way. But the black MC jacket was a staple of the eye-candy diet. They fit you perfectly, with silver zipper that could close the arms, side, and front to a snug fit extended to the very top of the waist. A couple of extra zippered pockets held your wallet, keys, drugs. Kinda punk, kinda 60s, very masculine, very sexy. Some had fringe down the sleeves, a few guys had silk-screened photos on the back. I liked them 'cause we could look like a cross between Madonna in the 'Borderline' video or Desperately Seeking Susan, and James Dean and Brando. Plus, a good MC jacket was thick enough to give you a little protection if someone tried to stab you on the way home, and you looked good in one gyrating around to the vibe of the music.

The greatest mix of music I'd ever heard used to leap from the jukebox at The Bar. A real jukebox with buttons and records at first, CDs later. Grace Jones, The Doors, Soul II Soul, Culture

Club, some Guns, a few Roses, Deee-lite and of course Madonna and if a writer named Gary Indiana was present, and endless supply of Marianne Faithfull — all kinds of music to connect all kinds of people. Moneyed, poor, wayward and stable. Sober and addicts. Everyone wanted the groove. Everyone wanted dick or something equally symbolic. Everyone wanted to be a part of something but retain a part of themselves.

The Bar was an escape for me, from the breeding, 2.3 kids and mortgage world and even the budding world of queer politics as well, which had started to confuse the hell out of me. Just because I liked 'same' didn't mean I wanted to 'be the same.' Greek: *homo* means *same*, not to be confused with the Latin *homo* which means *mankind*. Latin: *sexual* from the root word *sexualis*, which means acting on erotic impulses. Even the words don't really go together. The Romans and Greeks fought too much to have two of their words forced on one another. Like conjoined twins, things not intended to be attached. Same with the word 'gay.' Invented with the best of intentions, but used to lump an enormous group of people that don't fit together. Then the word 'community' pops up. Forced together with gay, I got lost. The only real reason people got together so strongly in the 80s was because of AIDS. A crisis like that can pull people together, and with good reason.

The 'we' I knew were a little of a lot of things, but something greater, something more — but the culture brokers from Washington to LA were starting to pick up on the catch phrases. Pride Day, a good idea based on visibility, had begun its descent into one big ad campaign for vodka, unbridled drug abuse and an opportunity for the news cameras to come take pictures of anything resembling a carnival show — guys wearing beards, panties and leather chaps. Community. Then somebody decides we need a flag. That god-awful flag. Not unlike the one Jesse

Jackson used for his Rainbow Coalition. Hrmmm. Somebody had obviously confused asserting the right to exist with sticking out like a circus clown. I guess it was better than the 'hate the sin not the sinner' bullshit: tempered vitriol courtesy of the compassionate Christians.

And woe be unto our best-kept secrets that got leaked to the capitalists. Just like how women's went from 'movement' to 'target market,' and black went from 'slave' to 'minstrel' to 'identity' and back to 'minstrel' for the entertainment industry. Gay was well on its way — kinda like Ghandi said: 'first they laugh at you, then they ignore you, then they fight you, then you win,' except America can't ever seem to get past 'laugh' and 'ignore'. Nobody wins. Instead of winning, we got 'tolerance.' I decided early on, with the half-baked smiles and pats on the back from North Carolina to New York, that I'd rather be hated than tolerated. Tolerated means just putting off a fight, or putting off leaving a place where you're not wanted.

Queers routinely put things where they don't necessarily belong. I belonged in the East Village because no one was tolerated — you just came there, and somehow it worked. And I liked hanging out at The Bar because it was frequented by a hodgepodge. Growing up, my sister called me an anomaly — the straightest queer ever. Which doesn't mean straight-acting. I have my nelly moments. It's a vibe, not a lifestyle. The guys who frequented The Bar had lots of vibes. Good ones at that. Several main characters ran the joint. Michael was the manager. A frail little guy, about 5'4 tall. Had the longest most New Jersey'd mullet in the world running down his back, which reminded me of the Lady Elaine puppet on Mister Rogers. Cropped on top, hair down the middle of his back. He kept a pair of fitted black leather gloves on the side of the long bar which he put on and pulled off in between making drinks. I figured they were part of some kind of leather S&M thing. The Bar survived because Michael was one of the meanest motherfuckers you didn't want to be on the wrong side of.

Everyone rumored the place was run by the mafia. The best ones were. Like The Monster in the West Village, which was probably owned by the same bunch. The Monster, the first place Seth had taken me, was more of a gentleman's club. Or ladies' parlor, depending on how you wanted to view a room full of older gay guys crowded around a piano singing show tunes at 5PM. There was a daily ritual of an older queen dressed to-the-nines in a pinstriped suit complete with fedora and pocket square, accompanied by armed goons, who came in to pick up a suitcase presumably full of money. Mafia cool. The Bar wasn't quite as dramatic. Michael had Al, the security man, who backed him up on everything. Al could have been Barry White's brother. A stocky black man who oozed Soul when he talked in a deep voice. Short cropped hair and beard, carrying a mean, heavy walking stick with a brass duck's head on top.

You didn't fuck with that duck.

Greg worked behind the actual bar with Michael. Greg was friendly and would talk to anyone. He usually wore a solid colored pocket t-shirt or the like, blue jeans and parted his short blond hair in the middle. People came to sit specifically at the side of the bar near Greg, 'cause he would chat to them.

Eddie, my one-time roommate *in absentia*, worked the floor as a barback. Picking up glasses and cleaning up. Gathering empty bottles in a box on his shoulder, sorting them by brand into boxes, stacked to the right of the squeaky front door. The walls were black. The interior lined by low windows, about five feet tall. A solid wooden bench surrounded the left side of the room, and a pool table in the middle. The physical bar Michael and Greg tended was to the right. Down the center was a makeshift wooden rail dividing the two sides for people to perch against. Straight back about twenty-five feet was the jukebox. To the left was an unused make-shifty closet, which also housed the air conditioning unit. Behind that, communal bathrooms, for men only. Eddie was responsible for keeping it all tidy. Even on jam-packed nights he'd have to make his way around with his token box on his shoulder collecting enough refuse to fill a small truck.

New York had a bad reputation before the yuppies moved in. It certainly earned it afterwards. But at this point, guys on the busiest of nights would let Eddie slip between their conversations, gossip and tongue kisses. Eddie was friendly and well-liked and well-lusted after. Eddie was also one of the best-looking corn-fed boys in the entire East Village. People came specifically to watch Eddie. He was 6' tall. Smooth alabaster skin. Framed like a model, chiseled stomach. Wholesome face, blue eyes, clear skin. Natural muscles and tone. A butt so round it should have had a globe painted on it. Perfectly plump, pouty Mississippi river boat lips.

My friend Scotty had kissing privileges with Eddie. Which meant, on a busy night or anytime he walked by, Scotty, a tall skinny blond from Seattle, would step in Eddie's way and make out with him like a bandit. The entire room would pause for it, this setting of the tone. This public display of male bravado something or other. Naturally, I decided I wanted privileges too. I wanted to be able to kiss Eddie on demand. You move up in rank with such a thing. So as not to make a competition, for Scotty and I were friends, I asked permission. 'Sure babe, he likes you, are you kidding? And his boyfriend won't care. Just as long as you know it ain't going nowhere else,' Scotty tells me. 'Yeah, that's fine...'

Scotty reached out and grabbed Eddie next time he came around the pool table. Planted one on him. Pulled back, grabbed me and pushed me into his face. The deal was done. I forgot who I was for a minute. I hear an 'oh' during the pause of those around. I'd never felt special like this before. I think I bought Scotty a beer or ten.

I had to watch the cash flow. Unemployment is like a heroin maintenance program — not enough to get you high, just enough to keep you from stealin.' In those days, fifteen dollars was a big night out. First beer: 3 dollars, 1 dollar tip. Second beer, 3 dollars, no tip. Third beer, 3 dollars, 1 dollar tip and you'd get a small shot of something — vodka lemons, Jaeger, Schnapps for free. Fourth, Fifth, Sixth beer, free, 1 dollar tip each.

I needed a cash supplement. One night, a slower Tuesday or the like, between make-out sessions with Eddie, I had an idea, probably as I looked over his shoulder back toward the jukebox and in the old closet beside the bathrooms. I went over and opened the door. Michael and Al didn't pay no mind. Inside was the a-c unit, and a bunch of coat hangers. An inch of dust had settled on the floor sticking down an old mop. The door itself had been sawed in two and a random piece of wood topped the bottom half laterally. Some hardware store rods had been installed. Just as I suspected. It had been a coat check room at some point. Or a coat check closet. I asked Michael if I could do something with it. Michael had been eyeing me from behind the bar all along, he didn't miss much the shrewd little mullet head. He stared me directly in the face to make sure I knew who's boss. 'Yes dear, you can do whatever you like with the closet. I thought you'd come out but apparently...' He liked the idea 'cause he didn't have to pay me a shift pay, got a built-in service and more action in the room.

'I'll do it right.'

'You'll do who right?' He shot a perverted grin. 'Why don't you just hustle hon? It'd be easier...'

'I'll be ready tomorrow night.'

'Come early if you're going to bother.' I was in business. I spent the rest of the night cleaning out the closet. Some middle-aged dude who had a crush on me helped out. Thought it might get him somewhere. New York was one big racket and I'd found one. My own gig. No stores, no bosses, no insurance scams. Just tax-free money. Reagan had gotten enough of my dough. I finally decided 'no time like the present' and opened right then and there. I had my tight jeans on and a tight white t-shirt and my leather MC jacket, and the best part: my youth. I begged a blank sheet of notebook paper and a ballpoint pen from Michael.

'Gimme that pen back or I'll kick your ass.'

'OK.' I put it down and traced the letters over & over so they can be seen: c-o-a-t-c-h-e-c-k-1-$. Fred Bidgood, one of the older regulars, who wore big-framed glasses and smoked a pipe, chimed in from the side, 'Going into business are we?' Fred liked to chat me up. Fred was good for ideas. And I liked Fred because he and the older generation who freely mixed with the younger in those days were good for us. They provided a stability, a security and a source of knowledge for a bunch of don't-need-nothing-from-nobody children from broken America. 'Hurry up, you've got customers.' Fred was probably one of the first in line. I appreciated the support. At one point, I decided to add k-i-s-s-e-s-$-2.

The first night, I made around seventy bucks. In just a few nights I could make double my unemployment and have reason to talk to the hottest guys in the neighborhood. I was a novelty, not a necessity, and I liked it that way. Although people told me I could have been a model, my reflection in the mirror said 'almost, not quite' to me. If you are born with no hope of fitting in, you can get on with doing other things. Some of the luckiest people I knew didn't have to worry about none of this shit. The rest of us learned how to paint, dress and reinvent ourselves new. Getting paid to receive kisses and compliments eased the trauma of young adulthood.

You take your coffee in one hand after pulling off the worn, limp, black tank top. You like how your body feels with nothing on it but the loose sweat pants. You like how they barely cling to your hips as you now formally begin the getting ready process. You like the tactical laissez-faire approach to clothing as a necessity. You like the possibility that one minute someone could sneak up behind you and be inside those sweats without warning, and get inside you the next. Ooh, a good fuck — the thought inspires you to music. You switch on the shiny black stereo, and put on your favorite getting ready playlist: 'fuck the pain away, fuck the pain away' starts and you hum along with the lyrics on your way back to the bathroom, swinging your hips for the cat, who watches without reaction or emotion. You've begun to feel cautiously fabulous. You know that in a mere hour or so you will transform yourself into something creative, something partially borrowed and something not-so-blue. A little makeup, a little shine, a little leather and you'll take your piece of that New York Doll and bring it to life. Buster will be pleased. So will the cat. But you're uncertain.

18. Together Apart

Even in summer someone had to store all those leather MC jackets while the restless natives carried on. Especially in summer someone had to kiss the lonely young tourists who either couldn't or didn't know how to approach anyone at one of the most friendly bars in New York City. Might as well have been little 'ole me. I was a prostitute for kissing and pimp for introducing people. Over time, I came to know most of the players, their likes and dislikes. Who was friendly, who was psycho, and who should be avoided altogether. Some guys just took turns coming over to talk to me in my little corner of paradise and I loved it. I could work whenever I wanted. That closet, ironically, set me free — and allowed me to do all the things I wanted: talk, chat, meet boys, get laid, make money, make friends. But freedom always has limits — you can leave North Carolina or North Anywhere, but your past and her problems are your traveling companions. I hid them behind the coats as best I could.

I made a career out of living in the East Village. When we weren't at The Bar, me and my friends frequented one of the few other haunts like The Tunnel — a shithole on First Avenue which tended to cater to a more 'let's get on with it now' crowd — as in sex. On special occasions a few of us would visit to the Michael Todd room at Palladium. Pyramid Club at least once a week, along with a new place on the scene, 'Wonder Bar,' a kooky joint on East 6th Street just up from Barney's apartment. Two of Barney's friends, Jeffrey and Tim, opened it as a dream project. They painted the outside like a Wonder Bread wrapper — white with blue, yellow and red circles. The inside was lit with black lights that brought hundreds of glowing paper cutouts of neon movie stars, cartoons and porno pictures suspended everywhere from fishing line to life. A small stage big enough for two people stood just ahead of a mini-movie screen, with a little private room behind it for more daring adventures — as in sex. Well, mostly fondling. Not that I'd know for sure. Not one inch of the place was left uncovered — sequins, glitter, lamé fabric, hanging things, tinsel. Not many Wonder Bar customers left uncovered. Some were stickier than others. A few I called close friends. The kind of friends that you went and talked to in between excursions behind the screen, or to the bar. Friends that you came with and, unless something came along, would leave with. Laugh with, talk and giggle about the rest of the crowd with.

One of my best pals Dan worked as a paralegal, but like the rest of us played like a party boy — I still don't know how we'd go out and drink to pollution until 4am then make it to work for 9. Dan was tall, with short, cropped dark hair. He wore the dark denim jeans you buy that are stiff as a board, and have to wash a hundred times just to get them on. He said he got a kick out of getting them cheaper. Flat-soled Converse tennis shoes and various collared shirts underneath the MC jacket treatment. He was Italian-Irish, and from Rochester. Ramon was from San Francisco, his parents from China. I think he might have been born in Mexico. Mexican for a few days — hopelessly international with a Northern California accent. Ramon worked three different jobs and was trying to start a clothing company. He had short black hair too — shorter than Dan's — and he kept glued straight up with enough gel to cover a giraffe. Kurt, a.k.a. Kurtie, was shorter, slightly stockier than the others. He had an Englishey face with rosy cheeks and spoke with a trained actor's voice until he got drunk. When he grew his hair mid-length, he looked like a Shakespearean courtier, which he played up with big blousey shirts topped with high collars, counterbalanced by leather daddy boots and a punk rock studded belt. I'm sure there was a kinky story behind the daddy boots. Kurtie was great that way.

Lawrence showed his face occasionally. He looked exotic, Aztec to me, with the darkest black hair and naturally tanned skin. He kept very busy with lawyers and doctors who liked boys with medium-dark skin, black hair, tight Lycra t-shirts and distinct features. I'd originally met him through Barney, who was his live-in boyfriend at the time. Lawrence liked to talk about some famous people he'd met. In turn, we'd piss him off by calling him names like Larry. It went like something like: 'The other night, I went to this fabulous party in a fabulous apartment in Soho, and you'll never guess who was there…'

'Who was there, Larry?'

'Ugh. Forget it.'

Truth was, we usually already knew the famous people he'd met. But we got a kick out of Larry, and let him stay. Maybe he let us stay. Who knows? He finally changed his name to Lorenzo at some point along the way. It didn't take much for me to irk Lawrence-Lorenzo because he thought I actually became one of 'Barney's Boys' when they were still together, and no amount of protest or convincing was gonna' change that. But it didn't stop a few escapades, like the night after I got my unemployment payout from Mario Cuomo.

Lawrence-Lorenzo and I met up at Boy Bar, where RuPaul was doing his new number 'Supermodel.' Before the show, Lawrence mentioned that he had a friend who'd gone up to Provincetown, Massachusetts for the summer, and we should go. Apparently it was this bohemian artist colony turned queer ghetto with sun and beaches. I agreed and the next afternoon we were on a bus to Boston, where we'd catch the ferry to P-town on the tip of Cape Cod. Unfortunately, we missed the last ferry by about an hour, and ended up roughing it at some dusty hotel near the harbor until the next morning. I got stuck with the bill. P-town was remotely interesting, if you're a closet-case banker from Boston in need of self-expression at any cost, but it wasn't for me. Lawrence's friend Mark kept trying to sell us on how bohemian and cool it all was, 'you could get a job in a restaurant and stay,' but all I could make of it was a small fishing town where the locals were ambivalently cashing in on all the desperately deprived-of-culture homos from Boston — something about as sad to me as the scene back down South, or anywhere besides Manhattan.

We knew, or at least I did, that we were the luckiest queers in America, and because people were dropping like flies from the big 'A,' we'd damn well better enjoy it before our turn came. Joey, who I'd kept up with since my Uncle Charlie's days, was still skinny as a toothpick, hung like a horse and popular with the boys. Joey was bopping in regularly from Bay Ridge. Once in a blue moon I'd venture out to his neighborhood and go to The Spectrum — the club where Saturday Night Fever was filmed, which still had the infamous lit dance floor, but he mostly came to the city.

I kept to the prowl around what had become our East Village, except on an odd Saturday night I'd sneak off to 'Roxy' with Lawrence to dance in a big way. Roxy with a capital 'R,' as in the original Roxy produced by Lee Chappell and Co. — before the onslaught of steroids, crystal meth, and muscle Marys clad in khaki, trying to be good little second-class gays and assimilate. I have never identified as, or been able to understand, or will ever be 'gay.' But I understand a thousand free people spread out across an enormous roller-skating rink, movin' and swishin' and swayin' — straight, not straight, who knew, who cared, all types in the groove.

Lawrence was a good Roxy partner 'cause he knew people there. I didn't call him by his other names at Roxy. Patiently, I'd listened to stories of his shenanigans if it meant I could get in free. If we were successful it meant I could afford a few cocktails, or maybe one-fourth of a hit of E from the 'It Twins' the dealers *du jour*. I really didn't care either way — the main focus of the evening was the scene: the music, the crowds, the fantastic outfits, the energy and sexual tension. Sure, drugs were everywhere and the entirety of Manhattan is an island floating on a river of alcohol — but in those days, just being out, to see and be seen, was the primary focus for me. If I got fucked up along the way, fine, but it wasn't a preset goal. Any boob could go to the suburbs and hang with a bunch of rednecks while senselessly pouring cheap liquor down their gut. Any Philistine could get loud.

On the big dance floor, you could become anything, or anyone. Me, along with a large number of young skinny queer twentysomethings, held the deep belief that we were the male Madonnas. I would wear the jeans, big black combat boots, big black belt with enormous silver buckle, t-shirt, and MC jacket. Desperately Seeking Sanity. A cross that hung from my neck on a long chain clanked the belt buckle when I danced, and followed my spins about three seconds behind me. It was dazzling, except for when it would jackknife and swing back and hit me in the head. Small price. The music was brilliant. The crowd was brilliant — and together we'd all sparkle.

Ramon would join in the monthly Roxy runs, but not Dan and

Kurt, because it just wasn't their thing. Dan and Kurt were good for touring the bars, or for Linda Simpson's Channel 69 Sundays at Pyramid. It was also home to punk rock nights, band nights and retro-queer nights. I think the Lady Bunny found the genesis for Wigstock there. I liked these downtown places 'cause they just seemed to like me back and that's all. Sometimes we'd live dangerously and Barney'd drag me into 'King Tut's Wah Wah Hut' on 7th & A where the hardcore crowd held court. I liked something about all the places where the people met. I could hide in them without hiding, know people without trying too hard. Breathe. All pretty good, except for the fact that I never felt like I fit myself. I didn't really fill out my own tall frame, bustling around inside my own skin like a kid trying on his father's clothes. For the larger picture, I wanted to live. As in, really live. Anyone could die. Dying seemed obligatory in those days, with AIDS in full swing. There seemed to be an honor among thieves: steal some life. It seemed, for me at least, that all of us were living our twenties to the hilt in overdrive, convinced we'd never see our thirties. Don't talk about it. No time to waste.

Although I'd run around the city collecting friends on every corner, I still kept up with Seth, Marilyn and Bari-G. My instinct has always been to never forget where I've been. But my social perspective, and all that came with it, had grown considerably. My first experience with New York City hospitals was at St Vincent's, one of the few places that would deal with the latest lepers on the scene. I don't know how I'd gotten the news, but I met Seth on the corner of Greenwich and 7th Avenues, just around the corner from Uncle Charlie's. Over a couple of years, I'd run into Marty Lipton a few times on the street, here and there. One pride day he made an effort to get across roving droves of queers to stop me. Now, he'd gone down real fast. Turned purplish on one side of his face and held his smile and eye contact unusually long with the other, as if to distract my attention from the horror he was living out. I tried my best to smile and not notice, and was quickly learning to numb myself against such things, but I usually failed at both.

I'll never forget the walk down the corridor and into Marty's temporary room. A corner room, all alone. Peter, Marty's boyfriend, sat to the left of the bed. Marty, with his beautiful muscular body, lay on the bed beside the window, a single white sheet haphazardly strewn over him like a deity in a Michelangelo fresco. Years of caked-on white paint covered the trim of the window which looked out on the avenue. Pastel-colored paper was stuck to the walls, the kind you only find in hospitals and old folks' homes. Marty grinned and sat up when we came in, 'Come on in guys! Hey!' he said, thrilled to have visitors. I squinted my eyes when no one was watching, and when I did Marty looked normal. I remember a sinking feeling, one that could not resolve how a hot young guy was stuck up in a place like St Vincent's. Except for the Karpoci's Sarcoma marks, he didn't really look sick. It was autumn and the purple had faded from his face a little since the summer. To me, Marty looked like an angel wrapped in his white sheet and blanket.

Someone commented on how Peter had just finished taking care of a certain itch Marty had. I didn't say anything. I couldn't. Marty was the first cool guy I'd known in New York. He knew I'd taken a shine to him the first time we met. He also knew I was just like any other young twentysomething from outta' town, beaming at anything on two legs. He rolled his sparkly eyes to the left from time to time to look at me and exchange a private grin as Peter and Seth chattered on and on about this and that. I also felt terribly uncomfortable just being there sharing this private experience with Marty. I didn't know him well at all, but somehow, when it came to AIDS in Reagan's indifferent 80s, everyone shared. 'Come here, chicken,' he said with his eyes at one point, lazily extending his left hand toward me. Or just letting it sit — I dunno', I felt like I was being drawn in. I sat motionless at first. This wasn't a drag show or a dress rehearsal. I had nothing to offer the deity.

I had to numb fear and rage and sadness. I was more confused than I'd ever been in my life. When I was sixteen my other grandfather, Miss Ruby's husband, passed away after a string of heart attacks and strokes. He was older and sick. He'd gone early by most standards — at sixty-five, after being ill for ten years. But grandaddy Belk had brought forth children, grandchildren, started umpteen businesses and had a life. I still miss him, but his story sort of made sense. The scene at St Vincent's fucked my mind. 'We shouldn't be here' I kept thinking. None of us, not me or Seth or Peter or Marty or any of the other guys I passed walking down the long corridor to Marty's room. We were young, goddammit. Healthy looking, mostly. Hadn't even gotten started good. In those days, it felt like every HIV guy with the strength to turn his head looked at me with a yearning, as if to ask if they could borrow my body, just for one day.

'Want some ice cream?' Marty said, reaching for a little styrofoam cooler on his nightstand. I didn't know what to say. Was I really sure that this thing, virus, wasn't transmissible through the air or on food or something? More important, how the hell do you take a dying man's ice cream? Further — how could you possibly refuse?

Although you've been accepted and can go in, enter — even after many years of trial, error and successful experimentation, you are never sure where you fit in. You can boast true friendships with some of the biggest rock stars of the day (although you rarely see them out of star venues) and the photographers manage to catch you off guard for a photo which will run in some pop-rag, somewhere. Your reputation supersedes you. Page Six gives you credit for things you never did. Unlike the fashion world or political arena — once you've made it inside one of nightlife's coveted cocoons: the messier life becomes. Then, you'll eventually grow old and go on VH1 to tell the world about the art of survival. A spiritual metamorphosis not unrelated to that of an incarcerated prisoner: there aren't many men in a prison who haven't found the Lord. They got caught. You are caught. All this, along with thoughts of who you'll run into tonight, who'll be fuckable tonight, who'll be fabulous tonight and how you'll get fucked up tonight, flash through your mind and squish through your belly. You feel sickly. You press on to press it on.

19. The Only Fear Thing We Have ...

Barney's East 6th Street garden parties kept going, although they were not as frequent as when I'd first met him. Otherwise, we were out six nights a week along with a whole host of East Village kids and downtown New York 'dinosaurs.' A dinosaur was a person in their thirties, forties or above, who'd ran around the previous generation's scene, as in actually been a regular at Studio 54 or the Mudd Club. I knew some of these guys from checking their coats at The Bar. To me, they just seemed like regular people. I imagined they all had day jobs and such, which many actually did. Like Marcus Leatherdale, another member of the grand family, would later remind me: 'If you read the press, you'd think we only ran around and did coke. People ran around and did a lot of coke, but there were eighteen other hours to each day that the press had no access to, where a lot of hard work went on.' Marcus was a photographer and had been connected with Robert Mapplethorpe and ran around with Andy Warhol. I envied him a bit because he lived more of what I'd come to see, except I was just barely a few years too late. My time wasn't panning out badly at all though, and Barney's parties afforded me a more comprehensive dip into the cultural gene pool. He had a big naked photo of Marcus walking away from a cross on his wall.

Although I first met Haoui Montaug a year or two before back at Uncle Charlie's and ran into him 'out and about,' I got to know him best in Barney's infamous garden. I realized he was very active in the arts and downtown scene, but I didn't know he was, like, all famous. Famous doorman guy. More than the ones at Boy George's birthday party or all of us goobers that worked the bars or at Pyramid or Wonder Bar, except for Willi Ninja, but he was in a different scene altogether. Apparently Haoui'd worked coat check with Madonna and introduced her onstage at Danceteria, the night she sang 'Everybody' she walked off stage with her first record deal.

Barney and Haoui knew most everyone on the planet between them. My other friends and me seemed to know the rest between us. If anybody got missed, they'd get picked up sooner or later. It was the culture, the New York pastime. Some people collected antiques or cars, we collected each other. A way of staying alive, being alive — an art in the pre-Giuliani pre-yuppie city. It meant something. We were all there to find each other — first and foremost. And we did. I think we all had a private collection of people, a guest list, stored in our heads, ready for instant retrieval. Changing moment by minute and in no particular order. One of the early trails went something like: Barney who introduced me to Haoui Montaug who was a Danceteria mogul and Madonnaman who was friends with Jorgé, a writer and a singer who worked a lot of doors to clubs like The Building and Quick, who was also friends with Grace Nemergut who I thought was the prettiest blonde girl in New York City — all of whom were friends with Paul Likins, a bartender at Boy Bar, and Kenny Scharf the artist who worked on Betty Badum's apartment, and certainly had beers at the Bandito's manager's table with David Russell on Greenwich Avenue just across from Uncle Charlie's and was very likely joined on a regular basis by Paul Garrity, a party boy who used to get incredibly wasted and talk about how one day he'd just like to disappear (which he one day did) to Barney and me at Boy Bar where Joey Arias (one day to officiate at Cirque Du Soleil), Sweetie B, RuPaul — 'StarrBooty' well on her way to becoming 'Supermodel of the World' — Hapi Phace and Taboo all performed or at Pyramid where Linda Simpson did Channel 69 on Sundays where Wendy Wild would coat-check and I met Hattie Hathaway who was a performance nun who hosted shows put on by Black Lips Performance Cult where I met Antony (soon to be of the Johnsons) and Lily of the Valley a.k.a. Michael (one day to guest star in Wonderboys) and Page Reynolds a performer who also lived down the street from me and Linda only nine blocks from Barney's garden where I got to know Michael Schmidt, a designer for Cher, Tina Turner and Debbie Harry, and Phoebe, a black-haired big girl, with her boyfriend Marc in tow who owned part of the triangle building at 14th Street and Ninth Avenue where we'd gather to watch the fireworks on Gay Pride with people like Calvin who kept the best Barbie collection and his boyfriend Larry who threw parties at their place in midtown, and in the center of the milieu was, of course, people like Haoui.

Haoui lived around the corner from CBGBs and kept a mountain home in Croton Falls, upstate, with his friend Cathy. He and his friends threw grand soirees up there. I was invited up three times. The first time was in May 1990, for, among other things the annual celebration of Barney's birthday — an outlandish party of misfits in the first warm, sunny weather of the year. Everyone partying, boozing, dancing and swimming in the lake. Fucking. Running around. Yelling out, thrilled to be alive — something you could be in those days. It went on all day, all night. Haoui followed me around some and teased me whenever he could. Haoui teased everybody relentlessly. If you got teased it meant he liked you. At the time, I was flattered beyond my size-ten-and-a-half boots being liked by someone who'd known Robert Mapplethorpe, Andy Warhol and knew Madonna. I didn't let it all get to my head — really. I didn't want anything from Haoui or any of the others, never have, except to be accepted, which they did. Those folks found me, awkward as fuck, funny. My prize was just to be there, make it, and be living among them. They encouraged my creative impulses and gave me room to be a stupid, clumsy kid.

Back in the city, with AIDS sweeping through the scene, we went out all the time. Fran Lebowitz used to say that the first reason they all went out in the late 70s was because their 'apartments were so miserably hot and disgusting.' By the late 80s I think it was that, and to distract ourselves. What in the 70s had been a great experiment in creative living became an 80s mandate in creative survival. And for the first big wave of the modern pestilence, no one cared.

Ronald Reagan, the greatest American president to some, phony bastard antichrist to others, wouldn't even acknowledge that he had a national health crisis on his hands. Of course, it was to minimize the liabilities of the insurance companies. The sluggish local authorities left it up to St Vincent's. NYC may have been progressive, but the big stuff was run up in Albany, where all things mean and right-wing began in the state. Before AIDS activism, the police would barely show up when faggots were getting beaten up, slashed in the face with razors or killed on the street. Like in the Tracy Chapman song: 'they always come late, if they come at all…' So, why would the government bureaucrats rush to help people just for being terminally ill? The greater city had amnesia and the God Squad now had another reason for its Armageddon. The people I knew just had a disease. A disease that I am forever convinced was either a military experiment gone wrong, or a government invention gone right. Like the continued involuntary mass sterilizations of poor blacks in the US even after Hitler was defeated and the Tuskegee experiments — a program for 'Hepatitis' prevention in the 70s remains suspect. Never in the history of the world had a naturally occurring disease selected certain groups of people more specifically — people whom society deems undesirable: queers, minorities, addicts. The people Jesus liked to call friends. Given the right-wing agenda of the time, it's all a bit 'coincidental,' as Gore Vidal says. The whole thing terrified me. Still does. I'd been a pretty patriotic, loyal American up to the point. I realized there were large numbers of fellow Americans who would just as soon see me dead, for no reason affecting them whatsoever. In all this, I needed no reason to party. To be distracted. To keep dreaming. I had to.

New York City had begun to die around me.

20. You Say Goodbye I Say Stop

Funny, how most of the people looking for themselves tend to stay lost. I did. The music was good, the scene on the streets wasn't. Goons from all over the outer boroughs of NYC had started queer bashing. It was sport. 'Roll a fag.' I never understood why people cared so much about 'fags.' Especially the teenaged blacks and Puerto Ricans who ran in mobs, hadn't they been shit on too? Not to mention all the time wasted in school growing up: who's a fag, you're a fag, fag-fag-fag.

Every weekend was met with some sort of incident: people getting slashed with box cutters, old men jumped and beaten in the West Village, many with AIDS. It was called 'wilding.' It was sick. I blame Reagan and Bush. They ran the agenda: anger and denial. Their fascist teen brigades followed suit. The tone had been set earlier, the preceding October. A group of kids attending a rap show across the street from The Bar decided to 'roll some fags' afterward. Nothing like that so-called 'Rap' and 'Hardcore' music, disguised as poetry and liberation — good for inciting people to get angry, real angry, and start a riot.

Some young guys walked in the squeaky gray door of The Bar bleeding profusely from their faces. They'd been slashed in the face. Greg killed the jukebox, jumped on top of the bar and announced to the crowd that they should stay inside until the cops got there. So naturally, the crowd of about a hundred went outside. The sight outside angered me: fifteen or so skinny juveniles laid siege to an entire bar full of adults.

The juveniles retreated across Second Avenue while a bunch of guys from Queer Nation screamed 'We're here, we're queer, get used to it.' I thought 'that's all you got, the best you can come up with?' and ducked as the kids responded by pelting us with glass bottles. I thought the hundred or so of us should go over and engage in a little eye for an eye. Instead, me and Jorgé ran over to the police precinct on East 5th Street telling them about the violence, the riot that was about to take place, the car that'd gotten hit with one of the bottles being thrown across the street. We were curtly told 'OK' — the reflections from the badges around the room shined with contempt. We were second-class. We returned. The scene had escalated. One cop car came, and went. It took forever for them to actually show up and actually do something. And what they did was take the perpetrators around the corner and tell them to go home. We later learned the kids did go home, and came back with bats. Only then were the police forced to arrest the little darlings.

It's amazing what you can get away with in the middle of chaos. The entire scene scared the fuck out of me, but strangely I didn't feel it. There I was, standing in my neighborhood, bottles flying, knives flashing, sticks swinging. Tenants throwing stuff at the perpetrators out the windows. I didn't want to fight. I didn't know how to fight. So I decided to put my hands in my pockets, and joined Jorgé as he and others led the way toward where the police were acting like they were dealing with the youths. 'Who's watching the police?' Jorgé shouted. People followed. With the Tompkins Square riots not so far in the past and Chris Connelly, a peaceful AIDS protester who'd been beaten into a coma by the NYPD, fresh in many of our minds, we crossed the avenue. This is when someone caught the sergeant telling the perpetrators to 'just go home, it's over, you made your point.'

The following week the police captain held his ceremonial hearing at the LGBT center on West 13th Street. The hearing was about as much fun as the incident. Worse actually. We didn't get to speak much. Tension filled the room with a coarse, grating air. The captain apologized to the community, and no one believed him. These hearings and public meetings were always a joke. We got a police van parked outside The Bar for a few weeks. It really helped my fears — bashers watching bashers watching us.

If it hadn't been for AIDS, the time would've passed like any other time. Problem was, people were dropping like flies in a DDT factory. I'd met too many guys working at The Bar who'd look great one day, not so great in a month, then would suddenly disappear. Back then, if you got HIV they poisoned you with AZT. Another one bites the dust. Killing you hoping it would save you. A lot of the guys I knew from the A-list crowd, Haoui's crowd, had long been activists. Jorgé helped to start ACT UP. There were others like Housing Works and God's Love We Deliver, a food program for homebound people who did not have hot meals. Most decent folks did something, anything, to contribute. I did AIDS walks and dances. Others made quilts in remembrance memorials to those who died.

Sometimes I went to the Monday ACT UP meetings, which frightened me. Sick people everywhere. I was caught between compassion, fear for myself and just wanting to be young and forget all of it. Guys in their twenties walked in with a cane in one hand, a lover on the other. Then, the reports and things would begin. They'd read the creed or whatever, ask for law enforcement people to identify themselves — which they never did. At first, ACT UP had been irreverently successful in getting the corporate media to pay attention to the guys with the canes.

The 'actions,' as they were called, like invading Dan Rather's newscast and shutting down Grand Central at rush hour were very effective. But in a short few years something had changed. The focus of the group shifted from fighting AIDS as suffered by anyone, to how this-group was more affected than that-group. And somehow all the racial disparity ever experienced in the US of A was now to be debated and solved in New York Fucking City by ACT UP. The Latino Caucus and the Asian Pacific Islander faction wasted much of the meeting time. Then came the angry black dykes. And then the people who blamed white men for everything. Every week the whole drama turned my stomach further. People were dying. That was my issue. AIDS wasn't killing a black any more mercilessly than a white one. AIDS does what I think it was intended to do: get rid of the fags and queers, coloreds, poor folks, make the pharmaceutical companies rich and wipe the African continent clean for new development.

I moved to the sidelines in ACT UP. I didn't want to be arrested like so many of the others. I didn't consider it a war badge. After the street riot outside of The Bar, I became equally terrified of the queer bashers and the cops. The best strategy I found: keep cool. Keep it on the 'D-L,' Down low — like the old schoolers say. A lot of brave people went to protests and got arrested for the cause, but they didn't need my panicky ass in a jail cell. I did my bit working for kids. All that had to be done was to go in front of high schools, the high schools run by the government and Catholic Church, who'd still not admit AIDS was a problem. Give the kids condoms. Tell them to watch out. This was my calling. My activism. And although I never actually made it in front of a school, I redesigned the cards that would go out with condoms and supported the meetings. Fear held me back and I'd never dreamed America the Beautiful would allow any of this

AIDS or meanness to happen. Nor did I fathom having to confront these issues on the street. I was discovering that from the Pledge of Allegiance to the story of the poor Puritan pilgrims to the Amber Waves of Grain, most of the America I'd been taught was a bald-faced lie.

People kept dying, including another of Barney's friends, Keith. Last time I saw him he was sipping a margarita in the garden. Paul Garrity fulfilled his wish, got high and just disappeared. One night I went to Pyramid. Most likely on a Linda Simpson's Channel 69 night — one of my favorites. Scott, a young new friend of mine, was up on the pedestal in the middle of the room. Dancing for money. His shiny, curly black hair adorned his smooth, perfectly tan skin. He looked like an angel up there, moving, becoming the oracle for the crowd to worship. I went over to him, he smiled with an unusually big smile as if it were a special occasion. I can still feel both of his hands touching my cheeks, pulling me close for a kiss. Then his hands dropping to my shoulders, keeping me there to dance close to him, an anointed friend of the object on the pedestal. The music was fast but we danced slow, grooving rather than bouncing. His white shirt was covered in sweat, the heat radiated from his body as I leaned in closer. I didn't know what we were doing, but we were definitely doing something. Thoughts raced through me: he's beautiful, and kind, why didn't we ever... I'd known that Scott liked me more than a friend. I felt so safe there, that moment, that it made me uncomfortable. I didn't know what to do with 'genuine.' Was it because he was mulatto? Or just that the whole concept of intimacy was foreign? I hated myself for that.

After a few songs I decided to walk around the club or leave and go somewhere else — I can't remember. I smiled really big and said 'See ya later.' We hugged and quick kissed. I thought he might say OK' OK,' back to me. He didn't. He just smiled without saying anything, waving as I walked to the front of the club. I looked back and smiled a time or two — we had a private moment over the crowds of dancing people. Looking back, I now realize that he'd probably forced just enough willpower into his legs to carry him there that night. And although he was weak and covered in sweat from medicine and fever, danced one last time, defiant that he too deserved life. And now I know all to well, that last look from people, the eyes of goodbye. I never saw Scott again.

On one visit back to North Carolina, I impulsively stopped off to see some friends, a couple who lived near Miss Ruby. I knew Stirl and Waynor through Timanrichard, the extended Charlotte crowd. Stirl, Waynor and I had once taken a getaway trip to Charleston, SC. They'd bought their house and were proud of it. They'd gotten it before I'd moved to New York and had begun fixer-upper-ing. New bathroom here, wallpaper there, stripped wood another place. Waynor was a district manager for a local fast food chain, and was forever proud of how he'd worked and earned his way up the ladder, in a state not known for its fine treatment of working-class black queers. I was excited to see them, say hi, and be the boy who made it out. When I got to the door I found a sign that said the place had been repossessed by government marshals. Like so many I knew in NYC, they too had apparently joined the legions of yesterday.

Haoui had AIDS too. It was no big secret. Silence = Death. When you ran half of Danceteria, had backed Madonna to stardom, people know things. I knew. He never complained in front of me. In fact, I don't know anyone who went down complaining. But we never talked about it either, for which I was grateful because our friendship on whatever level wouldn't be tainted by the plague. He was terrified perhaps, and rightly so: the only other people I knew who faced death on a daily basis, and were regularly mourning the loss of close friends, were much older, not twenty or thirtysomething young men. That first time I was invited up to Haoui's mountain party, upstate. The lake house was filled with the likes of record execs and club promoters, famous and not-so. I was coming in just as a transition in New York was underway, me a Freshman. Haoui's times were just before my time, but I felt we were there to keep things going. We all had places at the proverbial table, and if not, more could be found. I don't know anyone in the massive downtown circles of people who weren't affected by Haoui Montaug.

The parties were wild, and went on day and night. All the food you could eat, booze you could drink, pot you could smoke. Music from the massive speakers on the porch. Sun on the large lawn leading to the lake, highlighting people — all colors, shapes, sizes groovin' at their mountain beach. And I'm probably the only nervous one that didn't get laid. Too scared to walk into the great unknown of the surrounding woods. I had too much baggage to carry. Just because I'd made it to New York, and inadvertently gotten adopted by a very hip crowd of people, I brought all the insecurities of my South with me. Too many years and messages of 'repent' still needed to be let go. At the time, getting drunk was about the only way I could deal with what, for me, were high-pressure situations. Like back at Garinger High School, when me and my friend Mike would sit at the same lab table in biology class, and let our forearms touch while we were writing. What I believe for Mike was a big teenaged experimental nothing was a big deal for me — but every iota of excitement and pleasure was tempered with hellfire and damnation. Until I'd learn to send the devils packing back to their beloved hell, booze goosed away the guilt long enough to pretend.

The second year I was invited to Croton Falls was also in May, a more subdued gathering. The music was on, but not blasting.

Fewer people. Few drugs. Drinks, but not drinking with a capital 'D.' The crescendo of the afternoon was when a large, beautiful black woman sang a song called 'I Just Want You to Be What You Want Me to Be' or something like that while Haoui, now weaker and frail, listened from his chaise longue.

A Monday in June 1991. X—— calls. I refer to the person as 'X——' for obvious reasons — the so-called advanced Western World, particularly the God-fearing US, still cannot deal with people dealing with their own endings. Suicide, however morally challenging and outright frightening, was a last-source of empowerment in the face of Reagan and Bush's AIDS mess — dying by your terms, not theirs — and ending the suffering when you saw fit, not waiting to be poisoned by the cures. AIDS and the intended politics that come with it makes the preposterous plausible. X—— says Haoui's tired and says Haoui's only request is that he doesn't die alone.

Wednesday. X—— calls and says the chosen day is tomorrow. I need to meet him at Haoui's if I want to say goodbye. I do. I did. Haoui still smiled. Said he's cool with everything, he just doesn't want to go alone. I called Barney who agreed to meet me down at the Bowery and together we went for a visit. Everything was unusually normal. Haoui was weak, but could chat some. He said 'hi,' and he and Barney got to talking. I didn't say much at all — just like with Marty Lipton, what the hell do you say? I was afraid to touch or talk, afraid he might break somehow. I think he offered me a drink, or Barney did. Perhaps a beer. I'm pretty sure we got stoned. Barney was very studious about the whole thing. I hadn't yet become aware of cultures and options for handling death, other than the fearful 'til death do we die' routine of Western society. After a while things seemed almost like when we hung out in Barney's East 6th Street garden, except for Haoui being real sick, coughing and having to drift in and out of sleep. He was as sick as I'd seen my Grandaddy Belk, who I helped Grandma Ruby nurse for years after multiple heart attacks and strokes. Sicker even.

Thursday afternoon. *The day.* Closest friends only. X—— says he'll call and keep me posted. Haoui's to watch The Simpsons, say farewells on the phone. Then, *the time.*

Thursday early evening. X—— calls. Everything on course. Phone ringer turned off after Madonna's call. Watching Simpsons now. Soon.

Thursday evening. No word. I try to listen to music — never done anything like this, even from a distance — just nine blocks and one avenue away. I wonder if I'll feel anything when it happens. The wait was excruciating.

Thursday, very late. X—— calls again. Is it over? No. Problem. Haoui'd got stoned watching Simpsons then passed out before finishing even half of the pills. Everyone freaks out and tries to wake him up so he could finish dying. Shaking him, pouring ice water on him. He wouldn't wake up. X—— says it's the most surreal night he'd ever known, laughs even, and this coming from a person who'd been buddies with Divine.

Thursday, early morning. X—— calls again. Haoui'd awakened and become very upset that he was still alive. He sent everyone to go get breakfast and would decide what to do when they returned. He reassured them.

Friday, 7th June 1991. Morning. Last call from X——. Everyone returns. It's over. He'd gone alone.

Friday, 21st June 1991. 2PM. The memorial. St Mark's Church. The big beautiful black girl sings, just like at the lake. Haoui is lying beside her again. I was sure he could somehow hear her. They gave us a small card with names of people and Haoui's dates on it.

Inserted was a photo of Haoui, with a caption: *INSPIRATION.*

Haoui's memorial service at St Mark's Church was the first big one I ever attended in the city. The hall was the same one they used for the New Year's poetry readings, where Allen Ginsberg was a regular. I needed to be there, but didn't feel completely right about it. The place was packed. David Russell was real nice to me at the door. Barney made sure I had a seat. There was a video monitor playing tapes of Haoui as droves of people streamed in. I took a seat, but hadn't figured out how sad to be. How could I be as sad as people who knew him far better? Then again, who was I not to be immersed in sadness for every single person martyred by that useless, mean disease? I couldn't pretend to be a close friend, but I was a human being, and Haoui had been nice to me. That's all I needed. Many guys just faded away without a lot of fanfare — their family whisking them quietly, some shamefully, away to Iowa or Kansas for burial, removing the right to grieve in public.

Haoui had been cremated and his ashes sat on the spot where Ginsberg usually read. There were all kinds of people there. For some, it was a major event. A circus of crowned princesses, music industry people, and magazine publishers mingled with every-day-looking women wearing their Sunday dresses; club clowns from all over, who reminded me of the private-agenda people I detested at ACT UP meetings — there to be seen. Horribly underdressed, I didn't exactly belong, but I didn't not-belong. I had something to learn. Barney found me a seat. If Haoui could've worked the door for his own, last party, he'd have surely told me to 'come on in' for the beautiful black singer to sing the 'Just Want to Be…' song we'd heard at the lake.

Croton Falls, last time: September, almost melancholic mild day, almost warm, an intimate gathering — Haoui noticeably missing. Music playing quietly inside, lake water just too cold for swimming. The big beautiful black girl was there for a short visit, but didn't sing. The afternoon clouds and cool winds sent us indoors. Grace and I wandered around, someone told me to put on my shoes to be warmer. There was a derailed anticipation in the air: everyone wants to step outside, into the way things used to be. I put my shoes on, but I didn't feel warmer. As far as AIDS went, little did I know it was only the beginning of the cold.

Green Day blares at obscene levels from your stereo in the other room: 'No one here is getting out alive, this time I've really lost my mind and I don't care... to me it's noth-ing...' Fuck the neighbors. They'll live. Or at least they know it only takes you about an hour to get ready, and don't mind. Back in the bathroom, you pause for a moment to consider the face reflected before you in the mirror. You stare at the age you now think you are and shape the identity you want to be. All at once, at the proper musical crescendo from the other room, you see IT. The look, the feel, the vibe you'll be having this evening. The worry lines from your childhood disappear and the serious, respectable demeanor of your facial contours dissipates before your eyes, visually morphing into the entire being you shall create.

21. If You Like... As You Like...

Perhaps things were starting to make sense by not making sense. Like a scratched vinyl record — you're broken. Maybe your parents beat or abandoned you, drank or shot dope, ignored you; other kids beat you up, something, none, all. When you got to New York — the land of misfit toys — for the first time ever you could become part of a great whole, and find the others who also didn't make it to the top of whatever heap they used to call home. I was invigorated in my new place at the table, and the people I chose to dine with.

My friend Billy Corcoran was a Staten Island native. I met him on a night out at a new little dive called Dick's Bar, on the corner of 12th Street and 2nd Avenue. He'd started working there at the opening night, and stayed on as a bartender. I'd never much thought about having an older brother, but found one in Billy, and that was nice. There I was, running around the guts of Gotham like I'd been there all my life, thinking on my feet like a career criminal. Billy got me to slow down a little, relax a little, think a little. Old-schoolers could do that. Between him and Barney, and Marilyn, I was covered in the surrogate family department. And we didn't have to go to church every week or fight over Christmas plans to make it all legit. I pined for my family to have been from New York. Now one of them was.

Billy developed a loyal following at Dick's through his gift of gab. Some nights, the entire joint would be filled with people 'who'd come to see Billy.' He was friendly and had an accent and a smile that'd shine right through the most timid souls and somehow bring them to life. No one was a stranger when Billy worked, but Billy Corcoran was nobody's fool. When the owners of Dick's got jealous of all the attention Billy was getting and tried to order him around like a bitch, Billy walked and within one afternoon moved his nightly party to Reno — the Reno Bar, that is. 155 2nd Avenue between 9th and 10th streets. Just close enough for the Dick's crowd to watch as their former customers filed in without a further thought.

Billy was about twelve years older than me and I never saw him drink but he'd smoke pot better than any hippie. We talked every single day on the phone — recounting the happenings of the previous nights, who-did-whom-and-what. Billy was a tall, imposing, seventies-looking person, in an Aerosmithian tradition. Graceful, agile, deliberate on his feet — he could hunker down into small spaces and chat with you or just as easily tower over the crowd like a real-life Tommy standing atop his mountain of pinball machines.

Billy kept himself impeccably groomed. No dirty fingernails on this rock star. Woven cloth shirts that opened down the front. An assortment of chains with carved bones or amulets hanging on the end. Hair that would never un-feather. Tight jeans and leather belt. On his fingers he wore some of the most well-crafted rings I'd ever seen. Masculine angels, in polished sterling silver inset with shiny turquoise stones. Billy was friends with Ann-Margret and he used to describe some of the jewelry as 'gifts' so I used my imagination. He kept us downtown friends close, but not close enough to mingle with his quiet little circle on the

Upper East Side. He didn't like to play favorites, he just didn't mix people up.

From the minute he took it over, Billy's Reno Bar had become an instant addition to the underwater East Village scene just a few steps from St Mark's Church. The joint filled nightly with young freaks like me and Joey and Dan and Kurt and Ramón — and many of what could've easily been the children of the old Tenderloin, grandchildren of The Bowery.

The Reno Bar was pleasantly rustic. Barely painted. Strung with cheap Christmas lights and plastered with mirrors found on the street, but Billy kept it clean. The joint was a bit of a local secret, hidden by a narrow entrance on Second Avenue. Tourists and ignorant NYU kids had not a clue that at night, behind that innocuous storefront window, Reno Bar would come alive with some of the most eccentric and dangerous people in Manhattan. You might find anybody in Billy's culture kitchen: eighty-year-old drag queens putting away their Scotch with teenage run-aways; dancer girls down from their Broadway gigs, frightened boyfriends in tow; cute queer boys sipping blue drinks while debating Madonna lyrics in the back corner; someone having a loud screw in the bathroom. Everyone knew each other, or eventually did. Billy re-created in New York a scene from the bowels of Reno, Nevada. Paradise. Although no one was much interested in gambling.

Once, I even tried to do a performance night there called 'Martina Goes to Reno' in the tiny upstairs loft, but the wiring had been too faulty for the equipment to run, and I'd never really identified with the feminized version of my name. Total flop according to me. Not so bad according to most of the faithful, who were thankfully drunk upon arrival.

Reno, Billy, and our crowd. The center of the East Village. Heaven. Mecca. Shangri-La. Paradise. Transvestites, prostitutes, tranny-prostitutes, junkies, drug dealers, homeless people, old-school alcoholics, artists, poor folks, homos and cardboard poets shadow the sidewalks. The universe was meant to be chaotic, as was our little neighborhood. Transcendence through chaos. A haven, where you could live without being disturbed by squeaky progressive yuppie types who sell their souls to the god of baby strollers. The voice of the high school principal didn't reach here.

Out my front door and two left turns and Second Avenue appears underfoot. St Mark's churchyard is just a couple of blocks south, on the right in the direction of the Reno Bar. Tree-Man used to spend a lot of time traveling between that churchyard and Tompkins Square over on Avenue A. Tree-Man was a dark black man, about 5'7, usually wearing a red tank top and cut-off jeans in summer. Tree-Man walked around all day & all night, with his trademark tree branch tied to his head. Leaves sprouting everywhere. Lower limbs wilted around his scruffy-bearded face. He'd look straight ahead, with a toothy grin. He never asked for money, but would accept some if you felt the generous urge. Kept to himself, save an impulsive dancing jig, limbs over his head, leaves moving in rhythm. I imagined Tree-Man as one of the long-lost P-Funk All-Stars, a George Clinton original.

Tree-Man's path also crossed the one beaten by Quentin Crisp. Nearly every day you could see a small man, in a dark aubergine-colored velvet jacket, sparkly cufflinks and precisely placed fedora strolling the avenue, either to the small supermarket, or to the diner at Fifth Street. Quentin was listed in the phone book. A friend suggested I call him. One day I did. 'Hi, Mr. Crisp. I'm a fan and appreciate your work.'

'I'll meet you for lunch at noon on Thursday at the Cooper Diner. See you then.' And I did.

I nervously arrived, and took my seat in the busy diner — not my usual, this one was a bit plain. No tacky plastic plants or anything. What better place for an icon to shine? I brought probably thirty dollars to pay for anything, in those days before cash machines occupied the landscape like locusts. It was not my place to be generous, so at first I allowed Quentin to deal with the waiter: 'Toast, please.'

'Are you sure?'

'Yes, I'm sure...'

I'll never forget noticing how carefully he buttered and cut the pitiful white slabs of wheat. A beautiful gold ring with a shiny stone clicked against his knife. Little had I learned that eating was not one of his pastimes. And he told me his story, probably the same story he told everyone, but I got plenty to publish an interview in my first attempt at a magazine, which I named *BackTalk* and gave out in the neighborhood.

The 'family' embraced entrepreneurs back then, and people like Lucia, an older trannie who dressed in High 19th century Bo Peep Parisian glamour, strolling along in lacey hoop skirts, delicate white gloves, wide-brimmed parlor hat held in place by pink ribbon, all sheltered by a matching lace parasol with more pink trim.

I didn't get it. Any of it. And I didn't want to get it. I just went with it and loved it. There was nothing like it: living where people didn't breathe down your neck, announcing the rules every morning via an ominous loudspeaker mounted to the wall, and take it upon themselves to comment on anything and everything when they felt so inclined in the name of the Lord. New York provided autonomy before Giuliani's wrecking ball came to town. The phrase 'anything goes' should be saved for beach party movies. My anything became everything in the East Village. Your everything was your world, and belonged to you. Folks respected that. Nothing or no one needed dealing with — minding your own business was dealing with it.

You toss the coffee cup aside, rush into your living room and grab some white artist's tape from the shelf. You stretch out strand after strand onto the cutting board — enough for at least three shapes. 'It'll be a coarse-sharded salamander and two fine-ground silver glitter stars.' You trace out the shape in pencil and then cut them out with your X-acto knife, separating each one for individual application. One is a long salamander shape with three curves and a tail, made to crawl in the space from the outside corner of your left eye to the spot just above the corner of your mouth. The stars are two sizes, the larger one fitting directly on your right cheek, the smaller one just above your right eyebrow. Noticing the time, now 11:30, you peel up each adhesive stencil from the drafting table and run back to the mirror, placing them on the side of the sink for safe keeping. In front of them, you pull out all the accoutrements of painting your face. You don't do clown-face, so you don't need an inch of pancake fatch. You're an anomaly, a decorated boy, a peacock ripe for plucking.

22. Oh-Oh Aunt Betty. Bam a Lam.

I was blurring my way through the early 90s and heaps of new friends and acquaintances. Barney, Billy, Eddie, Scotty, Scott. E, ee, e. Names ran weird. I'd know six Michaels at any given time of day and twelve Stevens by nightfall. Billy, the one and only, had taken over The Bar. The old manager, Michael, had moved on — gloves, mullet and all. Things had become tense with the woman who owned Reno, as they always do when a queer comes into a dilapidated dump and turns it into a gold mine, so Billy moved the whole operation just a few blocks south. Scott, a light-skinned dancer, was working my coat check enterprise since I'd been bouncing from job to shit job. Scotty, the skinny blonde from Seattle, was a regular, who brought along his regular posse — Mikee, Jimmy, Tommy — to watch him snag tongue from Eddie. *Eee. eeee. eeeee.* All these 'E's.' How queer. Thank God there was a 'just-Bill' and Paach, a Pacific Islander, or of course Dan, Joey, Ramon and Kurt, in the crowd for a break in the name monotony. Some came with a wild-card past, like a man named Arif, who told me he was a Turkish Prince in hiding — who I was inclined to believe. Life was so colorful at that point, I wanted to believe everyone. One minute I'd be chatting with someone in a dump on the Lower East Side, the next I'd see them in a music video or on the cover of *Details*. From time to time I'd get an invitation to join Arif and a friend-girl of his out to dinner at fancy restaurants, and got picked up in a shiny Rolls Royce. Raoul, still my superintendent, was impressed. Many of us imagined the scene as a family of choice, and no family is complete, not ours anyway, without their own version of Auntie Mame.

John Badum's window overlooked St Mark's Church in the only medium-high-rise in the neighborhood. I knew John as Betty. Well, John sometimes, Betty, his nickname, others. Friends from the neighborhood called him Betty. Supposedly he had invented the first washable silk, was a founder of Go Silk company on 7th Avenue, and the world paid him dearly for it. He was no stranger to *Page Six*, the celebrity gossip page in the *NY Post*, and was known for lavish parties sprinkled with the likes of David LaChapelle, David Bowie and Todd Oldham. He dined with British Royals and Underground Queens. As far as eccentrics go, I'd certainly met some real characters along the way, But not even a crowned Prince could outdo a Queen like Betty, who complained about having to budget on ten thousand dollars a month. Somehow.

Betty-John Badum was about 5'10 tall, long dyed black hair that reached his waist, rather large. He wore black. All the time. A parade of the very finest luxury designer clothing — all in black. He gave Karl Lagerfeld a run for his money, all in black. He drove a black Volvo. Black wraparound sunglasses. It worked. 'Consistency is key,' he used to say.

Barney introduced me to Betty when he was doing some construction work in the apartment. I was hired to help put the electrical back together, and some lighting in the golden bedroom cabinets. I'd worked as an electrician's apprentice with my grandfather every summer for years, so would be putting it all to good use. After a while Betty and I became friendly, perhaps because my distant connections to the Klein Clan through my dad gave things an acceptable context. Betty kept me around for odd jobs and chores, odd mostly. He had stacks upon piles of old magazines and junk from the fashion world everywhere. I'd organize them into brand-new fold-up boxes by date, which would supposedly get taken to a storage facility in Brooklyn. Once, I asked why on earth he was keeping and paying money to store the last twenty years of runway pulp. 'Why not just ditch them, you'll never get these out of storage and read them… save the money…' I chirped, feeling clever. I didn't yet quite know how Grande, with a capital 'G' and french 'e,' worked. In response, Betty simply froze in his place, head tilted to 45 degrees, eyes hung low staring through me for the longest awkward pause of my young adult life. I got back to my boxes.

The entrance to Betty's apartment building was framed in green marble and had big brass and glass doors leading to a large foyer with drapes and bad mural wall paintings. The polished wooden elevator was the final over-baked-for-Second-Avenue before entering Betty's glamour abode.

The entrance was covered with thousands of broken pieces of mirror, black and white tile, set in place with a white grout. The immediate room interior was painted brown, the color of burnt umber you get in a Crayola box. To the right hung two bright David LaChappelle photographs, one in particular of a delicately tanned, loin-clothed Saint Sebastian with hands tied above and his midsection anchored by arrows to a large post. The ceiling of the room was divided into three parts, with a white background and bold, primary-colored American Indian symbols painted on each by Joey Arias. Kenny Scharf apparently designed parts of the rooms as well. In the corner by the air-shaft window was a five dollar bill in a red frame signed by Andy Warhol. The adjacent bedroom was, with the exception of a silver-sequined bedspread and matching disco ball, entirely covered in gold leaf — every piece of furniture, ceiling, frame, and inch of floor. The walls were papered gold with enormous sunflower prints — another Warhol original.

Further down the hall, which was painted in large green camouflage, was the living room. This room was as red as the bedroom was gold. Scarlet red carpet, drapes, walls, sofas, chairs, ceilings and furnishings. The kitchen on the opposite side of the apartment was equally loud, with more extravagant tile to match the foyer, black walls, a gel-sealed counter top with paper cut-outs and memorabilia glued in, and lacquered long-stemmed *papier mâché* flowers anchored above with pink flowers and light bulbs in the ends.

When I wasn't boxing magazines, I'd be invited for the occasional hang out and Chinese food, served all lumped together in a giant bowl with chopsticks on the side, which I quickly learned to use because I was afraid to ask Betty for a fork and spoil the mood. Other times were less formal, like after I'd gotten my very first VCR, I asked Betty to borrow some skin movies. 'Sure,' he said, 'come over, but you can't come up, and make it quick...' more special guests, I supposed. I ran and just made it down as box after box of Saving Ryan's Privates started falling from the sky. I caught as many as I could. One or two people glanced up as the dark angel above, with long black hair and flowing robe sleeves, tossed porn down five stories to the queer on the corner.

The rest of the passersby just dodged the plastic covers full of naked people that flew apart from the tapes as the boxes fell onto the Second Avenue sidewalk.

23. B for Barney, Billy, Betty, Birthday

One August, when my favorite international event known also as my birthday rolled around, Billy, Barney and Betty were reading and waiting. It was just before Billy took over The Bar, a last blowout for the Reno. Billy asked me what kind of flowers I liked. Barney asked me what I wanted as a present. I figure they were bored, because together they conspired to plan some big deal of a party.

I wasn't used to placing orders for my birthday with friends. Heck, I'd never really had many friends. Whenever anyone asks me, unless I do in fact have some thing I want in mind, I usually draw a blank and make something up. Anything is better than 'I dunno.' I told Billy sunflowers and Barney that I wanted a hustler, blond, on a leash like in the movie The Boys in the Band. Original, I thought. If anyone could swing it, Barney could.

I arrived on the night, and everything was just getting started. All the neighborhood friends were plodding in. Dan, Ramon, Kurt, Joey. I remember Joey being very excited, talking really fast 'Happy birthday, whaddya' want ta' drink?' in his authentic Brooklyn accent. Barney was already passing joints around, Billy was mixing cocktails. They took me upstairs to a room decorated in the usual birthday streamers, but with big sunflower stalks taped all along the walls. Another friend, Blair Schulman, was the token gogo boy, dancing with an open shirt and ripped jeans in his own rhythm next to the birthday cake. After a while, some cards and a present or two, more folks came in, some invited some not, and we started dancing the night away. I kept an eye on Barney, wondering about my special request. An hour or more went by and, nothing. We sang 'Happy Birthday,' blew out candles, had cake. Betty Badum even came by, which surprised me, as this was not his kind of scene. But just across the street nonetheless.

It was a Saturday night, so the neighborhood was hopping. Barney never brought in my blond on a leash, so I started to figure it was a no-go. I told a few guys about it, and they just kinda rolled their eyes and didn't say much. All of a sudden Barney and Joey came and got me, picked me up and everyone followed carrying me outside. A hired Lincoln Town Car, my favorite, was waiting. Everyone was laughing, joking, but no one would tell me what was going on. Joey stepped up, read a jingle from a birthday card, then started everyone throwing rice at me while the others picked me up and crammed me into the car, while stuffing money into my pockets.

'Where we going?' I asked the driver. No response. We ended up at 53rd Street and Second Avenue, just a hop away from the hotel I stayed in with Dad years earlier. The driver stopped in front of a notorious hustler bar called Rounds, and said 'go in there.' I was scared to death. My idea had been nostalgic, not operative. These places, like Julius,' the oldest gay bar in Greenwich Village, were serious. Boys worked and men paid, and a lot of craziness went down. A lot of sex went down. So did a lot of muggings, drugs and HIV.

I entered the place and I got the strangest looks from people. Interest from the gentlemen, scorn from the boys. Oh God. No one was saying anything, everyone was staring at something, watching every move, glance and motion. I found myself in the midst of what I found to be as tense as a spy bar in 1930s Berlin. I felt like saying 'no, no, you've got me all wrong, I'm not competition, I'm curious…' but of course that could not happen. I stuck out in the room, tightening my leather MC jacket closed as I walked in my combat boots toward the bar. The boys were all dressed like 70s porn stars — t-shirts with prints, Members Only jackets and jeans, or Oxford cloth button-down shirts with trousers. The Johns were mainly in suits — business casual. All created an orchestrated ballet of personalities, types and roles.

A panicky anxiety crystallized the mood. I found a seat at the bar and ordered a drink. The bartender was quieter than Billy or the others, who usually chatted you up to make you feel at home. This one stopped for a second, and I said hi. 'What brings you here?' he asked, which at first I took as 'What the hell are you doing here?' I sat for a long while, and reassured myself that any minute Barney, Joey, Dan and the rest would come bounding in the doors to continue my birthday laugh. They'd shoved around $200 in my pockets, certainly enough to afford one of the boys along the wall, obviously the point, but the boys would have nothing to do with me. Suddenly, I realized I'd never felt quite so awkwardly alone in all my life. An hour or more passed and no one bounded through any door. Or even strolled. When ordering my second drink, the bartender, realizing I wasn't on the game, chatted more and I told him the story, to which he laughed and bought me a round. Between us, I think we decided I was to keep the birthday money, but I couldn't go back to the party, that would mean being a failure. Someone as outgoing and, well, loud as me, the originator of the Second Avenue kissing booth, could not go back empty handed. But equally, I wasn't finished with my birthday, although somehow my train of things making sense had gotten thrown off. Outside, I hailed a cab and went to Roxy. Surely a few of my friends would be there. No dice. They were all back getting loaded at Reno. I danced a while, but couldn't really get into a groove, so I took the bartender's advice, kept the money, and went home.

The next day I got calls from all the usual suspects asking what had happened. Joey told me that he thought I would expect them to show up at Rounds, but they all got too wasted and just stayed downtown. Barney told me he'd planned to go two nights earlier and find me my blond prize. He'd met up with Betty in order to go uptown and do the scouting, but they too got stoned and never made it. There was just something about that Reno. So, they opted for the Lincoln and the cash in my pocket instead. Apparently Betty supplied most of the cash, because the others had spent theirs on sunflowers and booze. In the end, I opted for some new clothes and things for the apartment.

You only need the basics — some dust for base, eyeliner, shadow, etc. You apply the base dust evenly, so as not to make your look too phoney. Next come the eye shadows, applied with the softest pad of the ring finger. You mix the black, layer the indigo blues and follow with the grays — above and below. The result is a mix between rock star and football player. Dead football player. Following this comes the eyeliner — applied to the inside and upper outside rim of the bottom lid. Time for a cigarette and some air. The bathroom has become hot from all the lights and excitement. You go into the living room and change the song. You race back, against yourself, and start on your hair. Hair is easy, straight out in all directions. Lacquer. Lots of spray lacquer. Blow dryer. Pull. Spray. Twist. Blow. Spray. Blow. Stop. Finally the stencils: salamander on cheek, stars on right side. Check mirror. Looks good. Music blaring. Spirit gum-glue brushed inside the stencil areas onto your skin. Burn. Burn real bad. Red marks will be there for days, but no matter now, the world may or may not turn after tonight and if it does, the red marks tell the world you do glamorous things in your spare time. More spirit glue. More burn. Coarse shards of glitter picked up in patches with Q-tip and jammed into the glue on your face.

24. Lost & Found

Flashback: August 1971. My seventh birthday. Mama threw me a party in grandmother and Popey's front yard. Grandma Ruby and Grandaddy call me on the phone and wish they could be there. So does Daddy. Popey hangs streamers in the Magnolia trees. Aunt Sandy makes me a cake shaped like a fish with colored lifesavers on it. I get a purple bike. Lavender. I think I asked for purple.

My friend from grandmother's church, Jarrod Cline, is there. We were a put-together friend-couple. When there's no one else around but this other person and grandmother decides you'd make nice friends, you make friends. We actually liked each other. I first met him at Sunday School, then at school after Mama and Daddy had separated. Jarrod had a big head with brown curly hair and big eyes and he smiled a lot.

In a few weeks we would attended Mrs. Purser's second-grade class together. If I'd been asked I'd have probably predicted Jarrod and me getting popped almost every day with Mrs. Purser's ping-pong paddle. And it would be no surprise that Mrs. Purser got angry when the dentist man came and gave us dental floss and I tied knots in it around my big front tooth. The dentist had to cut it out with his pocketknife. They didn't have terms like attention deficit disorder back then — they didn't need it, I was just a rowdy boy. So, for my seventh birthday I got a bunch of toys and my purple sparkly bike and socks. I think the bike was that year, neither Mama nor I can pin it exactly. The socks came from Mama's friend Connie. 'Oh, socks, oh, thanks,' I said when I opened the box. Mama was embarrassed. Told me I should be too. I mean, I didn't not-like the socks. Connie gave the kind of gifts that would do you some extended good. She'd saved my Mama another trip to the store with those socks. And the money to buy them. But next to a screaming purple bicycle? Come on!

Mama and my sister Adrienne and me moved in with grandmother and Popey about a year earlier. Just after Mama decided she'd had enough of Daddy's shenanigans. Daddy needed to find himself — whatever that meant. He always did stuff on a whim that scared Mama. Which didn't take a lot because she had come from a family that'd come from nothing, or not much at all. After a short run in Brooklyn as a welder, my Popey had fought in the war, helped sink the ships in Le Havre harbor even, and settled near his kin in the foothills. Taylorsville. A lot of Scots around there. grandmother's people were Gunns and Montgomerys. Popey'd borrowed the furniture for his white, wood-framed house from the furniture man, who let him have anything he needed as long as he showed up every week and paid him something. Anything. Even a penny. They grew a lot of what they ate. Cows too. So Mama wasn't none too pleased when Daddy ran up the credit cards or ran off and left her without money.

Jarrod was killed when we were both sixteen. He'd been jogging along the highway, just beside the church cemetery, when he got hit by a car. He was buried right at that very spot pretty much. Jarrod has the only black tombstone at Antioch Church — his grave is beside the highway. I never knew Jarrod extremely well. I don't remember him as an extra smart guy, nor do I recall any tremendous hidden talents like music or art. But Jarrod liked me. I don't think he played for my team, but Jarrod was the kind of guy I know wouldn't have cared one way or the other. The kind of guy who'd kick someone's ass if they messed with me. I coulda' used some of ol' Jarrod after we moved to Charlotte. After I moved to New York.

25. Palaces, DC and Ritz

The phone rang followed with the usual dulcet announcement: 'Martin, it's John Badum.' As if I didn't ... well ... it was the game we played. Everybody else, Barney, Billy, Dan, just jumped in with 'whatcha' doin' or 'hey you.' Betty required an entrance, even on the telephone. I felt privileged when he called me 'cause I wasn't famous enough to be in the A-list crowd, nor were any of my immediate friends. But Aunt Betty tolerated we-waifs anyway.

'Hello, dear.'

'Hi. What's going on?' I said in my salt-covered voice, puzzled. I'd actually only been in Betty's apartment the night before — unusual to hear back so soon, but this is why we all called him Aunt, and Betty. I'd just broken up with someone again, with a Mr. Texas this time, and had called Betty for no particular reason. Within minutes he figured out the particular reason and had me come over for the sympathy minus the tea. No funny business. The good thing about back then was you didn't have to hurt alone. Fact was, Mr. Texas really didn't mean so much, he'd wandered off a long time before, and I knew it. What I was sad about was not really being alone, but lonely, as I was discovering could be possible in a sea of eight million. Some combination of Auden's 'loved alone' and Wilde's 'love that dare not speak its name.' Betty knew the growing pains.

Betty had held me as long as I could cry in the red room. The red room is where Betty entertained friends and celebrities. All a moist, sad red. He was probably calling from the same spot where I'd left him hours before. 'Me and some friends were thinking let's get outta' town for a bit. Get away. Something easy — DC — get a cheap motel room, play cards or something — whaddya' think?' 'Well, sounds great, but I don't have any money Betty, you know that — I can barely keep the rent going...' that, and I found the notion of playing cards rather dubious.

'Nevermind. I'll cover you — we can work something out.'

Having opened my heart and bled almost every secret I had to him the night before, I was vulnerable. It's hard to refuse a benefactor, emotionally or otherwise — especially when all they wanted was for you to play along. I couldn't be sure whether this was just about him being nice or what. Betty was a shrewd character. Ten grand a month and all.

'Sure, why not.'

'Be here at...' Click. From my point of observation, Betty always got what she wanted. I arrive at Betty's at 9:45. Doorman at 166 Second Avenue lets me in. I should be considered a regular by now, I think, waiting for the elevator. I get up to the front door, which is slightly ajar, but the heavy tiles cemented to its interior side keep it still.

Inside, the place didn't look as grand in the daytime as it did at night. Forward and to the right was the red room. I didn't want to go in there again — all that emotional stuff could stay in the red room. Steam carrying what must be gallons of expensive cologne and bath soap escapes from Betty's shower down the hallway and into the gold bedroom where I decided to sit. Nothing of high fashion ever looks comfortable, including the coarse gold sequined bedspread I laid back on — it's scratchy and cold against my skin. I tried to imagine why John, with all his money and influence and friends, didn't have a boyfriend, but then the entire abode, while undeniably stylish, seemed to scream 'Go Away.' Other guys show up. Joe and Bill. Joe was a wannabee magazine publisher. Bill seemed to be another one of us who was finding himself, at that particular juncture, and farted a lot thinking it was funny.

Whether they liked to admit it or not at the time, Joe and Bill were fellow B-listers. No matter, everyone was happy for a little trip to DC with Aunt Betty in the black Volvo. We'd all arrived on time, as instructed. Betty was busy with his bag in the gold bedroom. Some silk, of course, black, certainly, thin bag. Big enough for a pair of shoes. I guess it didn't yet get into my head that Betty Badum didn't pack for a trip. He purchased upon arrival. Anything he needed and then some.

Joe, Bill and myself had the usual twentysomething duffle bags. Combat boots or leather shoes, denim jeans, our MC jackets. And another jacket 'cause Betty had told us to bring one. Some toothpaste, brush and hair gel and we were set.

The Volvo had been retrieved from the garage. We piled in. I took a back seat of course. Joe was the second most favorite and would deal with co-piloting, opening snacks, checking maps and the like. DC was a straight shot down I-95. The most uneventful stretch of highway on the East Coast, with an on-ramp for every redneck town between New York and Virginia. They need love too.

As we left the city, lights, and everything behind us, I felt a simultaneous sense of relief and panic. Relief, at getting away. You don't understand how overwhelming the place can get when you're smack in the middle of eight million people with no easy way to crack a mental window for air. The feeling that comes when you live there. Panic because somewhere down in the recesses of my being I felt guilty for being there. Having it so good. AIDS, broken hearts, rent to pay, and all. Half of me felt fantastic about making it to the Big Apple. The other half a scoundrel, for leaving my old life behind, that I'd be caught and sent back. That the karma police would one day play a joke on me and prevent me from returning to my lovely city. I kept a third-eye watch for loudspeakers blurting the voice of my high school principal. 'Thought you got away, huh?'

Finally, we were off. On the same route I'd taken on buses with Marilyn for the anti-Gulf War protests. Betty was driving. The good thing about any activity with Betty is that it would be somewhat civil. I liked music, sometimes real loud, but not while driving in a car full of people screaming at each other over a cheap stereo. Betty's stereo wasn't cheap, of course, so you didn't have to play it loud. I noticed we were flying by the other cars on the roadway. I glimpsed the speedometer which is on like 97 bazillion miles per hour. I buckled my seat belt and figured when you're rich like Aunt Betty, you can drive as fast as you like 'cause you can afford the tickets.

We continued whizzing by the other cars. I didn't relax but I loved breaking the law. The karma police were after me — and not soon after, the state troopers were after Betty. Blue lights illuminated the rear window. Looked like something off the dance floor at Roxy. Betty pulled over. An officer walked up and asked him out of the car. Bill, Joe and myself sighed a collective 'Oh no.' Most folks going that fast in a 55 zone would go straight to jail. Betty didn't flinch. I took notes. Learn. We watched them both walk behind the Volvo. It was an overcast day, making it harder to see the action. Betty appeared very subservient, bowing his head, talking quietly. Chatting even. Not a nerve shown. I couldn't make out the words, only tones and murmurs. He opened his thin wallet with the mannerisms of a gentleman, handing the officer his papers. Joe told me and Bill to stop giggling, and to turn around. He didn't want us to look suspicious.

I was suspicious. I think I had a bag of weed on me. Bill definitely did. And our little gang of queers was not going to go over well in Virginia. The state with a slogan 'Virginia is for Lovers,' but should read: 'Virginia is for lovers of guns and god and whiskey and race cars. But not queer lovers. Especially queer yankees trying to zip down to DC for a party.'

Betty knew everyone in the music and fashion world. High roller he was. He also knew senators and statesmen. In fact, he was soon to be in the process of designing and planning a wedding for Adam, also known as Sister Dimension, and Beverly, a countess something-or-other of British royalty. I'd met the countess and her mother on another unsuspecting trip into Betty's red room. Before then, Beverly had been around, and I'd danced with the countess on the dance floor with Lawrence at what had been the old Cat Club.

As the officer read the license, Betty stood behind the black Volvo, hands moving openly, with more non-threatening head bows and accommodating gestures. The officer made a trip to the patrol car, apparently checking things out. He returned and handed the license to Betty with some minor talking-to. Betty was nodding in rhythm. Betty had begun thanking the officer. 'What?' I think. Joe, Bill and I are glued to the rear-view mirror. Betty's shoulder-length black hair falls from his ear as he nods and speaks — still in murmurs, but the tones are higher, cautiously polite and jovial. The license, now back in the wallet, is in his left hand with the black wraparound sunglasses. The officer turned and headed back to his patrol car. Betty waited diligently until he opened the door to make his own exit from the scene. Joe declared quiet as Betty eased out of the driver's side door. I already saw how the weekend was going to work. Bill and me were the bad boys. Betty got in, waited for the officer to leave and cranked the engine. There was a protracted silence. Betty was not even noticeably rattled. He signaled properly. Got back on the highway. I could tell he'd been affected by our little interruption, but only superficially. Bill and I make shrugging hands gestures to each other. We see an evil eye from Joe piercing back from the rear-view mirror. The officer had not so much as gave Betty a warning slip. Whatever Betty'd said, whoever he knew or was related to, must've meant something for this particular officer.

After a bit, the music came back on, the chatter returned. Betty never said how he'd gotten out of being arrested. Neither Joe, Bill nor I ever asked. Instead, Betty handed Joe the cell phone, a luxury at the time, and instructed him on some hotels to call in DC. Betty'd told me that we were going to get a cheap hotel room, play some cards, see the sights. It wouldn't be too expensive. Betty had agreed to pay for me then let me work it off. Probably by eating the food after one of his fancy parties. Joe busied himself calling here and there. Chatterin' on with Betty about who has a friend here and who knows who there. Social climbing on a cell phone. Me and Bill lumped in the back seats and made faces. I caught Betty catching us in the rear-view mirror. He grimaced. 'All set,' we finally hear after an hour of chatter about rooms and locations. I'd not been paying attention. I imagined it would be neat to see Washington without a tour bus. Just me, my adopted Aunt and some instant friends sticking out and touring the town that made nothing work.

We entered DC and passed a whole host of what I thought would be our final destinations. Holiday Inns and the like with signposted rates. I was ready to stop. I had to pee and wanted out of the black Volvo. We passed some of the monuments and all like the Lincoln Memorial. Washington Monument. The Capitol. Whenever I passed the White House I sent an angry vibe at Reagan's successor, King George Bush I — but it wasn't worth the energy to lift a middle finger. It seemed good to be out of New York for a little while, but DC was one big sterile nothing to me. No soul, no body, just a bunch of empty stone buildings and monuments and the air between them. Empty men in empty double-breasted suits gliding to and fro. DC has no Trafalgar Square, or Champs-Elysées, or Athenian Parthenon. It never will — it was slapped together too fast, with no time for it to be peopled with a meaningful legacy.

Joe and Betty were navigating. 'I think it's over there…' 'No maybe that way.' We had to pull into a few office driveways and circle some side streets. I knew nothing of where we were, and if I'd spoken my bladder would've burst. We make one more quick turn and pull into an oval driveway. A huge building with a magnificent facade. I figure to ask directions, but Betty sets the handbrake. I sit still, not knowing what we're doing here — a place with uniformed men all along the front. The others were gathering their things. I followed along curiously. It didn't look like no cheap hotel. Who knew, with this bunch, maybe we were stopping for a snack. I got out as the trunk pops open. The uniformed men start falling out of formation and toward the Volvo, unpacking everything. I looked up and saw the golden letters above: Ritz Carlton. The man with a slightly better uniform than the others came out the door and greeted Betty as if they've been friends for years. My stomach was on edge. The man looked back and gave our motley crew a once over, complete with obligatory smile. Combat boots go over well in the East Village, not DC. At that point I didn't even care. I just had to pee.

We entered a garish lobby room, with flowered wallpaper everywhere. Flowers in front of the flowered walls. Betty was at the desk, Joe one step behind. More A-list work. Bill and I had to plop down on one of the flowery gold-leafed sofas knowing they wouldn't have even let us in the place without Betty. I couldn't afford their air. The doorman was keeping an eye on us. I threatened to put my boots up on the furniture. We both gave each other intermittent 'oh shit' glances. Cheap hotel, Betty style. The same man who moaned about having to budget himself on ten thousand dollars per month. I should have realized.

We spent the weekend in much the same way as we'd traveled... unpredictably. I put my big black combat boots outside the beige hotel room door — they came back from the overnight shine service with a polish fit for the military. We toured the sites. Ordered from room service. A lot. Went out to a strip club. Got eggs thrown at us on the way. Bunch of kids driving by in a car yelling 'FAGGOTS.' Same kinda' side of town as Scorpios had been in Charlotte. When you get down to it, these towns are all the same. God, guns and slack-jawed culture. Inside the boys were on the bar wearing nothing but socks and sneakers, holding a small cloth in front of their privates, dancing for tips. Johns would come up and slip a bill in their white socks, the boy would kneel down, chat and give a peep show. I was impressed that they could keep the privates dancing proud for hours, in those days before erection drugs. Upon entering I went from excitably entertained to infernally bored in about ten minutes. The boys on the bar were for sale. Those watching them were hopeless. I didn't have anything against either, it was just that kind of desperate look-but-don't-touch-unless-you-can-pay scene. The lesson of Rocky Horror: a fine line between dreaming it and being it. And I didn't have any money. I shoulda' grabbed a towel and made some.

I got good and drunk because I needed something to do. My night was sleepless, with Betty sex-pesting and trying to convince me that mutual masturbation was in order. I didn't agree, and felt pretty well betrayed by the whole thing. He was friends with

Joey Arias after all. I was all for surprises and spontaneous fun, but my whimsy had fallen flat somewhere between the arrogant people in the hotel and Betty's desperation. I could've gotten off easier being chased by Joey Arias around Boy Bar. Bill and Joe were no help at all, and I'd come to realize that some ulterior plan must have been in place among the three of them, but I never figured out exactly what. Didn't want to know. Whatever the case, we all mixed like oil and salt water. I'd escaped suburbia too, but didn't equate a thirty dollar plate of eggs with fun. Or tacky wallpaper and the people who stick to it. In hindsight, I've since learned to remove some of the war paint against the world.

Betty drove us back the next day after breakfast. A little slower this time. I was so happy to see Second Avenue, and bounced up the sidewalk toward my apartment.

Later that year Betty threw a party for those of us who didn't actively mingle with super-famous rock stars and internationally famous fashionistas as an everyday affair. Lawrence-Lorenzo informed me he'd called us the 'B list.' I didn't mind. I was happy to be on the Betty B list. Better than in DC with farting Bill and giggly Joe. Being a 'B' kept me from having to put on a pretense, overspend on expensive clothing I didn't even want, and chase a pot of gold that didn't exist. I had lots of friends on the A list in my leather MC jacket and threadbare Levi's. I just didn't have their troubles. We B-listers ate goo-ood crumbs left by Betty. One holiday time, Betty rented half of an entire room at one of Michael Alig's clubs. The top of Club USA to be precise. Fancy. Had it roped off. Got ten or more 35mm slides made with the letter 'B.' Projected them on the walls. Had a dozen full-size brass beds brought in special for the occasion, covered with beaded bedspreads. Hired three drag queens dressed as beauty queens for waitrons. We could get Belgian chocolate-covered bites or some other crazy concoctions with a name beginning with 'B.' Bacardi cocktails. Sister Dimension stood high above us all atop a big black stone staircase, with turntables and records, DJing us into the night. A bunch of hired buff boys tied to podiums, slaves paid to dance, iced the cake. And there we lounged, all twenty of us in a room big enough for a hundred. Hedonists, the lot. If Betty's brainery for us Bs hadn't made us feel privileged enough, there was an added bonus — a packed room on the other side, held back by Betty's velvet ropes.

Apparently, *Paper Magazine* booked the other side of the room for their annual Christmas party. And they'd invited too many people. We were being ogled by a bunch of brooding, cramped bottom feeders. I can't say I wasn't uncomfortable being observed by the C, D, E, Z list, across the awkward space between us. Some of them looked attractive as they pressed against the ropes as far as they would go, just short of knocking the brass anchor poles over, while they peered and pointed. But most seemed to come from three peoples more loathsome than any other groups in a social setting: people who get tickets to fancy parties and concerts from their uncle, the people they invite to come along, and the ones that get in the door and act like they're all in-the-know. There are exceptions. There's nothing to know.

26. Back on the Chain Gang

After a long string of jack-jobs, and tour on the good-ship unemployment, I'd found something more promising at a little computer place called Userfriendly on Sixth Avenue by Greenwich Avenue, just down from Uncle Charlie's and the Jefferson Market Library. The internet hadn't yet dawned, but desktop publishing had. The store rented computer time so people could come do their stuff. All sorts of stuff — music, writing, resumes, applications, brochures. I knew very little about computers when I started, but the managers liked my retail customer service skills and hired me.

My friend Gaya Palmer, a fellow survivor from a previous crap job, recommended me to try there in the first place. I'd always trusted survivors — the real kind. Gaya and me had done some time in a sleazy architect's office, where she showed up for her interview wearing dark black cat glasses, black pumps, leggings, a long turquoise shirt-dress with a pressed-up collar, black belt, handbag and long 1920s cigarette holder. We didn't mix well with the big husky Greek man who drove a Jaguar and owned the business and enjoyed driving his employees crazy with pompous temper tantrums. He was too cheap to pay for a business account at the bank so we'd have to wait days for our paychecks to clear, and we were shamed for leaving on time in an intentionally belligerent, broken accent: 'we doan leaf ad sids o cluk on dee dot.' The hell 'we' didn't. And when he got violent one day Gaya and me got our next paychecks, stayed up all night calling the bank to make sure they'd cleared his personal account, and never went back. Mr. Jaguar apparently went wild the next morning trying to cancel our paychecks, but couldn't. And we both claimed on him for unemployment money. And it was good.

The day-to-day Userfriendly deal was simple: you greet the customers, seat them at a rentable computer, answer their questions. Pay was OK by the day's standards. No lunch break but got paid to stay on the floor while you ate a sandwich. In exchange, if you weren't lazy, you could learn all the software known to man at the time: Mac, PC, Unix. Benjamin, the owner, had it all and this was my ticket to something new. I absorbed the opportunity and every inch of the software like a sponge. Macs were the vanguard, and I was able to translate what I'd learned at design school at the community college in Charlotte into computer terms, and an art director was born.

I worked every shift I could get. Morning, noon, night. Ben allowed us to use any computer we wanted when we weren't helping customers, and he taught me everything he could. We'd get production jobs from the people who didn't want to rent time on the computers — resumes, wedding invitations, pamphlets… we did 'em all. I took to the technology with an unusual familiarity, and was made an assistant manager in about a month. I had access to everything Quark, Apple and Microsoft made. I knew them all in no time flat. All this from wandering in and telling them I knew how to talk to people, retail experience and all.

One afternoon, a funny-looking man walked in the shop. About 5'7 tall, balding, nice shoes, suit and tan-colored trench-style raincoat. The computers were all taken. He spoke to the receptionist with a stammering Jewish accent for a very long time.

I remember his distinct, thick New York vocal curve and phrases like: 'I-I don't want a computer. I wanna' know if somebody can do this here job... like professional and all.' He was waving a magazine of some sort, and I think speaking informally so as not to intimidate me. At first I took him for a flake — we'd had our share of crackpots asking us to forge bank registers and things, which we promptly refused. 'I-I lost the printing plates for it. Or, well, the vendor did. I need a carbon copy. Full four-color job...'

My first instinct was to go on break, but we got paid more if we did training and production jobs so I made eye contact with the receptionist and the man came over. He held the magazine under his coat until he got to my table. 'Ca-can you do this thing? I nee-need somebody who can do me up one of these things...' Sure I could, I thought. It was a 45-page expertly-done floor tile catalog. Bigger job than I'd ever seen, but I was ready. 'You bet I can.' I had no idea how, but I'd figure it out later. The man introduced himself as Michael.

For over an hour, Michael Pakula and I went back and forth over his job. Price, time, color specs and plates, film — all of it, to the point of repetitively driving me crazy. I kept speaking in the context of it being done in our little computer shop. He had other ideas. He kept asking me, over and over, 'You can do it right? You can do this?' To which I continued to assent. We got along well. There was something about his quirkiness I liked, although he repeated a lot of the same questions. I stuck with him, and figured it might be a nice feather in my cap to bring in such a big job to Userfriendly. Too big for the place really. After the fourth or fifth round, the conversation ended. We agreed he'd get back in touch. Less than an hour later, the phone rang for me. I never got business calls like that. Michael Pakula. What was I doing later after work? he asked. 'Can you do that job I showed you?' He went on to inquire something about me doing it at his office and how much 'I' would cost to do it. At first I began to redirect the conversation back to bringing the job to Userfriendly — I was, after all, loyal to Ben for teaching me in a year what they didn't yet even offer in colleges, but then my sixth sense kicked in and that 'don't be stupid' feeling ran up the back of my neck.

'Are you making me an offer?' I asked, quite surprised. I'd seen stuff like that in the movies, but didn't actually know it happened in real life.

'Why don't you come by after work and talk about it?' he invited. I think he'd also pushed for a time earlier than my shift finished. Nonetheless I finagled away to 740 Broadway. Corner of Astor Place. Mr. Pakula showed me into a modest yet quite comfortable office. He asked me about my work experience, and I knew straight away that I was at an interview, although I was dressed in blue jeans.

Within minutes I'd been literally hired off the floor as a new technologically-gifted art director for a small ad agency named Bryant Inc., which was even closer in walking distance to my apartment. I got my own office on the eleventh floor and around a fifteen thousand dollar a year pay raise. My office had a giant window that overlooked Astor Place and would actually open for air that to me smelled especially fresh.

Working for Michael Pakula and his creative director, Rudy, was probably the cushiest job I'll ever regret not still being at. In at 9, out by 5. The only agency I ever worked for that didn't include 'can you stay late' with 'good morning.' The summers were even better — most of the clients were seasonal, tile manufacturers or insurance, and the summer was their selling season, so no new ads or brochures from June to August. We'd show up, say good morning, and go hide in our offices. Everyone knew no one had anything to do. Everyone knew that Michael Pakula, and his father Randy, expected us to at least look ready and attentive. I started *BackTalk* magazine, other people read, we all went out to lunch. Rudy had us put in some time for one charity or another. Life was, well, not insane.

Bryant was designed as a big loop: in the door you could turn left or right, and circle the entire place, passing offices along the outside wall. In the center was where the production people, storage and archive departments were. We all had windows that would open, a rarity in what is now the open-plan-suffocate world. I got my first glimpse of Bill Clinton from mine. He'd come to speak at Cooper Union, just down the street, in the hall where Lincoln walked in an unknown and walked out President-to-be, and where ACT UP now met.

Times were pretty damn good. I didn't even realize how good, until one day at the office, when one of the few things actually got busy with deadlines, I started not to feel so well. All of a sudden my stomach felt queasy and bloated, and my head hurt. I thought it was the flu. Since we were busy, I decided to tough it out the rest of the day. I thought some spicy beef chilli from the famous Silver Spurs Diner would do the trick. I called up and ordered from Kiki, the owner's daughter. Kiki and I had many conversations over the months I'd been coming around for lunch. She was an attractive Greek girl, thin, long brown hair, high eyebrows. She used to take an unusual interest in whatever it was I was up to. It wasn't long until I figured out that Kiki was a dreamer. She'd ask me about advertising, or art, or writing after I'd given her a copy of my little copy machine magazine. 'You're something, aren't you. That's great, you see something and just go and do it,' she'd say. I'd encourage her, ask her what she wanted out of life. Little did she realize I was fantasizing how great it would be to have a family in New York City and a business and all that stability. Little did I realize she was probably fantasizing about how great it would be to live in New York without all the weight of family and their business. Little did she know that I had no choice, and if I sat still, I'd lose.

I got my chilli soup delivered that day, as I didn't even feel good enough to trek up the block. After about two bites I felt sicker than I'd ever felt in my life, like someone was inflating my stomach with air and stabbing the back of my neck with an ice pick at the same time, but nothing would give. At least if I could have thrown up I might have had some relief.

Rudy and Michael came in pretty excited about whatever job they needed to get out that day. I tried to listen, but my head became swimmy, I really thought something was seriously wrong. 'Michael, I'm sorry but I don't think I'm gonna' make it...' I explained. Michael just kinda looked at me like I was letting him down. Thing was, I rarely if ever called in sick to Bryant. There was no reason to. Great pay, easy day, summers practically off. I knew it and Michael knew it and Rudy knew it. So when I proclaimed my illness, it was but a minute when Michael seemed to realize that I was telling the truth, and all employer scrutiny turned to a get-the-hell-out-don't-spread-the-joy-now look. 'That's alright, Martin,' Michael said while Rudy nodded.

By the time I got home I was sick and confused. Nothing added up. Backache meant flu. Stomach meant, well, stomach something. Excruciating neck ache like I'd never had before. Hot and cold sweats meant a lot of things. I tried to take a bunch of ibuprofen and it made me sicker and I threw it up. Something definitely wrong. This was the age of AIDS, and no one was immune. The queer disease. I wondered if it was my turn. I'd been careful, but that wasn't a guarantee.

I called Billy and told him about my problem, we talked about these things. Everybody talked about these things, privately. Billy nailed the situation right off: 'you got Hepatitis honey, welcome to the world of Marigold. Your eyes and face will turn yellow, your shit will go pale gray and it's gonna' take you a few weeks… but you'll live.'

'WEEKS!?'

'Yes. Weeks,' he replied, before going into a litany of dos and don'ts about what to eat and how much water to drink. I was sure I had AIDS. I hadn't had a test. I didn't want a test. I didn't want to know. Billy told me plenty. I went to the doctor the next day, who confirmed Billy's original diagnosis. Hepatitis A. Possibly from food. I had no strength and no appetite. Walking from one end of the apartment to the other was the big activity for the day. Giovanni helped me get my cable TV turned on, and Chris, Billy's friend and ex-boyfriend of the notorious club promoter and leader of the Velvet Mafia Dean Johnson, came over and cleaned up the place. One Sunday afternoon, Dan, Ramon, Blair and Kurt came for a visit. I played it to the hilt, lying back in my bed as they fawned over me, until it hit me: they think I'm a goner! I looked around the room, everyone sitting around me, Dan staring out the window. I felt like a goner. Nothing to discuss, nothing to be done. Nowhere to go. No parties, no nothing. It wasn't too long before I was kicking to get out again.

Michael Pakula, still one of the best bosses I ever had, sent me money each week from an insurance fund he'd set up for employees a long time before. 'Use all you like, no rush, I paid for this,' he said. So I did. Rudy, my supervisor, and me had converted Michael P.'s agency from a traditional paste-up shop to computers. Saved Michael P. thousands. Then we made him tens of thousands. New technology. Somewhere, in a dusty accounting storeroom, sits an invoice with a line item for around $13,000, marked 'transvertical styrations.' I sure didn't know anything transvertical, much less anything close to a styration. Such was the time and technology. My job was the reward.

The illness messed with my head. In total, I'd ended up being in bed almost nine weeks. Christmas Day was a turning point, when my system finally kicked in and everything I'd been eating over the preceding two months decided to move out. By New Year's I was up and about, and Giovanni took me for a walk down the street. Being outside was weird. Being around people was weird. What I didn't know at the time was that I needed a few more weeks off, but I wasn't thinking straight.

I spent a lot of time on the phone with Billy. We talked about big stuff. We talked about people. We talked about the laundry. Usually an hour's worth of talk. On this particular night Billy reminded me of something he'd mentioned before. The only thing wrong with him was his stomach, he'd say. Bad stomach. He didn't drink alcohol because of it. Or at least I supposed that was why. He didn't do anything other than his pot. He mentioned his stomach, how it had been rough all day. I hadn't noticed that he should've been at work. And I didn't notice that he'd repeated the same stories three times.

I went from sick to stupid. Michael Pakula encouraged me to stay home and take the weekly money. I was itching precociously to get out. The illness, or something in my head, made me feel very guilty that I wasn't at work, doing something. I went back to Bryant, but things had changed. A freelance girl who I'd hired, and who'd come to fill my job while I was out, was doing everything. Rudy seemed to like her. For whatever reason, I decided it was time to move on. Stupid. Perhaps I shoulda just went home and ordered a premium movie channel.

One of the freelance agents, Monica Walsh, who'd built her business from scratch with her brother Kenny, took me on. Kenny had walked in one day giving out free mouse pads, flirting with everyone coming and going. I fell for it and started hiring their freelancers for jobs. Monica and Kenny were close to my age, movin' and shakin.' We all got along great, so the jump from client to employee wasn't hard. Before long I was teaching training classes for them and became one of their most sought-after freelancers, making anywhere from thirty-five to eight-five bucks an hour. I could work when I wanted. Perhaps not so stupid. Risky, unstable, but not stupid.

27. Nothin' but Time

After a while, the owner of Reno got greedy, and Billy moved on. Nobody's fool, he kept up with the comings and goings in the neighborhood, and was now manager of The Bar. He tried to spruce up the place, whatever that meant. He'd get flowers and such and plan some early performance things and poetry stuff. Business-wise, the weekends were stellar; the place would be jam-packed to the squeaky front door. Some of the weekdays needed help. Shameless Billy turned Monday nights, the worst business-wise by far, into a rival for Saturday — the best by far. He ran weekly 'Pot Brownie Night' ads in the *Village Voice* and baked trays of pot brownies at home and gave them out. No one noticed. Except the few hundred patrons and me, who still don't remember the walks home. But not the cops in the van outside. They were protecting us. When you don't matter, nothing you do really matters.

Business was booming, even though other, more sterile-chic queer bars were popping up all over town, particularly the no-man's-land called Chelsea. Even Misstress Formika had bonded with Billy and together they transformed the Monday night party into 'Hippie Chix.' Formika was a volatile drag queen from the neighborhood, who I'd known pretty much since she'd arrived from the South West. New Mexico I believe. Very political in performing, lots of anti-establishment stuff, but she also was a champion of people trying new things — whatever the schtick. Kindred spirit. Giovanni was working on a photography career and at one point had taken pictures of Formika for my *BackTalk* magazine. The local rag *Q* had turned to *QW* then turned boring. I thought something about our little Eastern enclave was disappearing and I'd try to fix that. The first issue of *BackTalk* had been twelve pages. Quentin Crisp on the cover. My interview with him inside.

One Sunday I went to Channel 69 at Pyramid with my friend Mark, who sported spikey Billy Idol bleached white hair. Linda Simpson was doing some special show with Formika, Lily of the Valley and the Blacklips Performance Cult. OK. I decide to go. Guaranteed good times. It was a holiday weekend, Easter perhaps, and I had the next day off. Mark and I showed up intent on doing nothing but dancing all night. We'd agreed we didn't want to talk to anyone. No gossip. No ki-ki. Just dance. Like good, all-American butch faggots in combat boots, leather MC jackets and t-shirts. I had some mushrooms left over from one of the Sixth Street parties. Just enough for a light ride. Just enough to dance on.

The good thing about Pyramid and Linda Simpson's Channel 69 party was that they still played good music. No one I knew could stand to go to Michael Alig's clubs in the first place, but certainly not anymore because Michael had what we kindly referred to as pots & pans music. Thump thump thump. Bang bang bang. Beats and noise. Same song playing when you went in and when you left. Even Roxy was starting to become the house of ear bleeds produced on a Radio Shack keyboard. No soul. No feeling. Just noise. Palladium had fallen long ago. Pyramid dance music was the best. Acid house. This is Acid. Black Box. Strike it up. Deee-lite. Groove is in the Heart. With the Lady Miss Kier who sang it dancing on the bar. The occasional Madonna song. A danceable rock track. This is what I considered to be real New York. The East Village dream that all the trust-fund NYU yuppies to come later can only wish for and will never get. And the crowd mirrored the vibe. Some of the biggest names in fashion and show business mingling with young people like me, and the whole thing leveled out into one damn fine party, and this house did not discriminate, as long as you knew the score.

Mark and I arrived a bit early, and it seemed like the night would have one of those can't get fully off the ground vibes. We split the mushrooms. 'Wanna drink?' I headed over to the bar at the same time as a guy I would soon know as Eric. He looked just like the guys in the Calvin Klein underwear ads. Marky Mark. Part Anglo, part Native American Indian. How I got him, I'll never know. My entire first encounter was a disaster, or so I thought. I can still remember my exact thought: let him go first so he doesn't cop an attitude… guys like that want nothing from me. By that time, a new breed of queers had slowly begun popping up in Chelsea — assimilation queers in khaki trousers, white t-shirts and self-hating haircuts. I wanted nothing from them or their new culture of loud. I incorrectly assumed Eric might be one of them. I motioned and half-smiled for him to go ahead. He did the same thing with his right hand, arm, and brown leather wristband. I was stunned. Maybe just a rare tourist with manners? Maybe the cutest most hottest bestest lookingest tourist I've barely ever seen with manners? 6' tall. Tan skin. Chiseled model features. An upper body like on the ads. Exactly. Lines and ab things and pec things. And a round butt that makes his jeans look the way jeans were supposed to look. Things I didn't understand or experience being tall and thin.

The scene: he further insisted I go first. I ordered. He glanced at me from the side, off and on. 'What the hell' I thought and say thanks for letting me go first. An hour later we were dancing and making out on the dance floor, with me trying to explain why I was about to become uncontrollably happy and possibly incoherent: the mushrooms. He told me not to worry. He's from Nebraska. He'd stay with me as long as I wanted him to. Ka-Ching. I felt more stunned than when we first ran into each other. 'I'll be keeping you' I thought as I did some sort of Madonna turn in the same spot I'd last seen my friend Scott the dancer alive. Eric was the first boyfriend I didn't literally meet on the dance floor. I'm a very good dancer. I'd always found communicating with my body easier than talking. I hated chat situations. Give me some good music and three feet of personal space, and I can tell you all you need to know.

Mark was across the dance floor, in the center of his own little gaggle. He broke form to shoot me an approving smile at one point. I'd never returned from getting us drinks. You could do that with friends. I danced toward him, he met me halfway.

'Sorry Mark...'

'It's OK! You're busy.'

Eric liked me for some mystifying reason. Now, I needed to go take care of business. He looked for real — 'bout time I had something other than these skinny, pale glow-worm twinkies. I went back over to be snatched up. Eric was strong. A real dancer. And yes, of course, model. He could've picked my skinny ass up and thrown me across the room without a thought. He treated me different. I'd rarely been treated like that. Like somebody wants you. Really wants you. Not just an object of lust, or someone to pass the time with. Or fuck. I'd been praying for a god to come my way with great looks and patience of a saint. Especially the patience. All I knew at the time was I had energy, in pretty much one direction.

Eric, the prince, kept up with me on that dance floor until way late. I usually left the place by 2:30—3AM on a Sunday. They usually closed at 4—4:30AM. But it was some sort of holiday, which the crowd always made their own. I'd been dancing for hours and had it not been for the nip of leftover mushrooms, I woulda' felt it. But all I could remember was the music, Eric's gorgeous face and his hands either gliding me or guiding me, keeping me on my center.

He walked me home. I had begun to fade, thinking of my nice cozy bedroom in the back of my apartment. It was about ten feet square — just enough for a double bed. And lots of pillows. And a cool breeze if the window was cracked. A breeze that smelled like fresh air and hundred-year-old mortar. We made out. Tried to make it. There I was, with Mr. Calvin Klein in my bed. There. And because I'd taken some of the noxious fungi, for the first time in my life I wasn't able to, well, dance anymore. Not for lack of effort. Eric tried everything. I pushed some button with the guy. I was happy to be whatever he thought I was for him. He'd certainly waited around for me to indulge my impulses earlier. I had time to allow life to travel round the corner and run into itself.

After things went from hopeless to almost ridiculous, I had him just lie down. Everything fit. Sometimes you don't have to try or talk. It just fits. I usually wasn't able to sleep with anyone strange. Even back home for holidays, as a kid, sharing beds wasn't my thing. I needed my pre-slumber futzing space. But not this particular night. Most guys sleep like statues. On top of you. Kicking you. But this time, I had Eric. A dancer. A Michelangelo type of statue. Certainly David's beautifully queerer brother.

The next morning everything worked normally. Made it better I think. Good things comin' to those who wait and all. Getting close to people, or rather letting people close to me, had never been my forte. And my experience was, when I did, they tended to leave. Eric stuck around for about six months, give or take. We made it through a snowstorm or ten, and loved to go out dancing. I let him come close, he left. But I was beginning to learn just how transient NYC actually was — you hadda' look out for the ones who were just 'in for the weekend,' or a few weekends.

For a few months Me and Eric had us a great time.

Little did I know that Eric had a lover back in Nebraska all along, who he also owned a house with. One day, the lover showed up in New York, and, well when a former lover comes calling, if it ain't done it ain't done and you get the sidelines. To make matters worse, Eric had this annoying friend named 'Chip' or something. The annoying ones always have annoying names — 'Chip,' 'Biff,' 'Skip.' These are the ones who hang around because they are secretly in love with their so-called friend, and since they, for whatever silly reason, cannot have the object of their affection, they stick around as 'friends' and torture those of us lucky enough to have the privilege. To make matters excruciating, I remember deciding to embarrass myself by inviting Eric and Chip to my birthday party, in hopes of a last hoorah with Eric. Or something. Little did I understand that I was going about it all wrong, but why wouldn't I? Do it wrong, that is. I'd been well trained and had come to believe in my status as a second-class citizen, I still had not shaken all the Jesus-infusions and my God did not like me very much. At times like that the line from Torch Song rang through my head — 'queers don't matter, queers don't love… and those that do deserve what they get!' Perhaps those that invite their soon-to-be ex to their birthday expecting something deserve to get the annoying friend acting like a complete jackass and rubbing their noses in defeat. I survived.

Martin Belk

28. Inventing the Reinvention

Michael Schmidt, who I originally met at Barney's, started coming around the neighborhood a bit more than usual. Schmidt was known for always being up to something. He'd been spending most of his time out in LA but some third-hand gossip put him in some drama with Cher or something equally trite so he'd appeared in New York. I never really cared about the gossip, I knew him as I knew the other famous people I knew. As people. At first he lived with our friend Paul Likins, a BoyBar bartender, in Phoebe's triangle building on West 14th.

I had brunch at 7A one weekend with Misstress. I think Blair either came along or wandered by. Blair'd gotten naked and done some goof doctor poses with Formika at the photo shoot for my *BackTalk Magazine* but I didn't end up using any. Formika was going on and on about how she was tired of doing drag and going to retire the character and just be himself. 'Sick of it,' she said.

'But you're just getting started, people love the Misstress' I protested. 'We need political people, leaders, anything!' This was in March.

In April, Michael Schmidt came through The Bar and handed me a tiny orange flyer, about 1" square, for his new club called SqueezeBox! 'Join your hostess Misstress Formika' was emblazoned on one side, along with a band name and address.

A boy in a Ramones t-shirt was on the other. What? Rock and drag? Blair was hanging with me. We decided the next Friday, we'd go check out this brave new scene.

Friday, April 15, 1994 to be exact, Blair and I went to check out SqueezeBox! at Don Hill's on Greenwich Street. As in, Soho. Sort of. Admission ten dollars. Misstress Formika was the hostess, and a whole crowd of our extended little family of dysfunction worked there. Miss Guy, a local DJ, spun the tunes. Lauren worked the door. Paul, the bartender from Boy Bar, worked as well — almost everybody from the old scene and the East Village and Haoui's crowd and everybody tied to them.

I'd arrived. My first night at that club was charged, hyper, chaotic, and although SqueezeBox! had only been open a week, I could tell it was special from the start. It had legs. The concept was rustic, and refreshing — queers and straights, high rollers and derelicts, gogo dancers, fortune tellers, drag queens, musicians and misfits of the second-class would come together under the banner of rock 'n' roll. As it should be. Sex, sexy and sexual. All lines blurred. Real music, authentic atmosphere, no one turned away. A place for the outcasts among the outcasts.

At first, Schmidt went around telling everyone it was just a new place just for our friends to hang out. But I think he knew better all along. His 'friends' included Cher, Tina Turner, and Sebastian Bach. The success of RuPaul had emerged from Boy Bar and Pyramid, and delivered lip synching into the hands of damnation. Local bands opened, then the house band featured a local drag queen doing cover tunes. Genius. SqueezeBox! took things to the next, higher level as every queen worth her salt was scrambling for a microphone and an angle.

It was the next logical step.

Your salamander emerges. Really, really burns. Same for the stars with the finer silver glitter. Beauty costs, you whisper to yourself. Your entire face is on fire from paint and glue, like a severe sunburn. Your eyes are red and you haven't had a drink or smoke. You feel like crying from the stinging pain, but the music erupting from the other room begins to carry you through: bite my lips and close my eyes, take me away to paradise. Right song and sentiment, wrong organ. You fan the pain with a washcloth. Finally, your epidermis numbs itself and you take a fresh look at your creation in the mirror. You love yourself as the cheap bathroom spotlights reflect your sparkly creations. Your painted features look truly deathly and fetching. You may proceed.

29. Rock 'n' Roll Over

Schmidt and me chatted at SqueezeBox! about the invitations and images and stuff he was using. He'd used one of the photos Giovanni had taken of Formika for *BackTalk* on the flier. Schmidt agreed to let me put some of the magazines in the club. Little did I know that Michael Schmidt was one of, if not the, smartest cats to spring from our extended contingent. Smarter, even, than say Betty Badum when it came to design style and innovation. And I'm sure Haoui'd taught him a thing or two about presentation. And of course Barney, who used to run Hurrah and had introduced me and Schmidt at one of his infamous garden parties had an influence. The story goes that years before Schmidt'd had dresses and clothes he designed and made in a boutique in Soho. One day, Cher came in and took a liking to his work. Although they weren't supposed to, a friend slipped Cher Schmidt's phone number, and the rest is history. All connected.

Early one weekday night, I hopped a cab down to Don Hill's, the name of the club and home to SqueezeBox!, with a trunk full of my magazines. I ventured inside and heard blurting from the back a strong, melodic voice. I thought it might be Don, but I'd met Don, who was about 5'7, thin, over forty, and soft spoken. Don couldn't make such sounds. Instead, a young guy with long brown rock and roll hair, about 5'11, with a badly worn dark-colored t-shirt, ragged jeans and painted fingernails came and opened the door. 'Who're you?' he billowed.

'Michael Schmidt told me I could bring these.'

'What's that?' He looked at my stack of hard work like it's a pile of useless rags.

'I got one for ya — who're YOU?' I wanted to fire back, but kept my cool. 'Where can I put these out?' I asked instead.

I don't remember exactly how, but I somehow learned his name was Patrick Briggs. My new friend Patrick had not completely decided to even let me in when I pushed up on him. I just kept dropping Schmidt's name, not knowing he was Patrick's ex-boyfriend, and actually Don's general manager. Paddling among sharks I was.

Pat had a history with Don Hill at the Cat Club, which had been on 13th Street and Broadway, a few years earlier. Sometimes I wished they were still there, a five minute walk from my house. Patrick'd been a singer with a band called 'Are You Ready.' I was ready. He took my magazine and flipped through it. 'Yeah, whatever.' He flung the door open and pranced back though the club, to the place where a manager goes.

A big, sandy blond-haired man I'd later know as Bobby, the head bartender, noticed me struggle my stack into the windowsill. In the meantime Patrick reappears, tosses his keys on the counter and quietly slides one over and takes a second glance. Without room for further bonding experiences with my new friends, I simply slinked back out the front door. The one thing I'd learned along the way was to not show your cards too soon. Especially when you don't know whether or not you have any cards. But as for Pat, I was actually impressed with the motherfucker.

The next Friday the 13th, in May, they recorded the SqueezeBox! CD, 'Sex, Drags and Rock & Roll!' A few weeks later this guy named Andy, one of Patrick's many boyfriends, had a video shoot at SqueezeBox!, rock-star style. All the drag queens did a song for the SqueezeBox! video and CD with the house band. Schmidt was quickly becoming a genius in my book. The place was brightly lit for the video, like we were on a big movie shoot or something. Well, we were on a set, actually. Sissy Fit. The Lady Bunny. Lily of the Valley. Misstress Formika. Patrick dressed up in drag, going by the name 'Torment.' He sang 'Rock 'n' Roll Nigger' by Patti Smith and Lenny Kaye. Figures. Angry young man. Yet I was developing a cautious liking for him. The crowd itself had grown over the weeks from one to several hundred and excitement had grown in the air along with it.

One week night I ran into Schmidt at The Bar. Billy was behind the bar, tending, although he'd told me his stomach was really bothering him. When I went over to Schmidt, he greeted me with his trademark 'hey' — a sound that starts mid-pitch and gravels its way down, the aural activity accompanied by my chin being held by the back of his turned hand for a kiss.

After I explained to Michael how I'd become a tech genius at the computer company and was now an art director with an agent freelancing throughout the city, he responded with a chirpy-yet-cool, 'Oh really.' Too cool actually. Michael Schmidt stood about 6,' thinner than me, in his early thirties with long dark brown Rock'n' Roll hair, but not like Billy's. Straighter, no feathering. Kinda like Axl Rose.

The thing was, I didn't realize Michael Schmidt was the type of cookie to probably already be aware of what I was doing for a day job. He was a master at people-finding, which is probably why he'd chatted me up longer than usual. We'd always been friendly, but we never had business of any sort. Somehow he asked me to help out or said that he'd call me or something — and I'd agreed. I thought the SqueezeBox! project was very cool, and this was a way of branching out beyond the East Village, although to his credit, Billy had been talking about doing a night with mixed music, a fortune teller and performances a while before Squeezebox! opened. Hippie Chix on a grander scale.

Schmidt now lived above Chelsea, in a large, west side building I'll call Charleville Towers. No man's land for me. I'd spent almost a year without going much above 14th Street, so this would be a nice change. I showed up at the address on the appointed day. I'd expected some redone slum building, as he'd explained to me he'd just moved in and everything was in disarray. He'd moved from Phoebe's building in the triangle at 14th Street and Ninth Avenue, the one where we'd always spent every Pride day partying and watching the fireworks before Haoui died. Nobody'd made any plans for it since, just like how the Croton lake parties had faded. What I found was a legendary apartment complex with a doorman — the kind of doorman that knows everyone in their building, what they're up to, and whether they're in or out. The building entrance was just average in decor and construct. Flat painted walls, a foyer, and the elevator. Mirrors and brass trim. 'Who ya' goin' to see?' the young man asks, I tell him the number. He's a young black guy, in a brown uniform. I think his name was Anthony.

He took me up in the elevator to the seventeenth floor. I didn't know what to do. In older elevators, with the crank levers and gated doors, you stand out of the way. This plastic-wood-veneered box had buttons. Anthony faced forward while he pressed 17, but I caught a peering corner eye every once in a while at my combat boots, jeans and freshly altered black t-shirt — Schmidt had already taught me some liberation: he cut the sleeves off his t-shirts. Little did I know that Anthony was well versed in things that rock.

The door was at the far end of the corridor, with a hay-colored doormat and green letters that read 'GO AWAY.' I rang the old-fashioned bell, and Schmidt opened the door to his palace. First I saw two odd-shaped seats just inside. Chrome with bumpy black rubber like on the neck of a dinosaur. They flopped over and recovered when you ran your hand across them. Next was an expansive living room, which joined a bar on the right with white walls and a small galley kitchen. Windows, with black iron window casings just like my Grandma Ruby had, lined the whole far wall and overlooked a groomed, quiet courtyard below. Not full of garbage like so many in the city. Further to the right was a short hallway. Schmidt walked me down. I paused to take note of a color photograph of Sid Vicious eating a hot dog covered with loads of yellow mustard. Further on the left, a small office. Just ahead, Schmidt's bedroom. There was another room combination down another short hallway he did not show me.

The office was long and narrow, with a large desk taking up most of the space. Trinkets and stacks of paper were everywhere. Autographed. A large poster-sized photo of Tina Turner sat beside the desk. Autographed. Thank you Michael or something. In the center of the desk was something familiar, a computer. Power Mac 600. Fourteen-inch keyboard. 500 megabyte hard drive. 256Mb ram. Around it were extras of the invites Schmidt had given out earlier. Black and white proofs. Printouts of trials, errors, tests and final successes. Just like where I worked. Blown-up copies of them on the other side. Intended to serve as posters and letters, I supposed.

Schmidt pulled out a bunch of large printouts of the SqueezeBox! CD covers and inserts, along with templates for the CD itself. He explained he didn't understand things about the software — how to get the computer to do things. I started going through it with him. Naturally, we both inched toward the computer, eventually sitting side by side, my sleeveless upper arm touching his. All four hands occupying a section of the keyboard.

I got from about the 'J' key to the mouse on the right. He took from the 'Y' key left. He got the artpad and quick keys.

The cover was to be a photo of Misstress Formika climbing the Empire State Building. A spoof of King Kong. Inside there were multicolored ghostings of that image, with song lists, credits and info about the club. I began to get very excited. At the agency I'd been doing floor covering catalogs and brochures... good work, indeed, but this was work with people I knew and music I loved and a club I wanted to support. It was different, innovative, unorthodox. Not your average come, dance, talk about it, leave kinda place. SqueezeBox! had started to stick with me since the first night Blair and I wandered in and saw Formika, standing tall on a makeshift platform stage, in a red dress, long black hair piled high, singing a live rock song. The music went inside our heads and inside our pants. Who'd have thought a bunch of nobody fags could rock out. Dance. Throw our MC jackets at the stage for Formika to trample and bless. Fuck giving the goddess a dollar like at lip sync drag shows. I'd been to plenty of shows at Irving Plaza, CBs, Academy and all kinds of other rock venues in the city. But queers had to watch their asses in those places. Oh, you could go, but you had to not give away the complete secret. Too many skinheads and leftover punks around. I wanted to play too. SqueezeBox! let me. And now, I was working for the motherfucker.

It was natural. It was odd. Two hard-headed, anal-retentive-acting, meticulous and slow grown up teenagers, agreeing to share the same computer in a stuffy room. The space became reassuringly weirder to me as the first hour passed. As we worked on the files, picking color, retouching faces, setting type. We began anticipating each other's moves with the art pen, mouse and key commands on the keyboard. We sat there, hour after hour, grinding out the artwork for the CD. An intense job. He was relentless, obsessively relentless in his attention to details. I respected this to the highest degree. It didn't matter if the line screening would make that one out-of-place hair unnoticeable, it must be fixed. We worked and worked, and although I had been doing the very same kind of work all day, the excitement kept me from noticing that it had become very late. Schmidt, a night owl, was right in his element. He came alive after 1AM, when I was getting cross-eyed; we agreed to pick it up later.

Schmidt put me on the guest list. The 'A' list. First time for everything. I started doing my Squeezing alone because my friends weren't getting the same rock-and-soul affirmations as I was going every single week. I needed the change of scenery, to feel that music, watch all the freaks. Word got out around town that something cool was going on at this dump on the Lower West Side — an unheard of location for a club at the time. There was absolutely nothing much on the corner of Greenwich Avenue and Spring Street in those days. A car garage was next to the club, some decent red-brick tenements across the street, a store two blocks up. The Ear Inn, one of the oldest in New York, is just across the block, where the water line for the Hudson used to come and people in boats could pull right up, long before Robert Moses injected Manhattan with his West Side Highway. Diagonally was the massive UPS weigh station, which spanned north for another three blocks. Otherwise, the area was littered with empty buildings and industrial storage. Perfect for punk.

Model types and celebrities began wandering in each week, but the cool thing about it was, they had to go through the same door and use the same bathrooms and dance on the same dance floors as everyone else. And most of them graciously paid for a place to party, rather than pose. Having worked in the clubs for quite a while I could get into the best parties. I used to live in the Michael Todd room at the Palladium or the upstairs at Limelight, a.k.a. Slimelight when I went to the occasional Michael Alig gig. Limelight had once been a church and gave me the creeps, but they had good VIP rooms. It wasn't a major feat to find them, favors among compatriots really. It's kinda' like I'd once read in one issue of *Interview Magazine* published before Andy Warhol died: one VIP room leads to another VIP room, which leads to an endless maze of dressing rooms, which leads to another door to the manager's office (filled with cocaine and the ghost of Steve Rubell). At each level, you were truly 54 times more special than at the one before. Better. Better until you got through that last hallowed door in the back of the manager's office, which lead to the alley, and the trash cans and the staff entrance where the bartenders and waitresses and dancers with pockets full of your money exit after a long night of your specialness.

SqueezeBox! was the new culture, the new vibe. There was a guest list. There had to be. Or you could just pay the cash. Our guest list maintained the mystique of a social strata. Humans don't function well without a pecking order, but beyond the door, it was every man for himself. No VIP rooms 'cause there was no room for one. The VIPs mixed with the folks who saw the ad in the *Village Voice*. Just like people said of the good ole' days when I'd first arrived in New York. At Mars or Roxy or Pyramid. Just like people said of the older days, before me, at Mudd Club or Max's Kansas City. Millionaire tycoons, movie stars and idols mingling with twinkies from the projects. Once I saw this middle-aged man dancing with total abandon in the middle of the dance floor. Spielberg.

Another night a young woman ran up on the big dancer pole in the front room, naked and having the time of her life, gyrating, swinging, boom-boom to the music, shaking to the guitar solos. Drew Barrymore. Once Marc Almond performed, the deal would be sealed. New York had done it again and our place was the place to be. No one was better. Better off, maybe, but that's how real culture happens — and the key to the 'Box!

My box.

30. Sometimes, I Feel

At the very next SqueezeBox!, I felt even more like I truly belonged, and Schmidt started introducing me around like a new foundling. Jayne County from the original Backstreet Boys, Bob Gruen, Stephen Sprouse. I'd been engaging folks like this for a while on the Lower East Side, but now, we'd come together to make something.

I knew, or knew of, most of the rest of the cast — from Miss Guy who had been DJ-ing around the East Village and performing at Boy Bar for years, to the queens from Lady Bunny, the Jackie 60 crowd with DJ Johnny Dynell, along with promoters like Howie Pyro were fixtures in the downtown rock world, and of course, manager Patrick practically lived at the club. The original SqueezeBox! band comprised some of the luckiest boys on a stage: Warner X played guitar, Stephen Trask sang and played keyboards, a cute Jack Steeb played the bass. A wild South African guy with a black mowhawk named Duard Klein hammered everyone home on his drums.

La, la, la, la, la-lala, la — we are the passengers.

Betty's B list had been great, but the permanence of such a distinction was defeating. I would never be a fashion designer. I wasn't a model. I didn't run with 'that' crowd, really. I loved Betty, but at the time his world wasn't what I'd moved to New York to find. I think if I had actually aspired to the same front-page leagues, I wouldn't have gotten to know so many of these people — celebrity, common or in the middle, as people, first. The rest is just, well, the rest.

SqueezeBox! was poised to be different, much bigger than anything I'd ever known. The scene was getting hot, and everyone in New York knew it. Even the *New Yorker* ran a cartoon of the place. Those times, just before the times that matter. That people remember. Anticipation resting on all the lips of all the children who'd come to worship their inner spirit for the first time in their lives. And for that moment, we held the keys.

I felt like I was catching up with my destiny, destined for somewhere, and something else. On that particular Friday night Schmidt paid more attention to me than ever. I got free booze. He'd told the bartenders I was working 'for us.' The place became more crowded than ever. I knew why, Marc Almond had been booked. Schmidt knew everybody. While not as savvy and experienced as him, I had skills. Some he didn't even know about. Even Patrick, the strapping young gent who'd greeted me when delivering my magazines, started treating me differently, with deep conversations like: 'You know computers, huh?'

'Yep.'

'Well, make us look good — okay?'

The night Marc Almond played swelled into one of the most packed crowds I had ever seen in New York City. Tighter than Pyramid on a holiday weekend. Hotter than the back room at Wonder Bar. Better than anything Irving Plaza could deliver. Louder than a Sunday afternoon matinee show at ABC No Rio. The roof almost lifted from its crossbeams when Misstress Formika took the stage. It surely shook when she announced Marc, and kept moving throughout the set. By the time he got around to singing 'Tainted Love,' the back doors were popping open and people were spilling out into the street. You could've heard the echos of the crowd billowing between the buildings 'get away, I got to, run away…' from across Sixth Avenue — the only thing separating the band and the dirty streets outside was a metal grate and a window glass, still there before Don had it covered over to appease the local community board.

Queers and straights and in-betweens and makeup and boys and girls and their pets, smoke, booze, laughter and kissing and corner sex made for one of the most incredible nights I'd ever experienced. This was what I'd come here for, I kept thinking again and again. This and a lover. And although I would have pretended to want to, I never forgot Eric and all the times we'd had before he faded away. We weren't really in love, or, I couldn't know 'cause I didn't even know what love was, and no matter, we were friends who made angels in the snow and ran around dominating dance floors and making people jealous. I never forget that he never asked me for anything and that he didn't ask me to be perfect, nor was he perfect — nor had I forgotten he was no longer there. Forgotten his boyfriend from Nebraska who I knew little about. Forgetting he wasn't my friend anymore 'cause I'd sent him roses to get him not to go back with the ex and him telling me 'it should never have happened.' I missed the friendship most of all. Eric made me smile. 'This tainted love you've given.' That night I ingested every note.

Over time I'd gone out and bought myself a few new articles to be wearing to my newly-found Rock 'n' Roll romper room. Schmidt had generally confirmed what Betty had told me years earlier — that 'consistency was key.' Betty had once advised me to scale down to one refined look. 'Two outfits for less that $300,' he explained, 'one, all black. Every shred on you down to the belt buckle, black. The other, same, but all white.' At the time I wasn't refined enough or moneyed enough. 'It's very Rock 'n'

Roll, if that's what you're into.' Now, I had a few dollars, more refinement from the battering I'd gotten from Macy's on down, and my place at the table. I went to Pat Field's, where they suited me up in shiny black plastic pants. A place further up 8th Street for black shoes. The t-shirts I bought two for ten dollars at David's Army Navy on Christopher Street. I continued to de-sleeve them, *à la* Michael Schmidt.

I usually stayed at the club until closing. In the beginning, anywhere between 4 and 5:30AM. Things were more fun as the crowds thinned. Dancing, more introductions. Cool people. The ability to actually talk. Some I knew, others I got to know. Always plenty left for next week. Painters, photographers, musicians old and new. Like at Haoui's lake parties. Patrick took a liking to my Southern accent. He caught me saying 'othern' and laughed hysterically for years to come.

'Othern,' short for 'other one.' I'd made an effort to clean up the twang, but after a hundred cocktails, anything could happen. I didn't think my little slip was all that funny, being that I was surrounded by a city full of Yankees who call pizza 'peetzer,' the floor 'fluhwa' and coffee 'kwoifee.' But I paid no mind 'cause Patrick, the manager, obviously took a shine to me and started inviting me out with the core group to breakfast. I, literally became, the othern'.

Miss Guy had gotten in the habit of playing Blondie's 'Union City Blue' as the last song of the night. Almost exactly at 5AM when the energy in the room was waxing electric. Couldn't be dissipated even by a legion of sage-wielding hippies. 'O-oh, O-oh whatta' we gonna' do? Uuu-nion, un-ion, Union City blue.' Blondie captured the energy, and put it in little invisible pockets along the walls, saving it for later.

Plenty of nights after closing, in the early twinkle of NYC Saturday morning, Schmidt, Guy, Patrick, me and Lisa — the girl who drove Patrick around 'cause he couldn't drive, ride a bike, or use public transport — would pile into Lisa's red, slightly used Chevy Cavalier. The same kind of shit-Chevy I'd had back home. Lisa apparently worshipped the ground Patrick didn't walk on, and was with him almost all the time. They knew each other form Warwick NY, upstate. Some might have called her the old cliché 'fag hag, but actually Lisa served a crucial role in our little group of rock 'n' roll numbskulls, keeping us grounded, wanted and from killing each other. Some might even call her manager. Either way, we'd end up at a glorified diner on Greenwich Avenue. The Greenwich Café.

On a typical night, we sat at one of the big tables on the right side of the place. The air from yesterday mingled with the brick walls. Daylight was threatening to appear from behind in the east. Guy talked so softly I couldn't hear what he ordered. Lisa got a hamburger. Other people would wander up, dragging chairs behind them. Schmidt and I got cheeseburgers. Patrick always ordered a croque-monsieur. Everybody chattered about the people from the night. Did you see so & so... what was so & so wearing... the show was good... Marc Almond was amazing... Misstress was fantastic... she rants about politics too long... so & so got thrown out by Kevin and Carl... so & so was there... I chimed in when I felt like it. I was usually too drunk to say anything spectacular, but not too drunk to take it all in. One of the first nights I noticed, for the first time since I'd been working in bars, that the conversation was missing something. Missing gossip about the ins and outs of running the place. Who's the boss. Who did who wrong. It's because these people actually had something besides shop to talk about. We had our own thing, and a challenge to stay on top of the game. The kind of things the rest of the world wants but can't have. OK, sure, Schmidt would piss everyone off in the coming weeks for taking a huge amount of cash in pay and buying a Harley Davidson motorcycle, and Guy would storm out throwing his measly pay at the door, but even that would blow over, eventually.

Years before, back in North Carolina, we'd go out to eat as well. Much earlier though — the clubs had to close at 1AM. We'd all go to the Athens Diner near the really, really bad part of town. If you were an outcast, for being a queer or colored or dork or whatever label the God Squad threw your way, and live in Middle America, you could hide easier in the rough parts. But now there I was, week-in week-out in New York City, dressed in my shiny black plastic pants, sleeveless black shirt and all, hiding from no one. Surrounded by a group of even more outlandish people, who outlandishly, thankfully, put me to shame. The first shame I was ever thrilled about. Inside-out in New York. There's no fear when you stand out enough to make them think.

Typically, Schmidt didn't touch his cheeseburger, but sometimes paid for everyone else's. He loved pulling out his two-inch-thick wad of money. Patrick teased me relentlessly, kinda like Haoui used to, but in a much more aggressive way. He cajoled me to keep saying things in Southern like 'Mama' and 'othern' and he actually laughed for real when I did it. Patrick was riding the AA wagon and prompted me for comic relief.

There's something really satisfying about being taken out to dinner by your bosses after work. Lisa got up and came back from the restroom. So did I and a few others. Upon my return Pat was already outside in the red Cavalier. Lisa sometimes offered me a lift home, but more often than not she waved me off with an air kiss. Lisa wasn't stupid, she was just gaga over Patrick. So were a lot of us. She would take him back upstate to where Patrick lived in Warwick. He had a house and a garden there. For me, I'd moved away from house and gardens and the novelty hadn't quite yet returned.

I usually left alone as the others drifted and drove with some tune throbbing in my head, compressed from the hours before. Hyper, but more relaxed than I'd ever been in that city. I'd wave for the cleanest, newest, shiniest cabs I could see. Which usually blew right past my shiny pants for the yuppies a block ahead. Older, dustier ones usually stopped for me. I liked them better, this new usual.

The colors are best in New York City between five and eight in the morning. Purples, deep blues and gold bounce off the buildings. A shadowy haze covers the trash in the street. I would feel sexy walking up my dilapidated staircase. As if I wanted someone to come out of his apartment just to see how sexy I was. I never felt like going in. The mornings played tricks on me — like I could just jump into work mode and head for the office; take a shift with the trash collector working my block; do a round of early-bird shopping. I felt like going out. But not to party. I dunno'. To just continue this feeling that I've never had so completely before. Everything looked so, real.

When I'd get inside my apartment, my kitty-cat would give me a once-over. I imagined her thinking like Grandma Ruby, in that all-too familiar humorous-yet-serious Southern tone, 'Mmmm-hmmm.' I'd fall into bed. I could've closed the shutters. I didn't want to. I wanted to sleep in the daylight. It was like I was getting away with something. Eric wasn't there. If he had been, he'd be getting ready for bed with me, complaining 'why am I the one who always has to be naked?' Answer: because you're the pretty one. He'd dumped me. Eric was destined for a stint on the tepid new Chelsea scene. Who was I to stop him? He had the body. They had the spandex.

I imagined myself lying there, an outer-body daydream, a reflection in the mirror on the wall opposite. I'd become pretty. Pretty with a capital P. I'd put on 'Union City Blue' — not being able to get it out of my head since Guy played it. I'd listened to it a thousand times before, but then I felt it — lying on my bed, floating on the music. Arms extended extravagantly to either side. Heavy silver rings weighting my fingers against the pillows and sheets. Hair thrown every which way, in unkempt abandon. Just like I'd always felt 'Dreaming.' I didn't undress. I stank of smoke. Eyeliner running. I was a pretty boy. Finally. Pretty and it meant something.

31. Flesh and Fantasy

After one of our wild Friday nights the phone rang. Billy. I was hung-over, still high probably. Head throbbing. Adrenaline still at full tilt. He told me to get it together and meet him in a half hour. His tone was unusually abrupt.

I got up. I still looked pretty. Needed a shave, definitely a shower. But I didn't want to wash off yesterday just yet. I did a cloth-in-the-sink freshen-upper. Glued my hair back into place. I considered wearing my R 'n' R outfit, but decided to save it for official purposes. I grabbed some sunglasses and headed out. A 24 hour diner. All-day food. Food, good. Plenty of room at off-hours but it wasn't off-hours, for once. The sun was warm, streets packed. I was glad I didn't wear my last-night outfit. Skin needed air. I got to the place, Billy'd beat me down from the Upper East Side, before starting his shift at The Bar.

Right off, Billy noticed I'd had an energetic evening, and a newly inflated ego. Billy could see that I was about to burst my seams to tell him about my new night life. I started babbling about rock stars and people and outfits and music. Billy had known for a while I needed something to spice up my life. I think he was a bit surprised with this particular scene though. He grabbed my attention mid-rant-and-hand-gestures.

What I tried to tell him was:

'Imagine yourself in a dark, crowded room surrounded on all sides. The air so humid you forget to breathe. Marc Almond, Green Day, Boy George, Nina Hagen, RuPaul, Jayne County, Joey Ramone, Joan Jett, Lene Lovich, Courtney Love or Evan Dando is onstage. Toss in the likes of John Waters, Gus Van Sant, Tim Burton, Greg Gorman, Marilyn Manson, Henry Rollins, Perry Farrell, Sandra Bernhard, Drew Barrymore, Liv Tyler, Stephen Dorff, Kathleen Turner, Naomi Campbell, Stephen Sprouse, Thierry Mugler, Calvin Klein, Donatella Versace, Patty Hearst and JFK Jr. Then imagine being smashed so tightly against even more hot sweaty bodies that you are forced to let your beer drop. You imagine hearing the glass shatter on the floor. The music is louder than you've ever imagined music could be. It's like front row for a rock show at the Garden. But better. A hand gropes your crotch, and you can't do shit about it. The exit is miles away. You imagine licking the runny eyeliner off the queen to your left. The boy to your right has wet hair matted to his head and pulls your hand between him and the girl he's making out with. The music dominates your ears, the backside of the go-go boy consumes your eyes. Someone licks the back of your neck. You reach for the hottie two people ahead of you. You can't tell if it's a boy or girl. You don't care if it's a boy or a girl. You've forgotten about care. The crowd sways to the left and so do you. Your thighs twitch from the electricity in the room. You want everybody. Everybody wants you. Labels do not apply. Your second-hand shirt gets caught on the super-model's thousand-dollar jacket. You look at each other, smile, and begin to dance. You're there...'

Billy sat and smiled and ate and listened just like always — except for the occasional interruption for clarification or to correct something I'd said. Billy had long become my keeper. He decided it. He'd sat in my seat before. Billy was just about the only person out of eight million that I would listen to. He'd met my mother on her second trip up to see me. They'd gotten along well. Almost too well.

Billy said he knew Ann-Margret. Billy had a way about him that he was able to have friends like Ann-Margret. He used to tell me stories of his younger days. Early-twenties or something. As Billy was somewhere in his forties, this would have occurred in the 70s. He said he was at either The Anvil or Boots & Saddles or one of those classic joints. Hanging out, having a drink, about to go home. In walks a tall, lean, big man with long curly black hair. Said he musta' been 6'7 at least. Billy was quite tall, and for him to describe someone as tall meant t-a-l-l.

He said the guy walked in, checked out the place and the crowd, wandered to the bar next to Billy. Ordered a beer. Gets it, paid. Began to sip and give Billy the once-over from the side. Billy turned around and tossed him a Staten Island attitude. The guy poured half his beer on the bar. Looked at Billy. Extended the longest tongue he'd ever seen on a human being, and lapped up the beer. The next morning, Billy woke up to the old King Biscuit Flower Hour on the radio, with the mysterious tongue guy lying half asleep next to him. He got up to pee, paying no mind to the guy or the radio, but noticed the radio announcer saying something like, 'We have a surprise caller ladies and gentlemen, Gene Simmons from KISS is on the line, Good Morning Gene!'

Then he said he became aroused by a certain sound, as if he had a second radio on in another room or something. At first he shrugged it off, thinking it was the night before coming back to haunt him, which in essence, it actually was. He heard the tone again and went back to the bedroom to find his friend with the tongue on the phone. He heard the announcer ask Gene another question, and his friend, the guy, was answering, on Billy's phone. 'Oh my GOD it's HIM!' he shrieked. I'll never know how true this was, but my experience in the naked city had become that if it were too weird to actually be true, it had a high probability of nonfiction.

Billy said he handled himself well. Billy was known for keeping his cool. The man with the tongue turned out to be the man with the tongue. Billy didn't seem displeased with either. Billy liked to know stuff. He knew a lot of stuff. Protectively, Billy asked me about who ran SqueezeBox! and more specifically Don Hill's. Billy was from Staten Island. Very connected. Typical Billy. He knew half of Manhattan. The other half knew him. And Billy wasn't known for tall tales about tall men, but you never know.

When Billy and me went out to a restaurant, we took turns with the eatin,' talkin' and eatin.' That's how we were as friends. One talked, the other ate. Switch. On the phone, we could hang for hours. Ever since Billy had taken over The Bar, incidents outside had eased. I didn't notice until later that no one, absolutely no one ever fucked with me. Not even the guy at my local deli. I'm glad I didn't notice until later. Maybe just lucky.

More likely, connected.

I chattered on and on about Squeezebox!, my new Shangri-La, realizing in the back of my mind I'd not mentioned a word about

Dan, Ramon, Kurt, Joey, Barney or the rest of my East Village gang. I was too busy with the rock stars. Billy knew Schmidt from the old days — overlapping downtown social circles from Hudson river to East. 'That's all cool,' he said after a minute or so. Suddenly, on an impulse, Billy stopped and pointed at me. 'Ya know, I think it's cool and I want you to go have some fun, make some cash... go run around with rock stars and all — it'll be fun... but, and don't you ever forget it: these people are, not—your—friends.' He poked at my chest with his index finger once to emphasize each of his last three words. Not. Your. Friends.

On the surface, I thought, How dare he? I felt betrayed, like when Mom or Dad, or any other of a plethora of well-intended individuals, found it their calling to ruin my manic upswings. And I knew he was talkin' generally. For guys like me, you crash as hard as you fly. But way deep down I knew Billy was right. I rationalized that I could keep my real friends in compartments. I didn't want to admit it at the time, but I knew at that point while I was a proper misfit, I was no rock star. At the time, I was only the computer-geek, adman and media dude. 'Producer' if I needed a proper name. I can admit it now.

32. Breakfast in Leather

During the day I worked freelance as an art director, at night, two or three times a week — I went back across town to Schmidt's apartment. He always wanted to work more on the CD cover and on some ads or something. I was more than happy to oblige. Plus it was very hot out and Schmidt had a new air conditioner installed in the office. The building management put it in. The. Building. Management. Things like that didn't happen on the Lower East Side.

I got there in the afternoon. Anthony greeted me, didn't even ask me what button to push. The front door opened. The chrome and black chairs were in the same spot. Some new magazines had been strewn about in the chain mail chair opposite. Things were always different. 'Hi, Doll,' Schmidt would say to me, and everybody. He knew he had neat stuff hanging on the walls and in the rooms. Sometimes he gave me a minute to browse from a distance.

I got into the office around 4PM. Schmidt launched right into a question. He was all serious, all work, doing the print artwork plus some leather outfits for someone's wedding. He said he's a bit behind on the project and was taping folded-over segments down out of the same piece of black suede for a vest. The result was supposed to look like black-suede gills of a shark or something. At first, I was left alone to work on the files. Then he stopped his project to jump in. We did another duet on the keyboard. Then he naturally took part of it over, and I swapped and began holding the black-suede gills.

My Grandma Ruby taught me a few of the basics of sewing. I'd always been good with my hands. I studied the meticulous folds Schmidt was making in the suede. I tried to help as best I could. 'That's good. Keep goin,' he prodded. And that was it. For another entire night we sat there, pasting photos of Misstress on the artwork. Texturizing scans. Working on the leather back and forth, naturally taking turns on the keyboard.

One night Michael ordered cheeseburgers from the Moonstruck diner. They had great food there. I'd been going in & out of the kitchen to get sodas. After the burger, I needed a change of atmosphere. We'd printed out the A-list invitation letters for the next week, which had to go in the mail quickly. I was to fold them and stuff them into the envelopes. The letters were fluorescent pink, orange, green or yellow, as were the envelopes, which we had to run around town finding, week in, week out. They had a plastic feel to them, and were supple, making them slippery and harder to fold and stuff.

I took the stacks into the living room. More space. Spread out. I started the job. There were almost a hundred letters. Handwritten notes from Schmidt had to go on most of them. Waiting for Schmidt is like waiting for damp bread dough to rise, it happens when it happens. Schmidt's A list was by far more impressive than Betty's to me. At least I recognized most of the names on Schmidt's — local faces I knew from the scene, musicians and artists from all over the world. Kate Pierson, John Waters, Sebastian Bach. Cher. Drew Barrymore. Joey Ramone. John Cameron Mitchell, a guy I'd met while working at The Bar. At the time, an actor for PBS.

I didn't react to the names on the list. I'd been trained for such things at Sotheby's. Cher had been in their databases. Barbra Streisand would come through. I broke the rules one time and walked by the entrance to the showroom just to get a glimpse of her. Big deal. I've never been impressed with fame anyway. I am entirely impressed with the process of success. His list would be treated with the same integrity as the one at Sotheby's. I didn't realize how much I could gain by observing the movements of these people. Just like at our early-morning Greenwich Café breakfasts, where no one reacted differently if the conversation went from a local person to a celebrity. This is how I'd quickly learned things worked. This is how I liked it. I learned the art of the introduction when Schmidt entered the dressing room the night a performer named Pussy Tourette was booked. Inside was a bit of a tense situation, not unlike the one I'd encountered at NBC when Cobain played. Pussy sat to the side, in a black and white outfit, alone, dealing with pre-show nerves. Band members and wannabees buzzed around. I think Misstress was down there, on the other side of the room. Michael Schmidt seemed to glide across the room with a stealthy saunter, uncurling his right arm in time with each step and opening his hand precisely upon arrival at the outer perimeter of the performer's personal space. 'Pussy Tourette, Michael Schmidt,' he said, without missing a beat, and with that they were instant friends. Working so closely behind, I witnessed the delivery, the timing, all of it many, many times, which elevated Schmidt and his subject to a new personal plateau, where they would forever remain.

Schmidt continued to assert that Patrick and he had gotten the club as a place for our friends — a haven. Apart from maybe The Bar and a few other remote places, New York was getting taken over by the worst wave of soulless music ever. Yuppies had overwhelmed most of the regular rock clubs. CBGBs was a tourist dive. The gay Chelsea circuit offered little in the way of 'new,' and had started its descent into self-hatred, cocaine and crystal meth. We needed a place. Now, we had it. And no one person would be 'the' person. SqueezeBox! was becoming a collective of talent, a movement and would remain so, as long as that talent collectively held together.

Schmidt was certainly the catalyst and the ring master. Patrick the horse trainer. And a cacophony of people made up the rest of the weekly Friday circus. From the minute you walked in the door the tone was set. A beautiful young blonde woman named Lauren stood with Don at the door to take the money and check the guest list. Thing was, lending to Schmidt's genius, the Squeezebox! guest list was not like the others — a list for the appropriation of free passes to VIP's. No one was a VIP at Squeezebox!, not even the biggest rock stars, who had to mingle freely in the crowd. And people like Lauren knew how to carry it, holding a small clipboard in hand, wearing the latest clothes from Pat Fields or Pat-Whoever, makeup painted with the stroke of an artist, and in her hands was the key to a celebration. Style sans arrogance, something not common on the doors of many clubs. The guest list served more to put said 'VIP's' on notice: that they were role to play, for us. It was one of the biggest mind-game I've ever seen, and it worked.

A man named Nick Zedd showed movies he made in the back of the club. Crazy fuck. Crazy cool, yet crazy as fuck. Movies of girls getting porked by an octopus. And live births. And such. Len Whitney from BoyBar made videos which played on three or four old televisions that sat on top of speakers. Mostly queer porn and motorcycles. Rafaelle and Viva were two of the best go-go girls around. A bunch of alternating go-go boys danced on the bar — all set the scene. Local bands played the first sets. Drag queens played with the house band for the second, late night set. Miss Guy kept everyone dancing in between. The DJ booth was originally not a 'booth' at all, which I believe was another ket to the successful setup. Guy, who was naturally aloof, but had a glamourous sincerity about him, stood on the same floor as the dancers, with two turntables on a roller cart. Everyone could see his hands move, his thoughts percolate, and his big glistening eyes as they scanned the room while chatting in someone's ear between record changes. Not even the hacks who study retail customer service could get this many things right.

There were video directors and CJ, a record producer. And a ton of other people. Some famous, some, like me, on their way somewhere if only they knew where somewhere was. The two key ingredients to the genius of this club were that it required and would remain a true collaboration as long as it ran, and the talent, stars, music and sexiness were equally accessible to everybody. The press and VIPs stood at the same distance, on the same floor, breathing the same air, as the general public. Bands with names like Turbo AC's, The Goops, Special Head and Lovemaker played the early sets. Queens of all shapes and sizes like Antony, Ebony Jett, Lady Bunny, Sherry Vine, Lily of the Valley, Justin Bond, Sissy Fit, Sweetie B, The Duelling Bankheads, and a litany of others blasted forth from the serious New York drag brigade.

Don provided the bartenders, who knew the art of cultivating their own loyal crowds. Two Tommys and a large curly haired man named Bobby at the front bar did the job. Because I came in a few weeks after the initial start, I wasn't yet familiar to a lot of people. Except for Friday nights, the entire group was never assembled — which, although it made me skeptical, was one of the first things I noticed about successful projects: lack of corporate bullshit. Nonetheless, I had to win over people like Bobby, and rightly so. I'd watched Schmidt go up to the bar and order a tray full of drinks, and freely distribute them to people in the crowd, who in turn, felt extra special. Being that I was walking in Schmidt's shadow, I decided I'd like to follow suit. After a while, I apparently had proven something along the line, and got drink privileges, bestowed with no fanfare except a smile and a wave of a hand. Before long, Schmidt and me and god-knows-who-else were giving out and drinking enough booze to float a barge down that big Hudson River just a stone's throw away. And Don, being one of the lasts to know how it all worked, let us. What we gave away, he got back tenfold in sales, and Bobby and the rest made in tips.

Safe to say, ours, collectively, was a major hit. I thought about all this each week as I stuffed the envelopes in Schmidt's living room. I was very tired, most of the time, but remained exhilarated. Schmidt loved to buy toys to keep me motivated. The first couple of weeks Pat and Howie Pyro handled all the mailing the hard way, but with my up-to-date technical savvy I kept him interested in the latest gadgets. When we needed a color printer, we went down to the big store at City Hall and paid $1756 in cash out of his pocket wad — after a brief stopover where he took a nap on the grassy knoll across the street as I sat impatiently. When he got the idea for official t-shirts, he ordered a huge flatiron to make them on, and I got to learn to use it. When they came out with 33.6k modems, we were some of the first to order, and he bought me one as a present. We thought we were travelling high and mighty on the Information Superhighway. We were becoming more and more automated. For the letters, I'd found a folding machine, but only folded a few letters at a time, which had to be hand-fed. It was OK. I had nowhere else to be.

33. Who's Afraid of Debbie Harry?

Once, I casually asked Schmidt about his roommate. Just makin' conversation — really. The curious kind you have when you spend a lot of time working with someone. 'She'll be around, you can meet her. Her name's Debbie,' he replied. OK, I think. Roommate. Debbie. Debbie from the bank or something. There'd never really been any reason to chat about it. Debbie. I imagined a woman in a skirt, Italian maybe, hip, trendy, but well off. I didn't give it much more thought, except whoever she was, I was in her space too, and she must have been very understanding to agree to live in a club production factory.

Another Monday night at Charleville Towers, I was over working on a guest-list mailing when I heard the front-door lock turn over and open. It shut, locked again. I had most of my back turned. I thought it rude to look over quickly.

The person shuffled some bags and went down the opposite hallway toward the office. Schmidt had gone to the foyer to greet whoever — I overheard the conversation...

'Hi, Peaches!' Schmidt says.

A pleasant, low woman's voice responded. They continued jibber-jabbering. I continued putting letters through the paper folder, which made a giszh-giszh noise on each insertion. The chatter came nearer. Because of the paper folding I can't figure out if they are heading into the little kitchen just behind me or nearer to me in the living room. I keep folding and stuffing, *giszh*. Out of respect for Debbie, the waitress or banker who paid for one-half of this nice little palace Schmidt lived in, I decided just to keep at my work until called on. Maybe Debbie'd had a hard day at work and didn't want anything to do with new people. I start feeding pages pretty quickly through the folder machine — *giszh giszh giszh*. The noise got louder and faster. I lost track of their conversation, but look just ahead as two female feet approach, in red pumps. I realize I'm going to meet the roommate. As I stop folding, Schmidt says, 'I'd like you to meet my roommate, Debbie.'

'Sure, OK,' I nonchalantly reply — the good worker bee — slowly raising myself up, head last, extended right hand to shake, following the female body from her feet up to her waist, chest then head. I freeze but don't choke. *O-K.* 'That's a great system you've got going.' I opened my mouth and attempted a 'yes.' Debbie gave Michael a familiar grin, they were obviously having fun with me. 'This one is a computer genius,' Schmidt told Debbie, and about how I am working for the club and all. Debbie's tone was soft, smooth yet crystal clear. It's as if her voice comes forth, surrounds the note to be uttered, and delivers it fresh to your ears, each aural piece an independent creation. Like on all her songs. In her sound I heard the contemplation of 'Union City Blue,' the confidence of 'Dreaming,' the chutzpah of 'Atomic.' Maybe that's why people like to hear singers speak, at concerts, on TV. It provides a road back to the music. On that particular night, her voice and her face provided a mental road back to my Mama's basement and one of three albums I could afford in my high school days: A Night at the Opera, The B-52's and The Best of Blondie. Debbie's face was an apparition — a montage of all I'd ever seen now before me. I questioned the reality of what was happening. The air felt barometrically sublime, like just before a massive summer rainstorm back at Popey's, when these things happened to me. Her hair was lightish brown, but the moment turned it platinum in my eyes. I didn't get especially nervous or anything — more curious. I stared her way, she stared mine.

Schmidt teased me with something like, 'now you, get back to work,' as they walked away still talking. I'd seen Debbie at Wigstock and heard of her comings and goings all over town. Only made sense that in such a close-knit rock scene that existed at the time I would eventually get a close look. It made sense but felt so surreal. Then again, much ado about nothing. Just people, doing people things. In this case, a singer. But it would take me a long time to learn to separate image from existence.

Things were movin' but Billy's voice frequently rang in my head: 'not your friends.' What did he mean? I can still feel the thumps he'd put on my chest with his finger. What could he have meant, beyond the obvious? For the first time I was part of something truly new. Something I thought would make a mark. Make a difference. This would make the difference. Debbie had to be right, dreamin' is, in fact, free.

Pretty Broken Punks

II. Art Likes Life

'All of old. Nothing else ever.
Ever tried. Ever failed. No matter.
Try again. Fail again. Fail better.'

– Samuel Beckett

Your cat sits directly in front of you now, on the toilet seat, unchallenged. You wonder what goes through her mind as she watches you, towering over her, working yourself into a frenzy. A friend once suggested that animals have no concept of the other side. Once you close a door, they have no sense of the depth into which you've ventured. You know better.

1. Queers in Your Kwoiffee

Time moves fast when you're swimming in Rock 'n' Roll, barely come up for air. Swimming with its people. And its stars. Weeks flew by. Friday to Friday. SqueezeBox! opened in April 1994, and by July had erupted like Krakatoa. Lines ran down the block reaching toward Canal Street, where the city became a freeway then turns itself into a tunnel which plunges below the murky Hudson River.

No one else had a gig like our little artist collective — not Marc Berkley, who, in my humble opinion, turned the dance scene into a spandex tink-tink nightmare, not even Michael Alig — we were live. No soul-destroying pots & pans music, no drug-infested beats. Schmidt told me Debbie would soon do a gig with the SqueezeBox! band — a major event, which would kickstart our kinda' nocturnal 90s New York. While all the other clubs were stepping on each other to become bigger and bigger, turning creative culture into a cattle-drive, SqueezeBox! became better. It's all about cool. Mass production is not cool. Style is. Cultivated, not packaged. The very mention of a singer like Debbie Harry taking the stage conjures images of Warhol, CBGBs and Max's Kansas City in the minds of the willing — creating an excitement that does not transmit on MTV — times that the 'I Love NY' marketers have been prostituting ever since.

Usually a small venue couldn't touch the likes of Debbie Harry or Marc Almond — but we did. And I watched people like them and Joey Ramone as they discovered a loyal, new, young audience who could dance just as hard in '94 as they did in '74. And I observed people much older than I, as they'd come in the club with an expression of relief, as if to say 'phew, we can go out again...' And for me, it was hilarious to watch so-called celebrities saunter in with their model fuckbuddies of the moment, looking around grandly for attention from the crowd, perhaps a photographer, only to get shoved out of the way by a big trannie in six-inch heels then gulped into the dance floor by sweaty rock kids. Bump.

At some point around 1AM, that little former diner called Don Hill's would be so crammed with bodies that no one, literally, could move. One big bottleneck, waiting for some folks to fall out the back door so the crowd could shift. Perpetual rock motion. I remember getting stuck in the back corner by the bar, sometimes having flukey conversations with strangers I'd get smashed into, other times using my status as a producer to jump up, on and over the bar to hide for some crowd relief. I used to think of it like some of the stadium or Madison Square Garden shows I'd been to — this crowd could have been the five hundred or so people smashed up against the front railings to the stage — the true fans, the ones who worked at it.

Couples consummated marriages in our crowd — no Supreme Court decision necessary. Funny how it is, while politicians and the media argue about telling people how to live, they've been living all along. And we kept living. Despite all the efforts to the contrary, God kept making us and we keep living. That's what I liked best about the early years of SqueezeBox! It was about partying and all that, but it was also about free expression — the likes of which I'd not seen since the early Roxy days, and never with a masculine slant. Boys could be boys at this club. Being queer didn't make them girls, and being boys didn't necessarily make them queer. Some were just queer boys. Too many of the gay rights people had fallen into narrow definitions until SqueezeBox! came along. Yes, punks with red mohicans could be queer. And straight punks with blue Mohawks could dance with them without the queer rubbing off. And if they had money and a successful venue, they had to be acknowledged. And yes, major rock stars, symbols of our culture, could like them, love them — heck, in Schmidt's case, live with them. But this troubles some people. Our queer punks with red mohicans were no more welcome at spanky-fresh Chelsea bars than they were in the towns they'd run away from.

I'd become a regular at Charleville Towers. Two or three times per week to do the ads, another night to do the letters, flyers, invitations — a weekly routine. Debbie was quiet with me at first, but warmed over time. As for me, the mystique of the album covers and my shock from our introduction was wearing off. We had things to see and people to do. The Debbie in the music was not the Debbie at home, where she was a more chatty, regular person. I pretty much came and went as I pleased. And even though I had absolute access to the most private place of one of the biggest names in Rock 'n' Roll, I never fully took the left turn into her side of the apartment. Forget the invasion of privacy — to do so on any level would have changed me, and in turn changed her towards me — whether she'd ever know it or not. I wanted to learn, not be a snoop. I'd bleached a blond streak in the long hangy-down front of my hair. She'd reach and stroke it in passing every now and then, and look at the color in a sister-like manner. 'Not bad,' she'd sometimes say, before turning away.

We started promoting Debbie's first show at SqueezeBox! right away, weeks in advance. I'm not sure what she'd been doing over the preceding few years. There was a jazz group she'd played with — The Jazz Passengers. I think it's safe to say SqueezeBox! gave us all good reason to do a lot of fresh things. This was one aspect of Schmidt's genius — if you plop Michael Schmidt in the middle of a desert, he could manage to find a crowd, put people together and make something happen. And it will be more interesting and artistically valid than anything Hollywood, MTV and HBO could ever devise, combined.

The pressure was on. 'Such '70's nightclubs as Max's Kansas City and Club 82 are long gone, but a new punk-glam scene has emerged with SqueezeBox, every Friday night.' ranted the *New York Post*.

The Village Voice upped the ante: 'How many of us, tired of house music all night long, have daydreamed about a dream club that mixes Studio 54 and CBGB? These Fridays at SqueezeBox! are making those dreams come true.' And Rolling Stone turned up the heat: 'On the edge: an emerging genre spearheaded by club theme nights like New York's Squeeze Box.' And even the fashion world rang in with a clear directive from Gianni Versace: 'On Friday nights you frolic at Squeeze Box in Tribeca.'

Suddenly, there was a ton of extra work to be gettin' on with. Immediately, the press were like bumble-bees, flyin' around and stingin' whenever they could. Suddenly, most of New York City's Rock 'n' Roll scene became VIPs, and then more real VIPs started swarming by the bucket loads — photographers, writers, singers. Deborah Harry brought them all out. This would be the first event in a long time that was a must-see.

Since I didn't know, or care for that matter, who the throngs of press and industry people were, I could be around them as needed, without the jitters of a record label person or back door groupies. I didn't want anything. If someone had broken into my Mom's basement while I was choreographing one of a hundred dance-rock operas and told me that one day I'd be helping produce shows in New York City with the very people I had playing on my stereo... well, all the rest was gravy. I'd dreamed of getting to New York, doing something cool. Little did I realize that my present situation had nothing to do with luck. Maybe timing. And maybe because I had something to offer. But not luck. It's like the Swamis and Buddha say, you are exactly where you are supposed to be, doing exactly what you are supposed to be doing at this very moment. And I didn't even have to look for this thing. It chose me — but I didn't quite know this yet.

2. Run On the Band

July 15, 1994. A hot summer. Debbie showed up for rehearsal in the late afternoon. She had her hair tied up. Jeans, t-shirt. The barbacks and bartenders and porters and people were all there setting up. SqueezeBox! was and always would remain a dedicated group effort. Patrick managed the stage. CJ, a friend of Pat's, had produced Andy's videos and our CDs and was stacking them up to sell. Lisa, Pat's friend and driver, ran errands and willingly took on all the tough go-fetch jobs any of us could not have handled. Blake did the lights. Formika and Paul warmed up the band. Schmidt was back in the office making tickets and badges and backstage passes and guest lists. It was like setting up for the prom none of us never had. I was excited: a real prom or formal, where we could wear black and kiss boys and girls and where the music would be the best motherfuckin' show ever. Everyone was jumpy and hyperactive. Showing it a little was allowable. How could you not? One of the biggest stars in the world was about to get on that rickety little stage and sing.

I was shaking and in a cold sweat while going up and down the ladder. I should have been in bed. Debbie started working through her set. I loved watching the band watch her. Tense, so as not to miss a direction, a cue or something. They too had no time for excitement; they had to play. These kids, barely in or out of their twenties, had the gig of a lifetime. I liked watching Jack the best. I always watched Jack, with crushed eyes. He was a cute skinny, pasty-white boy from Jersey. Big pouty lips, brown hair, and eyes so reflective you could see yourself in the right light, and they'd change color from gray/blue to brown.

Debbie was incredibly pleasant to everyone... if she was nervous, you couldn't see it. Occasionally she'd stop the band and ask for a little more of this on sound, little less of that. Less drums, more keys, more sound in her stage monitor. I was impressed by the relaxed nature of it all — knowing every single one of us wanted to pee our pants and squeal like schoolyard children. It really was work, a job — with tasks and goals and quality control. But her voice was the unmistakable magic, that sound that had come from that person and projected through radios, cassette players and stereos around the world for over two decades. And there she was, roughly running through a set, on a stage, just beneath me.

After rehearsals, I rushed back to my apartment to change clothes and grab a nap. The world outside of any gig appears rigid, the air thick and sifted by concrete, boxed in from the workaday world — as if there will be no more time after the big moment, you and yours alone are bringing to life. One time, when I was sprinting home, I looked into the face of an older black woman who regularly sat on the corner of Second Avenue and East 11th Street by St Mark's Church, across from Betty's, shaking her cup in front of the graveyard for money. She wraps colorful cloth on her head and wears lots of sweaters. I've given her money whenever I saw her because she doesn't attempt to evoke pity in solicitation of her handouts. She just asks, and looks as if she will never be phased by anyone's responses. I don't read auras or anything, but no doubt this woman is spiritual, mystical even. Once, I asked her what her name was as I dropped a handful of change into her worn paper coffee cup. She only stopped jingling the cup long enough to say, 'Thank you.' I wasn't taken aback. Mystics do not easily reveal themselves. I decide to contribute a few dollar bills instead of coins. With them, I offered her my own made-up name. 'Here you go, Mama,' I said as I stopped to dig clumsily into my wallet, amid the crowd of people jumping out of the way to avoid her. 'Thank you, baby,' she replies. She did not mind her new name and I felt honored to get one in return. We were now 'Mama' and 'baby.' Not bad. Not *cliché* either. On the New York avenue of working-class life, addressing a black woman over 30 as 'Mama' is in high regard, and showing respect. For an older woman to address a young adult man as 'baby' is also in high regard — an offering of protection. I was reassured.

I made it back to the club in my shiny black pants, with determination and my blessings from the mystic Mama on Second Avenue. People were running around, distracting me, asking me for this or that. Poking thinly-veiled questions about Debbie that I couldn't answer. I worked hand in hand with Schmidt, which must've meant I had answers. I tried to psych myself out. Whatever it took. I was high, on life. The club opened at 10. People were already lined up outside. Debbie was to go on at midnight, which meant 1AM. Debbie drove up around 11:45PM. I just happened to be outside surveying the scene with Schmidt. 'Hey, Peaches,' he says to her as she handed him a bag. They start chatting. People were watching. No one got within five feet of us. Some kids called to her from the line, she smiled. The security guys became more alert, loving the moment. I followed them into the massively overpacked club. At the front she took her bag back from Schmidt, and a little cardboard box I'd been handed. They say a few more things, and Debbie turned directly into the mob to head down to the basement where people got ready. 'Should I go with her?' I ask Schmidt, just generally concerned and not knowing my place or what on earth to do. 'She can take care of herself, don't you worry,' he replied in high, affectionately patronizing tone. I observed the legend gingerly make her way.

The place was utter chaos. No one could dance for all the posturing to get a good look at the stage — which was another of SqueezeBox!'s charms. VIPs had to mingle with the nobodies, which is why I think so many other people in the New York nightlife business hated us so much. They had to peddle the illusion of substance while we, simply, had it. The first band went on and off before a packed room awaiting their goddess. Blonde wigs were everywhere. Drag queens and trannies in full regalia. Like one local who called herself Aqua had boobs made of clear plastic, filled with water and goldfish. Boys took the time to layer on extra eyeliner and mousse in their hair. All waiting, expecting. Guy was hurling the anthems from the rollercart DJ booth beside the stage. Every once and again someone would bump it, skipping the record, which only invigorated the crowd even more. I'd been out thousands of times in the naked city, clubs, arena shows, public events. Never had I felt such energy in a crowd, air fueled with silver anticipation.

Suddenly, through the crowd, my elbow got pulled. Schmidt motioned for me to come to the top of the staircase leading to the basement. Debbie and her band are on the step. Schmidt turns me around and says 'Let's go.' I'd learned how to work through the crowds over the preceding weeks. Something about how you hold your head, touch people with a detached air of belonging. You have to kill, numb a part of yourself to belong, the part that makes you want to run naked through flower fields with excitement. Kinda like the lyrics from one of Prince's songs, made before he got weird: 'the reason that you're cool is 'cause you're from the old school, and they know it.' But it came at a price — one that I didn't know I'd begun paying. When you work at a place, it's not about being above anyone, but the greater responsibility of being with them. Schmidt pushed ahead, everyone follows.

There was no room. We worked our way out the big side door, and up to the corner of the building and the single side door to the stage. Kevin, the bouncer, opened it. People who couldn't get in are on the street watching, a loud murmur ensues. I heard them begging Kevin to keep the door open as I jump on the stage and head to the other side. Schmidt, Debbie and the band follow. I squatted down far stage right, just between the edge and Guy's DJ stand. Schmidt joined me. The crowd went wild. Our weekly sea of faces cascade as far as I can see, back and to each side. The girl with ginger hair and light complexion. The tan boy with dark eyes and black hair pushed up into a spike. The tall, skinny guy with blond messy hair, Clark Kent glasses and sweaty, white short-sleeved shirt open down the front, revealing a smooth alabaster chest. The big football-player-sized drag queen with hair twisted into thick black Medusa snakes, and black contact lenses in her eyes. The heavyset computer guy with a geeky striped polo shirt and brown thick hair, clipped to outline his face. The model girl with prefect makeup and long auburn hair. The black girl with dreads and orange mystic eye shadow. And on, and on. This was America to me. This was the real New York. Everybody, nobodies, chaos. The people from the land of music and make believe — within reach of those who loved to sing along and believe. Everyone was safe here, at this SqueezeBox! — me, Schmidt, our friends, Debbie, the crowd — all bound in our own unequal.

A big push came from the rear, people in front literally had to bend forward and catch themselves with their hands sprawled out on the stage next to Debbie's feet. Joey Ramone came out and did the intros. She did a long set and at least two encores. The songs were a blur to me, but I caught 'Rip Her to Shreds' in full audible connection. That and 'Call Me.' The crowd refused to stop screaming for more. But this show had to stop. People were on the brink of passing out. Someone knocked a beer bottle out on some boy's head while doing the opening warm-up number, and he was bleeding from the forehead down the front of his white t-shirt. After one of the bouncers determined the wound to be superficial, Schmidt introduced him to Debbie and they let him sit stage left for the show. I don't think I've ever seen a pretty boy singing along with a rock show covered in real blood. Although he used a towel-compress, the red liquid seeped from the top of his head, mixing with the sweat of his brow, and ran over his soft lips, finally dripping to his lap. I don't think I'd ever sat onstage for a real rock show.

An audible gasp of relief came from the crowd as the side stage door opened. Air, much cooler than before, swirled in and swept the sheet of smoke and show pus from the interior. I jumped up and followed the entourage outside. Lightning colored the black sky over the top of Greenwich Street. Debbie stood with Michael and Joey Ramone. I was a few feet away, hands on knees, breathing. I was watching them, and to my complete surprise, people were watching me. The stress of the day rolled off me with the heavy raindrops that had started to fall. The wetness quickly went from playful drips to a permeating downpour. Debbie reached in the stage door and got her bag. No big hurry. Debbie, Michael, Joey Ramone, the boy who had been superficially bleeding, Patrick, the band, me, and a whole crowd of people hung out on the street. Breakfast that morning was especially tasty.

3. More, More, More. How do you like it?

The next six months were a rapid fast forward to New Year's Eve. Goodbye 1994. The second Debbie Harry show. While we were busier than ever before, little did I realize my city had begun a slow, deliberate fade. SqueezeBox! had opened on the cool Friday night of April 15th 1994 — the day the US shot down its own helicopters over Iraq. Four months later, Rudolph Giuliani raised his iron fist to be sworn in as Mayor of New York City. Little did we realize that our 'black outfits at midnight, guitars screeching 'til dawn, and the glitter in our breakfast cereal' was soon to be at the center of Rudy's war on culture. But that was OK, those of us who worked there instinctively created it, lived it, and made love to it. Second-class counter-culture became my career. In America, the back of the bus suited me just fine.

Debbie, the SqueezeBox! encore , was a much bigger build than the July gig. Unfortunately, I was also in the throes of a flu — but you didn't call in sick to this job. I felt like absolute shit, but the adrenaline and cold pills kept me going. One of my main responsibilities was to decorate the dance floor — another opportunity for my practice in Mom's basement to pay off. I rigged a massive fishnet above the stage and dance floor, then filled it with black and white balloons. You couldn't have a New Year's rockout without balloons falling from the sky like on American

Bandstand. The club itself was run down, with old, cracked plaster walls, sagging tile ceiling and peeling paint. An air exhaust grille covered with dust webs hung above the fifteen- by ten-foot stage. Schmidt and I had arranged some sort of sign and special decorations to hang. I timed it to be on a ladder, stage right, just as Debbie's band started rehearsal. Things had to be done... no one cared and I wasn't stupid. I fumbled with the same decorations over and over, so as to keep my bird's-eye view.

The rehearsal was filled with the loud stops and starts of people who knew exactly what they were doing. I remember Debbie wearing denim, and patiently waiting for sound technicians to call out settings to each other, make adjustments and signal the band when to start again. Eventually, I wrapped up what I was doing and hailed a taxi home to shower and change. In any other job I would have called in sick, stayed home. This was no job. I arrived back at the club while the house band played a set. At midnight, Misstress Formika did the countdown, and I dropped our black and white punk rock balloons on the dancers. After, as we drank our champagne toasts, the room began to swell with more and more revelers, eager for the main event. And there I was, December 31, 1994. Around 1AM. New York *fucking* City. Squeeze *fucking* Box! — Boy makes it up from North Carolina to the hottest stage since Max's Kansas City. Sweating from the flu, adrenaline and the five hundred people packed in a room meant for seventy-five.

Later, as the band took to the stage and Formika screamed into the mic announcing the moment we'd all been waiting for, the crowd surged forward and Debbie appeared. The band started rockin' their first song. Suddenly, people in the front of the stage started reaching for the keyboard stand and speakers to steady themselves against the uncontrollably moving mass of bodies. Schmidt crouched just beside me, holding onto the keyboard to keep it from being detached from its base. On the other side, I leaned in to help. Simultaneously, we noticed Debbie's sound monitor disappearing into the audience. Schmidt jumped over and grabbed it, pulling it back onstage. He was holding the monitor with his left hand, the front of the keyboard stand with the right. I had both hands on the keyboard itself. It took all my strength to hold it down for the duration of the show.

Physically, I felt horrible, afraid I might throw up at any moment. The club was hotter than the West Fourth Street subway station at rush hour in July — easily over 100° Farenheit. Plus, the air was thick with smoke, but as Debbie sang, all this seemed to evaporate. Mind over matter. Collectively, we began a metamorphosis — the sound of Debbie's crystal-clear voice ushered me, Schmidt, the entire crowd to rise above it all. We all came to SqueezeBox! for this. And I was a part of it, needed, belonged.

After the last song, the crowd relented and Schmidt gave me a huge smile and a big hug. 'Look what we did,' I said. For some reason I remember him wearing new leather jeans, with white stripes down the sides. Following the band, Formika, Schmidt, Debbie and I fell out the side stage door onto Spring Street. Oblivious to the drizzle, everyone lingered outside, chatting, congratulating and talking about whatever you talk about after one of the biggest shows to date in downtown Manhattan. It was now January 1995.

With no energy left, I didn't quite know what to do with myself. I expected Debbie, standing nearby with Schmidt, to just say goodnight or something — if that. Whatever rock stars do when it's time to split the scene. Just when I was about to wander off, Debbie asked me if I wanted a ride home. There was only one relieved, grateful, elated answer. She retrieved her things from the club, came back over and gestured 'c'mon, let's go.' The sidewalks were wet and reflected our shadows, the street lamps and traffic lights.

The rain beat on the metal roof of Debbie's car. Older cars sounded better like that, the drops had resonance. Modern cars look like eggs and sound like they're made of cardboard when the rain hits them. Hers, I'm almost certain was a light creme late 70s Chevrolet, the shape of which kinda' reminded me of my Grandma Ruby's 1967 Buick. Debbie started the engine, and put her bag in the back seat, and fiddled with some of the instruments on the big black panel. I was trying not to shake but the vented air was making me. We needed it. I knew I'd be done for — working sick, getting hotter than the 15th of July and then drenched in cool. Death by Rock 'n' Roll. She put the car in drive and edged up Spring Street. Our heads were full of the past few hours. Mine still full of over-the-counter dope. She was quiet. 'It was a great show,' I shivered across my lips, partly so as not to be rude, partly to distract myself from the shivers. 'Yeah,' she starts, 'it was. The crowd was really into it.' The understatement of the century. She'd put on glasses. For a minute, she became my imaginary friend — a girl I always wanted to know. The cool girl from the cool high school I never went to.

I spoke cautiously, like a kid trying to keep from scaring the pretty bird off his windowsill. You want to be friends. You want her to like you. 'I-I've never seen anything like that before.' She smiled, no comment. 'It must be fun right? I mean work, sure, but fun too?' My question came in the middle of a left turn off Houston Street onto First Avenue. She'd heard it. Took her time to respond. This was the Debbie I was beginning to appreciate more than the one on stage. The one that, with no apologies, took her time, thinking before she spoke. Surely a sign of years dealing with a massive career, tours, press, clubs and upstarts like me. A quality I needed to learn. We moved quickly up First Ave.

No traffic. As she made the turn onto my block, 13th Street, she came out of her head to say 'It was a lot of fun.' And smiled. She stopped in front of my building. 'Now, go get better.' Ten different expressions of gratitude raced through my head. The one that came out was 'Thanks for this' — the weakest, but most honest one. I closed the door. The rain was still coming down in buckets, the only movement on my block except for Debbie's car disappearing just ahead — the off-white Chevrolet took on the colors of the traffic signal at Second Avenue as it disappeared into a cool new year.

4. Tossing Tea Leaves

I woke up, officially, two days later out of my flu-and-show-induced coma. Excitement from the event had made it really hard to relax. SqueezeBox! had gone from something big to something historical, mammoth in an NYC sense. As I was lying there for those two days, I took inventory — like you do when you're sick. Sometimes I think being sick is God's way of just getting us to have more time for REM sleep so we can figure things out. Another year. Something. Something big. Part of something.

One day, the phone rings, it was Billy. He asked where I've been. I made a futile attempt to explain my neglect of my neighborhood friends. We laughed and he started into what I figure is one of our regular jibber-jabbers. One of the reasons I loved Billy is 'cause he never held a grudge. If he had something to say, he'd say it and move on. 'Well I got somethin' ta' tell youse,' he continued, increasing his Staten Island accent. 'Things ain't so good with the boys' — meaning the boys working at The Bar for Billy. He always kept me up to date on the goings-on. Recently he'd hired a new guy, Paul, to work with Greg and Eddie. Eddie'd moved up to bartending. 'So I'm at work yesterday, and I told them that I wanted them to have the bar stocked a different way than usual. And Paul takes it upon himself to tell the others not to, and directly undermine my authority.' Billy didn't like undermining. He just didn't understand the concept. And he hated 'bar drama' which was why I found the whole thing strange.

He went through the story, which I thought had been complete. Then he told me he had a doctor's appointment later in the day because of his stomach problems. I figured it was because he'd partied too much or something, like on Pride Day earlier in the year. He'd had a gang of us up to his house for lunch, then we went to a rally in the park, then saw some of the parade on Fifth Avenue. Then Billy begged off and went to two big dances and then the fireworks on the pier like a tourist. I didn't like Pride *per se*. That particular year everything was further tainted because it was the 25th anniversary of the Stonewall riots, and some bunch from California had apparently come in and railroaded the local Empire State Pride group, taking over the planning and turning it into one giant cock, booze and breath mint advert.

I had nothing in common with most of those people. Pride had become all too commercial, too spandex, too drugged out. The only thing I liked about it was the idea of being able, for one day, to walk around and not be conscious of my sexuality — in a sea of a million queers where no one was looking, for once. I think me and Ramon and Dan and Joey from Brooklyn had found all of Billy's festivities rather strange — Billy wasn't one for the tourist traps or Pride. We figured he'd just gotten an urge or something, acting like he'd never have the chance to go to a parade again.

The day he called, we chatted for another half hour or so, but it naturally became time to go and I tried to wind up the conversation. Billy seemed to follow, like we always did, until he said, 'Wait a minute, man, have I got something to tell you. So I'm at work yesterday, and I told them that I wanted them to have the bar stocked a different way than usual,' and to my complete surprise, he launched into the same story about Paul he'd told me a half hour before. I started to laugh it off, 'OK-OK, I gotta go,' thinking he's joking.

'What?' he said, surprisingly. I was stunned. I stopped and listened to the exact same story as before, told as though I'd never heard it. I found this very strange but went along with it. He seemed to finish again, and I made a second attempt to get off the phone. It'd been an hour at that point. Heck, I'd been planning to go down and see him at work later anyway. Again, he seemed ready to say goodbye, and then started right back in the middle of the story about Paul and the bottles again, at which point I literally had to apologize, say goodbye and finally hang up on him.

Something strange had been going on down at The Bar for a while, and I knew it. Paul, the new guy, and Eddie, who'd been there for a long time now, had become cagey about Billy. Where Billy and I used to see each other all the time for lunch, going out, dinners, etc., Eddie and Paul now injected themselves, as if they'd become his keepers or something. Weird. Were they protecting him? In hindsight, probably. People did what they had to do, as best they could in those days, and usually it didn't make much sense at the time. We were fighting a plague, after all.

I decided not to go down that afternoon. Instead, I went to Schmidt's to get a jump on the promotions for the club.

Pretty Broken Punks

You switch off the hot bathroom vanity lights. The packages and containers of makeup and glues lie in a pile like spent bodies after an orgy, contemplating their next endeavor. Time for a third cigarette and a caffeine-filled Goody headache powder. No headache, but a good speed-up nonetheless. Maybe the aspirin helps the remaining tinges of fire vibrating around your face.

Another afternoon at Charleville Towers. Five bucks in a cab, exactly. Anthony the elevator dude took me up. Schmidt and I got along some. We argued some. Fought a lot over layouts and type and color usage. But on screen, the collective work grew into brilliant pieces of art. The atmosphere was just as charged creatively as the shows at the club each week. Schmidt paid an obsessive commitment to detail and style. I paid obsessive commitment to color, function, format. He encouraged me to break the rules I'd learned about typesetting back at the community college. I encouraged him to abide by them so the work would be effective. No matter which way the ball bounced, the shit looked amazing. On our CD, Misstress did, in fact, climb the Empire State Building. Queen Kong. Vibrant yellow and pink and green duotones splashed across the inside of the CD liner.

The weekly invitations were black and white, but Schmidt managed to make them look like crafted silver, with shiny type and dark hollows on one side, photos of hot naked boys on the other. Our invites could melt the eyes as good as a Bill Graham poster on one side, and, placed on the tongue properly, would melt from the other. Rock was historically sexy. Our posters were sexual, luring you into a humid, free world where imagination was worth more than money.

We worked way up into the night again. The situation on the phone with Billy had creeped me out, and I was still weak from the flu. I decided not to make a stop at The Bar and was happy to be occupied. I just wasn't in the mood for drama.

One of the nights Dan called. Apparently Billy had to be rushed to the hospital. I called him back before the message even finished playing. He told me that apparently something had happened, he wasn't sure what, but when he'd gone to The Bar for a nightcap Greg told him that Billy'd been taken in. They didn't know for what, and he didn't know the location. I didn't know how concerned to be — Billy never mentioned anything but his stomach. I figured an ulcer or something. Billy was strong. I was told they'd call me as soon as they knew something.

I knew the 'sick drill' all too well, but you-know-what hadn't even crossed my mind. When I was in my teens I stayed a lot at Grandma and Grandaddy's in Charlotte. Mom didn't mind too much. Grandaddy'd had around nine heart attacks and three strokes by the time he passed away. He was one of the sickest people I'd ever known before moving to New York. Grandma had a full plate with him, so, just because it seemed natural, and the thing to do, I helped however I could. I felt it to be almost an honor to be able to care for an elder. I'd learned to give him insulin shots, medicines, bathe and feed him, even the necessary enema and catheter if need be. I didn't think twice about it. It was what you did. I learned to numb out the part that found things foul or ugly or inappropriate. And I learned from Grandaddy's many trips to the hospital that when people went to the hospital you had to wait and see. A lot.

I'd had marginal experience with New York hospitals. Haoui'd passed away at home, and I wasn't present for any of the others I'd known. I thought about St Vincent's and Marty Lipton who'd gone down real fast. But I kept numbing myself mentally.

You take yourself back into the bedroom, dancing to the music still blasting from the front of your apartment. The difficult work is done. You're not a fancy wardrobe-er, so getting dressed is easy — your canvas is painted, all you need is the frame. You reach into the closet and pull out the heavy black leather pants Greta and Duard made for you. They're tight as possible and accessorized with silver zippers which retract the legs over the entirety of your calves. A black leather belt, completely covered with silver studs, cinches the waist just below your danger line, allowing your closely trimmed pubic hair to peek out for the inquiring viewer. Your top is a black concert t-shirt, sleeves adequately removed — the middle, midriff adequately cropped so your navel and pubes can breathe a little. A not-so-subtle invitation to anyone with the wherewithal to notice. To a rock punk the only thing more satisfying than having a sexy middle is having people notice your sexy middle.

I'd been unable to get Billy at home, so I called down to The Bar. Paul answered. Told me Billy was in the hospital for tests and things. He'd been in a few days apparently. Paul acted cagey. Resentment burned in my veins. I didn't like being informed about one of my closest friends from strangers and co-workers. Bad enough that the rug I'd trod so many times before was once again being yanked from underneath me, I didn't need blinkers to hide it. I grew numb. I started meandering over how I'd just spoken to him days before.

Paul reluctantly told me that he was in a psychiatric ward at Lenox Hill for his own protection. They were afraid he could wander off and hurt himself. They didn't know what the prognosis was. I hung up, stunned. Billy'd only mentioned things about his stomach. Never his head or anything. Unless, there was something... I put my head in my hands. I wanted desperately to cry, but couldn't. I'd numbed out that part. 'Not again, not again,' was all I kept thinking. But nothing had officially been confirmed so I held on to a sliver of hope.

Paul told me that while he was in intensive care only close relatives could visit. He told me to check back. Days went by. I didn't hear anything from Eddie or Paul. Not surprising. I made a stop down at The Bar to try and catch one of them. It was a busy night. All I got was that he was still in the hospital, and they didn't know anything. I was furious. One of my closest friends in the whole world had been taken by some strange illness, and then was being hoarded by people who'd only known him a fraction of the time I had. Finally, I got ballsy and called the Lenox Hill Hospital myself. I found out the information and visiting hours.

When I hung up the phone I decided I was going up there. I could talk myself into any room in Manhattan, and now this hospital would be no exception. I was sick of second-hand information. I wanted direct contact. No more in-betweens. I called Billy's sister Linda and got an answering machine, and I left my number. I think Kurt had squirreled her number from Paul or something. Linda called back, saying she'd wanted to call me for days, but didn't know my number. She said Billy talked about me to her. Billy'd told me Linda was a real sweet person, and she proved it that day. She worked to keep herself from crying. She told me she'd put me on the list, and I could go visit anytime I wanted. I thanked her and hung up.

My nerves became swollen with rage and devastation. Again. I knew how fast this shit went down. I got Barney, Dan, Ramon, Kurt, Giovanni and Joey together, our old crowd. We were at the desk at Lenox Hospital within an hour. The woman at the desk told us the floor. The psych floor. She said we would have to leave our things with her at the reception and then go in. I gave her everything but my wallet. They said it was to protect the patients. We went up the elevator. The place was clean and all, but it might as well have been a sewer; it still spooked me. I never understood why they decorate hospitals with burgundy.

We got up to the proper floor, stepped out and followed the signs to the psychiatric ward. A black nurse wearing a white uniform and cream-colored homemade-looking knit shawl or sweater buzzed us into another reception area. The walls up there were light pink. She explained to us that Billy'd had a good day, and would be up walking around in a minute. We could visit with him in the sitting room. She pressed another button and another door opened across the room. She waved us into another room with heavy wooden chairs and brown plastic couches and heavy doors with windows that led to a bathroom and patient rooms. Billy was peeking his head out. His hair was flat. His gorgeous jewelry missing, replaced by a white hospital bracelet. He had a light yellow robe covering his white hospital gown. Both hung ajar on his shoulders. One foot stuck out around the corner, his white sock jutting out in front, not quite on, not quite off. They could only let us in three at a time. Giovanni and Dan had come in with me. They sat down on the plastic couch.

Studying them, I could tell by the way they acted they'd never been around or seen this type of thing — the thing when people's bodies don't keep up with their spirit. Or, they'd seen so much of it they were completely overwhelmed. Who the fuck knows? We were present. I sucked it up, ignored the smell of recently-clean coming from the bathroom, and walked over to Billy. I reached my hand out. I didn't know what I was dealing with. Was he being his usual funny self? Maybe he was almost well, ready to go home and trying to play a major goof on us long-faced faggots. Yeah, I looked in his eyes, saw the laughter, the reason half of the population of downtown made stops to see him whenever he worked.

Quickly, he spooked back to the other side of the door. A voice of another nurse comes from one of the bedrooms in a high, put-on happy tone, 'Billy! These are your friends. Come on out now!' He emerged slightly, looked down at the floor, ashamed. He sat down and took my hand. I knew what I was dealing with. When he sat down he came to life. Started chatting like normal. However, his timing, the duration of syllables and sentences, was slipping. 'Hey guys, how yous' all doin? Some mess they got me in here, right?' We chatted back. He talked about work, The Bar, asking if we had gone by. In an erratic gesture he suddenly got up and went to the security door. 'Hey, hey,' he said to the nurse on the other side. 'I know, I don't want out I want to know where their drinks are? Don't we have anything for the guests?'

'We'll work on it, Billy,' says the nurse.

'Billy, we're OK, really,' Dan tries. Tears seem to be appropriate in my eyes, I work as hard as I can to decide whether to let them through. He can't see me do it. He's as bad as Marty Lipton giving me his ice cream. It's always the same, the sick ones taking care of the well ones.

'No, you're not OK, you don't come to visit me and sit empty-handed,' he tried to say. Billy was still Billy, no matter what was wrong with him. His guests always well cared for. He seemed to be starting to get really tense. I suggested he wait and we go check while the others could come in and talk to him a while. Dan and Giovanni went out, Ramon and Joey in. I was left. Nudged back in, even. We all rotated in and out over the next hour, trying to talk to him, see how he was doing. I was happy Barney came along, he too knew the drill. But I also wondered how it all would affect him, having lost so many. In any case, he stood by us all.

On one of my trips out to the internal nurses' stand I tried to get my hands on his chart. I saw it on the counter. It bugged the crap out of me that I had no confirmation of what was wrong with him. I thought I knew, but still hoped I was wrong. Maybe for once it wouldn't be it. The thing. The Plague.

Eddie and Paul were on their way in as we approached the glass front-entrance door to the hospital. They didn't notice us at first, but looked annoyed when they did, like somehow we'd broken some rule by coming up there. 'Fuck you,' I thought as I walked past, not even blinking. They heard me. What's the big secret? My friend was sick. Period. Dan or one of them hung back and talked a minute, perhaps trying to smooth things. I just walked down 77th Street, tears rolling, fists clenched. No one to hit. None of us should have been there, in the first place. We should all be back at the bar, selling beer and kisses, figuring out our next phases of life. But no, the clearances were underway. I swallowed the rage like a warm, leathery, raw oyster which scraped down my throat and then boiled in my stomach.

The only thing more satisfying than having people notice your sexy middle is having them indiscriminately kiss, touch and feel your sexy middle. The middle, as is known to the Brahmin, is the root of the soul, the chakra from where all life emanates. Rock 'n' Roll, musically and in attitude, emanates from your middle. You check your outfit by raising your arms in Christ-like reverence, and check your middle. It works. Boy, girl, girly-boy, superstar, macho-leatherman, nobody, gatekeeper, being.

5. And You Are?

Each week Squeezebox! grew stronger and stronger. The front door seemed like the Academy Awards, only the people looked better and had a reason to live. Some of them anyway. Bands were booked through the next year. Before SqueezeBox!, drag queens merely mimed other songs. Now, they had their own voices, and graduated from clowns to performers. The house band and the queens would whip the crowd into a frenzy. The dance floor became a mosh pit. Bodies wrangling and banging into each other, sweat flying. I'd been in plenty of mosh pits down at places like ABC No Rio. They were mostly full of skins and straight fucks. There you'd very well leave with a bloody nose or blackened eye. I'd been into bands like Murphy's Law and DRI. What I found cool about those pits was that, even though dangerous, if you fell on your ass you'd be grabbed back up by anywhere from two to five people in a matter of seconds so you wouldn't get trampled — the antithesis of real life. There was an etiquette to beating the crap out of each other. At SqueezeBox!, one of the bouncers had to make himself available when the crowd started moshing. Problem was, at a punk club you'd get punched but not trampled — in a crowd full of queers and newbies you wouldn't get punched, but if you fell, you'd die. No one had gotten the memo about picking up your fellow man — the love was in the sweat and bruises. Many of the guys there had never played sports, never had testosterone-driven contact with other males besides full-on sex. All guys need outlets to be guys. Some girls do too.

Carl, a bouncer, used to grin at band time, as did his secure counterpart Kevin Brennan. Kevin had his own band and sang brilliantly, but Carl didn't quite get us freaks, yet went along like a perfect gentleman. He treated me like a gentleman. He was a 7' tall giant black man from Barbados with closely trimmed hair, baby face and size sixteen shoes. The nicest guy you'd ever want to throw you out of a club. Calm, easy-going, he liked an occasional joint and some chill reggae.

Mosh time seemed to confuse Carl, a.k.a. Carlisle. Carlisle didn't pay no mind to queers kissin' and carryin' on. But I'd watch him from time to time, standing like a statue on the side, smirking in anticipation as the band would start to play a fast song. It only took one bozo to start it, sometimes me. Push some folk forward and back, and within seconds everybody pushin' everybody else every which way. Sooner or later, some fag would fall and Carl, cool as a cucumber, would reach into the swarm of bees without a thought, grab the him-her-it by the shirt, and hurl the poor slob ten feet in whatever direction was open — like plucking feathers off a goose. 'Oh Lord,' he'd chant after things calmed down to just making out and groping on the dance floor, and say something like: 'What's wrong with you people?' and we'd share a good laugh. Something was wrong?

And of course, there's always the angry yuppie girl who'd clamored for a place at the front of the stage so she could stand there bobbing her head with arms crossed. Being boring. And of course, she'd get really pissed off when mosh time started. This girl is and has been at every show in the history of rock music. Her Uncle Dave works in PR. She came in all shapes, and sizes, but was always there in her jeans, not-really-rock t-shirt and made-for-daytime hairstyle. And of course she grabbed at and complained to Carl relentlessly. Usually, Carl or Kevin would shrug her off and try to get her to go get a drink and calm down. On one occasion, maybe an off night, she started complaining in Kevin's left ear while he plucked a skinny young queer up off the floor with his right hand. Without a thought he took the girl by the arm and sent them both sailing.

Schmidt had been working his 'A' list. All manner of superstars were either coming to or performing in our little hovel on Greenwich Street. Word travels fast when someone has an original thought in the US of A. It does still happen from time to time. The owners were pleased. Don Hill had a supreme hit. They never figured on success of such scale. We had news cameras from Tokyo. Steven Spielberg was a regular by then, and headed straight for the dance floor, and stayed there the entire night dancing like a school kid at the gym, harder than ever, t-shirt drenched. John Waters unassumingly held court by the back double doors. Some of Betty Badum's fashionista friends like Thierry Mugler, Stephen Sprouse, Donatella Versace made regular appearances. The angel Rafaella was the key female dancer of ceremonies and her and her fellow dancers role cannot be underplayed. Unlike other clubs, if the dance floors wasn't moving, all you had was dead space. With dancers, the no one in the crowd had to worry about being 'the first' and all joined in. Raf also sang with a band called the 'Cycle Sluts from Hell,' so she did double duty.

The crowds came from all over. Word traveled up and down the east coast, out to California and over the pond to Europe. We got the old-school rockers and new-school neophytes. Businessmen chatting about politics with trannies. Trannies giving them the business. Then there was the small gaggle of under-agers. I identified with them in particular. These were the ones who'd heard about the place, and were able by hook or crook to sneak out of Mom's basements and get there, and live it. They got to be queer and be punks or whatever iteration of the culture they wanted, or all of them for that matter. Some of them would even thank one of us, 'cause they just couldn't fathom the Chelsea scene, where you had to be perfect, dressed in spandex, and into really bad pots & pans music. This was one of the main keys to the success of SqueezeBox! — the music, go figure. Music with soul, meaning, power. Music that didn't pit races or generations against each other and divide them into tidy little target markets. Music that talked of love, sex, power, politics, fucking, sucking and death. Religion experientially, rather than egotistically. From Blondie to Bowie, AC/DC to Guns N' Roses, with Nina Hagen, Marilyn Manson, Boy George to make it all stick. At the same time the angry children joined from the West Coast and vomited themselves across America — Cobain and Courtney, and some little darlings called Green Day and L7.

Michael Alig, Marc Berkley and their respective bands of clowns were tink-tink-tinking their way to nowhereland. How original. I'd done that a few years before when you could still get real MDMA back in Dallas at the Starck Club, owned by Grace Jones and Stevie Nicks, among others. It was a novelty that should have gone the way of the name-game. To my knowledge you couldn't even get real MDMA anymore, all these two-bits were prancing around with lunchboxes full of heroin and rat poison. I'd gone by Limelight a few times. Berkley was doing something called Club Mall at the Tunnel. Both bored me to tears: non-artists struggling to make art into a parody of the suburbia that sought to destroy it. Nothing like a few years earlier at Roxy. I remember standing on the dance floor, feeling rather plain because I hadn't painted myself up to look like

Ronald McDonald like the rest of the rabble. And, I stood with absolutely no reaction to the music, which is rare. My hips move to soul music. My feet pivot to 70s disco. My heart sings to Rock 'n' Roll. I could be caught anytime listening to anything in a range from New Order to Beethoven's Ninth but on that particular night I might as well have been standing in the middle of a cornfield waiting for the second coming. The energy was so negative all I could think about was leaving. Little did I know that someone had made a major mistake, as Limelight, a former Episcopal Church, had not been properly deconsecrated. Me and my friends called the place Slimelight because it championed the soulless cattle-call in New York. A place for the uninspired and unoriginal to come decorate themselves. Masses of roaming drugged-out children, looking for a home or a fuck or a home to fuck up. One or two were found dead under the pews from time to time.

SqueezeBox! wasn't irreparably saturated with dope at first. Unless you consider alcohol a drug. It was about finding your own joy, in a group of others doing the same. Sure, people were doing whatever they wanted — boozing, smoking, tripping, and they certainly got wasted throughout, but they didn't come to SqueezeBox! just-to-get-wasted. You could do that at any corner saloon. People came to SqueezeBox! to be at SqueezeBox!, anything else that happened was secondary. As for the club kid idiots, ecstasy and rock don't really mix — thank God. Nothing more boring than a room full of people standing around chewing their lips, unable to talk, and trying to hump everything that walks by. I even knew plenty of twelve-steppers who told me SqueezeBox! was the only place in the city they could come and have a good time without being relegated to the sidelines.

My little job got bigger week by week. I was office-trained, I knew protocol, how to prioritize. I could also talk the business talk. Not perfectly, but well enough to reach out across the outcast wall and deal with the outside world. Early on, Schmidt had been paying me, but soon he formalized it. 'Well, if you want this little job, Mr. 'Producercomputergeniusperson,' you can have it.' Was he kidding? Producer? What is this producer? 'Producer' was a glorious title given to someone who worked like a dog to keep the misfits in line and make the thing and things happen. He told me I was already doing the job, and gave me one of a few tips of a lifetime: the true power is one step behind the stage. He'd already put my name on the CD credits without my even having to fidget, along with a fellow partner-in-typesetting, Edward O'Dowd. I appreciated being appreciated and I appreciated Michael Schmidt 'cause he appreciated me. One big cluster fuck. Nothing shady going on. Business. I was both wanted and paid for it. What a concept. 'How do you know all this??' he'd say. Schmidt could see my value, as did Michael P. back at the ad agency. Too bad I couldn't.

Not long into it he entrusted me with most of the finances of the club as well. All above board, no Gatien-style shenanigans here. The first time he counted me out over three thousand dollars. The wad was large because he'd given me the fives and ones. The folks at Sotheby's had taught me to dull my senses when it came to values, 'just more zeroes...' like my co-worker Cathy had once told me. I remembered when Cathy'd taken to schooling me on a few things: 'Just put it in your pocket and walk down that street like you got nothin.' I trusted Cathy 'cause Cathy was from the old school. She was a black woman from Brooklyn. And I knew that since she'd been a regular at the Paradise Garage, 'My favorite all-time dance floor,' she'd known people or known of people from Haoui's old crowd. That's how New York City used to work, one day dancing, one day sitting at a desk opposite the kid who'd been adopted by the people you used to dance with. Nice. I kept Cathy's lessons with me when Schmidt would stuff my plastic pockets with the money.

Over the following few days I'd run around distributing pieces of the cash to places we owed for ads and things. My favorite was the *Village Voice*. A woman named Carol worked there and we hit it off instantly. She told me to call her Kitty. Kitty had been booking club ads for years. She was about 5'7 tall, nice-looking gal from the Midwest. Light brown hair when she didn't give some arrangement of blues or pinks. Had been in the city for a long time, run the club gamut. She didn't have much use for them anymore, unless they were running ads. The first time I took money to her I could tell she got a kick out of my excitement. She took me to her cubicle and indulged me with a grin as I counted out a few hundred in ones, fives and tens. 'You know, postal money orders work well?'

News from Billy wasn't good. His sister Linda kept me up to date, without ever revealing the actual cause. 'Something neurological…' Linda was sweet, but Billy'd kept each facet of his life separate — family, uptown friends, me — a divide that was becoming impossible for me to straddle.

6. Can You Repeat the Question?

One morning, I woke to a funny feeling. A familiar feeling. Heavy and familiar. The same feeling I'd gotten with my Great grandmother Montgomery, Grandaddy, Marty Lipton, Haoui… For some reason I've always known. I wake up not quite rested. Feeling like I've just cried and need to throw up, like I might be coming down with something. But then, when I can't find the reason behind it all, I get on with the day anyway. Later on, I took my lunch hour to go back uptown.

The Lexington Avenue trains were fucked as usual. All redecorated, but ran slower than the old red ones. The city stank of summer — discarded food and body odor. The slow steady rain outside makes the scent and my shirt stick to me. I get on a #6 local. The air conditioning is on full blast. I shivered. I thought about how much I hate architects and the people who design public spaces and services. They aim to take away all our working windows, fresh air and self respect — freezing us in the summer, boiling us in subtropical temperatures throughout the winter. I should have taken a cab, but the Upper East Side is notoriously gridlocked.

The train finally pulls into the 68th street station. A combination of habit and complete exasperation inspires me to sprint for the concrete staircase. I walked fast, up to 77th Street, like something was pulling me along by a rope. I blew past the main reception. There were people there, no one noticed. I got up to the psych floor. I felt like I would walk in on something traumatic, but what I found was much the same scene as when me and the boys had been last time. The main nurse in the cream-colored shawl at the desk, other visitors milling about. Patients going about their business. Other patients were making unusual noises intermittently. 'Billy's in his room,' the nurse kindly told me.

When I went in, Billy was in the bed and clutching his covers with his left hand and has them pulled and bunched toward his chin. He looked out at me, semi-blankly, and smiled. I saw his face starting to form the Billy I know; I expected the greeting I was used to, but it didn't come. Nothing came easily. A letter here, a word there. His hair twisted and pushed up on his head. I did my best with the brush.

After a while I took a seat on the wooden chair toward the foot of the bed. Outside the security window I can see life, heat, summer. The rain stopped. A bluish-gray New York light crept through the leaves of the tree outside. I've since learned to recognize the moment: the last time you're to see someone in his body.

I talked for a while to Billy like nothing had changed, nothing was wrong. It only frustrated him, so I stopped. He desperately tried to make a sentence. A word here, a phrase there. 'I, was.' His face lit up, he flipped back his hair, reached his hand up as if to signify being upright, stable. 'And now.' He lowered his hand and flipped his wrist over and waved it over the length of himself with the grace of a gypsy dancer. He repeated the movement again and again, kinda like the last time we were on the phone. 'I was,' hand up, 'and now, I, now.' I thought of Bob Fosse, one of my favorite choreographers, as I watched him. The movements continued for a while. His spirit wanted to tell me that the whole thing had come on him as a surprise. That he'd had no warning. That if he had, he woulda' talked to me first. He woulda' talked to all of us.

I don't remember if tears were streaming down but it felt right for that moment. At some points you can become unaware. Billy motioned back and forth with his hand. I don't know how long I sat there. I don't know how I told him I had to leave, and resolved that no matter how long I sat there, I would have to, at some point, in fact, leave.

7. Such, Such Were the Toys

As rock stars go, Debbie inspired me on quite a few levels, impressed me as a person on more. She seemed to know something about life. Grass roots and the like. It is no secret that when Chris Stein, one of the major forces behind Blondie, got threateningly ill over a long period of time, she threw her career to the wayside to be with him. This is what outcasts do. She understood when I told her a friend was in the hospital. She'd spent long days in one with Chris.

Chris was a regular at SqueezeBox! Him and his girlfriend Ila, whom I became friends with as well. He had a reputation for dumpster-diving, saving perfectly good yet forsaken items from an eternity at Fresh Kills, the Staten Island landfill. Apparently Chris had a house full of junk, from lamps to electronics. The place was located just down from the club. One big yard sale waiting to happen. Rumored a total mess at the time. A few weeks earlier, during the afternoon, I'd gone to the club to drop off some posters, and when I came out I noticed this shorter blonde woman, in a blue jean jacket, denim jeans, hair tied up in some kind of work-scarf-looking thing, rubber boots, sunglasses and carrying a toilet plunger. At first, I just took it as another New York City eccentric, but as she approached I realized it was Debbie. She slowed down in front of me, I wanted to giggle but didn't. She looked like a character from Coal Miner's Daughter. Puzzled, I said, 'Hey girl, what are you up to?'

'Chris's basement is flooded again. I have to go see about bailing him out, literally.'

'Gee,' I said, flabbergasted. Don't rock stars have plumbers? I think. 'Need any help?' I sheepishly offer, and swing my keys as if in a big hurry somewhere.

She graciously declined, although I did owe her for the ride home a few months before. I'd been invited over to Chris's plenty of times, but just never quite made it. Didn't need to start now. Chris and Ila and I kept our friendliness in the club and on the block. He liked to chat me up about technology — something I was always up for.

Having worked at the computer place and now being hooked up with ad agencies all over town, I had access to the new systems and software. The marketing machines from Apple to Microsoft fueled a frenzy of competition, to the point where most products weren't even out of beta test mode when released. Somehow, all the computer manufacturers had found a way to convince an eager public that buying buggy software and shoddy systems was a good thing — and then paying for the updates and fixes was a better thing. Because of all this, while computer science students at NYU were still clamoring to get their heads around BASIC, I had access to just about everything on the market. And I took it. And used it.

Chris was amazed by technology, Schmidt was obsessed by it, and I was his cyber whore. Just like him knowing to get his dresses in a certain shop window in Soho, he knew to get his club onto that computer. Somehow. I had my mouse. Debbie, her microphone whenever she wanted it, her plunger whenever she needed it.

Back at the office, Schmidt usually did most of the on-screen grunt work. The final design was so intricate and layered I couldn't match it. He knew every precise pixel to click to select just the right text. I handled them once they were ready. I prepared the files, took them to be printed large-scale, copied, cut. A lot of the time they wouldn't be ready until 10PM or later on a Friday. I'd go to Kinko's on Twelfth Street and University all done up in my black plastic pants, sleeveless black t-shirt, eyeliner. Standing in the line with people late from work getting a last-minute job out, college kids using the computers, girls getting wedding party invitations. No one paid me any mind. Schmidt and I had come in and charmed the boys and other workers many times before. They liked talking to people they saw as rock stars, getting bright flyers done announcing rock stars, with pictures of naked boys who looked like rock stars. It's been a long time since New York had any real celebrity, accessible celebrity. Something other than hyped names of club kids and club creeps.

Then there's the paper. The fluorescent paper. The damned fluorescent dayglo paper. The paper that cost about thirty cents per sheet, didn't hold ink properly, was always in short supply across the city, and jammed up the printers. This is, of course, the paper Schmidt just-had-to-have for the A-list mailings. I guess famous people liked dayglo. Pink, green, yellow and orange. You could've spotted a piece of this stuff from the Space Shuttle. And this was dayglo before they'd outlawed most of the cancer-causing dyes used to make it. But no one in town ever had more than a pack or two, nor, for some odd reason, would they order in quantities of less than a case. So, I ran, and ran and ran around the hot steamy streets of Manhattan to get it each week. 'And I am well paid to do it,' I reflected along the way, although I hated doing it.

I told him about Billy. Schmidt wasn't happy to hear the news.

Schmidt reached into a paper bag and whipped out some boxes of bleach. He'd been playing with a photo of himself on the computer — turning his hair white. I don't know if he asked or I offered, but that day I was drafted into turning Schmidt platinum. Schmidt and I had more in common than we liked to admit. Things like moodiness, insecurity. We didn't talk about it much.

This was also the time of the dawn of big prescriptions. Once I was referred to a psychiatrist by my own psychologist. I think my dear patron saint, Yvonne, who patiently listened week after week to me try to figure out life, wanted me to get the urge for meds out of my system, and move on. And that I did.

The psychiatrist asked me a quick battery of questions, and within a half hour wrote me a prescription for lithium. A week later I was a walking zombie and felt like I was on E. She changed the prescription to another massively strong drug. Two days later I was having dizzy spells. I didn't want to get out of bed, but was twitchy. I decided that not feeling like getting out of bed was better than not getting out of bed due to the cure for not wanting to get out of bed. The end.

At the time, SqueezeBox!, Schmidt, the project, engaged a part of me that elevated, gave me purpose, distinction and desire. The kind of thing that takes you really high, feet off the ground, but can, in turn, make walking difficult. Such is the definition of mania, pain and the bluest blues making you want to die one minute, but not dying 'cause you can't wait for the next high. Imposed, absorbed or inflicted. Both of us knew what 'having a slow day' really meant. But on this particular day we would bleach his hair. It never occurred to either of us that he could go to a salon for such a task. I'd been helping my mother do her roots every other Sunday night since I was little. It was one of my favorite things as a kid. Something about actually being involved when a person makes a major change that brings you closer. Like going with your friend to get a tattoo or new piercing, things that don't easily go away. Things that form the person they present to the world, day-in, day-out.

I knew the box and the instructions by heart. The same Mama used back in the 70s. Born Blonde. The smell fucked with my head. I'd been using another brand — something geared for teenagers — to do my streak — not Mom's brand. They're for two different things. Schmidt had unknowingly taken me back-home, once again. Truthfully, I think he was just humoring me and giving me somewhere to be after dealing with Billy.

We applied the bleach, box by box. It'd take about an hour or so for the peroxide to stop working. I knew how to use these kits, but I had no idea they were probably the weakest bleaches you can buy. They're not meant for radical change. After about three hours we had Schmidt from dark brown to a summer gold, and took a break before putting the next kit on. I was tiring of the little joy ride. I thought it would have been an hour or so then down to club for a celebratory drink — not an all-night affair.

I heard the front-door lock turning — the sound of Debbie's keys. She came in with Greta Brinkman, her bass player. Miss Harry, well, she defined blonde. Greta followed suit with absolute platinum resolve. I'd met Greta not long before, and we were slowly becoming friends — a thin punk-rock girl, like 5'7 or so tall. Spikey platinum hair. Jeans and colored Converse sneakers, tattoos, armbands, leather wristbands. Both came over to the kitchen where Schmidt and I had been putting on bleach all day. Greta was from Virginia. 'Hrmm. Getting there,' one of them said. Debbie ran a comb or implement through Michael's hair and checked the color. One of them made a gesture when they saw the Born Blonde boxes. Debbie picked up her keys and walked with Greta back out. 'Back in a minute.' Schmidt and I just sat around, like two school kids waiting on their lessons.

About a half hour later I heard Debbie's keys again, and two sets of feet. They both came in, each carrying a bag. Debbie sat hers on the counter and told me to unpack it. Inside were packets of powdered bleach, a huge plastic bottle of peroxide with a number stamped on the side, and some tiny little brown bottles with a picture of the hair color on the front.

I left the project in Debbie and Greta's capable hands, with the thick scent of bleach in my nostrils. A chemical and menthol openess. Schmidt was well on his way to a scorched scalp and platinum locks as I finally decided to leave.

I took a walk down to 23rd Street. I noticed the same stores and lots of people. Moonstruck Diner. None of them had just watched a lesson on how to bleach hair by the woman who made the process an international institution. It was one of those few moments I've felt like the only person in the world doing the only thing that anyone anywhere would ever have wanted to be doing. It all meant new things to me, the glamour, the music, life, connections… my mother, peroxide, Blondie, Debbie. Little things, they meant the most.

8. Just, No

One time, back home in my building they'd just painted our hallways white, doors black. Like the tile in Seth's bathroom that matched my Grandma Ruby's. I opened the entrance door. The place stank of oil paint. I looked for my new kittens, which I'd named Saturday and Tuesday. One was there, one gone. I noticed the screen on the middle-room window had been pushed out.

Raul had given me those kittens from the same litter. White with gray-patched coats. They liked to run and pounce all over me when I came in from the club, then snuggle under me for my sleep. A neighbor knocked on my door and said Saturday had fallen out my window. A pet rescue lady who lived next door had taken Saturday to a veterinarian. She'd left word that I could pay the bill off in installments. I ran out, leaving the neighbor standing in my doorway. I had nothing much of value then except my leather MC jacket and my kittens. I jumped in a taxi. The vet was on the other side of like Sixty-fucking-Fourth street. I got there, paid the taxi and went into a fancy building. I handed the nurse the receipt the neighbor had given me. I hear someone upset crying back in the examination room where I'm told to have a seat. This was not my kind of vet. Some girl who looked kinda like Brooke Shields with fat legs was sitting next to me. I tried to start a conversation with her to break the ice of the woman crying in the other room. She said something completely nasty to me. I got the vibe that she was an animal dealer. Always about money. They called my name, brought my Saturday out in a box.

The paper receipt they handed me said 'treated for shock.' I acted relieved, even though I didn't know what a treatment for shock was and knew deep down it was a hustle. I didn't look at the rude fat-legged woman as I left. She reminded me of a relative I don't like. I taxied back down to my house, cooing the frightened little kitten as I went. Got home, let her out of the box. I felt really bad 'cause Tuesday came up to check her out and I think that if I'd had to choose I would have chosen to reverse the situation. Saturday had been my buddy, she'd sit around quietly, gently, playing, but very cool and sweet. Tuesday was a spaz. She reminded me of myself. Uncoordinated, anxious, too playful at times, too fussy at times.

The vet bill was seventy dollars. I didn't have seventy dollars. I still didn't know what the fuck treated for shock was. And I was beginning to suspect that the spaz had been playing too rough and pushed Saturday out the window, to fall five stories below.

A few nights later I was awakened by a loud shriek. It was the kitten, Saturday. She had been lying on the bed like she always had done, keeping me company. I jumped up. She seemed to be choking, trying to catch her breath. I think, air, air, air. I tried to stand the little thing up in my hand, and get her moving thinking she was just blocked or something.

'Not this one, not this one,' repeated over and over in my head as I tried to revive the kitten. She looked at me, went limp, life set in her eyes. I looked on the place she'd been sleeping where a dense pool of blood had drained from her. I fell apart. I screamed. Yet another lesson in me loving something; it goin' away. I sat there for a while or so holding the little corpse as it started to stiffen. I called Giovanni and woke him up for reassurance, I had to talk to somebody. I arranged her so that she was lying as when she sleeps.

I found a suitable plastic bag and sturdy shoebox. If I had been back home I would have proceeded to the backyard, shovel in hand. But I was in the concrete jungle. Not knowing what else to do at four in the morning with a dead kitten, I did what any other devastated, exhausted New Yorker would do — put it in the freezer.

I remembered the story of Saturday on another day when the phone rang again. Not a normal ring. A sublime, reluctant, pausing ring. I felt a shiver come over me — the cool that comes with calls like that and precedes all manner of life storms. 'Hello,' I answered, cheerily, in hopes that my usual intuition was incorrect.

It was that faraway, distant voice on the other end, the one you never want to hear, the one with the final word.

'Billy's gone.'

III. Find the Frequency

'To be alone
is an act of choice,
while loneliness,
has another voice...'
—John Calder, *Solo*

You grab your shoes — some version of black Pumas with white stripes, or black Pumas with any manner of stripes. They work. Next comes the jewelry. You put the heavy chain-link necklace that came from your dead friend around your neck. It is held on by a small, solid silver lock. In remembrance to you, dear whatever your name was, in homage to Sid. The chain looks just like Sid's. The one he wore before Nancy came along and ruined everything. Or was it after... Next come the leather bands around your forearms — very intimidating to the average John Q. Public. Very jack-u-off male. Music at an all-time high. 'Bodie-eeees, fucking bloody mess.'

1. Don't Look Back

We were living our twenties convinced we'd never see thirty. AIDS or something else would surely get us. By the Summer of 1995, thirty was just around my corner. I booked the SqueezeBox! band at special events with as many of the queens as I could get — Misstress, Guy, Lily of the Valley, Sherry Vine, Joey Arias, and a milieu of others who were taking their turn joining in. We got the B stage because the main stage was reserved for dance tracks and drug music, yet another appearance by Cyndi Lauper or one of the holdover 70s disco legends. I had nothing against Cyndi, the 70s or 80s — I'd enjoyed them very much. I did, however, have something against the queer establishment that had engaged the same narrow thinking as our greater society in defining what it meant to be queer. Some would have us believe that nothing queer, gay, homosexual had happened before Stonewall or after 'It's Raining Men,' when in fact some of the most intelligent thinking on the subject comes from the previous century.

To make life even more confusing, I kept getting haunted by this little anomaly known as the 80s. See, the 80s didn't produce the same kind of talent as other recent decades. People I knew were still suffering from the Reagan identity crisis. For some reason, Boy George, the pinup puppet of the 80s kept appearing in my life as well. At some point I got invited to a taping of the John Stewart show, which featured Chris Isaac and George. Adrienne and I stood outside the studios waiting to be herded with the rest of the cattle when a limo approached and George got out. He was wearing some big hat, a red feathery boa-scarf, and round John Lennon glasses, and skipped quickly up to the door as if a marauding crowd of Beatles fans were about to set upon him. As he stopped in front of security, three or four girls hopped out of the line and went over to accost him. He seemed satisfied at this, having been given his moment, and after one or two 'Thank You's' he cocked his head back demurely and lunged inside. Perhaps Mr. DeMille was waiting within. Perhaps I hadn't gotten the memo that he was still as famous then as he'd been in 1985. Once the show got underway, we were further underwhelmed. Stewart never addressed the crowd, and we were sat behind a lot of scenery. Typical of MTV, no one even attempted to build excitement in the room. I guess we were supposed to applaud because the big bad keepers of culture had let us in where the magic happened. George did a song, 'Everything I Own,' a cringeworthy little ditty to a reggae drum machine beat. I didn't get it. We sat and watched him do his trademark dance moves in slow motion, while sort of singing one of the most boring songs imaginable. Adrienne kept looking through her periphery with a 'are they kidding' expression. Perhaps we were just too spoiled with our own fun to appreciate what the outside world had been left to endure.

On a brighter side, in September, we took the bands out to Wigstock. In many ways, Wigstock was a model for a lot of things we did at Squeezebox!, and the "Lady" Bunny, the founder and friend of just about everyone on the entire downtown scene — from Pyramid to Jackie 60 to the Alig crowd, captured something very extra-special year after year in Thompkins Square park. A fellow transplant from North Carolina, Bunny's careful curation of Wigstock was never lost on me. Sure, it was a party. Sure people got high. Some didn't. But whatever they did, it was within the context of a naturally non-judgemental, highly creative environment. The talent came from the community, from within. And the entire show was political, but nowhere near correct. Bunny kept it upbeat, positive and I can only reason that she is either a shining light on the world of misfits, a genius marketer, or both. She brought wigs, and a lot of peace, love and disco music. At Squeezebox!, we leveled the party field with punks and rock 'n' roll. Before the electronic *coup-de-crap* short circuited tangible human interaction all this was easy: you smell the wind, grab the vibe, and run with it. Funny how most people struggle with the concept.

The first year we took the bands, Lady Bunny had to move Wigstock to the West Side piers because of an on-going scrape with the local city councilman and his cronies yet another vibrant community event ruined by dirty New York City politics. Little did anyone know it was evidence of things to come well into the next century.

A politician named Antonio Pagan got himself elected to City Council on a so-called progressive ticket. I figured he got himself put in by the real-estate developers, landlords and yuppies who were moving into the Lower East Side in droves. He also got in because none of us that I knew bothered to vote. The agenda: to drive out the existing residents and replace them with fine, upstanding citizens. It wasn't enough that they had Boston, Charlotte, Indianapolis and Houston to breed like rabbits in. Push their strollers through. Crowd the streets with their cars that looked like purple eggs. No, they needed to be in Manhattan, because it was 'cool.' And if they could just get rid of the undesirables and get in some Starbucks and other fantastic chain stores, they'd be set. Pagan was strike one, laying the ground work for another, bigger henchman, Rudolph Giuliani. And along with Pagan's and Giuliani's neighborhood council puppets — parading as a friend of the queers, alternatives, and downtrodden, they would double-speak their way right through the center of the middle class and its culture in downtown New York City.

In front of the camera most of these people championed family values and decency to the remaining native middle class, and those living in subsidized housing. Behind the scenes, some were rumored to frequent public toilets on their knees, at the altar of gentrification. So Wigstock moved to the piers — the other side of the highway. Tracks.

For the audience, Wigstock was one of the best outdoor parties the East Village had ever seen — a place to wear a wig and hear music and see acts like French Twists, Baby-Doll Head, Barbra Patterson Lloyd, RuPaul and her StarrBooty, and Deee-lite — right around the corner from where Charlie Parker was born. Things all young Americans should be able to do. The thing about Wigstock was that it was just pretty. In an area surrounded by eight or nine million people, where folks were dropping from AIDS and a Presidency that couldn't care less, Wigstock gave respite. Anyone looked good in a wig, dress, flashy sequined top or adorned with all manner of garden vegetables from the local bodega. Even our black-wearing, sometimes angry, always loud little band of misfit SqueezeBox! toys fit into the Wigstock lifeboat. Well, once anyway.

We arrived on the piers with tons of gear. Bunny had other acts on as the band set up. I think it was the same year they filmed Wigstock: The Movie. Guy, Sherry, Lily and all the regulars would open; Misstress, the star of our show, would bring up the rear. Bunny'd asked her to do rock songs that were positive, that

Wigstock should be a celebration. Misstress didn't do positive. Michael Ortega became Misstress Formika to be a political rebel-rouser, thankfully, and had a mouth the size of New Mexico. Her weekly torch songs included 'Shitlist' and 'Killing in the Name.' She wasn't giving anything less for Wigstock — stinging the audience from the stage in her black-and-yellow-striped bumble-bee dress.

Misstress did her anthem, a slightly modified Beastie Boys song: 'You Gotta Fight, For Your Right, To Be Queer,' and with the likes of Rudolph quietly amassing his power down at City Hall, she'd handed us a prophecy. But Bunny didn't see it that way, and supposedly banned her from ever performing at Wigstock again. The crowd got it, and the crowd looked stunned as all the queens sang, live, with the band, playing live. Real music made right before their eyes. By freaks and queers. If coming out of the closet included music, this was it. Glam and drag went hand in hand, and had always meant taking something ugly and making it beautiful, new, your own. Deee-lite, Debbie Harry and others had set the stage years before. Bunny was a genius at it. SqueezeBox! went one more by showing you could be ugly or pretty, and do it live, which is an act of ownership in and of itself — if you own your art you owned yourself, and gentrification couldn't take it away.

2. Goodbye to Billy

Back down on the corner of Greenwich and Spring, the club was off the charts. And so Friday nights went, week in, week out. I barely saw the light of day. By the time I got the money and got out of SqueezeBox! at 5, sometimes 6 in the morning, I was utterly exhausted and usually drunk. Up to then I certainly would tie one on every now and again, but the scene was so exciting and the booze so free, I took to bingeing. As long as I could walk and count at the end of the night, no one seemed to care. I was having the time of my life, and in the land of outcasts, there were not many big no-no's. A lot was happening, and I was but one cog in the gears — again, the charm of the place. Patrick managed the stage and the bands and had started a new project called Psychotica. Schmidt kept designing and bringing in the sparkle and celebrity. Misstress kept up the hosting, loud anthems, and the politics. Guy kept the music on the edge. Lisa shuffled Patrick to and from Warwick, about an hour's drive north. Stephen Trask, Jack Steeb, Duard Klein and Warner X kept their band tight. We booked whoever was good and could fit on that stage — from Angela Bowie to Nina Hagen to Antony Hegarty. Don kept the place from burning down, sound proofed it for the neighbors and the crowds deluged it every week.

The so-called 'mainstream' tried, but couldn't ignore us. While the Slimelights and Tunnels and other gigantic places of repetitive musical possession and common sexual ambiguity were happy to get a few celebs, our little crowded hole had 'em lined at the door. They came for the show, the dancing, the people, and I think they mostly liked the even-ing aspect. As in level. The first time Boy George came through I was in the basement, and word literally came from above. Schmidt and I worked our way to the door to meet him — being that he was Boy George and all. Aside from the occasional TV appearance, I hadn't seen or thought a lot about Boy George since my first night out in New York at Lee Chappell's party years earlier. I'd been to plenty of other things Lee did, which were actually better, namely dancing at Roxy. Even though I didn't know him well, Chappell exuded a certain charm, and sophistication I admired, someone who could mix the best of old school with new style.

I expected as much from George, but he came in wearing a shabby brown sport coat and disheveled cropped wig. Odd. Schmidt got chatty with him. He ignored the rest of us, and had more attitude than a trannie from Harlem. Didn't look at me when I was introduced and shook his hand. I went and got him and his guest some beers. We were body-locked on all sides. The only reason I could hustle my way through the crowds was because folks knew I worked there, or, for the occasionally challenged yuppie, I had Kevin and Carl to back me up. George and his guest inhaled the beers, and without so much as looking at me, handed back the empties and said 'Two more.' I began to wedge a path back to the bar doing my duty, but then decided he could get his own beer, I wasn't in the mood to tumble. Sure, he was Boy George and all, but in our colorful crowd, to me he was just another drag in a badly pressed wig. And most of the crowd out-dressed him that night. Even me. His attitude could get him to the bar.

Other famous people weren't so grandiose. At the back side of the room was one of the most congested but popular spots in the club by the rear double-door exit. The spot John Waters stood when he came. There were two steps leading to the exit doors, and John would stand on the bottom one, just enough to see above the crowd, but not enough to be ostentatious. For some reason, I found Waters intimidating, like some mad scientist scouring our club like a laboratory for new subjects. Schmidt had introduced me at some point and we chatted here and there. I'd seen a lot of his movies, and he appeared to me as one of his own characters — camp as Christmas, but carrying a canny poker face, and cards held tight against his chest. One night I told him I was going on a business trip to Las Vegas, and asked him for ideas on places to go. 'Fuck Vegas,' he replied. 'Go to Reno, that's where the real sick shit is. Vegas is ruined. Nothing left.' Keeping in mind that this was the man who'd gotten Divine to actually eat dog shit on camera I said 'thank you' and just kinda' slinked away, leaving him to his scan of the room, without venturing further into his definition of 'shit.'

Although the club was raging, shiny things began to lose a little luster for me after Billy died — almost like a part of me went with him. Perhaps, as many have suggested, I take things too serious, to heart. Perhaps I needed a reason to justify the uncontrollable onslaught of depression. Sure, people die. But not before their forties, *en masse*, of a disease spawned by hate. My days became crowded and cloudy. Between the haze and the gentrification going on, my connection to the old neighborhood was flickering. We weren't safe anymore. Jesus said to walk amongst the prostitutes and thieves. And I did. And I found it peaceful, and safe. I didn't fear drug dealers. I loathed the influx of the soulless yuppie masses. It seemed I'd run all the way from North Carolina and my high school principal was following me, creeping up like a cancer from the South. Misstress Formika screamed her head off every week against Giuliani, corporatism and families that didn't include her values. She knew we were losing our home, our lives. This is why she sang about fighting for rights. Queers from all over were banding together under that God-awful rainbow flag and dressing themselves in khaki pants and white t-shirts. Hiding amongst the masses. 'Assimilation' they called it. Out of the closet and into the woodwork, I called it. I hated the bigots. I hated the establishment. I hated the politically-correct gay scene. I might as well have been locked in Mom's basement. I drank too much. I ran around too much. Fucked every cute boy I could get my hands on. One for every night of the week was a goal. I would be calm and at ease when we'd arrive at my apartment. A little emptier, lonelier and scared each time the door would shut behind them an hour or so later. Many times, while waiting for sleeping pills to kick in, I pretended what it would've been like if one had stayed. I kept an extra set of pillows on the bed, just in case I found one I liked who liked me back. One who'd want to stick around for a while like Eric had done years earlier. Booze and sleeping pills invaded the sad thoughts. I loved slowly drifting out of consciousness. I didn't have to think about being alone, or the fact that we were all probably going to be dead within five years so it didn't matter anyway. Subconsciously I'd decided that back in 1991, standing in The Spike, when they came on the microphone and announced Freddie Mercury had died. I was too young to be losing heroes, and I decided that if it could take Freddie down, it would surely get me. Now, in 1995, the stupid, yuppified world was encroaching from every angle and I didn't want to see it coming. Sometimes I wondered what it would be like not to wake up. A few times I took an extra half of a pill. I didn't want to die, and made sure not to screw around too much, just remain asleep like a modern-day Lazarus waiting for his messiah.

I started working at an internet company. Out of the frying pan, into the inferno. I tried not to think about Billy. For me, AIDS only happened to people I knew or knew-of, not people who became a part of you. But this was silly and I knew it. But I couldn't help feeling it. Billy wasn't supposed to die, because I had gotten close to him. At that point, absolutely everyone I got close to in life left me. I imagined it must have been my fault. No one had ever officially confirmed he had AIDS. Paul and Eddie had lorded over the aftermath, and I'd never gotten so much as a trinket to remember him by. Since he died, I'd wanted one of his rings. Not even an expensive one, just something silver that would fit, so I could carry a piece of him around with me.

Calls to Paul and Eddie weren't fruitful. I dropped it. It's one thing to lose your best friend, another to be forced to beg permission to grieve. If it weren't for Billy's sister I might have never made it to the wake. But bless her, she called, and I've always felt like a fool for telling her to hire the big Italian funeral home on Bleecker Street. I thought that masses would've surely come for the service. Thinking of Haoui's memorial, I told her she'd need the space. It was very embarrassing when me and Dan, Kurt and Ramon arrived to a nearly empty room. I was still learning Billy's lesson on party people — 'not your friends.' It was hot outside. We waited though, for more people to come. I think a few showed. The rush of the icy air conditioning left us reddened in our borrowed suits. I think Dan was the only one who owned a real suit.

We wandered down the hallway to the chapel. There were Catholic icons all over the place. Billy'd never spoken of religion that I knew of. He was just very loyal and true to his friends. Lived-it as opposed to talking-it, I guess. Once my eyes adjusted to the indoor light the mint-green wall color faded to the background, and Billy, lying in a long narrow box, came into view. On the left at the back of the room were some of Billy's relatives. A short, blonde-haired lady got up to greet us. There were many empty chairs. 'I'm Linda, welcome...' I introduced myself and got distracted into a whispering chat with Linda. I wanted to grab her, hug her and fall apart, but I realized I didn't really know her. I wanted to apologize for encouraging her to rent this big room, although when alive Billy would have packed it with three hundred people on word of mouth alone.

I wanted one particular lady to show up, to do him top justice — I imagined her pulling up in a black Lincoln Town Car visible out through the large glass doors; the driver opening the back door where she'd emerge, dressed in a dark navy-blue suit, hat and black sunglasses; taking delicate charge of the sidewalk in the ten or so paces from the curb to the glass entry doors; walking in and being greeted by one of the suited workmen; the workman leading her to Linda on the opposite side of the room from us; a conversation between her and Linda; the room overhearing 'Thank you very much for coming' repeated a couple of times; at last the lady walking up to the coffin, paying her respects slowly, turning, and going back down the hallway and out to her car. I didn't say anything to the others about who was or wasn't there — it wasn't appropriate and I thought Billy might hear me thinking — but Ms. Margret sure would have done Billy right. Who knows, she might have and I just missed her.

All I could think about was where was Betty Badum, Misstress, Tree-Man, Al and the other half of the East Village? But deep down I knew that a lot of folks just couldn't deal anymore. Ten years on and all that dying was wearing folks out, losing its charm — acknowledging a lost friend was to acknowledge another lost part of yourself, one step closer to your own destiny. Now, departed, no brownies to offer, Billy just lay there motionless, in a black suit. He did not look dead to me as I approached the box. I think I touched him on the hand. Cold, like Grandaddy. I observed the rosary beads wrapped in his fingers. I didn't know what they meant. I didn't care what they meant. I never knew Billy's Catholic side. He was supposed to have his rings on.

I turned on the numbness. Not feeling: my artform. I didn't even pretend, this time, that it would be the last time, again. It's as if you can open your own brain and pull a lever, dispensing heroin throughout your aching veins and body. I just stood there, looking at my friend, the big brother I never had. This was the first time I actually said goodbye to someone that close — other than Grandaddy. Most folks looked awful when they died. Marty Lipton would have looked terrible all laid out for the world to gawk at. People must have been scared that the AIDS could jump out or be carried around by air or something so they cremated everyone. We spent years saying goodbye to urns full of ashes, leaving the people still kind of alive out there, somewhere. Scott, Haoui, Marty, Keith…

Kurt sniffled off and on. I remember his look of solemnity, a copy of what he'd seen his Mom do once. Giovanni studied the corpse inquisitively. Dan and I spent our time in the big room pretty much motionless. It's all still a blur. I knew the hurting wouldn't start until I got home. It never stopped. How are twenty-something kids supposed to know how the fuck to bury their friends? My grandparents hadn't really even started doing it. We didn't know then and I don't know now. I just did the best I could.

Billy's family watched politely — this was apparently one of those guess-who funerals. The kind where the family doesn't talk about or know certain details about their real loved one until a gaggle of queers show up to say goodbye. And it wouldn't have even hit me in that place had Dan not broke first. We finally said our thanks and goodbyes and started back out through the long hallway when Dan stepped to the side. I saw a water cooler nearby and thought he was after a drink, but instead he just stood there, stunned-like, placing his bent elbow across his eyes. We stopped and asked what's up, thinking the moment had passed. 'That's Billy in there,' he said, and burst into tears, putting the corner of his right elbow over his face and breaking into a real cry. Kurt reached and held his shoulder. Then I don't remember if I just thought it or Kurt actually just said 'Yes, yes it is.'

3. Time for a Cool Change

Somehow we kept at it in the land of the living, for me, a bit slower perhaps. Something about another friend, a close friend, rotting in a box underneath the soil of Staten Island made it strange for me to party 'til the break of dawn. SqueezeBox! charged ahead. Some nights were good. Some were great. Other nights, well, they were just nights. Each one was a hit in its own right, but when you do something every week for going on two years, the lines become fuzzy. You only pay attention to the space between whatever's not predictable. At first things are fresh, new. Then, just like Teletubbies, we want 'Again! Again!' In the beginning, I thought that the albatross of repetition couldn't choke us. There's safety in repetition until the repetition devours consistency, then you have to fight like mad to reinvent, night by night, week by week.

I decided to try and import a little bit of home. Billy's death left me floating, with an arid feeling of disconnect, so that second summer of SqueezeBox! I convinced my sister to move to New York. I was working in an internet company. Whatever that meant. I think it was supposed to mean that we all had an enormous new frontier on which to plant our seeds and reap our fortunes. We're still figuring out what it meant. Adrienne had come from North Carolina to get her feet immersed — in anything.

I'd have given just about anything to transplant some of my people to the city. There was more than one Sunday afternoon I sat watching movies, jealous of my native friends who'd run to Queens or Co-op City to hang out with Mom, Aunt Lila, or go bowling with Cousin Gerry. I didn't even realize I had fallen completely off track. I wasn't finding a boyfriend to have fun with, live with, live New York with. It just didn't seem to happen. Queers come to New York in droves to fill that empty spot of autonomy, self love and real love — and when they get here, they get completely sidetracked. "Loved alone" as Auden said. But it went further. Party, party, party. Drugs-this, trick-that. Cocaine was starting to make a scene-wide comeback, followed by its insidious step-sister crystal meth. AIDS was nowhere near done decimating the American capital of free culture. Shopping! Fire Island! In my case Rock 'n' Roll — my entire lifestyle got in the way of life.

Adrienne had an instant Twiggy effect on New York. Or better yet, Holly Golightly. Folks took to her without need of a double-take. Adrienne does Holly better than Audrey did Holly. Capote would've loved this gal, at Tiffany's or Lord & Taylor. Tall, thin, with high cheekbones, long dark hair, an enviable American 90s New Yorker. Adrienne looks as if she'd been pulled from a Degas painting — a dancer who glides like a silicon sculpture through the atmosphere. Thin arms branching from her carved torso, which glides and cuts and makes the atmosphere bend to her will. She kept her skin slightly tanned, her wardrobe current, and long, dark, polished hair almost to her waistline. The kind of hair that people pay a lot of money to try to have. Downtown designers would soon be giving her all the clothes she wanted, 'Just mention who you're wearing.'

The good thing about New York in the 80s and 90s was when you had the style, grace and presence of an Adrienne, you have places to go. People to see. And do. Such beauty is wasted in other places. Only New York City eats *Breakfast at Tiffany's*. Adrienne became Holly, but better. All dressed up, for what? The mall? To get in your car and drive to the 7-Eleven? She was no courtesan, and didn't need trips to Sing Sing — the Sallys of our world offered their tomatoes willingly. And Hollywood wouldn't be screwing up this ending, and we wouldn't be listening to that awful 'Moon River' on a loop.

I had plans. I'd decided it was my job to help Adrienne shake off the South upon arrival: the highways, traffic, fast food, chain stores and television. I'd decided she'd become a New Yorker from the start. It was a Thursday afternoon, when Patrick rehearsed his band Psychotica down at the club. You'd think Patrick, the Manager, would have his pick of time slots, but Don's had a lot of hit nights since SqueezeBox! had put it on the map below the enormous UPS warehouse, and time was tight.

Adrienne had incredible patience with my whims. As goes with most siblings, I really didn't know her very well growing up. We coexisted. When Dad left everyone around made the mistake of telling me that 'you're the man of the house now.' This, when I hadn't even mastered being a six-year-old boy. Adrienne knew I wasn't the grown-up, but I never figured this out until later. Many, many years later. In contrast, Adrienne was the smart one. She knew how to sit back and let people take her places.

After heaving her bags up my four flights to the fifth floor, a pee break and a quick cab ride west, Adrienne and me stepped out at 511 Greenwich Street, Don Hill's. It was a Thursday, around 5PM. The outside of Don's was like a rusty, overpainted beer-joint-looking place your mother would never have allowed you to go for a pee in: 'Let's keep looking' 'But Mo-om, I ha-ve to go-oooo!' The front glass door of the club creaked and pivoted on and off its hinges, which had probably been there since Don Hill's was Munson's Diner. An aluminum-cast 60s door frame held a thick piece of storefront glass littered with band stickers, ASCAP stickers and marker graffiti. The place looked different in the daytime than the palace of kitsch it became at night. Somehow, the filth seemed intentional. You entered a tiny foyer, where the money-desk sat, along with Don on a wobbly stool when the place was open for business. A second wooden do-it-yourself door hung to the immediate right, leading into the club. If this were a SqueezeBox! night, we'd have been met with a waft of cigarette smoke so thick that your eyes would catch fire, like with tear gas. But this was early evening, before opening, and the scent that greets you is a standard in the clubs and bars of New York city — a mix of Lemonex attempting to mask the scent of old smoke and yesterday's beer, a scent that sticks in your nostrils. Sweet and stale. Like when you do stop on a road trip to use the restroom, and get bombarded with acrid urine waltzing with spicy room freshener shooting from a can mounted on the wall. Adrienne wrinkled her face in an attempt to cover her nausea. I pretended not to notice.

The sound from the band distracted us immediately. Patrick's voice was better than any rock singer around at the time. Better than Axl Rose, certainly better than all the bands from the ME-2 Generation, whose musical transgressions on MTV hid all the sins of my Generation X. Psychotica was to be our Velvet Underground, and little did I know that by watching them, and others, I'd already begun the next big phase of my life.

Unlike the majority of Pop musicians, Pat had the talent and the balls to walk up to a microphone and entertain. Move. Dance and force you to dance with him. Fuck Kurt Cobain. This was it. The world just didn't know it yet. You don't need grunge and gimmicks when you have the words of a poet, voice of a choir like Stevie Nicks, and the soul to go with it. True rock. Heart.

Bootsy Collins knew about this. So did James Brown. And Pete Townsend and Robert Plant and on and on. Folks who don't need sampling, computerized vocals or slobs who call themselves producers remaking the sound. Give a real musician a stage, and they instinctively make art.

Pat Briggs was about 5'11 but on the stage at Don Hill's he was three extra feet in the air. He had beautiful long brown hair. The lucky hair. Hair that moves with you. Medium-framed body. Perky butt for anyone who wanted to stare. Lightly freckled face for anyone who wanted to flirt. When he sang he cocked his head to one side and closed his eyes. Except he didn't sing. He flew. Most singers try to hit notes, or reach for notes. Patrick opened his mouth, allowed his voice to fly to the proper note, and like a delicate bird — lighted on top of it and pushed it into you, through you. Like an organ. No screeching and scrambling. No need for backup singers to take the place of skill. Ena Kostabi — brother of the famous painter, blond, thin, very Warhol, guitars. Rikka B — tall, skinny, Swedish Rastafarian chick, dreads that stick up, vocals. Tommy — about 5'11, long black hair, natural tan, probably American Indian mixed with California, bass. Buz — about 5'7, perfectly sculpted little white gym body, rosy puffy pink lips, wore nothing but pants barely covering his bubble butt, biggest cock tease on the scene, drums. Enrique — 6,' Latin, reminds me of someone from a vogueing house, always laughing, cello. The band.

You can always tell when musicians are having fun — they sound good and aren't relying on pre-recorded material or battery-powered machines from the local gadget store. This band was loud, and tight. Enrique began with a haunting cello solo, as if resurrecting the dead. Tommy's steely bass kicked in. Ena's guitar builds the eruption. Rikka screeches above it all, ushering in the gods for the ceremony. Buzz drives everything from behind. Suddenly the lonely, empty, stinking little cavern is vibrating off its moorings. Then Pat, unassumingly shooting me a wave, walks up to the mic as nonchalantly as a cook at Burger King going to the french fry bin, and rips out his lyrics in the octave above the octave that people try to reach. *'Phoenix, rises, from the ashes... will you sell your soul?'*

He left me hanging in the band's propulsion. Then he answers with ultimate vibrato *'no-oooooooooooooo-ooooooooo.'* He looked liked an archangel declaring something official at the rapture.

I was in love, but didn't know with what. When they played, the air took on that texture of when you're fucking just before you cum. But it was more than that — I'd known them as people, watched them rehearse, and then mesmerize a young audience at our club. Psychotica was one of a few projects that I'd witness emerge from literally nothing, and in turn would stir something in me stronger than my teenage urges to get out of the South and explore. I'd put it all together, beginning, start of the middle, and the end — who knew? But what I did know was that this was the way Rock 'n' Roll happened. I wanted my own.

Adrienne's reaction was immediate, 'Yeah! They're fucking great!' The band leaped into song after song, with some fits and starts — rehearsal. Patrick channeled lyrics like *'Sometimes when we walk, sometimes when we talk, sometimes when we cry I feel alone...'* Adrienne closed her eyes and moved in her seat — sign of acceptance from a Southern-rock chick with a palate for everything from Zeppelin to Dokken to Tool — and all manner of hair rock. Pat continued belting *'...but sometimes when we walk, sometimes when we talk, even when we FUCK I FEEL ALO-ONE!'*

My head spun. I was dreaming, as Debbie would say and sing. Dreaming is free. She'd thrown her star power behind the club, and all of us misfits, for the first time, dreamed together in every direction. Patrick dreamed of doing what he was doing right there, right then, in front of millions. For millions. I dreamed of this, belonging for the first time in my life — having somewhere to be. We were making web sites and online junk as quickly as it could be invented. We'd already pulled a few what we called 'coups' at SqueezeBox! We'd certainly brought Debbie out of downtown hiding. Her first show, like every other one to follow, had been a complete sellout. The room capacity of Don Hill's, as determined by Rudolph W. Giuliani's fire marshal, was 189. On a regular Friday night almost three or four times that came and went. On Debbie's first show night, even more. In the summer some people just hung out on the street. Before Don renovated, the old diner with a huge plate-glass window covered by a curtain for a stage back, overlooking Greenwich Avenue, had become a mecca. A side door to Spring Street was operating stage left. From center point, the performers from the stage looked out onto a rank joint, with yesterday's covered windows and last year's coat of paint. One large room in front, a narrower one to the left. Red booth banquette seating lined the place, and Guy's DJ booth was a rollercart on the floor, stage right. The stage was still the color of whatever the place used to be — a yellow ochre. Behind it, the front door where Don sat and took the money. A long bar spanned the room to the right, empty space for people to the left, leading to a stunted service bar. The place worked for our crowd of outcasts, primarily because it too was an outcast — a business that had been intended to be something else. A space designed for other purposes. It wasn't like the big joints like Tunnel or Roxy designed for the masses, where, A list or B, you paid to be herded like cattle. Your night predetermined. If you didn't like the space or couldn't find your perch — on the dance floor or in the mingling spaces or dark rooms, you were screwed. Paid money to be uncomfortable. The crowd would go with you. One of my favorite things each week was to anticipate the time when the place became completely body-locked. That is, where so many people were jammed like sardines that the crowd literally had to stop moving for a few minutes. Not unlike the downtown #6 train at rush hour — you don't hold on 'cause you can't hold on. You just stand and let everyone around you hold you up. Faces would lift from the dense mass of humans and grin at each other upon the realization that they were helpless to move and free to not move. Something of a liminal situation where life is suspended for a few brief, sensual moments. Like sex, crying, or the seconds just before your head hits the softness of your familiar pillow. When Don Hill's was empty it seemed lost, crying for gyrating bodies and music and light. When it was filled, it became its own cosmic entity. Things started moving at warp speed — months flew out and back again. By holiday time, Pat and Psychotica had gotten signed to a record label right off the stage. Just like Madonna at Danceteria, which I think Haoui had a hand in. SqueezeBox! was gaining international notoriety. The press loved us. We had *Page Six*, the *New Yorker*. Next stop: the cover of the *Rolling Stone*?

4. Look Back, Don't Stare

Grunge exploded on the scene, and, just like any other shred of originality that happens in American culture, the jackals in the boardrooms, otherwise known as corporate entertainment execs, had already scrambled their legions of Pharisees to either get rid of it or to get control of it. Time was of the essence. Pat was striking when the time was right. He'd already made one attempt back when Don owned the Cat Club up on 13th Street, none of us were getting any younger, none were immune to AIDS, and for some reason, the vibe of city seemed to egg on an accelerated sense of urgency. Page Six of the *'Daily News* was running gossip on us. A cartoon in the *New Yorker* magazine, 'A Night at Don Hill's,' exposed us to the 'outside' world, and I wasn't so sure this was a good thing. But overall, the gig was not a bad showing for a bunch of loser outcasts. We'd managed to piss off the rock establishment, alternative establishment, gay establishment, and last but absolutely not least, the government establishment — bringing in another side of tragic Americana — jealousy. For me, frustration. Had the publishers of the local queer magazines like *HX* not passively shunned us, we might have instigated some new, progressive political conversations. Cookie-cutter faggots in spandex might have had something to gain by chatting with rock-cloned faggots in t-shirts, jeans and leather accessories. But just north of Don Hill's in a neighborhood known as Chelsea, all that most of the queers would do is turn up their noses for another line of crystal meth.

Creatively, George Clinton and David Bowie had some things in common, as did SqueezeBox! and Jackie 60 which was run by former BoyBar DJ Johnny Dynell and Chi Chi Valenti, who had, literally a cult following. We did rock and punk, they did cabaret meets Weimar Berlin. Hot stuff. All our paths crossed considerably back through the old Pyramid, Wigstock, BoyBar, and our two clubs might have complimented each other better had the twisted head of petty rivalry not gotten in the way.

Squeezebox! promoters were barely allowed through Jackie doors. Not the work of the Jackie 60 high-creatives like Hattie Hathaway, who I'd known over the years and was one of the most diplomatic people I've ever met. But the fight for the bottom clouded the air, like in any human subculture. Freaks segregating freaks. Someone, somewhere along the line hadn't gotten the memo that subdivisions are lethal to all things alternative, especially in a city where the fangs of trickle-down corporate culture had begun devouring everything in sight just a few blocks away.

I learned early on that the best way to piss off people who hate you is to have the tenacity to just exist — walk, talk and smile. You infuriate them if you claim validity. You become valid if you dare to breathe. 'Fukinfagits.' SqueezeBox! did more, the club reinvigorated a cultural legitimacy that not even the old-school, straight rock venues could claim. Everyone was forced to take note. Good or Bad, I wanted to bring more than just a party drama to bear. I wasn't alone, but didn't quite have a plan. Michael Alig was busy doing party. Party, party, party. Only party. Yippee, facepaint, party. How about some culture, culture, heck maybe even something else… We didn't know our limits because, aside from probably Schmidt, we were still stunned at the success. Magazines from LA to Tokyo had SqueezeBox! articles. According to pretty good rumor, people from Paris flew in just to attend a Friday night. Schmidt had Debbie, Tina Turner, Sebastian Bach, Guns N' Roses, Cher and many others as clients. When the world becomes an oyster — an oyster that happens to belong to you — they slide down your throat with ease — so easily that you might question how they even got there. A salty residue remains on your lips, sweet, sweat taste on your tongue. A drug, sex…

At one big show we carried Patrick to the stage through a raging mob tied to a pink cross. The first sign he was getting weird. I'd always thought the music stood on its own merits, but he was determined to challenge the Bowies, Nicos and Iggys of the world. He used Queen Helene's green facial mask and ran it through his long hair, which made thick strands like alien tentacles. Stephen Sprouse designed the band logo and got him using all sorts of dayglo paints — an orange band across his eyes. The next big show we carried him out in a silver egg, which I think they'd found down in Chris Stein's basement. Blake Burba, the lighting designer for a new off-Broadway show Rent, lent his skills for Pat and the club. Psychotica was inducted into the Rock and Roll Hall of Fame as 'The Future of Music' before many people outside of New York knew about them — and I think even before the album was finished. Weird got weirder. Who cared? Pat invited me to the ceremony, but I didn't have the cash. Then he got booked on the Lollapalooza tour as his drag persona Torment. The press was going mad. For Psychotica, Pat had perfected a *genitalia-absentia* look with surgical skin over his cock. We helped circulate rumors that he was either born sexless or a hermaphrodite. The press'll devour anything, and they ate his smooth crotch for lunch. Marilyn Manson stole the look. The whole idea really. I'd met Manson with Schmidt one night. 'Martin, this is Brian.' I shook his hand, taking him for another eccentric in the crowd, no real idea who he was. I'd stopped watching MTV a long time before. Brian had come to the club in less makeup than usual, trademark long black hair. Schmidt was going to surprise everyone and do the drag set as 'Heidi Hole.' While I was standing with them, he asked Manson if he'd sing with him. Then he said I could do it too. I didn't even know the words to 'Ace of Spades.' They had to read them off a note card. Pat screeched about Manson stealing his look to the press, who apparently put the story in the news cycle. Lisa told me that there was a curt answering machine message left up in Warwick: 'Pat, this is Brian, we have to talk' click… Rock 'n' Roll.

Schmidt and me went to Lollapalooza with Glenn and Stevin, friends from the old Pyramid days. Stevin had a cable TV show named Azo's Small White House, drank enough Coca Cola per day to float a small river craft and shake nervously, but did manage to book very big names on his show. He was obsessed with Jackie Kennedy and did a drag character named Jackie Offie, dressed in a black suit and black pillbox hat. Glenn did Glennda Orgasm and together they did duets with the band at the club. Glenn was also an activist. He wore tight-fitting dresses and a giant blonde bouffant wig, and marched with a group called the X-X-X Gays at Gay Pride — people who weren't buying the whole khaki pants-wearing, assimilating, be-just-like-Mom-and-Dad rainbow thing. Glenn was making a statement. At the time I think Glenn knew, as all of us knew, we weren't just like Mom and Dad. The rainbow crowd responded by pelting Glennda and friends with bottles and stones. Rock 'n' Roll.

One night a group of us went to an early show in the main sanctuary room of the Limelight. I got the same bad feeling I'd always gotten in the place - spooked. Nothing inside made it not look like a church. Psychotica and some other bands played the big stage, the same stage Alig used to romp around on. The one they hoisted Angel Melendez up over wearing huge angel wings.

I'd dabbled plenty in Aligland. Jorge set me up with Alig when they were opening Club USA, and interestingly, some with the first master of ceremonies I'd known, Lee Chappell. Alig and a few others videotaped me in my leather jacket. Alig seemed still high from the night before — blue paint lined the insides of his ears and the entire group scared me to death. He pranced around with a tin lunchbox. He tried to hit on me, told me I was 'so sexy' in my ear while the makeup artist dobbed my face with powder, but he was finding it hard to stand still. I felt weird, being lavished with a lot of attention for not being the typical type they dealt with every day. Alig paid me fifty bucks out of the lunch box and the video played at the entrance for the life of the club.

Not many Fridays before Alig took a hammer to his head, Angel made an appearance at SqueezeBox! Probably making a delivery, or maybe he was scene shopping. I'd always seen Angel traveling alone. He knew Guy and Schmidt. He was standing up front. I took time to check him out. Angel noticed me checking him out. He's wearing his angel wings — small ones, trademark leather jacket with stripes, elevating boots. Alig-boy trademarks. The usual New York smile-or-attitude is suspended for a second. I catch a weird vibe from him. He just stands there looking out toward the dance floor. Looking somewhat lost. 'What are *you* doing here?' I think, feeling predatorial — not realizing our club had yet to have the honor of being graced with a permanent drug dealer. I get interrupted with a grab to my right elbow and someone yelling uninterpretable language into my ear over the music. When I look back, Angel's no longer there. A few weeks later, I am over at Schmidt's, working. I see an email from Guy...

'There's been some trouble. Freeze and Michael are in jail and Angel's gone missing…' Rock 'n' Roll.

On the Lollapalooza tour, Pat made friends with Billie Joe, Tré and Mike from Green Day, a band I particularly liked because somehow through them I relived the teenagehood I'd always wanted. Later that year, Pat invited me out to their show on Long Island. Kevin Brennan, our Squeezebox! bouncer and the only singer I knew who could absolutely cover Robert Plant on stage, drove us out to Nassau Coliseum. Pat went in drag as Torment 'cause he thought Billie Joe would call him up onstage. But Tim from Rancid was already there and something was weird with the stage or something and they just wanted to get through the gig. Sitting in an arena full of virile, moshing Long Island kids with a bouncer the size of Kansas and a drag queen with a big red wig wrapped in plastic wrap wearing white knee-high go-go boots was an experience. Backstage, we were the only ones in the dressing room apart from the band. I'd already learned backstage was one of the most boring sought-after places on earth. It was kinda' like going over to some cousin's basement and watching teenagers take turns talking and banging drums. After sitting as a silent observer for a long time, Billie Joe plopped down beside me on a metal folding chair and asked me if I was a drag queen too. God, I wanted to fuck him. I just sat, as he stared at me with a shit-eating grin, my face melting into an animated pool of drool. He knew I wanted to fuck him like Prince once said on 1999, to a Lady Cab Driver 'I'm not saying this just to be nasty, but I sincerely want to fuck the taste out of your mouth.' If I had been drunker I would have gone for it. If I'd have been a drag queen I probably would have gotten it. I had a crush on Billie Joe the size of Yankee Stadium, although he repeatedly talked about how small his dick was. I must have looked like a horny puppy at a beef jerky factory. Pat died laughing and almost split the sides of his saran-wrap dress. Billie kept contemplatively staring at me. Everyone wanted to fuck Billie Joe, even the straightest guys found themselves going for a tongue kiss while jumping on stage for a mosh pit dive. Why? Billie is one of our James Deans, the other side of rebellious masculinity, the ones we can get close to, but never actually fuck, because to do so would cause our youth to be completely over.

The next night Green Day played Madison Square Garden. I couldn't go because there weren't enough spots. I was green with jealousy, but Garden shows are historically a drag, in the classic sense of the word — a security nightmare, dull crowds that stand and stare, the arena filled with people who got free tickets from the phone company and really didn't appreciate the music. I'd see them all again later anyway — although it was a Monday night, not our usual Squeezebox! gig, we opened for an invitation-only after-party. The place stayed pretty packed 'til the band finally arrived around 5AM, but admittedly, I was beginning to fall asleep. Green Day played a set for us. Awesome. Then Courtney Love showed up. The plague. I never liked her. She was a charlatan in my book. Stole everything she did. Cooked out of her brains. Jumped onstage, grabbed the instrument from around our guitar player Warner's neck yanking the strap repeatedly before he could get loose. She acted like she'd accomplished something, raised her hands for cheers from the crowd for assaulting someone. Nice. I've hated her and her crappy music ever since. I remembered Kurt from the Saturday Night Live show, shooting a chilled glance at me over a pizza box. Ever since, I had a hunch he was a homo. Certainly more sensitive than the Nancy Spungen-wannabe brute Courtney aspired to be — but isn't that the way it works? Sid & Nancy, Kurt & Courtney. Just like high school. Everybody dies.

We stayed way into the wee hours that Monday morning at

our little Green Day party. We got tattoos from an artist in the basement. Most folks got stars on the right ball of their wrists. This scared me — way too Mark of the Beast for me. I got an iron rose on my left upper arm. Kind of a Paul Stanley tribute, kind of like some ink I saw on Billie Joe. Imitation is the highest form of flattery. We'd been hanging out there since midnight. I was intoxicated beyond repair and wasn't going to make it with them to the Empire Diner. The place mostly cleared by around 8AM. Billie Joe was sitting talking to Lily of the Valley. On my way out Tré came up to me with two girls. The girls shot me evil looks. He grabbed my crotch and asked me if I wanted to go play. I'd always fancied the thought of fucking a rock star. Alone. Ronnie, the newest and cutest bartender, caught the scene. I liked Ronnie better than Tré. And there was no way I could deal with pussy that night, especially the evil kind. I just said no, and stumbled to the door while Tré looked at me with a 'whatever dude' expression. I was OK. Sometimes, being an idiot is simply OK.

Stop, Drop 'n' Roll.

Every now and again you take a second glance into your mirror — is this really real? Is my life actually happening? Yes. But you know you can't explain anything, don't want to explain anything. Hard to explain when the wheels are turning. Careful not to fall under. You're sure the music, somebody, anybody, will keep you safe. There's no return.

5. Search and Destroy

Life in New York City got tougher. Giuliani was everywhere, like pus dripping from a leper. Like my high school principal on the loud speaker. He and Pagan were well underway in sweeping the East Village clean of all the middle-to-lower-class people they could, and Giuliani used his fire marshals and police as his battering rams. All of the old neighborhoods were being harassed. If a joint didn't have a violation, Mr. Giuliani's teams would make one up. They dusted off the 19th-century cabaret laws to tell people when they could and could not wiggle in place. They threw dust over the rent laws. The city housing departments were stacked with Giuliani cronies. No one had a chance.

Giuliani stacked every city agency with henchmen, and his culture war didn't stop with nightlife or entertainment. He forced community libraries to close; museums to cut back on hours. All over town, historic landmarks like the Palladium Theater were falling to the wrecking ball. New York University, a private institution originally founded for working-class young people — now the second-largest landowner in New York and most applied-to college in the US — was allowed to run rampant through the Lower East Side over Washington Square Park and beyond the West Village — buying up every piece of property it could get its greedy purple hands on. Thousands upon thousands of arrogant, binge-drinking, yuppie adolescents were being herded over the rivers and into our woods to enroll for thirty grand a year at NYU. Mommy and Daddy back in Cleveland, Fort Wayne and Nashville took out second mortgages to send junior to New York City so he could pretend to be trendy, drink bottled water and complain about things. They tore down the Palladium just about a month before it got landmark protection. Just in time to slap up another dorm, for more rich kids. They had the nerve to name it 'Palladium Hall.' Inspired surely, by Giuliani, who modeled himself after Fiorello LaGuardia. Charlatans like to steal from credible predecessors, to give the appearance of legitimacy.

Only a generation earlier, LaGuardia and Robert Moses notoriously bulldozed half the Bronx, Queens, Brooklyn and downtown Manhattan to make way for highways. And with them, displaced hundreds of thousands of families. That ugly World Trade Center was their doing. And if it hadn't been for Bella Abzug, they'd have taken out the West Village as well.

Winks, nods and blind oversight camouflaged what I will forever maintain is the biggest case of housing fraud in the history of New York. Rent regulations and housing department codes were ignored; inspectors paid off. Landlords turned seven-hundred-a-month tenement shitholes into fifteen-hundred-a-month 'Renovated Sunny Apartments' — with a cheap coat of paint and forged paperwork.

My hunch is that Giuliani did it for spite first, profit second. He was a probable rat, an overgrown kid who probably never got picked for the baseball team, probably grew up with Mommy as his only friend and probably never got laid until he was a sophomore in college — and even then had to pay for it. Now, the rest of us were paying for the mercy fuck he never received. Any why not pick on queers, freaks and drag queens in nightclubs?

Bullies always choose vulnerable victims. According to the news media and salesmen from St Louis, Giuliani 'Cleaned Up New York.' Bullshit. Crime dropped everywhere because Bill Clinton had balanced the budget and people had jobs to go to. Because of AIDS, the credit for almost everything noteworthy on the downtown scene since Studio 54 was up for grabs. Cheap new club promoters used the same kind of spin as Rudy to crown themselves the new Kings and Queens of nightlife — almost everyone jumped in on the me-me ME-2 hustle.

SqueezeBox! got regular visits from the police and fire marshals. Things like needing to measure the widths of the door for regulation compliance and check the licensing. At 1 and 2AM. Giuliani used safety and so-called quality-of-life issues to convince the general public he was acting in their interest. From where I sat, the only real interest he acted on was real estate — developers, schemers, loan sharks. Manhattan was once sold out from under the Indians for some beads. We didn't even get the beads. We got double-talk and harassment. And just like Orwell described, the ones who considered themselves wealthy sided with the few who actually were wealthy to get rid of the so-called scum. Problem was, they didn't know who the 'scum' was. Giuliani took credit for everything positive in New York and the press let him get away with it... even conspired to help perpetuate the myth.

To further my melancholy, Giuliani's 'Quality of Life' troops were still hemorrhaging throughout the city. I've never stopped picking the wounds. They'd harassed Coney Island High almost out of business several times. A fun night during the week popped up at a place called Cake on Avenue B — and, of course, the Quality of Lifers set their sights square on it. 'NO DANCING' signs popped up all over the city. Giuliani's cronies found a loop in an ancient cabaret law used to discriminate against the blacks in Harlem, and used it to discriminate against queers, trannies, hip-hoppers and ethnic parties in the boroughs. He took the fireworks away from the Chinese New Year. He sanitized Times Square so it would be 'just like home' for all the squeaky tourists.

I suspected someone at the club had to keep paying off the cops and the firemen but it didn't matter. They kept shutting us down. One night during a raid, Misstress, in six-inch heels, tight leopard dress and long black wig, rallied the employees to the stage. Scanning our little mob, I wondered if the marshals were familiar with the word 'Stonewall.' Our situation was the real deal. Not a bunch of Chelsea fags in Gap clothes. Freaks have nothing to lose. We were allowed to stay.

Misstress, along with a whole contingent from SqueezeBox! and other clubs like Coney Island High, Lakeside Lounge, Cake, The Cock in the East Village, jammed into a Community Board meeting. I spoke on behalf of venues, and accused the city of targeting queer clubs and anything that was non-yuppie. I got booed by the board members. Some yuppie girl that had moved from Iowa, or wherever, into the apartment above Coney Island High, another rock club on St Marks Place, stood up played innocent and complained of the noise and not being able to sleep and that her husband was having trouble at work. 'So why the *fuck* did you move on top of a rock club for!?' somebody yelled out. Thunderous applause.

What people didn't get, and never got, is that little Lower East Side dumps were a cornerstone of the NYC commodity. People didn't come to Gotham to shop at chain stores back then. They wanted rustic, original and imperfect. This was one of the deadliest of Giuliani cocktails: ignorance and hypocrisy. He shouted 'commerce' to anyone willing to suffer his shrill voice, and stamped out the roots of autochthonous culture at every turn. Little did anyone, even me, realize that our extended group would produce major international celebrities, Carnegie Hall performers and bestselling authors, to name but a few.

I was also concerned with people like the nicest Chinese couple who owned the Marlboro Cleaners at the end of my block, on the corner of 13 and First Avenue. You could take in a shirt to them and have it back in two hours for no extra charge. Their children played on the block. When their lease came up for renewal, the greedy bastard landlord increased it from fifteen hundred to three thousand eight hundred a month. Six weeks later a chicken franchise opened at the location. I watched our food stores, tailors, antique shops and shoe-repair places closing by the dozen. The arrogant NYU brats started arriving in droves. 'Lost Our Lease' signs went up everywhere. The dry cleaners, butchers, bakers and, yes, even candlestick makers were disappearing underneath the fists of progress.

The Second Avenue Deli, landmark since 1954. The Palladium, c. 1927. Even CBGB had one foot in the corporate grave, another on a banana peel. Nail-painting salons, which seem to be very money-launderingly peculiar, and cheap, bad, restaurants opened and closed, and the entire downtown flavor evaporated with every mayoral news conference, where Giuliani delivered a distinct message to the rest of America: New York City was up for grabs. As I watched the daily invasion of wide-eyed wannabees, I sometimes wondered if the problem was just me, afraid of change? No. Historically, the last refuge of East Coast American bohemia went through several metamorphoses over a century — Tenderloin, Bowery, Harlem. One hundred years' span, or more, not ten. But then, weren't we all once new, green and wide-eyed in Gotham? Yes, but with one distinct difference: this new 90s crowd wanted to control New York. We just wanted to keep dancing with her.

6. Living on the Ceiling

Bennington College, Vermont. What in hell? Bennington College wanted us which was beyond me. Stevin Azo, a.k.a. 'Jackie Offie' when in drag, drove one van, I drove another. I never realized this was where Jack Kennedy types frolicked and 'found themselves.' We arrived after a seven hour drive and unloaded the vans. While the bands unpacked and did sound checks, Schmidt and I absconded to shop at the local discount store — a place with fishing rods, candy, tools, children's clothes and sewing notions. He bought a dayglo-orange plastic hunting jacket two sizes too large. Schmidt could make anything 'work,' and turn everything into fashion. Stephen Sprouse would have been envious of that one — the color almost like those we'd seen at his Barney's show.

This was different than the times we went shopping in Manhattan, where he knew absolutely everyone. We spent a lot of time in Charivari one afternoon. And Bergdorf's, where ironically I found an expensive leather MC jacket — a top-of-the-line knockoff of our downtown originals — with playing card emblems and things that I really wanted. For a second, Schmitty acted like he might buy it for me. Schmidt would occasionally buy me nice things. A new modem, a silver and crystal kaleidoscope from Tiffany's. But the jacket was in the thousand-dollar range, about one-sixth of the money Schmidt had earmarked for his new designer couch. I respect that: better to have one nice place to sit than a bunch of cheap chairs.

Like the City Hall grassy knoll nap hour on our way to buy a printer, outings with Schmidt were always engaging. On Charivari day, we ran into the black men who dress as super heroes in Times Square, who claim to be the 'real Jews.' They were reading something out of a Bible about how only righteous people had kinky African hair. I thought we'd sweep by, but of course, Schmidt stopped for a chat. 'Hair is just hair' he said to the massive seven-foot tall man towering over us.

'No, it's not the right kind of hair. It has to stand up on your head.' With this, I pulled off my baseball cap, under which a 24-hour birds nest had been congealing. My hair stood straight up, even with the warmish early spring breeze. The big black superman was forced to crack a laugh, all I was after, but he quickly regained piety when he saw his minion standing puzzled behind him. Schmidt tried to argue, but I bored of it all and we went to the Paramount Hotel for lunch. We did not fit in. I was in raggedy black leather, as was Schmidt, save some carefully placed and expensive pieces of jewelry and accessories. At first, I thought I might die: other diners gave 'hhmmph' looks across the restaurant. But Schmidt proceeded to teach me another lesson, carrying yourself 101.

Through direct eye contact, sincerity, and a refusal to be accelerated by any peer pressure, real or perceived, Schmidt had the *Maître d'*, waiters and servers hopping to our beck-and-call. We sat and drank and ate snack after snack until salads and burgers arrived. And we outlasted everyone in the place. And no one looked twice when Schmidt settled back in his Philippe Starck chair and took a cat nap while I ordered more fries. We walked out slowly and deliberately, defining ourselves the stars of the afternoon.

At first I expected hordes of drunkard college jock kid lunatics at the Bennington gig but the cool thing was, I quickly realized was that the student body was only a few hundred or so. We were used to throngs of people crammed into Don Hill's. We'd arrived late overall, so there wasn't much time between rehearsal, break, show. I took a nap on a wooden crate in the corridor of the cafeteria while the bands rehearsed. Sherry Vine had come along, as had Misstress, Patrick, and Lily of the Valley. After dinner, I wandered around while the queens packed on the pancake makeup. I noticed small groups of kids watching all of us, running around from dorm to dorm hurriedly in preparation. Only a deaf mute would have missed the excitement spiraling through the air like slivers of asbestos.

Finally, show time approached and the students began to arrive, and we were all shocked: apparently, this gig had become more than a come-in-your-jeans party on campus. The students had read all about SqueezeBox! and our notorious reputation, studied photos, and endeavored to construct their own outfits, costumes, and personas in honor of the event. My feet became tingly as the young people wandered in, one by one, with makeup and extravagant outfits and hairdos.

How could this be? It'd never dawned on me that the club, the people, friends, the music was anything more than a goof — a parody of the life we wished to escape. These kids saw us, and it all, as their own means of escape, maybe even transcendence. Not unlike me, barely 16, sneaking out of the house and into the Plaza movie house on Independence Boulevard for the Rocky Horror Picture show. Who wouldn't? 'Don't dream it, be it.' And these kids were lucky — we had celluloid, they got flesh.

The room filled and the bands started. The queens played the set, followed by unstoppable screams and applause. So, they played the exact same set again. More applause. The kids went mad — dancing, moshing, posing and singing along. I don't know who what was more fun to watch, the looks on the kids faces or on ours. We were being taken seriously. Now we all had to somehow walk away, and take ourselves seriously.

After a second set, groups of young people divided up and cornered each one of us. Again, where I thought the night would turn into just another party-night train wreck, but I was thankfully wrong. The kids wanted to talk to everyone, at length. They took us back and showed us their projects in their rooms, some had more sensual intentions. Although the queens and the musicians got the most attention, there was plenty of admiration to go around. As I chatted to some hip girls and cute boys, I winked at Stevin in the other corner of the room, who was equally engaged. I'd never been wanted by younger people for being a freak before. After growing up in Charlotte, any assembly of young people in a setting resembling 'school' made me nervous.

There we were, searching every Friday night and now in the far reaches of Vermont looking for deliverance, and this group of young folks were looking to us for the same thing. I was overwhelmed. Come to think of it, maybe I'd never imagined that I wasn't that good of a freak. It would have made sense — I wasn't that good of a queer either. Maybe this made me more real, attractive.

Back in New York, each Friday night took on a unique personality. Loud, happy, messy, sexy. A chaotic cacophony of misfit organisms. Unlike too many other clubs that had become HIV factories, we never opened a sex room because Don, nor Pat or me or anyone, wanted the responsibility of it. Schmidt would have liked it I think, but I'm glad it didn't happen 'cause it would have changed the night — made it about the same tired shit as all the fag bars: get laid, fuck, drink, start all over. No culture there. Too much AIDS still going around. Pat almost beat the shit out of a skinny guy I'd gone home with who'd lied to me about his HIV status. Better not to know than lie. Safe sex was relative. On one hand, you could get it by buttfucking without rubbers on. I rarely did that. Well, sometimes. At least I knew Pat cared kinda' like a brother. Things happen. Life happens. AIDS was only supposed to happen to the old guys, so, if I was with a young guy who seemed cool, like he didn't whore around with older guys, my standards slipped a little.

On another hand, professional opinions were that you might get it by sucking, especially if you had cuts in your mouth. Oral sex was one of my favorite pastimes. You weren't supposed to do oral sex within three hours of brushing your teeth, so I used to brush my teeth early in the evening before I went out just in case. But no one knew for sure. There were guys who claimed to only have had oral sex and got AIDS anyway. Then, there were other guys who swore to have never had anal or oral sex and had it. By the end of the night, all this would wear me out. I understood dying, had seen it too much. I thought I understood grieving and loss. Late in the evening, drunk, tired, lonely, all I really understood was that I wanted the here and now, and someone to help me forget it all.

This particular skinny guy was a rogue of Schmidt's and hung around a lot. It was no love interest, just what we'd call a 'why not.' He was cute. Now I know why not. But then, I why-notted. I think asking someone their HIV status made me feel better about taking some futile responsibility for myself. I'd read the reports in *HX* or some other marginally credible rag that over half of all homosexual males in Manhattan had it and should be treated as such.

I hadn't even realized the self-hatred I choked down because of AIDS. Outcast, undesirable, second-class citizen. Because we wouldn't wear Raymond Dragon spandex and sit quietly with the rest of the infidels. 'Gays' and 'party' — 'til death do they part. And somebody in the war-disease labs got hip. All the righteous world needed to do was to invent a disease that would force barriers between ourselves and those we loved — if even for a little while. Psychoimmunomeltdown. Same thing they do to black folks in the ghettos — take away hope and watch 'em kill each other.

Sex for me was not only a driving internal passion, but a form of social protest. Like Rimbaud. As long as they had laws on the books saying I was wrong, I'd fuck anything that moved. Or at least act like I did. Most of the time I even enjoyed it. Fuck, fuck, fuck. Why? 'Cause fuck them. Fuck anyone who'd tell me otherwise. Existing wasn't enough. Carrying rainbow flags and a sissy lingo did nothing. Fucking, shoving who I was inside of another person — this, to me, was living, alive. The world, religious charlatans, and my government forced me to take something sacred and turn it into a metaphysical weapon. Sad thing was, all I started to want, really, was to find a way to walk away from all of it. Stop fucking, start making love. What a concept. Could there be a more subtle way of connecting? Before AIDS I connected — I actively remembered a time when passion could just be passion, and be left there. I was an adolescent fool to think that by being queer I didn't have to worry about getting anyone pregnant — one upside to being a freak.

Unfortunately, men lie. So do women. The skinny rogue lied. The morning after the morning after I got a phone call. He had something to tell me. Apparently his conscience was getting to him. Poor thing — a closeted son of a high-ranking police captain. I should have outed him so I could enjoy watching the cuts and bruises his dad would've beat into him. Pat offered to do likewise. Adrienne, Pat, Lisa and Schmidt stuck by me as I waited the ten days for my results. Midnight panic attacks. Daily bouts of anxiety — live, die, live, die. More than the usual depression I'd known all my life. I was terrified, but figured my time would be sooner or later. Maybe this was the time I had waited for: my time. I'd always thought I'd see thirty, but no matter. It didn't matter. Me and my friends lived like every day was our last.

Getting my results was the most traumatic experiences of my young adult life. Adrienne was terrified for me, but didn't show it. After the two-week waiting period, I called Dr Jeffrey's head nurse, who told me 'You don't have any reason to come in,' which was code for 'you're OK.' They weren't supposed to tell us over the phone. I needed to go in and hear it anyway, see the charts, look him in the eye. This was all going to change my life.

Dr Jeffrey Wallach was one of the first practitioners in Manhattan to take on AIDS patients. He'd been dealing with the plague from the gitgo when it was called GRID. Gay Related something or other. Related. Jeffrey'd held and let go of thousands. That morning, I begged the nurse to let me come to the office. 'OK but hurry up, I have rounds at the hospital.' It wasn't just about the test for me, it was about the whole God-forsaken disease, my life, my sex, my love. I didn't realize until I was halfway over to Twelfth Street that this was actually my first complete test.

I got to Dr Jeffrey's office and buzzed the door. To my right was the entrance to the copy shop I used to make Squeezebox! fliers. For the first couple of years, I'd show up on Friday nights around 10pm to pick up our orders on the way to the club — East 12th Street was rough at night for jittery young punks all made up, the sidewalks filled with a combination of bridge and tunnel partiers, bankers and young Puerto Rican males on the prowl to prove their manhoods. Each week I just wanted to get in and out alive. Now, in the light of day and one door to the left, the same held true.

I didn't know what to expect. My friend Michael Fernandez once told me that Jeffrey treated a lot of AIDS patients for free in the mornings. He said he walked in one time and there was all manner of guys with IV drips and the like. Guys who didn't have money or insurance. Jeffrey treated them for free. I had no health insurance — not big news in the wealthiest country in the world, 'the greatest nation. Jeffrey treated me for little, or free. He kept a closet — me and Fernie called it the candy closet — bursting at the joints with samples. He'd load you up with your full prescriptions in two-to-a-box samples. Fuck the system. It has to come from somewhere. Reagan let the drug companies loose — an equal and opposite reaction to every action. Medicinal anarchy. God bless America.

God bless Jeffrey Wallach.

I didn't know what to say, I was happy, then stunned, then dumbfounded on what to do next. Jeffrey didn't see me that morning, one of his big butch male nurses in a plaid shirt and jeans did. Everything, thankfully, had been blown off course. How can you live like you're gonna' die if you ain't gonna' die? I thought as I strolled back home, in shock. Life was getting to me. Nothing seemed simple anymore. And AIDS wasn't the only thing that could get you. The next night at SqueezeBox! I kept an eye on some shady characters who'd started camping out in the club. A new coke dealer had hit the scene, except this one wasn't as discreet as Angel Melendez. This asshole paraded around like the scene was all his, like he was the reason everyone came. I'd seen it all before — coke taking people's minds, hearts, dreams. I pointed the dealer out to a friend one night, and told him to mark my words: it was the beginning of the end. 'When cocaine hits a scene, it's over.' The dealer and his followers stuck to the walls of Don Hill's, taking over, preying on the willing and not-so-willing. Some dealers are dealers because of money. Most like the power to destroy.

The club started seeing more rumbles of its own. That particular Friday, Pat confronted the skinny rogue who'd almost killed me and then Schmidt got involved and then I ended up with the guy, alone, in the kitchen. He spewed everything he could from his sour mouth to defend himself. I feel like I should have just picked up a broomstick and beat him. No one would've known. I coulda' killed him, saved him some suffering. The guy, and I honestly can't remember or just have his name blocked out, deserved a beating for what he'd done, but in hindsight, so did I. Nice. Just like the inventors of HIV intended: queer-on-queer violence. Instead of escalating it, I let him have his say. I was actually afraid of him — this guy, the type Larry Kramer would call 'murderers,' had wielded a certain mortal power over my life. So had I by being a dumbass. The outcome: I would live, he wouldn't. And unless they got him the cocktail, he probably didn't.

Rumble rumble. Another Friday, at closing, 'Union City Blue' time, I sat on top of the bar, just listening and talking to Tommy, the bartender. I watched Guy pack up his records and CDs. I usually missed out on the good cruising time every week 'cause I was in the basement counting money. No cute boys were left, so I was doing a few shots of Jägermeister and contemplating how good my head would feel as it hit my pillow. The dancefloor had cleared out except a few couples making out and having a slow dance. I actually hadn't drunk as much as usual. Taking it easy. I can always feel change approaching, there'd been a weird vibe in the air all night. Just some average dude — the kind I didn't want to be let in the door in the first place. He was wobbling on his feet, had apparently been asking Tommy for another drink. Tommy said he couldn't, that it was after hours. In those days, Don could let us stay open after 4AM, but wouldn't serve booze. Fair enough. He looked at my fresh drink and walked away. The guy came back again, and again Tommy said no. Tommy and I shrugged and had a grin at his persistence. Bobby, the head bartender, joined in. The bushy-haired guy lingered in the empty room opposite, peering over. I was hoping Carl would see him and chat him out the door. Instead, the guy picked up a glass, walked toward me and threw it at me and Tommy. It barely missed my head and barely missed Tommy and broke the big mirror behind the bar.

I was a frustrated young man. If this guy was going to play the fool who'd light my fuse, so be it. Without flinching I dove off the bar and threw my entire weight in his direction and the big double back door. Within seconds Carl and Gary, one of the owner's relatives, were there to help. We jousted the guy against the door, which flew open, and threw him on the pavement. I thought sure Tommy was going to beat him, but Carl cooled things down, like only Carl could. Sometimes I wished Carl hadn't talked everyone out of it — I had twenty years of queer, religious and outcast rage built up inside me and this guy would be perfect to unleash it on. Someone needed to pay for the sins of society. But I didn't unleash anything. We let the guy scramble up and scream a little. Turns out he lived in the building just next door, so he ran inside.

We all laughed it off as best we could, and stood outside for a minute. Nervous male laughter. Gary and I had turned our back to the guy's front steps. I heard the door open, some shuffling, and noticed something long, gray and shiny pointing from the direction of my right periphery. I slowly prepared to move, thinking the guy was going to get his moment of glory — the kind you get with guns in the good ole U-S of A. The kind that really proves something — that's for sure.

Things went weird in my head, life morphed into slow motion. I think the sound came, the one I'd only heard in movies and when skeet shooting with my cousins. Schisk-schisk. Only two. Gary and I turned around and stared up past the sights and the shiny barrel of a shotgun. I don't know what is supposed to go through your mind at gunpoint. This is it? No music? No shrill sound of an orchestra? No. It's how you know the shit is really happening. I'd never been so blatantly gun-pointed. I remember calculating the potential trajectory of the buckshot and the size of the barrel — which made it a twenty gauge. I was aware that every one of us was in the spread, and with one pull of a finger me, Gary, Carl, Tommy and now Don would be history. I also figured the fact that he hadn't already blown us away showed he wasn't as serious as he'd have us believe.

Time caught up with me. Seconds splitting into individual, liminal, subatomic particles. Gary saying to the guy, 'What you gonna' do then? Shoot me?' in his Irish accent. It finally dawned on me that this was really happening, but I couldn't feel anything. My internal numbing machine kicked in without my even knowing it. I was back in school. Stop, drop and roll. A shotgun was close enough to nukes for me, so I got myself back inside. At the same time, cop cars came screeching from all directions, guns drawn. The Giuliani Administration was known for placing cop cars outside of the club to try and catch us for violations. They sought to shut down offenders as part of their so-called 'quality of life' campaign, but now they were forced to do their real job.

I was frightened of the cops — a historically unpredictable bunch. Nothing had really much changed in New York since the draft riots. The town was run by sharks and was now headed by a dictator. I'd seen the NYPD beat up a handcuffed person right outside my bedroom window. I'd seen footage of them beating blood out of unarmed, innocent people during the Tompkins Square riots. They'd beat Chris Connolly, an ACT UP activist, into a brain-dead coma at an AIDS protest. I expected a hail of gunfire or tear gas or something.

The gunman ran into his building and bolted the door behind him. The cops screamed 'everyone else back inside' while riot police smashed in the door with a battering ram. A legion of them ran into the building, their boots pounding up the stairs. Then crash, bump, followed by an eerie silence. I felt pale. Me and Carl and Gary and Adrienne and Tommy and Don stood like stone statues. All this over a fucking drink, I thought. I figured the guy had been hanging with our charming hardcore coke crowd.

Next, we heard some shuffling and yelling. The front door burst back open, glass panes rattling everywhere. They hustled the guy out in handcuffs. They got him in the back of the car, and the officers started mumbling to each other, while passing around the guy's ID. The sergeant said something to Don, then they all got in their cars and left.

The next day, I stopped in to ask Don what had happened. Good rumor had it the guy just happened to be Police Commissioner Bratton's son or nephew or something. More trouble from cop spawn. According to Don, he had gotten a call of apology from someone high up at City Hall. Told he could either go ahead and press charges, or the commissioner would personally see to it that our business was never again interrupted, hint-hint, and that the boy would be relocated and forever barred from coming anywhere near the club or any of us ever again. Deals were invented to be made: this was Giuliani's game.

If I had spent time thinking, I might have pressed for more action. I didn't know how many 'probablys' I actually was from having my face blown off. At least I did notice, thereafter, neither the police nor fire department ever bothered us much again. They just turned up the heat on every other queer venue in town.

7. The Men Who Sold the World

By 1996, Blake Burba got nominated for a Tony award for the lighting design of the Broadway smash 'Rent.' A fucking Tony award — the real deal. Pat was in the Rock and Roll Hall of Fame, strangely but we went with it, and set for a proper tour on Lollapalooza with Psychotica. Steven, the SqueezeBox! band director, had begun working with John Cameron Mitchell on something named Hedwig. Our mothership was afloat. The band and the queens went to Japan. Things were looking possible for a global expansion.

In the quest for global Rock 'n' Roll if there's one type of person I particularly learned quickly to detest it's those, who, because of the onset of cheap technology, pride themselves on being Artists, with a capital 'A.' And in the mid-90s, as soon as blue type appeared on a gray page of a computer screen, the race to the bottom was on. Along came a litany of computer nerds turned geniuses, most of whom quickly turned into con artists. The problem was, they could make things spin, speak and twirl, but none knew how to really work, few knew the value of integrity. The worst: the Steve Jobs types who, because of an ignorant public, would sell shitwater to flies given the chance. Wait, perhaps the actual worst were those who bought their crap. All in all, a marriage made of maggots in my humblest opinion.

Cue the big Gigabit grifter show, when all smoke becomes fact, and it sells for a price. Starring: every sociopath that ever hid behind a rock while your kids played in the park. I mean, what I saw, and what came was one hateful scam. I'd gone freelance years earlier, because since working for Michael P, every job I ever had was for people who forced 'social overtime' — unpaid work by peer pressure. Somehow, they'd made leaving on time a sin, and a sign of non-commitment. Clients were being charged for every second you sat working to sell their crap, but we weren't paid for it. Reagan's America. I call it: the great 'crap.con'

From five feet away I watched millionaire CEOs gleefully paraded in front of empty steel boxes hanging from 'Silicon Alley' office walls (the area West of 7th Avenue, and below Houston, NYC, so named to be the East Coast's answer to California's 'Valley' - which didn't seem to stick) as they were told they were somehow standing in front of the greatest fiber optic connection to the universe. In turn, these giddy CEOs whipped out checkbooks, tossing paper in all directions. Again in turn, the geeks ordered lobster for lunch, and seemed to actually believe they were changing the world.

I knew of tens of thousands stolen in the way of commissions on sales that never materialized, and never were intended to materialize. Rule #1: lie now, make it later. I observed insidious post-pubescent nerds stand and create lavish fabrications over things like 'bandwidth,' 'server capacity,' and 'hits.' No one was checking. No one ever makes-sure when the great deceivers wave the wand of 'NEW!'

Everyone from Vice President Al Gore on down was buzzing. Although I didn't have the words, or the effective language at the time, the 'Information Super Highway' frightened me, as I was convinced on all sides that it was giving birth to a new breed of sociopath the world had never seen. I did the best I could to mitigate the muck, even bought into some. Fine. But deep down I hated it. After years of ad agency bullshit, I knew where it was going. But, easier to innovate than fight.

I was calling it the 'internet,' and began working with a little internet startup company. Schmidt, the seer, was relentless for news and developments of the new technology, and wanted a piece of whatever it was we thought we had. The group I was with sold Procter & Gamble their first web site through ad agency connections. Somehow, surprise-surprise, the job got botched.

Once, when we had no money, I went over to my friend Andy, who had a store in the East Village called Body Worship. He had a thriving business, doing tour clothes for Madonna and fetish wear for uptown customers. I came back with around six thousand dollars in cash to build his new web site. That job, too, got botched. This taught me rule #2 in the internet business, if rule #1 doesn't work, blame the customer and confuse them with technical jargon. Then re-package it and call it 'new and improved.'

Schmidt did his homework and found out about projects like the one the Rolling Stones did — an audio-only event over the internet. He wanted SqueezeBox! to be the first to do a real event, with audio and video. These possibilities were the good side of the great con.

Optimism was in the air. We got a team of companies together, and put together one randy-dandy network of computers and engineers for one show, the likes of which the world had never seen. We gave the event a name: *Live @nd InConcert*. got Schmidt, who got Debbie and Don over to the crappy little internet company. She signed on to do the show. Then Schmidt got the Lunachicks and Joan Jett. Of course, Patrick was ready with Psychotica before we even got the ink dry on the proposals — which were easy, no money, just cool.

I was beside myself. I literally thought we were going to change the world and make our little corner of the society a global reality. I believed that people — you, me, us kind of people — could, for once, have their own way of getting out. Fuck the big conglomerates. Fuck the boardrooms full of record execs who sit in their fat chairs with their fat desks covered in pictures of their spoiled fat kids. Most of all fuck MTV and its faux pop culture — in my opinion all we were getting from them was a new and improved blackface Al Jolson show. Sad. Plenty of black, white and purple musicians, poets and writers were out there who actually had talent. I wanted to cut some of the middlemen and actually reach people.

Sun Microsystems, Real Audio and companies from DC to LA signed up — refreshingly professional in the face of the 'cons' — and on January 6th, 1996 we shook, or more like, precociously pissed off, the online entertainment world. This was what I called fun. And on the night, one hour before, it didn't work. Well, the computers worked. The people manning their stations in Washington worked. The network seemed to work. The microwave dish connecting the club to the office — the only link to put it out on the net — wasn't working. I held the show, and decided if we'd waited for Green Day 'til 5AM, *The New York Times*, CNN and *Washington Post* could wait too. The club was packed to the rafters, everyone a bit calmer than usual, checking out all the equipment, watching the geeks run around. The show had sold out in a matter of days. We all had press badges and walkie talkies, like a real gig. It only took about a few minutes and a few trips of me running back to the offices on Hudson Street and back down to the club to figure out and correct an encoding error on the main distribution computer. God bless the geeks — it's a love hate thing, like all good affairs.

Schmidt always wanted to have the ability to say we were the first. And as I ran from the office back to the club while ten thousand hits per minute were coming to our servers, and a lot of people were getting immediate, uncensored audio, and plenty were getting the first real-time video, and Misstress screamed something in Japanese and 'What the fuck's up, we are live, worldwide from New York Fucking City!,' we became the first ever live audio and video webcast the world had ever seen. And sure, it didn't work perfectly: neither did the Model-T, but that didn't stop Henry Ford.

While the Lunachicks and then Psychotica played I argued with Kenny, Joan Jett's manager. To hear him talk, you would think that Joan Jett was the biggest rock star, ever, in recorded history. Demanding this and that every second of every day. I'd only wanted Joan because we were a queer club and we wanted some appeal for dykes, which was rare. Sure, we'd all rocked out in high school to 'I Love Rock 'n' Roll.' And OK, 'Crimson and Clover' was kinda catchy. But this guy needed to chill. He had the nerve to act annoyed when I gave him the index finger and 'one second' when someone came by and gave me a kiss. That someone would be Debbie.

Debbie was the real star and he knew it. And this kind of crap was precisely what I hoped the internet could make inroads against. But behind it all I felt there was something very sinister about all this free tech. I knew it would only be a matter of time before the ad agencies and the big brands of Corporania™ grabbed it like a newborn guinea pig and squeezed every inch of life out through its nostrils.

The audience waited patiently for their goddess Deborah as she took the stage in her lime dress, smart glasses and long hair. Chris Stein joined her. Chris was particular about his guitar picks. The ones he had to have. Once we had to hold a show while Ila ran back to their place and got new ones. Misstress chattered to the audience 'til she got back. No one cared. I caught Misstress's eye a few times, as if to say 'Look what they're up to now,' as if talking about family members who'd saved all their best peculiar behavior for a Thanksgiving dinner.

I felt half the world was watching us that night and the other half wasn't hip enough to know about it. Debbie was the show just in and of herself, moving gracefully around the stage, the side I'd admired from the ladder the day we set up her first gig. The whole world seemed to stop as she sang the theme from 'Taxi Driver,' read a monologue, and then went into Leonard Cohen's 'Waiting for the Miracle.' I'd never seen, heard or dreamed of such a set. We all experimented. We all succeeded. The next day, press outlets from London to Tokyo and back to the Big Apple were abuzz. With good reason.

8. Highway to Hell

The great crap.con was plugging along. Many of the so-called young entrepreneurs seemed to worship a guy named Tom Peters, who'd written a book called *Wow* or something — one of those hallmark narratives of the new ME-2 generation which convinced everyone that the only way up was through a hole they'd blast through decades of proven business methods. Things like, standing by your product, respecting the customer seemed irrelevant to the wow cattle. Mr. Wow also advocated offices without walls or privacy. Personal desks even. Very Victorian workhouse. And anyone worth a crap knows that people don't do well in situations without things that are familiar, consistent and stable. This was very typical of the new ME-2s, the suckled-on-cable TV generation: recycle old mediocrity and claim it to be the 'new original.' To this day there are huge rooms full of workers in Manhattan, London, and all over the world, sitting at rows of desks, sweatshop style.

'Open plan' equals open heart surgery after your first attack after enduring the stress is more like it. Not even the benefit of the dreaded cubicle. Not even an ounce of privacy to make a call to find out about your HIV test or pap smear. It's trendy. We're no longer humans, we're 'resources.' And for us, with the *décor du jour* came stories of high-transmission satellite dishes on the roof, and some convoluted tale of how the construction up and down the entirety of Hudson Street was to install the biggest fiber-optic network in New York. Bullshit reigned supreme in the early days of the internet, and everyone was doing it. Thousand-dollar web pages, hundred-dollar hourly fees to make a stick figure jump across the screen. The technology was exciting, but the Dodgers of the world were determined to oversell it before it could even get off the ground. Having worked in advertising for a long time, I knew what would eventually happen: the big agencies and software firms would sit back licking their incisors while the little startup companies devoured each other. And that is exactly what happened. And as the pressure grew, so did the taller-than-tall tales.

When the Feds started sniffing around Hudson Street, I got a little nervous. Adrienne and I stumbled upon questionable dealings all over the place — pricing that fell from the sky, funny clients, strange computer purchases — but I didn't freak. I started distancing myself from all this soon after the big SqueezeBox! internet show. The press was up my ass for a celebrity angle — I didn't want them down my throat for some sort of racketeering nonsense I didn't even understand. People from Microsoft and MSNBC came posing as clients to try to find out what we knew. A war broke out among all the fledgling software companies, from RealAudio to Pseudo - incidentally run by another Squeezeboxer, who went by the name of 'JudgeCal™' - to Sonicnet — suitors of the infant internet airwaves. Battles to 'carry' music concerts, programming and venues ensued. No one bothered to find out whether the public even gave a shit. But the important thing was we did, and we really wanted to change the conversation. A very tall order.

Sometimes I wished we never had done the January netcast — all it did was turn up the heat on a big nothing. Nothing but some fun which should have just sparked more fun and some new innovations. Don Hill had gotten some friends-of-friends to toss a little development money our way, to see what we could do with this thing, this broadcasting something or other. We'd been told by the geeks that we had all these fancy computers on a big fiber-optic pipe down to Washington. It had a fancy name — 'Mae East.' Whatever that meant. Apparently it was a million-zillion-gabillion miles big and everyone up to the President wanted space on it. According to the crap.conmen, our lines were connected to all the big telephone companies, from AT&T to US Sprint.

It's true: dreamin' is free, and after a while, I too drank the kool aid and became determined. To hell with just music and all that — if I could find a low-cost, global medium for the chumps-like-us of the world to use, we could cut the rug from underneath the big broadcasters. People, left, right or wrong, could have a say. Education could take new forms. Autochthonous cultures could compete with the influx of corporate bilge. There were like minds. JudgeCal, already had a lot of shows going on Pseudo and we spent many nights in the back of the Don's with bands raging, discussing algorithms, data compression and video software. In hindsight, we really shoulda' joined forces. Nonetheless we put out a mini-broadcast, live, from Greenwich Street, every Friday night for over a year.

Some friends and SqueezeBox! regulars owned a hip salon just a few blocks away in Soho at Mudhoney, where Michael and Alicia cut hair for all the rock stars in town. They played MC5 all day long. They did my hair. They employed a lot of the wayward SqueezeBox! children. They let me set up shows in their salon. They did hair, the rock stars sang, we put it out on the net. *Paper Magazine* covered it. A few months later I did the first ever online global conference of the European Union, and

Vice President Al Gore sent me a congratulatory email for trying new shit — not his words. We did a huge charity event for Design Industries Foundation Fighting AIDS, DIFFA — a heavy hitter in the charity business. They'd rented an entire pier facility on the West Side and called it 'Maximum Exposure.' Famous photographers from all over like Annie Leibovitz, Herb Ritts, Greg Gorman and William Wegman donated their time. Rich people donated money in exchange for photos by their favorites. Calvin Klein sponsored the event, and Cindy Crawford did our promo. On the night, we found ourselves on a couch interviewing a range of people like Herb Ritts to Greg Gorman to Harrison Ford. The heat got hotter, and none of us seemed to know exactly what to do with it.

At another event for DIFFA, a tribute to Edith Head for which I'd also typeset the posters and print ads, the paparazzi let loose with the flash photography at the door. I'd never had them take my picture like that. Then I heard one of them ask another 'Who is he?' and another one sorta said my name and mumbled something about the club — or at least that's what I thought I heard. At first it excited me. Then it frightened me. Somehow I got seated at one of the main tables right beside one of the Directors of CBS television. Life became more surreal when the runway started, and the most iconic costumes from the silver screen came to life. I particularly recall Bette Davis' dress from 'All About Eve' — those fur tails dangling from the shoulders, for which I could never quite figure out a purpose.

I showed up at a PETA benefit with Greg Gorman. My friend Dan Renehan came along. He'd never been to one of these 'dos.' I knew Dan Mathews, the PETA guy, from SqueezeBox! He had us wooshed down to the VIP room. Only then I realized I was dressed head to toe in black leather, surrounded by people concerned for ethical animal treatment. Ooops. Chrissie Hynde, standing right next to me, didn't say anything. Dan let me off the hook with 'well at least it's not fur, everyone has to start somewhere.' Dan, my friend, laughed at my expense. When Pamela Anderson reached for Greg and said 'are you Greg Gorman? THE Greg Gorman?' we giggled at her expense. Funny us.

Another crazy evening found me in a private event at the old Barney's department store with Patrick and Lisa for Stephen Sprouse's fashion showing. Barney's had put his entire dayglo collection in for the season. Sprouse and I used to chat a lot by the back bar at SqueezeBox! — music, art, crowd-spotting — one of those rare people I just clicked with and loved talking to. He brought his kid nephew along a lot. Stephen designed Psychotica's logo. I would have been hurt that Patrick went to someone else except Sprouse did such a great job with it I didn't care. Plus he had the name.

At one point I walked into Don's in the middle of an afternoon, with horrible sounds of destruction coming from all angles, but this time, it was not a thrash band. Inside, dust permeated the air, and I waved my way through to find Patrick standing in the middle of the dance floor, overed from head to toe in dirt, holding a sledge hammer, with what used to be the ceiling collapsed all around him. 'Hey...' he said nonchalantly.

'Hey, Patrick, wh-what are you doing?' I replied gingerly, unsure what I'd walked into.

'We're re-decorating. Wanna' help?' He asserted as he eyed up his next piece of gypsum to whack. Anger management perhaps.

Truth was, the ceiling was very close to the stage, and performers had to be very careful up there. Pat's remodeling would give everyone at least three feet more clearance — which was great for the likes of Dean Johnson. Perhaps Bunny would do a big gig now that her hair would fit. Around the same time, a young guy who called himself 'Mr. Tim' showed up and Don hired him to re-do the lights, and re-do them he did. Suddenly, we had not one but probably fifteen mirror balls of all sizes, special effect to rival a Star Wars convention, and a stage that reminded me a bit of Bootsy Collins, George Clinton and Parliament landing the Mothership. In time Mr. Tim became a friend, and was always excitably interested to show me the latest flashing gadgets.

With all this, I respected that Don kept a modicum of classiness about that old diner-turned music hall. Mr. Tim even devised a way to construct a two-sided video screen that caught projection from two directions. The whole place just kept transforming and evolving into something I never thought possible, sans the tackiness of CBGB or sterility of big mega-clubs.

Every delectable minute was beginning to run together. Candy, candy everywhere. Schmidt, Debbie, and a bunch of us went to one of Marc Berkley's nights at Tunnel 'cause Debbie had a walk-on gig there. Club Mall or something. They had different themes for different rooms, but the same tired-old music — they hadn't locked it away with Michael Alig. Upon arrival, we quickly made our way through the throngs of young, jumpy people, as Debbie was due to be performing on the main stage within minutes. As dance beats so loud that the vibrations knocked my equilibrium surged through our bodies, security swept us through the dance floor full of thousands of tripping teenagers. Without warning, a strange hand grabbed my arm hard. At first I figured it might be someone wanting to come along to get close to Debbie, but after a second to focus, I stunned to realize it was Tim, my old friend from Charlotte, minus Richard.

It had been years and many lives before that I'd known him. He was dancing alone in the crowd, sweating in a white tank top and red Scottish tartan kilt. He must have been on one of his weekend jaunts with the boyfriend, and boy oh boy was he flying. His black hair was pulled back in his signature ponytail. We gave a deep, brief hug but then I quickly broke away, lest I get separated from my group. If you get left behind in a place like that, you'll never find your way forward. He wouldn't stop dancing long enough for me to talk to him, but kept grabbing me hard, giving me a begging look to get me to stay with him and dance. I yell over the music 'Follow me! Come on!!' I wanted to chat for a minute, introduce him to Debbie and my friends, but he wouldn't stop twirling around. I would have relished knowing he would carry the story of me working with rock stars back to the Scorpio Lounge with him. I wanted him and everyone else to know I'd been making it for years. He tried to get me to dance with him. I saw the entourage slipping away ahead of me. I left Tim, looking both betrayed and stunned, in front of the DJ booth.

Debbie took the stage in front of the tweaking masses. She stunned them further into their denial — forcing their brains to break from the repetitive beats and noise for one simple, expertly delivered song. It may have been one of the songs from the new album, but I can't remember for sure. I tried in vain to find Tim in the crowd.

Little did I realize at the time, I'd already begun drowning in my own excitement. Later I met a hardcore kid at one of the hair salon gigs. He got high, real high, all the time. I wanted the Kid to be my boyfriend, but he couldn't. Sex was out. He could, however, sleep with me and cuddle. That was OK with me. I'd become expert in loving people I couldn't have, and having people I could never love.

9. Road to Nowhere

The Kid came, went, and got lost sometimes, which was good because I couldn't deal with him every night. He was the best cuddle ever, but inconsolable when he was tweaking. He swore he didn't do smack, and I chose to believe him. He was company, and I loved him for what he was — I had no room to judge. The mind fuck of it was that I was just as whacked as he was. He got high to ease his pain, check out. I got high on him. The Kid was cute, blond hair, gymnast's body. What a waste, I'd think when he was sober, hyper and annoying. What perfection, I'd think when he was floating above the clouds, a perfectly passionate, delicate being. We both psychologically fed our addictions.

Another guy I'd always had a crush on was Jack, the SqueezeBox! bass player. Jack had kept me at a safe distance since the club opened, primarily because, it turned out, he was in love with John Cameron Mitchell — who was working with Stephen Trask, our band manager, on the music for a new project called Hedwig and the Angry Inch. Together and with a few others, like Mike Potter who invented Hedwig's wig and makeup, they formed their own little subculture. I was jealous of Mitchell for some reason. He spoke with a cool composure my jumpy young nerves hadn't yet discovered. Although I'd met Mitchell at The Bar years before, he carried himself in a way that got my goat, although he was never rude. Just...something. He had that trained-actor way of speaking that made people stand and swoon on every word. Or something.

These were confusing people to me. I remember one Friday night, a couple of years earlier during the first winter of the club, a major blizzard had set in. Those were some of my favorite nights — truly unpredictable and barometrically enhanced. I got silly drunk, as did the rest of the house. In the few hours we were in there a foot of snow had fallen — we'd nowhere to go... another reason to laugh and get loaded. Jack was pretty hyped up too. More chatty than usual. We started talking after the show. Apparently he and Mitchell, the boyfriend, had taken a break. My ears pricked up, but I didn't even think of trying anything — I'd lost interest in Jack. I'd been watching some of these characters for quite a while, and they could be so narcissistic that even they didn't realize it when they were playin' you. It was what I'd call a 'weird energy night' — which always come when you least expect them. He lived in Hoboken and couldn't get home, so I invited him to my place. Something about him struck me strange that night, something amiss. We ventured out in the calf-deep snow, and a near whiteout. Full-on snowstorms in New York are the best: the cold white stuff keeps falling from the mouths of the gods above, the streets fall silent, the airports shut, the tourists hide in their overpriced hotels and jam telephone lines worrying about how to get back to Tallahassee, and for a short time the city belongs to the people who truly love it; and we get the still, quiet, majestic city — lonely, empty, replicating for a brief allegorically merciful moment, the caverns in our hearts that drove us there.

The wind cut down Spring Street hard, like Mother Nature's infantry laying waste to all who dare travel. The snow stung as it laced my cheeks. Jack had his bass guitar on his back, thin plaid pants on, brown corduroy jacket with fleece collar. I plowed quickly ahead of him in my leather pants with zippered legs, scarf and leather coat. I was hammered-drunk and was trying to get a good start when I noticed Jack had fallen down in the middle of the Hudson and Spring Street intersection. I looked back and yelled something, but he just flopped his arms up in the air and back down as if giving up. As if he just couldn't — helpless — someone who needed to pull himself up, but only knew to wait for someone to save him. His bass guitar was covered in slush. Jack had revealed his entire story to me in those few moments — intriguing and frightening to me. Like Andy, when he'd get high and sit up playing on my computer in the room on the opposite end of my apartment. Without warning he'd get scared, realizing he was alone, and begin to call my name while shuffling into my bedroom and under the covers.

I went back and helped Jack stand up. His brown corduroy jeans were wet. Luckily, a cab-turned-snowplow chugged by and we took it to my place. I took notice of his smooth alabaster skin and cute, boyish feet. I think I puked the night up like usual. He didn't mind I was sick. I always thought it kind of brotherly when someone was willing to kneel down beside another, holding them around the middle — helping the lover to release their demons. Jack didn't go that far. There's something really terrible about getting sick, even worse getting sick alone. I'd made it a regular practice: out to indulge in all I couldn't handle, back to purge it from my system. The thought had occurred from time to time — why bother?

Later on Jack and I fell asleep after sort of fooling around. If I had been less ill, him less cold and the time less late, we might have kept it up. We rolled up in a ball of blankets and comforters, and the next day woke up and rolled around a little more. It was more like a curiosity thing than a sex thing. Out of nowhere he broke into a massive cry — which lasted the rest of the afternoon. He talked some, revealing a major love for Mitchell. Really loved him. I didn't really know a lot about John Cameron Mitchell, except I usually tire easily of people with three names, but this boy had it bad.

I didn't quite know what to do, but I did know that letting this guy leave in a crying fit wasn't the answer. So, what else was there to do but put him to work. Jack spent the next few hours helping me put stickers on the SqueezeBox! letters, and telling me all about his troubles. He tried to run away in an anxious fit, but I kept handing him things to do. The remnants of any crush I'd had on him faded after that, but I respected what kind of thing he was going through. I thought I wanted that kind of thing. The closest I'd gotten so far was Eric.

I started needing some distractions, so I tagged along with Patrick in the big van with Psychotica down to DC for Psychotica's Capitol Ballroom gig. It was the first time I'd been to Our Nation's Capital since the trip with Betty Badum. The van wasn't as nice as Betty's black Volvo. The trip wouldn't be to the Ritz Carlton. Down and back the same night. The Capitol Ballroom wasn't very queer at all. Hostile even — filled with a bunch of jarheads for a Ska band. I didn't exactly like leaving Manhattan once I was away. Some boy with stars in his eyes grabbed me on one of my trips between the dressing room and the bar. I got him a wristband. I bought shots of Jägermeister. We made out beside the stage during the show, and I knew how the rest went: either an attempt to find a dark corner for a desperate tryst, or an 'oops-we're-too-drunk' scene filled with 'come back with us' chants on repeat. I rode the entire way home with my head lying across Enrique, the sympathetic cello player's lap, staring out at the night sky as it guided us back up I-95. Enrique, whom we called 'Henry,' stroked my hair like an understanding mother figure, for which I was grateful — it saved me the usual anxiety attack.

Jimmy James hired me to go with him to help put up his show in Provincetown. Blake Burba, the 'Rent' boy, and his boyfriend Keith went to rig the lights and video, I did the print ads and the promotion. We stayed in a big house in the main part of town — not one of those cute New England cottages like the rich queers all had, ours was a Spartan gray new build over a converted gas station, with cheesy black and mauve 80s furnishings, banker-green sofas and cheap copies of Erté prints hanging on the walls. We went for a long weekend, stayed for a week.

I'd scarcely left Manhattan in years, much less ventured above 23rd Street. I tried to relax in Provincetown. It was a nice change of scenery. The booze flowed. The boys romped. The drug music thumped. The dykes argued over everything. Soon it all ran together just like Manhattan, and I got bored. Blake and Keith took the spare bedroom, so I slept on the huge chair in the living room. It was a tepid, misty few days, but the scent of New England fog crept through the crack in the window near my hung-over head, and the passing rain showers massaged my insides for our final three days.

When Patrick started on the big Lollapalooza tour, the whole club crowd got to go to Randall's Island to launch the US tour. We had to wait at the gate because Pat's mom, Judy, wasn't on some list. Pat had to come out in full makeup and scream at the guards. I never understood the screaming. Most of the big stars I met were the nicest people and they always got what they wanted. Soundgarden and the Ramones were also on the tour.

Backstage, Pat had a trailer where we hung out. I laughed 'cause although I never lived in one, I'd moved a thousand miles to New York to get away from any notion of trailers, and there I was, backstage at one of the most coveted tours in rock music, sitting surrounded by wood paneling, metal doors and amber-tinted light fixtures. Trailers, too, are a state of mind. Joey Ramone's trailer was beside Pat's. I went over but didn't stay long 'cause the scene among them was too tense. Joey and I chatted outside of the trailers for a minute. Joey lived a few blocks away from me on 9 Street back in the East Village. We'd been introduced by a mutual friend at our internet gig, plus I met him briefly outside when he had introduced Debbie's first show at SqueezeBox! He'd been enamored with the tech stuff since we'd done the internet show at SqueezeBox!, and we talked many times about producing one of his birthday bashes from Irving Plaza. He wanted me to put his party out on the net. I wanted to, but the problem was finding the money to pay for it. Plus Joey wanted money. There'd been meetings with his manager, Arturo, and a man named Ira Lippy, and we were all trying to find a way to do it. I'd cooled on making any major promises because I'd begun to suspect that some of the computers we'd been told were at the fancy Mae East place down in DC weren't actually in DC, or anywhere for that matter. I didn't rush into anything with Joey. One night at dinner Joey took a special liking to Adrienne, and we all talked and chatted for a very long time, and no matter what I did, I could never get over sitting there, watching Joey F*ing Ramone, innocently flirting with my sister. Nothing happened. Nothing was going to happen. Although we were at the same table, we were world's apart. But we all seemed to need each other that night, and somewhere across the tables we just had a good time.

Aside from what myths the tabloids were telling the ME-2s, being backstage at concerts is only surpassed in boring-ness by the loading docks filled with garbage. Dreams of champagne on ice and cozy party pads are quickly smashed by metal folding chairs and a plastic dish tub filled with water from melted ice and lukewarm beer. And the people, ugh, the people — standing around, saying nothing, building unnecessary tension, waiting for their moment to try and fuck a star. Sure, Schmidt was right — the true power is one step behind the stage, but not in the party room. And aside from my time hanging out with the Green Day boys, backstage is also, without a doubt, one of the most revolting places on earth. Stars are working, or should be, if they're actually stars. So are the stage men and the producers. You don't go have beers with Aunt Minnie in the middle of her shift at the bank. The others are record label people and cousins of record label people. And if any one of them had a chance at being center stage they'd drool and trade every wholesale deal in the world for three seconds of it.

That year at Lollapalooza, I liked wandering through the actual paying crowd, watching the shows, wandering backstage at my leisure only for the one redeeming part of backstage: the porta-potties. I never got off on the power an 'all-access' pass brings, except getting through to the toilet at will, for a long, undeterred piss.

When the Ramones went on, I edged my way up through the crowd. Of course, a mosh pit ensued. I kept to the fringes. I'd some time earlier traded my Pat Fields plastic shiny pants for Tino Trevino's leather jeans from the big daddy shop on Christopher Street, and didn't have a lot of energy dressed in cow under a beating sun. The mosh pit for the Ramones was different from the usual madness. People were falling and no one helped them up — and this was supposed to be the 'civilized crowd' — not like the rooms full of Giuliani's so-called degenerates of the Lower East Side. Some people started getting bloody. In years of the occasional Saturday hardcore matinee I'd never seen blood. Not on Rivington Street even. I became concerned. These *poseur* preppies were beating the crap out of each other. I watched as big jocks rammed into the crowd of other jocks and younger dudes trying to have a good time. One kid looked like he'd been mauled by a bear — busted nose, blood everywhere. I retreated from the stage some and watched to see if Joey noticed it while he was singing. I actually found it both disturbing and hot. Young, writhing, sweaty, bloody bodies - 'I just wanna have some kicks, I just wanna get some...' dick? Rock 'n' Roll High School.

On another outing, Patrick and Psychotica opened for Tool at the Roseland Ballroom. We tried to put it out on the net. Tool had the same managers as Patrick — Nikki and Ted from California, two of the nicest people I've ever met in the business. Tool was a massively popular band, but I didn't like them so much. My sister Adrienne loved them. My first notice of our slight generation gap. Angry music. No point. The lead singer wasn't nice or even pleasant to me. Rather, what I found to be a bigger asshole than the lead singer for Oasis, which took doing. All this angry music popping up everywhere... America was angry... but this guy called it art. Tool brought their record label people with them from LA and I've never met phonier people in my life. Bad karma. Together, we made a disaster out of the net show, and the computers that the crap.conmen had sworn were the best on the planet failed. I began to lose interest, fast. I'd given enough to shyster internet dorks and some of the plastic people exported from Cali. They weren' t all bad, but I had a love for music and our crowd. These people were not our crowd.

I felt lost with everything in general — between the parties and the business and the internet and a whole string of boyfriends. I'd remained friends with Marilyn from the old neighborhood. In my eyes she was a Mother of the New Age. If they made it, she tried it. And I was her willing guinea pig. Yoga, Feng Shui, Reiki. She rebirthed me and channeled my energy. Years before, on a dare, I followed her to a yoga class on a Friday evening before the club. It was at the Integral Yoga Institute, started by the guru who'd chanted for the million-or-so crowd at Woodstock. A man named Surya taught our class. 'Surya' means 'sun' in Sanskrit. 'Just try one, if you don't like it, you're only out eight bucks,' Marilyn reassured me. So, I tried it and loved it, and started meeting her regularly, and going back on my own. I felt so much better after the classes, but after a while fell out of the habit of going. One night, during one of my more acute anxiety attacks, I turned off the TV and sat in my dark front room of my apartment. 'What can I do?' I thought to myself. Then, I remembered the yoga, and the things Surya had tried to teach me... peace is your true nature. And I remembered that Marilyn had made me a cassette tape of some of the music from the chanting groups they had, so I switched the punk music for some spiritual, and started doing all the yoga I could think of. And it worked. After that, I went back to the Institute, and Surya was there, teaching and ready for me. I jumped in head-first. They reminded me, over and over, to breathe.

Alicia from the Mudhoney salon, whom we all called 'Sissy,' bleached my hair totally platinum. Something about the act of bleaching my own hair transcended my life. Alicia is the only person I know who can cut one persons hair, bleach mine, and all the while maintain a perfect dancing rhythm — with sassy red hair and head swishing back and forth, in tandem with her hips to the MC5. At the same time. Oh, this, and pause every few minutes to give her loyal pet beagle a doggy treat. Style? Rock 'n' Roll style. This girl defined it. Shaking, her booty, stirring, every rock star in town.

By contrast, the yoga people wore white. I felt more connected than I had in a long time. I was leery of the whole hippie thing — memories of Dad's big leather hat and apartments that smelled of perfumed incense and had cork walls never left me, along with how sad I had been during that time of my life. But these people seemed harmless, and a nice change from constant clubs and bars and booze and drugs. In fact, it was the first purely physical thing that I was good at. And the mental part — that was a bonus. But the yoga ran in direct conflict with the scene — somehow lighting up a cigarette after all that breathing seemed a sacrilege, as did going on to the club, for another night of all things predictable, and telling everyone how great I felt as I poured beers into my cleaned-out veins with all the denial I could muster. It just wasn't making much sense.

On my thirtieth birthday, August 23rd, 1996, to be exact, the very day Osama Bin Laden issued a jihad against the US, I'd began my first official, event-of-a-lifetime identity crisis. Perhaps it was in the air, all this upheaval. That particular birthday also just so happened to be a SqueezeBox! Friday. Greta encouraged my idea to sing a number with the band to mark the occasion. I had to. I didn't even know if I wanted to be a singer. But I knew I had to do it. Not backup as I'd done several times, me, alone, for three or so minutes. I had no idea what this meant. I wanted energy on that stage, power, fun, rock. So instead of choosing something practical, fun, and within my vocal range... like a Ramones cover or so... I made the pristine decision to try a long, hard ballad to embarrass myself with.

On stage, I sat, ready to be announced, overcome with nerves. It was all over in the longest 3 minutes of my 30 year old life. See, I could have picked something I could've easily sang and had fun with. But I was all caught up in the 'conquer the stage' headspace, and chose to give 'Enter Sandman' by Metallica a try. I didn't even consider that James Hetfield probably could no longer cover himself on that song, let alone me, a lost, unrehearsed amateur. The song wasn't mine, the look wasn't mine. It was fun and all, but not mine. Patrick told me that no matter what you want to do you just have to keep getting up there. Adrienne and Giovanni stood up front and to my left. Gio snapped photos. They both panted until I started, then sighed a relief when I didn't completely choke.

Of course I barely made it through. If it hadn't been for Kevin Brennan singing with me, I would've died right in front of 300 of my closest friends. Adrienne and Giovanni would've died with me. But on many levels, that's what Squeezebox! was all about — a voice and a mic for anyone willing to make an honest try. We'd certainly seen much worse on our stages, but supported right along. That's what you did in those days. We all had a story to tell. As for me, that night I discovered I'd find a different way of telling mine.

After I finished, Misstress, sitting in my usual spot at the side of the stage for the show, jumped up unaware I didn't have the standard 3-song set and yelped 'Oh! That's it!?' and Patrick came up onstage from the other side and said to the crowd 'I just wanna say, if James Hetfield knew that fags were now covering him he'd roll over in his grave!'

The crowd cheered, and I was grateful for the quick diversion from me. But in that split second, as the applause subsided and Misstress prepared for her song, I realized: they accepted me. Bad singing, awkward outfit and all. Nobody died, and people had my back. I could possibly work with this being imperfect thing. I just needed my own medium to work with.

10. Time May Change, Me

7AM. The phone ringer sounded serious. You can just tell. Dad. Grandma Ruby had something wrong. They didn't know what. He said they couldn't get her to go to the doctor. Their church had a doctor that came around. I'd known this church doctor man ever since I was a teenager when my Grandaddy had been sick and then passed away. The man was very nice, but Grandaddy had a doctor in a normal practice as well. Grandma didn't. 'Make her go!' Silence.

A few months later my aunts and uncles were completely worn out from minding shifts with Grandma. It was difficult to get her to talk on the phone — the one thing she'd always done very well. Even after I moved to NYC we'd spend hours talking for as long as we wanted. I felt guilty for not picking up and going down to stay with her. She'd stayed with me when I needed it. I remember as far back as three years old, and Grandma Ruby and Grandaddy coming to visit before Mama and Dad broke up, and Grandma Ruby taking me down to the spare room for a nap after I'd become inconsolable at all the commotion, and she sat with me in the sunlight helping me touch the glistening dust particles in the air with my fingers. Now, years later, it wasn't like I had an incredible career going or anything — I was living the life of the downwardly mobile. But something told me that this time, it just wasn't my place. I stayed with them as a teenager when Grandaddy was sick, and moved in with her after my Dallas burnout. I remember the last time I'd spoken to her before the stroke. She told me to do the right things, be persistent. I didn't catch on at the time.

The year before Grandma had a heart spell. They'd always claimed she had a weak heart. That time, I flew down to see her, but I knew it wasn't anywhere near over. Grandma and I were bonded some way besides the usual — she'd let me know when it was finally time. My Uncle Ronald had been staying with her. I considered taking him a picture of me and Boy George and the club. Maybe even hiding it in the heavy old oak desk drawer.

When I arrived she was in her room, quiet and tired but stable. Uncle Ronald said they didn't know if she'd pull out of it. I knew she would that time. He, on the other hand, was riddled with anxiety. He told me about some big blowup at his work and a fuss with people in his church. He fidgeted in his wooden seat, across from Grandma's feet. The hiss of the oxygen tank never let silence fully master the air. Uncle Ronald's polyester-blend slacks rode up on his legs, revealing his navy-blue nylon socks and bare calves. He looked like my Dad, but a little heavier, a bit older. He had a more definite look about him than Dad did as he mumbled about his work situation. He left room for me to respond — something I was not expecting. Once in a while you get those precious moments when you can just be with the person in front of you, and are no longer uncles, aunts, sons or queers.

They always said that my Grandaddy had 'worried himself to death,' referring to his heart attacks. True enough, I knew him to be obsessively anxious at times, qualities that might befit an artist or designer. Uncle Ronald resembled his father that day, sat in the very room where Grandaddy spent most of his last days. I searched for some words of my younger wisdom for

Uncle Ronald, I told him that as I had it figured, his generation was a group of people who'd forgotten how to believe in themselves. That's why they elected people like Reagan to put on a show for them and then got upset when life didn't come out like 'Ozzie and Harriet' or 'Leave It To Beaver' on TV. He thanked me, the queer who liked Boy George, in earnest for listening. I held back a little concern for my nervous uncle. Something was really rocking his soul.

There was talk of moving Grandma out of her home. My home. Our home. 1643 Medford Drive was one of two consistent addresses throughout my life. I told Dad that if they did she'd be dead in a matter of weeks. She didn't like to stay away from home too long — there were exactly, and only, three reasons in the preceding fifteen years she was what I call 'out at night.' Out to a restaurant once, when we'd forced her — Chinese food at my aunt's former-boyfriend Dick Wing's place, the Hong Kong East; my Aunt Janice's for Christmas Eve a couple of times; and once, when I lived there, she'd let me have a party — a very big deal. Miss Ruby was my first biggest fan.

Determined not to see her moved, I crammed on the internet and telephones trying to find any resources to help get her at-home care. She'd had a day nurse after the heart spell, why not now? I became very aggravated with my father and my family. I didn't want to play the backseat driver, I'd hated it when others did it when I'd cared for Grandaddy, staying up all night giving injections and changing bedpans. Listening to the man cry because he was freezing cold in the middle of summer. So as diplomatically as I could, I fought her being moved. But the powers that be were turned against me and her. Somehow between that church business, not going to the doctor properly and being moved, somebody was resigned to Grandma's downfall. The leader of the yoga center had taught me that 'where the mind goes the body will follow,' and this I believed. It stood to good reason that if everyone around you acts like it's your time to go, well, you just might accept it and go. Not a far stretch if people really die of broken hearts. Truth be told, Grandma Ruby disliked doctors and refused to go get treatment unless absolutely necessary. It could have had something to do with Grandaddy, or the fact that some quack stripped a bunch of veins out of her legs when she was young to treat her anemia, which left her knees and calves swollen. Either way, it's like one of the lyrics Pat wrote, 'so you do what you're told and you swallow your bitter pill...'

I was having none of it. I flew down straight away. Took Adrienne with me. Dad was scared of Adrienne, who never played her trump cards too quickly. We went straight from the airport to Grandma's house. The air inside smelled of stress. She looked like Grandma, but she acted like Grandaddy after his stroke. Daddy gave me the drill of all that was going on. I was ready to jump right in, take a shift, clean something, do anything. But it was clear I wasn't being asked. Part of me hated the helplessness, part of me figured it was OK. As a teenager I'd taken a large responsibility for the care of their father. As a young adult, I'd lived with Grandma and we helped each other in all sorts of ways, some I'll take to the next life.

This was Dad, Uncle Ronald, Aunt Janice and Aunt Susan's to deal with. I felt powerless, but justified. I'd been born early in the family, I was more like a little brother to these people. I took a step back. Adrienne and I took Dad out in the back yard for a talk. I was going to try to see if there was any getting him swayed from moving Grandma. I had my familiar, nauseous feeling in my stomach — the same one I got whenever internet people lied to customers, or Dad, over the years, lied to me. I was convinced that if she got the new stroke medicines and a live-in care worker she'd be fine. She'd taught me to persist. I was persisting. Dad asked me 'Who you think you are coming all the way down here from New York City tellin' us anything.' He tried to country up the accent when he said the name of my hometown. Noo Yerwark Ci-a-dy. Funny how he could pronounce it properly when he'd worked at Calvin Klein, but the guy was stressed and that was all he had. I argued back. He'd run off and married some woman who wouldn't even allow me in their house and had done everything she could to distance my Dad from his family — and moved off to Atlanta, then Texas, then Atlanta, then, God forbid, Tennessee. Hell, I'd been around Charlotte and my Grandma more than he had over the years. Who was he to tell me anything? I hadn't come to pick a fight, but got one. The one we should have had years ago. The one I should have won. The one where I told him what I really thought, without reservation, and got my self-esteem back.

We stared at each other. The anger which veiled the pain in his eyes frightened me. He threw his glass of tea at the ground while looking at me. I'd always suspected he could get physical. Adrienne jumped in to make peace.

Later on I came back over, and suggested that Dad take a drive, get out of the house. He went in and told Grandma he'd be back after a while. 'You not gonna' leave me with him!' she said, looking directly at me, locked on my gaze with a look demanding I read between the lines, I knew all too well. The 'don't say a word' look. The 'go along with it' look. 'That boy ain't fit to sit with me, what if something happens?' Dad laughed, I knew what she was doing. Her voice was shaky, her thought not in line, but no matter what anyone believed, she had control. Even from behind the clouds of a stroke she set me free.

Some weeks later I got word that they all had a talk with Grandma. Asked her what she wanted to do. In fairness, there is no tired like the exhaustion that comes with caring for another person. I still didn't see why they didn't just take out a mortgage on the house and hire full time help, but that isn't ideal either. They said she wouldn't say anything. I can picture her, sitting at her dining-room table, looking at the placemat, arm on one side, pad of her thumb running back and forth across the pads of her fingers. There was no way she'd agree to leave her home. The next day uncle Ronald came and took her down to the old folks' home run by their church. They said he sat and cried uncontrollably on the back porch while my aunts got Grandma's things ready to leave.

A few months later still, me and Adrienne went back to visit her in the nursing home called the Mill House, a converted mill renovated by her church people. She was there with her sister Rachel so at least that was somebody familiar, and to be fair, she'd known most of the people there. The great thing about her church community is they look after their own. She had her own private brick room with big windows in a side wing of the house. She was well cared for, more than I can say for most of the poor old folks in America, but she was out of her element and I think embarrassed for us to see her there. She wore one of the many beautiful dresses she'd made for herself before the stroke.

I went to the house on Medford Drive. Almost everything was gone — someone had scavenged the whole place. I took some remaining furniture, a few pictures that were lying about, and packed them with the incredible guilt I'd amassed over leaving her. As I departed, the walls ached to know where Miss Ruby had gone, and why I wasn't staying.

Back in New York, the city slowly stumbled toward a new millennium. By early 1997, the DNA was hardening on Monica Lewinsky's blue dress, the right wing and the Republicans were doing everything they could to attack Clinton, the evil white horse reared its ugly head even higher, and its hooves hit the scene like asteroids — trampling everyone in site. I'd thought the nostalgia for the diabolical white powder had gone to the grave with Steve Rubell and Bianca Jagger's stallion, but was so very wrong. One night, I stood in the back of Don's watching people digging at their noses while exiting the bathroom. The beginning of the end, I thought, over and over. I'd watched cocaine ruin so many friends and so many scenes I didn't care to count. That drug in particular steals the center of any situation. The guts. Rock 'n' Roll requires guts, and soul. Some of our most exquisite drag queens turned to lip-chewing, teeth-grinding sideshow gimps. It seemed like everyone was jumping on the lily-white snowmobile. Some went off the deep end. Walking zombies. But then again, I dabbled for a month or two while I was working on becoming the town drunk. None of it worked.

Apparently Patrick had broken his sobriety by starting to take pain pills for back problems on Lollapalooza. He told me he needed them because he'd injured his neck diving backwards into the drum kit on the last number of every show. 'Why do you have to drum-dive every show then?' I asked, menacingly. One afternoon I walked into Don's because Patrick had called me to come down, despite my protests. Some band was on something or other. I found him sitting at the bar with a martini glass. 'Uh, Pat, what are you doing?' I griped. 'Having a drink,' he countered. So much for things holding together. He stared into his glass as if squaring off with a dear old demon, which frightened me.

As time had passed, John Cameron Mitchell had quietly perfected his new play, Hedwig, and had enjoyed a successful run at the Westbeth Theatre in the West Village. Schmidt booked Hedwig for one of the drag slots. Every week I sat on the side of the stage with Patrick and Misstress during the shows. I wanted to be on stage, but I couldn't sing, except a few backups here and there. I wasn't a drag queen. I was press, production and computer dude. I didn't have anything of my own.

The coke dealers and their crowd nauseated me like LA-style pariahs. I didn't know any of them from the early days, although they acted like they'd been there from the start. Johnny-come-lately charlatans. They don't blend, they just show up and assume. They tried to get Carl to throw people out at their beck and call. They thought of themselves as big, important people carrying their little plastic bags of hate-powder. They menaced and harassed people and mostly got away with it.

They bullied Alicia from Mudhoney which angered me a lot — none of the people involved were from the old neighborhoods like her, came every week to support us like her, or were even remotely interesting like her, and the atmosphere began to take on a distinctly vapid, Hollywood overtone. One night I flopped myself on the bar right in the middle of their little gaggle, in the same spot I'd done for years, in the middle of their drinks and purses. Like a bunch of immature teenagers, they ran right to get Carl to tell on me, and one tall bitch dragged him over to get him to throw me out — something I hadn't yet realized was their latest pastime. I'll never forget seeing Carl come through, looking down patiently as he listened to the chick telling him whatever, and then he looked up as she pointed my way and said 'him!' The look on his face was priceless, deer in headlights. 'Ohhhh no!' he said out loud. We looked at each other and started laughing, and I sat and gloated in the faces of the nobody patrol, and sat in the middle of their little ego party and had a nice long chat with my friend Carl. Stupid fucking loser nobody hipsters. And if it had been a year earlier I would have gotten Don to ban them once and for all. But I didn't feel good about any of it. We had the world at our feet and had started to forget what to do with it. Stupid fucking me. Little did I realize that these irrelevant people with irrelevant, uninteresting lives would eventually take over our town. Everyone started losing.

Things kept getting uglier. One night, Adrienne passed out in the middle of the room by the back double doors from heat and too much drink. Schmidt grabbed me off the side of the stage during the show 'something's happened to Adrienne!' and I climbed over people in the crowd with my combat boots to get out to the back doors. Carl held her while she came to. I was on my way to the corner phone to dial 911 when I heard her scream 'Dammit I just got hot, don't call nobody' in her raucous Southern accent, the one we didn't use in the city. I sent her home in a cab. I'm pretty sure somebody had GHB'd her drink. Roofied, knockout drops — whatever — someone deliberately slipping drugs in your cocktail so you will fall on your ass. The same kind of thing happened to Schmidt a week or so later. Patrick and I hid him in the basement office until closing. Lisa, Pat and I drove him home and put him to bed in his black boots and blue jeans. Another time someone, from what I gathered, came close to sexually assaulting Adrienne right there by our bar stand, and whoever it was is very lucky she chose not to tell me his name. I'm very lucky she kept the secret, because I was becoming very frustrated, and looking for someone to take it out on, and I don't mean with words.

To me, the whole fucking place was becoming a mess. I worried about Schmidt and whatever he might be doing. Pat was partying. I was a binge boozehound. On yet another night, someone had given me a joint. I'd been asked if I wanted 'some,' but nobody got around to tellin' me that 'some' probably included heroin. Or angel dust. Being a lightweight anyway, I stumbled down the stairs, double vision, flopped in a seat next to Greta and Duard, the Squeezebox! drummer. Greta had not been working with Debbie because after the internet show, coincidentally,

Debbie and Chris went to work putting Blondie back together. So, Greta had taken Jack Steeb's place in the SqueezeBox! band playing bass. Jack had disappeared off the scene, hanging with John Cameron Mitchell while they put 'Hedwig and the Angry Inch' together at the Jane Street Theatre. Greta and Duard had started dating and opened a leather clothing business. One time I was fucked up beyond belief and must have said some nasty things to Greta and Duard. They were justifiably furious with me, and I regret it because these were two of a very few who'd encouraged me to get something together for myself. They'd let me rehearse with the band. Greta told me I had a singer inside me. You cannot buy that kind of creative devotion. I think it's called love. They pushed me toward something. But I didn't have a clue or know what that something could be. I needed to know.

Greta and Duard had made me fancy leather clothes and kept me all pretty. Black leather jeans, silver leather pants. Studded belts for my waist, studded crosses for my arms. They kept my outsides up to par. I needed to keep trying to fill the insides. I should have been trademarking the name, opening the SqueezeBox! record label, opening clubs from LA to Montreal to London. But like Schmidt, my life, the scene, the booze, the coke, the drama, got in the way. Now I was pushing away the few people I could trust.

One night while the show was on, I was standing at my usual spot by the back bar — the best spot in the house for the stage view. I'd done a couple of lines in the bathroom. I never really liked the high cocaine gave me. Jittery, hyper, pensive, depressed. I'd ordered a few shots of Jägermeister from the bar. It gave me a false sense of connection, like the first night Michael Alig shoved a bottle of it in my face. I was bored. Bored and sad, and didn't know what to do. A drag queen friend wandered next to me, laughed, then sighed and said, 'I just feel like a pig in a wig,' and then went on 'but you're a genius and look what you're doing with it.'

Schmidt and I'd stopped talking as much as we had in the past. Everything went from exciting to necessary and regimented. We fought a lot about getting things done, keeping the club going — things we'd relished in doing together previously. The money wasn't pouring in like the first few years. Another reality set in. He'd always said 'Everything's cyclical' but never made plans to deal with the ugly hand of monotony.

My internet company fell to pieces. So did I. In a private strategy meeting, the investors discovered mathematically, that there was no way the computer servers that the crap.conmen supplied down in Washington could do what they swore they could do. I was devastated, and frightened. One was a bigwig with a Fortune 5 outfit, the people who made the entire backbone of the net. A few of the investors had Tahoe connections. You don't fuck with Tahoe. Or connections. I'd almost made the mistake of vouching for the line of bullshit that had been thrown, but my gut instinct told me not to. Thank God, for once, I listened. Even though I wanted things to work real bad, I wasn't about to take the fall for two-faced computer nerds, the type of people I started to loathe because I was beginning to see, merely by way of their unique skills, what the world was ready to allow them to get away with.

The Kid was still coming around from time to time. I didn't like being alone. I guess I felt safer when he'd get high and sit up all night and play on my computer and watch me sleep. He came over and helped me clean out the remains of my office. It was one of the worst experiences of my young life. I'd been forced to fire two loyal employees. One girl, Cheryl Compton, a dear friend from the East Village and a veteran of the film industry, who'd tried to help us get things going. She cried. She, too, saw the potential. It broke my heart.

What did I learn? That being first doesn't get you paid and doesn't make you win, it just makes you first. I saw a world, finally, where, if we could have turned out a few more events like the one with Debbie, we could have blown the whole nasty American media machine wide open. We could have had real talent, fresh talent, people who believed in their dreams singing and dancing and talking their way around the world. But everyone, from the greedy record execs to my two partners, conspired to make sure these dreams would never be realized. I despised all the crap.conmen because most were conspicuous bullshit artists, not even good ones at that, fabricating the story as they went along. We even tried to get some money-partners to offer them a lump sum to buy them out, but like the little toddlers they truly were, they were more interested in their egos than success. They could have taken the cash for that broken lump of an operation, and wasted it all the same by joining the legions of new startups, or shoving it up their asses for all I cared. Instead, after being tipped off by one of their patsies, they came in and fired everyone, Adrienne included. She responded by accidentally deleting their entire accounting system file in a panic, which probably only helped them cover more of their shenanigans from the IRS. In any case, it was over.

The Kid pushed the cart. I followed, watching my career and dated computer equipment going down Spring Street — career didn't pay, equipment didn't work, boy wouldn't put out. We stored the equipment in Don's basement and went across the street to the Ear Inn. It was owned by a friend of Don's and our club. I got on well with the guys in there — all from Ireland. They fronted me a bottle of scotch. I sat outside with the Kid at the wooden spool table that was held together with rusty bolts, and drank it.

11. I'll Be Seeing You

Fall 1997, or so. In the days following my first internet collapse I filed for unemployment. Full circle. At least I still had the club, but things there had become more hectic. Pat was turning angry. He'd signed a bad record deal. The record label wouldn't provide proper promotions, Marilyn Manson had his look. Schmidt became reclusive. He moved into another apartment across the hall from Debbie and painted the walls black with silver criss-crosses and candles everywhere. It was smaller, but had a better view of downtown, you could see the World Trade Center and everything in between.

We should have gotten out of our ruts a little more. While we were suffering the effects of several years of a hot scene, plenty of our friends had hot scenes of their own. Justin Bond and Mo Fischer ignited the East Village in a little former bakery on Avenue B called 'Cake.' And they were packin-'em in as good as we were. Justin started a successful lounge act, 'Kiki and Herb,' with Kenny Mellman at a restaurant-turned nightspot on Second Avenue called Flamingo East, oddly enough, owned by a friend of Barney's. Little did anybody know that Kiki would go all the way to Carnegie Hall and back. Mo, who also did a drag king character called 'Mo B. Dick' would find her way from the East Village stages to John Waters' film 'Pecker' and back. Little had I begun to realize that I might play too, but differently.

Soon I got a call from Dad that Grandma Ruby wasn't doing well. She'd taken to her bed. I could feel something was up. She was calling for me, a sense thing. Just like when I lived with her and she'd think to tell me something and before she ever said a word I would go to her and ask what she wanted. The first couple of times we felt funny but then took these little extrasensory experiences as a matter of course. Same with when she'd talk about Grandaddy in a sublime moment. How she heard him walking the hallways like he did when he was sick and stayed up all night and played tricks on me like sneaking in my room and setting the clock ahead.

Another early morning the phone rang and Dad told me they didn't know how long. Grandma had stopped talking since the day before. Something happened and Dad called the ambulance and had her taken to the hospital. They were making her comfortable. I told him to put the phone to her ear 'cause I knew she'd hear me. I talked to her for a minute. I told her thanks for trying to get me to stop worrying about what other people thought of me. Then I went and woke Adrienne up and got her to talk to her too. I know how these things go. Billy just disappeared, as did Marty Lipton and a whole bunch of other people. You better take the time when you've got the time — no shame in it. Just as Dad took the receiver away from her ear, she said my name out loud.

I got on the phone and found a cheap air fare. It was time to go. Dad told me they didn't know whether she'd last a week or a day. I knew. Dammit, I knew. 'It'll change you. It'll change everything,' someone told me. I called Schmidt and told him to handle things while I was gone. He was surprisingly more supportive than in recent months, perked up, encouraged me as the occasion required, as he had when we first started the club.

When I got to LaGuardia I had time for a double scotch. Got

on the plane. Ordered another, and another. The cabin crew reminded me of the crew when I first flew up to the city when I was sixteen. One tall, thin black woman was the only one who took care of me. I had a seat in an empty part of the plane. I sat there and let the tears run down, mixing with the acrid whiskey — salt, alcohol, a taste I'd become very used to. Life was catching me, no matter how fast I ran.

I thought about how I'd run away so long ago. I thought about my birthdays when I lived with Grandma. I got off from work that day. I got up to a full Southern breakfast: grits, fresh baked biscuits, country ham, eggs and on and on. Grandma made a big fuss over me all day. 'Anything you want for lunch! You got a phone call! Your mama and them's here! Your daddy's on the phone! You got a package in there!' If you didn't have fun she'd have it for you. She'd done much the same thing every year at Christmas, when I'd ride my bike over after school — lookin' for Dad's Christmas-in-a-box to come from the postman. Sometimes it would take extra days to get there. On those days I got vanilla ice cream.

Dad and some relative-in-law I don't think I'd ever met picked me up at the airport. Dad looked like a stunned little boy when he reached out to hug me. The relative drove fast from the airport. They both briskly walked me into the new facility, which had an air that comes with places which hadn't yet established a routine of life and death. I felt like a secret agent or something. Dad told me folks were ready to go home and such, that they'd been there all day. He asked me if I would be OK if something happened that night. 'That's why I'm here.'

The rings come next. At this point, you're bouncing harder than ever. The coffee, Goody powders and nicotine are at full strength, pulsing through your circulatory corridors. You pull the solid-silver celtic dragon on your left pinkie — protection. The silver cross with inlaid turquoise fits on the left ring finger — married to God. The one with the gospel carvings never leaves the right thumb — summoning ancestral spirits.

January 1999. I looked into the face of my grandmother as she lay on her deathbed. We were alone in the brand spanking new hospital room, which still contained the smell of plastic builder's wrapping and fresh sheetrock. Gypsum was such a trite discovery. Color had left her face, the blue was creeping into her feet and up her legs — true signs that this life was coming to a close. All of my cousins, my aunts and uncles, my father had left me to do my job. I felt like the Angel of Death, because I've been through this process so many times. I do not fear it, I never have. It actually intrigues me. The process is a new frontier in my opinion. My grandmother had been many things to me: extra mother, teacher, best friend, debate partner, ally, companion — why shouldn't I be intrigued? She unquestionably encouraged every single one of my intrigues in life. Now, she lay there, clearly speaking without motion. She had waited for me. No conversation necessary. I had to sign the do-not-resuscitate forms, which Grandma thanked me for because she was very tired. I could feel it. I sent the nurses away when they came to take more blood. Grandma taught me how to send the nurses away when she and I helped Grandaddy. My family — Uncle Ronald and all of his children, others — all left when I arrived, which I found bizarre.

These people never left me alone, and this was the one time I kinda wanted them around. I was completely alone with her, except for my Uncle Bill, whom I liked although he was a Republican. Grandma liked him too. He was an old-school Republican — not one of those new Neocon bastards.

Uncle Bill had originally left with all the others — aunts, cousins, Dad, in-laws I didn't know or recognize — but he came back and popped his head in the door and told me he figured this was too much to leave with a 'young boy' — he'd be in the waiting room just down the hall. He could call me a boy 'cause I was just thirty or so and he was over sixty. I'd forgotten how it felt to be called young.

The scotch on the plane got to my head, had made me tired. I nodded off. I timed my attention to her gaspy breathing and willed myself to wake up with any change. 'So, it's come to this,' I thought. Johnny Carson said that on his last night on television. I remembered because when I was a kid I used to sneak and watch 'The Tonight Show' at Grandma's — she kept a TV hidden in a closet just to watch the news.

'Haup, hap, haup,' her labored inhalations continued. In my restlessness I imagined I could have been wrong about the timing, miscalculated, when suddenly I found myself beside her bed with no explanation of how I'd gotten there. I felt like she had already left her body and was in the room with me. She had snatched me up and flung me to the bedside, to go through the motions. Some monitors began to alarm, and in came the nurses. I told them not to touch her, please. They began to disconnect the cables and cords to my satisfaction. Grandma's body was still delivering beats from her heart. I shouted across the corridor to get my Uncle Bill who was resting in the waiting room. He bounced across the hallway and into the room, grabbed the telephone and began to call relatives. After finishing his calls, he took the opposite side of her bed, and Grandma's hand.

I watched her face as the blue crept through it like the lights on the final moments of an opera. One large vessel in her neck would pulse occasionally, which became the focus for my uncle. Funny, how the heart they'd always claimed was weak had become her bodily champion in the end — it just refused to quit.

Uncle Bill and I started talking to her. 'Hold on, grandmother. They're coming,' my uncle said, referring to her children he'd called who were rushing to her bedside.

'Go. Go ahead. It's OK. Let go,' I interjected, at my turn.

'Hold on.'

'Go ahead.'

'Hold on.'

'Go ahead.'

'Hold on.'

'Go ahead.'

Soon Uncle Ronald, Aunt Diane, my Dad, Aunt Janice and Aunt Susan came running in the room, in that order. The instant Susan arrived, the heart went still. I remember my Dad looking at me with a terrified, little boy expression.

I got up and left the room to go out of doors and get some fresh air. It was 5AM and the sky was turning an ugly suburban crimson. I had come, done my job, and now I was ready to leave, although I was destined to spend the rest of the day going through all of the rituals of death. Someone suggested we go down and eat breakfast — the first time in a long time all of us had been at the same table.

Their familiar conversation frightened me terribly, but that was one of the merciful lessons of elders: grandmother died, not us. It was as macabre as it was sensible. Surreal as anything to do with any theatrical 'scene.' She was with us. Breakfast: do what you know when you don't know what to do. And that's when it began to occur to me: this thing, what some call 'liminal' place, a suspended reality that is used in performance — but it had been there all along, right in front of me as well — this contract we make with life; and absolutely applied, if not moreso, to everyday life as any stage, fiction not required.

Half of me was at that table with my family, toast and eggs. I'd done what I'd come to do. The other half just wanted to run, again.

12. Missing

We showed up at the church that very afternoon. I was completely exhausted. I'd gotten into a fuss, again, with Uncle Ronald because they all believed in same-day burials, but I had to get my sister down there. I thought there'd have been a day's grace at least. But he was determined.

Besides taking on the government, one other thing I'll give Grandma Ruby's church is the way they keep to themselves and work to keep themselves. Almost Amish in some respects. Like most Americans, plenty of them believed the Puritan myth and the Thanksgiving myth — they came for religious freedom and brotherhood with the Indians. Yeah. A bunch of apocalyptic fascists maybe. At least they were pacifists when it came to war. I also remember Grandma bragging on them when a member who was also a woodworker decided to make the coffins by hand. 'Just as fine a piece of work as you could buy — better in fact...' she'd say. Other members pitched in and did the funerals. Grandma liked that too. She and I'd agreed over and over that Grandaddy's two-thousand-dollar, three-day funeral cost too much and ran two days too long.

So it didn't bother me when I arrived and the little man apologized for having to use a bit of tape on her eyelids to keep them shut. I knew Grandma would have found it practical.

I'd always considered death a doorway even before I met any Buddhists or Swamis. Instinctively, I knew it as a transformation. A lot of folks think of it as the ultimate end. And then some nasty judgment follows — God sits up like our mean high school principals and condemns us, except for the few perfect ones. And they're wrong. I know they're wrong 'cause if they were right they wouldn't have to scare people and make them feel bad about themselves. They would use fire to ignite people's passions instead of having it fall from the sky like in superhero cartoons. And if they weren't very wrong, people like the reverend Tricky Dick wouldn't have the need to stand over my Grandma's grave and say: 'Well, we don't know where she went. We'd like to believe a good place, but we have no way of knowing. That's between her and the Lord,' which he mispronounced 'lard.' I think people like him mispronounce certain words on purpose so they'll sink in better — and we sit back and grin at the simple *faux pas*, while simultaneously every syllable etches itself into our brains. Who needs brainwash drugs?

The reverend stared straight at me when he shot his words at our grieving family. I seriously considered throwing my chair at him. I wanted a fight, but thought of my Grandma calling across the wind. It doesn't matter, it doesn't matter. And she was right. It didn't matter. He was talkin' from what he knew. Fear-monger. To me, just like all the other mongers — Giuliani, Hitler, the Puritans... I once heard a Lakota Indian once say — 'Religion is for people afraid of going to hell, spirituality is for people who've been there.' And because of Grandma's great, great, great grandmother, the Cherokee blood boiled inside my veins.

Later, the family was led back into a community building, where the entire congregation had brought prepared food. I never understood why people want to eat at such a time, but we do. That's the mind fuck about the conservative right wing, you find a lot of good people trapped inside it. Fine people. If it weren't for queers and abortion and the apocalypse, they wouldn't need the scary reverends of the world. Yet again, as time passes, I see value in a world where children aren't addicted to sugar, phones and shopping.

I stayed behind at the graveside. I always stay behind. The boys lowered her, put on the cover — all stressed out because I was watching every move. The reverend was nearby, directing. There, I just stood, talking to Grandma's best friend Mildred to my left, watching them fill in the grave just three feet ahead on my right. One blond-haired boy kept looking back at me after finishing a segment of his tasks. He must have been around sixteen or so. His expression sought approval, acceptance, as if to show me the care he was taking. As if to say 'See, everything is going perfectly.' I've since learned to appreciate the angels in our midst. Grandma'd always bragged on those boys, how conscientious they'd been at other funerals, the loyal worker bees.

Soon all the others retreated, and me and the blond boy were the only ones left. He placed each piece of sod back in place, then joined the edges with a little water. Finally, he brushed the remnants of crumbly red earth away from the plot, as if we'd never even been there. Life to ashes to dust. And back.

13. Reprise

Holding Grandma's hand as she left one world for the next had transformed me. I'd not been able to shake the tingling feeling. Didn't really try. My nose felt a permanent, menthol, strange kind of open. The air back in New York was a satisfyingly familiar irritation to my nostrils. My eyes felt like the first time I went to an optician, who put that big contraption on my face and with a click or two: I could see better.

But, I didn't know where to go.

14. Smiling Faces

Late spring, 1999. I start arriving at the club later and later each week. The sheer repetition of my life wore on me — work, out at night, drink, sleep, work. My own little rut on top of the world. Unemployment money ran out long before, I was living on freelance, diner food and the club. People in the scene became more petty — childish turf wars continued. The coke drama filled the air. I was doing some, hell, everybody was. A nice slip into denial. What was once interesting conversation, artistic energy and creative juice turned to jittery lip-biting. I didn't want to talk to anyone, I would just stand at the back after doing a few lines and down shots of Jägermeister, surrounded by people whoring free drinks out of me. I'd started a shot count for myself and I tried each week to do one more than the week before — the same liquid heroin Alig had given me on my first real night out in the city. And each week, I got just as sick as I'd been on that long D-train ride back to Brooklyn. Mornings filled with nasty yellow bile, body exhausted from the wrenching stomach, finally, the ability to rest.

Patrick stopped being my friend for a time. I'd invited an investor around to talk to Don about possibly doing a night of some sort. Don pushed me toward taking Saturdays, which Pat had a retro night of his own booked into. I never asked Don for

Saturdays, nor did I want it; he just put me in. Justifiably, Patrick went ballistic, calling me on the phone and swearing out every speck of anger he had on me. The tour, the bad record deal, pain killers. I never hated him for it though. I knew we were all undoing each other — it was part of the natural process. The building of an original idea is the exciting part, the getting ready. After, the clock of the world starts ticking, awaiting demise. I think that's why we all worshipped the likes of Blondie, Bowie and George. One way or another, time takes a cigarette — but you and me, we know we got nothin' but time.

And times got weirder, and in my mind I became a bystander, an audience member and witness to the movie in which I was starring, and which played out in front of me at the same time.

I remember one night Adrienne, Stevin Azo and me went to the old Trammps Club for a crazy bill of Vaginal Creme Davis, Miss Guy and the Toilet Boys, and headlined by one of the greatest performance art bands ever, The Voluptuous Horror of Karen Black. It was a weird night — Trammps was not a traditionally mixed place, so the air in the room was hostile, but this also provides an edge. Nobody messed with Vag, doing a set dressed in an army uniform covering her almost seven foot tall, massive black frame. Guy's set was fun until he misjudged the poorly marked edge of the stage and fell flat forward into the crowd. Luckily, he got right back up and kept singing.

When T.V.H.O.K.B. came on the crowd got rowdy. I usually loved to mosh, but this particular crowd — probably comprised of a bunch of loser yuppies — just wanted to fight for space. As Kembra, the lead singer, came on and did songs intended to bring attention to the plight of women and feminism, two girls at the very front, who'd apparently been at-it for a while, began to fight and grabbed large chunks of each other's hair, and stood like that, pushing back and forth. The crowd became more and more violent, not my thing, and I pushed out the back, until I noticed Vaginal had demanded her space in front of the stage. I made my way over and danced in front of her, under her arms, protected from weekend warriors. I didn't get it, and kept not getting it.

Another night I attended a party at either Linda Simpson's house or around the corner at our friend Joelle's house. In any case both were there, as was RuPaul, who Joelle had begun working with. At whatever point the party folded, an early affair as I recall, and we all made our way to Second Avenue to hail taxis to the next stop. As the grouping turned out, I was left with Joelle and Ru and two others. Ru stood up, hand at least eight feet in the air, and empty taxis kept whizzing by. At first I paid no mind, until Ru turned around and exclaimed 'a black man still can't get a cab in New York City.' One of us obliged. I'd never seen such a thing first hand, like that.

Don't get me wrong. On the surface life hummed by. I don't know if the world had become more fucked up, or I'd just started paying more attention. As for the club, anyone walking into SqueezeBox! in those days for the first time would've found it as dumbfoundingly outrageously amazing as I had. They just didn't have to come every week, work it, be it. If I'd been emotionally mature enough and not been on the go–out–booze–get–laid–recover hamster wheel, I would have found a way to turn that place into an empire. It was all a mess, but maybe that's exactly what it was meant to be, nothing more, nothing less.

15. Another One Bites the Dust

Sometimes I'd go out and hang with Mike Potter and Justin Bond at the Cake parties on Avenue B. Mike wore black patent leather outfits and a huge blonde wig and called himself Emmanuel Labor. Justin was a natural, almost like a mythic hermaphrodite, pretty as a boy, pretty as a girl. Justin got off on taking boys in the bathroom and photographing their dicks, which he then put in a contest at the end of the night. He has one of mine.

I fell in love. Justin came to Spring Street to meet me for lunch at the Ear Inn. He had his own long, blond hair; long, tan, suede coat with wool collar and clear violet 70s sunglasses.

If Justin had been single, and I the least bit capable of handling it…well… Instead I kept a string of drinkers and party boys going in and out of my personal space. One would come, another would leave. They all played tricks. I pretended I needed trickery. I didn't possess the confidence to have relationships that weren't sordid, episodic, manipulative. A product of living what you think is close to your end. I wasn't ready for a Justin; he could have been a beginning, but surely a rollercoaster in his own right.

Betty Badum had returned to New York the preceding summer after a long stay in Europe. He'd sold the 2nd Avenue apartment before he left, and taken to living abroad. The grapevine reported that he'd become a loathsome houseguest from London to Lisbon. Marcus Leatherdale told me he had to keep Betty from making his housekeeper-boy wash his feet — apparently in India, boys who do so are either to be immediately married to the person or stoned to death or something. They worked something out eventually.

Betty was house-surfing with this-designer and that-person. He'd changed a bit since I'd known him previously; his airs had become as large as his head. Nonetheless, he was still good ole' Aunt Betty to me.

He'd become close friends with Jimmy James. They ran around town in Betty's black Volvo, the same one we'd taken to DC. Jimmy had weekly gigs on Christopher Street at a club called Pieces. I was doing Jimmy's artwork, posters and CD covers. I went to the shows regularly, and kept a standing table reservation. Betty came every week and shared the seats.

One week Betty brought in a person he unceremoniously announced to the table as his new lover. A tall, intimidating young man he'd met in Morocco, with large facial features and bushy eyebrows. They sat together. Betty cooed, the Moroccan didn't stop him.

A few weeks later they both came in again, but didn't sit beside each other. The Moroccan sat beside me and didn't drink or talk or move. A few weeks later still, Betty came alone. Jimmy had told me of troubles in Moroccan paradise. Just to be cruel, he put 'Over the Rainbow' in the lineup, done in Judy Garland voice. Betty ran out of the club crying.

Adrienne planned an Easter lunch at Cowgirl Hall of Fame on Hudson Street. We'd been Cowgirl regulars for years. I invited Jimmy and Betty. Jimmy showed up in his usual sweatpants and parka AARP style lounge outfit. Betty had on some designer flowing black sweater. Something was amiss with Betty, as he turned his snippy, shallow side on and directed it at me, things like: 'Well, well, still an urchin. Do you have a job?'

Responses like: 'Nice to see you too, Aunt Old.'

'Oh, original as usual. How delightful you are.'

Betty made a yawning gesture and a fake giggle at Jimmy. I knew Betty well enough to know that something bad was eating at him. I pretended to play along in my B-list role, although I'd started the day eager to see Aunt Betty again. He sat beside me at the table, acting like a defensive school child. Jimmy complied, as if they had some inside secret. Betty's black sweater pocket flopped open beside me as we ate. Inside I could see his credit cards and some money. After a few more shallow insults, I think 'Fuck her, bitch gonna' sit here and act like an ass to me on Easter...' It wasn't the insults disguised as joking that bothered me, it was the teasing from a place of unfamiliarity — like we'd never been to DC together, or spent hours in that old apartment, or that I'd not once been high enough on the list to come to his B party. To deny someone is the cruelest sin. I reached in when he wasn't looking and stole the money. Twenty dollars total. Jimmy and him had a hushed chat about getting the bill paid. I considered fessin' up and paying him back, but they just kept smart-assing up Hudson Street, so I paused.

A month or so later, Jimmy had a birthday party at Penang restaurant in Soho. His friend Bhan ran the place. It was a great space, a pillar of Soho's restaurant scene that has since fallen to the axe of the greedy landlord. Jimmy's mom flew in for the event. Aunt Betty came. Some other random friends of Jimmy's came. We took up the biggest round party table in the back room. I hadn't eaten out at a restaurant with Betty since our DC trip years earlier. Betty was acting weird again, and uncharacteristically swiggin' back the whiskey. He kept yelling 'Wet nurse, wet nurse!' at the waitress, while holding his wrists limp and giggling, wanting her to bring him more. I thought Betty was losing it. Very anxiously he chattered through the meal. Drink after drink came for him.

After the main course, most of us went up to the front for a smoke. Jimmy had friends coming in and out and was preoccupied. Betty came rumbling up to the bar beside me. I thought about giving him his twenty bucks back. He asked me for a cigarette — Betty never smoked. He acted troubled. Jimmy had filled me in that Betty had pulled some strings in Washington to get the Moroccan guy into the country legally, and once he got here, the guy turned mean. Betty got him a place to stay upstate and paid his tuition for college, but the guy wasn't happy and started being abusive. I don't think Betty fully realized he was being hustled by one of the best. He stalked Betty from place to place, in and out of the city. Some said he was trying to beat Betty up. As he clumsily puffed the cigarette, I cautiously offered: 'Ya know John, er Betty, if you ever want to talk, hang out, shoot the shit like we used to…'

'Oh honey, thanks. But this is big. This is 'bigger' than big. Bigger than you and me put together.' I just let it go. He was drunk, acting weirder than even the usual high-drama he was capable of. Maybe it really was something big.

A few nights later on Memorial Day I got a phone call from Jimmy. He was in hysterics — inconsolable. The Moroccan had broken into Betty's sister's apartment upstate where Betty was hiding. He had a huge knife and a meat cleaver. He'd tried to kill the sister while she dialed 911. He stabbed her a few times but she got away. Betty wasn't so lucky. Hacked over and over all over his body with a meat cleaver, left to die in a pool of blood. They said he probably didn't die immediately. The Moroccan ran out of the house, onto the highway, and into an oncoming truck. He was killed instantly. Some say suicide. I don't really believe it. I'd sat next to the cold bastard. Others say that the guy wasn't even a fag — that they go with queers to make it out of the country, then extort money from them. All I know is that Betty was dead and I owed him twenty bucks. And I wasn't invited to the memorial party all the top designers threw at some fancy hotel in midtown. Still B list and happy to be there.

16. Save Me

SqueezeBox! kept going. So did I, spending daytime consulting for yet another internet startup company. At least this one had computers that worked and the paychecks wouldn't bounce. I'd long tired of the work though — bitchy clients, attitudes, haggling. Advertising as a whole is one of the most un-creative, self-destructive industries on the planet, and is helping our planet self-destruct. It's all about lies. Everyone burns out except the agency owners who can afford weekend sabbaticals. Same crap I'd found at Macy's, or even Sotheby's to some extent — Robert Woolley got to be the big antique-dealer homo-about-town. We got to work for nineteen-five a year and say we'd been employed by Woolley and Alfred Taubman. It got me places. 'It' always gets me to lots and lots of places. Really. No, really. If I listed all the advertising agencies I'd ever worked for you'd have the Yellow Pages of Madison Avenue and then some. From the Saatchi's up the street from the club, over to Peter Arnell's place in Soho and straight up Madison Avenue.

By summer 1999, if I'd lined up every Friday SqueezeBox! night back to back I could've filled an entire calendar year. Practically one whole year of my life had been spent at 511 Greenwich Street, watching bands, making out with pretty boys and hot supermodels. Stumbling out, loaded with money. Falling into a cab. By then I could count the exact wait times at each stop light. Spring and Sixth Ave. Sixth Avenue and Houston. The drive across Houston, and my fantasies of ripping down all the hideous mile-high billboards that covered every inch of free space. Especially the DKNY one. I'd been to a party on the top floor of that DKNY building. I envisioned going back with a group of people and hundreds of gallons of paint, climbing on the roof, and carefully pouring each bucket over the edge to run like a cancer over the face of the tacky, building-sized billboards.

The age of the corporation had slammed into New York like a tidal wave. Giuliani had weakened all resistance with an intoxicating 'quality of life' campaign — the Statue of Liberty his lone Siren. My New York was disappearing before my red, swollen eyes. First my friends, now the city. To cope, I started going out almost every single night, and of course Squeeze on Fridays. The days when Schmidt and I made magic on his computer were long gone. I missed that.

I was suffering from the other side of the new New York state of mind. Booze only got you drunk and cocaine only kept you up to be drunk — all of it useless. Seemed like everybody had psychologists, psychiatrists, pills and shrinks. It's like reaching for a cube of ice that burns your fingers, or speaking and no sound coming out — those bad, terrible nightmares you fear as a child. Life melting all around you, and not a damned thing you can do about it. You envy the thick, stupid ones who are able to just stay high through it all, or ignore it altogether.

As the glum slowly drowns you, the nerves set in. You can't sleep because the anxiety surges up from your middle as if you were connected to a TENS electro unit, so you go out trying to run away, only to thicken the glum with more chemicals or booze to ease the shock. The vicious cycle goes on as long as you are happy being married to the real devil. Once or twice a week you see your shrink and cry your eyes out and feel a little better. Then your shrink asks you to come more often, to make more progress, which means you have to find a way to get out of bed more, to go to work more, so you can make more money to pay her, so you can come to her more, and feel better more. I've never been so frightened in my life. So unsure, so lost. And I couldn't look to the 'old crowd' for a lot either, Kenny Scharf and others from Haoui's extended family had been moving to Miami, and it began to be proclaimed as the new creative Mecca. Jorgé even went down for a while. People were searching, I was confused.

I had no idea who to trust. There was a good chance that any friend I made would drop dead. There was a better chance that my neighborhood would fall under the rent hammer. There was every chance that at every turn I'd run into the trust-fund jackals that were invading the city from every bridge, tunnel and waterway. I built up more resentment than a rooster that'd just been hit with a water hose, and because of this, the few steady friends I had began to tire of me. I was tired of me. Depression is a vicious, nasty trap. You have to act like a victim to get empathy, then when you try your best to let out the rage, no one wants to be around a victim. Truth was, I'd built up a base for a lot of this stuff pre-Big Apple. Can't blame everything on Gotham.

So what's to do? Just keep going, somehow. Get out of bed, make some money, see your shrink, repeat. A good time mercifully sneaks its way in between sad and sick every once and a while, giving hope that an answer lies out there, somewhere. Once I got a call from my old friend Giovanni, who I'd lost regular touch with. After chatting for a bit, he interrupted my thinly veiled attempts at a front with 'When are you going to do something beside all these robotics?' to which I became defensive, angry, and confused, finally arriving at a defeated 'I don't know.'

And I didn't know or feel or anything. So I just kept going, actually believing that the scene, the people, the New York would somehow save me. Save us. It had to. In that state, there was nowhere else to go, so I scraped my fingernails holding on desperately to the chalkboard sidewalks of New York, as they slowly slipped away.

17. Mama Said There'd Be Days (Like That)…

Around the holidays, my Dad came to visit. Adrienne and me got excited, like we used to when we were little kids. He'd gotten a new job which required him to travel to New York, like when he was with Calvin Klein. There's no question of my Dad loving us — he tried and tried and tried as best he could. He just didn't have the word 'father' in him, I don't think. Neither had his father, I don't think. One summer, when I was about twelve, Daddy took Adrienne and me on a trip. He rented a camper and we drove all through North Carolina and Virginia. I think Dad had as much fun as either of us. He frightened me. If I accepted too much, would he leave again? The first summer I was living in Brooklyn, Dad came up for Pride. That frightened me. Supportive, but unusual. Even my Grandaddy was known as an eccentric, moody, unpredictable type. It must run in the family.

We took my Dad out all over town the first night. Fighting through the crowd for a table at Virgil's for ribs and tequila. Dad and I had a tequila-drinking contest. After-dinner drinks in Soho. Nightcaps at the wine bar around the corner from my apartment. The next afternoon I came home to him, Adrienne and Giovanni getting stoned together in my bedroom. I threw a fit.

The next night we took Dad down to Don's. Don had on some instrumental rockabilly bands which almost drove me crazy —

no vocals, just rockabilly. Good for some I suppose. It wasn't Patrick's disco night so Pat wasn't there so I didn't have to worry about his attitude.

I don't know why but it seemed Pat had crossed over. To what side I don't know. He was angry with the world; everybody. He fought with everybody. One afternoon Schmidt and him were in the basement of the club screaming at each other. 'You can go straight to hell, and Lisa can drive you there!' Schmidt squealed.

I can't say I blamed Pat. He got shit from his record labels; been apparently ripped off by Manson. I built a lot of his first web stuff until a loyal fan took it over. Record labels for the most part were just like ad agencies to me — all wanting something for nothing. We put Patrick out on the net real-time for call-in shows. As low-tech as you could get, but Don's phone rang for weeks after — little vampire queers all over the country wanting to talk to Patrick. Pat and I hadn't spoken since Don had tried to get us competing over the same night. Pat used to call Don his 'surrogate father.' Not too long after the incident, Don admitted to me that underneath it all he was a businessman and needed to do whatever he could to keep things going. I guess that meant slamming two guys, two very good friends, into each other like oncoming traffic.

In any case that night, my Dad had a good time partying with us. It felt odd to me though — watching my Dad dance with my friends. I wondered if he'd ever had any of his own. He and Adrienne did the father-daughter thing. That was cute. We all got loaded.

Adrienne and I took Dad back to his hotel on the Upper East Side. Stopped off in the lounge for a nightcap. It was very quiet compared to Don's. Dad got scotch. I ordered some Jägermeister. The room was painted dark green with matching carpet and red-stained wooden tables.

Dad was really loaded. He mumbled something to us about having another sibling. Adrienne freaked and went outside. I slammed the rest of my drink and followed her. She was shaking. The comment hadn;t really registered with me. I remembered how Mom had sheltered her from a lot of this stuff. That and that she was too young to remember a lot of it. We got a cab home. Adrienne looked out the window as if she would explode at any minute. I wished she would have. I wished somebody had the guts. I was glad I was drunk.

18. Dot Bomb

My sister got me a job with a successful internet company called Interactive8. I was working night shifts. Adrienne had started working with them a couple of years before. Or, rather, they started working for her. Adrienne's place among the Gotham icons had only gotten stronger. People tend to gravitate to her. Right after the crap.con company went under, she'd been asked to 'I8' for an interview, and showed up to meet the bosses wearing crazy print pants from Pat Fields and carrying her little Yorkie dog, Zoë in her designer purse, who she allowed to prance up and down the long conference room table eating puppy treats throughout the negotiations. Adrienne had long become a Native New Yorker: when you stop giving a shit, and make the city dance for you. For her, style is the currency.

My creative wind, if I ever had any, had been knocked out of me by the collapse of my internet broadcasting venture, so I ran the tech support at I8 from 6 at night to 3 or 4 in the morning. Tim, the guy I reported to, was a loner like I'd become. He stood about 5'11 and was an all-American type. I wasn't the least bit attracted, but let him think I was. Straight boys get a kick out of it sometimes. He liked Kiss as a kid, and rock, so we had something to talk about. Soon after we made friends, he'd stay all night after being there all day. Just geeking out, playing with hundred-thousand-dollar computers, ordering hundreds of thousands worth of software and stuff. Setting up new workstations for the poor slobs who had to come in and made the clients happy the next day by being creative. 'Put some lipstick on a pig — the public'll kiss it...' was the inside joke. I liked the gig, just like the first geek job I had over a decade before at Userfriendly. Access to all the latest technology, plus no one bothering me. Except Tim, and his wife Rachelle, who took to calling me to find out if he was ever coming home. I buddied up to Rachelle pretty quickly too. The offices were just barely in Chelsea, west of Sixth Avenue. Plenty of times Tim and I stayed up all night — I got a kick out of being on my way home just before everyone else was rushing to work. One early morning, I was glad I wasn't there. A construction crane malfunctioned and fell straight up Sixth Avenue and crashed into the apartment building next door. Killed one woman, hurt a few other people. The twenty-story crane looked like a mangled erector set, twisted along the sidewalks. Since Mr. Giuliani had taken power, construction sites littered the city and accidents were on the increase, but the brain-dead media didn't seem to mind.

Interactive8 had grown better than most during the internet boom — also known as the time a lot of people were spending a lot of money on things no one could identify or explain. Schmidt and I'd hired Thomas, an assistant to help me cover the work at the club so I could work more in the dot com boom. If I thought the crap.conmen had been bad before, I was in store for a rude surprise.

The good thing about Thomas Onorato was that he was serious. Enrolled in the public relations program at NYU, he wanted to work in a way that wasn't as affected by life trials as the rest of us. He brought a positive attitude to a weary table, and management skills that I didn't think could be applied in a club. I'm not sure where Schmidt found him — he'd probably found Schmidt for that matter. In either case, one night Schmidt pulled me aside and introduced me to Thomas with a keyword that meant a full vouchsafe for someone, a 'keeper.' The best part, he could handle himself. The better part, he could handle me, and in a way that freed me up and helped me refocus.

I'd been waiting for something to come along after my first internet broadcasting venture — for me it was akin to losing a child. We were supposed to change the world: birth does. After a few months, the partners at Interactive8 announced a merger. Since my sister was the third-in-command of the place, I knew it ahead of time. Eight companies from all over would get together to form what I'll call 'Supercompany.' Everyone would get a chance to cash in the shares of the company they'd been given for all the extra hours worked over the years. This seemed real to me. I got excited. I8, as we called it, was a real company, with real awards on the walls, much like the recognition I'd gotten from Al Gore for working with the European Union. Most of the people used the word 'can' a lot. It just worked. They did major television launches on the air in conjunction with the web. There were interactive sites for Fortune 5's and non-profit work for charities. The place started to get my juices going again. Cautiously, I asserted myself, and cautiously, they let me do a few things.

Then, we merged. The new union formed. We had become one in name with a part of an ad agency down in Washington — and even celebrities got involved as investors. Eight-hundred-million-dollar deal apparently. I'd gotten in on helping the auditors, allocating budgets — all the stuff I'd learned from the agencies. It started to hum along, until two major problems occurred: they slammed four hundred people who didn't much like each other together into our offices on the same day, and some Texas bureaucracts showed up and thought they were going to come up to 'Noo Yerwark Ciady' and show 'them people' how things should be done. Instead of building on the strong teams we already had, they started replacing them with paperwork, jargon-laced computer systems and second-rate business school rhetoric. To make matters worse, a bunch of low-level locals went on a political power sweep. Needless to say, my stomach sank. Another beginning of another end.

I seriously began to question how I kept getting involved in these situations where the man comes in and shuts everything down just when great things get going. Of all the motherfucking places for the henchmen to come from — Texas.

Giuliani was turning New York into the same humdrum kind of place as Cleveland, Cincinnati or Dallas. The sick thing was, these people actually believed they were doing us New Yorkers a favor. That somehow Disney, McDonald's and Starbucks would replace hundreds of years of autochthonous culture. Making money bossing a bunch of New Yorkers around, rolling in their Hugo Boss suits and hiding behind their email.

I knew it couldn't last. Every day on my way to work on East 14th Street I passed the demolition site of the famous Palladium Theatre, another victim of the great NYU land grab. My city was fading. Interactive8 was gone. Supercompany was a joke. Resentment ran through my veins, not just for a workplace, but for signs that the once impenetrable New York culture, work ethic and robust ability to produce had been compromised. I thought it cultural, but in reality, what we'd run up against was the ramifications of what Allan Bloom identified as the dark side of the MBA. From where I sat, the deal-makers hadn't merged anything but paper, money and hype. Then ran off with the kitty. You can't put four hundred people in a room and just say 'get along.' They made my sister get rid of clients we'd had for years

— apparently, they weren't big enough for the blowhards. Then they tried to convert the entire company to a dry, pedantic computer consulting operation. Nobody bothered to notice that almost all of the awards that hung on the walls were for artistic ingenuity. Advertising agencies had been making truckloads of money for over a hundred years off the model we'd been using. And no one knew how incensed I was for having to defend Madison Avenue.

I guess I was ready for my meltdown, so I rolled my dice. I befriended the CEO — a man from DC. Mr. 'C.' was a businessman who I feared was put in place because he wasn't from Texas and could smooth the north/south relations. I asked for a meeting because he had already appropriated money for me to bring in massage therapists and throw parties — anything to keep the staff working and from going off their rockers.

I approached Mr. C. with an idea: instead of just talking about the technology, let's demonstrate it. I'd already met with a dude from the scene who'd done lighting for some of the biggest events and parties in the northern hemisphere. Together, we met with a company from Canada, which had some never-before-used lasers that, with the help of a massive water mist, could project a hologram one hundred feet in the air of a person shot by a special camera. Blondie had the new album out. Debbie was no stranger to new tech — after all, she'd been 'painted' by Andy Warhol on an Amiga computer back in 1985. She was perfect.

'Mr. C., a quarter of a million won't get you shit on Madison Avenue, we both know that. But it could get you Debbie Harry, who loves new things, projected bigger than life over the West Side piers. And a concert — the biggest netcast the world has seen to date. *You in?*'

Mr. C. gave me a good answer, the kind I like. Some corporate go-ahead slogan along the lines of 'make it happen' or 'put the plan together.' I felt alive for the first time in a long time. I felt warm, I felt excited. I felt. Maybe, just maybe, my little dream of rock and tech and the world could happen. Maybe, the world could change. Little did I know, my world would not only change, it would collapse.

I felt uneasy about bouncing between two people I considered superior. Co-dependant parental figures. No matter my plans, over time Schmidt bascially disappeared. The genius who showed me hope, had become lost. I felt abandoned by him, like so many others in my life. I wanted, for once, to pull something together on my own. Prove I could handle the big time. Prove something to myself. I'd done tons of events so far, surely I could handle it.

What did I learn?

Lesson number one — don't approach rock stars with a business deal without Michael Schmidt. I pitched the idea: 'You can sing on one stage and be projected as a hologram a hundred feet into the sky…' Debbie liked it. She agreed to do it, subject to agreement. Mr. C. had given me a budget. She said in total, it would probably cost something in the range of a hundred thousand dollars. She referred me to her managers, who also agreed. I went back to Mr. C. and asked for the check.

I bought Debbie one of the fancy new tangerine-colored laptop computers. I had to pay almost double to get that color, but bondi blue just wouldn't do for the poster queen of downtown punk. I'd seen her working in the office on an old laptop, with a picture on the lid drawn in what looked like pink nail polish. Old as the hills. The tangerine one would propel her into the current state of the art, and prove we were serious. After I sent it, a week or so later, she called and thanked me for it. Mission accomplished. I was no longer the kid from the club. With shaky knees and a dream which included the woman who'd introduced me to the concept of 'dreamin,' I figured things were right on track.

Lesson number two — don't deal with opportunists. Antonio Pagan, the city councilman who, as far as I could tell, played a hefty part in selling out the entire Lower East Side, lost his re-election, but had since gotten an appointment in the Giuliani administration. One of Antonio's enthusiasts, had always kept a toe in our scene, trying to recruit me for this or that cause. With others, he did some things which seemed real good — things for neighborhood children, festivals, charity work. People from the club scene even supported this to an extent, but the endgame was always unclear to me.

Some of these people were the ones that contrived to getting the 'Lady' Bunny and Wigstock evicted from the East Village and Thompkins Square Park. They promised an effort to 'take back the neighborhood,' but this always seemed to fall short. Some of them snuggled up to the Manhattan Borough President, who was throwing some Gay Pride event at City Hall. I was very weary of people trying to make a name for themselves. I couldn't blame them, everybody wanted a place at the table, and everybody in fucking New York worked the scene like this. But I remained cautious. One Friday, after the show, I'd noticed one of the Lower East Side progress brigade talking to Schmidt and Debbie, but I didn't get involved. Later, I was told that Debbie had agreed to come to a Pride *soirée* as an invited guest, for which they wasted no time in publicly announcing.

Lesson number three — no good deed goes unpunished. I'd been dealing with Debbie's management company at the time, about the internet contract. We'd not agreed on the final fee even — but I trusted that it could be all sorted in the wash. Mr. C. had given the go-ahead on the hundred grand. I was working on good faith to make the event happen. One day, when I returned to my desk I had two voice mails. One from the Lower East Side bunch, and one from a chick at the management company. I dialed the bunch first, who told me that there'd been angry phone calls from Debbie's management in regards to the party at City Hall. Although my gut told me otherwise, I then called the management company thinking I could somehow smooth things out, thinking it was all a misunderstanding. The same angry chick answered the phone, talking fast. I told her to calm down. It was all about the stupid event which had nothing to do with me. I told her that I thought it had been set up directly with Debbie, and I thought it was a friendly thing. I faxed her the fax I'd gotten. I believed all was fine.

Lesson number four — expect nothing, from anyone, and like it.
About a half hour later the phone rings. It's Debbie. Very quiet but terse. 'I will *not* be at that event.' I just agreed with what she said, but tried to explain the same thing to her that I had to the others — I thought they had a deal all on their own. I should never have gotten involved. 'Make sure everyone knows I will not be at that event…' — 'OK, Done.'

She hung up. I jumped right back on the phone…

'WHAT THE FUCK is going on here!?!' I seethed. The entire office around me felt my rage I did not give a rats' ass. The anger began to creep up my spine like fire ants. 'What have you gotten me sucked into?' The other side mumbled on & on about how Debbie had agreed to come. About how Debbie said so. Blah blah blah. I asked who had spoken to her, sent a proper letter of confirmation explaining the event, or anything?

'No. She said she'd be there…' they maintained. I was convinced someone knew exactly what they'd done, a flim-flam. They'd published Debbie's name based on a flimsy conversation at a club, and never confirmed anything. Anyone knows you don't list major rock stars' names on announcements without official confirmation. And everyone knows not to rely on club conversations. I'd gotten sucked in the middle. By calling her manager, it looked like I was in on their side.

Lesson number five — the silence, don't be surprised by the insidious silence. Over the next couple of days I tried Debbie's line a couple of times and left a few messages for the management people. No one answered or returned a call. All I wanted after years of working with and around her, priding myself on safeguarding the relationship, was three stupid minutes to explain I had no idea things hadn't been handled right, it was a mistake and had nothing to do with my event. And I was about to get a certified check for one hundred thousand dollars, for the real project. I didn't fucking care about any gay-assed Pride event. For the first time since our original internet show, I wanted to demonstrate more technology. Demonstrate, instead of all the talk-talk-talk — but I got no talk and no demonstration.

Lesson number six — don't expect help. Everyone gets skiddish when the social dragnet rolls through town. It became clear: I was good enough to do grunt work others got credit for. Good enough to be a Rock 'n' Roll sucker. But not good enough to have something of my own. Who's fault? My fault.

I'd come out of nowhere with a promising event and a lot of money to work with. How stupid could I be? I could have just offered Schmidt a grand as a consultant and had no problems. Hindsight, perfect. But he had one foot in NYC and one in LA — back and forth. I just didn't see it at the time.

And fame never mattered to me either, nor did people who played that game; the craft, the music, the possibilities and ability of making a change in the world did — the rare opportunities we get in this life to achieve excellence.

Billy tried to warn me long before. 'They, are not, your friends.' I guess I really didn't listen. Listening would have to come later. Grandma Ruby always said 'If you don't listen, you'll have to feel…' And I was suddenly feeling a lot. At times I cried uncontrollably — not about a silly rock star or the stupid internet, but about losing. Losing so many people. Having to constantly restart. Losing one of the best opportunities available, because of stupid club gossip and an opportunist. I questioned whether I was in the right place anymore. Under the King Mayor G, the city had become an impersonal, hateful place. My stomach turned more sour with the sight of every chain store, chain bank and arrogant, entitled yuppie. I was just about to give up.

What I didn't realize at the time was that I was right on track. And that Billy's advice may have been more sage than first anticipated: sure they were not my kindred, soulmate friends from the old neighborhood, but there was also no way they could be, because I'd either forgotten, or never finished learning how to be a friend to myself, making the proposition of others nearly impossible. But I've since heard 'rejection is God's protection.' And it was. At the time, all I could do was mope around and seek the comfort of anyone who'd sit still for the story. But this was my ticket. None of the little scenester sycophants got angry calls from Debbie Harry, or even a cold shoulder by Schmidt. Maybe I was actually onto something. Perhaps I had a role in looking for other people to be my higher power. Although it didn't feel like it at the time, perhaps Debbie actually did me a big favor.

A few months later Supercompany started going belly-up. They got rid of all our clients to make room for bigger 'A-tier' clients — whatever the fuck that meant. Problem was, there weren't any. I'd heard it before — 'A' tier, 'A' list — it's all the same shit. People wanting something for nothing.

Supercompany was rumored to have ties to Enron. An accounting firm called Arthur Andersen was the trusty goalkeeper. Surely you've heard of them, the proverbial camel, straw, and his back. And an industry, as nutty as two fruitcakes on speed, along with the entire US economy came tumbling down. Or something like that. As Supercompany fell, they took a lot of our small suppliers out with them, not to mention laid off a large chunk of the staff. Including my sister, me, and most of our colleagues.

To make us all good and nuttier, word was spreading about a superbug called 'Y2K.' Sometimes I wished we could have just returned to the simpler Reagan years, when decisions were made by astrologers.

19. Time Won't Give Me Time

As Supercompany collapsed, after talking about it for years, I enrolled at SUNY, Empire State College and was placed with a woman named Mary Folliet, a senior writing teacher, as my mentor. I didn't know what I'd do, but I had to do something because I was sick of it all — advertising, the internet, clients, people. At the very least I'd collect some student loan money, and give myself a break. I was one big walking anxiety attack. I'd always had obsessive-compulsive tendencies, but they became overt. Locking and unlocking and then back again before I could go to sleep at night. And then fifty times before I could leave the house. Counting lines in the pavement. Stepping on every other step leading to the subway platform. Washing my hands. Crying for not very good reasons. I think it's called a nervous breakdown. The only somewhat calm places I had were in my night classes and at the yoga center. When I went to the college and wandered in the classrooms with gray walls and uncomfortable chairs, I felt so stupid, out of place, and insignificant. So very awkward, new. And it was invigorating. Folliet introduced me to literature, and Professor Flynn, a dyslexic genius, got me addicted to Socrates.

In time, she'd also lead me to another mentor John Calder, notorious British friend and publisher of Samuel Beckett, and the man who'd fought and overturned the Obscenities Act in

Britain on behalf of Hubert Selby Jr's *Last Exit to Brooklyn*. Vidal, Dostoevsky, Plath, Baldwin, Fitzgerald, Whitman, and The Beats. She took me to see Mike Daisey in his debut play '21 Dog Years: Doing Time at Amazon.com' at the Cherry Lane Theatre — a monologue performance that inspired me in ways I hadn't yet thought of, like I'd also foung in Jack Kerouac's radio shows.

I started networking in new circles, and people introduced me to theatre methods and performance techniques I'd use the rest of my life — from Boal to Turner. All of this kept my wobbly knees carrying me to class each week, incidentally just a few blocks away from Don Hill's and SqueezeBox!

One day I got a call from Dad. Uncle Ronald had gone to the doctor with a sore throat. Antibiotics didn't work. It chilled me to the bone and reminded me of Grandma. How she might still be around if she'd been under proper care. They had new medicines for strokes and things. And now uncle Ronald, who, to me, was always the mouthpiece of their church and beliefs. I admired a lot of the frugality, their attempts to live simply — but not when it came to health.

Uncle Ronald had in some ways been like an older brother, role model. He'd always shown me more than a modicum of respect. But now, barely five months after burying Grandma, he was given three months to live. Eaten up with cancer from his head down all the way one side of his neck. Maybe they could have caught the cancer, maybe they should have caught it — but they didn't, or he hadn't availed them the opportunity. Whatever the case, it was too late. I started another honest attempt to stop smoking. This would make every male on Grandma's side of the family a cancer victim, except Dad. So far. All my great uncles and now Ronald.

I flew down for a visit in the fall and left an entire afternoon free for uncle Ronald, if he were able. I drove the hour to his house down in Mint Hill. When I walked in, my aunt was nervously working in the kitchen. Their house was very country-French, white walls and raw wooden furniture and wooden floors. Printed wallpaper with light flowers in the kitchen. An iron-wood stove, red with warmth in the living room. Uncle Ronald sat in a big chair. Pillows propping him this way and that. Hot autumn sun beat through the windows that surround him, and down his freshly pressed ecru oxford-cloth shirt. He stood, stepped forward, hand extended for me. My vision blurred, blood rushed to my head, I touch his hand and became disoriented. I knew that feeling all too well, and with no denying his fate, was certain what it meant. I took my uncle's hand, the touch was my Grandaddy. He looked like Grandaddy and Dad and all my great uncles. He was surrounded by an aura I don't quickly recognize, one of someone who's going somewhere, in motion. After I sat down, my senses came back. The air was charged. I'd come for Grandma. She sent me. She was there too. They all surrounded Ronald. They'd come around early to help the younger ones make the transition.

We talked for over two hours. About life. About Grandma and Grandaddy. About his church, Jesus. We talked to each other as if Grandma were sitting over us with a ruler. It came naturally for me and I think for him. He made no comment to make me feel other, less than. My Aunt listened from the kitchen. He knew I'd stood with both his parents at the same door he was fast approaching. He needed me to tell him something. I've never felt qualified at these particular moments. I told him he was fine. I told him I respected his strength. I told him he knew what he had to know. He told me he did his best with Grandma. All he could. I told him I knew he did. As I watched him talk, his movements faded into the sunlight and back, I knew this would be the last time I would see him. I always know.

Uncle Ronald passed away, surrounded by his family, not far from that very spot. Apparently he refused all medical treatment, including pain medicine. Daddy was with him. I didn't attend the funeral. I'd already said goodbye.

20. Chicken Little has Left the Building

By the turn of 2000, we'd all survived 'Y2K.' For me, thirty had come and gone. So did a few more. The years faded one after the other, as did my city, as did part of my sanity. And I felt there wasn't a damn thing I could do about it — I couldn't get away from it, from them, the high school principals and the Giulianis and the preachers and the fear-mongers. Here I was, living with what I thought was an overdue appointment with the other side. I never sought to die, but I fantasized on not being here.

I tempted fate at every turn. Drank as much as I could hold as often as I wanted, although I couldn't stand the taste of alcohol and the hangovers got worse and worse. When I went to pay the Squeezebox! advertising bills, a friend at the *Village Voice* told me that before she got sober, she used to 'trick herself into believing that the hangover was just an extension of the high.' I tried it. Didn't work. Then I got a prescription for headache pills, which I took before going to bed at night to avoid the hangovers. The result was I was pretty fucked up a lot of the time.

At the club, just like the night of the shotgun incident, if a fight broke out, I was the first to jump in to break it up. Honor in peacekeeping. I went to see Iggy Pop at Irving Plaza, and moshed my way to the front and back over and over, just to see if I could. It's almost as if I wanted someone to stop me, I prayed for someone to get in my way, shout at me, challenge me, wake me out of my own head.

What I did not see at the time that while my wallow in the pigpen of self-pity was entirely of my own doing, some of the sadness I was reacting to was beyond my control. The ME-2 generation was now in full effect — everything had turned to an atmosphere of hazy beige. Anyone could become a native New Yorker overnight, as long as the limit on their credit card was high enough. It's like Dorian Corey said in Paris is Burning — 'Society has gone from what you can create, to what you can acquire...' and I didn't have a damn clue about how to deal with it except get angry.

By the end of the year 2000, the club had been going for almost six solid years. I'd only missed five Fridays in total — a better work record than I'd ever had anywhere else. One particular Friday night my disco nap ran too long. I woke up at midnight. Groggy, I drank some coffee. Started getting ready. I dragged myself in front of the mirror. I didn't recognize the person. My head hurt. I debated on going to the club or just back to bed. It was unseasonably warm. My cat was sprawled out in the bathtub. She shot me a look as if to say 'are you ever going to shock me and do anything new?'

Thomas could handle most things, but I had nothing better to do. Something still tugged me. I pulled on my leather jeans. A black t-shirt. Poured myself in a cab. As things got tougher Schmidt told me he would rather proactively close the club than to let things fizzle. I felt it important that if I was going to quit or even take breaks I needed to arrange, rather than just disappear. We had all become overwhelmed. No one had any intention of pulling the plug.

My last few 'official' nights at the club run together for me. I'd been arriving later and later, like 2AM each week: Carl says 'hi' to me, I walk into the club, 'Glad you could make it,' he teases. The crowd is lighter than usual. Must have been the weather, or any one of a million other rationalizations club producers and promoters tell each other and themselves when they don't get the crowd they want. A band is on. Something really rotten. We'd been having trouble getting good bands for some time. It doesn't matter, I couldn't hear it anyway. All a blur. I find the same people in the same places. The crowd in the back corner were trying another 1950s turf war. Kids I'd never seen before are running around like disheveled mongrels ready to fight over scraps of a lost vibe.

I go to my spot by the back bar and ask for some shots. In fact, I tell him thirteen. He started pouring. I wandered over to the coveted corner, push the ring-leader bitch out of my way. I wanted a fight. Say hey to about twenty people on the way to the back bar. Adrienne had gotten there earlier than me. We'd stopped traveling together quite some time before. She had her own friends by now. She'd been partying already. I noticed her watching me down a few shots of Jäger and swig my beer. Our eyes catch for a minute, we both stop and grin. 'I do love you, ya know…' I smile and tell her I love her too. I don't know what happened, but something definitely happened. We hugged.

I start on my fourth shot. Then number five. And on. I wanted to feel something — anything. I'd been overstimulated to the point of dullness in that place. Like too much sex — the first time not enough, the next time amazing, the next time overwhelming, the next time you start thinking about that hobby you've been meaning to get to and want to leave.

I think of my Grandma, how right then and there I'd give almost anything for one more minute with her. Or Billy. Maybe even Betty. Or the others I've loved and lost. So much god damned loss. I'd come to NYC to escape the bulldozers of progress, but they haunted me and followed me, all the way up the east coast. Instead of my high school principal, or the cops, or kids in the streets with baseball bats it was now Giuliani. And myself.

I stood near the spot where a girl had passed out cold in the floor months previously. The bouncers weren't right nearby, so I picked her up and ran her out back through the double doors. Her eyes were rolled in the back of her head. Her body limp. She was struggling to breathe. I scream at people on the corner to dial 9-1-1. Someone does. I hear an ambulance up on Houston Street. In the same second her body seizes, then relaxes. Carl was out there now, telling me I did the right thing before he runs over to the pay phone to make sure the call was made. I start noticing the girl'd stopped or was barely breathing. She's a sandy-blonde white girl. Her plasticky silver dress barely covers her body in this position. She looks like an erotic Greek messenger, a female Hermes. I can tell by her hairstyle she was new to the scene — it didn't match the tiny, shiny dress and strap sandals. She looked real young. Ten seconds later two thugs burst out of the back doors. One looks Italian or something, telling me 's'OK s'OK' in a heavy accent. 'No, we got an ambulance!' I screech at him. He looks greasy, and has on sleazy clothes like his partner, who's at the curb hailing a cab. He starts wrestling the girl out of my hands — I can barely hold her up anymore anyway. His partner joins, and they get her away, rushing her limp body into the taxi, slamming the doors, and tearing off. I stand there, stunned, as the cops drive up and then the ambulance. The cab with the girl is already gone — it tore up Spring Street. At least in the direction of St Vincent's. I figure they are either two shady characters who'd roofed her and didn't want to get blamed for it. Or they were two friends rushing her to the hospital — a party gone out of bounds. Either way, that shivery feeling had come over me, right when her body had let go. I'm almost sure she died. I couldn't save her. Carl tells me I did the best I could.

I down more Jägermeister. Liquid heroin. I'd pretty much gotten the reputation as the blithering town drunk. Don tried to make good out of it — 'At least a drunk will never lie to you.' I guess they trusted me. I ordered more shots. Everything started whooshing around me. I had a pretty high tolerance at this point. The coke made the anxiety rocket up my spine, the booze met it and calmed me down. I considered what if I just didn't do anything, instead of trying to maintain a proper balance to cancel each other out. But then, I wouldn't have anything to do now, would I? Fucked up and alone was better than not fucked up and knowing it. All the things that I had numbed myself to over the years were coming back to square up. Anesthesia does, eventually, wear off.

The next part is even more a blur, but I've tried over and over to piece it together. Schmidt comes over to me as the next round is being poured. He grabs me by my black t-shirt and pulls me back toward the bathroom. We jump the whole line. We can do that. He gets me inside. The chrome fixtures beat holes in my retinas as they reflect the incandescent lights above. The black walls make it difficult for me to know where to grab and hold myself up. I start to giggle — 'Finally something new,' I think.

Schmidt is swaying a bit himself. He's no stranger to the chemicals. He turns on the faucet — it has a tall neck, Don must have found it cheap at a kitchen dealer or something. He waits for the water to get less cold. 'Put yer finger down your throat…' he tells me as he pushes my staggering body toward the toilet. I barely have to, the mess of pee and shit and tampons is enough to make me gag. 'What?' I ask him. I was the one who'd carried him home before, and gotten him up and out before. I was supposed to take care of him. I felt criticized.

'Don't argue with me. Put your fingers down that throat,' he persists. So I do. It takes no effort. I knew the drill — just like every night at home for the past year. The venom comes back, separated into sugar and paint thinner. The burn goes up your nose if you're not careful, singes the back of your throat. I heave from the depths of my guts... Half a bottle of that wicked poison. Poison I didn't even like, introduced by Alig, the wicked cherub. I want to cry, but can't. After I'm done, he pulls me toward the sink. I start inhaling some water, swishing the bile from my teeth.

'Now,' he motions to my nose, 'rinse it.' At this point I got it. I complied. I could see his face, two actually, in the cracked mirror above as I inverted my head under the running tap. I was very out of it, but he mumbled things to me like 'This has to come to a screeching halt. You're too smart for this.'

'Patrick won't talk to me. I'm sick of it. Everybody I get close to leaves, fucks me over or dies. *Fucking sick of it Michael!*' I don't remember if I had him by the lapels or was holding him or what. I wanted him to know I never wanted a competition. Perhaps it was all in my mind. Michael had been telling me to 'relax' from the beginning. I hadn't yet learned how.

'Patrick won't talk to anybody — don't flatter yourself.'

'It's just too much, Michael, just too fucking much, man.' I started blubbering. Not in a self-pity way, just the first sincere expression of pain I'd managed in a long time. We hadn't really spoken in months.

'I-I know. I know a-aall about it. Trust me.' I figured he'd written me off as another soon-to-be casualty, but here he was with a 3AM intervention.

Billy was right. Schmidt and I'd been thrown together to work out some karma on each other. We'd come full circle — working together, creating something, then perhaps destroying it. I was fast coming to the realization that this was how it, life, worked.

Traffic was light, I got home in no time. I staggered up the five flights to my apartment. The bastard landlord had poured concrete over them to make the place look better kept for his new, high-paying NYU tenants. Each step had become a chore to remember and re-learn.

I was used to feeling nothing. I had no answers. I used to gobble a couple of the headache pills Dr Jeffrey gave me before curling up in my bed. I knew it was dangerous. I didn't want to die, just check completely out. Sometimes I left the curtains open so I could watch the moon. I frequently began to cry a long steady trail of tears. Sometimes unable to stop. I didn't bawl, choke or the like, I just laid there, arms extended, water pouring out of my ducts like open spigots.

I missed everyone. I ached for Billy and Grandma Ruby. I missed Haoui, Marty, Scott and a laundry list of others I couldn't even articulate because they spin so fast in my head. I missed Eric, or having someone like him. I thought of how we used to run around and play in the snow, making angels on the Second Avenue sidewalks in front of Dick's Bar. I thought of what things would be like if he were around. I thought of the New Year's we spent dancing at Billy's party. I imagined my Grandma holding my right hand. I was falling harder than ever before, but before passing out, I remember the feeling of something catching me. I said a little prayer just in case I didn't wake up. More symbolic than real. But I wanted to wake up so badly. I'd been aching to come back alive for a long, long time. But at that moment, I just drifted.

21. Just the Way It Is

Flashback to Summer, 1978.

As good as I can remember, I am twelve. Donna Summer Live is my favorite album. It has two full-length records in it. Saturday Night Fever is my favorite movie. My Dad took me with his mean girlfriend. I didn't know what a blow job was and embarrassed Dad by asking him in the theater. Everybody's acting funny 'cause that Jim Jones guy took a bunch of people to some country and they all drank Kool-Aid and died for the People Temple. I just got back to my Grandpapa's — my favorite place. I call him 'Popey.' It's in the mountains, sort of. It's hot out. I don't have to wear shoes. grandmother makes good food. The spring was a bad one for storms they say. That's why I have a pet cow. He used to be a he and now he's an it. That's what Popey says anyway. I named it Sam. Every morning I get to go early and help give Sam a bottle. Its Mama cow got killed by lightning. Popey's been feedin' him before I got here. It's tame and lets me hold him and lead him around on a rope.

By 1979 I am thirteen. I just got to Popey and grandmother's. I still like Donna Summer. 'MacArthur Park' is my favorite song now but I don't know what it means. My cousin Robin says it's stupid. Everybody's acting funny 'cause some people set fire to a nuclear power plant and a dude in a black hat is in Iran. I'm starting to like this other 'Heart of Glass' singer. Her hair is the same color as Mama's. She's pretty. Mama's always been pretty. I snuck and watched HBO at my Aunt Mittie's. I saw All That Jazz. They thought I was watching Dance Fever or something usual. It showed this really cool guy getting dressed at a mirror in his New York apartment. He took pills when he got ready to go to work to get the people to dance. He had got two boys dancing together in their underwear. It's hotter this summer. Popey lets me go to work with him some. He's a welder and an electrician. We get up at 6:30AM but I don't have to feed Sam. It's big now. As big as Popey's truck. Really, really big. Popey gets me to move him. He still lets me put a rope around his neck and walk him and sit on him. He's my buddy.

Around Christmas 1979. I am now fourteen. We get to Popey's late. They've been waiting for us. It's pitch dark. No streetlights in this part of the mountains. We all say hey. Popey has the grill going. I go inside to get the strong flashlight so I can go see Sam. Popey catches me and gives me an order: 'Here, go wash up, it's almost time for dinner.' 'OK, Popey.' You don't question Popey. We go in and sit at the rectangular blue and gold table. Everybody's talking. Popey brings in the steaks from the grill. We all say grace and start eating. Remembering I had been on my way out to the barn when I first got there, I ask 'How's Sam?'

Cue everybody acting funny.

22. Wicked Little Town

Back to 2000. Life was beyond my covers. The hangover passed in a couple of days, but I just couldn't bring myself to go out and face the world, a real conundrum: since I wasn't a rock star, I didn't have to die, but what on earth to do? Thank God I had a line of credit with the deli. I'd made friends with Victor, the delivery guy. He brought me sandwiches, juice, cigarettes, and potato chips in the morning, canned soup, soda, more smokes in the evening. 'You call me if you need anything...' Kitty stood guard on the edge of my bed. Over and over, filling in the square shapes of the tin ceiling of the bedroom with scenes from my flickering brain. I couldn't get my thoughts around my life to date, all the people I'd met and known, and slept with and loved. The whole thing seemed as it always had — out of reach. Me, a modern-day Tantalus: reaching for life, again and again, refusing to believe it somehow keeps slipping out of reach.

I'd come to New York just to be a homo and be left alone. Now, surrounded by nine million people, I was just alone. I wanted to find a lover. Have a life. Go out once in a while. Once, I reached for the phone and dialed Grandma Ruby's number. Some girl's voice picked up on an answering machine. Then she called me back a few minutes later in a horrible Nascar Southern twang 'Uhm, ye-us. Thee-uss numbar cawlled mah house...' A friend tells me I need to get away from losers, I need to get things on track. He tells me just like I told Uncle Ronald, that I need to believe in myself, or something — I just don't know what.

Thomas took over my job completely, allowing me to withdraw with a little dignity. He brought me the money each week, which I distributed as usual. He told me I was not missing anything by not coming for a while. Every time he left, I think: 'I'm not ashamed, I just can't.' Thomas was smarter about it all than I was anyway, he paid attention more, didn't get all caught up in the drama as deeply. He never said 'us' when it came to Squeezebox!, he kept himself separate, 'what I can do for you guys...' Smart.

Winter came. I called Mike Potter, who'd gone from hosting parties with Justin Bond to designing the hair and makeup for Hedwig. He asked me why none of us have been to see their hit play. I had my head buried so deeply in my own sand I didn't even really know that Hedwig was such a smash hit. Apparently, John Cameron Mitchell, Stephen Trask and company had become huge off-Broadway celebrants. Toast of downtown. Obie Awards. Madonna and Bowie came to the show. From bit parts on PBS and cop shows to making art on Jane Street, John made it. Big, in my eyes. I could have kicked myself too — John and Stephen left the door wide open at the git-go for me to do something with them, a web site maybe. Just be involved. Yet there it was, Hedwig: the first thing I knew to make it big out of the underground hopper since RuPaul, and I was in the middle of a nervous breakdown. Talk about timing. If I'd had it in me, maybe I could have contributed. These people got up in the morning, had contact with the outside world, were making an album, had a fan base and interest outside our circles of sycophants. I didn't understand why our extended band of clowns hadn't run to see it. Eventually, I decided to go. How dare I. Hedwig had been going strong two years on Valentine's Day.

Wait a minute: *Madonna* came? *Bowie* came? All manner of folks came. Except 'us.' The big musical debut at SqueezeBox!, circa 1997, had been a smash hit but somehow the 'inside' crowd wasn't making it to the play. Crowds went ape for the music and were going ape for it. And why wouldn't they? It had a glam drag-queen transsexual, and a story that touched every generation from the Boomers on. By putting a band on stage with Greek myths, offering a new angle to the Berlin Wall, and floating the whole boy-becomes-girl meets boy-loses-boy who then becomes a redeemed rock god taking the entire audience on a glittering catharsis, Hedwig raised the bar. Who needed Vagina Monologues when Mitchell & Company tore the roof off with his Angry Inch?

I knew Mike since he'd landed off the boat, so to speak, then started doing drag as Emmanuel Labor. He cornered me at the old Cake parties a few times and shared some insecurities about working in those rooms full of lizards. He found it condescending when I assured him he'd make it big. I just had a feeling. I had those feelings about certain people, like Justin, Thomas and a few others.

I waited to go see Hedwig and the Angry Inch because I was angry, then lost in the scene. Then hurting, but didn't know it. And at the time I just wasn't able to add another layer. My life was running five feet ahead of me, and no matter which way I jumped, I couldn't catch the shadow — due in part to sheer overstimulation.

I could get laid left and right, but somehow couldn't find anybody to watch bad TV with on Sunday afternoons. I could walk straight into any club in Manhattan, but didn't really know why I was there. Everyone else I knew had reasons — they performed, acted, sang, promoted, decorated, did lights, wrote — tangible things. I was computer dude. SqueezeBox! dude. I was advertising man. Computer dude. I was the one who ran around covering up messes. I had the money, but nothing to spend it on. Except booze. Food. Clothes. On top of it my neighborhood had disappeared before my eyes, and with it, too many friends. I went to the loudest hardcore shows in Manhattan and threw myself into the moshpit, but couldn't hear. Couldn't feel. Didn't care. Sometimes I woke up with bruises and fat lips, and hadn't a clue how they'd gotten there. I thought about heroin, but wanted something to live for, not to live for me. I'd lived my whole life, from seventeen on, absolutely convinced I would never make it to thirty. Isn't that what we all deserved? Just like Harvey Fierstein's line — 'queers don't matter, queers don't love, and those that do deserve what they get' — right?

The Jane Street Theatre was part of an SRO hotel in the far reaches of the West Village. It was once a nice hotel by the looks of it, and was the place they took the Titanic survivors. I'd been to a Dean Johnson party there about ten years before — The Comeback Club. Dean had erected a huge bullpen made from eight-foot sheets of plywood in the center of the basement. Me and Paul, a friend of Haoui's who worked with David Russell on Greenwich Avenue across from Uncle Charlie's, went one night. We entered through the side door, which led to a cavernous hallway, got drinks, and proceeded to stand against a wall and chat while acclimating to the roomful of boys and makeshift walls. The ceilings were low, the lights dim, but we could see. Out of nowhere two pasty-white cute boys approached us. One said my name. I'd never had anyone approach me in such a determined way. Before I could turn my head to act astonished and see what Paul would do, the boys fell to their knees and attacked my belt buckle. I looked over to Paul, who was grinning from ear to ear, shrugging as we giggled. Paul and I just stood there, continuing our conversation except when time for our momentary climax.

Pretty Broken Punks

My boy got up, smiled at me, said 'thanks,' and walked away. Paul and I just laughed. During our little interlude, I thought I would have to make plans to take him home, feed him, etc. — which was exactly what I wanted. A boyfriend. I was still under the impression that when you do things with people it meant something — something permanent. But this boy, like all the others, had no such intentions. As he walked away, I wondered who'd had whom.

Now, over a decade later I entered the Jane Street Theatre from the front. Potter met me in the lobby at the top of the stairs, and whisked me in the glass doors and to our seats. I didn't recognize anybody in the packed theatre except for Potter and Jack Steeb, who was mulling around the sound booth. I was happy to see a room full of people I didn't know patronizing people I did. For the first time in a long time I saw a tangible connection between reality and what I considered real. John took the stage as Hedwig and for me, summed up most of what I'd ever wanted SqueezeBox! to be, say, stand for. A place to exist while searching for ourselves. He sang of 'other halves,' 'lost parts.' As I watched John onstage, something welled up inside me. Something woke up. Something moved for the first time in many, many late moons. Not only was the play outstanding, something about John being onstage... John, onstage...

He'd not lived as a drag queen for years to get there. He was playing a role he created, not putting on an impersonation sideshow. He'd been at the club a lot, but he didn't live there. He got his story, and put together a play. A story. His.

A few days later I took Adrienne. I wanted to see it happen again, the play — sure, and the connection. Adrienne was an instant fan. I'd experienced some of this excitement with Debbie then Patrick all those years before. Or watching Joey Ramone or Soundgarden at Lollapalooza. Or goofing around with the

Green Day boys. For me, split-seconds where whatever had held me back all my life eased its rage. And sure enough, it happened again, and I knew I wasn't alone when I glanced over at my sister during one of the ballads and saw what I was sure was a lone, heavy tear contouring the front of her cheek. Adrienne beamed. We saw you, me, we, us, and them on that stage. It was alive. So was I. It was tangible. People I knew had moved from the masses, up five steps to center stage — there was a map to be had. Finally, I could put 'a' and 'b' back together. Rock 'n' fucking Roll.

The following weeks I kept with the invigoration. I started doing more yoga — two or three times a week. Something about those rose walls and the mystic teacher Satchidananda inspired me further, propelling to where — I didn't know. 'Let go, have faith,' he'd say. 'Play, play, learn, learn.' I hadn't 'played' in a long time. Yet, although I felt lame, the momentum was building inside me. I considered not going down as a failure. I completed my first courses at Empire State College — the place where adults used to go to get their shit together. One lonely night, instead of getting drunk for the millionth time, I went to the local bookstore. A copy of Louise Varèse's translation of *A Season in Hell* stuck out of the poetry section. I plucked it and read, then took it home and re-read. Arthur Rimbaud beckoned me — 'I sat beauty upon my knee and found her bitter.' I could relate. I'd scarcely read a book in my life, but I devoured Arthur from back to front and back again, an eager pupil of the teenager of the holy clandestinity.

Things went the same way when I met with Mary, my assigned mentor at college. An eccentric, self-described 'old-babe' from the Plath years; a fixture on the New York Jazz scene. A poet. The first time we met she basically went through the motions. Forms, loans, paperwork. Her office overlooked the yellow and blue community swimming pool at the corner of Varick and

Clarkson Streets. The sound of young children squealing and splashing over the impatient traffic waiting for the Holland Tunnel set the background for our chat. At first, I didn't think Mary liked me at all — another desperate, lost puppy to be coddled and pushed. 'Sign here, take that to the finance office.'

The second time we met, I was surprised to find Mary had a laundry list of things for me to start doing. A test. I'd sent her a letter demanding we get something happening faster than later. Problem was, I didn't know what the something was. But for the first time in my life I'd chosen something before it chose me. I was searching, all over the place. Anything but be who I'd become, this person I no longer knew. The void in the mirror.

A few days later I went with a friend to Café Carlyle. Old-school. Eartha Kitt playing. We got sat right up front. Eartha bantered during her shows, usually about rich men and things. Eartha took an unplanned break between songs, and told us in her rolling, trademark staccato voice, 'You know ladies, and gentlemen, once I recorded a disco song, something for the younger ones, something they could dance to… now, twenty years later they've finally shown up to my show.' She pointed to us and laughs. The old people smiled in patronage as they slowly massaged their cognacs.

23. This is The End, Sort Of

May, 2001. The club was punking along. I was still waiting for Schmidt to kill it off rather than watch it fizzle. No one had the heart. No one knew what to do next. What do you do when one of the greatest times of your life, not to mention a definitive era in the capital of the world, is over? You hide. At least for a while. Thomas was still doing my job and starting to earn a high perch on the social climb. I should have stayed on top of things, but decided to let him have the glory. I hadn't been to the club in ages. Schmidt eventually moved out to LA. Miss Guy decided to throw a 'Last SqueezeBox! Ever!' party. It was more to promote his new band, the Toilet Boys, but a last hurrah nonetheless. I ask to be put in to do a number: 'Animal Boy' — by the Ramones.

When I arrived for rehearsal, I discovered that Lyle, a go-go boy, had decided to get a movie made about the club. I gave him credit for effort, but knew this was really the end — of 'cool' anyway, like when the vultures show up to crunch the bones of a decaying carcass. I guess he hadn't tried to hire Blondie for a hundred grand, therefore was in good favor with what Annie Lennox called 'all those fake celebrities and all those wicked queens.' Lyle booked interviews with all the stars — from Waters to Jayne County to Debbie. When I showed up for rehearsal, Greta was handling the band. She'd recently been signed to do a tour with Moby. Some skinny kid with zits was walking around with a camera and release forms. He approached me: 'Uhm, and who are you?' Indeed. Like the SS in Nazi Germany, the ME-2s had come to seize the day.

Who the fuck are you, asshole?, I thought, looking at the desperate starfucker before me. I left no room for patience. I'd been working on myself for a while, in the daylight. I was nervous to be back there to begin with, I didn't need some pimply-faced starfucker getting me off on the wrong foot. 'I'm the director of this movie we're making about SqueezeBox!, and if you're going to be in here we need you to sign this. It's about the club…' Yeah, the club. I think back to the first day I showed up. Patrick greeting me at the door — the manager. I shoulda' punched the guy, but all my spiritual work helped me just grin and dismiss him.

'OK got it,' I said with a sigh, looking down at my shoes. I started killing him with enthusiastic questions like 'Out of curiosity let me ask you, did you ever make it to a real SqueezeBox! Night?' Like, when it was going strong? Did you ever see a celebrity here, hanging in behind a booth making out with teenage boys? Did you ever lose your shit in a mosh pit? Did you ever chat up John Waters in the corner, make out with a drag queen, or do anything that would require an original thought? I implied, so the whole room could hear.

'Uhm, no, but they've told me all about it.' Right then and there that boy became everything I'd grown to hate about New York. He was Giuliani, the yuppies, the baby carriages, Disney, Starbucks, NYU and ten thousand of their arrogant, brainless students all rolled into one. I think twice about attacking him. My right hand ached to punch him and punch him and keep punching him until the blood covered both of us. But I don't. Lyle walks up, I sign their little paper, and walk like a grand old swan onstage ready to rehearse my song.

Greta had stopped band rehearsal for a break. No one said anything — the original people didn't want to admit to being older, the twerps surrounding our new film director didn't want to admit to being wet behind the ears. This guy didn't care anyway, who knew what deal he had with Lyle and how I was sure they'd whore us all out to the highest bidder. Hooray for Hollywood.

That evening the club was packed with reporters. The entire mosh pit where people used to dance was overrun with people shoving cameras every which way. Nowhere to stand, move, talk — a bunch of hacks throwing attitude and jockeying for the best vantage point.

Adrienne came in with me this time, just like when she first moved to New York. I needed her to make it through the night. We didn't know half the people in there. Debbie slid by me in the basement. I refused to move or cower, even though she was five feet from me, and five feet from a place she'd kissed me all those years before. It felt like the high school reunion I never went to — or wanted. An excuse for a lot of people to dress up and act like assholes. Too many had decided that they were famous, or on their way to be, and did that 'ruin the photo' face in the few photos I tried to get. Nothing more revolting than someone who's a legend in their own mind. Nothing more pathetic than big fish in a puddle.

Guy practically set the roof on fire with his show. Sparklers and fire bombs and flaming guitars and all. We almost choked from the dense, sulfurous smoke. I was truly in hell. The camera people and newbies flocked in packs all around the place. For a minute, I regretted not trying to prevent all this Disneyfication of the hottest rock club in New York City, but I just didn't have it in me anymore.

I do my number, 'Animal Boy.' It's a short one — which I liked because I'd come to admit I wasn't trained to sing. Metallica: just say no. I wore the leather pants with zippers up the back of the legs and a black t-shirt. I didn't make a special effort, I didn't need to overdress for a trip home. Greta said I can sing, especially enough for punk. She'd always been on my side. I actually had fun up there, in front of all those people again. A sea of faces had managed to mosh their way up front and shove the yuppies back. One boy, who'd made an effort every single week for almost seven years to say hello to me, mouthed the words I Love You, and snapped my picture. That was a first. I was getting into it, but realized something was still amiss — something about it didn't belong to me, felt strange, awkward. Schmidt, who'd flown in from LA for the event, pulled me aside and grabbed my left hand, pushing it down and in front of him. He pried my fingers open and I felt something hard and smooth pushing on. He closed my palm around it. He pushed my hand back, kissed me, and twirled into the next room. On my third finger is one of his famous rings he'd been making recently. Only a few of us got them. Mine was a big silver skull encrusted with the brightest rhinestones I'd ever seen. The ring was too big though. I had to go in the back storeroom and swipe gaffer's tape off of a speaker to put wind in it and keep it from slipping off.

For old time's sake, I got slightly hammered. No coke though. I managed not to do that — never liked it anyway. Lyle, now a.k.a. the latest Mr. Important, came and got me for my interview. I had a whopping five whole minutes. In the basement, I was seated on a metal chair, and the girl doing the interview looked at me with a lost stare. She barely knew who I was, which convinced me they'd never produce anything worth watching — the ME-2s were only concerned with starfucking, not getting laid. Lyle was flitting around in the room behind us, reassuring people I won't take too long. Lyle didn't even have the first clue what I actually had been doing at that club for almost ten years.

The whole thing irked me, but I was already far beyond the parade of what Patrick liked to call 'maroons.' Like Rimbaud wrote: 'And springtime brought the idiots' frightful laughter.'

I glazed over every time we saw someone spouting off about how great they were. I talked about all the connections and people and talent that had fed SqueezeBox! over the years — as much as I could. I was allowed five whole minutes to talk about the club I'd spent years upon years building, to a couple of kids who'd never really been there, who thought they were going to tell our story. I sailed into a litany of names and dates and times, and pointed out to the camera that SqueezeBox! was a collective effort, knowing the camera would quite probably be the only recipient of the footage.

Back upstairs, I noticed the place emptied out rather early — as soon as the photographers were satiated. I was staggering out the door with some posters and memorabilia when a kid stopped me. I recognized him from the old days. 'Great song man!' he said and flittered away back to the boy he'd been chasing. I envied him. I wanted a boy to chase. I just didn't want to be alone. I must have looked terrible as the 5AM sun was coming up. No cabs were around — they'd gotten scarcer and scarcer since the city officials had started harassing them. No one was waiting to go to the Greenwich Café either — most just got their money and left. You know it's over when no one wants to stay longer, go somewhere else, and imbeciles are running things. There's no free breakfast.

I stood there on the corner looking at the warped green and white street signs, Greenwich, Spring, and the crust of band stickers, posters and flyers taped on the signpole below them. Bob Gruen and his pretty companion came up behind me as their black Lincoln pulled up. I smiled at him and said goodnight. Part of me wanted to be left there, completely alone on that corner.

Part of me wanted to move on. 'Take it man, you've certainly earned it...' Bob said as he motioned me to the car. I thanked him and got in, relieved the night was over. A decent guy, finally. I couldn't wait to get home to have a shower and rinse the assholes away, knowing full well they'd do another one of these high school reunions I'd have to live to endure.

24. The New World to Come

September 9th, 2001. After a few months I began to feel like things were turning good for a change, like my feet were touching the ground again. I was in the writing program with Mary at college. Me, in college at my age… I was giddy with excitement. I'd been freelancing for money. Jed Root, one of the hardest working men I've ever met, hired me to design his first web site about sixth months earlier, and since then I'd been taking on new clients. The weather was nice, I felt like I could breathe again. It looked like they might investigate Florida, so that criminal Bush couldn't stay in the White House. Things were looking up.

Ever since the Supercompany disaster, I'd been doing my yoga faithfully. I thought of Marilyn every time I arrived at the center. She'd since moved away to DC, NC, and then Florida. I listened some more to Swami Satchidananda, who started the yoga center: 'where the mind goes, the body will follow…' So I made my mind up to make my mind up to go somewhere. I sat in the audience of the Dalai Llama in Central Park. I took classes in Thai yoga massage therapy. I went vegetarian. I started giving up smoking, and all but stopped drinking. No more drugs. I didn't know how long each piece would last, or even if I wanted it to, but trying everything was better than trying nothing. I still had days I could barely get out of bed. I still had anxiety attacks.

September 10th, 2001. I took my Monday evening yoga class. Sivani was the teacher and had a loyal following. It was held on the top floor of the center, with a full view of downtown. Usually, the class is one of the most peaceful groups of people I encounter each week. However, on this night, the class is agitated — people are fussing over their space on the floor. Helen, an Auschwitz survivor with the tattoo still on her arm, called the girl next to her a 'n–ger.' Helen was a little off, generally. People had complained about her to the management, but someone pointed out that whatever hate she had was put there by Nazis. After the class we usually dispersed pretty fast. Sometimes I'd stay for the evening meditation — but I didn't want to this time. For some reason though, I found myself standing with my yoga friends — Rhada, Jerry, and our teacher Sivani, at the window — gazing at the cold twilight falling over downtown, a crisp fall evening air filling the sparkly city. Just a mile or so in the distance, the World Trade Centers were shimmering a dusty pale blue-gray. The red lights decorated the top. 'What a sight,' Rhada said. We stood there, in a collective contemplation a very long time for a group of people who usually went about their business after class.

The night of September 10th was filled with nightmares. I'd heard that when you 'tuned in' spiritually, a lot of things could happen. That night was no sleep, toss, turn. I dreamed I was in the desert in the middle of a raucous game of some sort. Men surrounded me, desert men wearing robes. They yell a bit, then cheer. I am handed an ax and told it's my turn. I am pushed toward the center of the mass. A lamb is placed before me. 'Your turn,' says one man. I am to chop off the lamb's head. I woke up with a quick 'NO!'

September 11th. I get up after a fitful night, but happy nonetheless, about a meeting with a new freelance client I had for 10AM. I started getting ready, but absolutely everything was taking longer. Kitty was acting needy, agitating me. I was still sleepy but down some coffee to boost me into my swing. The phone rang, my friend Fernandez was on the line, I found it odd, Fernie and I usually talked at night. He told me to turn on the television. Oh, God. A few minutes later I was on my roof with the rest of my neighbors. Another plane hit. People were crying. You could see the burning towers, the smoke, tops of the buildings. One appeared to lean. 'That thing is going to fall,' I thought to myself. I didn't share my thoughts with the neighbors. The tower collapsed. A few minutes later, I had the same thought, the second tower collapsed. Then for no reason at all, a third building just collapsed.

September 12th, I found it hard to leave my apartment. At the hands of Rudy Giuliani, my beloved New York had begun a freefall. Now, it had fallen. It was over and anyone with half a brain damn well knew it.

A few weeks later I couldn't take anymore. I'd been assisting people, pitching in and assisting wherever I could through the yoga center to provide help to families, police and firemen. I became friends with a police captain from ground zero, who was supposed to send some of his men for classes and massage therapy. Everyone was freaking out. I spoke to him when he was very upset one Thursday. He began confiding in me. Telling me they'd gotten some bad news, some intelligence — he couldn't tell me what, but the coming weekend could make September 11 look like a tea party.

Before September, Giuliani was one of the most hated, divisive men in the city. After, he used the whole thing to boost his ratings, just like he always had boosted his ratings — on the backs of everyone else. The media touted him as 'America's Mayor' just for doing his job. Bush, the criminal who had never even been elected, had his Reichstag. The game was on. Giuliani started his 'get back to work' and 'keep shopping' and 'show them we don't cower' campaigns. Governor Pataki was in on it, and since then the new mayor, Bloomberg, followed suit.

In my eyes, New York was dead long before 9/11. This was just the party to gather the spoils — Bush got his reason to be President, Giuliani invented himself a legacy. Rents were doubling, tripling — corporations replaced locally owned businesses on every corner. Now, those of us who remained were to walk around and pretend like nothing had ever happened, unless at an officially-sanctioned flag-waving rally. America fell for it. America was stupid. I developed a nice case of Post-Traumatic Stress Disorder. Panic Attacks and all.

I loaded up Kitty and my few belongings that were worth something, and drove down to North Carolina. At that point, I didn't know whether there would be a Manhattan to come back to. Months later, I saw where *Time* magazine delicately reported they'd pulled a 10-k Russian nuke off a barge in the East River, four blocks from my house. I stayed in NC for a few weeks and visited relatives I hadn't seen in many years. I sat in Mom's new living room because she didn't have a basement in her new house. I asked her not to turn on the TV news. I spent time with grandmother and Popey. They were glad to see me. I'd sent Adrienne upstate. Popey didn't have a lot to say about the whole thing, just like he never had a lot to say about WWII. I knew he'd served in France, sinking the ships in Le Havre and in Germany — fighting all the way to Berlin. He got a purple heart for breaking his arm playing softball with the 'Jerries' they'd rounded up. Popey'd always been my hero. A stand-in father after the day I came home to our house and found Mom dressed in her best glen plaid suit, crying. Dad had left, we would move.

The day before I drove back to New York I talked to him about a lot of things, life, whatever. He never asked me about girlfriends, he knew. He knew and didn't care. He'd always known and never cared. He'd planned on me spending one of my last nights that trip with them at their house, but I wanted to get back to Mom's instead. I hugged grandmother, and then Popey at their back door. 'I thought you was goin' to spend the night,' he protested, with a disappointed look. I got that feeling again.

The following Spring, May 2002, I was at the Roxy for the first time in ages. Thomas and some other post-Squeeze kids started a club called 'Motherfucker.' Lyle and his director were debuting the trailer for the SqueezeBox! movie. I'd met with Lyle a couple of times earlier, to compel him to put a real narrative behind the project. While we were doing the internet broadcasting, I'd collected around six hundred or so hours of footage from the internet broadcasts, and offered to share it. I told him of how many of the people who made Squeezebox! happen met through Haoui and the old Danceteria/Studio 54/Hurrah crowd, not to forget Pyramid and the old Avenue A scene, and how *that's a story in itself* — the New York lineage: how we, even him, were all connected through a very fine creative thread.

That night, most of the old guard showed up at the Roxy, except Schmidt. Bob Gruen had a big booth up and took our photos. I'd gone alone. Some MTV rock star named Andrew WK went on. I'd never heard of Mr. WK, I didn't watch MTV. But the regime had changed. We'd brought out Debbie, Nina Hagen, Marc Almond, Joey Ramone, Angela Bowie, Jayne County, Lene Lovich, Vaginal Creme Davis and a litany of what I considered an ecclectic mix of super-talented performers to a downtown audience. Now, the future stood before me: a shrieking Neanderthal surrounded by children who spoke with a Valley Girl accent. I had a few cocktails. And then a few more. I'd not been drinking much for quite a while, but in that crowd, my old habits came creeping back up. I ran into some people I knew.

The space was too big for any intimacy. DJ Adam, my friend from Avenue A, was there, along with a few more of the club regulars. Debbie came in with Miss Guy and Sherry Vine, and stood right across from me. Everyone said hello but Debbie. Kids were all popping around our little circle, getting a glimpse of her, with stars in their eyes. Debbie kept her eyes engaged. No one else in the group knew what could be going on. I felt a great distance between me and her. Truth was, it was between me and me, perhaps wanting all the right things in all the wrong places.

For what I knew, the whole 'pride' incident had blown over, like my friend Clark from the Duelling Bankheads used to tell me, 'everything is forgotten in 72 hours.' But I remained conflicted. The thing was, that the withering downtown scene as we knew it was no longer able to sustain itself, and it grabbed people to blame and ostracize. No one knew exactly what to do, especially after 9/11. Had any of this happened before the big Giuliani meets dot-com bust, everyone would've just gotten high and gone for a dance. But like Jamaica Kincaid once said about the Studio 54 bust: 'The thing about the 80s is that everyone got serious,' something that doesn't mix well with creative juices.

After years of work, therapy, and yoga, I thought I finally knew the meaning behind Billy's fingers poking me in my bird chest, with his words: 'Not. Your. Friends.' He wouldn't have taken crap from anybody, and I could almost hear him shouting in my ear from the grave *'Uh-uh, no, I marched right over and said hello anyway...'* as I continued chatting with passersby. Debbie locked onto me. I nodded my head forward like Popey used to do. It showed respect, she repeated my motion.

I couldn't much handle that room, the crowds, and the ghosts haunting it. I just couldn't find my groove, and felt like some merciful release had taken place. The whole night seemed like one of those days that no matter how much you want it, or how many cups of coffee you drink to accelerate, your rhythm remains one step behind the clock of the world. Was New York telling me something?

At a recent party at Linda Simpson's apartment next door — I lived in 324, she in 326 — all the downtown divas came. From Sweetie B to Sultana, pieces of New York's soul. Page came along as well. Page Reynolds: with a Grace Jones vibe, and a blonde flat top. She used to perform at Linda's Channel 69 at Pyramid. One of the songs she sang was called 'In My Cubicle' — a testament to the cells we called our homes, our apartments, our minds. She'd been on my block before I'd been on my block, and had caused a scandal in *Vogue* magazine before most of us could afford one. On that particular evening, Page seemed more introspective than usual. She took a seat in the corner of Linda's tiny living room and started talking to me. We chatted about life, the city, friends, everything disappearing. How it had started well before 9/11. I shared how I'd gone back to school, stopped going out for the most part — except the occasional Saturday night to hang with DJ Adam in his DJ booth at the Cock bar. Without him I don't think I'd had much social life.

'When life gets down you gotta' get up, Mister. *You know it—* you gotta' just keep going!' she asserted. It was a good party.

I was being as 'up' as I could when the DJ announced the SqueezeBox! movie trailer. Three minutes of quick cuts of people from the scene, all saying how great the club had been. Friends dancing, singing, a long segment of me making out with Justin Bond at the last Squeezebox! 'A' for effort, but the whole fucking thing annoyed me. It was like trying to get people to feel what we felt, when we felt it. Moved by music that was no longer playing. The only thing that'd mattered to me was the people, where they came from, where they were going, what they were doing. The action, the motion. The Patricks, who made a stir around

America. The John Cameron Mitchells, Barb Morrisons, Blake Burbas, Mo Fischers, Lily of the Valleys — all in music, movies or with long-runs Off Broadway. Things that channeled the energy. Hell, even our internet shows sparked plenty of imitators — this, to me, was the magic of Squeezebox!, and the magic of what is possible when human beings are allowed the space to consider their state of being. I didn't need a movie to tell me anything — it needed to show something, stand for something. Make sense in a hundred years. Debbie and others had been the name, the catalyst, the reason for our notoriety, but, SqueezeBox! was about the little people — the nobodies who could hang stars, and make the moon smile. The little ones. The celebrities were our cannon fodder — if it weren't for the freaks, they'd have had nowhere to prance and parade.

To me the movie trailer also came across like an infomercial. I was too worn out with it all to be objective. These kids didn't get ... *did they?* Lyle ran over to me, looking for approval, 'Whaddya think?' 'It's pretty good, a good start,' I told him as he ran away into another conversation. The screen rolled up. Big mean security guys were everywhere. Thomas had whooshed me in the doors and put some armband on me. I stuck it out as I walked straight for the goons. I figured they'd either jump me, or move. They moved. Schmidt had taught me how to talk and walk my way into almost any door. I went out on the stage. My friend Randella, a sweet, giggly little blonde drag queen from the neighborhood, watched me. Smiling. We'd danced many times on the floors of Avenue A, the good days. The days when we'd crowd into the Pyramid on a Sunday night and make out while Lady Miss Kier danced on the bar and Wendy Wild cheered us on from the coat check. The days when I could meet people like Eric, and others hodge-podge into comfortably unfamiliar circumstances — black walls, hot bodies, lipstick and leather jackets and white t-shirts. The days before Willi Ninja would get asked for ID at clubs he used to run.

The dance floor at Roxy was pretty full, but not like in the old days. I went over to Randella and extended my hand. *Waltz with me, darling...* She grinned bigger and grabbed me, climbing up on the stage in a tight black sequined dress and heels, and a cast covering her broken leg. The security goons watched me with evil eyes — these were no kin of Kevin or Carl, these were big angry monsters who'd love to smack queers around. This only inspired me more. I climbed up on top of a stack of speakers and took Randella with me. Twenty feet in the air, the music went through me. I'd spent plenty of nights in that room, the large, expansive roller rink and dance club. I rarely left the dance floor once in. It'd always been about the music for me. The speakers were enormous, like the ones on Lollapalooza. Randella and I had a private ballroom, and we danced like two escaped convicts. I twisted and turned, the moves familiar. This is what I loved. Dancing, all night.

The energy took me, consumed me. The alcohol left me. We kept going for a long time. I remember glancing at my watch. Around a quarter past 4AM. I felt like laughing, I think I was crying. I kept dancing, moving... a feeling of euphoria had come over me like never before, like this big rush of energy, like someone going inside me, like I was steady and grounded but about to fall from the top. Everything started moving in slow motion — the lights, smoke, hundreds of people. I felt like I'd woken inside a dream, the kind I have in the early morning — when people come to visit me. I imagined Lorenzo, Ramón and Dan on the dance floor — Billy too. Even Barney, who I saw get up one time in all the years I knew him, when they played 'Just Can't Get Enough,' one of his favorites.

I saw yesterday sitting on the giant swing that used to hang in the middle of the floor. Excitement, like when Madonna's new song would come on. Boys of all shapes and sizes dancing around, sporting their tight jeans and jewelry. Cheers for the stage filled with drag queens and go-go dancers and performers. The queen with the big pink Chinese fan waving a breeze over the thirsty crowd. Another rush of energy, a surge up my spine, out my head. Then, dizziness.

I came around when I noticed Randella ready to move on. You could trust your friends in those days. Although I didn't know her all that well, I remember being very glad she was there. We climbed down from the speakers high in the air. Only a few groups were dotted around the massive dance floor beneath. I was drenched in sweat. 5AM. DJ Adam and another boy were waiting for me on the side. They exchanged eye signals with Randella, the kind when people are keeping something from happening to a friend, like rampant laughter at how awkward he is. They asked me if I wanted to go soon, share a cab. I agreed. My body was buzzing from head to toe. I felt sublime. We stepped outside and there were a lot of people waiting for cabs. None to be found. We walked over to Ninth Avenue, and without discussion, continued. A warm breeze engulfed me. The humidity was too high for me to get dry. A fog had settled over downtown. We could tell day was near breaking by the cobalt-blue glow in the east — the way home. We walked all the way. Adam walked on one side of me, the attractive blond guy on the other. I knew they were looking out for me. Something like that. Friends do that, even the ones you don't yet know. Adam left me and the other guy at Second Avenue. The guy, Robert, followed me home and up to my apartment. He came in for a while, but I told him I needed to be alone. I had a strong desire to be alone.

Just five minutes after my eyes shut, the phone rang. My hand shook as I reached for it. 'Hi son, it's your Mother. I have bad news honey: your Popey's gone.'

I was still reeling from my night out, energy pulsing, thinking that I wasn't hearing right. My auto-numbing mechanism kicked in. 'Wait, huh, what? How?'

'Well, apparently he woke up about a quarter past four in the morning, complaining of his legs hurting. He told grandmother that it was worse than he'd ever felt. He got up to walk around, and went to the kitchen and took a quinine. Came back and sat on the edge of the bed, still saying how bad they felt. Grandmother reached down and started rubbing them as he laid back on the bed and was gone.'

Quarter past four. I'd felt it. It was Memorial Day, the same holiday Betty Badum died on. Mom had told me earlier in the week to make sure I called Popey real soon. I was going to. I meant to. We keep in touch, our family. I remember part of a letter of his he'd sent back home during the war.

March 26, 1945, Germany

Dear Mom,

The going's been hard the past few days, but we've been pulled off the front line for a rest. It's the same old thing, war everywhere, affecting everybody... But it looks like this mess will soon be over...

Love, Bill

25. Back, in Black

Adrienne and I got on a plane a few hours later. She'd been out to the Hamptons and I had to wait for her. She had moved up in another company, just like always, and was running the joint. Making major money. She was on a boat, still sleeping. I'll never forget how her cries echoed in that hull.

I was so distraught I forgot to pack any nice clothes. I just threw some jeans and a pair of black pants in my bag. I felt like I'd lost my father, even though I had one. My Dad even thought of Popey as a father. It was so confusing. My Dad loved us, I didn't question, but Dad just didn't seem to know how to go about it. Popey knew. He showed me a lot of things.

When I was a kid back in high school, and was wasting my life away, Popey confronted me. 'I thought you told me you wanted to be in a rock band..?'

'I know, Popey. It's just…' I stood stunned. He took me seriously. Popey knew how to believe in me before I did. He did that for people. He did it quietly, precisely. He'd hold up a mirror or hold you up, whichever was required.

Some knew Popey drank. Quite a bit, at night. Not that you'd ever notice. He was a quiet drinker. Mainly just put away a third of a fifth, and fall asleep at night on the left side of the couch — his spot. The boys in the family knew where he hid liquor all over that mountain, in tree trunks and tool boxes. Just in case. I thought Popey had been doing all right to be in his eighties. I calculated he had another good ten years or so. He'd survived bladder cancer, and the doctors in Winston Salem said he checked out good. He'd even stopped drinking completely after his surgery, which I found miraculous until learning the reason. A local quack doctor gave him an open-ended prescription for Xanax and Lord knows what else, which Popey had been eating like candies — unaware of what they really were.

I could have gotten furious about the doctor and pills business, but I didn't have any fury left. Back in New York the queer scene was getting swallowed whole by crystal meth. Hundreds upon thousands of guys seemed intent on getting fucked up, getting fucked, and getting AIDS. Some even went after the disease without drugs, so they could be part of what they described as the 'AIDS club.' And a whole new generation of young, invincible kids had hit the scene — under the impression that AIDS was something you now just had to take a pill for. I wished Billy or Marty Lipton or Scott or Haoui or any number of the hundreds of thousands who had died could have come back and kicked the shit out of every last one of these assholes and taken their bodies to finish their lives.

Even AIDS charities were running sexy ads of models carrying a 'Living with AIDS' message — which would have been OK, I guess, if they'd shown the other side. And drug companies intent on promoting their new cash cow followed suit. Dolce and Gabbana had been replaced by Retrovir and Cyclaplex. The airwaves became cluttered with drug ads. Don't do drugs unless you get them from your doctor. Popey was right — war everywhere, affecting everybody.

Mom picked Adrienne and me up from the airport. Together we drove up into the mountains. You can tell when summer is approaching, the nighttime dew becomes more pungent. That night was the family viewing at Adam's Funeral Home.

Everyone assembled in the reception area. Grandmother held my Mom and uncle Jimmy's hand. I was numb, as usual. Grandmother looked at me. 'I don't want to do this again,' I said. The entire room was silent. 'You think I want to?' she said back. We went in, everyone took a turn filing by. I went up and kissed him on the forehead. As I pulled away, I noticed something was amiss. Not that the no-longer-living should look alive, but something needed fixing. Nobody gave me a second glance — they all knew I was weird. They had no idea how much experience I'd had in scenes like this. I looked up and noticed there were two spotlights on him, one red, one blue. I spent time explaining to the funeral director how you don't put a fucking blue light on anyone, alive or not alive.

The funeral was the next day. I told Mama I wished to speak at the service. Dad had become a born-again Baptist and came in for the service. He got insulted when I didn't want to hold hands and pray before breakfast at the Waffle House. The local veterans would bring the military colors and the drums and the twenty-one guns. My cousin Reese, a professional trumpet player, and his brother David prepared Taps.

I stayed up almost all night, working on what I would say. I wanted to honor Popey, and in doing so, honor the respect he always showed me. He knew I was queer, but that didn't change one thing between us. The hard thing for me was sucking it up at a straight funeral — we wouldn't be clapping or camping out or anything at this one. Not that anyone would mind. I wished for some professional wailers. The only odd thing I'd ever brought up was a few years earlier when I decided to start hugging Popey. He didn't mind, he just wasn't used to men hugging him. I think some of my male cousins later followed suit.

Around 11AM I started up to the pulpit with my prepared statement. The sanctuary was filled with Popey's friends, war veterans, church members, family. Dad sat back with the guests. I was nervous, just like I had been every time I'd ever gotten up in front of people. But as I mounted the steps, almost by mistake, I noticed something had changed, something new. I felt a strength, although my Popey lay just in front of me in a little gray box. My arms didn't twitch. My palms weren't sweaty. In my right hand was my scratchy, messy, marked-on paper I would read. This wasn't someone else's song, cause or anthem. It was just me, with my thoughts on a piece of paper, getting up in front of a large group of people, and it felt right.

After the inside part, we carried Popey to the outside part. After the graveside ceremony, and the trumpets, and the guns salutes, everyone went inside the fellowship hall to eat. Food after funerals seemed to be the trend. I waited outside for them to lower the casket. I showed a few of my cousins how to toss on the first dirt. I stayed out there until the job was complete, just as I had with Grandma Ruby. The gravediggers don't like it 'cause they have to be real careful and not shake things. I get a kick out of that. I felt a little funny because before they closed the casket for the last time, I stood over Popey in my borrowed clothes, took my pack of cigarettes, and pushed them down beside his right leg. Popey loved to smoke. I told him he could have those, and take them with him. I had to move on.

I joined everybody inside the sanctuary-turned fellowship hall. I sat up at the front where the entrance used to be, where Grandma would drop off my Great grandmother Blanche on Sunday mornings before parking the 1957 Rambler. Where Jarrod Cline and I used to play. Just across the road from where Jarrod was buried. It all smelled the same — fresh-cut grass, budding rosebushes, damp sandstone — like I'd never even left

26. Sodacracker Redemption

Back in New York once again, I spent most of that summer and fall floundering. In life, with people. I could barely leave the house anymore — except for yoga and my night classes — too many panic attacks otherwise. Somehow I'd managed an almost straight-A average — first time, ever. I'd gathered Rimbaud, Tolstoy, Brecht and Plato around to keep me company. *Bartleby the Scrivener* my new hero. Mary, my mentor and patron saint of writing, kept encouraging me. She told me maybe I needed a gestalt therapy, where you get a friend to lock you in a room or something while you scream and cry for a couple of days. I needed something.

At first, I went back to the familiar — exactly what I didn't need. Boozing, not at all like years before, but too much anyway. And I found a nice little alcoholic loser boyfriend — emotionally vacant, selfish. We said 'I love you' but I think I loved not being alone and he loved my centrally located apartment and high-speed connection to the internet. Good for slutting around downtown on the net.

All this made me more miserable than ever. I fell almost completely apart. I didn't want to die, but I didn't know how to live. Mom worried about me. I guess it was one last breakdown before I faced whatever it was I had to face. The mirror is always waiting.

The bright silver skull ring covered in bright rhinestones gets the index finger — power. The silver Sanskrit one from your sister gets your right-third finger — blessed by the sage. The ankh engulfs the right pinky — dare. All covered, the energies correct. One final cigarette before you go, so you can admire your look, your face, your jewelry in your dim East Village hovel. You've become the triumphant phoenix about to arise from his destitution, if only for one night. In a mad dash you turn out the lights, grab your leather MC jacket, phone a taxicab and fly down your stairs. Your hands sparkle while grasping the iron turns of the rotten old staircase. You get outside on your stoop — 12:30. Perfect. While sitting down to wait for your taxi, you have an encounter with one of 'them,' who hasn't made it inside yet. You despise 'them.'

A friend referred me to a man named George Mcavoy. George was one of the best cognitive therapists in New York City. He'd held hands with hundreds of palliative care patients, mostly men dying from AIDS. Probably some of my friends. At least I had something in common with him. He lost his brother, a fireman, on 9/11. He knew the deal. I figured it worth a shot, since I was as isolated as ever, barely able to leave my apartment.

The first time I went into his office, I told him an overview of my story. He told me he could help. After a few visits I learned I was obsessive-compulsive and the post-traumatic stress disorder was confirmed. But mine wasn't just because of 9/11. That only sealed the deal. I'd been building it up for quite some time. I thought I was bound for a hospital and all sorts of things. None of this surprised me. My friend Jorgé once told me that I 'reminded him of his friend Robert Mapplethorpe, but unfortunately most artists end up — crazy.'

Falling apart was no problem, it just came to me like breathing. 'I, just don't know why... How can people... I am so wrong... I-just-don't-understand...' I couldn't even make complete sentences without choking. George quickly interrupted, and told me to clam up and just accept it.

'Just accept it, just accept everything.'

'But, I...'

'But nothing... just accept it.'

'But what if...'

'The future will take care of itself. Reduce, reduce, reduce. Let the drama go. Just accept it.'

For some reason I trusted George. Really, I had no choice. Billy would have appreciated him. He was just a few years ahead of me. Salty, nice-looking guy. Kinda like the character Robin Williams played in 'Good Will Hunting,' that came from whence I came. Drugs, booze, people, flashy scenes. He knew the deal. He'd survived. I wanted to. He had an office and a nice cell phone and a car. Between him and a Monday Al-Anon meeting, I began to feel like my legs were attached to me again, and no one told me I had to regret and lament the past, so I looked to the future for the first time in a long time. It hurt my eyes.

I spent the next winter of 2002 in the Rose Reading Room of the New York Public Library doing my work for Empire State College. It's big and airy, with long tables for anyone to use. Warm, incandescent light flowed from the chandeliers above and radiated from the lamps on the tables. And the most comfortable wooden chairs ever made. The gigantic windows look out onto

Bryant Park. Some days the sun beat in like a beacon from the gods. Other days, our reflections littered the dry side of the rain-soaked glass. This was the only room in Manhattan where my memories didn't haunt me.

I used seat number 203. I lived in that room. No one there knew each other; no one allowed to talk. Only the scraping of chair legs on the floor was permitted. The people who use that room form a congregation, which tourists quietly tiptoe by while touring the hall — the only barrier between them and us is the will to take a seat. The ceiling is a mammoth 19th-century painting surrounded by hundreds of carved Tudor roses — one of which is tilted just slightly to the left from the others. I took the slow bus up Third Avenue, every day, and finished manuscript after manuscript for my undergraduate degree.

Going to twelve-step meetings, yoga, and seeing George was better than staying depressed. 'Gay' now meant back rooms, crystal meth and bad TV sitcoms about rich fags on the Upper West Side, and I needed my own groove. I needed a new place to live, but Mayor Bloomberg was more concerned with slapping a football stadium in the middle of Manhattan than places for people to live.

For a diversion, Linda Simpson invited me to a corporate party for a watch manufacturer. 'Let's go get a free watch.' Capital idea. I needed a new watch. I needed a new anything. Linda and me hadn't hung out much since Page Reynolds' funeral — the last time I heard 'In My Cubicle.' Antony did a great job singing it, alone, onstage with his mini-synthesizer. The lyrics, 'Living! Dying! Laughing! Crying! In-my-cub-i-c-u-hul...,' reducing my vivid imagination to resolve the sour spaces we'd been inhabiting for years, haunt me to this day.

At the watch party, I was seated beside a young guy who was starting a golf magazine. He had stars in his eyes. The beautiful blond, blue-eyed boy from Luhrmann's La Bohème sang. This inspired me. Afterwards, I walked through the security, the way Schmidt had taught me, and into the backstage area. People around him gave me the icky looks and the who's-he stares. They hadn't yet gotten the memo that I was immune to bourgeoise bullshit. I shook the guy's hand and told him he had inspired me. I stood there and made him shake my hand back. I still had it.

Earlier that year I'd gone to see Hairspray. Harvey Fierstein had the starring role. I took a notion and wrote to Harvey, telling him how Torch Song had inspired me to come to New York — and how I was still inspired with his tenacity. He wasn't a politically-correct queer. He'd had the courage to get on TV and blast the party pushers, the drug culture and bug chasers — people who deliberately got fucked by people with HIV so they too could join the AIDS party. Harvey wrote me back and told me to keep it up, don't stop, don't ever stop. And I didn't. My mentor Mary Folliet from SUNY started hooking me up higher on the food chain with events like 'Poems Not Fit For the White House' held at Avery Fisher Hall in an ice storm after Mr. Bush cancelled the program in Washington — he couldn't handle the heat. We went to hear Gore Vidal speak on his book *Perpetual War for Perpetual Peace* at Society for Ethical Culture, and sat a handful of seats over from Senator George McGovern. What I hadn't completely realized that my life transition had already begun in a big way, beyond my wildest dreams.

You look into the face of the loud, babbling girl who's passing your stoop. Looks right at you with her tired, drunken, red eyes. She stops just long enough to notice that you see her secrets spilling out of her brand-name clothes. Demurely, you light a cigarette.

She wants you to see that she is a conforming participant: proper shoes, navy jacket, gold jewelry, big hair — a rubber-stamp twenty-two-year-old. All she needs is a macho-pig boyfriend with an IQ of 12 on her arm to complete this lovely package. She looks back at your expressionless face with an aristocratic sneer as she trips over a cardboard refrigerator box. She's trying to hide the fact that she hasn't got an original thought in her head. She wishes she were anybody else, and hates you for it — while you sit there, the person you created. She wants you to skip over. Just move on and not notice. Her sneer lingers as she works her foot clear from the cardboard, like a raccoon caught in a steel trap. What she really wants is for you to react: either to help her laugh, to laugh with her or to laugh at her, so she can know what she's dealing with. You don't budge.

You don't care about the plight of drunken college students. You owe her nothing. 'What?' she says aloud after finally breaking free from the refrigerator box. You continue smoking your cigarette through a

sadistic, expressionless face. 'Fuck You!' she screeches with the voice of one who's been handed everything, and walks away. She did good. She can now truthfully tell her friends back home that she told off the freak. She won't probe farther, she's frightened of your decoration, now turned to war paint. You've never budged. She'd rather give you her soul. You don't even consider responding because you know she doesn't have any idea where she is going or even wants to go, now or tomorrow, and she'll probably spend her entire life owing somebody something. Pathetic. The bright lights of the late-model Lincoln Continental suddenly bathe you in midnight sun. Everything on you shines and sparkles. You're fabulous. Your carriage awaits...

27. Just Gettin' Started

May 21, 2004. My prediction came true, surprise, surprise. The very last ever, really official SqueezeBox! came a second time — Jackie Beat, Lady Bunny, Jayne County Five and Boy George. Earlier in the day I took a birthday cake down to the club for Jimmy James. Jayne was rehearsing, Boy George was wandering around. Schmidt flew in from LA again. Rumors fly that Courtney Love might show up, another about Chrissie Hynde. Jimmy told me that I should jump onstage and beat Courtney up and cause a publicity stunt. Yeah.

I meandered around after dumping the cake in the fridge, and decided to hang around and listen a bit. That's the part I liked the most — preparing, planning... I remembered the days all those years ago, me up on the ladder, hanging stuff before Debbie's New Year's Eve show. The place seemed much bigger then. The world, more fertile. Now that I'd quit smoking, and all but quit drinking, the place smelled extra rank — more Lemonex and beer. Lily of the Valley and I had a catch-up conversation outside the front door. Boy George, who was on the bill, wandered over to join us. The irony was not lost on me that the man who'd appeared throughout my life for over 20 years showed up out of nowhere, again, as I prepared another major life change, had been the guest of honor of my first big night out in Manhattan, and would headline one of my last.

I told Lily about my plans for Europe and the writers' program. I hadn't bothered to introduce myself, but when George heard 'Scotland' he jumped in the conversation: 'It's very beautiful there, you'll love it. Just wear a bit of eyeliner and the boys will love you!' And for the first time since I'd heard of him, mid-80s back in High School, I was able to appreciate good old George. He'd calmed down a lot since the night I first met him at the club, and was simply standing there, a regular person in a pair of sweatpants and a t-shirt, encouraging me to create myself anew. I couldn't argue with it. And this reminded me that there's many sides to people, and strangely, we were wandering ahead of ourselves, in spite of ourselves. Now, I'd fetch him drink anytime.

That night, the front of the stage was filled with the same old photographers, groupies, and tired music-industry lackeys — all afraid they'd miss something. Fact was, they had, by about ten years. Remnants of the old-school crowd was in the back of the room. The death of a club is never glamorous. And, the movie people were back. Lyle and his new friend Zach had apparently fired the previous team and taken the project over. I'd spent some more time talking with Lyle trying to put together a story in his head about the club — loaned them hours of footage. I even had footage of the last time Joey Ramone had been onstage at Don's. Rare stuff of Debbie, Nina Hagen and all of them.

Everything about the night was too forced, staged, the crowd too eager, the place too clean. Don had renovated, moved the bathrooms around, changed the hallway. Chi Chi Valenti and the usual band of phantoms plopped down in the middle of everything — getting in line for the cameras. They'd be sure to tell the world they were there.

Debbie showed up. I acted like nothing had ever happened between us, like everything was just as it had been the first day she showed up for rehearsal at SqueezeBox! I walked right around her like I always had. I'd spent a lot of years working to make the club popular and these people famous. I'd earned my place, although my knees were still shakey.

I saw people I hadn't seen in years. Alicia-Sissy came with Justin Bond, and both waited patiently for me to get my new digital camera to work. Adrienne was a hit, drawing the usual crowd around her wherever she went. The boys from Psychotica made it — Ena, Tommy, Buz, Enrique. All except Patrick, who had run away and was hiding out on the West Coast. Schmidt had flown in for the occasion. He gave me charge of Jimmy's birthday cake, which I took to him onstage just before he started his cover song, 'Maggie May' by Rod Stewart. The lyrics bounced over me like falling pebbles. 'Wake up Maggie I think I got somethin' to say to you.'

I was awake, very awake. Standing in the same spot I'd stood in all those years before, behind Debbie. This time, I wasn't behind anyone. My closed hand was planted on the hip of my black leather jeans which Greta, just across the stage, had custom altered for me. In the front pocket was the top page of my Bachelor of Arts transcript, with nearly perfect grades. Along with it, my entry pass for my graduation ceremony and an acceptance letter from the University of Edinburgh. In just a couple of weeks I'd be crossing a stage at Lincoln Center, dressed in black again. 'It's late September and I think I should be back at school,' the lyrics continued. I stood in the same spot where I'd been hanging decorations at Debbie's rehearsals for some of her first SqueezeBox! shows. The same spot I'd held the keyboard from flying off the stage. The same stage I'd stood on and tried to sing backup for Schmidt and Marilyn Manson. That space, my spot.

'You led me away from home, just to save you from being alone, you stole my heart and that's what really hurts…' As the audience screeched along at the top of their lungs, I realized the tune was one of the main songs from Torch Song Trilogy — the scene where Arnold meets Ed. The movie that convinced me New York was to be my town. 'You stole my heart, but I love you anyway,' the lyrics rise into the microphone from the crowd.

I looked out at the sea of people in front of the stage and imagined the room as it once was, unrenovated and full of our original family of misfit toys. For all my falls, there'd been plenty to catch me, catch each other. So many people gone, missing. Hearts and souls. They made up a vibe that had been passed down from old times. The old Bowery, Tenderloin, Harlem, Max's, 54, Danceteria, Mudd Club, Pyramid, SqueezeBox! everybody worth an ounce of salt knows rock isn't new, it's just a 20th-century incarnation of tribal storytelling — right up there with old-school soul and jazz. And I have to give credit where it's due: without Dean Johnson, who'd originated 'Rock 'n' Roll Fag Bar' at The World in the late 80s, Squeezebox! might never even have been imaginable.

I considered all this, standing there, sober, the first time ever on that stage. I got a pang in my throat that's been there ever since. I couldn't decide whether to wish for one more night — an orgy of lost spirits making out with each other to save the world — or to let it all go. I reached in my pocket and felt the heavy stationery, from Scotland. It was a different-sized paper than we had in the States. The folded shape felt unnatural poking into my thigh. I became lightheaded — that feeling again, like when someone is going to die, or when something is about to change.

After the show, the energy in the room transformed to petty nostalgia. To me it felt like the Studio 54 reunion parties sponsored by local radio stations. Absolutely everyone was armed with pocket cameras, and more interested in snapping than dancing.

It was like another prom we'd already been to, but decided to have again. The scene was over, the world had shifted. We had illegal wars going down, a pathological liar in the White House. The city was lost to real-estate developers. Giuliani was gone, but not the scars from his unmitigated reign of hateful progress.

Late in the night, I ran into one of the film guys, who looked embarrassed, and started chattering, LA style: 'Oh, man. I'm so sorry! Did you get a turn in the interview van? Everybody was supposed to be filmed. We were doing second interviews. Let me see if they're still there. Someone was supposed to find you.' He ran to the van and stayed a long time then came back with a perfected drawn expression. I'd followed him outside but realized I'd been overlooked by the idiot parade again.

'It's OK,' I lied before he could say much. 'You got the first one of me, right — from a year or so ago?' I let him off the hook so I could get away without another wasted moment.

'Yeah, yeah for sure man...' he muddled on.

'Good. Just use that. It's not important.' film dude stopped mumbling, stood and looked a little baffled, as if there could be nothing more important in all the world than his little movie. 'You can take all the pictures you want, try to piece something together...but I *lived* the story motherfucker...' I smirked to myself. No need to waste my breath.

'You can't make chicken salad out of chicken shit...' recalling once again what my high school orchestra teacher used to say.

At the end of the night, which had collided with the next morning, a contingent of original Box! people and their admirers hung around. Chatting, talking. I'd never really gotten lucky at SqueezeBox! — always too busy at the end of the night running around collecting money or whatever. This time, I had nothing to do. I sat up on the bar, a couple of cocktails in my head — I hadn't been drinking hardly at all for months — getting misty.

I felt the earth moving under me, just as I had all my life before a big change. I was about to say some goodbyes and go catch a cab, when Guy put on the end-of-the-night song — I think 'Union City Blue' — ten years, and it all ran together. I decided to stay 'til the end.

Everyone else had someone to make out and slow dance with. I started to back up toward a bar stool when I saw a tall, dark-haired boy, with camouflage pants, combat boots and no shirt is smiling at me.

He had paint all over his body. Dark war stripes on his face. I'd noticed him earlier and incorrectly figured he was too young, too pretty, too perfect for me. He was most definitely a model type. Dark, black hair, piercing black eyes. Smooth alabaster skin. He pulled me toward the dance floor and wrapped his arms around me. He told me his name, Xavier.

I rested my head on his shoulder, and thought, 'Where the fuck were you thirteen years ago?' We slow danced the entire song. Guy must have been busy, a few more songs played, then silence fell on the room for our last time.

I left by myself. There was no Bob Gruen outside to loan me his Lincoln; no Debbie to shuttle me in her Chevrolet. Not even a faint drizzle of rain to make the pavement look sexy. At that point, I didn't even know where 'home' was.

Greenwich still collided with Spring Street, and although I imagined the cackle, roar and coo of the voices of the last great decade, the entire area was deserted — not even another lost soul to reassure me. Where a gaggle of yellow taxis once lined up beyond daybreak to await the *connoisseurs de l'artiste* to emerge, an eery silence now mingled with the dew.

As I passed, the warm light of the all-night diners beckoned for the company of the nowhere to go people, presenting a familiar urge to oblige — but the golden glow, however devastatingly seductive, had forgotten my song.

As I continued and Gotham slept, I suddenly went from fearful loneliness, to merely alone; and became delighted at the notion of preparing my own breakfast.

> *Once, when you were younger, the nighttimes ran together into one big glorious haze, glossing your periphery like a candy-coloured twilight glow from the gilded carousel in Central Park. Now, seventeen years later, just as you've finally arrived in the eye of the great people-storm called New York City, it's time to go. You sell everything you have, including the keys to your coveted rent-controlled apartment, and walk with your knees wobbling, to deposit the ten grand in the bank. The landlord was happy to see you go — loyal tenants mean nothing to those who've sold their soul. He'll get three times the amount you pay after a cheap coat of paint and some forged paperwork. But no looking back: you have to leave. It's one thing for a corrupt mayor to sell Gotham out, but too far for a corrupt president to let it get bombed out. Clearances. 'Goodbye' has been a central theme for your time on fanatic island — Marty, Haoui, Billy, Scott and so many others gone — with Seth, Marilyn, Raul, Page, Dean and Jack and others soon to follow. You realize it never stops. Life. The war is lost, New York*

to you is dead, and you cannot survive in whatever they're pretending it still is. Soon, Bloomberg will throw out the term limits you helped fight for, and continue Giuliani's rampage throughout the city, with an army of ambivalent masses inspired by a stupid TV show. You know better. You've chosen a non-fiction life. Acceptance is the key. There're Queens to meet, stories to write, First Ministers to befriend; cities from Paris to Rome to frequent, writers' festivals in Prague to host; and a close relationship to be had with a notorious publisher who'll join you in prison. You'll do just fine. You're from New York, the old-school state of mind.

They've reinvented our gods at
Saint Christopher Street, the downtown side.
Funny, it all looks the same.
Saint Vincent stopped taking the damned,
the market will handle them now.
If I walk the streets where I once loved Blondie,
she can no longer be found.
Instead: jackals who'll swear they've seen the deity.
Funny, it all 'looks' the same.
I made it there. The love is genuine.
Now I can leave.

—MLB

epilogue

> 'You know how they always say: *Everything happens first in New York?* Well, it's true, and this time the city is dying. We're going to be the first modern city to die. You're going to get to watch us die.'
>
> –Kembra Pfaeler, The Voluptuous Horror of Karen Black, Antony's Meltdown Festival, London 2012

So, where'd everybody go? Well, if they're alive, they're all online. Find them. Along with their photos. Better still, go outside and find them. None of our stories, your stories, stop here. For every page in this book, there's ten more on the floor under my desk and ten more out there yet to be written.

The people? Well, in no partulcar order, Michael Schmidt, forever the creative culturist, is on top of his game in LA, his designs, literally, are on the cover of the *Rolling Stone*. And Debbie, well, she's giving lessons on how to take yourself from icon, to iconic — an unmistakeable face and voice of our entire generation. Antony is an international singer-sensation with his band The Johnsons. Lily of the Valley co-starred in one of my favorite light hearted movies, 'Wonder Boys,' and has gone on to bigger roles in the theatre. Blair Schulman is an arts critic in Kansas City. Marcus Leatherdale lives between Portugal, Canada and India, and recently sold out another show of his work in NYC. On occasion I contribute to his new *Omen magazine*, and his friendship has been invaluable to me. Thomas Onorato, the man who kept me from going completely crazy back in the day, owns his own successful PR firm 'O-W' in Manhattan with Max Wixom, and has his own story out, *Confessions Behind the Velvet Ropes* written by Glen Belverio, my longtime friend-in-crime. Justin Bond, who's since added a middle name of 'Vivian,' and Kenny Mellman toured the world with Kiki and Herb, and impressively played Carnegie Hall not once but twice, and are now on to new projects. Justin Vivian since played a poignant gender redefining role in the movie 'Short Bus.'

Pat Briggs is still touring with Psychotica, and is working on a new record. And it would be easier to name the bands Nite Bob didn't do a recent tour with. He's spread like butter. Mo Fischer has her own specialty catering business out in California, and still does shows coast to coast. Lisa Carbone must have finally dumped Pat off at a bus stop, and started driving school buses for cash, and her own custom Harley Davidson for pleasure — 'Big Bad Mama' as Formika used to say. Bunny is still doing shows, writing political commentary, doing a lot of work on television and had a movie done on Wigstock. Rumour has it that John Cameron Mitchell and Steven Trask are writing a sequel to Hedwig which means Mike Potter should be back in the mix as well. Greta Brinkman is still playing gigs and seems to be the Rock 'n' Roll queen of Richmond Vee-A. James F. Murphy is performing in Berlin, as is Vaginal Davis, and touring with her new band Tenderloin. Linda Simpson is still at it — hosting all sorts of parties in New York along with her infamous Bingo. Tim Mclusky went back to F.I.T. and with the best of us, is playing 'catchup with our new careers.' I keep up with a lot of these people better now than back in the day.

Some others weren't so lucky. My friend and first NYC roommate Marilyn, well, just didn't make it. Seth reportedly died of liver problems in '05. Raul, my friend and 'Supa' went to a great big tenement buidling in the sky. JudgeCal™ Chamberlain, well, he didn't make it either. Nor did Jack Steeb from the original Squeezebox! band. Page Reynolds also passed away around ten years ago, and last year Don Hill dropped dead while walking down the street in Soho — the legendary club finally closed. I can think of worse ways to go, while the rest of life goes on.

In February 2009, my art director agent, Monica Walsh, sent out an email to thousands of contacts from her very successful business, with the subject 'Monica's Health.' She always shot from the hip. 'I want the information to come directly from me...' — a hopeful message about a brain tumor, operable, and prognosis of a tricky but full recovery. In the 'biz Monica and I'd had ups, downs and we'd kind of grown up together since my days working for Mike Pakula. We were contemporaries. She fought like hell — just as hard as she'd worked to build a woman-owned business, but alas, less than a year later, well ... you know.

Rest peacefully, people.

As for the Squeezebox! movie, just before the Tribeca Film Festival premiere I was in the city for another project. I got an email: 'We have you a ticket on hold as you are a cast member in the film.' I sat in Queens NY with my new partner Jonny with the worst flu I'd had in years. In the old days I would have loaded up on medicine and gone running. But I just couldn't. The emotions were too crazy for me. Jonny, who isn't from New York and had never been to Squeezebox! took a friend instead, and said the crowd applauded when I came on screen, which surprised me. The reviews were mixed. Tough business, this storytelling.

As for the rest my original group, Dan is a high-faluting lawyer at a big fancy firm, and has a house in Queens. Full of refried beans. Ramón owns his own apartment building in San Francisco and splits his time with NYC. He's worried about having a job when this book comes out. Kurt is lost in Seattle, writing about music and hosting a radio show. He still owes me a look at the pair of trousers Robbie Williams took off and gave him. Giovanni is a photographer, with work published in several major magazine outlets, and DJ's all over the Hudson Valley. Lorenzo seems to be happy, which makes me happy. Jorge is a writer and back in the meatpacking district, where we get regular reports of the yuppie vs. tranny hooker turf wars. Barney, fixture of a heart and soul of a lot of what I held dear in that city; and some of the extensive 'old crowd' are still in NYC doing just fine, but others still are spread out all over the world, doing their thing — Paris, Berlin, London ... even Egypt, just in time for the Spring.

Adrienne runs an online marketing agency for action sports, which means she's surrounded by surfer boys all day long, and lives on a beach with her dog and well-trained boyfriend. We're both grateful that Dad seems really happy for the first time in a long time, and Mom is living the golden life to the hilt. Separately, mind you. Thankfully, mind you.

As for me, well, with Bloomberg setting aside a popular vote and granting himself an illegal third term, Giuliani's legacy of untenable rents, and NYU now formally taking over the last scraps of the village for it's entitled hipster students — I've never really looked back at NYC to live. I've been gone almost a decade. But I do gratefully keep in touch with all my New Yorker brethren who are too many for any lists, but collectively we keep pushing the creative envelope.

After R.E.M. came out with 'Leaving New York' I cried for about a month, and was sad for another two years. But that city, like so many others, now belongs to billionaires and the working poor. New York City is dead, while New York, the state of mind and passion of the people who once knew her live on. It's kind of like Medgar Evers said 'You can kill a man, but not an idea.'

Well, Rudy, you accomplished neither. You can start a culture war, but you will never silence our culture. Silly, little, man. We're stronger now, and will outlive, out love and out shine you and yours completely. That best revenge: living well.

In the words of my literary publisher-mentor-friend John Calder: *'You've got all of eternity to do nothing after you're dead, until then you have to go on – On – ON!'*

And I'm still dreamin' — last time I checked, it's still free, and so am I — and, again, this book ain't even the half of it, just gettin' started.

But I've also tried something new — I woke up.

Martin Belk

Pretty Broken Punks

1982 photo: Dad

"Doing what I'm doing, feeling out of place..."
– Grace Jones

Pretty Broken Punks

1992, West Village
photo: Giovanni DiMola

c. 1993
East Village,
7th Street & Avenue A

1995 Wigstock,
West Side Piers, with
Candace Cayne &
Edward O'Dowd

photos, reviews, audio books,
additional chapters & stories online at
www.prettybrokenpunks.com

MARTIN BELK is a writer, performer and expat New Yorker.

Belk's first monologue, '105° Peach,' premiered on the Edinburgh Fringe Festival in 2006. In Paris, December 2011, he presented the first reading of the stage version of 'Pretty Broken Punks,' which is also scheduled for the 2013 Prague Fringe Festival, and other projects in London.

Belk is currently the Writer-in-Residence and director of the creative writing program at HMPYOI young men's prison; a host for the Prague Writers' Festival; and editor of *ONE Magazine*. He earned a B.A. from SUNY Empire State College and a Master's degree from the University of Edinburgh.

He is also an advocate for youth education and has been recognized by First Minister Alex Salmond and Her Majesty The Queen for his work with young people in custody, detailed in his feature article in the *Scottish Review of Books*. He has also appeared on BBC Radio – 'Scotland Live,' and 'The Lesley Riddoch Show.'

In New York City Belk was a producer for Squeezebox!, the New York rock venue where Blondie reigned supreme, 'Hedwig and the Angry Inch' had its musical debut and the first-ever live, NYC webcast - *Live @nd InConcert* starring Deborah Harry originated. Belk was also a producer for the Multimedia Application of the Year award winner *Will Europe Work?* — the first-ever live, global conference of the European Union.

@MartinNYID
PrettyBrokenPunks.com

"I was 32 when I started cooking, up to then I just ate."
– Julia Child

EP, Multimedia *and* Communications *Glossary*

David Penfold

Published by
Pira International
Randalls Road
Leatherhead
Surrey
KT22 7RU
UK
Tel: (+44) (0)1372 802080
Fax: (+44) (0)1372 802079
E-mail: publications@pira.co.uk
http://www.pira.co.uk/

The facts set out in this publication are from sources which we believe to be reliable.

However, we accept no legal liability of any kind for the publication contents, nor for the information contained therein, nor conclusion drawn by any party from it.

No part of this publication may be reproduced, stored in a retrieval system, or transmitted in any form or by any means, electronic, mechanical, photocopying, recording or otherwise, without the prior permission of the Copyright owner.

© Copyright Pira International 1997

ISBN 1 85802 113 8

Printed in the UK by Arrowhead Books, Reading, Berkshire

Preface

There are two questions raised by a publication of this type. First, given the nature of the content, why a book at all and not an electronic publication and, second, will it not become out of date very quickly? The answer to the first question is that people still often find it easier to refer to books than to access their computers for information; and anyway, there are still a significant number of people who do not always have easy access to a computer but still need to look things up. This glossary is at least partly for them. After all, if you did not have the book, you would not be reading this — and an electronic version may yet be forthcoming!

The answer to the second question is probably yes and there are three ways in which this is true. First, some of the entries will become unnecessary because the term considered, and even the concept described, becomes obsolete or unused. This matters very little and the glossary may still provide a useful retrospective reference. Second, there will be new terms, concepts, software, etc. and this problem will be overcome with future editions (and remember that, while an electronic version has the potential for faster updating, this may be an illusion because the updating still has to be done and there is no guarantee that an electronic reference is actually more up to date than a printed one). Third (and in many ways the same argument applies as for new terms), terms may change their meanings. In such cases, obviously the intention is to provide updated information, but if in you are doubt, I suggest that you go back to the primary source (see below).

Content

The title of this glossary states that it is concerned with electronic publishing, multimedia and communications. This combination was chosen because the three areas seem to be symbiotic: electronic publishing cannot be discussed without including multimedia and, of course, there can be no electronic publishing without communications. With the ever-increasing importance of the World Wide Web (WWW), there are obviously very many references to the Internet and related topics and, of course, to computers. However, while this is not intended to be a dictionary of computing — there are a number of excellent ones already available (both on paper and on the WWW) — inevitably computing terms have been included. The difficulty has been where to draw the line. I have thus included terms that I feel are of direct relevance to the topics of the glossary, but excluded more general computing terms, particularly hardware, although doubtless not everyone will agree with my choice.

Just as there may be computing terms that have not been included, there will almost certainly be even more relevant terms that I have overlooked. Those who have reviewed the glossary have suggested additional terms and I am grateful to them for that. However, I would welcome any additional suggestions for terms that could be included, as well as comments on, and corrections to, the explanations given, and even suggestions of what could be omitted.

I have consulted a very large number of publications and Web sites in compiling this glossary. It is impossible to list them (and even to remember some of them), but I am grateful to all those who have written them. However, I have tried as far as possible to use my own words to discuss the concepts involved and, if I am guilty of plagiarism at all, I hope that those I have plagiarized will take this as a compliment, in that their definition may be the best available. Indeed, there are some, the more simple, definitions that really allow very little latitude in how they may be expressed. I have also added a large number of cross-references (indicated in italics), which I hope are useful.

I have noted above that, if in doubt, it is wise to go back to the primary source. My experience is that today this more often than not means using the WWW. Very few URLs are given in the glossary (look up URL if you do not know what it means), although that may change in future editions. Part of the problem is that in many cases identifying *authoritative* Web sites is not easy and, in addition, Web sites appear and disappear. On the other hand, there are very many search engines available. I use

Preface

AltaVista (http://www.altavista.digital.com/) most often, although other people may find that other approaches suit them better. I hope that enough information is given in the glossary to allow an intelligent search of the Web for any information that is related to a particular topic.

As far as has been possible registered trade names have been given with an initial capital letter. If, in any particular case this has not been done or if there are any errors in such names, they will be corrected in future editions if brought to my attention or that of the publisher.

Finally, I would like to thank all those who have helped with this project. Francis Cave, Principal Consultant, Pira International and David Richards, Production Director, Readers Digest, have extensively reviewed the first draft and I am extremely grateful to them, although of course the final responsibility for what is included here is mine. I have already thanked the very many authors whose writings have been of benefit to me, but my other source of information has been those with whom I have come into contact during my work over the last 10 (or maybe it should be 30) years. I am grateful to all of them, but especially to my colleagues in the British Computer Society Electronic and Multimedia Publishing Specialist Group, and those who have spoken at the Group's meetings, for helping me to keep abreast of developments.

I would also like to thank both my long-suffering family and Gail Murray, Ingmar Folkmans and Lewis Marshall of Pira International for their help and patience. Finally, as one who works both as an editor and in production, I would like to thank those who worked on the editing and production of this glossary. I believe that, however advanced the technology involved, the skill and expertise of the editors and production staff make a major contribution to the quality of a book — or a Web site.

David Penfold
(penfold@eps-edge.demon.co.uk)
Huddersfield
June 1997

1-bit, 8-bit and 24-bit colour The number of bits of information (*colour resolution*) that can be represented in the *pixels* (dots) on the screen. The higher the number of bits, the more colours or *grey scales* you can have. In turn, the higher the number of bits, the more memory is required to handle them, so the number of colours depends on the size of the computer memory, rather than on the monitor used. 8-bit and 24-bit are the most commonly used. 1-bit colour is *monochrome*.

1.TR.6 A control protocol for *ISDN*, which is a national standard in Germany. However, it is being replaced by *Euro-ISDN*.

2B1Q See *two-binary, one-quaternary*.

2B + D See *basic rate ISDN*.

3DO A games system including animation, which will also play audio CDs, allow *Photo-CD* to be viewed and will eventually play video CDs using *MPEG*.

8-bit colour See *1-bit colour*.

10Base2 A type of *Ethernet*, in which computers are connected by thin coaxial cable, commonly known as *thin Ethernet* or *thinnet*. (See also *cheapernet*.)

10Base5 The original *thick Ethernet* cabling standard, which uses thick yellow cable.

10BaseT A type of *Ethernet*, in which computers are connected by *twisted pair cable*.

16-bit Describes hardware or software that manages data, program code and memory address information in words that are 2 bytes or 16 bits wide.

24-bit colour See *1-bit colour*.

32-bit Describes hardware or software that manages data, program code and memory address information in words that are 4 bytes or 32 bits wide.

100Base-FX Part of the *100Base-T* standard, requiring *fibre-optic* connections.

100Base-T A 100 Mbps *Ethernet* standard, which is based on *CSMA/CD* technology, also called *Fast Ethernet*. Includes 100Base-TX, which requires two twisted pairs and 100Base-T4, which requires four pairs (but of lower-quality cable).

431A The type of plug that fits a standard 'type 600' *BT* telephone socket.

A

AAL See *ATM adaptation layer*.

ABI See *application binary interface*.

acceptable use policy (AUP) The official policy applied by networks concerning the use to which the network may be put. For example, *NSFNet* does not allow commercial use. Different networks have different AUPs.

access class In *SMDS*, the type (or *bandwidth*) of access. Different types of access line offer different access classes, ranging from 1.17 Mbps to 34 Mbps.

access control list (ACL) A list giving the services available on a *server*, showing which *hosts* are permitted to use which service.

access provider See *service provider*.

Accunet A switched 56 kbps service provided by AT&T in the USA. A forerunner of *ISDN*.

ACK (Acknowledgement) The *ASCII* character with code 6. An acknowledgment that a previous transmission has been correctly received. Also an acknowledgement number in a *TCP* header giving information about the receiver to the sender.

ACL See *access control list*.

ACN See *Advisory Committee on Networking*.

acoustic coupler A device that permits data transmission through a telephone handset over the public switched telephone network by modulating audible (*analogue*) tones.

Acrobat A technology produced by Adobe Systems that allows documents created on one computer system to be read and printed on other systems. The technology uses *portable document format (pdf)* files, which are produced either directly as a print option in the source application or by running *PostScript* code through a program called Acrobat Distiller. All formatting information is embedded in the compressed file and graphics and font information can also be included. If the fonts in the document are not present on the system where the document is viewed, *Multiple Mastering* technology is used to simulate those fonts. Acrobat can be used for proofing (particularly in conjunction with *ISDN*) and for *electronic publishing*, although the facsimile of the printed page is not always an ideal format for viewing onscreen. The latest version (Acrobat 3.0) was described as *Amber* during development and allows more flexibility in viewing documents over the *World Wide Web*.

active document The part of an electronic document that is displayed in the current window and therefore receptive to commands from the keyboard or mouse.

active matrix A design of *liquid crystal display*.

ActiveX A set of utilities developed by Microsoft as an answer to *Java*, so as to allow interactive content to be run over the *Internet*. ActiveX is an implementation of *OLE* and thus limited to Microsoft *Windows*.

AD See *administrative domain*.

adaptive answering The ability of a *fax modem* to decide whether an incoming call is a fax or data call.

adaptive digital pulse code modulation (ADPCM) A *compression* technique in which the difference between successive samples is encoded, rather than their values. This increases the amount of audio that can be stored on a CD about 16-fold. ADPCM is used on *CD-Rom XA* and *CD-I* discs.

ADB See *Apple Desktop Bus*.

ADCCP See *advanced data communication control procedure*.

A/D conversion See *analogue to digital conversion*.

add/drop multiplexer A device that can extract certain specified lower-bandwidth signals from a high-bandwidth signal and insert other lower-bandwidth signals.

additive colour The production of colour by blending different colours of light. Colour (*RGB*) computer monitors and television sets use additive colour. Blending equal amounts of red, green and blue light gives white light and other combinations give other colours. This should be contrasted with the way in which we normally see, using white light, when the colour perceived is made up of the wavelengths reflected by an object, with those absorbed subtracted. *Subtractive colour* is used in printing (see *CMYK*). It should also be noted that devices using additive colours have a *colour gamut*, which does not include all the colours that can be viewed in nature. (See also *1-bit, 8-bit and 24-bit colour*.)

address The sequence of bits or characters that identifies the station to which a message or packet of data must be routed. (See *electronic mail address, Internet address, MAC address, memory address, network address, on-line address, SCSI address*.)

address checking A security procedure in which the *router* checks the *network (IP) address*.

address mask Used to identify which bits in an *IP address* correspond to the *network address* and which to the *subnet* portions of the address. This mask is also referred to as the subnet mask because the network portion of the address can be determined by the *class* encoded in an IP address.

address resolution Conversion of an *Internet address* into the corresponding physical (*Ethernet*) address. (See *address resolution protocol*.)

address resolution protocol (ARP) The TCP/IP protocol used to find an *Ethernet address* from an *Internet address*. An ARP *packet* containing the Internet address of a host is transmitted and the Ethernet address will be returned by that host or by another host. Each host *caches* address translations to reduce delay. ARP allows Internet addresses to be independent of Ethernet addresses but only if all hosts support it. ARP is defined in *RFC 826*. Hosts that do not support ARP use *constant mapping*. (See also *proxy ARP, reverse ARP*.)

address screening The procedure in *SMDS* by which a user can control the destinations and/or the sources of information.

ADMD See *administration management domain*.

Administration management domain (ADMD) A public *X.400* Message Handling System telecommunications provider. Examples are *MCImail* and ATTmail in the USA and British Telecom Gold400 mail in the UK. Together, the ADMDs in all countries provide the X.400 backbone.

administrative domain (AD) The *hosts*, *routers* and network(s) managed by a single administration.

Adobe Photoshop See *Photoshop*.

Adobe Systems, Inc. The company that created the *PostScript page description language* and the *Acrobat* technology and the *pdf*.

Adobe Type Manager (ATM) A program that uses Type 1 *PostScript* fonts to display type on the screen to provide the best onscreen rendition that the resolution of the display screen allows. ATM will also allow output of Type 1 fonts to a non-PostScript printer. (See *fonts, outline fonts*.)

Adonis A pilot document delivery service based on the supply of scanned images of the full text and graphics of 219 biomedical journals stored on CD-Rom. The service was initiated by a consortium of European scientific publishers.

ADPCM See *adaptive digital pulse code modulation*.

ADSL See *asymmetric digital subscriber line*.

advanced data communication control procedure (ADCCP) An ANSI-standardized bit-oriented synchronous data link control protocol equivalent to *hdlc*.

advanced peer-to-peer networking (APPN) An IBM procedure that routes data in a network between two or more *APPC* systems.

advanced program-to-program communications (APPC) An implementation of the IBM *SNA/SDLC* protocol which allows communication between interconnected systems so that the processing of programs is shared between the systems.

Advanced Research Projects Agency (ARPA) An agency of the US *DoD* responsible for the development of new technology for use by the military (for some time called *DARPA*). It funded development of *ARPANET* (which was the basis of the *Internet*) and *TCP/IP*.

Advanced Research Projects Agency Network (ARPANET) The predecessor of the *Internet*, funded by *ARPA*. It became operational in 1968 and was used for early networking research, as well as providing a central *backbone* during the development of the Internet. The ARPANET consisted of individual computers interconnected by *leased lines* using *packet switching* to communicate. Protocols used included *ftp* and *telnet*. ARPANET was superseded by *NFSNET*.

Advisory Committee on Networking (ACN) A committee of the Information Systems Committee of the UK Universities Funding Council.

AFS See *Andrew file system*.

agent A program that acts as an intermediary in *client-server* computing, preparing information and handling information exchange on behalf of *client* or *server*. (See also *intelligent agent*, which implies that the agent is involved in some decision-making process.)

AIFC, AIFF See *audio interchange file format*.

Albert A name given by *British Telecom* to a machine intended to combine telephone, word-processing, *teletext* and *Telex*. It has long since been abandoned.

alias A method of allocating an easily memorable name to an *email address* (if perhaps the actual address is hard to remember, for example *CompuServe* email addresses). Alternatively, if the mail software allows, a group of addresses, so that you can send a message to a group of people while apparently only using one address.

aliasing A possible result of displaying or printing an *analogue* or continuous image in a *digital* format, so that the image is split into cells. This can create a jagged or 'pixellated' image and is particularly noticeable on low-resolution devices and in fine detail (see Figure 1). (See also *anti-aliasing*, *moiré*.) Aliasing also occurs in the conversion of *digital sound* to *analogue sound* using a *sound card*. If the *sampling rate*, that

Figure 1 Aliasing
A simple example of aliasing. The left-hand letter is a bitmap at the maximum resolution available for the printer used, while the resolution of the right-hand letter has been reduced to 25% of the maximum

is, the frequency of extraction from the digital sample, is too low, the sound is distorted. To avoid aliasing, a sound card with a sampling rate of around 40 kHz is required.

ALOHA A system of *contention resolution* devised at the University of Hawaii ('aloha' is a Hawaiian greeting). *Packets* are *broadcast* and the sending system listens to see if they collide and, if so, re-transmits after a random time. *Slotted ALOHA* forces packets to start at the beginning of a time slot. Basic ALOHA is particularly appropriate for networks with long propagation times, for example those including satellites.

alpha channels A feature used in the storage of 24-bit images on the *Macintosh*, which uses 32-bit *QuickDraw*. The remaining eight bits are used by the alpha channels to hold information on other aspects of the image, such as masks and layering effects, for use by *bitmap editors* such as *Adobe PhotoShop*, in much the same way as in drawing programs. The effect is that different parts of the image can be handled independently.

alt A *Usenet* newsgroup category, which stands for 'alternative' and includes many of the more unconventional, not to say controversial, topics.

AltaVista A search engine for the *World Wide Web* and for *Usenet* newsgroups. AltaVista was mounted by *DEC* to demonstrate the power of the alpha chip, on which it runs.

AM See *amplitude modulation*.

Amber The development name for *Adobe Acrobat* version 3.0, especially designed for accessing *Acrobat pdf* files via the *World Wide Web*. With this version it is possible to view a document page by page as it is downloaded, whereas previously, with earlier versions of Acrobat, it was necessary to download the whole document before any of it could be viewed.

American National Standards Institute (ANSI) Creates standards for a wide variety of industries, including computer programming languages.

America On-Line (AOL) A US on-line service provider based in Vienna, Virginia, USA. AOL offers *electronic mail*, interactive newspapers and magazines, conferencing, software libraries, computing support, on-line classes and services such as hotel and plane reservations and shopping. Since 1996, it has also been operating a European service. (See also *Prodigy, CompuServe*.)

American Standard Code for Information Interchange (ASCII) An agreed method of representing alphanumeric characters by 7-bit binary numbers. ASCII represents the characters that can be keyed on a standard PC keyboard, plus some characters which provide certain functions, such as 'Bell', which produces a bell or 'bleep'. Although there has been no formal agreement, 8-bit characters are often described as *extended* or *high-level ASCII* and include many of the commonly used accented characters and some other characters. Note that the values for individual high-level characters differ from the *ANSI* character set, which is used by *Microsoft Windows*. (See Table 1.) (See also *EBCDIC*.)

amplitude modulation (AM) A form of transmission in which the level of a *carrier frequency* is changed to determine the encoded information. (See also *frequency modulation*.)

analogue Information that can vary in a continuous fashion (e.g., loudness of sound), containing no discontinuous elements. (See also *digital*.) The conventional telephone system uses analogue signals and thus *modems* are required to convert digital signals for transmission over telephone lines. Newer methods, such as *ISDN, frame relay* and *asynchronous transfer mode* are digital.

analogue loopback A self-test for *modems* to check the frequencies they are using.

analogue to digital conversion Conversion of information from *analogue* form (such as the loudness of a sound) to *digital* (so that it can be represented in a computer). (See also *sampling, digital modulation*.)

anchor A marker for the beginning or the end of a hypertext link. Also used within word-processing and DTP processes to indicate where a graphic or other imported information is linked to the main document text flow.

Andrew file system (AFS) The distributed file system developed in the Andrew Project, a distributed system project at Carnegie Mellon University, subsequently adopted by the *OSF* as part of the *DCE*.

animation Displaying a series of images with slight differences between them, at a speed that is fast enough to create the illusion of smooth movement. (See also *cell animation, Gouraud shading, morphing, Phong shading, tweening*.)

anisochronous data channel A communications channel in which data, but not timing information, is transmitted. Also called an *asynchronous data channel*.

annotation In *hypertext*, a new *node* linked to an existing node. If the software allows it, this provides both authors and readers with the opportunity to add additional information, which can be *text, graphics, audio* or *video*.

anonymous ftp The facility to transfer documents, files, programs and other archived data over the Internet by *ftp* to a standard guest account with login name 'anonymous' or 'ftp' and the user's electronic mail address as password. Access is then provided to a special directory hierarchy containing the publicly accessible files, typically in a subdirectory called 'pub'. It is not possible to access other directories on the system.

ANSI See *American National Standards Institute*.

ANSI character set The character set adopted by *ANSI* as the standard for computers; also the character set used by *Microsoft Windows*. Unlike the *ASCII* character set, ANSI uses all 8 bits, so that the character set comprises 256 characters. The printable characters of the ASCII character set have the same code in both the ANSI and ASCII character sets. ANSI characters that are not displayed on the keyboard are accessed using the 'alt' key on a PC keyboard and the 'option' key on a Macintosh keyboard. In Windows, the characters can also be accessed using the Character Map utility. (See Table 2.)

ansi.sys A configuration file needed in MS-DOS to be able to display *block graphics* and other effects.

answer-only modem A *modem* (usually a very cheap one) which can receive messages but not send them.

anti-aliasing Ways of improving the display of *analogue* or continuous images in digital formats by reducing the 'pixellated' appearance or reducing the creation of artefacts when the *colour resolution* is low. Can use either *dithering* or *grey levels*. (See also *aliasing, jaggies, hinting*.)

AOL See *America On-Line*.

APDU See *application protocol data unit*.

API See *application program interface*.

APPC See *advanced program-to-program communications*.

Apple Computer, Inc. Manufacturer of the *Macintosh* range of personal computers as well as the earlier Apple I, Apple II and Lisa. Founded in 1983 by Steve Jobs and Steve Wozniak.

Apple Desktop Bus A system for connecting input devices to the *Macintosh*.

Apple File Exchange A utility that allows a *Macintosh* to write disks in IBM-PC format.

AppleLink An electronic mail and information service reserved for Apple employees, developers, universities, user groups, dealers, etc., which provides product announcements and updates (for third-party products as well as for Apple products) and technical information.

AppleShare File server software from Apple for handling networked or connected *Macintosh* computers.

applet See *Java applet*.

AppleTalk A proprietary *local area network* protocol developed by Apple Computer, Inc. for communication between Apple products,

ASCII coding

Table 1 ASCII coding
The printable ASCII characters. Characters 0 to 31 represent 'control codes', such as tabs, *ACK*, *NAK*, carriage return and backspace; 32 is a space and 127 is delete

ASCII Character (decimal)		number ASCII Character		(decimal) number ASCII		Character (decimal) number		ASCII Character (decimal)		number ASCII Character	
32	[space]	48	0	64	@	80	P	96	`	112	p
33	!	49	1	65	A	81	Q	97	a	113	q
34	"	50	2	66	B	82	R	98	b	114	r
35	#	51	3	67	C	83	S	99	c	115	s
36	$	52	4	68	D	84	T	100	d	116	t
37	%	53	5	69	E	85	U	101	e	117	u
38	&	54	6	70	F	86	V	102	f	118	v
39	'	55	7	71	G	87	W	103	g	119	w
40	(	56	8	72	H	88	X	104	h	120	x
41	)	57	9	73	I	89	Y	105	i	121	y
42	*	58	:	74	J	90	Z	106	j	122	z
43	+	59	;	75	K	91	[	107	k	123	{
44	,	60	<	76	L	92	\	108	l	124	|
45	-	61	=	77	M	93	]	109	m	125	}
46	.	62	>	78	N	94	^	110	n	126	~
47	/	63	?	79	O	95	_	111	o		

Table 2 ANSI character set
For ANSI numbers 032 (space) to 0126, the characters are the same as the ASCII character set, while 0127 to 0129, 0141 to 0144, 0157, 0158 and 0160 are undefined

ANSI Character		number ANSI		Character number		ANSI Character		number ANSI		Character number	
0130	,	0154	š	0177	±	0197	Å	0217	Ù	0237	í
0131	ƒ	0155	›	0178	²	0198	Æ	0218	Ú	0238	î
0132	„	0156	œ	0179	³	0199	Ç	0219	Û	0239	ï
0133	…	0159	Ÿ	0180	´	0200	È	0220	Ü	0240	ð
0134	†	0161	¡	0181	µ	0201	É	0221	Ý	0241	ñ
0135	‡	0162	¢	0182	¶	0202	Ê	0222	Þ	0242	ò
0136	ˆ	0163	£	0183	·	0203	Ë	0223	ß	0243	ó
0137	‰	0164	¤	0184	¸	0204	Ì	0224	à	0244	ô
0138	Š	0165	¥	0185	¹	0205	Í	0225	á	0245	õ
0139	‹	0166	¦	0186	º	0206	Î	0226	â	0246	ö
0140	Œ	0167	§	0187	»	0207	Ï	0227	ã	0247	÷
0145	'	0168	¨	0188	¼	0208	Ð	0228	ä	0248	ø
0146	'	0169	©	0189	½	0209	Ñ	0229	å	0249	ù
0147	"	0170	ª	0190	¾	0210	Ò	0230	æ	0250	ú
0148	"	0171	«	0191	¿	0211	Ó	0231	ç	0251	û
0149	•	0172	¬	0192	À	0212	Ô	0232	è	0252	ü
0150	–	0173	-	0193	Á	0213	Õ	0233	é	0253	ý
0151	—	0174	®	0194	Â	0214	Ö	0234	ê	0254	þ
0152	~	0175	¯	0195	Ã	0215	×	0235	ë	0255	ÿ
0153	™	0176	°	0196	Ä	0216	Ø	0236	ì		

principally the *Macintosh*, and other computers. AppleTalk is built into the Macintosh and is independent of the *network layer* on which it is run. *EtherTalk* is an implementation of AppleTalk on an *Ethernet LAN*. (See also *LocalTalk*.)

application Software such as a word-processor or spreadsheet that is used to perform a specific type of work.

application binary interface (ABI) The interface via which an *application program* accesses the *operating system*. Binary-compatible applications should run on any system with the appropriate ABI. (See also *API*.)

application layer The top layer of the *ISO seven-layer model*, which handles aspects such as *network transparency* and resource allocation. The application layer is concerned with the user's view of the network, areas such as electronic mail, directory services and file transfer. The *presentation layer* (the next layer) provides the application layer with a local representation of data that is independent of the format used on the network.

application-level gateway A *filter* or series of filters specially written to permit and prevent the transmission of specific *applications* through a security *gateway* or *firewall*. Provides a high level of security as it also allows all traffic to be monitored.

application program interface (API) The interface that an application program uses to request operating system and other services. An API can also provide an interface between a high-level language and lower-level utilities and services. For *Windows*, the API also helps applications manage windows, menus, icons and other *GUI* elements. For a local area network and on the Internet, an API provides applications with routines for requesting services from lower levels of the network or from communication protocol stacks. (See also *ABI*.)

application protocol data unit (APDU) A *packet* of data exchanged between two application programs across a *network*. This is at the *application layer* of the *OSI seven-layer model* and may actually be transmitted as several packets at a lower layer including extra information for *routing* etc.

application service element (ASE) Software in the *presentation layer* of the *OSI seven-layer model*, which provides an interface to handle *APDUs*. Because *applications* and *networks* vary, ASEs are split into common services and specific services.

APPN See *advanced peer-to-peer networking*.

Arachnophilia A *Windows freeware HTML* editor, available from *ZDNet*, that can also be used to create Web pages from *RTF* documents.

Archie A system to automatically gather, index and serve information on the *Internet*. The initial implementation provided an indexed directory of filenames from all *anonymous ftp* archives. Later versions provide other collections of information. (See also *archive site*, *Gopher*, *Prospero*, *wide area information servers*.)

archive site An *Internet host* where files are stored for public access via *anonymous ftp*, *Gopher*, *World Wide Web* or other file handling tools. There may be several archive sites for, say, a *Usenet newsgroup*, where one may be recognized as the main one and the others act as *mirrors*. Archive sites are also know as ftp sites and ftp archives. (See also *Archie*.)

ARCnet See *Attached Resource Computer Network*.

area composition See *page make-up*.

ARP See *address resolution protocol*.

ARPA See *Advanced Research Projects Agency*.

ARPANET See *Advanced Research Projects Agency Network*.

ARQ See *automatic repeat request*.

AS See *autonomous system*.

ASN See *autonomous system number*.

ascender The part of a letter extending above the *x-height*, as for example in b, d, h, k and l. (See also *descender*.)

ASCII coding See *American Standard Code for Information Interchange and Table 1*.

ASDL See *asynchronous digital subscriber loop*.

ASE See *application service element*.

ASN See *autonomous system number*.

ASN.1 Abstract Syntax Notation One. The *OSI* language for describing abstract syntax, used in the *presentation layer* of the OSI *seven-layer model* to describe the sort of information being exchanged.

aspect ratio The ratio of width to height. Common uses are to describe a *pixel*, a display screen or a *graphic*. Although square pixels (1:1) are considered preferable, most displays use aspect ratios of about 5:4. The aspect ratio of graphics will not always appear to be the same on paper as it does on screen (partly because the pixel aspect ratio is not 1:1). When graphics are transferred from one software package to another, care needs to be taken to preserve aspect ratios.

assigned numbers The *RFC* in which the currently assigned values used in network protocol implementations are documented. This RFC is updated periodically and current information can be obtained from the *IANA*. The IANA assigns numbers to new protocols, ports, links, etc.

asymmetrical modulation A scheme in which the use of a communications line is maximized by giving a larger share of the *bandwidth* to the *modem* which is transmitting the most information.

asymmetric digital subscriber line (or loop) (ADSL) A digital telecommunications protocol that allows transmission of VHS quality video over standard telephoe lines. This means that VCR-quality video could be delivered to homes without the need for rewiring. (See *video on demand*.) Uses the principles of *asymmetrical modulation* with upstream bit rates measured in kbps and downstream bit rates of up to 9 Mbps. Will also effectively provide a greater *bandwidth* for access to the *Internet* to those using *dial-up* connections over modems. Note that this provides an alternative to *ISDN*. In the USA provides part of the *National Information Infrastructure* (NII).

asynchronous Not *synchronous* (or synchronized). Most often refers to data communications in which the sending and receiving devices do not have to be synchronized and thus the data is sent in groups or blocks, rather than as a steady stream, between two devices. The data must include *start* and *stop bits* to indicate the beginning and end of each group or block. Asynchronous can also refer to events that occur at different times rather than concurrently. For example, *email* communication is asynchronous. Similarly, a telephone conversation is asynchronous, in that signals are recognized, equivalent to start and stop bits, which indicate when to transfer control of the conversation.

asynchronous assignment In *asynchronous transfer mode*, the manner in which individual cells are allocated to different users in response to the varying demands of the traffic.

asynchronous data channel See *anisochronous data channel*.

asynchronous transfer mode (ATM) A high-bandwidth method of transporting information in short, fixed-length cells, designed to integrate the transport of all services on a single network. Defined by the *ITU-T* for public broadband-ISDN. Also known as 'fast packet' and generally associated with a fast packet switching technology called cell relay, in which information is handled in fixed cell lengths of 53 *octets*.

AT command set A set of commands developed by Hayes Microcomputer Products for software control of *modems*. This set was emulated in *'Hayes-compatible'* modems and is now regarded as standard for modems used with PCs.

ATM See *asynchronous transfer mode*, *automatic teller machine* and *Adobe Type Manager*.

ATM adaptation layer (AAL) The interface between services and the *ATM* switching protocol. AAL 1 provides constant bit rate at source and destination, thus emulating a *private circuit* or *leased line*. AAL 2 emulates a variable bit rate service (e.g., voice). AAL 3 emulates a *connection-oriented service*. AAL 4 emulates a *connectionless service* (e.g., *SMDS*). AAL 5 is a null adaptation layer.

AT&T American Telephone and Telegraph, Inc. One of the largest US telecommunications providers. The *Unix* operating system and the C and C++ programming languages were developed at AT&T Bell Laboratories. Until 1983, AT&T had a monopoly on the supply of telephone services in the USA.

Attached Resource Computer Network (ARCnet) Originally a proprietary *network* developed by DataPoint; now no longer proprietary. Uses a star topology and a token-passing protocol. Slower than *Ethernet* at 2.5 Mbps but allows different kinds of transmission media (*twisted pair*, *coaxial cable* and *fibre-optic cable*) to be mixed in the same network. A revised specification called ARCnet Plus will support *bit rates* of up to 20 Mbps (see *bits per second*).

attachment A file sent with an *email* message. May be compressed or encoded using *BinHex* or *uuencoding*. In most cases uses *MIME* to enable the attachment.

attribute Property or characteristic. Within the *DTD*, attributes may be defined for *SGML* (and *HTML*) tags or elements, as well as possible values for an attribute. Within a *document instance*, a tag may include a particular value for an attribute. Attributes are also used within SGML to define the position of cross-references and their targets. Within typography, attribute is used to mean type style, such as italic or bold, while in *paint* and *draw programs*, attribute refers to line weights, colours and styles, as well as to the colours and styles of fills.

audio Sound on computers (and on audio *compact discs* and *digital audio tape*). This is handled by storing a sequence of discrete samples. The continuous (*analogue*) sound waveform of the original is sampled tens of thousands of times a second. Each sample represents the intensity of the sound pressure wave for each frequency at that instant. The quality of the digital encoding is also affected by the number of *bits* used. The encoding may be linear, logarithmic or *mu-law*. Audio is replayed through a *sound card* which converts the digital file back into an analogue waveform. Sound is one component of *multimedia*. (See also *Audio IFF*, *audio formats* and *aliasing*.)

audio bridge A way of connecting a small number of telephone lines in order to provide an audio conference. Audio bridges over *ISDN* are more effective than those over the *PSTN* because there are fewer problems with varying audio levels and background noise conditions.

audioconferencing A multi-party telephone conversation. (See also *conferencing* and *videoconferencing*.)

audio formats The most common audio formats are given in Table 3.

Audio IFF See *audio interchange file format*.

Audio interchange file format (AIFF, Audio IFF) A sound format developed by Apple Computer for storing high-quality sampled *audio* and musical instrument information. It is now also used by Silicon Graphics and some professional audio packages. AIFC is a compressed version of this format.

audiographic teleconferencing Use of an *electronic whiteboard* or shared screens as part of *teleconferencing*.

audiotex A system in which it is possible to access a database of audio messages using a *touch-tone* telephone. Is widely used as part of *voice mail* systems.

Table 3 Common audio formats

Name	Extension	Comments
Amiga MOD format	.mod or .nst	Contains partly audio and partly *MIDI*-type information
Audio IFC	.aif(f)	AIFF with compression
Audio IFF	.aif(f)	For Apple and Silicon Graphics
Audio U-LAW (or μ-law)	.au or .snd	NeXT, Sun (.snd is an ambiguous file extension)
Audio-Visual Interleaved	.avi	
HCOM	(none)	Apple Macintosh — Uses *Huffman compression*
IFF/8SVX	.iff	For Amiga
MIDI	.mid	Not strictly an audio format, but see *MIDI*
MIME	(none)	*MIME* type
MPEG	.mpg, pm2, mpeg	Note that MPEG can be used for audio as well as video
VOiCe	.voc	Developed by *Soundblaster*
WAVE	.wav	See *WAV*

audio video interleave (avi) Alternative expansion to *audiovisual interleaved*.

audiovisual interleaved (avi) A *video format* used within *Windows*. Files using this format can be replayed using the Windows *Media Player*.

AUP See *acceptable use policy*.

authentication Verification of the identity of a person or process. In a communication system, authentication verifies that messages really come from their stated source. (See also *digital signature, encryption*.)

authoring Creating a *hypertext* or *hypermedia* document. There are a number of authoring languages, such as Apple's *HyperCard*, as well as an ever-increasing number of *Web* authoring tools for creating *HTML* documents for the *World Wide Web*.

Authorware Interactive Studio Software from Macromedia for developing interactive multimedia applications. Takes a more structured approach than the same company's *Macromedia Director*. (See also *Shockwave*.)

auto-answer A feature supported on many *modems* and all *fax* machines which allows incoming calls to be answered automatically, even if the user is not present.

auto-dial A feature of advanced *modems*, usually used for *callback*, so that the modem can call automatically without human intervention.

automatic repeat request (ARQ) An error control protocol used in *modems*, in which the receiver asks the transmitter to resend corrupted data.

automatic teller machine (ATM) Cash dispenser which uses credit or debit cards, authenticated by the use of a *PIN* number.

autonomous system (AS) A collection of *routers* under a single administration using a common *interior gateway protocol* for routing *packets*.

autonomous system number (ASN) Used for *routing* on *Internet*. (See *autonomous system*.)

auto-redial A feature supported on many *modems* which allows redialling until a connection is made. The redial time can usually be set to a value to suit the user. This is a particularly useful feature for *dial-up connection* to *bulletin boards* and *Internet points of presence*.

autotracing The conversion of a *bitmapped image* to a *vector* or *outline image*. Most autotracing programs are able to trace images in *tiff* or *pcx* format and output as *Encapsulated PostScript*. Autotracing is useful for converting images which have been *scanned* to images which can be manipulated using a *draw program*.

avatar A computer-generated figure, intended to represent a human on a computer screen. In the early days of *videoconferencing*, it was suggested that such an approach might be used to reduce *bandwidth* requirements.

avi See *audiovisual interleaved*.

B

BABT approval Approval by the British Approval Board for Telecommunications, indicated by a green circle. Any equipment, most commonly *modems*, requires this approval before it can be legally connected to the UK telephone system. A red triangle means that approval has not (yet) been obtained.

backbone The primary connectivity mechanism of a hierarchical distributed system. All *stub* and *transit* networks which have connectivity to an intermediate system on the backbone are assured of connectivity to each other.

backbone site A key *Internet* site, which processes a large amount of third-party traffic, especially if it is the home site of any of the regional co-ordinators for the *Usenet* maps. (See also *rib site, leaf site*.)

back link A *link* back to the point from which the last link was made.

backoff Where a *host* that has experienced a *collision* on a *network* waits for a (random) amount of time before attempting to retransmit.

backslash The slash character '\'. It is used to separate subdirectories in DOS commands. Note, however, that *Unix* uses the forward slash command for this purpose and, as most *Internet hosts* run on Unix machines, it is necessary for DOS users to remember this when using such programs as *ftp*.

Backus–Naur form (BNF) A grammar of grammars (or metasyntax) for specifying the syntax of programming languages, command sets, etc. *SGML* and *HTML Document Type Definitions* can be regarded as BNF grammars.

BackWeb A *push technology* that enables *Web* site owners to create their own controlled *Internet* channels to deliver targeted and personalized content directly to end users. This is rather like *PointCast*, except that PointCast sends only public information. BackWeb's patented Polite Agent unobtrusively monitors an Internet user's on-line activity and, when bandwidth is available, BackWeb incrementally *downloads* user-requested information using *UDP*. Because the downloads take place when data-transfer levels are otherwise low, they do not affect a user's other activities and real-time delays appear shorter. Users are able to schedule deadlines by which time files should be available. (See also *Castanet* and *Netscape Netcaster*.)

banding An effect seen on low-resolution printers when *graduated fills* are printed, in that the transition is shown in distinct, contrasting bands rather than in one continuous flow. The higher the resolution of the printer, the less banding will be visible. It is also possible to observe banding onscreen, depending on the screen resolution, but this does not mean that the bands will necessarily print.

bandwidth Technically, the difference, in *hertz* (Hz), between the highest and lowest frequencies of a transmission channel or the range of frequencies required to transmit a signal. However, as typically used, the rate at which data can be sent through a given communications circuit. For example, voice over the telephone network requires a bandwidth of 3 kHz while uncompressed video requires a bandwidth of 6 MHz. (See *broadband*, *voice band*, *wideband*.)

bandwidth top-up The opening up of an *ISDN* channel when a *private circuit* becomes congested. The channel is closed again when the traffic subsides.

bang path A way of describing a *UUCP* electronic mail address naming a sequence of hosts through which a message must pass to get to the addressee. So called because each *hop* is signified by a bang sign (or exclamation mark '!'). Now that *Internet* addressing is available, this notation is rarely used, although the terminology is used to described the sequence of *hosts* through which a message may pass before it is delivered to the intended recipient.

barcode A horizontal strip of vertical bars of varying widths, groups of which represent characters. There are various different standards but each symbol typically contains a leading 'quiet' zone, start character, data character(s) including an optional check character, stop character and a trailing 'quiet' zone. In addition to conventional barcodes, there are also radial and two-dimensional coding systems, which are used for specialized applications such as automatic warehousing. Barcode readers usually use visible red light with a wavelength between 632.8 and 680 nanometers.

baseband A transmission method through which digital signals are sent without modulation. In general, only one communication channel is available at any given time. Most *local area networks* are baseband networks; e.g., *Ethernet*.

base-level synthesizer The minimum capability required by the Microsoft *MPC* specification for a music synthesizer within Microsoft *Windows*. It must be capable of playing at least six simultaneous notes on three melodic instruments, together with three simultaneous notes on percussion instruments. (See also *MIDI*.)

baseline The line on which characters are based, that is, the line along the bottom of characters, such as a, b and c, which do not have descenders (as in j, p, q and y). Line spacing is measured between baselines. *Leading* is extra spacing added, based on the strips of lead (the metal) which compositors used to add between the blocks of type.

basic bandwidth unit (BBU) The smallest unit of bandwidth which can be allocated.

basic rate interface (BRI) See *basic rate ISDN*.

basic rate ISDN (BRI) This is a UK version of *ISDN* which consists of two 64 kbps channels (B – 'bearer' – channels) for speech or data, plus a 16 kbps channel (D – 'delta'– channel) used for signalling and control purposes. The aggregate data rate is thus $2 \times 64 + 16 = 144$ kbps. Basic rate ISDN is often referred to as 2B + D. BRI is the kind of ISDN interface most likely to be found in a residential service.

Bath Information and Data Services (BIDS) A data provision service at the University of Bath, providing bibliographic and electronic *document delivery* services to the UK higher education sector.

baud The information-carrying capacity of a communication channel in terms of the number of changes of state or level per second, that is, the frequency of electrical oscillation. This is the same as the bit rate only for two-level modulation with no *framing* or *stop bits*. Many people confuse the two, probably because many lower-speed modems have the bit rate and baud rate (also called *symbol rate*) identical. It is, therefore more usual to use the term *bits per second* (bps). The term baud was originally a unit of telegraph signalling speed, set at one morse code dot per second and named after J M E Baudot (1845–1903), the French engineer who constructed the first successful teleprinter.

baud barf The apparently random characters which appear on a monitor when a *modem* connection is used with some protocol setting (especially line speed) incorrect, when voice communication occurs on the same line, or when there is really bad line noise. Baud barf is not completely random, and experienced *hackers* (in both the good and bad senses) can extract information from it about the sending modem.

Baudot code Five-bit code developed by the French engineer Emil Baudot in the 1870s (see *baud*); still used for *telex*.

baud rate See *baud*.

baudy language A graphical language for conveying feelings, also described as *emoticons* and *smileys*. Obviously a pun on *baud* (and of course 'body language'), e.g., :) = smile, ;) = wink, : (frown. The possibilities are limited only by imagination and the *ASCII* character set. Has to be viewed sideways, which might be regarded as an appropriate view of the whole approach!

bboard See *bulletin board system*.

BBS See *bulletin board system*.

BBU See *basic bandwidth unit*.

BCC See *block check character*.

B-channel The main type of component channel of ISDN services, used for carrying data or voice. B stands for 'bearer'. (See *basic rate ISDN*.)

Because It's Time NETwork (BITNET) A wide-area academic computer network in the USA based originally on IBM mainframe systems connected via leased 9600 bps lines. Operates as a single network with *earn* in Europe and other networks in different parts of the world.

Bell 103 The variant of *V.21* created by *AT&T* when it had a telephone system monopoly in the USA.

BER See *bit error rate*.

Berkeley Internet Name Domain (BIND) An implementation of a *domain name server* developed and distributed by the University of California at Berkeley. Many Internet hosts now run BIND.

Berkeley Network (B-NET) *Unix Ethernet* software developed at the University of California at Berkeley, which is regarded as the *de facto* standard and distributed by Unisoft.

Berners-Lee, Tim The leading developer of the *World Wide Web* at *CERN* in the early 1990s.

best effort A classification for low-priority network traffic, used with reference to the *Internet*. Different kinds of traffic have different *bandwidth* requirements and therefore different priorities. For example, certain types of real-time communication, such as *videoconferencing*, need a certain minimum guaranteed *bandwidth* and *latency* and thus need a high priority. Electronic mail, on the other hand, has no real-time need and is classified as a 'best-effort' service.

Bézier A collection of formulae for describing curved lines (Bézier curve) and surfaces (Bézier surface), first used in 1972 to model automobile surfaces and named after Frenchman P Bézier. Curves and surfaces are defined by a set of 'control points' which can be moved interactively, making Bézier curves and surfaces. The control points indicate where the line starts and stops, the points where a curve changes direction (known variously as the anchor points, handles or nodes) and the control points for each of the anchor points (sometimes called BCPs, Bézier control points). Related to the anchor points (actually on the curve) are dashed lines which extend out on either side, ending in the control points; the direction and length of these lines indicate the angle of the curve at that point and the curvature. Moving the control points alters the curve.

Bibliographic Retrieval Service (BRS) An *on-line* information service providing indexed access to scholarly, scientific and technical publications. Two leading suppliers are BRS Information Technologies and DIALOG Information Services. While these providers can be accessed via the *Internet*, most companies use direct *dial-up*, as they have done since long before the wide spread of the Internet.

BIDS See *Bath Information and Data Services*.

biff To notify someone that they have incoming mail. Named after a Unix utility, which was in turn named after a golden Labrador at the University of California at Berkeley which barked when the post arrived.

big-endian The ordering of the components of a hierarchical name in which the domain name is specified first, e.g., uk.ac.warwick rather than warwick.ac.uk. This system was established on *JANET* in the UK before *Internet* hosts' names were standardized and has led to much confusion. However, it is now being superseded by the *little-endian* approach used elsewhere. The terminology was taken from Jonathan Swift's *Gulliver's Travels*: the Big-Endian and Little-Endian parties debated over whether soft-boiled eggs should be opened at the big end or the little end.

bilevel bitmap, bilevel coding A black-and-white *bitmap*, in which each *pixel* is either on or off. Thus the two levels of a bilevel bitmap are black or white. A bitmap can, however, have many shades, or grey levels, because it can deal with more than just one bit of data. (See also *1-bit, 8-bit and 24-bit colour*.) Bilevel coding is used in fax where each pixel in a scan is represented as either black or white with no representation of a degree of greyness. Grey levels can be simulated on output by a mixture of black and white pixels in appropriate proportions.

binary See *binary system*.

binary file Any file that is not ordinary text, that is, which contains more than just standard (7-bit) *ASCII* characters. This includes spreadsheet files, databases, executable programs and most word-processing files.

binary newsgroup A *newsgroup* concerned with *binary files* (usually image files).

binary synchronous communications (BSC, bisync(h) or bisynchronous communications) A protocol developed by IBM for *half-duplex* links and widely used in networks on mainframes. Bisynch communications need the clocks on the computers sending the information and receiving the information to be synchronized before transmission begins. (See also *asynchronous transmission*.)

binary system (base two) A method of working with numbers based on only two digits, 1 and 0. Used in all *digital* computing systems because 1 and 0 can represent 'on' and 'off', or 'connected' and 'disconnected'. All data input into computer systems and transferred over communications links is therefore converted from the everyday decimal system to binary. *Octal* and *hexadecimal* systems (based on 8 and 16) are also widely used in computing, essentially because they are based on powers of 2.

binary transfer A *File Transfer Protocol* which allows *binary files* to be transferred between computers.

BIND See *Berkeley Internet Name Domain*.

BinHex A *Macintosh* format for representing a *binary file* using only printable (i.e., *ASCII*) characters. Because BinHex files are simply text, they can be sent through most *electronic* *mail* systems and stored on most computers, although it is necessary to obtain appropriate software for non-Macintosh computers in order to read and use these files. The suffix 'hqx' usually indicates a BinHex format file. (See also *BinHex 4.0, uuencode*.)

BinHex 4.0   A 7-bit wide representation of a *Macintosh* file with *CRC* error checking. Bin-Hex 4.0 files are designed for communication of Mac files over long paths. Some Macintosh mailing systems will put *attachments* into Bin-Hex 4.0 automatically, which can cause problems if the receiving machine is not also a Macintosh.

bipolar signal   An electrical line signalling method used in *digital communication*, where the signal alternates between positive and negative polarities.

B-ISDN   See *broadband ISDN*.

bisync, bisynch   See *binary synchronous communications*.

bisynchronous communications   See *binary synchronous communications*.

bit   An acronym for *binary* digit, the smallest item of information which a computer can hold, being either 1 or 0, essentially representing a switch being open or closed. More meaningful information is handled by using combinations of bits, called *bytes*. In *serial communications*, bits are transferred one at a time.

bit bang   *Serial* data transmission by rapidly changing, in software, a single output bit at appropriate times. Bit bang was used on certain early computers, presumably when *UARTs* were expensive. The technique is now being used again on some *RISC* architectures because it takes very little processor time.

bit error rate (BER)   The number of bits received with errors relative to the total number of bits received, given either as 1 in 10^6 or as 10^{-6}, indicating that 1 in 1 000 000 (a typical error rate) have errors.

bitmap   A two-dimensional array, in which pixels are either on or off, i.e., black or white, or 1 or 0. Can easily be stored in a computer. Often used to describe the image itself. Unlike *vector graphics*, bitmaps cannot be resized without loss of quality. If a bitmap represents a coloured image, there will be more than one bit for each *pixel*, i.e., each colour will have its own bits. (See also *raster, 1-bit, 8-bit and 24-bit colour*.)

bitmap display   A screen on which each *pixel* displayed corresponds directly to one or more bits in the computer's video memory. Such a display has fast updating compared with a terminal connected via a *serial line* where the speed of the line limits the speed at which the display can be updated. Almost all modern personal computers and *workstations* have bitmap displays, which means that *graphical user interfaces* can be used, together with interactive graphics and choice of onscreen *fonts*.

bitmap editors   See *paint program*.

bitmap font (raster font)   A *font* in which each character is stored as an array of *pixels* (or a *bitmap*). Such fonts are not easily scalable (see *aliasing* and Figure 1), in contrast to *vector* or *outline fonts* (like those used in *PostScript* and *True-Type*). In practice, bitmap fonts need to be stored in all the sizes required, which not only limits their functionality but also takes up space on the storage medium, particularly at large sizes. Of course, all fonts are bitmapped when displayed onscreen or printed. The difference between outline and bitmap fonts is that the bitmaps for outline fonts are created 'on the fly'.

bitmap graphics   See *bitmap*. Compare with *vector graphics*.

bitmap image   See *bitmap* and *bilevel bitmap*.

BITNET   See *Because It's Time NETwork*.

bit-oriented protocols   Protocols that deal with information transfer at the bit level.

bit pipe   A path using *circuit switching* which provides unrestricted transfer of information. The user is responsible for protocols above the physical layer.

bit rate   The rate at which digital information can be sent over a communications system, measured in *bps* or kbps or Mbps.

bits per second (bps)   A measure of *bandwidth* or data transmission speed. Often quoted in kbps (1000 bps) or Mbps (10^6 bps). The *ITU-T* has set a number of standards for data transmission over analogue networks (*V series*).

bit stream A sequence of bits, usually regarded as potentially endless and occurring at regular intervals. Note also that BitStream is a company supplying fonts and related software.

bit stuffing A method of ensuring *data transparency* in *bit-oriented protocols*.

BIX A US on-line service owned by *Delphi* but operated independently. Offers *email* and conferencing, as well as its own *Windows* access to the *Internet*.

beeper See *pager*.

block Transmitted information regarded as a discrete entity, often identified by starting and ending delimiters.

block check character (BCC) A character which is added to blocks in *character-oriented protocols* to indicate that they contain codes.

block graphics Use of the graphics characters defined in the IBM extended *ASCII* character set to create graphics on a PC screen running under MS-DOS (rather than *Windows*). Each graphics character takes up the space usually used by an alphanumeric character and therefore detailed effects are not possible. In order to use block graphics, the file *ansi.sys* must be included in the config.sys file.

Blue Book One of the four standard references on *PostScript* (*PostScript Language Tutorial and Cookbook*, Adobe Systems, Addison-Wesley, 1985). The other three official guides are known as the *Green Book*, the *Red Book* and the *White Book*. Also the *JANET Coloured Book Protocol* on file transfer or one of the 1988 standards issued by the *ITU-T's* ninth plenary assembly, which include the *X.400 electronic mail* specification, the standards for *Group 1 fax* to *Group 4 fax* and the *I series* standards for ISDN.

blue ribbon campaign A campaign run against censorship on the *Internet*, prompted principally by the US *Communications Decency Act* of 1996. Support is shown on *Web* pages by a looped blue ribbon (similar in style to the red ribbon worn by those supporting AIDS research).

bmp Microsoft *Windows bitmap* graphics format. BMP files may use *run-length encoding*.

B-NET See *Berkeley Network*.

BNF See *Backus–Naur form*.

body type The type used for text, rather than for headings, usually between 8 and 12 point. Conventionally, a *serif* typeface, but this is not always the case in modern typesetting. For electronic publications, there is much controversy over the most effective typesizes and styles for screen viewing.

Bongo A visual interface builder for *Java*, developed by Marimba, Inc., a company formed by four of the original developers of Java. Marimba has also developed *Castanet*, and Bongo is principally a tool for creating Castanet channels.

bookmark A mark to indicate a position in a document (used, for example, in *Acrobat* files). Also used to describe a *WWW* reference to a document, which may be on the same server or a different one. It is possible with most WWW browsers to save a file of bookmarks and thus allow quick location of frequently referenced documents.

Boolean search A search formalism using operators such as AND and OR. Used in most searching programs on the *Internet*.

bounce The return to the sender of an *electronic mail* message that is undeliverable, together with an error notification (a *bounce message*) usually explaining why the message has not been delivered. The terminology is presumably based on the analogy of a bouncing cheque.

bounce mail See *bounce message*.

bounce message (bounce mail) A message returned to the sender of *email* explaining why it has not been possible to deliver the message to the intended recipient or to the next link in a *bang path*. Reasons may include a non-existent or misspelled user name or a relay site that is *down*, i.e., not accessible. Bounce messages can themselves fail, with unpredictable results.

bps See *bits per second*.

branching coupler In *optical fibres*, a device for splitting the signal from one fibre into two or more fibres.

Bravo A new *imaging model* being developed by *Adobe*.

break To send an *RS-232* break (two character widths of *line high*) over a *serial line*. (In general computing the term is also used in other ways.)

break-out box A test device, which is inserted into a *serial communications* connection to test the signals on each wire.

breath-of-life packet An *Ethernet packet* that contains bootstrap code (i.e., code which will allow a computer to reboot or restart), sent out periodically from a computer on the network to infuse the 'breath of life' into any computer on the network that has crashed. Computers which rely on such packets must have sufficient hardware or firmware code to wait for (or to request) such a packet during the reboot process.

BRI See *basic rate ISDN*.

bridge A device which transfers traffic either between homogeneous or between network segments using *datalink layer* information. These segments would have a common *network layer* address.

brightness A measure of how much light is perceived by the eye. The more correct term is luminance, but brightness is important in the *HLS* method of representing colour in computer graphics.

British Telecom The largest telecommunications provider in the UK, formerly part of Royal Mail. Now known as *BT*.

broadband This can be defined in a number of ways. It is generally used to describe networks faster than those in common use, so exactly what it means depends on the date. In 1995, the boundary between broadband and narrowband was often considered to be at 2 Mbps. However, higher speeds are becoming common, even for *wide area networks*. If 20 Mbps is taken as the boundary, then most *local area networks*, principally *Ethernet* and *Token-Ring*, are narrowband; while *FDDI* (at 100 Mbps) is broadband. This is also a useful dividing point because the much-vaunted *information superhighway* will require these higher frequencies to support such services as *VoD* and realtime access to information sources.

broadband ISDN (B-ISDN) A broadband network in which *ATM* and *SONET* transport are used to provide four service classes delineated according to connection orientation, the need for an end-to-end timing relation, and whether the service bit rate is constant or varying. This proposed successor to *ISDN* will operate at broadband speeds, even to the home (but not over the existing phone cabling). Should be distinguished from primary rate ISDN which works at 2 Mbps, but is actually made of 64 kbps ISDN circuits and is not a fully integrated service. The two main proposed broadband ISDN rates are 150 Mbps and 600 Mbps.

broadband network A *network* that can support a wide range of frequencies, typically from audio up to video, and employing *frequency division multiplexing* on a *coaxial cable*.

broadcast A transmission either addressed to two or more stations at the same time or a transmission to multiple, unspecified recipients. (The terms *narrowcast* and *personalcast* have been coined to describe more focused transmission.) On *Ethernet*, a broadcast packet is a special type of *multicast packet* which all nodes on the network are always willing to receive.

broadcast quality video Flicker-free video (more than about 30 frames per second) at a resolution of about 800 × 640 pixels.

broadcast storm A *broadcast* on a *network* that causes multiple *hosts* to respond by broadcasting themselves, causing the storm to grow exponentially. (See also *network meltdown*.)

brouter A device which bridges some *packets* (that is, forwards them based on *datalink layer* information) and routes other packets (that is, forwards them based on *network layer* information). The *bridge/route* decision is based on configuration information.

browser A program that requests, interprets and displays *hypertext*, or *HTML*, documents available over the *World Wide Web* (although it is often also able to use other *Internet* tools). Also provides tools for *navigating* and for following *links*. Another name for a World Wide Web *client program*. Commonly used browsers include *Mosaic* and *Netscape*.

BRS   See *Bibliographic Retrieval Service*.

BSC   See *binary synchronous communications*.

BT   The current name for *British Telecom*.

BUBL   See *Bulletin Board for Libraries*.

buffer   A temporary storage area for data.

bulletin board   See *bulletin board system*.

Bulletin Board for Libraries (BUBL)   A *Gopher*-based information service of interest to the library and information community (and others) running on the UKOLN machine at the University of Bath. It was originally a bulletin board service, hence the title.

bulletin board system (BBS, bboard)   An electronic message centre, accessed by *electronic mail* and by *dial-up* over a *modem*. Bulletin boards (named after real notice boards) are usually devoted to specific topics. They are in many ways similar to *newsgroups* on *Usenet* (which is essentially a distributed BBS). There are publicly available areas and areas accessible only by password, or other form of checking system, so that 'private' bulletin boards can be set up for group discussions. Increasingly, BBSs are connected to the *Internet*.

burstiness   The ratio of peak to average *bandwidth* required by a telecommunications service.

bursty traffic   Where a *local area network* device takes over the whole bandwidth for a very short period, which means a sudden burst of activity.

bus   A communication path (usually a series of wires) along which information is passed from one part of a computer to another. The devices are connected in *parallel*. A PC, for example, may have a number of buses so that internal communication takes place at a speed similar to that of the processors themselves. Recent developments have been *local bus*, *PCI* and *VESA* local bus, all intended to prevent communications bottlenecks within systems.

Bush, Vannevar   Author of the original paper (1945) which suggested a *hypertext*-type system, called memex.

button   An image or *glyph* on a screen, designed to be 'clicked on', as a method of user input. This may be to start a program, change the display or, in *hypertext* viewers, to indicate a *hyperlink*, from which a link or jump can be made to a different part of the same document or to another document. Hyperlinks are also often indicated by using a different colour, font or screen attribute, such as underlining.

byte   A combination of eight *bits*, generally used to represent a character. There are 256 permutations of the eight 1s and 0s and therefore 256 characters can be represented in principle. However, in the official *ASCII* character set, only the first seven bits are used, so that 128 characters are defined and of these some are used for control purposes (see Table 1). Bytes, kilobytes (1 kb = 1024 bytes) and megabytes (1 Mb = 1024 kb = 1 048 576 bytes) are also used to describe the size of both computer random access memory and disk storage memory. Transmission speeds, however, are given in *bits per second*. In networking, the term *octet* is usually used in preference to byte, because some systems use the term byte for things that are not eight bits long.

C

cable   Although in the past cable has meant any kind of electrical wiring, the term is now almost always used, at least in the communications industry, to mean *fibre-optic* cable.

cableless LAN   A *local area network* using radio, microwave or infrared links in place of cables.

cable television (CATV)   Supply of television signals via cable (originally copper *coaxial cable*, but now *fibre-optic* cable), rather than by broadcast signal.

cache   To store documents or images, usually locally, after they have been accessed over the *Internet* in order that future access can be achieved more quickly. If a document or image is not available in the cache, the *browser* has to return to the Internet to retrieve it. Cache is also used as noun describing the place where the files have been 'cached'. In computing generally, cache has the meaning of storing temporarily, usually to allow other information or programs to be loaded into memory.

CAD/CAE Computer-aided design/engineering.

CAJUN See *CD-Rom Acrobat Journals Using Networks*.

CAL See *computer assisted learning*.

callback A user authentication scheme used by some computers running *dial-up* services. The user dials in to the computer and gives his login ID and password. The computer then breaks the connection and uses an *auto-dial modem* to call back to the user's registered telephone number. If an unauthorized person discovers a user's password, the callback will go, not to him or her, but to the owner of that login, who will then know that his account is under attack. However, by sending a dial tone it is possible to fool some *PABXs* into thinking that the original caller has hung up. When the computer tries to call out it will still be connected to the original caller.

caller ID (CID) A feature of some *modems*.

calling line identifier The telephone number of the device originating a call.

CALS See *Continuous Acquisition and Lifecycle Support*.

camera-ready copy (CRC) Pages produced by typesetting or by other means, which are subsequently photographed to produce printing plates. This method is gradually being replaced by sending a *PostScript* file which is output directly on a high-resolution *imagesetter* or even on a *digital printing press*.

campus wide information system (CWIS) Information and services made available at university sites via *kiosks* running interactive computing systems, possibly via campus networks. Services routinely include directory information, calendars, *bulletin boards* and *databases*.

canonical name (CNAME) A *host's* official name as opposed to an *alias*. This is the first hostname listed for its *Internet* address in the hostname database or the *NIS* map. A host with multiple network interfaces can have more than one Internet address and each address will have its own canonical name (plus any aliases).

CAP See *Columbia AppleTalk Package*.

cap height The height of the capital letters in a particular *typeface* or *font*. (See also *x-height*.)

capture To transfer the text accessed from a remote host and appearing on screen or in a window into a disk file. Unlike *downloading* a specific, complete file that already exists, the capture feature will save everything that appears on the screen, wherever it comes from, including any text typed at the keyboard. *Screen capture* refers to taking a quick picture of the computer screen. *Acrobat* Capture is a program produced by *Adobe Systems* which allows text to be *scanned* and then transferred via *OCR* directly to form a *pdf* file readable with an *Acrobat* viewer.

CARL A document delivery service set up by the Colorado Alliance of Research Laboratories.

carrier sense multiple access/collision detect (CSMA/CD) A method of access control used to resolve contention between stations wishing to transmit on *Ethernet*. If two nodes transmit at once, the data is corrupted. The nodes detect this and continue to transmit for a certain length of time to ensure that all nodes detect the collision. The transmitting nodes then wait for random times before attempting to transmit again. This reduces the amount of *bandwidth* wasted on collisions compared with simple *ALOHA* broadcasting. (See also *collision*.)

carrier signal (carrier tone, carrier wave) A continuous signal of a single frequency which can be modulated by a second, data-carrying signal. In radio communication, there are two common kinds of modulation: *amplitude modulation* and *frequency modulation*. In *modem* communications, *phase modulation* is also used, often in combination with amplitude and frequency modulation.

carrier tone Another term for *carrier signal*.

carrier wave Another term for *carrier signal*.

cascade The arrangement of *windows* in a *graphical user interface* so that they overlap in a regular fashion, usually with the underneath window in the top left-hand corner of the screen and each overlapping window offset down and to the right.

cascading style sheets (CSS) A method by which layout and typographic information can be encoded into *HTML* documents, so that the document provider, rather than the user, has control over the design. Requires a browser that is CSS-compatible, but CSS are supported by the latest versions of both *Internet Explorer* and *Netscape Navigator*.

case Refers to whether letters are capitalized (upper-case letters) or not (lower-case letters). The term comes from the days when typesetters used metal type and stored the letters in wooden typecases: the capitals were usually kept in the top, or upper, case; the small letters were kept in the bottom, or lower, case.

CASE Data Interchange Format (CDIF) An emerging standard for interchange of data between CASE (computer aided software engineering) tools.

Castanet A *client-server* framework developed by Marimba, Inc., a company formed by four of the original developers of Java, for the *broadcast* distribution of software applications, *applets* or any other form of content. The information is selected on the basis of channels, similar in structure, although probably not in content, to conventional TV channels, and these channels can be personalized on a subscriber-by-subscriber basis. A Castanet transmitter runs on the server and a Castanet tuner on the client machine, probably integrated with a *Web* browser, with which the channels required are selected. Whenever a selected channel has been updated, the tuner instigates the download of an updated version, although it is not necessary to be permanently on-line. *Bongo* has been developed as a tool for building channels. Castanet is essentially a *push* technology, extending the *Pointcast* metaphor. (See also *Net TV*, *BackWeb*, *Netscape Netcaster*.)

CATNIP See *common architecture technology for next-generation internet protocol*.

CATV Community antenna television. (See *cable television*.)

CBDS See *connectionless broadband data service*.

CCD See *charge-coupled device*.

CCIR See *Consultative Committee on International Radio*.

CCIRN See *Co-ordinating Committee for Intercontinental Research Networks*.

CCITT Comité Consultatif International de Télégraphique et Téléphonique (International Consultative Committee for Telegraphy and Telephony). Part of the United Nations Organization through which national telecommunications organizations coordinate their activities. CCITT produces technical standards, known as 'Recommendations' for all internationally controlled aspects of *analogue* and *digital* communications, including *modems*, *ISDN* and *videoconferencing*. In several areas its activity overlaps with that of *ISO*, but the two agencies endeavour, generally successfully, to avoid conflicting standards. CCITT changed its name to *ITU-T* on 1 March 1993; all other references herein are to ITU-T. (See *I series*, *H series*, *V series* and *X series* ITU-T recommendations.)

cc:mail Commercial *electronic mail* software for Microsoft *Windows* from Lotus Corporation.

CCS See *Common Communication Services*.

CCTA The UK Government Centre for Information Systems. Originally 'Central Computer and Telecommunications Agency' (the letters were retained as customers were familiar with them), CCTA is part of the Office of Public Service and Science, which works to improve government's services to the public. It is responsible for stimulating and promoting the effective use of information systems in support of the efficient delivery of business objectives and improved quality of services by the public sector.

CD See *compact disc*, *compact disc interactive* (CD-I or CD-i), *compact disc-recordable* (CD-R), *compact disc-read only memory* (CD-Rom) and *CD-Rom eXtended Architecture* (CD-Rom XA).

CDA See *Compound Document Architecture* and *Communications Decency Act*.

CDDI See *copper distributed data interface*.

CD-I, CD-i See *Compact disc interactive*.

CDIF See *CASE Data Interchange Format*.

CDM See *Content Data Model*.

CDMA See *code division multiple access*.

CDPD See *Cellular Digital Packet Data*.

CD-R See *compact disc-recordable*.

CD-Rom See *compact disc-read only memory*.

CD-Rom Acrobat Journals Using Networks (CAJUN) A project at the University of Nottingham investigating the use of *Acrobat* for publishing scholarly journals.

CD-Rom XA See *compact disc eXtended Architecture*.

CEEFAX Trade name for the *videotex* or *teletext* system used by the British Broadcasting Corporation (BBC).

cell A fixed length of data for transmission, as used in *asynchronous transfer mode*. Also used in other ways, for example to describe parts of tables or spreadsheets.

cel (or cell) A single background image within an *animation*. (See *cel (or cell) animation*.)

cel (or cell) animation An *animation* technique in which the background is kept constant and transparent sheets containing images, which are perceived to move, placed in front. This is easier than drawing a new background for every frame and has been incorporated into some computer animation programs.

Cellnet One of the principle providers of mobile communications networks in the UK.

Cello *World Wide Web browser*, or *client*, for IBM PCs. Runs under Microsoft *Windows*.

cell relaying See *fast packet switching*.

Cellular Digital Packet Data (CDPD) A wireless standard providing two-way, 19.2 kbps *packet data transmission* over existing *cellular telephone* channels.

cellular radio A low-power radio transmission system with a cellular network of base stations which may be used by stationary or mobile users for voice or data communication linking into the *public switched telephone network*.

cellular telephone A telephone which uses *cellular radio*.

CELTIC French *digital compression* equipment for *telephony*, which uses *voice activation* to assign an active channel only when one of the parties is speaking. (See also *digital speech interpolation*.)

Centronics interface An alternative name for a parallel interface. (Centronics was an important printer manufacturer in the early days of microcomputing.)

CEPS See *colour electronic prepress system*.

CEPT European Conference of Posts and Telecommunications, the European grouping of *PTTs* which undertakes in Europe functions similar to that of *ITU-T*.

CERN (Centre for European Nuclear Research) Now The European Laboratory for Particle Physics in Geneva, Switzerland, where the *World Wide Web* was first developed in order to allow physicists to take advantage of *hypertext* technologies to share information.

CERT See *Computer Emergency Response Team*.

certificate authority A body that attests to or confirms the identity of a person or an organization and issues digital certificates. Used in secure communications.

CGI See *Common Gateway Interface*.

CGI-script Language in which *scripts* can be written using the *Common Gateway Interface* to allow users to interact with external data and applications, thus creating dynamic *HTML* documents.

CGM See *Computer Graphics Metafile*.

challenge-handshake authentication protocol (CHAP) An authentication scheme used by *PPP* servers to check the identity of the originator of a connection. Once a link is established, a 'challenge' message is sent from the server to the originator, which responds with a value calculated using a *one-way hash function*. The server also calculates the value and if the values match, the authentication is acknowledged; if not, then the connection is usually terminated. CHAP is one of the more secure authentication procedures.

channel A path for the transmission of information, which may be physical or logical. The concept is particularly important in some *push technologies*, such as *Castanet*. Also the basic unit of discussion on *IRC*. Once one joins a channel, everything typed is read by others on that channel. Channels in IRC can be either named with numbers or with strings that begin with a '#' sign and can have topic descriptions. One well-known channel is #report, which at times of international crisis has hundreds of members, some of whom summarize international news or even give first-hand accounts of the action, for example Scud missile attacks in Tel Aviv during the 1991 Gulf War.

channel op Also *chanop* or *chop*. Someone who has privileges on a particular *IRC channel*.

channel service unit (CSU) A type of interface used to connect a terminal or computer to a *digital* medium in the same way that a *modem* is used to connect to an *analogue* medium. If a CSU is used, the user must supply all of the transmit logic, receive logic and timing recovery in order to use the CSU, whereas a *digital (or data) service unit (DSU)* performs these functions.

channel service unit/data service unit (CSU/DSU) A device that performs both the *CSU* and *DSU* functions.

channel status table A table indicating the current status of all physical and logical channels at the user interface to a network.

chanop See *channel op*.

CHAP See *challenge-handshake authentication protocol*.

character A representation of a single unit of meaningful data, e.g., a letter or a number, usually using *ASCII* or *ANSI* coding.

character-based interface The traditional user interface, where all screen images are made up of text characters. Commands are input as standard text strings, followed by a carriage return. Alternatively, *menus* can be used. Compare with *GUI*. Also described as *command interface* and *command line interface*, although these imply that menus cannot be used.

character entity A way of describing a character, using only *ASCII* characters, which is used in *SGML* and *HTML* (see *entity*). The character is usually delimited by '&' and ';', so that, for example the Greek letter alpha (α) might be represented as 'α'. The *delimiters* can be changed in the *SGML declaration*.

character formatting The application of a format or style (including such factors as typeface, typestyle, indents, space before and after) to a single character, or group of characters in a *desktop publishing system* or *word-processor*. Compare with *paragraph formatting*.

character graphics See *block graphics*.

character set An abbreviation for *binary coded character set*, a collection of characters, that may include letters, digits, punctuation, *control codes*, graphics, mathematical and other symbols, which can be stored or transmitted as binary data. Each character in a character set is represented by a character code, which has a one-to-one correspondence with a unique *bitmap*. Different character sets have different mappings between codes and characters. The most widely used character sets are *ASCII* and *ANSI*, although others are also used. In particular, *Unicode*, which uses a 16-bit coding, is intended to provide a completely international character set including Chinese and Korean ideograms. If a computer is to handle a particular character set, it must be possible to enter all the characters from the keyboard and to display the *glyphs* (or the equivalent character coding) on the screen and to reproduce the glyphs on a printer. While most modern *operating systems* include support for multiple character sets, some still have problems with ones which require more than seven bits to represent a character (see *eight-bit clean*). A character set defines the representation of characters as binary data whereas a *font* defines how characters appear on the screen or printer. A glyph may correspond to one or more characters, while more than one glyph may correspond to a single character (see examples under *glyph*).

charge-coupled device (CCD) An array of light-sensitive transistors, arranged across a *scanner* head, one for each *pixel* or unit of resolution. They convert the reflected light signal into *bitmap* information. Sensors may be only *bilevel* or they may measure levels of *grey*.

Chat A *Windows* for Workgroups (Windows 3.11) interactive *talk program* operating over a *local area network*. Also generally used (without the initial capital) to describe real-time interaction of the *Internet*. (See *Internet Relay Chat*.)

cheapernet Also known as *thinnet, thin Ethernet*. Colloquial term for thin-wire *Ethernet* that uses *coaxial cable* instead of the full-specification *yellow cable*. (See also *10Base2*.)

checksum A computed value which depends on the contents of a *block* of data or *packet*. This value is transmitted or stored along with the data. The receiving system recomputes the checksum based upon the data received and compares the computed value with the one sent with the data. If the two values are the same, the receiver can have some confidence that the data was received correctly. If the two sums do not match, there was probably an error in the transmission. (See also *digital signature, cyclic redundancy check, validation*.)

Chicago The development name for *Windows 95*.

CHILL CCITT HIgh-Level Language. A realtime language widely used in European telecommunications. (See also *CCITT*.)

Chimera A modular, *X windows* system-based *World Wide Web browser* for *Unix*.

chop See *channel op*.

cicero The basic typographical unit of the *Didot point system*. (See *font size*.)

CID See *caller ID*.

CIE The Commission Internationale de l'Eclairage (International Commission on Lighting). The body responsible for standards on colorimetry and photometry. In particular, there are two methods of graphically representing *colour spaces*, called *CIELAB* and *CIELUV*.

CIELAB A method of graphically representing *colour spaces* by plotting luminance against values representing the colour axes yellow–cyan and yellow–blue. (See also *CIE* and *CIELUV*.)

CIELUV A method of graphically representing *colour spaces* by plotting luminance against values representing the colour axes yellow–cyan and yellow–blue. (See also *CIE* and *CIELAB*.) CIELUV gives a more uniform distribution than CIELAB, following a transformation of the colour coordinates, but provides the same information. In addition, its origin is transferred to the reference white.

CIM See *CompuServe Information Manager*.

ciphertext Encrypted information, which will require a *password* or *key* to decrypt. The converse of ciphertext is *plaintext*. (See also *encryption, public key, private key, Clipper, DES, RSA encryption*.)

CIR See *committed information rate*.

circuit A transmission medium linking two or more electronic devices.

circuit-level gateways A *gateway* in a *firewall system* which controls transmission of traffic at the *TCP port* level to prevent unauthorized access to a *host*.

circuit switching A paradigm in which a dedicated communication path is established between the sender and receiver along which all *packets* travel. The telephone system (*PSTN* and *ISDN*) is an example of a circuit-switched network. Circuit switching is also referred to as *connection-oriented*. (Contrast *connectionless* and *packet switching*.)

CIS, CI$ See *CompuServe* and *cooperative information system* (CIS only). The (rather sarcastic) use of the dollar sign is a reference to what some see as CompuServe's rather steep charges.

CIT See *computer integrated telephony*.

CITED See *Copyright in Transmitted Electronic Documents*.

CityScape A UK re-seller of *Internet* connections to the *Pipex backbone*. Now part of *Demon Internet*.

CIX (Commercial Internet eXchange) An international cooperative grouping of the major commercial *IP* network providers which have agreed to interwork their networks. The member organizations provide *TCP/IP* or *OSI* data internetwork services to the general public, providing unrestricted access to other world wide networks. The CIX also takes an interest in the development and future direction of the *Internet* and provides a neutral forum to exchange ideas, information and experimental projects among suppliers of internetworking services, often leading to consensus positions on legislative and policy issues of mutual interest. It also provides technical and other support to its members.

CIX (Compulink Information eXchange) A company offering Internet access in the UK.

class The type of a network, depending on its size and structure. There are four types of network on the *Internet* and these are distinguished in the *IP* addresses. Class A networks are usually large government or educational organizations (over 16 million hosts); Class B is for smaller organizations, but still leaves room for growth (over 65 000 hosts); Class C is for small organizations and individuals; while Class D is currently reserved for *multicast* experiments. The term is also used in many other contexts, for example in *object-oriented programming*.

clear to send (CTS) Response in a communications system to message *RTS* (request to send).

click Pressing a button on a *mouse* or other *pointing device*. This generates an event and specifies the screen position, which is processed by the *window manager* or *application program*. (See also *double-click*.)

clickable image An image displayed on a screen, which when pointed at with a *mouse* (or other *pointing device*) and the mouse then *clicked*, initiates some action on the computer. (See also *button*.)

click-and-drag Pressing a button on a *mouse* (or other *pointing device*), holding it down and dragging the mouse to the required position before releasing the button. (See also *drag and drop*.)

client A computer system or process that requests, usually over a network, a service of another computer system or process, called a *server*. For example, a *workstation* requesting the contents of a file from a *file server* is a client of the file server. (See also *client-server*.)

client-server A mode of network computing in which a *distributed computing system* is split between one or more *server tasks* which accept requests, according to some protocol, from (distributed) *client* tasks, asking for information or action. There may be either one centralized server or several distributed ones. This model allows clients and servers to be placed independently on nodes in a network. Client-server computing allows more effective use of computing resources, higher performance, greater flexibility, simpler upgrades and (for some applications) greater reliability and data integrity.

client to client protocol (CTCP) A type of *protocol* created to allow structured data such as *font* information to be exchanged between users on *Internet Relay Chat*. It is also used to send a query to a user.

clip art Computerized art, often copyright-free, but created by professional artists and designers, which can be used in both conventional and electronic publications. A successor to the book of clip art, from which illustrations really were 'clipped'.

clipboard A temporary storage area to which text and/or graphics can be *copied* or *cut* and from which the stored material can be *pasted*. In most systems only one item can be stored at a time, but there is software which allows more items to be stored on a longer-term basis.

Clipper An integrated circuit, or chip, on which the *SkipJack encryption* algorithm is implemented. The Clipper chip, which is manufactured to encrypt telephone data, can also be decrypted by the US government (although using a trusted *escrow* scheme), which has tried to make use of the chip compulsory in the USA. This has led to a great deal of controversy, with criticism from the civil liberties lobby.

clock A regularly occurring signal that provides a timing reference for a transmission and is used to synchronize reception of a data stream.

closed user group A subgroup of users on a *network*, who can communicate only with other members of the subgroup.

cluster controller A device which provides a remote communications capability to several terminals located in a cluster.

CLUT See *colour look-up table*.

CLV See *constant linear velocity*.

CMC See *computer mediated communications*.

CMIP See *Common Management Information Protocol*.

CMIS See *Common Management Information Services*.

CMYK The subtractive colour system used for printing. A coloured image is 'separated' into the three secondary colours — cyan, magenta and yellow — together with black (K = 'Key' or blacK, so as not to cause confusion with the B – Blue – in *RGB*). Each of these is printed with a separate, transparent ink (four-colour printing) to build up an image which resembles as closely as possible the original. In order to produce the secondary colours in their appropriate percentages, the original is subject to four-colour separation. CMYK should be compared with the additive *RGB* (red, green, blue) system which is used on computer screens. Partly because of the differences between RGB and CMYK, and partly because of the technical limitations of the media concerned, it is not always possible to represent faithfully on screen a colour which can be printed. Note that using CMYK and colour separation is different from using *spot colour*, in which each colour is printed in a separate, opaque ink. (See also *Pantone colours*.)

CNAME See *canonical name*.

CNI See *Coalition for Networked Information*.

Coalition for Networked Information (CNI) A consortium formed to promote the creation of, and access to, information resources in networked environments in order to enrich scholarship and enhance intellectual productivity.

coax See *coaxial cable*.

coaxial cable (coax) A cable with a solid or stranded central conductor surrounded by insulator, in turn surrounded by a cylindrical shield, which is solid or woven from fine wires. It is used to carry high-frequency signals such as television, video, radio and other telecommunications transmissions. The shield is usually connected to electrical ground to reduce electrical interference. It is increasingly being replaced by *optical fibre* or *unshielded twisted pair*.

code division multiple access (CDMA) Also known as *spread spectrum* and *code division multiplexing*. A form of *multiplexing* where the transmitter encodes the signal using a pseudo-random sequence also known to the receiver so that it can decode the received signal. A different random sequence corresponds to a different communication channel. Motorola uses CDMA for *digital cellular phones*.

code division multiplexing See *code division multiple access*.

CODEC COmpressor/DECompressor. Covers a variety of software products that determine how a *video* file, such as *QuickTime*, should be condensed, or compressed, to save space on the hard disk and to make the video run faster. A different CODEC would be used for video images than for still photography images. The choice is intended to create a balance between picture quality and the size of the file.

codec *Coder/decoder* (analogous to modem = *modulator/demodulator*). A device which translates between *analogue* video and a compressed *digital* format. The bit rate of the digital signal from a codec is usually between 64 kbps and 2 Mbps, depending on the efficiency of the codec and the degree of degradation of the video signal which is acceptable.

COLD See *computer output on laser disc*.

Collabra See *Netscape Collabra*.

collision The outcome when two *hosts* transmit simultaneously on a *network*, so that their *packets* collide and are corrupted. The *CSMA/CD* protocol used on *Ethernet* specifies that each host should wait for a random time before retransmitting. (See also *carrier sense multiple access/collision detect*.)

colour Colours are usually represented on screen using the additive *RGB* system, in which either a colour image may be stored as three separate images (one for each of red, green and blue) or each *pixel* may encode the colour using separate *bit* fields for each colour component. Subtractive *CMYK* and/or *Pantone* representations of *spot colours* are used for printing.

colour correction Matching the colours onscreen to those that are produced when an image is printed. Includes adjustment of parameters such as brightness, contrast, mid-level greys, saturation and hue. The *CMYK* subtractive process and the additive *RGB* process work on different principles and have a different reproducible *colour gamut*. This means that the colour shown on screen will not match the printed colour from the same file. Matching the two, so that the correct colour is printed, remains as much an art as a science. It is perhaps worth noting that because, in general, printing on paper requires images of much higher resolution than those which are required for *electronic publishing*, i.e., viewing on screen, it is not the same files which are used. It is therefore possible to adjust the high-resolution image for printing (even though it appears 'wrong' onscreen), while keeping the low-resolution image so that the colours appear correct in an electronic product.

Coloured Books A set of protocol definitions for the different aspects of networking developed and used on the UK Joint Academic Network, *JANET*, for open systems communication before the definition of international standards. Each protocol is usually referred to by the colour of the cover of the publication defining it.

colour electronic prepress system (CEPS) An image-processing system used in the publishing and prepress industry for designing, laying out and editing colour pages for printing.

colour gamut The range of *colours* which can be produced in *subtractive colour* printing by combining inks of the four *process colours* (*CMYK*) or can be displayed on a screen using additive *RGB*. Note, however, that there are some colours which cannot be made up of a mixture of red, green and blue phosphor emissions and thus cannot be displayed on a screen.

colour look-up table (CLUT) A software palette or set of 256 colours, which is used on a computer with 8-bit colour (which can only display $2^8 = 256$ colours) to determine which 256 colours, out of the 16.7 million ($=2^{24}$) colours available with 24-bit colour, it can use at one time. Many applications allow a choice of the 256 colours to be used and a palette can be set up for each particular file to suit the subject matter of the image being handled, so that, for example, flesh tones would be appropriate for an image of a face, while a different, probably green-based palette would be more appropriate for a landscape.

colour resolution The number of *bits* per *pixel* in a colour image. (See *1-bit*, *8-bit* and *24-bit colour*.)

colour separation The process of separating artwork into the four basic process colours, *CMYK* (or sometimes into *spot colours*) for printing. Starting with a colour photograph, it must be scanned by a machine that can separate the colours into CMYK and save the image in five files, a file for each high-resolution version of each of the four process colours (cyan, magenta, yellow and black), plus a fifth file containing a low-resolution-screen version to be used in the page make-up procedure. This fifth file displays faster onscreen and takes up much less space on disk. Once the page has been made up and is ready for output, the high-resolution files are substituted for the low-resolution image, often using the *Open Prepress Interface* (OPI) and four films will be output, one for each of the process colours. Alternatively, both an image and a colour separation can be generated by software. Note, however, the problems of *colour correction*.

colour space A graphical or pictorial method of representing colour distributions in terms of combinations of single colours. Used in analysing *colour gamuts*. (See *CIE*, *CIELAB*, *CIELUV*.)

Columbia AppleTalk Package (CAP) An implementation of Apple Computer's AppleTalk protocols for the Berkeley version 4.2BSD of *Unix*.

COM See *computer output on microfilm*.

Comdex The communications and data processing exposition held in Las Vegas, which is probably the biggest trade show in the world on any subject. Many manufacturers use the show as a platform for product announcements.

command interface A user interface that requires the user to enter commands at the command prompt. Also called command-line interface, command line interpreter or *character-based interface*, although the latter can include *menus*.

command line interface See *command interface*.

command line interpreter See *command interface*.

committed information rate (CIR) The guaranteed bandwidth over a *virtual circuit* although, if the network has spare bandwidth, devices can go higher for short bursts.

common architecture technology for next-generation Internet protocol (CATNIP) An *Internet-Draft* designed to provide a compressed form of the existing *network layer* protocols and to integrate the protocols currently in use.

common carrier A private company that offers telecommunications services to the public. Can also be described as a telephone company.

common channel signalling A networking procedure in which a special channel, separate from the user channels, is devoted to signalling information.

Common Communication Services (CCS) The standard program interface to networks in IBM's *systems application architecture* (SAA).

Common Gateway Interface (CGI) The standard interface between *HTTP* servers and external programs. External programs are known as *gateways* because they provide an interface between an external source of information and the server.

Common Ground A document exchange system, which has similarities to *Acrobat*, although fewer features.

Common Management Information Protocol (CMIP) The part of the *OSI* body of standards that specifies the protocol elements that may be used to provide the operation and notification services described in the related standard, *Common Management Information Services* (CMIS).

Common Management Information Services (CMIS) The part of the *OSI* body of network standards describing the services used by *peer processes* to exchange information and commands for the purpose of *network management*. It is similar to the *Simple Network Management Protocol* (SNMP), but broader and more complex.

Common Object Request Broker Architecture (CORBA) A standard way of describing the interface between *objects* in *object-oriented* applications.

Common User Access (CUA) The user interface standard of IBM's *systems application architecture* (SAA).

Communications Decency Act (CDA) An act passed by the US Congress in February 1996, intended to prevent the transmission of indecent material over the *Internet* and thus to protect minors. The act was challenged in court by the American Civil Liberties Union and the American Libraries Association, among others; and in June 1996 the District Court for the Eastern District of Pennsylvania issued its opinion that the CDA violated the First Amendment and was, therefore, unconstitutional. The US Department of Justice then filed an appeal to the United States Supreme Court, which on 26 June 1997 decided that 'As a matter of constitutional tradition, in the absence of evidence to the contrary, ... governmental regulation of the content of speech is more likely to interfere with the free exchange of ideas than to encourage it. The interest in encouraging freedom of expression in a democratic society outweighs any theoretical but unproven benefit of censorship.' (Justice John Paul Stevens.) (See also *blue ribbon campaign*.)

communications protocol A set of signals that computers can use when they want to exchange data. These signals make it possible for computers to send and receive information and to check that the information has been transmitted and received correctly. There is more than one set of protocols and a computer, or group of computers, may use different protocols in different situations. (See *full duplex*, *half duplex*, *handshaking*, *parity*.)

communications speed This is normally specified in *bits per second* (bps) or multiples such as kbps or Mbps. Often described as the *bit rate*.

communication system A system or facility providing information transfer between persons and/or equipment. The system can consist of a combination of individual communication *networks*, transmission systems, relay stations and tributary stations, together with terminal equipment capable of interconnection and interoperation, which forms an integrated whole. The individual components must serve a common purpose, be technically compatible and employ common procedures and protocols; they must respond to some form of control and generally operate together.

COMNET A commercial simulation tool for analysing wide-area voice or data networks.

compact disc (CD) A disc (note the agreed spelling with a final 'c'), about 12 cm/4.5 inches in diameter, developed by *Sony* and *Philips*, that can store, on the same disc, still and/or moving images in monochrome and/or colour; stereo or two separate sound tracks integrated with and/or separate from the images; and digital program and information files. The same fabrication technology is used to make both audio CDs and CD-Roms for storing computer data, the only difference being in the device used to read the disc (the player or drive). The disc is made of aluminium covered with a transparent plastic coating. Microscopic pits etched by a laser on the surface of the metal are used to store the data in binary code. The image is recorded from the centre outwards. During playback, a laser beam reads the code and produces signals that are near-perfect replicas of the originals. (See *compact disc interactive* (CD-i or CD-I), *compact disc read-only memory* (CD-Rom), *compact disc-recordable* (CD-R).)

compact disc eXtended Architecture (CD-Rom XA) A compact disc format being jointly developed by *Philips*, *Sony* and *Microsoft*, which will allow the storage of, and simultaneous access to, audio and video data. Uses the *White Book* standard.

compact disc interactive (CD-i or CD-I) Format of compact disc developed by *Philips* for storing a combination of video, audio, text and pictures, allowing the user limited interaction with films, games and educational applications via a special controller. It was aimed at the consumer market, to be used in systems using a combination of computer and television. An alternative format is *Digital Video Interactive* (DVI).

compact disc read-only memory (CD-Rom) A data provision (rather than data storage; compare *CD-R*) medium using the same physical format as audio *compact discs*. Up to 600 Mbytes of data can be stored on one CD-Rom. Access times are slower than with magnetic media. There are several formats used for CD-Rom data; *ISO 9660* defines a standard file system. (See also *WORM*.)

compact disc-recordable (CD-R) Type of compact disc on which data can be overwritten (compare *CD-Rom*). The disc combines magnetic and optical technology so that during the writing process, a laser melts the surface of the disc, thereby allowing the magnetic elements of the surface layer to be realigned.

companding *Com*pressing/ex*panding*. Amplitude modulation process for manipulating a telephone signal to improve the *signal-to-noise ratio*. Allows voice signals to be transmitted at a lower *bit rate*.

composite video A way of broadcasting video or television signals with the colours and the horizontal and vertical registration information integrated. Gives poorer quality than *RGB*. Used in the USA for television.

compound document A document file that contains embedded and *linked data* that was created in other kinds of applications. Particularly used with reference to Microsoft *Windows*. (See *Object Linking and Embedding*.)

Compound Document Architecture (CDA)
DEC's standard for the creation, storage, retrieval, interchange and manipulation of compound documents.

compressed video The result of *video compression*.

compression The coding of data to save storage space or transmission time (*decompression* is the reverse process). Data can often be coded more efficiently (using fewer bits). For example, *run-length encoding* replaces strings of repeated characters (or other repeated units of data) with a single character and a count. There are many compression algorithms and utilities. When several similar files are to be compressed, it is usually better to join and then compress, rather than compress and join, files because most compression algorithms build up tables based on the data they have already compressed; they then use this table to compress subsequent data more efficiently. *PKZIP*, for example, allows compression of multiple files, while other programs may require the files to be joined first. (See also *tiff*, *JPEG*, *MPEG*, *Lempel–Ziv Welch* (LZW).) Compressed data must be decompressed before it can be used. However, utilities, such as *Stacker* were developed which allow compression and decompression on the fly, so that disk capacity appears to be doubled. In addition, there are storage techniques, such as *Megafloppy*, which allows data to be searched and used without decompression; this also provides data security. Compression can be *lossy* or *lossless*.

CompuServe (Formal name CompuServe Information Services — CIS.) A commercial on-line service that can be accessed via *modem*. Widely used for *electronic mail* and *bulletin boards*, it also provides on-line conferencing, business news, sports and weather, financial transactions, travel and entertainment data, as well as on-line editions of computer publications.

CompuServe Information Manager (CIM) The official off-line reader and navigation tool for *CompuServe*.

computed tomography (CT) A medical-imaging technique in which a sequence of X-ray images is used to build up a three-dimensional representation.

computer assisted learning (CAL) In education and training a computer displays instructional material to a student and asks questions about the information given; the student's answers determine the sequence of subsequent lessons.

computer conferencing Collaboration and discussion between people who do not physically meet. All discussion is carried on using *bulletin boards* or *email*.

Computer Emergency Response Team (CERT) An organization formed by *DARPA* in November 1988 in response to the needs exhibited during the *Internet worm* incident. The CERT charter is to work with the Internet community to facilitate its response to computer security events involving Internet hosts, to take proactive steps to raise the community's awareness of computer security issues and to conduct research targeted at improving the security of existing systems.

computer game Computer-controlled game, in which the computer (usually) opposes the human player. Computer games typically employ fast, animated graphics and synthesized sound.

computer graphics The use of computers to display and manipulate images and drawings. Images can be stored as either *raster* (*bitmap*) or *vector graphics*. Computer graphics are used in a wide range of applications, as well as in publishing.

Computer Graphics Metafile (CGM) An international standard file format for graphic images. Most CGM files are *vector graphics*, although it is possible to store *raster graphics* in the CGM format. The standard was created to enable users of different systems and different programs to exchange graphic files.

computer integrated telephony (CIT) A specification for the integration of computers and *PABXs*, so that applications such as screen-based telephone systems, call centres and *voice mail* can be used. (See also *computer telephone integration*.)

computer mediated communications (CMC) Computer conferencing, *electronic* *mail*, access to remote databases and related applications.

computer output on laser disc (COLD) A document storage technique in which scanned images of documents are stored on optical disc, rather than on microfilm. Replacing *COM* (computer output on microfilm).

computer output on microfilm (COM) (Or computer output micrographics.) Direct output from computer onto microfilm or microfiche. Is gradually being superseded by *COLD*.

Computer + Science NETwork (CSNET) The networking organization which combined with *BITNET* to form *CREN*.

computer supported collaborative learning (CSCL) The use of computer systems (such as computer conferencing) to facilitate collaborative learning. Similar to *computer supported cooperative work*.

computer supported cooperative work (CSCW) The use of computer systems to facilitate cooperative working including *workflow* automation and documentation management. Systems to support this include *electronic mail*, *computer conferencing*, group scheduling systems, databases and shared desktop systems. Also described as *groupware*. (See also *Lotus Notes*, *teleconferencing*, *videoconferencing*.)

computer telephone integration (CTI) Using computers to handle and control telephone functions, such as making and receiving calls, directory services and caller identification. (See also *computer integrated telephony*, *TAPI*.)

computer vision See *vision system*.

concentrator A kind of *multiplexer* where many inputs may be active simultaneously so the output *bandwidth* must be at least as great as the total bandwidth of all simultaneously active inputs. May be used to connect a group of terminals to a mainframe or other multi-user system.

concurrency control The controls built into a program running over a *network* to handle the situation where more than one person tries to access a program or data at the same time.

conditioning The provision of filters on leased *analogue* telephone lines to permit higher-speed data transmission.

conferencing A generic term used to cover various types of system which link people together. The main types are *videoconferencing*, *audioconferencing* and *computer conferencing*. All except the last link people together 'synchronously', that is, the people are present simultaneously, even if not physically together.

Configurable Unified Search Interface (CUSI) A collection of indices to various *World Wide Web* and other *Internet* documents. Also describes a tool for searching the Web.

ConflictNet A network connecting those concerned about global conflict. (See *Institute for Global Communications*.)

connectionless A mode of data communication in which *packets* are sent from the user to the *network* without the need for a connection to have been established previously to the destination of those packets. Each packet contains its own destination address and is routed individually. Connectionless operation is also known as *datagram* operation and *packet switching*. Examples include *LANs*, *Internet IP*, *UDP* and ordinary postcards. (Contrast with *circuit switching* and *connection-oriented*.)

connectionless broadband data service (CBDS) The term used in Europe for *SMDS*.

connection oriented A type of *transport layer* data communication service in which an end-to-end logical channel is established prior to the start of communication, allowing a *host* to send data in a continuous stream to another host. The transport service will guarantee that all data will be delivered to the other end in the same order as sent and without duplicates. Communication proceeds through three well-defined phases: connection establishment, data transfer and connection release. The most common example is *Transmission Control Protocol* (TCP). This is the opposite of *connectionless*. (See *circuit switching*, *datagram*, *packet switching*, *virtual circuit*.)

connector Connectors are the parts on the ends of cables that actually make the connection to another piece of hardware. Both the part on the end of the cable and that on the hardware that it plugs into are called connectors, and they are described as either male or female.

constant linear velocity (CLV) A technique used in *CD* drives to ensure that the linear velocity of the disk is always the same at the point being read. This should be compared with constant angular velocity, which is used on magnetic disk drives.

constant mapping A method of describing an *Internet* address used by some *TCP* systems, in which the Internet address is not independent of the *Ethernet* address. (Contrast with *ARP*.)

Consultative Committee on International Radio (CCIR) Of the *ITU*. Recommends standards and procedures for radio and television broadcasting.

container An *HTML* element that contains text. The term can also be used in *SGML*, with the same meaning.

Content Data Model (CDM) An *SGML*-based US *Department of Defense* specification for interactive manuals.

contention A condition in which multiple users compete for access to a shared *channel* or computer port.

contention period See *contention slot*.

contention scheme A method of multiple access to a shared medium, such as a *LAN*, in which access units compete with each other for bandwidth.

contention slot Also described as *contention period*. The minimum time for which a *host* must transmit before it can be sure that no other host's *packet* has collided with its transmission.

Continuous Acquisition and Lifecycle Support (CALS) Note that what the acronym stands for has changed several times. Originally a US Department of Defense standard for electronic exchange of data with commercial suppliers. Now, more generally, a global strategy intended to bring about more enterprise integration through the streamlining of business processes and the application of standards and technologies for the development, management, exchange and use of business and technical information. Includes *SGML* for the documentation aspects; a CALS *Document Type Definition* has been defined. This gives particular attention to coding tables and is widely used outside CALS applications themselves.

continuous tone An uncountable range of colour variation or shades of grey such as occurs in a photograph or painting, which cannot be directly reproduced. All such images must go through a *halftone* process in order to be reproduced. In the halftone process the image is broken up into a series of discrete dots which, when printed, give the illusion of continuous tone.

continuous wave (CW) A term dating from the use of circuits containing thermionic valves. The term is still used to mean transmission by means of a signal at a single frequency, which is either on or off (e.g., Morse code), as opposed to a carrier which is modulated in amplitude, frequency or phase.

control code A character which provides a control or function, rather than being part of the text or data. These include tab, carriage return, etc. Different operating systems and programs have different conventions for what control codes are intended to do. Control codes are also used to control transmission between *hosts*. In some cases, their function is specified as part of the *ASCII* character set, e.g., *ACK*, *NAK*.

cookie A *World Wide Web* mechanism through which servers can obtain information stored on the client side, usually as part of a *browser* implementation. Storage of such information is an automatic process that occurs as the Web is accessed. A common use of cookies is to identify registered users of a Web site without requiring them to sign in each time they access that site.

cooperative information system (CIS) A network of computers which support individual and/or collaborative human work, as well as managing access to information and computing services. Computation is done concurrently over the network by using cooperative database systems, expert systems, multi-agent planning systems and other software application systems ranging from the conventional to the advanced. (See also *computer supported cooperative work*.)

Co-ordinating Committee for Intercontinental Research Networks (CCIRN) A committee that includes the United States *Federal Networking Council* (FNC) and its counterparts in North America and Europe. Co-chaired by the executive directors of the FNC and the European Association of Research Networks (*RARE*), the CCIRN provides a forum for cooperative planning among the principal North American and European research networking bodies.

CopiCat A project, which has developed from *CITED* and other projects, to investigate the use of *encryption* in the control of, and compensation for, *intellectual property* rights in electronic material.

copper distributed data interface (CDDI) An *FDDI* network running over conventional copper cables. All FDDI connections, *single-attached* or *dual-attached*, can be either fibre or copper.

copy To transfer a copy of text and/or graphics to the *clipboard*, while leaving the original in place. (See also *cut*.)

copyleft (A play on *copyright*.) The *copyright* notice applying to the works of the *Free Software Foundation*, granting reuse and reproduction rights to everyone. Those who pass on a program must also include the rights to use, modify and redistribute the code; the code and the freedoms become legally inseparable.

copyright The exclusive legal right of the author of a work (or whoever he or she transfers that right to) to make and distribute copies, prepare derivative works, and perform and display the work in public.

Copyright in Transmitted Electronic Documents (CITED) An EC project aimed at addressing the issues of control of and compensation for intellectual property in electronic information.

CORBA See *Common Object Request Broker Architecture*.

Corporation for Research and Educational Networking (CREN) An organization formed in 1989, when *BITNET* and *Computer + Science NETwork* (CSNET) were combined under one authority. CSNET is no longer operational, but CREN still runs BITNET.

country code A two-letter abbreviation used for a particular country. The codes are based on *ISO 3166* and used as the top-level *domain* for *Internet hostnames* in most countries, although the code for the USA, us, is hardly ever used.

cps Characters per second. Used to measure the speed of a printer or communications device.

crawler See *spider*.

CRC See *cyclic redundancy check, camera-ready copy*.

CREN See *Corporation for Research and Educational Networking*.

crop marks Marks printed on a printed sheet, which indicate the edge of the intended physical page. They can also act as *registration marks* if more than one colour is to be printed.

cross-posting Sending a news article to several different *Usenet newsgroups* simultaneously. It is recommended that a 'Followup-to' line should always be included, directing responses to a single follow-up group.

crosstalk Unwanted coupling of electrical signals between two adjacent transmission media.

cryptography The study of *encryption* and *decryption*. Usually involves taking *plaintext* and applying various encryption algorithms to produce encrypted *ciphertext*. The security of a cryptosystem usually depends on the secrecy of (some of) the keys rather than on the algorithm itself. (See *Clipper, RSA, DES*.)

CSCL See *computer supported collaborative learning*.

CSCW See *computer supported cooperative work*.

CSLIP Compressed *SLIP*, producing faster transfer rates than with uncompressed *Serial Line Internet Protocol* (SLIP).

CSMA/CD See *carrier sense multiple access/collision detect*.

CSNET See *Computer + Science NETwork*.

CSS See *cascading style sheets*.

CSU See *channel service unit*.

CT See *computed tomography*.

CTCP See *client to client protocol*.

CTI See *computer telephone integration*.

CTS See *clear to send*.

CUA See *Common User Access*.

cursor The screen symbol that indicates where the action initiated by the next keystrokes or *mouse click* will take effect. Cursors in *character-based interfaces* are either a block or an underline (sometimes flashing), while in a *GUI* the cursor can consist of any icon chosen by the software developer or the user.

CUSI See *Configurable Unified Search Interface*.

cut To copy text or graphics to the *clipboard* but, unlike *copy*, also to delete the original from the current file.

CW See *continuous wave*.

CWIS See *campus wide information system*.

cybercafé A café where not only coffee, but also *Internet* access, is provided. (See *Cyberia*.)

CyberCash An electronic payment method using *RSA* encryption. (See also *Digicash*, *Ecash*, *Mondex*.)

CyberGlove A *data glove* sold by Virtual Technologies. The glove houses 18 sensors to track accurately just about every move the hand is capable of making. The accompanying software includes a three-dimensional model of the hand that can be added to any *virtual reality* application.

Cyberia The first *cybercafé* in London (and in the UK).

cyberspace Meanings are many and include: the universe of computers, both hardware and software; the perception of and habitation of this universe as *virtual reality*; society from this perspective. Cyberspace inhabitants include cybernauts, cyberpunks, etc. The first popular usage was by William Gibson in his novel *Neuromancer*. Can, in some senses, be equated with the *information superhighway*, but enthusiasts see it almost as a way of (virtual?) life. The implementation of cyberspace on the *World Wide Web* is one of the aims of *VRML*.

cyclic redundancy check (CRC) A method used to detect errors in transmitted data whereby a polynomial algorithm is used to generate a CRC code, which is transmitted with the data block; this code is compared with a code that is calculated at the receiver. If there is a discrepancy, then it will be clear that an error has occurred. A *parity bit* can be considered a one-bit CRC for a string of bits. A single corrupted bit in the data will result in a one-bit change in the calculated CRC but multiple corrupted bits may cancel each other out. *Ethernet packets* have a 32-bit CRC. Many disk formats include a CRC at some level. (See also *checksum*.)

D

D2-MAC A standard for satellite TV signals. It will probably be superseded by digital technology.

DAB See *digital audio broadcast*.

DAC Digital to analogue converter. (See *digital to analogue conversion*.)

D/A conversion See *digital to analogue conversion*.

DANTE A European network company set up by the national research networks.

DARPA See *Defense Advanced Research Projects Agency*.

dash A character, similar to but longer than a hyphen. An en dash is the width of 'N' in the *font* being used and an em dash the width of 'M'. While the hyphen has clearly established uses, how em and en dashes are used depends on the style of a publication and on the country in which they are being used. Regrettably, many *electronic publishing* ventures tend to use a hyphen indiscriminately, this being a carry-over from *character-based* screens, where the hyphen is the only such character available. With *graphical user interfaces*, there is no reason why screen typography should not reach the same standard as that used on paper.

DAT See *digital audio tape*. The abbreviation is also used within computing generally to mean dynamic address translation.

data Information, usually recorded in a quantifiable, i.e., *digital*, manner. Data is the plural of datum (Latin for 'given') but is today almost always used as a singular collective noun.

database A structured container of data of any type. There are several different types of database, which are more or less appropriate for different applications. *Relational databases* are not always appropriate for text-based applications, while *object-oriented databases* are being developed which will handle *multimedia* applications. *SGML* and *HTML* can also be regarded as linear databases. The hierarchy implicit in SGML is more descriptive than a text database, although it requires tools to manipulate it. Databases which will encompass SGML are at a late stage of development.

database query language A language in which users of a *database* can (interactively) formulate requests and generate reports. The best known is *SQL*. Such requests will often be made over a *network* using a *client-server* approach.

database server A computer in a *network* that holds and manages a *database* (the back end), while the user only manipulates data and applications (the front end). Database servers should be distinguished from *file servers* in that with file servers, it is necessary to download large parts of the database to the user or *client* because the database software has not been designed for a network. It was the development of later, network-aware software which allowed the use of the database server.

data bus The internal connections in a computer that carry data, essentially between the processor, memory and peripherals. Data buses are able to transfer 8, 16, 32 or even more bits at a time and the width of the data bus is an important factor in determining the processing speed of a system. (See *bus*, *PCI*, *VESA*, *local bus*.)

data circuit-terminating equipment See *data communication equipment*.

data communication equipment (DCE) (Or data circuit-terminating equipment.) The devices that provide the interface between the data source and the transmitting/receiving equipment (the *data terminal equipment* or DTE), so that in an *RS-232*, or *serial*, interface the *modem* or line interface device is usually regarded as the DCE. In an *X.25* system a network access and packet switching node is regarded as the DCE. DCE and DTE need to be distinguished in order to ensure that they are wired correctly.

data communications Sending and receiving data via any *communications* medium, telephone line, satellite or *wide area network*. Less usually the term refers to *local area networks*, when the term *networking* is more commonly applied. Data communications are increasingly *digital*, although transfer over the *PSTN* is still *analogue* and *modems* are required to convert the signals from and to digital signals at the end of the line. (See also *analogue to digital* and *digital to analogue conversion*.)

data compression Techniques used to reduce file size in order to cut down either the amount of storage needed for a given amount of data or the time taken to transmit it over a communications link. Often (but not always) this data is text. (See *compression*.) On a dial-up line, the *ITU-T* standard data compression technique for low-speed data transmission is *V.42 bis*, which is gradually replacing older and more proprietary techniques. V.42 bis will yield up to 4:1 compression.

Data Discman A Sony trademark for a portable *compact disc* player with a *liquid-crystal display* for data discs.

Data Encryption Algorithm (DEA) An *ANSI* standard identical to the *Data Encryption Standard* (DES).

data encryption key (DEK) Used for the *encryption* of text and to calculate integrity checks (or *digital signatures*). (See *cryptography*, *public key*, *private key*, *EDIFACT*.)

Data Encryption Standard (DES) The *encryption* algorithm developed at the US

National Bureau of Standards. It operates on 64-bit blocks of data and is based on a 56-bit key. DES is identical to the *Data Encryption Algorithm* (DEA). DES has been implemented in both hardware and software. DES is not supposed to be used outside the USA and US companies are not allowed to export equipment in which DES is implemented. However, companies outside the USA have implemented DES and there has been a suggestion that this puts US industry at a disadvantage. This has led to the development of the *Clipper chip* and *key-escrow encryption*. (See also *triple DES*.)

data glove An device used to interact with *virtual reality*. The data glove contains sensors, which measure the movements of the wearer's fingers and transmit them to the virtual reality system. Some data gloves also measure movement of the wrist and elbow and contain control buttons. They can also output signals, such as vibration. The related software is set up so that the user knows what he or she can do and is doing with the glove. (See also *CyberGlove*.)

datagram An independent data entity that carries all the *routing information* it needs to reach the destination computer without relying on other communications between the source and destination computers and the transporting *network*. The basic unit of information transferred over the *Internet* using the *IP* protocol. See *connectionless* and *user datagram protocol* (UDP).)

Data Interchange Format (DIF) A standard file format for spreadsheet and database applications, in which the information is structured in columns and rows. It was originally developed by Software Arts, the company that produced the first spreadsheet, VisiCalc, created for the Apple computer.

data link connection identifier (DLCI) In *frame relay*, the part of the frame header that distinguishes a particular frame of a particular *virtual circuit* in a *link*. As a frame passes from link to link, the DLCI may change. Similar to *Virtual channel* identifier (VCI) in *Distributed Queue Dual Bus* and *asynchronous transfer mode*.

datalink layer (DLL) The second layer in the OSI *seven-layer model*, which is responsible for establishing, maintaining and releasing data link connections between adjacent *network* stations.

data pabx A private (telephone) exchange switch which allows data users to establish connections to host computers or other data users.

Dataphone Digital Service (DDS) The first private-line digital service that was offered by AT&T, with data rates up to 56 kbps. Other suppliers now offer similar services.

data privacy In a *local area network*, the restriction of access to a file so that only authorized users are able to view and/or edit it. In more general terms, applied to personal data, it is concerned with the right of individuals to have both access to and control of data concerning themselves. Subject to legislation in many countries. (See *data protection legislation*.) Privacy can also be ensured by *encryption*. (See *passwords*, *Pretty Good Privacy*.)

data protection legislation Legislation that seeks to protect persons from three potential dangers: the use of personal information that is inaccurate, incomplete or irrelevant; the possibility of personal information being accessed by unauthorized persons; and the use of personal information in a context or for a purpose other than that for which the information was collected. The legislation usually covers only personal data in digital form and is concerned with three general categories: factual data about an individual; subjective judgements and expressions about an individual (judgemental data); and statements of intent, rather than statements of opinion (intention data). (See also *data privacy*, *privacy*.)

data rate See *baud* and *data transfer rate*.

data service level (DS level) A measure of data service rates used to classify the user access rates for various point-to-point *wide area network* technologies or standards, such as *X.25*, *SMDS*, *ISDN*, *ATM* and *PDH*. In North America the DS levels are classified as DS-0 (64 kbps); DS-1 (1.544 – used, for example, on *T-1* synchronous ISDN lines); DS-1C (3.15 Mbps, using 48 *pulse code modulation* channels); DS-2 (6.31 Mbps, using 96 *pulse code modulation channels*); DS-3 (44.736 Mbps – used, for example, on *T-3* synchronous ISDN lines).

data service unit Another term for *digital service unit*.

data terminal equipment (DTE) The device, acting as the source and/or destination of data, which controls a communication channel. This includes terminals, computers, *protocol converters*, and *multiplexers*. Generally, DTE is connected via an *RS-232 serial line* to *data communication equipment* (DCE), most probably a *modem*. DCE and DTE need to be distinguished in order to ensure that they are wired correctly.

data terminal ready (DTR) An *RS-232-C* signal raised by the *data terminal equipment* to indicate that it is ready to receive data.

data transfer rate (Or *data rate*.) The speed at which data travels from one device to another. This can vary greatly, in that data transfers within computers using internal *buses* are very fast, while transfers via *modems*, over *analogue* lines, can be many orders of magnitude slower. Any transfer which involves a mechanical device, such as a disk drive, is always very slow compared with internal transfer rates. (See also *bit rate*.)

data transparency Transmission such that a signal is not modified by the communications system in any way.

dB See *decibel*.

DBM See *dynamic bandwidth allocation*, *dynamic bandwidth management*.

DBS See *direct broadcast satellite*.

DCA (Defense Communications Agency) See *Defense Information Systems Agency*. (Also see *Document Content Architecture*.)

DCC See *Direct Client to Client Protocol*.

DCE See *data communication equipment*, *distributed computing environment*.

D-channel The control/signalling channel in ISDN. (D stands for 'delta'.) (See *basic rate ISDN*, *primary rate ISDN*.)

DCM See *dynamic channel management*.

DDCMP See *Digital Data Communications Message Protocol*.

DDE See *Dynamic Data Exchange*.

DDES See *Digital Data Exchange Standard*.

DDIF See *Digital Document Interchange Format*.

DDN See *Defense Data Network*.

DDP Distributed data processing. (See *distributed computing*.)

DDS See *Dataphone Digital Service*, *digital data service*.

DEA See *Data Encryption Algorithm*, but see *Data Encryption Standard* for more information.

DEC Digital Equipment Corporation.

decibel (dB) A logarithmic unit of measurement used to express the ratio of two amounts of power = $10\log_{10} P_1/P_2$, where P_1 and P_2 are measures of the powers being compared. Used in *communications* to measure response, it is often expressed as $20\log_{10} V_1/V_2$, where V_1 and V_2 are the voltage levels measured.

DECnet Networking protocols proprietary to *DEC*, which are used instead of *TCP/IP* and are not compatible with the *Internet*. Used on DEC machines such as the VAX.

decompression The reverse of *compression*.

decryption To restore information that has been encrypted, i.e., to restore *plaintext* from *ciphertext*. (See *cryptography*, *encryption*.)

dedicated circuit or line A line reserved for only one user. Also called *private line* and *leased line*.

Defense Advanced Research Projects Agency (DARPA) Former name of *Advanced Research Projects Agency* (ARPA).

Defense Data Network (DDN) A global communications network used to connect US military installations. It is made up of *MILNET*, some other portions of the *Internet* and other classified networks. The DDN is managed by the *Defense Information Systems Agency*.

Defense Data Network Network Information Center (DDN NIC) (Also known as 'The NIC'.) The organization which provides services to the *DDN*, although it used to be responsible for coordinating the *Internet* as a whole. This has now been taken over by *InterNIC*. DDN NIC has now been renamed DISA NIC. (See *Defense Information Systems Agency*.)

Defense Information Systems Agency (DISA) Formerly called the Defense Communications Agency (DCA), the US government agency responsible for managing the *Defense Data Network* (DDN) portion of the *Internet*. Currently, DISA administers the *DDN*, and supports the user assistance services of the *DDN NIC* (recently renamed DISA NIC).

DEK See *data encryption key*.

delimiter The character used at the beginning and end of *SGML/HTML tags*. In the *reference concrete syntax* (the usual way of encoding using SGML, also used by HTML), the opening delimiters are '<' for a *start-tag* and '</' for an *end-tag*, while the closing delimiter is '>' for both start and end-tags.

Delphi A US and UK *Internet service provider*. Also used to describe a form of iterative discussion and decision-making, often carried on using *computer conferencing*. Finally, it is an *object-oriented* rapid application development package for Microsoft *Windows*, written by Borland in the Pascal language, using visual, component-based design.

demodulation The extraction of information from a *modulated carrier signal*.

Demon Internet Ltd The first company to provide public low-cost full *Internet* access in the UK.

demultiplexer A device which separates *multiplexed* signals.

DES See *Data Encryption Standard*.

descender The part of a letter extending below the character *baseline*, as for example in j, p, q and y. (See also *ascender*.)

descriptive markup *Markup* that describes the structure of a document in a non-system-specific manner, independently of any processing that may be performed upon it. For example, *SGML* descriptive markup uses tags to express the element structure.

desktop In a *graphical user interface* the representation of the working area, showing *icons*, folders and dialogue boxes, which can be accessed using the mouse.

desktop conferencing A *conferencing* utility, in which users on a *network* are able to share a *white board* and transfer files between them.

desktop publishing (DTP) The use of computers to make up pages including text and *graphics*. DTP began in the mid-1980s with the almost simultaneous appearance of the Apple *Macintosh*, the Apple LaserWriter (effectively the first low-cost laser printer) and the Aldus *PageMaker* program. With this combination it was possible to produce *camera ready copy* which was adequate for many publications and, what became even more important, to output a *PostScript* file that could be proofed on a low-resolution laser printer and then sent for output on an *imagesetter* or typesetter at a much higher resolution. The technology has taken over from conventional typesetting approaches in many areas, particularly magazine production and advertising, where it is the layout that is important, and *QuarkXPress* has virtually become the standard program for these applications. During the late 1980s, the term *electronic publishing* was almost synonymous with DTP, but as 'true' electronic publishing (on the screen as opposed to on paper) has developed in the 1990s, there is a clear difference between the two, although there is still some confusion, particularly amongst those still concerned with the production of conventional publications.

desktop video The use of a personal computer to view and control still or moving *video* images. Mainly used in the context of *videoconferencing*.

destination address The part of a *packet* header that specifies the destination to which the packet is to be sent, using an address that is unique throughout the whole network, whereas the *data link connection identifier* and *virtual channel* identifier apply only to a given link in a network.

device driver The program which provides access to a particular device, for example a printer or a *sound card*.

device independent files/fonts Files or *fonts*, which can be output on any output device, subject to its *resolution*. Examples include *PostScript* files and fonts and *TrueType* fonts whilst devices include *printers* of many types, *imagesetters* and *screen displays*. Device independence was an important factor in the successful development of *desktop publishing*, in that low-resolution proofs can be checked before files are output on a high-resolution device. Before the development of device-independent fonts and file formats, output (and also *page make-up*) was generally specific to a particular output device, i.e., device dependent. In one sense, no file or font is truly device independent in that it relies on the output device having the ability to interpret the file. However, so many devices now use a subset of output programs that many formats are effectively device-independent.

DFS See *distributed file system*.

DG XIII Directorate General (Section XIII) of the European Union, which is responsible for the information market and for innovation.

DHCP See *Dynamic Host Configuration Protocol*.

dial-in IP Running *IP* direct from a computer linked to an access provider using *dial-up*. The computer remains a *host* for the time it is connected.

DIALOG An on-line information service which can be *dialled-up* directly to gain access, via a *modem*, to *on-line* databases.

dial-up A temporary, as opposed to dedicated, connection between machines which is established over a *public switched telephone network*.

DIANE See *Direct Information Access Network for Europe*.

DIDOS A *RACE* project to describe, realize, test and evaluate a services environment for distributed technical documentation, using a framework of standards, services, products, agreements, business models, networks and applications.

Didot point system A method of measuring typesize, used in Europe. (See *font size, cicero*.)

DIF See *Data Interchange Format, Document Interchange Format*.

differential line A two-wire electrical connection. One wire carries the normal signal and the other an inverted version of the signal. A differential receiver subtracts one from the other with the aim of cancelling out any noise induced in the wires, assuming that the same level of noise will have been induced in both wires, often configured as a *twisted pair*. The two wires may be connected at the receiver to separate *analogue to digital converters* and the subtraction performed digitally. The *RS-422 serial* line standard specifies differential drivers and receivers, whereas the *RS-232* standard does not. (See also (the opposite) *single ended*.)

differential phase shift keying (DPSK) A version of *phase shift keying* (PSK) in which the difference between the signal and the preceding signal is transmitted, needing fewer bits in total.

digest A selection of messages that have been posted to a *newsgroup* or *mailing-list*, prepared by a *moderator* who standardizes the format and produces a contents list. The digest is then posted to an alternative mailing-list or alternative newsgroup.

DigiCash A company developing products to support electronic payment methods. *Ecash* is its trial form of software-only electronic money. (See *Mondex, Cybercash*.)

digital Meaning 'coded as numbers', digital signifies the use of two states — on and off, low and high, black and white — to encode, receive and transmit information. Should be contrasted with *analogue*, which implies continuous variation.

digital audio broadcast (DAB) The broadcast of audio information, particularly stereo hi-fi, using digital transmission at 128–384 kbps to provide audio quality equivalent to that produced from an audio CD.

digital audio tape (DAT) A format for storing music, in *digital* form, on magnetic tape, developed in the mid-1980s by *Sony* and *Philips*. In order to cope with the *bandwidth* requirements, DAT uses a rotary-head (or *helical scan*) format, where the read/write head spins diagonally across the tape in the same way as in a video cassette recorder. Tape speed is much higher than for conventional audio tapes and the tapes are single-sided, with a capacity of 120 minutes. DAT technology is also used for storing digital computer data, although the interface is usually different from that used for audio. (See also *Exabyte*.)

digital camera A camera which records images in *digital* form rather than on photographic film. There are both video digital cameras and still-image digital cameras. Images are often stored on standard 3 inch diskettes using a standard bitmap format, such as *tiff*. Digital cameras work in a similar way to *scanners* using *charge-coupled devices*.

digital carrier A *multiplexer* and *codec* combining several *pulse code modulation* (PCM) encoded channels on one transmission path. If the path is copper telephone wire, the digital signal is amplified and called *T-1, T-3*, etc.

Digital Data Communications Message Protocol (DDCMP) A *DEC* datalink layer protocol using character count.

Digital Data Exchange Standard (DDES) A standard which may find application for exchanging the high-resolution image files between colour electronic prepress systems produced by different manufacturers.

digital data service (DDS) The class of service offered by telecommunications companies for transmitting digital data as opposed to voice.

digital display A display that shows discrete values as numbers (as opposed to an analogue signal, such as the continuous sweep of a hand on a clock).

Digital Document Interchange Format (DDIF) A *Compound Document Architecture* (CDA) specification for representing compound documents in revisable format; a *DEC* standard for document encoding.

Digital Equipment Corporation Network See *DECnet*.

Digital Lempel–Ziv 1 (DLZ1) The *compression algorithm* used on *digital linear tape*, which maps variable length input strings to variable length output symbols. During compression, a dictionary of strings is built up, which is then accessed by means of a *hash table*. Whenever an input data string matches a string in the table, it is replaced with the output symbol.

digital linear tape (DLT) A magnetic tape drive format developed by *DEC*, based on the *Digital Lempel–Ziv 1* (DLZ1) *compression algorithm*.

digital modulation Encoding analogue signals as a series of discrete or pulsed signals. (See *digital signal processing, sampling, analogue to digital conversion*.)

Digital Network Architecture (DNA) The *DEC* communications *network* architecture.

Digital Object Identifier (DOI) An identifier and a routing system for *electronic documents*, being developed for the Association of American Publishers by R R Bowker and the Corporation for National Research Initiatives (CNRI). The system is *URN* compatible and designed to provide a persistent way of identifying and linking to electronic documents and their constituent parts. The system is based on CNRI's *Handle System* and will have some resemblance to the *International Standard Book Number* (ISBN), in that the first part of the number will identify the publisher or similar body, while use of the second part will vary depending on the publisher and the type of document.

digital press A printing press in which the image is transferred to the drum by electronic methods, directly from a *PostScript* file. This means that, in principle, every page printed can be different, as on a *laserprinter*, but in practice means that short-run printing becomes economic. (See *Indigo, Xeikon*.) The *DocuTech* provides a similar effect but uses xerographic techniques rather than ink.

digital service unit (DSU) (Or *data service unit*.) A device used in *digital communications* to connect a *channel service unit* to *data terminal equipment*. Performs a similar function to a *modem* in *analogue* communications, so that on transmission the DSU translates the outgoing signal into bipolar pulses, while on receiving the DSU both extracts timing information and regenerates the *digital* information from the incoming bipolar signal.

digital signal processing (DSP) Manipulation of *analogue* signals (often in *sound* or *image* files) that have been converted to *digital* form (by *sampling* or *digital* modulation).

digital signature Data at the end of a message that both identifies and authenticates the sender of a message. Uses *public-key encryption*. With a *one-way hash function* the sender generates a hash-code from the message and then encrypts this with his or her *private key*. The receiver decrypts the received hash with the sender's public key and compares it with a hash-code generated from the data. If the two hash-codes are the same, this confirms that the sender is who he or she claims to be and that the message has not been corrupted. (See also *digital signature standard*, *EDIFACT*.)

digital signature standard (DSS) The *NIST* standard for digital signatures (authenticating both the message and the signer). It is based on an algorithm using discrete logarithms. Its security is comparable to that of *RSA* and is based on 1024-bit keys.

digital speech interpolation (DSI) A *sampling* technique that improves the efficiency of digital voice transmission by using the transmission channel only when someone is talking.

digital to analogue conversion (DAC, D/A conversion) Conversion of information from a *digital* form (as information is held in a computer) to *analogue* form (such as sound), for example in a *modem* for transmission over analogue telephone lines.

digital versatile disc (DVD) (See *digital video disc*.) The change to the name digital versatile disc has been proposed because the discs will carry more than just video. Thus there will be DVD-Video, DVD-Audio, DVD-Rom, and DVD-R (recordable).

digital video disc (DVD) A new form of disc. Unlike the CD, which is single-sided and contains only one layer, the DVD can be dual-layer and double-sided. Its maximum storage capacity is 17 Gbytes, equivalent to four full-length feature films. (See also *digital versatile disc*, which is the proposed new name for this format.)

digital video interactive (DVI) A technology used for storing video images. Uses special processors for *compression* and *decompression*. (See also *compact disc-interactive*, *JPEG*.)

digitize To convert an *analogue* signal, such as *video*, *graphics* or *sound*, into a digital format so that it can be input, stored, displayed and manipulated by a computer or transmitted over a *digital* communications system.

dingbat A term for typographical characters, such as arrows, stars, hearts and snowflakes (for example, ❊ ✱ ❤ ➝ ✝ ① ✎ ⑨ ⊃), also called *ornaments*. *Zapf Dingbats* is a font which is provided as standard with most *PostScript* printers.

DIP (See *document image processing*.) Also used in computing to mean dual in-line package, describing computer chips that are fastened to a printed circuit board.

direct broadcast satellite (DBS) A satellite which transmits video signal directly to the standard satellite *dish*, usually sited on the sides of buildings.

Direct Client to Client Protocol (DCC) An *Internet Relay Chat* (IRC) protocol which allows private interchanges (including file transfer) between users rather than going via IRC servers. This means that conversations cannot be logged and it means a much more efficient use of *bandwidth* as the data does not need to be *broadcast*.

Direct Information Access Network for Europe (DIANE) Information search and retrieval services offered over the *Euronet* system.

direct memory access (DMA) Transfer of data between computer memory and external devices without going through the central processing unit. This speeds up transfer rates. DMA is used for devices such as scanners.

Directory Access Protocol An *X.500* protocol used for communication between a *Directory User Agent* (DUA) and a *Directory System Agent* (DSA).

Directory System Agent (DSA) The software providing the *X.500* directory service, usually for a single organization or some smaller unit.

39

Directory User Agent (DUA) The software that accesses the *X.500* directory service for the user, which may be a person or more software.

DISA See *Defense Information Systems Agency.*

disc The traditional British spelling of *disk*. It has been formalized for use in the term *compact disc*, this spelling being part of the CD standard, although magnetic disks are almost always spelt with a 'k' (see *disk*). While the difference does seem to be an unnecessary *attribute*, it is sometimes useful for clarifying what is being discussed (as long as both parties have agreed the convention).

disk The US spelling, which has become standard for (magnetic) computer disks. (See also *disc*.)

dispersion The spreading (over time) of a wave packet as it propagates through a medium, such as *optical fibre*, which is not free space, as each wavelength has a very slightly different speed of propagation.

Display PostScript A form of *PostScript* which makes it possible to display a true PostScript image onscreen (strictly *WYSIWYG*). However, it is much slower than *QuickDraw* for the Macintosh and various screen drivers for the PC. It is implemented on the NeXT computer.

display type Type used for headlines, titles, etc., rather than for text (see *body type*). These typefaces are usually 14 point type or larger. Some typefaces are designed specifically for this use, while other *expert sets* have special versions of particular typefaces intended for use as display faces.

distortion A corruption of a signal as a result of changes to the waveform.

distributed computing (distributed data processing, DDP) The dispersal of computing power, storage and applications throughout a number of computers connected through a *network*, rather than concentrating computing on a mainframe. (See also *client-server*.)

Distributed Computing Environment (DCE) A computer architecture based on *open systems* and promoted and controlled by the *Open Software Foundation*.

distributed database A logical *database* that looks like a single database to the user, but which is divided among several physical locations. An example is the *Internet Domain Name System* (DNS). (See also *distributed computing*.)

distributed data processing (ddp) See *distributed computing*.

distributed file system (DFS) A file system which, while accessible to any user and appearing to be local, is actually distributed over a number of computers. (See also *distributed computing*, *distributed database*.)

Distributed Operating Multi Access Interactive Network (DOMAIN) A proprietary network protocol used by Apollo (now Hewlett Packard) *workstations*.

Distributed Queue Dual Bus (DQDB) An *IEEE* standard for the control of access to networks, so that access units queue until bandwidth becomes available. DQDB also allows bandwidth to be reserved in advance for voice or video traffic. DQDB is used in *metropolitan area networks*.

dithering A technique used in computer *graphics* to create the appearance of additional colours and shades of grey. As a *bit* can only be on or off, depending on the *colour resolution* (bits per *pixel*) or number of *grey levels*, there will be a limit to the number of colours (or grey levels) that can be displayed. However, as the dots which make up a conventional *halftone* illustration are much larger than a pixel, pixels are grouped in ways which fool the eye into thinking that it is seeing more shades of grey (by using pixel groups making up different shapes) or additional colours (by combining pixel combinations of different colours which the eye integrates). Dithering is also used in *antialiasing*.

DLCI See *data link connection identifier.*

DLL See *datalink layer, Dynamic Link Library.*

DLT See *digital linear tape.*

DLZ1 See *Digital Lempel–Ziv 1.*

DMA See *direct memory access.*

DNA See *Digital Network Architecture.*

DNS See *Domain Name System*.

document A term which is not generally defined. In some circumstances it is equivalent to a computer file, while in others it may be what can be viewed or even what is printed. Also used for a *hypertext node* or a collection of nodes on related topics. *Multimedia* documents, by definition, contain more than just text and graphics. Unless the context is obvious, the term should not usually be used without additional information making clear what is meant. (See also *document instance*, *structured documents*, *SGML*.)

document architecture Rules for the formulation of text processing applications. These are not part of *SGML*, but may be used in conjunction with SGML to control the structure and semantics of a document. (See also *DSSSL*, *ODA*.)

Document Content Architecture/Revisable Form Text (DCA/RFT) A document format used by IBM's DisplayWrite program. It should not be confused with Microsoft *Rich Text Format* (RTF).

document delivery The supply of individual documents, usually copies of already published articles, following a request which has been delivered over a network. The supply of the document may be in electronic form, effectively a *download* (either including format commands for printing out, such those provided in T_EX or *RTF*, or as an image from a *DIP* system); or it may be sent by fax or even via the postal service. It is important not to confuse document delivery with *electronic publishing*, where information is delivered in digital form, in most cases formatted so that it can be accessed and searched using software supplied with the document or separately available, e.g., a *World Wide Web browser*.

document image processing (DIP) The scanning of (usually large volumes of) documents and subsequent storage on *CD-Rom* or *WORM* discs, which are indexed. Many companies are using this approach both to reduce storage space requirements and to provide better customer service in that the documents are much more easily accessible. The software used generally also includes facilities for *optical character recognition* (OCR), so that the text of the documents can be extracted for use in other applications.

document instance The actual content, i.e., text and markup, of an *SGML* document corresponding to a particular *Document Type Definition*.

Document Interchange Format (DIF) A standard file format used by the US Navy to interchange documents between different computer programs.

document reader An input device that reads marks or characters, usually on specially prepared forms and documents, such as cheques. These devices use *optical mark recognition* (OMR), *optical character recognition* (OCR) and *mark sensing*. (See also *MICR*.)

Document Style Semantics and Specification Language (DSSSL) An *ISO* standard (ISO 10179) which defines how to transfer information about the presentation of an *SGML* document to formatting software, associating *stylesheet* information with a *document instance*. SGML, by definition, says nothing about how a document is to appear, either on paper or onscreen. DSSSL is intended to formalize the process of associating appearance information with the SGML structure.

Document Type Definition (DTD) The definition of a document type in *SGML*. This is a formulation of the hierarchy of the document (see Figure 2) and the definitions and relationships of the *elements* that make up that hierarchy, together with their *markup tags* and their *attributes*, the rules for applying the tags and definitions of *entities*. The DTD actually forms part of an SGML document, but in many SGML applications is not seen by the user, for example in *HTML*, which is defined by a DTD. Other well known and widely used DTDs are the *CALS* DTD and the American Association of Publishers (AAP) DTD, which has been revised and published as *ISO 12083*.

DocuTech A high-speed *laserprinter* from Xerox, which produces print-quality output. This makes short-run printing economic. (See also *Indigo*, *Xeikon*.)

Docuverse

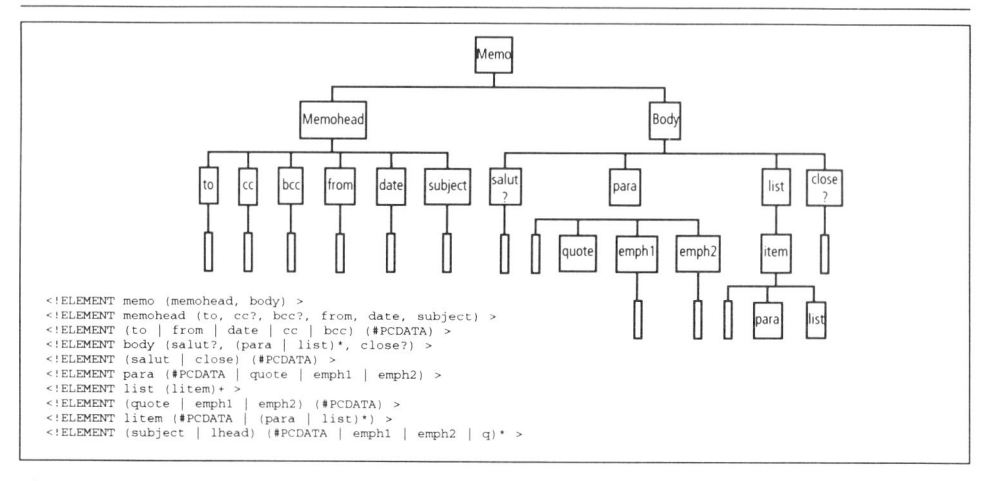

```
<!ELEMENT memo (memohead, body) >
<!ELEMENT memohead (to, cc?, bcc?, from, date, subject) >
<!ELEMENT (to | from | date | cc | bcc) (#PCDATA) >
<!ELEMENT body (salut?, (para | list)*, close?) >
<!ELEMENT (salut | close) (#PCDATA) >
<!ELEMENT para (#PCDATA | quote | emph1 | emph2) >
<!ELEMENT list (litem)+ >
<!ELEMENT (quote | emph1 | emph2) (#PCDATA) >
<!ELEMENT litem (#PCDATA | (para | list)*) >
<!ELEMENT (subject | lhead) (#PCDATA | emph1 | emph2 | q)* >
```

Figure 2 Document Type Definition

The structure of a simple memo together with the Document Type Definition representing it (see *mark-up* for an example of a memo marked up to conform to this DTD). Each element is defined in terms of the (sub)-elements that it may contain. The usual computing conventions on symbols are followed, so that '|' means 'or', '?' means 'optional', '*' means 'any number of (including none)', '+' means 'any number of (but at least one)'. #PCDATA (represented by the narrow empty boxes in the structure chart) is an example of an *SGML* 'reserved name' which here just means the actual characters, i.e., the letters and spaces used to convey the information

Docuverse A concept, of the whole world being one document, put forward by Ted *Nelson* in connection with *Xanadu* and one which is embodied in the way the *World Wide Web* has developed.

DoD The US Department of Defense, whose *Advanced Research Projects Agency* set up *ARPANET*, the forerunner of the Internet. (See also *CALS*.)

DOI See *Digital Object Identifier*.

DOMAIN See *Distributed Operating Multi Access Interactive Network*.

domain A group of computers on the *Internet* whose *hostnames* share a common suffix, the domain name. Domains often indicate a country, e.g., '.uk', or a type of organization: '.com' (commercial), '.edu' (educational), '.net' (network operations), '.gov' (US government), and '.mil' (US military). Although the '.us' domain includes subdomains for the 50 states, they are rarely used. Within the .uk domain, there is the '.ac.uk' subdomain for academic sites and the '.co.uk' domain for commercial ones. Other top-level domains may be divided up in similar ways. (See *administrative domain*, *Domain Name System* (DNS).)

domain address The name of a *host* on the *Internet* which is part of the *hierarchy* of Internet *domains*.

domain name See *domain*.

Domain Name Server (DNS) An alternative name for *Domain Name System*.

Domain Name System (DNS) (Also Domain Name Server.) A hierarchical method of naming *Internet* addresses, based on the domain and subdomains. DNS is also used to describe the distributed data query service which is used for translating *hostnames* into *IP* addresses. (See also *Berkeley Internet Name Domain*, *Network Information Centre*.)

Domesday Project A *multimedia* project run by the BBC in the late 1980s. Information was gathered, mainly through schools and local communities, about places and their communities (in analogy with the original Domesday Book). This information was put onto two *laser discs*, one of which included *video* material. The project was significant because it was almost the first large-scale multimedia project.

DOOM A popular three-dimensional monster-hunting action game published by id Software.

drag and drop

DOS See *MS-DOS*.

dot address An *Internet* address in *dot notation*.

dot gain The increase in the size of the dots in a halftone illustration when they are printed on the paper (using a printing press, rather than a computer printer). The magnitude of the dot gain will depend on the characteristics of the press, the paper and the ink. If there is cooperation between the originator of the artwork and the printer, it may possible to use software to adjust the colour curves and even dot size to obtain the image which is desired.

dot notation The usual notation for *IP* addresses, consisting of one to four numbers most often given as a decimal (also known as *dotted decimal notation*), e.g., 158.152.28.130 (but can be given in *hexadecimal* or *octal*). Many commands will accept an address in dot notation in place of a *hostname*.

dot pitch A measure of the spacing (and by implication the size) of the individual dots of phosphorescent material that provide the image on a screen when irradiated by the electron beam. On a colour monitor, each spot of light is made up of a group of three separate dots which glow red, green and blue (see *RGB*). In general, the smaller the dot pitch, the sharper the image below a certain dot pitch threshold, although there are other factors involved. The screen *resolution*, in *pixels*, is determined by the electronics of the display and a single pixel may be made up of 4–16 separate phosphor groups.

dots per inch (dpi) The *resolution* of a printer or scanner is measured in dots per inch. For a printer it is the number of dots of toner placed on the paper (in both directions), while for a scanner it is the number of *charge-coupled devices* per inch.

dotted decimal notation See *dot notation*.

double-click To *click* twice on the button of a *mouse*. While single-clicking usually means selecting an icon, double-clicking almost always means that the command associated with the icon or with a file name should be executed. If a file name is double-clicked, then this is equivalent to (single-) clicking on the name to select it and then (single-) clicking on the 'OK' button.

down Not functioning or not accessible. The term is applied to *hosts* on the *Internet*, as well as to computers in general.

downlink A satellite earth station that receives signals (such as television) from a satellite. (See also *uplink, TVRO*.)

download To transfer data from a distant computer to a local one, often over the *Internet*, using *anonymous ftp* or other technique. The opposite of *upload*, although the distinction between downloading and uploading is not always clear, except that downloading often refers to transfer from a larger 'host' system (especially a mainframe) to a smaller 'client' system. (See also *downloadable font*.)

downloadable font (Also called *soft font*.) A *font* (or *typeface*) that is not resident (permanently stored) in a printer, but has to be sent, or *downloaded*, from disk to the printer before it can be used. It may be necessary to download fonts before sending the file to be printed, but increasingly applications will download the required fonts as part of the printing operation. Exactly how this is carried out depends on the types of fonts used (e.g., *PostScript* or *TrueType*), whether *Adobe Type Manager* is used and the printing interface.

dpi See *dots per inch*.

DPSK See *differential phase shift keying*.

DQDB See *Distributed Queue Dual Bus*.

drag To move the *mouse* cursor while holding down the mouse button and then, at a new position, to release the button. Used on scroll bars, to move icons, to resize drawings, to select text and for many other tasks. (See *drag and drop*.)

drag and drop A method for handling files in a *graphical user interface* or a *WIMP* environment. The user drags either a file name or on an icon representing a file to another position, either an icon for an *application program* or a new window (representing a directory or a disk drive), and then releases the button (dropping the file or icon). The effect is either to trigger the application to act on the file which has been 'dragged and dropped' or to move the file's position in the directory structure. (Drag and drop is also

43

used in some word-processing programs to move text.) While the advantages of this technique seem self-evident to a novice, it needs to be used with care, in that sometimes it means move a file, and sometimes it means copy a file and which of these is not always intuitive or obvious. Often, confirmation of the action is requested by the system before it is implemented.

Drawing eXchange Format (DXF) A *graphic file format*, similar to *IGES*. Commonly used by *CAD* systems.

draw program A program used to create and edit objects (lines, circles, squares, etc.) using a *vector* approach, such as Bézier curves. Should be contrasted with a *paint program*, which is used to edit and manipulate *bitmaps*. It is usually possible to import bitmap graphics into *draw programs*, but not to edit them. If a bitmap is *autotraced*, then a *vector graphic* is produced, which can be edited in the draw program.

drop cable The wiring between a computer and its *Ethernet transceiver*.

dropout Characters lost in data transmission for whatever reason.

DSA See *Directory System Agent*.

DSI See *digital speech interpolation*.

DS level See *data service level*.

DSP See *digital signal processing*.

DSS See *digital signature standard*.

DSSSL See *Document Style Semantics and Specification Language*.

DSU See *digital service unit*.

DTD See *Document Type Definition*.

DTE See *data terminal equipment*.

DTMF See *dual tone multi frequency*.

DTP See *desktop publishing*.

DTR See *data terminal ready*.

DUA See *Directory User Agent*.

dual-attached An *FDDI* interface where a device is connected to both FDDI *token-passing rings*, so that uninterrupted operation continues in the event of a failure of either of the rings. While all connections to the main FDDI rings and a some critical devices such as *routers* and *concentrators* are dual-attached, *host* computers are normally *single-attached* or *dual-homed* to a router or concentrator.

dual-homed A connection to an *FDDI* network in which a *host* computer is simultaneously connected to two separate devices in the same FDDI ring. Normally, one of the connections becomes active while the other is blocked. However, if the first connection fails, the backup link takes over. The difference between a dual-homed device and a *dual-attached* device is that while the former can tolerate a fault in one of its 'homes', the latter can tolerate a fault in one of the FDDI rings.

dual tone multi frequency (DTMF) (Or *touch-tone*.) The method employed in telephony throughout the USA to communicate the keys pressed when dialling. Pressing a key generates two simultaneous tones, one for the row and one for the column.

Dublin core A core of *metadata* elements proposed (at a 1995 conference in Dublin, Ohio) as a basis for searching for information available over the *Internet*.

duotone A black-and-white photograph (or other artwork) that is reproduced using two colours, both near to black. Two halftone images are generated, one of which is slightly underexposed and the other slightly overexposed, and they are printed one on top of the other. The effect is to give a more striking image, together with more control to the designer, who can vary the proportions of the two images. *Tritones* and *quadtones* are also possible.

duplex See *full duplex, half duplex, simplex*.

DVD See *digital versatile disc, digital video disc*.

DVI See *digital video interactive, device-independent file*. In particular, a DVI file, which contains a device-independent description of the formatted document, is the usual output of T_EX.

DXF See *Drawing eXchange Format*.

dynamic bandwidth allocation, dynamic bandwidth management (DBM) The allocation of bandwidth as and when it is required by users, depending on the *burstiness* of their traffic. All *packet-switched* networks provide dynamic bandwidth allocation.

dynamic channel management (DCM) Allocation of the *channels* available as and when required by users.

Dynamic Data Exchange (DDE) A Microsoft Windows *hotlink* protocol that allows *application programs* to communicate using a *client-server* model. DDE is mainly used to include live data from one application in another, for example spreadsheet data in a word-processed report by reference, so that whenever the latter is processed the latest version of the spreadsheet data is included. In version 3.1 of Windows, DDE was enhanced by *object linking and embedding* (OLE).

Dynamic Host Configuration Protocol (DHCP) A protocol in a *Windows NT* server that provides dynamic allocation of *IP* addresses to PCs running on a Microsoft *Windows local area network*. (See also *Reverse Address Resolution Protocol*.)

dynamic IP address A temporary *IP* address, which is allocated when a user connects to the *Internet*, usually over a *dial-up* connection. (Compare with *static IP address*.) Dynamic IP addresses allow a more efficient use of IP addresses, the number of which is finite. (See *TUBA*.)

Dynamic Link Library (DLL) An executable program component for Microsoft *Windows* that can be loaded and linked as required at run time, and then unloaded when no longer needed. Windows itself uses DLL files to handle such aspects as international keyboards, while Windows word-processing programs use DLL files for functions such as spelling and hyphenation checks. Other operating systems — such as SunOS (the Sun Microsystems version of *Unix*) and the RISC OS on the Acorn Archimedes — also use dynamically linked libraries.

Dynatext A viewer for *SGML*-based documents, together with the related *graphics* etc., produced by Electronic Book Technologies.

E

E-1 A European leased line service, used by *primary rate ISDN* with a bit rate of 2 Mbps. The equivalent of the US *T-1* service. (See also *E-3*, *E-4*.)

E-3, E-4 European *PDH* services running at 34.368 Mbps (E-3) and 139.264 Mbps (E-4). For the USA, see *data service levels*.

E164 The worldwide number plan of the *ITU-T* for identifying network connections via *ISDN* and *SMDS*.

EARN See *European Academic and Research Network*.

EBCDIC See *extended binary coded decimal interchange*.

Ebone A European-wide *backbone*.

Ecash A trial form of *electronic funds transfer* over the *Internet* (and soon by *electronic mail*). Each user withdraws money from his or her bank account and, using Ecash software, stores it on his or her own computer. The money can then be spent over the Internet at any shop accepting Ecash. Security is provided by a *public-key digital signature*. (See also *Cybercash*, *Digicash*, *Mondex*.)

echo In telecommunications, the reflection of part of the signal energy from the remote end back to the transmitter. Also a kind of *newsgroup* on *FidoNet* and a *Unix* command that just prints its arguments.

echo cancellation A process that isolates and filters out unwanted signals, resulting from *echoes* of the main signal, on a telephone line. Also a technique which permits *full duplex* transmission over two wires.

echoplex A communications procedure in which a receiving station acknowledges receipt of a message by echoing it back to the transmitting station.

ECHT European Conference on *Hypertext*.

ECMS See *Electronic Copyright Management System*.

Econet A network connecting those concerned about environmental preservation and sustainability. (See *Institute for Global Communications*.) Also a network produced by Acorn Computers for the BBC Microcomputer and its successors.

EDI See *electronic data interchange*.

EDIF See *Electronic Design Interchange Format*.

EDIFACT See *ISO 9735*.

edutainment The integration of interactive education and entertainment services or software. In Europe usually on *CD-Rom*, while in North America often supplied via a cable network. (See also *infotainment*.)

EEMA European Electronic Messaging Association.

EFF See *Electronic Frontier Foundation*.

EftpOS See *electronic funds transfer at point of sale*.

EGP See *Exterior Gateway Protocol*.

eight-bit clean Describes systems that take advantage of all eight *bits* of a *byte*, using extended character sets (unlike *ASCII*). In programs and *communications* only using the first seven bits (that is a character set from 0 to 127), the eighth bit is often used as a *parity* bit or to contain a flag. If *binary* files, including most word-processor files using *ANSI* coding, are sent over a communications link that is not eight-bit clean (and this is many communications links), the files will be corrupted. Coding approaches such as *uuencode* and *BinHex* can be used to convert to *ASCII* for sending such files over systems such as the *Internet*.

EIS See *executive information systems*.

E-journal See *electronic journal*.

Electronic Copyright Management System (ECMS) A system that will allow the electronic submission of copyright registration to the US Copyright Office and electronic notification of registration. Many of the transfers performed in the ECMS will use *Privacy Enhanced Mail* (PEM).

electronic data interchange (EDI) (Or electronic dissemination of information.) The exchange of certain business documents — such as orders, invoices, bills of lading — in standard format between organizations, using *electronic mail*. Can include *electronic funds transfer*.

Electronic Design Interchange Format (EDIF) A format to transfer data between *CAD/CAE* systems.

electronic dissemination of information (EDI) See *electronic data interchange*.

electronic document Any *document* that is held in electronic, as opposed to print-on-paper, form.

Electronic Frontier Foundation (EFF) A foundation which is concerned with the possible social and legal impact of the *Internet* on society.

electronic funds transfer The use of telecommunications or a *network* to send payments from one organization to another, usually via their bank accounts.

electronic funds transfer at point of sale (EFTPOS) Transfer of funds between bank accounts by electronic means, usually implemented at a point-of-sale computer terminal (or check-out) in a supermarket on the basis of information supplied on a debit card; telephone lines are used to make an automatic debit from the customer's bank account to pay a bill. (See also *electronic data interchange* (EDI), *Mondex*.)

electronic journal (E-journal) The electronic equivalent of a paper-based journal (or magazine), available either over the *Internet* or by direct *dial-up* (see *OCLC*, for example). The journal may be an electronic version of a print-on-paper journal, but an increasing number of E-journals exist only in electronic form and are regarded by some areas of the academic community as the most efficient way of communicating the results of research. Over the Internet there are many different delivery methods, for example via *email*, by using an *ftp* archive (with the 'contents page' distributed by email or mailing list), or over the *World Wide Web*. Most E-journals are free but some require a subscription to be paid for access. Those available by dial-up usually have a proprietary *browser* program, such as *Guidon*, which was used by OCLC, and these are available only by subscription. There is much discussion over whether electronic journals will eventually replace printed journals and over the related question of the importance, or otherwise, of peer review (the refereeing of academic papers before they are published), which is a significant element of conventional printed journals but may or not be part of the operation of an E-journal. The role of the commercial publisher in E-journals is also much discussed.

Electronic Libraries Projects (e-Lib) A series of projects in the UK concerned with electronic access to information in UK higher education.

electronic mail (email, e-mail) (There seems to be no general agreement on which is the correct abbreviation; 'email' is used in this glossary.) Messages sent from one computer user to another, either on the same site or in different parts of the world, often through computer *networks* and/or via *modems* over telephone lines. Email is almost always used in *asynchronous* mode, i.e., without the sender and recipient needing to be directly connected. Originally, email was text-based but most modern email systems (see *MIME*) can transmit arbitrary data including image, audio and even video messages (if the bandwidth is sufficient). Lotus' *cc:mail* is probably still the most popular email software around for local area networks, while between organizations and individuals email is transmitted using either the *Internet* or a commercial provider, such as *CompuServe*. Over the Internet the *Simple Mail Transport Protocol* (SMTP) is the most widely used mail protocol, but there are many *message handling systems* and probably even more user programs for handling email, some of which are free and others which are not. (Contrast with *snailmail*.)

electronic mail address The address that is used to send *electronic mail* to a specified destination, usually based on a *domain name*, or on *UUCP* or *IP* addressing. On the *Internet* the *RFC 822* standard is probably the most widely used, although *X.400* addressing is also in used. (See also *bang path*, *fully qualified domain name*.)

electronic money A method of payment without using cash. A card, for example *Mondex*, is inserted into a machine (a form of *automatic teller machine*) at a bank and an amount of money is transferred onto the card. This is equivalent to a cash withdrawal in that the money is taken from the user's account. Money is then spent by passing the card through a trader's card reading machine, so that the requisite amount is transferred from the card and credited to the trader. *Ecash* provides a similar facility, but over the *Internet*.

electronic publishing (EP) The publication of information to be viewed on a screen rather than on a printed page. During the 1980s, the term was also used to describe the use of computer techniques for producing the *camera ready copy* (CRC) for printed publications and some people still use the term in this way. A clear distinction should be made between EP and *document delivery*, in that EP implies that the information provided has viewing and access programs associated with it (either provided together with the information files or assumed to be available on the recipient's system), whereas document delivery only provides an electronic version of a printable document. Because EP provides functionality over and above that provided on the printed pages, the information has to be organized and formatted by the information provider (or publisher) using a structured approach, such as a *database* or *SGML/HTML*, in that all viewers, such as *Dynatext*, *Guidon* and the *World Wide Web* browsers (*Mosaic*, *Netscape*, etc.) require files to be *generically coded* in order to provide the functionality required. In very general terms, the more structure that is coded into the source file, the greater the functionality available to the user. An alternative approach is to use *Acrobat* but, unlike the other viewers mentioned, Acrobat restricts viewing to a page format, which has its limitations for screen viewing. EP information is accessed either from a *CD-Rom* or, via a *wide area network*, such as the *Internet*, from a remote database.

Electronic Publishing: Origination, Dissemination and Design (EP-ODD) A journal published by John Wiley & Sons Ltd.

electronic transfer of funds See *electronic funds transfer*.

electronic whiteboard (EWB) (Also described as *audiographic teleconferencing*.) A method in which users can share a writing area over a communications link. Originally this was a device based on a whiteboard, so that the pen movements at one end of the link could be transmitted to a pen at the other end, but the term is now often applied to screen-sharing systems with similar functionality.

element A structural part of an *HTML* or *SGML* document. The name and usage of an element, together with its *attributes*, are defined in the *Document Type Definition*. Elements are coded within the *Document Instance* by using *tags*. For example, within this glossary, the element for 'SGML' defined as 'entry' would be coded as '<entry>SGML</entry>'. (See also *start-tag*, *end-tag*.)

e-Lib See *Electronic Libraries Projects*.

Elm A full-screen-based *Unix mail* (or *electronic mail*) program.

email or e-mail See *electronic mail*.

email (or e-mail) address See *electronic mail address*.

em dash An elongated hyphen (the width of capital 'M' in the *font* in use), which is used within printed (and electronic) documents as a form of punctuation. Different publishers and different nationalities have different conventions about how the em dash and *en dash* should be used. (See *dash*.)

EMDIR The *CERN Electronic Mail DIRectory* utility.

emote icon See *emoticon*.

emoticon (Or emote icon.) An *ASCII glyph* or group of characters used to indicate an emotional state in *electronic mail* or *news*, also described as a *smiley*. (See also *bawdy language*.)

emulation Setting up a computer, a terminal, a network or communication equipment in such a way as to make it appear to another computer etc. as a different device. For example, it is possible to make a PC appear as a *terminal* to a mainframe.

Encapsulated PostScript (EPS) A *PostScript* file format that has special structure, which will allow *application* programs that do not have the facility to edit PostScript to view an EPS file and manipulate it in certain ways (crop, scale or rotate), but not to change it otherwise. The EPS file format consists of two parts: the first is the PostScript code which will generate the image on an output device, while the second is a low-resolution *bitmap* image for viewing and editing in the other applications. There are different versions of the EPS format for the *Macintosh* (using a *PICT* format for the bitmap image) and for the PC (using a *tiff* format).

encapsulation In *communications*, a technique that is used by layered protocols such that a layer adds header information to the *protocol data unit* (PDU) received from the layer above. For example, an Internet packet will contain a header from the *physical layer*, followed by a header from the *network layer* (*IP*), followed by a header from the *transport layer* (*TCP*), followed by the data protocol from the *application layer*. The term is also used (as in *Encapsulated PostScript*) to describe a way of giving users a well-defined interface to a set of functions in a way that hides their internal workings. Also used in *object-oriented programming*, to describe how data structures and the procedures which act on them are kept together.

Encarta The *Microsoft multimedia* encyclopaedia.

encryption Conversion of a *plaintext* file to *ciphertext*, so that it can be used or understood only by those who have the information to decode or *decrypt* it. The two most widely used technologies are *Data Encryption Standard* (DES) and *RSA* (an abbreviation based on the names of the inventors). (See also *cryptography*, *public key*, *private key*.)

en dash An elongated hyphen (the width of capital 'N' in the *font* in use), which is used within printed (and electronic) documents as a form of punctuation. Different publishers and different nationalities have different conventions about how the en dash and *em dash* should be used. (See *dash*.) There are two almost universal uses of an en dash. The first is to indicate a range, as a substitute for the word 'to' (or 'through' in the USA), for example 'pp 20–30' (pages 20 to 30), while the second is to denote a relationship, for example 'speed is a time–distance relationship'.

end-tag The tag which indicates the end of an *element* in *SGML* or *HTML*. For example, this entry could be represented as '<entry>end-tag</entry>', where '</entry>' is the end-tag. Although this syntax is that usually used, it can be modified in the SGML declaration, if so required. The logical structure of a document may mean that end-tags are not always necessary, because they are implied by the next *start-tag* or another end-tag. Whether or not end-tags should be included for particular elements is defined in the *Document Type Definition* (DTD).

end-to-end performance A measure of network performance, which will be related to *bandwidth* and other factors.

entity A code used in *SGML* and *HTML*. There are two types: the first is the *character entity*, used to code non-*ASCII* characters using ASCII coding, while the second use is as a kind of macro and inclusion facility. The second use is not currently implemented in HTML.

Envoy A document exchange format, originally part of the PerfectOffice package, which also included the WordPerfect word-processor. Now distributed by Corel. Has some similarities to *Acrobat*, but so far is less widely used. Also a *Personal Digital Assistant* produced by Motorola, which incorporates two-way wireless communication.

EP See *electronic publishing*.

EP-ODD See *Electronic Publishing: Origination, Dissemination and Design*.

EPS See *Encapsulated PostScript*.

equalization Compensation, in high-speed *modems*, for the differences in attenuation at different frequencies on a telephone line.

erasable optical disc See *compact disc-recordable, floptical*.

erlang The standard unit for measuring telecommunications traffic. One erlang of traffic indicates continuous 100% loading of one circuit or 50% loading of two circuits.

error correction See *error detection and correction*.

error detection and correction Detection of errors in transmitted or stored data and the correction of them. The simplest form of detection is to use a single added *parity* bit, a *cyclic redundancy check* (CRC) or a *checksum*, which will indicate that an error has occurred. Use of multiple parity bits will also indicate which bits have been inverted and should therefore be corrected to restore the original data. The more extra bits that are added, the greater the chance that multiple errors will be detected, and therefore be correctable. (See also *Hamming code, forward error detection*.)

escrow Deposit of information with a third party for safe-keeping. The practice is used for the deposit of software source material to ensure that it will be available should the supplier cease to trade. It is now being used for deposit of *encryption* keys by the US government. (See *Clipper*.)

ETC/ACK handshaking A *handshaking* technique in which the end-of-text character ETX (*ASCII* value 3), also called Ctrl+C, is used to pause transmission.

Ethernet A *local area network*, developed by Xerox, *Intel* and Digital Equipment Corporation, for connecting computers together with *coaxial cables* or *twisted pairs* so that the computers can share information. (For cabling options see *10Base2, 10Base5, 10BaseT*.) Within each main branch of the network, Ethernet can connect up to 1024 personal computers and workstations, uses *CSMA/CD* access control and runs at 10 Mbps. It is specified by the IEEE 802.3 standard. Ethernet is not very suitable for the transmission of real-time signals such as speech or compressed video. *Fast Ethernet* runs at 100 Mbps. (See also *cheapernet, EtherTalk*.)

Ethernet address A six-part *hexadecimal* number identifying a controller board. This number, in which the parts are separated by colons (':') indicates that an Ethernet communications board is installed in a PC and is used to identify the PC as a member of the network.

EtherTalk An implementation of *AppleTalk* on an *Ethernet LAN*, allowing a Macintosh to connect into Ethernet networks; the Macintosh must have an Ethernet interface card installed.

ETSI See *European Telecommunications Standards Institute*.

Eudora *Electronic mail* software for mail operations using *TCP/IP*, available for a number of operating systems.

EUnet The European part of the international network that links Unix systems running *UUCP*. It is the largest European component of the *Internet*; also provides for *X.400* access.

Euro-ISDN An *ETSI* standard for *ISDN* introduced in 1994. Euro-ISDN will allow full transparent interworking between all European countries which are members of the *CEPT*. It is available on a commercial basis in most European countries.

EuroNet A company offering *Internet* connection from Amsterdam.

EuropaNET A combination of pan-European *network backbone* services run by *DANTE*.

European Academic and Research Network (EARN) A network for universities and research in Europe, originally set up by IBM. It uses *BITNET* protocols and connects to BITNET in the USA.

European Conference of Posts and Telecommunications See *CEPT*.

European Laboratory for Particle Physics See *CERN*.

European Telecommunications Standards Institute (ETSI) An organization set up in 1988 by the European *PTTs* with the support of the European Commission. ETSI is taking over much of the standardization work previously carried out by *CEPT* and other bodies, including the harmonization of *ISDN* standards across Europe. It can be regarded as a European version of the *ITU-T* (formerly *CCTIT*).

EUTELSAT EUropean TELecommunications SATellite organization. Owned by the European *PTT*, it runs the main European communications satellites.

EWB See *electronic whiteboard*.

eWorld An on-line system from Apple, based on the *America On-Line* system.

Exabyte A tape format (based on the company name) for computer data back-up and transfer, using data-quality 8 mm video cassette recorder tape. Exabyte tapes can store between 5–14 gigabytes of data and are most often attached to *Unix* workstations. (See also *digital audio tape* (DAT).)

executive information systems (EIS) Software which extracts data from an organization's computer applications and files and presents the information in a form required by management. How the information is presented depends both on management requirements and on the software used; graphical information tends to be preferred.

expert set (Or expert collection.) A *font* with an extended *character set*, including such characters as true small capitals, non-aligning (or oldstyle) numerals and additional accented characters. The term 'expert set' is used by Monotype, while Linotype and Adobe use 'expert collection'.

extended ASCII An alternative term for *highlevel ASCII*.

extended binary coded decimal interchange (EBCDIC) An eight-bit character code set developed IBM, mainly used on mainframes. Within IBM a number of variants of EBCDIC are used but more generally *ASCII* is the standard.

extended-level synthesizer An extension to the minimum capability required by the Microsoft *Multimedia Personal Computer* (MPC) specification for a music synthesizer within Microsoft *Windows* (see *base-level synthesizer*) so that it is capable of playing at least 16 simultaneous notes on 9 melodic instruments, together with 16 simultaneous notes on 8 percussion instruments. (See also *Musical Instrument Digital Interface* (MIDI).)

eXtensible Markup Language (XML) A simplified version of *SGML*, developed under the auspices of the *W3 Consortium*, with the aim of enabling SGML to be served, received and processed on the *Web* in the way that is now possible with *HTML*'. XML has been designed for ease of implementation and to be interoperable with both SGML and HTML. One area in which XML has an advantage over SGML is that it is designed to handle international character sets corresponding to *ISO 10646*.

Exterior Gateway Protocol (EGP) A protocol which distributes routing information to the *routers* which connect *autonomous systems*. (See also *gateway*.)

external modem A *modem* which has its own housing, cables and power supply, which is usually connected to a computer via a *serial line*, as opposed to an *internal modem*. While using an external modem means having an additional piece of equipment, there are advantages in that it is possible to obtain an indication of the operational state from the configuration of the indicator lights and, on some modems, it is possible to control functions by using push buttons.

extranet The extension of an *intranet* to allow access to other, authorized, users and organizations.

F

facsimile transmission (fax) A technique for transmitting graphic or text documents over the telephone network. *ITU-T* standards define four facsimile representations: Group 1 defines analogue transmission taking 4 or 6 minutes per page; Group 2 defines analogue transmission taking 2 or 3 minutes per page; Group 3 defines digital transmission taking less than 1 minute per page; Group 4 defines digital transmission over *ISDN*. While Groups 1 to 3 are for black and white only, Group 4 will also handle colour.

fall back When two modems which experience data corruption, for example as a result of line noise, can renegotiate to use a lower speed connection. (See also *fall forward*.)

fall forward When two modems which *fall back* to a lower speed because of data corruption later return to the higher speed if the connection improves.

FAQ Frequently asked question(s); selected, sometimes summarized and specially listed to help newcomers to a particular topic. Probably originated with new users of *email* and *Usenet newsgroups*, but now appears in many contexts.

FAQ list See *FAQ*.

Fast Ethernet A *networking* protocol which provides *bandwidth* of 100 Mbps, as opposed to the 10 Mbps of ordinary *Ethernet*. (See *100Base-T*.)

fast packet switching (Also called cell relaying.) A *wide area network* technology based on the high-speed transmission of fixed-length short packets (or cells). Operates at the datalink layer of the *OSI seven-layer model*, and is capable of handling data, voice and video.

Fast SCSI A variant on the *SCSI-2 bus*, which uses the same eight-bit bus as the original *SCSI* but runs at up to 10 Mbps, which is twice the speed of SCSI-1.

fax See *facsimile transmission*.

fax modem A *modem* that is designed for sending and (usually) receiving faxes via the computer, in addition to its usual *communications* facilities. This means that, using special *fax* software, documents produced by any *application* can be sent as faxes without the need to print them out. Documents can also be received, but this means either leaving the computer switched on continuously or using some special hardware to provide a storage buffer until the computer is used again. (See also *voice modem*.)

FBS See *flexible bandwidth service*.

FCC See *Federal Communications Commission*.

FCS See *frame check sequence*.

FDDI See *fibre distributed data interface*.

FDM See *frequency division multiplexing*.

FDMA Frequency division multiple access. (See *frequency division multiplexing*.)

FDX See *full duplex*.

FEC See *forward error correction*.

FECN See *forward explicit congestion notification*.

Federal Communications Commission (FCC) The US government body responsible for regulating communications.

Federal Information Exchange (FIX) One of the interconnection points between the US government *networks* and the *Internet*.

Federal Networking Council (FNC) The co-ordinating group of representatives of US federal agencies concerned with federal networking, especially those networks using *TCP/IP* and the *Internet*.

feed The active electronic part of an antenna where the signal is either originated or is concentrated for reception. (See also *Newsfeed*.)

Fetch A program for the *Macintosh*, which enables the transfer of files using *ftp*.

fibre-distributed data interface (FDDI) A *local area network* standard that is based upon *token* passing and uses a *token ring*, made up of *fibre-optic* cable at 100 Mbps (although copper cable can be used, in which case it is called *CDDI*). It is suited to data traffic and is being introduced at many sites to replace *Ethernet*. FDDI 2 operates at 200 Mbps and incorporates voice and video as well as data. Generally, because the dual ring passes through each connected device and requires each device to remain continuously operational, *routers* and *concentrators* are *dual-attached*, while host computers are *single-attached* to the routers and/or *concentrators*. Alternatively, devices such as *workstations* can be *dual-homed* to make the connection doubly resilient. (See also *optical fibres*.)

fibre-optic(s) See *fibre-optic transmission*.

fibre-optic transmission A transmission method that uses modulated infrared or visible coherent light, which is transmitted down dozens (or hundreds) of strands of glass fibre (or other transparent material – *optical fibres*). Optical fibre is less vulnerable to external noise than other transmission media and is cheaper than copper wire, although it is much more difficult to connect. In addition, it is more difficult to tamper with the signal (to monitor it or inject data in the middle of a connection), which makes fibre-optics appropriate for secure communications. The light beams do not escape from the medium because they are totally internally reflected. Each fibre can carry many signals (a single fibre can transmit 200 million telephone conversations simultaneously) and, as the frequency is high (10^{14}–10^{15} Hz), the information transfer rate is also high. Fibre-optics will be a vital element of the *information superhighway*, because fibre-optics is one of the few methods that can provide the *bandwidth* necessary for such services as *video on demand* (VoD) and full real-time *videoconferencing*. (See also *FDDI*.)

FidoNET A World Wide hobbyist network of personal computers which offers similar services to the *Internet* and *Usenet*, but is accessible from a much wider range of (small) computers, so that there are FidoNET networks in Africa and parts of the Far East where the Internet is virtually unknown.

file compression The *compression* of *data* in a file, usually to reduce storage requirements or transmission time.

File Request The *FidoNet* equivalent of *ftp* and an option of the *BBS* mailer.

file server A computer in a *network* that holds files, which can be accessed by users on the network. File servers often also act as *print servers*, while *database servers* provide database intelligence such as transaction processing, indexing, logging, security and so on. Storing files on a file server means that it is unnecessary to have multiple copies stored on individual computers, which both saves disk space and makes controlling and updating files easier, particularly for software upgrades.

file transfer Copying a file from one computer to another computer over a network or a direct connection. (See *File Transfer Protocol* (ftp), *Kermit*, *Network File System*, *rcp*, *UUCP*, *Xmodem*, *Ymodem*, *Zmodem*.)

File Transfer, Access and Management (FTAM) An *application-layer* protocol for file access, transfer and remote manipulation (ISO 8571).

File Transfer Protocol (ftp) A *client-server* protocol that enables a user on one computer to transfer files to and from another computer over a *TCP/IP* network (often over the *Inter-*

net); ftp is also used to describe the client program that the user executes to transfer files. (See also *anonymous ftp, FSP, tftp*.) There are of course other file transfer protocols, such as *Kermit* and *Xmodem*, etc.

fill   The pattern and the colour inside an object produced in a *draw program*. The parameters controlling the fill are almost always handled separately from those controlling the *outline* of the object. Fill is also used in some text processing programs to indicate whether lines should be run on to make a single paragraph or set line for line as keyed in. This is to allow for editing programs which do not allow *soft carriage returns* onscreen.

fill-out forms   Often abbreviated to 'forms'. The principal way in which *World Wide Web* sites request information from Web users. Users enter appropriate data within a form (as with conventional printed forms) or they select options from amongst a number given and this information is transferred back to the *host*.

film recorder   An output device that captures data and records it onto film, usually at high resolution. (See *imagesetter*.)

filter   An electronic or optical device which removes unwanted frequencies from a signal. A program which converts one file coding structure into another, for example in converting from one word-processor format to another or from a word-processor format to a *desktop publishing* format. A control within a *firewall* machine that blocks transmission of certain kinds of traffic. (See also *packet filtering*.)

Finder   The file and memory management system generally used in the Apple *Macintosh*. Finder allows only one program to be run at a time. *MultiFinder* allows *multi-tasking* and is built into the System 7 *operating system*.

finger   A program which can be used over the *Internet* to obtain information about a particular user, or about all users logged on to a system, local or remote. Typically shows full name, last login time, idle time, terminal line and terminal location (where applicable). May also display other information; for example, if mail facilities are accessed from a mail server over a *dial-up* link, then it is possible to see what mail messages are waiting to be downloaded to the local computer.

firewall   Any kind of security barrier to prevent external changes to a system, by *hackers* etc. (See *firewall code, firewall machine*.) Often a system that prevents external access from the *Internet* to an organization's computers. Internet access may, however, be provided using a *proxy system*. The firewall is intended to protect other machines at the site from potential tampering via the Internet.

firewall code   Code put into a system both to ensure that users cannot cause any damage and to keep the *user interface* friendly. Also used to limit the damage which a known programming bug could cause if not correctly fixed.

firewall machine   (Or firewall system.) A system that isolates an organization's computers from external access, for example through the *Internet*. An organization sometimes provides some Internet access through use of a *proxy system*. The firewall is intended to protect other machines at the site from potential tampering by external users. (See also *application-level gateway, circuit-level gateway, packet filtering*.)

First Virtual   A US bank that provides a method of secure payment over the *Internet* by issuing an identification number that references back to a credit card number, avoiding the necessity for the credit card number itself to be transmitted.

FITS   See *Flexible Image Transport System*.

FIX   See *Federal Information Exchange*.

flag   In general, a variable or quantity that can take on one of two values (often 'on' or 'off'). May be a *bit* (within operating systems) or a *byte* in some programs. In communications bit-oriented protocols, a unique bit pattern used to identify the beginning and end of a frame.

flame   An *electronic mail* or *Usenet* news message that is the equivalent of an angry retort or a strong opinion, intended to rebuke or even to insult or provoke. Also used as a verb to describe the sending of such a message.

flame bait   A message which is intended to provoke a *flame* or even a *flame war*.

flame war An acrimonious dispute consisting of a series of *flames*.

flat ASCII A text file that contains only *ASCII* (seven-bit) characters and uses only ASCII-standard control characters. Thus it includes no (eight-bit) embedded codes specific to a particular program or output device, and no *meta-characters*. Also called *plain ASCII*. SGML files are flat-ASCII in that all non-ASCII characters are represented by *character entities*. (See also *flat file*.)

flat file A representation of a database or tree structure as a single file from which the structure can be rebuilt. The file will often be in *flat-ASCII* form, but may also contain accented characters represented by eight bits.

flexible bandwidth service (FBS) An alternative to *leased lines* and *multiplexers*, allowing changes to the *bandwidth* available to any site.

Flexible Image Transport System (FITS) The standard data interchange and archive format of the astronomy community.

flight simulator A computer-controlled device for training pilots. It consists of an artificial cockpit mounted on hydraulic legs, so that the pilot feels that he or she is flying a real aircraft. Also, a popular computer program giving a similar onscreen display.

floptical discs A removable *optical disc* which is the same size as a 3½ inch floppy disk, but has a capacity of up to 25 Mbytes. Floptical disc drives can often also be used for conventional 3½ inch disks. (See also *SyQuest disk*.)

flow control The techniques used in serial communications to indicate when the sender begins and ends sending data and when the receiver is able to accept it. May be either *software* flow control or *hardware* flow control. Typically, received data will be written to a fixed-size *buffer*. When the amount of buffered data reaches a certain level, a signal will be sent to the transmitter to stop transmission until sufficient data has been read from the buffer so that another signal can be sent to start transmission again. (See also *x-on/x-off*.)

flush centre, left or right In word-processing or *DTP*, alignment of text to the centre, left or right of the column or page. (See *justification*.)

FM See *frequency modulation*.

FMV See *full-motion video*.

FNC See *Federal Networking Council*.

FolioViews A viewer, mainly for textual information, although links can be made to graphics etc. Requires *structured documents*, but not necessarily *SGML*. Can provide its own *database* structure.

follow-on posting A contribution, to a *newsgroup* or *forum*, that is a public response to a previous *posting*.

font A set of images representing the characters from some particular *character set* in a particular size and style (*typeface*), although today, when a font is referred to, the typeface is meant regardless of the typesize. The image of each character may be encoded either as a *bitmap* (in a *bitmap font*) or by using a description in terms of lines and areas (a *vector* or *outline font*). There are a number of different ways of coding and handling outline fonts; *PostScript*, *TrueType*, *Type 1 PostScript* fonts and *Type 3 PostScript* fonts. A new font specification, *OpenType*, has recently been developed with the aim of removing font compatibility problems. (See also *Adobe Type Manager* (ATM), *font metrics*, *font sizes*, *hinting*, *Metafont*, *QuickDraw*, *scalable fonts*.)

font metrics The detailed design specifications of a font, which include the widths of individual characters, the *x-height*, how tall the capital letters are, the *kerning pairs* and many other items. Different font descriptions store this information in different ways: for *QuickDraw* on a Macintosh, the metrics form part of the screen fonts, while the font metrics for a *TrueType* font are stored in the TrueType font file itself and for *Type 1 PostScript* fonts are stored in PFM (PostScript font metrics) files. Type 1 fonts usually also have corresponding AFM (Adobe font metrics) files, but these are not used by most applications.

font size In the UK and USA, font size is usually given in *points* (1 point = 0.351 mm) and 12 points make up a *pica*, the basic unit of typographic measurement. Elsewhere in Europe, point sizes and measurements are given using the *Didot* system, based on a 12-point *cicero*, which measures the same as 12.8 British points, so that 1 Didot point = 0.376 mm.

font substitution Printing an *outline font* to replace a *bitmapped* screen font. For example, when output is sent from a Macintosh to an Apple LaserWriter printer, the driver will substitute Times, Helvetica and Roman for the New York, Geneva and Monaco screen fonts. In a slightly different context, Adobe *Acrobat* will use *Multiple Mastering* technology to generate a font if the font called for in a *pdf* file is not present on the system where the Acrobat file is being viewed.

footer In conventional books the running footline that sometimes appears at the bottom of each page. (See also *header*.)

Format Output Specification Instance (FOSI) An *SGML-marked-up* document that uses the *DoD's CALS* output specification as its *Document Type Definition* (DTD). A FOSI contains formatting information structured according to SGML. FOSI styles define all features of composition: font, leading, quadding, spacing, etc. (about 125 characteristics in all). FOSIs map SGML documents to appearance-based mark-up ready for composition by a FOSI-capable system. FOSIs were originally intended for print but can equally be applied to composition onscreen. FOSIs use the same constructs as documents but apply them to format instead of to structure and content. Likely to be superseded by *DSSSL*.

forms See *fill-out forms*.

forum A discussion group accessible through a *bulletin board* system, a *mailing list*, or a *Usenet newsgroup*. Users submit *postings* for all to read and discussion follows. A forum is both *asynchronous* and available to all (or all those authorized) and can be contrasted with both real-time *Internet Relay Chat* (IRC) and point-to-point personal *email*. Note that both 'fora' and 'forums' are used as the plural of forum.

forward error correction (fec). An *error-correction* technique which adds extra bits to a transmission over a communications link. This allows errors to be detected and corrected without any retransmission of data.

forward explicit congestion notification (FECN) A notification, in *frame relay*, that a network node is congested. FECN allows the receiver to reduce the traffic in certain circumstances, for example by delaying acknowledgement messages.

FOSI See *Format Output Specification Instance*.

four-colour process See *CMYK, colour separation*.

four-colour separation See *colour separation*.

fps Frames per second. See *frame rate*.

FQDN See *fully qualified domain name*.

fractal An irregular fragmented geometric self-similar shape. The term was invented by Benoit Mandelbrot in 1975. Fractal objects contain structures that are nested within each other, so that each smaller structure is a reduced version of the larger form, although not identical. Many mathematical structures are fractals, but fractals also describe natural objects, such as clouds, mountains and coastlines, which do have simple geometric shapes and generally cannot be described using conventional Euclidean geometry. Fractals are also not definable in terms of specific numbers of dimensions. Fractals can be generated using a number of easily obtainable programs. (See *fractal compression*.)

fractal compression A *lossy* method of compressing images by expressing the image as an *iterated function system* (IFS), which can then be expanded to generate the required number of levels of (synthetic) fractal detail. Generating the IFS from the image is the most difficult step and involves running a (patented) compression algorithm on the bit pattern of the image.

frame -A sequence of contiguous bits, enclosed by opening and closing *flags*, transmitted over a *serial link*. A frame generally contains its own addressing and error-checking information and is sent between datalink layer entities. The size of the frame will depend upon the protocol used. Also a single image that forms part of a series that make up either a *video* or an *animation*. (See *video capture card*.)

frame check sequence (fcs) A field containing error-checking information which is added to a frame in *bit-oriented protocols*, such as *frame relay*.

frame grabber A device which allows a single *frame* of a video to be captured and subsequently used as a still image.

frame rate The number of *frames* of an animation, video or television picture displayed every second. The higher the frame rate, the smoother will be the movement although, for an animation, more processing power and system *bandwidth* will be required. About 30 fps is necessary to give the impression of smooth movement. A European standard (*PAL*) television signal displays 25 fps and a US standard (*NTSC*) signal displays 30 fps. Various kinds of compressed or simplified video (such as *QuickTime*) often use fewer frames per second but the results may not appear natural.

frame relay A *connection-oriented wide-area network* interface standard which caters particularly for 'bursty' data communications. It includes error detection but not error correction, and is suited to the interconnection of *LANs*, and to the connection of dedicated lines and *X.25* to *ATM*, *SMDS* and *B-ISDN*.

frames A facility available in *HTML-3*, implemented by current *World Wide Web browsers*, which allows the browser screen to be broken into several different areas, some of which may remain static, acting as a menu, while new information is downloaded into the main screen area.

frame switching An extension of *frame relay*, in which the full *datalink* protocol is implemented, including frame acknowledgement, *flow control* and *error correction*.

Freenet A US community-based bulletin board system. Freenets are funded and operated by volunteers; they are part of the National Public Telecomputing Network (NPTN), an organization based in Cleveland, Ohio, devoted to making computer communication and networking services as freely available as public libraries.

Free Software Foundation An organization devoted to the creation and dissemination of software that is free from licensing fees or restrictions on use. Its main work is supporting the *GNU* project, which has produced replacements for many Unix utilities and other tools. Software is distributed under the terms of the GNU General Public License, which also provides a good summary of the Foundation's goals and principles. (See also *copyleft*.)

free-text search Searching text files for any combination of characters, often words. *Search engines* which are able to carry out free-text search often include *Boolean* facilities and *proximity searching* so that, for example, one can search for the ocurrence of a group or string of characters within, say, 20 words of another group or groups. Such engines are usually based on *indexing* and the approach should be contrasted with *keyword search*.

freeware Software made available by the author at no cost, often over the *Internet*. The author still retains copyright and thus it is not quite the same as *public domain software* (PDS). (See also *shareware*.)

frequency The number of repetitions per unit time of a periodic waveform. The number of cycles per second for an electromagnetic waveform is expressed in *hertz* (Hz, kHz, MHz or GHz).

frequency division multiple access See *frequency division multiplexing*.

frequency division multiplexing (FDM) The simultaneous transmission of many separate signals through a shared medium (such as a wire, *optical fibre* or light beam). The separate signals are modulated at the transmitter into separable frequency bands, which are added linearly either before transmission or within the medium. The combined signal can then be treated as a single signal for transmission purposes, while at the receiver the multiplexed signals are separated by means of filters and demodulated. Standard radio, television and cable services are examples of FDM, and it was the principal method used for long-distance telephone calls, although *time division multiplexing* is increasingly used for digital data. Also described as frequency division multiple access (FDMA). (Contrast with *SCPC*.)

frequency modulation (FM) A method for encoding a *carrier signal* by changing the *frequency* according to the data being transmitted.

frequency shift keying (FSK) A *modulation* technique in which two different tones are used to represent the 0 and 1 states of binary data.

FSK See *frequency shift keying*.

FSP A *connectionless* protocol for moving files around networks, rather like *ftp*, with protection against server and network overloading. It is probable that FSP is an acronym for file server protocol.

FTAM See *File Transfer, Access and Management*.

ftp See *File Transfer Protocol*.

ftp archive See *archive site*.

ftp by mail A service offered by *DEC* so that people without *Internet* access can obtain copies of files which are available by *anonymous ftp*.

full duplex (fdx) Communication in which it is possible to transmit and receive at the same time. The usual data communications channel (the *V.24* interface) between a microcomputer and a *modem* is full duplex. (See also *half duplex*, *simplex*.)

full-motion video (FMV) A system used to deliver moving *video* images and sound on a computer. Also used to describe video which plays back smoothly at 30 fps and a video signal before it has been compressed. However, as FMV is often used to denote a *digital* signal, the exact meaning depends on both the sampling and the TV standard used. Some form of *video compression* is used to reduce the amount of data and to ensure that it can be read from disk quickly enough. While compression can be relatively slow, decompression has to be done in real time, so that the picture quality and *frame rate* vary with the processing power available, the size of the picture and whether it appears full screen or in a window. Compression formats include *QuickTime* and *MPEG*.

fully qualified domain name (FQDN) The full name of a system, including its local *hostname* and its *domain name*, so that 'eps-edge' is a hostname and 'eps-edge.demon.co.uk' is an FQDN. An FQDN should be sufficient to determine a unique *Internet address* for any host on the *Internet*. FQDN is also used for *electronic mail* addressing on some hosts which are not on the Internet. If a host does not have an FQDN, it must be addressed using a *bang path*. (See *network, network address*.)

FYI For your information. A subseries of *RFCs* which convey general information about topics related to *TCP/IP* or the *Internet*.

G

Gates, Bill William Henry Gates III, Chief Executive Officer of Microsoft, which he co-founded in 1975 with Paul Allen.

gateway A communications device or program that passes data between networks which have similar functions but dissimilar implementations. Should not be confused with a *protocol converter*. Thus, a *router* is a layer 3 (*network layer*) gateway, and a *mail gateway* is a layer 7 (*application layer*) gateway. The term 'router' is now used in place of the original definition of 'gateway'. Also an interface between an external source of information and a *World Wide Web server*. Common Gateway Interface (CGI) is a standard for such interfaces.

Geek of the Week A program, broadcast over *Internet Talk Radio*, in which *Internet* experts are interviewed.

GenCode A *generic coding* project set up the US Graphics Communications Association. An important precursor of *SGML*.

Generalized Markup Language (GML) The *generic markup* language developed at IBM in 1969; the principal precursor of *SGML*. The acronym originally comprised the initials of the three inventors, Charles Goldfarb, Edward Mosher and Raymond Lorie.

generic coding The use of codes or *tags* within text to describe the structure of the text, for example heading types, lists, footnotes, etc. The codes are subsequently converted to typesetting commands and only then is the actual appearance of the page revealed. This approach can be compared with the *generic markup*

WYSIWYG or *desktop publishing* approach, in which the page is made up graphically onscreen. Generic coding, as widely used in the publishing and printing industries, does not indicate that the document concerned has a formal, hierarchical structure and there are many different systems used. A development from generic coding, at least in part, is *Standard Generalized Markup Language* (SGML) or *generic markup*, in which both generic coding and hierarchical structure are defined. (See also *FOSI, DSSSL, Rich Text Format*.)

generic markup A method of adding information to text, indicating the logical components of a document, such as paragraphs, headers or footnotes. *SGML* is an example of such a system. Specific instructions for layout of the text on the page do not appear in the markup. Essentially the same as *generic coding*; the difference in emphasis between the two terms is more one of usage than of any real difference in meaning.

geographical information system (GIS) Software that makes possible the visualization and manipulation of spatial data, and links such data with other information such as customer or maintenance records.

geosynchronous orbit The position where communications satellites remain stationary in orbit above the same point on the equator. This is about 23 300 miles above the earth's surface. Such satellites may be described as geostationary.

geosynchronous satellite A satellite in *geosynchronous orbit*.

Ghostscript The *GNU PostScript* interpreter with previewers for a number of systems.

Ghostview An interface to the *Ghostscript PostScript* interpreter, which allows PostScript files to viewed in *X windows*.

GIF See *Graphics Interchange Format*; '.gif' is also the filename extension for files in Graphics Interchange Format.

GIS See *geographical information system*. Also used to mean global information society.

GKS See *Graphical Kernel System*.

GKS-3D The three-dimensional version of the *Graphical Kernel System* (GKS).

Global Network Navigator (GNN) A collection of free services provided by publisher O'Reilly & Associates. 'The Whole Internet Catalog' (based on the book by Ed Krol) discusses the most useful *Internet* resources and services and provides live links to those resources. The 'GNN Business Pages' list companies on the Internet. The *Internet* 'Help Desk' provides help in starting Internet exploration and '*NetNews*' is a weekly publication that gives news about the Internet.

Global Network Service (GNS) The service which connects national *PSS* services. Formerly known as *International Packet SwitchStream* (IPSS).

Global System for Mobile Communications (GSM) The standard for *digital cellular* communications, which is in the process of being adopted by over 60 countries. The GSM standard is currently used in the 900 MHz and 1800 MHz bands.

glyph The actual shape of a character, as opposed to its identity within a *character set*. Whether two representations of the same character in two different *fonts* constitute one or two glyphs is not agreed, as long as they are basically similar, so the sans-serif 'g's in the typefaces Arial (g) and Helvetica (g) can be regarded as two glyphs or two representations of the same glyph. However, the letter 'g' in the Times typeface (sideways spectacles) is definitely a different glyph. It is possible for several characters to make up a single glyph (for example, a ligature), while equally a single character may be composed of more than one glyph (for example an accented character such as 'ë').

GML See *Generalized Markup Language*.

GNN See *Global Network Navigator*.

GNS See *Global Network Service*.

GNU A recursive acronym which stands for 'GNU's Not Unix!', the *Free Software Foundation's* project to provide a freely distributable replacement for *Unix*, including GNU Emacs, the GNU C compiler, *gzip* and much more. GNU software is available from many GNU archive sites.

go back *N* A *datalink layer* communications protocol which allows retransmission of faulty blocks.

Gopher A menu-driven hierarchical document retrieval system, which began as a *Campus Wide Information System* at the University of Minnesota and is now available over the *Internet*. Gopher allows a single *Gopher client* to access information from any accessible Gopher server, providing the user with a single 'Gopher space' of information. Gopher has been largely superseded by the *World Wide Web*, which includes access to Gopher documents as one of its protocols.

Gopher client A program which runs on the local machine and provides a user interface to the *Gopher* protocol.

GOSIP See *Government Open Systems Interconnection Profile*.

Gouraud shading A method of surface shading or *rendering* used in *animation* to make the surface of rounded objects look smoother and more natural. It is based on linear interpolation of the normals to adjacent polygons. (See also *Phong shading*.)

Government Open Systems Interconnection Profile (GOSIP) Used by both US and UK governments. A procurement specification for *OSI* protocols, although the protocols used by the two governments are not identical.

graduated fill A gradual shift from one colour to another, from a dark tone to a light one in an object *fill*. An ideal graduated fill avoids *banding*. (See also *Gouraud shading*, *Phong shading*.)

gradient fill Another term for a *graduated fill*.

Graphical Kernel System (GKS) A standard for *outline* graphical input/output. (See also *PHIGS*.)

graphical user interface (GUI) (Pronounced 'goo-ey'.) An interface that allows users to choose commands and other options by pointing to a graphical icon or by pulling down a menu and then activating the choice, either by using the keyboard or by *clicking* with a *mouse*. Provides what is often thought of as a more *user-friendly* approach than a *command line interface*. A GUI runs under a *windowing* system, such as *X windows*, Microsoft *Windows* or *Macintosh*. Although the Apple Macintosh *operating system* was the first commercially available GUI, the concept originated in the early 1970s at *Xerox PARC* with the *Xerox Star*. (See also *WIMP*, *WYSIWYG*.)

graphic file format The format in which graphics are stored and transmitted. There are two main types: *raster* or *bitmap graphics* (in which the image is stored as a bitmap) and *vector* or *outline graphics* (in which the image is stored using geometric formulae). There are many different file formats, some of which are used by specific computers, *operating systems* or applications. Some formats use file compression, particularly those which handle colour. Some common graphic file formats are shown in Table 4.

graphics The creation, modification and manipulation of (usually static) graphic images. The two basic forms are *bitmap* or *raster graphics* and *vector graphics*. In general, bitmapped graphics are handled using *paint programs*, able to access individual *pixels* or groups of pixels, while vector graphics are handled using *draw programs*, which allow the manipulation of graphics as mathematical *objects*. A third way of representing images uses *fractals*. Graphics are stored in a wide variety of *graphic file formats*.

graphics-based software Software which requires a *graphical user interface* (GUI) for it to be able to operate, unlike 'character-based' or 'text-based' software, which can be operated using a *command line interface*. The *Macintosh* is graphics-based, while PCs and Unix require *Windows* or *X windows* software to allow them to be run in graphics mode. Graphics-based software allows operation in *WYSIWYG* mode, so theoretically anything can be shown on the screen, subject to resolution and colour limitations. This requires a powerful computer in order to provide acceptable operating speeds.

Graphics Interchange Format (GIF) (Pronounced with a hard 'G', as in 'gift'.) A *graphic file format* in which images are compressed with the *LZW* algorithm. It was originally developed by *CompuServe* and is widely used for images on *on-line services* and particularly the *World Wide Web*.

graphics primitive

Table 4 Common graphic file formats

Name	Extension	Type
Adobe Illustrator (subset of eps)	.ai	Vector
Apple Macintosh vector format	.pict	vector
Autodesk, used by most CAD systems	.dxf	Vector
Computer Graphics Metafile	.cgm	Vector
CorelDraw	.cdr	Vector
Encapsulated PostScript (eps)	.eps	Vector
Gem (used by Gem GUI)	.gem	Vector
Graphics Interchange Format	.gif	Bitmap, compressed
Hewlett Packard Graphics Language	.plt	Vector
IBM vector format	.pif	Vector
JPEG	.jpg, .jpeg, .jfif	Bitmap, compressed
Lotus Picture File	.pic	Vector
Microsoft PowerPoint (not strictly a graphics format but widely used for graphics)	.ppt	Vector
Paintbrush	.pcc, .pcx	Bitmap
Portable Bitmap Graphic (or Portable Pixmap)	.pbm, .pgm, .ppm	Bitmap
Portable Network Graphic	.png	Bitmap, compressed
Tagged Image File Format	.tif, .tiff	Bitmap
TrueVison TarGA picture	.tga	Bitmap
Windows BitMap	.bmp	Bitmap
Windows MetaFile	.wmf	Vector
WordPerfect Graphics Format	.wpg	Vector
X-window BitMap graphic	.xbm	Bitmap

graphics primitive In a *vector* (*object-oriented*) *graphics* program, one of the basic graphic units, e.g., circle, rectangle, line.

graphics scanner An input device, which allows *images* on paper to be input into computer systems as *bitmapped* graphics files.

graphics tablet An input device in which a stylus or cursor is moved by hand over a flat surface. The computer keeps track of the position of the stylus, making it possible to input drawings or diagrams. Graphics tablets are generally used with *graphics* programs, though they can be used instead of a mouse with most programs. Some graphics tablets are sensitive to pressure, so that with appropriate graphics software the line thickness can be recorded. Recent developments in handwriting recognition may lead to wider use of graphics tablets.

gray scale See *grey scale*. 'Gray' is the US spelling and is widely used.

Great worm See *Internet worm*.

greek, greeking Method used in *desktop publishing* and other page make-up systems to show type below a certain size (which may be specifiable by the user). Instead of the actual characters, grey patterns or graphics symbols are used, which speeds up the display of a page onscreen. Greeking is also employed when an overall impression of the layout of one or more pages is wanted. Greeking is more traditionally, although now less common, used when a document is filled with nonsense text so that the page design can be seen. Usually the text is not actually Greek (because most designs use Roman type), but something which looks like Latin words, but is probably meaningless, the idea being that the operator (or compositor) could focus on the design without being distracted by the meaning of the text.

Green Book A standard *CD-Rom* format developed by *Philips* for *CD-i*. It can only be played on drives which are *XA* (eXtended Architecture) compatible. Green Book discs may contain *CD-i* applications that can only be played on a *CD-i player*, but may also contain films or music videos. Videos in this format are usually labelled 'Digital Video on CD'. Green Book was superseded by *White Book* CD-Rom in 1994. The Green Book is also used to describe the document listing the protocol known as *Triple-X*, used for remote login in the *JANET Coloured Books* software suite. Also used to describe any of the 1992 standards issued by the *CCITT's* Tenth Plenary Assembly. Finally, the Green Book is one of the three standard books describing the *PostScript* language (*PostScript Language Program Design*, Adobe Systems (Addison-Wesley, 1988)).

Grey Book The document defining the electronic mail protocol used in the *JANET Coloured Books* software suite.

grey levels The levels of grey in a *grey scale*.

grey scale The use of (discrete) shades of grey, from black to white, to represent an image. If the *pixels* of a grey-scale image have N *bits*, then 2^{N-1} levels can be represented. If N = 1 the image is *monochrome*, i.e., black and white. Grey-scale monitors represent pixels by using different intensities, often with up to 256 different levels. Grey scaling is used to represent *continuous tone* images. (Note the difference from *dithering*.) The US spelling of grey is 'gray'.

ground An electrical connection or common conductor connected to the earth. Also known as the *earth wire*.

grounded Connected to the earth.

groundstation (Also known as earth station.) A communications and control installation on earth for a satellite relay.

Group 3 fax The standard which is currently widely used for *facsimile* over *PSTN*. It operates at 9600 bps and the average transmission time of an A4 page is about 30 seconds.

Group 4 fax The *ITU-T* standard for facsimile over *primary rate ISDN*. Compared with Group 3, it offers better resolution, more grey levels and improved error-correction and data-compression facilities. It also provides colour. (See also *Joint Bi-level Image Experts Group (JBIG)*.)

group addressing Addressing a message to a group of addresses. Makes *multicasting* possible.

groupware General applications software intended to help groups of people working together over a network to coordinate and organize their activities (*workgroup computing*). Such software usually includes *electronic mail* facilities and scheduling programs and may also allow computer conferencing and *audioconferencing*, *audiographic teleconferencing* and *videoconferencing*. (See also *CSCW*, *Lotus Notes*.)

GSM See *Global System for Mobile Communications*.

GUI See *graphical user interface*.

Guide A *Unix hypertext* system developed at the University of Kent and supplied for the PC by OWL (Office Workstations Ltd).

Guidon Viewer software for *SGML* documents, developed for *OCLC* and used for the world's first purely electronic refereed journal, 'Clinical Trials'. Now no longer used by OCLC, which is moving journals to the *World Wide Web*.

gunzip Decompression utility for files compressed with *gzip*.

Gutenberg Project See *Project Gutenberg*.

GWHIS A commercial version of *NCSA Mosaic* for Microsoft *Windows* 3.x and Windows for Workgroups, released by Quadralay Corporation.

gzip The *GNU* compression utility, developed by the *Free Software Foundation*. Uses *Lempel–Ziv LZ77* compression. Compressed files can be restored to their original form using gzipd or gunzip. All GNU compressed files available by *anonymous ftp* are in gzip format and their names end in '.gz'.

H

H.120 An *ITU-T* standard for *video compression* at transfer rates of 2 Mbps, now superseded by (and not compatible with) the newer *H.261* set of standards.

H.261 A *video compression* standard developed by ITU-T to work with *ISDN* principally to support *video phone* and *videoconferencing* applications. Data can be compressed on the fly at the rate of 64p kbps, where p is the number of ISDN channels used (from 1 to 30). The standard includes a system of frame difference, so that each frame in a video sequence is encoded only as the differences between it and the preceding frame, thus saving space. Now part of *H.320*.

H.320 A recent *ITU-T* standard embracing the *H.261* video compression standard. Used in most *videoconferencing* systems.

hacker Originally, a computer enthusiast who was willing and able to work (often tediously) at understanding computer programs. Subsequently, the term has acquired derogatory overtones, so that hackers may be considered to be people who gain unauthorized access to remote systems, often belonging to large organizations, and may corrupt and/or steal data. There is an ongoing debate about the ethics of the practice of accessing remote systems if no damage is done. Indeed, some hackers inform systems managers of the weaknesses of their systems, so that the practice can even be considered as providing a service. It can be argued that development of the *Internet* to its current state is in large part due to the willingness of hackers to share information and software. (See also *Free Software Foundation*, *GNU*.)

half duplex *Asynchronous* communication in which data can be relayed in only one direction at a time. Two-way transmission is possible but the transmissions must be alternate. Also used for *local echo*. (See also *full duplex*, *simplex*.)

halftone A *screened* image derived from a *continuous tone* original (usually a photograph), in which levels of grey are represented by dots of different sizes. This is necessary if a continuous tone image is to be printed (on a printing press). Traditionally this was done photographically, using a *screen* calibrated in lines per inch (lpi). However, now that images are more generally being scanned and handled by computer, very high-resolution images are required for printing. This does not mean that images need to be scanned at high resolution (measured in dots per inch or dpi), but with an appropriate number of *grey scales*. The relationship between the number of grey scales that can be seen on the final image, the resolution of the output device and the equivalent half-tone screen is:

$$\text{number of grey scales} = \frac{(\text{output resolution in dpi})^2}{(\text{halftone screen ruling in lpi})} + 1$$

while the relationship between the halftone screen and the scanning resolution is:

input resolution in dpi
= scale factor × halftone screen ruling in lpi × resolution factor

where the resolution factor is usually 1.5 because it gives acceptable results without making file sizes too large. It is important to keep clear the difference between the input resolution (which will generally be quite low at 150–300 dpi), the halftone screen ruling and the output resolution (which may be as high as 3000 dpi).

HALGOL A simple language developed by Hewlett-Packard for communicating with devices such as *modems* and *X.25 PADs*.

hamming code Extra *bits* added to transmitted data in order to improve *error detection and correction*. Hamming codes are used with data sent from space probes, since requesting retransmission is not very practical because of the long delays involved.

H&J Abbreviation used for *hyphenation* and *justification*.

handle A nickname used on-line. The term is taken from CB (community broadcast) radio.

Handle System A distributed and scalable system developed by the US Corporation for National Research Initiatives (CNRI) for storing the names of digital objects and the information needed to locate those objects via the *Internet*. (See also *Digital Object Identifier*.)

handshaking An electronic exchange between two devices which confirms that they are communicating with each other and establishes the communications channels and protocols necessary for the devices to send and receive data. *Hardware* handshaking uses voltage levels or pulses on wires to carry the handshaking signals, whereas *software* handshaking uses data units, that is, *ASCII* characters, carried by some underlying communication medium. Handshaking is also used to control the flow of data: two devices use a handshaking signal to stay in sync with one another.

hard carriage return A carriage return that is inserted by the user, i.e., the end of paragraph, rather than the *soft carriage return* inserted by software.

hardware flow control An alternative term for *hardware handshaking*.

hardware handshaking (Also called hardware flow control.) A technique for regulating the flow of data across an interface by means of signals carried on separate wires. A common example is the use of RTS (*request to send*) and CTS (*clear to send*) signals on an *RS-232 serial line*. (See also *handshaking, software handshaking*.)

hash An index number, otherwise meaningless, that is generated from a list or series of *pointers*.

hash table An array of *pointers* used to provide rapid access to data items which are distinguished by some key. Used, for example, in *compression algorithms*.

Hayes AT command set The *de facto* standard according to which almost all *modems* are designed today. Each command is preceded by the attention code (AT). A listing will be found in the manual of any modem which is *Hayes compatible*.

Hayes compatible The term used to indicate that a modem is able to understand the *Hayes AT command set*, which has become the *de facto* standard according to which almost all modems are now designed.

HCI See *human–computer interaction, human–computer interface*.

HCOM An *Apple Macintosh* audio format. Uses *Huffman* compression; hence HCOM.

HD-MAC See *high-definition multiplexed analogue coder*.

HDLC See *high-level data link control*.

HDTV See *high-definition television*.

head end A broadband network component that converts the transmit frequency band to the receive frequency band, making it possible for stations to transmit and receive over a single-cable network.

header The portion of a *packet*, preceding the actual data, containing source and destination addresses, error checking and other fields. Also used to describe the part of an *electronic mail* message or *news* article that precedes the body of a message and includes the sender's name and email address and the date and time when the message was sent. In conventional books it is sometimes used to describe the running headline appearing at the top of each page. (See also *footer*.)

HeadLiner A *World Wide Web push technology*, similar to *BackWeb* and *Castanet*, providing personalized delivery of public information, such as news. Similar, but not identical, to *PointCast*.

head-mounted display (HMD) A stereoscopic set of goggles, with a separate display for each eye, used in *virtual reality* systems to give the user the impression that he or she is actually in the virtual world created by the virtual reality application.

helical scan A way of writing data to a *video tape* or *digital audio tape* (DAT).

help A method of providing information to the user. Often *hypertext*-linked to the *application* itself and to an index. Usually also includes a search facility.

HEPnet An association concerned with networking requirements for high-energy physicists.

hertz (Hz) A measure of frequency. One hertz is one cycle per second; 1 kHz = 1000 Hz; 1 Mhz = 1 000 000 Hz. (See also *bandwidth*.)

heterogeneous network A *network* running more than one *network layer protocol*.

Hewlett-Packard Graphics Language (HPGL) A *vector graphics* language originally used by Hewlett-Packard plotters. Now HPGL has been incorporated into *PCL* Level 5, used to control HP LaserJet printers.

hexadecimal system A counting system based on 16, widely used in computing, essentially because it is based on powers of two (see *binary system*). The hexadecimal digits are 0–9, followed by A–F so that, for example, the decimal number 12 is written as C, while hexadecimal 10 is equivalent to decimal 16.

HF See *high frequency*.

hierarchical addressing and routing When a network is divided into a hierarchy of smaller networks, each level can be made responsible for its own routing. *Internet addresses*, or *fully qualified domain names*, have a hierarchical form, which reflects this hierarchical routing. Names on the Internet are *little-endian*, while names on JANET are *big-endian* (although, in order to avoid confusion, JANET addresses are often given as little-endian). (See also *Exterior Gateway Protocol, protocol, Interior Gateway Protocol*.)

hierarchy An inverted tree structure. Examples in computing include a directory hierarchy where each directory may contain files or other directories; a hierarchical *network* (see *hierarchical addressing and routing*); a *class hierarchy* in *object-oriented programming* (OOP); and the structure of a *Document Type Definition* (DTD) in *SGML*.

high-definition multiplexed analogue coder (HD-MAC) A high-definition TV (*HDTV*) standard used in Europe. (See also *MUSE*.)

high-definition television (HDTV) Has twice the resolution of normal television, giving a very clear picture at about 1200 lines per screen with a height-to-width ratio of 3:4. HD-MAC is the standard in Europe, while commercial *MUSE* services are run in Japan.

high frequency (hf) (Also known as the short-wave band.) The part of the electromagnetic spectrum between about 3–30 MHz, which is used mainly for long-distance communication.

high-level ASCII (Or *extended ASCII*.) The term often used to describe characters with code numbers from 128 to 255, as the true *ASCII* character set only includes the characters from 0 to 127. Because there is no standard for these characters, *DOS*, *Windows* and the *Macintosh* each assign different characters to these high-level ASCII code numbers, although generally they are used for accented characters and other commonly used symbols. (See *ANSI character set*.)

high-level data link control (HDLC) A bit-oriented *datalink* control protocol specified by *iso* for transmitting variable-length *packets* over a datalink. Functionally equivalent to *ADCCP*.

high resolution High density of detail. Is often used to describe the numbers of *pixels* or dots per unit area in an image. The higher the *resolution*, the more information there is in a given amount of visual space.

High Sierra A standard defining the file system for *CD-Roms*. It is equivalent to *ISO 9660*. The name derives from the name of the hotel where a significant meeting to agree on the standard took place.

hinting A method, developed by *Adobe Systems*, to reduce the effects of *aliasing* when *outline fonts* are printed. It uses a series of priorities, either encoded as extra information in the font or applied using set mathematical formulae, to correct noticeable distortions, such as uneven stem weight. *PostScript Type 1* and *TrueType* fonts are hinted. Hinting is only required for small characters or for printers with a low *resolution* when the presence or absence of a single dot makes a visible difference to a character.

HLS See *hue, lightness* and *saturation*. A method of representing colour in computer graphics. (See also *RGB, HSV*.)

HMD See *head-mounted display*.

holography A method of recording and then reconstructing three-dimensional images (holograms) using coherent light beams from lasers. The laser beam is split into two and one part used to illuminate the object. The light waves scattered by the object are then recombined with the other, reference part of the original beam and the interference pattern thus created is stored as a hologram on a photographic plate. When the hologram is illuminated a three-dimensional image is created. It has not so far been possible (and it may not be possible) to create such an image digitally.

home page (Sometimes called a welcome page.) The first page accessed on the *Web site* of an individual or institution on the *World Wide Web*. This may have a *URL* that consists of just a *hostname*, e.g., 'http://www.pira.co.uk'. All other pages on a server are usually accessible by following *links* from the home page. There can also be links to other home pages. It is also used to describe the page that is fetched when a user starts his or her browser.

hop One of a series of file transmissions required to get a file from point A to point B on a *store-and-forward* network. On such networks, e.g., *UUCPNET* and *FidoNet*, an important metric is the number of hops (number of network segments or *routers* passed through) in the shortest path between machines, irrespective of their geographical separation. (See also *bang path*.)

host A computer system which provides services to users of a network. Also a computer to which one connects using a *terminal emulator*. (See also *hostname*.)

hostname (Also called sitename.) The unique name by which a computer is known on a *network*. This is used to identify it in various forms of electronic information interchange, including *electronic mail*, *Usenet* and *news*. On the *Internet* the hostname is an *ASCII* string, such as 'eps-edge.demon.co.uk', which consists of the local part ('eps-edge') and a *domain name* ('demon.co.uk'). The hostname is translated into an *Internet address* by the *Domain Name System* (DNS) or other name *resolver*. Although a host will have a *canonical name*, it can also be described by various *aliases*. Hostnames can be found by searching using various *Internet utilities*, such as *Archie* and *AltaVista*, and checked using *Ping*.

host number The *host* part of an *Internet address*. (See *hostname*.)

HotJava A *World Wide Web* viewer developed by Sun Microsystems and written in the *Java object-oriented language*. Its outstanding feature, in which it differs from all other browsers, is that it is able to pull down *applets*, applications also written in Java, from the server on the fly in order to perform specific tasks, such as viewing an *MPEG* movie, if no MPEG viewer already exists on the client system. Note that Java is now implemented in viewers such as *Netscape Navigator*.

hotlink See *link*. Also a mechanism for sharing data between two *application* programs where changes to the data made by one application appear instantly in the other's copy. On the *Macintosh* 'Create publisher', it is used in the server and 'Subscribe' on the client, while in Microsoft *Windows* 'Paste special', it is used to link into client applications that are able to act as servers.

hotlist A list of documents which the user wishes to access frequently, stored as part of the set-up in a *World Wide Web* viewer, such as *Mosaic* or *Netscape*. Clicking on the name of the document (strictly speaking, its *URL*) will activate a *link* to that document and fetch it to the screen. (See also *bookmark*.)

HoTMetaL Editing and parsing software from SoftQuad which enables the user to create and edit documents coded in *HTML* and conforming to the HTML *Document Type Definition* (DTD). HoTMetaL is a specialized version of the more general Author/Editor software for creating and editing *SGML*-conforming documents.

hot spot The active location of a cursor on a *bitmap* display. Also described as a *screen* region that is sensitive to *mouse clicks*, which trigger some action, often to activate a *link* to another application or another part of a document. Used widely in *hypertext* applications and now in *World Wide Web* viewers to access other documents or applications, such as *email* or *ftp*.

HPGL See *Hewlett-Packard Graphics Language*.

hqx The filename extension for *Macintosh BinHex* format files.

H series The series of *ITU-T* recommendations governing audiovisual services, including *video compression*. Some of the most signicant are given separately.

HSV *Hue*, *saturation* and *value* (or *brightness*). A method of representing colour in computer graphics. (See also *RGB*, *HLS*.)

HTML See *HyperText Markup Language*.

HTML3 The current (1997) version of *HTML*.

HTML+ A proposed new version of *HyperText Markup Language*, intended to supersede HTML2. Now absorbed into *HTML3*.

HTTP See *HyperText Transfer Protocol*.

HTTPS See *HyperText Transmissiom Protocol (Secure)*.

hub A device or computer to which several other devices are connected (like spokes to the hub of a wheel). The central *node* of a *network*. Hubs provide flexibility in logical interconnection of networks and data equipment.

Hubnet A 50 Mbps *fibre-optic network* developed at Toronto University.

hue Essentially, a representation of how colour is perceived, based on the artist's colour wheel from violet to red (red and violet then being adjacent). The relationship between hues is thus represented in terms of the number of degrees separating them on the colour wheel.

Huffman coding A data *compression* technique, first described by D A Huffman in 1952, in which the length of the encoded symbol varies in inverse proportion to its information content. Thus the more often a symbol or token is used, the shorter the binary string used to represent it in the compressed stream.

human–computer interaction (HCI) The study of how humans use computers and of the design of computer systems to make them easy, quick and productive for people to use. (See also *user-friendly*, *human–computer interface*.)

human–computer interface Any tool or utility which allows a user to interact with a computer, for example *WIMP*, *command line interface* or even *virtual reality*.

HyperCard Software for information storage and retrieval on the *Macintosh*. Consists of a 'stack' of 'cards', each of which can hold text, graphics, sound, animation, etc., together with *links* to other cards. HyperCard is very similar to *hypertext*, although it does not conform to the rigorous definition of hypertext. (See also *HyperTalk*.)

Hyper-G Now called *HyperWave*. An advanced *World Wide Web* server technology, based on an object-oriented database, developed especially for hypermedia at the University of Graz, Austria. Hyper-G provides tools for structuring, maintaining and serving heterogeneous *multimedia* data, including automatic hyperlink consistency and advanced navigation tools. As HyperWave, it includes authoring utilities (Harmony for *Unix* and Amadeus for *Windows*).

hyperlink A *hypertext link*. A reference from some point in one hypertext document to (some point in) another document or another place in the same document. A hyperlink is usually displayed in some distinguishing way, such as a different colour, font or style, or even as a symbol or graphic.

hypermedia A combination of *hypertext* and *multimedia*, or the extension of hypertext to include graphics, sound, video and other kinds of data. (See also *HyperText Markup Language*, *World Wide Web*, *HyTime*.)

HyperNeWS A *hypertext* system developed at the Turing Institute, Glasgow, based on *NeWS*.

HyperTalk The programming language which can be used to control *HyperCard* stacks.

hypertext A term, used originally by Ted Nelson as part of his vision *Xanadu* in the mid-1960s, to describe a collection of documents (or *nodes*) containing cross-references or *links* so that, with the aid of an interactive *browser* program, the reader can move easily from one document to another in a non-sequential manner. Although Xanadu is still in existence, the *World Wide Web* is now probably the most widely used implementation of hypertext. (See *hypermedia*.)

HyperText Markup Language (HTML) The underlying *hypertext* language of the *World Wide Web*. HTML is based on an *SGML Document Type Definition* (DTD). HTML can be viewed using one of a number of viewers, or clients, the best known of which are *Mosaic Navigator* and *Internet Explorer* and *Netscape*. The 1995 version of HTML is HTML2, but this is fairly limited in what it can display. HTML3, released in early 1996, has much greater functionality. In addition, Netscape extensions provide functionality not included in HTML2, while *Panorama* allows any SGML document to be viewed on the Web. A fairly recent development is *Cascading Style Sheets*, which allow typographic and layout information to be embedded in an HTML document. (See also *XML*.)

HyperText Transfer Protocol (HTTP) The client-server *TCP/IP* protocol used on the *World Wide Web* for the exchange of *HTML* documents. It conventionally uses *port 80*. (See also *uniform resource locator* (URL).)

HyperText Transmission Protocol (Secure) (HTTPS) A *URL* access method, used by *Netscape*, for connecting to *HTTP servers* using *SSL* (*secure sockets layer*), which runs underneath HTTP. (See *secure HTTP*.)

HyperWave See *Hyper-G*.

Hyphen The (UK) company which produced the first commercial *PostScript* clone. This was principally used for high-resolution output on *imagesetters*.

hyphenation Literally, the use of a hyphen to connect two words or numbers. In typography, however, it is usually employed to mean the use of a hyphen at the end of a text line (often when *justification* is also used, whence *H&J* as an abbreviation for hyphenation and justification) to indicate that a word does not fit completely on that line and the remainder is at the beginning of the next line. There is much discussion of the merits of hyphenation in printed documents. In electronic documents, particularly those where the lines *wrap* on screen as the *window* or *typesize* is changed, justification, and thus in most cases hyphenation, is not used.

HyTime Hypermedia/Time-based Structuring Language: an emerging *ANSI/ISO* standard which is essentially a *hypermedia* extension of *SGML*. (See also *MIPS*.)

Hz The standard abbreviation for the unit of frequency. (See *hertz*.)

I

IAB See *Internet Architecture Board* (previously stood for Internet Activities Board).

IANA See *Internet Assigned Numbers Authority*.

ICBM address (Or *missile address*.) The longitude and latitude of a *Usenet* site, which can be used in address blocks. (A real missile address would also include altitude.)

ICI See *Image Compression Interface*.

ICMP See *Internet Control Message Protocol*.

I-Comm A *shareware* graphical *World Wide Web* browser for use with a *modem* on MS-DOS, which does not require a *SLIP* or *PPP* connection.

icon A small picture representing something (a file, a directory or an action) in a *graphical user interface* (GUI). When the user *clicks* on an icon, a program is run. Icons are usually stored as *bitmaps*.

I-D See *Internet-Draft*.

IDEA See *International Data Encryption Algorithm*.

IDN See *Integrated Digital Network*.

IEC See *International Electrotechnical Commission*.

IEE See *Institution of Electrical Engineers*.

IEEE See *Institute of Electrical and Electronics Engineers*.

IEEE 802 The *IEEE* standards for local area networks (LANs). IEEE 802.3 covers *CSMA/CD*, IEEE 802.4 token bus and IEEE 802.5 *token ring*.

IEN See *Internet Experiment Note, Individual Electronic Newspaper*.

IEPG See *Internet Engineering and Planning Group*.

IESG See *Internet Engineering Steering Group*.

IETF See *Internet Engineering Task Force*.

IETM See *Interactive Electronic Technical Manual*.

IFF See *interchange file format*. IFF/8SVX is an Amiga audio file format.

IFS See *iterated function system*.

IGC See *Institute for Global Communications*.

IGES See *Initial Graphics Exchange Specification*.

IGP See *Interior Gateway Protocol*.

IINREN See *Interagency Interim National Research and Education Network*.

ILMI See *Interim Local Management Interface*.

image A two-dimensional rectangular array of *pixels*, each pixel consisting of one or more *bits* of information, representing brightness, colour, etc. (see *RGB, HLS, HSV*). Images may be created on screen or taken from an image capture device, such as a *scanner, digital camera* or *frame grabber*. (See also *image compression, image file formats, fractal*.)

image compression The reduction of the amount of information required to represent an *image*, so that the file size is smaller, which means that it will require less space in computer memory and storage and that it takes less time to transfer over networks and communications systems. Is used in *fax* transmission and in *videophone* and *multimedia* systems. (See also *JPEG*, *compression, fractal*.)

Image Compression Interface (ICI) A standard interface to compression algorithms, produced by C-Cube Microsystems.

image-editing software See *paint programs*.

image file formats There are many formats used to store images in files: *GIF*, *tiff*, *pcx* and *JPEG* are common; a recently developed format is *PNG*. A list is given under *graphics formats*.

image map An image in which different computer actions are initiated when part of the image is selected. (See *ISMAP*.)

image processing The manipulation of *images*, usually using algorithms, for example to enhance contrast, reduce noise (remove spots) or change colours.

imagesetter A *high-resolution* output device that usually provides output on photographic material (either bromide or film) or even directly on printing plates. The software technology is essentially the same as that of the laserprinter, although the hardware will probably be different. Resolutions can be as high as several thousand dots (or spots) per inch, which are necessary to achieve the output of high-resolution *halftones*. Most imagesetters today use *PostScript*. Imagesetters were previously called typesetters.

imaging model How output is represented on screen, for example in a *GUI*. (See *QuickDraw GX*, *TrueImage*.)

IMEI See *International Mobile Equipment Identity*.

imposition The arrangement of pages on a printing plate so that, when a publication is folded and bound, the pages are in the correct sequence. Traditionally, this was done by physically arranging the film or bromide before creating the plate, but now either computer or photographic methods are frequently used. Software is available to impose *PostScript* files.

IMSI See *International Mobile Subscriber Identity*.

indexing The creation of ordered lists of entries or terms. Most *World Wide Web search engines*, such as *AltaVista* and *Yahoo*, use indexing in order to speed up access to data, as does most *database* software.

Indigo One of the leading *digital presses*.

Individual Electronic Newspaper (IEN) Part of the *Telepublishing* project, set up under the *RACE* initiative and involving Pira International and participants in other European countries, in which a pilot newspaper was set up according to a profile of an individual's interests. The intention was subsequently to deliver this electronically.

Infobahn A term (taken from the German 'Autobahn') for the *information superhighway*.

Information Engineering A research programme of the European Commission, concerned with how information and data are created, stored, distributed, changed or manipulated, and used. A major area of interest is *electronic publishing*.

information highway See *information superhighway*.

information retrieval A term used in the context of obtaining information from *on-line databases* in response to a query formulated in an appropriate way. Large companies and libraries still access on-line databases in this way, usually by directly dialling into the database provider and, for structured information, this is still a very efficient way of obtaining information, particularly for someone familiar with the data structure and query syntax. However, for the individual, access to information via the *World Wide Web* and indexes and search tools, such as *AltaVista*, *Yahoo* and *Lycos*, is now a real alternative.

information superhighway (Also called *information highway*, *Infobahn*, *infostrada*, *National Information Infrastructure*.) A term first used by US Vice-President Al Gore in the early 1990s for high-speed communications networks carrying *multimedia* applications and information around the world. The term is widely used but rarely defined, meaning different things to different people. For successful implementation it will require high communications *bandwidths*, generally not currently available over the *Internet*.

infostrada   A term (taken from the Italian 'autostrada') for the *information superhighway*.

Infosync   *Software* that is used to download updates to information at the *bit* level. Information is *downloaded* from a *database* to the *client*. Then, whenever the client accesses the server, either via the *WorldWide Web* or over a *dial-up* connection, Infosync checks the local database (on the client) against the master database (on the server) at the level of the bits stored, and downloads any changes since the last access. In this way the amount of data transferred is kept to a minimum, but the database can be accessed locally, both of which keep down communication charges.

infotainment   The integration of interactive information and entertainment services or software. In Europe usually on *CD-Rom*, while in North America often supplied via a cable network. (See also *edutainment*.)

infrared   The part of the electromagnetic spectrum with wavelengths between about 0.7–100 µm. It is used extensively for *fibre-optic* communications.

Initial Graphics Exchange Specification (IGES)   A standard for the exchange of *CAD* (computer-aided design) files.

inkjet printer   A printer that sprays very fine droplets of quick-drying ink onto the paper. The quality of printed text is not as good as that on a *laserprinter* at the same resolution, but inkjet printers provide a relatively cheap way of printing both monochrome and colour images of acceptable quality.

INRIA   The French National Institute for Research in Computer Science and Control, which is working with the *World Wide Web Consortium* in developing standards for *HTML* and the *World Wide Web*.

INRIA Videoconferencing System (ivs)   A *videoconferencing* tool for the *Internet*, developed at *INRIA* and based on the *H.261 video compression* standard.

Institute for Global Communications (IGC)   A provider of networks and networking tools for international communications and information exchange. The IGC networks – *PeaceNet*, *EcoNet*, *ConflictNet* and *LaborNet* – are the only networks dedicated solely to environmental preservation, peace and human rights.

Institute of Electrical and Electronics Engineers (IEEE)   (Often known as 'I triple E'.) US professional society, which is involved in academic publishing, organization of conferences and formulation of standards. IEEE standards are widely used in computing and communications. In particular, IEEE 802 standards are concerned with *local area networks* (LANs) including *EtherNet* and *Token-Ring*.

Institution of Electrical Engineers (IEE)   UK professional society (not to be confused with the *IEEE*). Publisher of *Physics Abstracts* and the INSPEC databases. Also publisher of 'Electronics Letters', the first refereed journal to be available in both printed and electronic forms (via *OCLC* and based on *SGML*, using the *Guidon* viewer).

integrated digital network (IDN)   A network which uses digital technology with the switching and transmission functions integrated.

integrated services digital network (ISDN)   A network that provides end-to-end digital connectivity to support a wide range of services, both voice and non-voice, e.g., *fax*. ITU-T standards have been recommended for interfaces and operating procedures. More simply described as a *digital* telephone service as opposed to the *analogue* service, which has been used ever since telephone services were introduced. *Bandwidths* vary from 56 kbps in the USA and 64 kbps in Europe upwards. ISDN has the advantage that lines can be combined to increase bandwidth. (See also *basic rate ISDN*, *primary rate ISDN*.)

integrated services local network (ISLN)   A local network technology that can handle voice and non-voice services on the same network.

Intel   Company that designs and manufactures the microprocessors used in most PCs. The range 80086–80486, used from about 1980 on, has now been extended with various versions of the *Pentium*.

intellectual property rights The rights of an author or creator to the use and re-use of material created by him or her, including *copyright*. How such rights can be protected in an age of *electronic publishing* and the *World Wide Web* is the subject of much debate.

intelligent agent An automated network information gathering tool, which searches the *Internet* either to locate documents on subjects specified by the user or to create indexes. Sometimes referred to as a *knowbot* or *spider*. (See also *AltaVista*, *Microcosm*.)

intelligent character recognition A form of *optical character recognition* (OCR) in which logic or fuzzy logic is used to aid recognition of letter forms and combinations of letter forms, making up words.

intelligent terminal A computer, with its own memory and processor, but not necessarily storage memory, which is used as a terminal to another system. (Compare with *dumb terminal*, where all the processing is carried out on the system accessed.) (See also *client-server*.)

INTELSAT See *International Telecommunications Satellite Consortium*.

interactive Being able to accept and react to user input. This is generally applied to a program or to a communications medium. Thus almost all computer applications are interactive, while normal television is not and *teletext* is only interactive in that the user can choose the page to go to.

Interactive Electronic Technical Manual (IETM) A *hypertext* standard developed in association with the *CALS* initiative.

interactive video See *video*. Applications in which it is possible for the user to interact with and control information (including text, sound or moving images) stored on video disc. It is widely used for training purposes, but also forms an intrinsic part of *CD-I*.

Interagency Interim National Research and Education Network (IINREN) A still-evolving high-bandwidth US network, part of *NREN*.

Intercast A hardware and software technology, developed by *Intel*, which allows PC users to watch television and simultaneously receive broadcast Web pages related to that cable or television programme.

interchange file format (IFF) Type of *audio file format*. (See *Audio IFF*.)

interface The physical boundary between two systems or devices (hardware interface). Also used to describe the specifications for the protocols, procedures, codes, etc. (software interface) that enable communication between two dissimilar systems or devices. (See also *user interface*: how the user is able to interact with the computer.)

Interim Local Management Interface (ILMI) A *network* management specification for *B-ISDN/ATM* networks, based on the *Simple Network Management Protocol* (SNMP).

Interior Gateway Protocol (IGP) An *Internet* protocol which controls the *routing* of information to the *routers* within an *autonomous system*. (See also *Exterior Gateway Protocol*, *Routing Information Protocol*.)

interlacing A technique for increasing resolution on graphic displays or screens. The electron beam traces alternate lines on each pass, providing twice the number of lines that would appear on a non-interlaced screen. However, screen refresh is slower and screen flicker may be increased over that seen on an equivalent non-interlaced screen because any given *pixel* is only refreshed half as often.

Intermedia A *hypertext* system developed by a research group at Brown University, USA. Also a UK company which pioneered disk format conversion in the early 1980s, when there were many more disk formats than there are today. Provides hardware and software conversion solutions used widely in the UK typesetting industry.

Intermedia Interchange Format A standard *hypertext* interchange format based on the *Intermedia* hypertext system.

internal modem A *modem* which takes the form of a card or board which is situated within the computer. (Compare with *external modem*.)

International Data Encryption Algorithm (IDEA) An encryption algorithm used by *Pretty Good Privacy*.

International Electrotechnical Commission (IEC) An international standards body at the same level as *ISO*.

International Mobile Equipment Identity (IMEI) The 15-digit serial number which identifies the *GSM* handset (sometimes found on the back of the phone).

International Mobile Subscriber Identity A number which is used by the *SIM* card in a digital mobile phone to identify itself to a *GSM* network.

International Organization for Standardization (ISO) A voluntary organization, founded in 1946, responsible for creating international standards in many areas, including computers and communications. These include the *seven layer model* for network architecture, *Open Systems Interconnection* and *SGML*. Some important standards are listed under their ISO number. (See also *International Telecommunications Union*.)

International Packet SwitchStream (IPSS) The service which connects national public data network *PSSs* to other national networks operated by *PTTs*. It is now known as *Global Network Service* (GNS).

International Phonetic Alphabet (IPA) A system that provides special characters (IPA characters) and *ASCII* equivalents for phonetics (how characters or combinations of characters are pronounced).

International Standard A standard which has been approved and published by the *International Organization for Standardization* (ISO).

International Standard Book Number (ISBN) A 10-digit identification number, individual to each book (and edition) that is published. While there is no legal requirement for books to carry these numbers, they are used by both librarians and booksellers. The numbers are allocated on a national basis and part of the number is unique to the publisher of the book, while the last digit is a check digit. (See also *ISSN, PII, DOI*.) (Should not be confused with *ISDN* – integrated services digital network.)

International Standard Serial Number (ISSN) An eight-digit identification number that is allocated to each journal that is published. It remains the same for all issues and volumes of a journal. Unlike the *ISBN*, it does not contain any information that identifies the publisher, but is an arbitrary number made up of seven digits plus a check digit. The *PII* has been developed partly to make it possible to identify individual articles within journals.

International Telecommunications Satellite Consortium (INTELSAT) Established in 1964, it launched its first communications satellite, Intelsat 1 – or 'Early Bird' – in 1965. It currently has over 30 communications satellites in orbit. (See *satellite communication*.)

International Telecommunications Union (ITU) An international body, part of which, the telecommunication standardization sector (*ITU-T*) is responsible for making technical recommendations about telephone and data (including fax) communications systems. Before 1 March 1993, ITU-T was known as *CCITT*. Plenary sessions are held every four years and new standards are adopted and published (see, for example *Green Book*, used to describe any of the 1992 standards issued by the Tenth Plenary Assembly). ITU-T is responsible for the *H series*, *I series*, *V series*, etc. of standards widely used in communications.

Internet (With a capital 'I'.) The largest *internet* in the world, made up of a three-level *hierarchy* composed of *backbone networks*, such as *ARPANET*, *NSFNet* and *MILNET* —, mid-level *networks* and *stub networks*. These are connected using the *Internet Protocol* (IP). Access to the Internet can be either from a network such as *JANET* or via a *point of presence*, provided by such companies as *Demon*, *CityScape* and *Pipex* (although there are many others). Although the international links within the Internet operate at high *bandwidth*, the bandwidth available to the individual user will usually depend on the speed of the local connection. Many utilities and services, such as *email, newsgroups, ftp* and *Gopher,* are available on the Internet, but the *World Wide Web* is rapidly becoming the most important way of distributing and accessing information. There are several bodies associated with the running of the Internet, including the *Internet Architecture Board,* the *Internet Assigned Numbers Authority,* the *Internet Engineering and Planning Group, the Internet Engineering Steering Group* and the *Internet Society.*

internet (Without a capital 'I'.) Any set of *networks* interconnected with *routers.*

Internet address (Or *IP address, TCP/IP* address.) The 32-bit host address defined by the *Internet* protocol and usually represented in dotted decimal notation, e.g., 158.152.28.130. The address can be split into a *network number* (or network address) and a *host number* unique to each host on the network, and sometimes also a *subnet address.* The way the address is split depends on its *class.* The Internet address must be translated into an *Ethernet* address by, for example, *ARP.* The term 'Internet address' is sometimes incorrectly used to refer to a *fully qualified domain name.*

Internet Architecture Board (IAB) The body that is responsible for the development of *Internet* protocols. It has two task forces: the *Internet Engineering Task Force* (IETF) and the *Internet Research Task Force* (IRTF) and also includes the *Internet Assigned Numbers Authority* (IANA).

Internet Assigned Numbers Authority (IANA) The central registry for various *assigned numbers,* such as *port* and *protocol* numbers, and options, codes and types. Part of the *Internet Architecture Board* (IAB).

Internet Assistant An add-on for Microsoft *applications,* which allows the user to edit *HTML* files and to convert word-processing and other formats to and from HTML. Can also act as a *World Wide Web browser.*

Internet Control Message Protocol (ICMP) An extension to the *Internet Protocol* (IP), which allows for the generation of error messages, test packets and informational messages.

Internet-Draft (I-D) A draft working document of the *Internet Engineering Task Force* with no formal status and valid for a maximum of six months. Very often, an I-D is a precursor to a *Request For Comments* (RFC).

Internet Engineering and Planning Group (IEPG) A group set up to promote a technically coordinated operational environment of the global *Internet.* However, the IEPG is not a group which conducts activities of a technical developmental nature.

Internet Engineering Steering Group (IESG) A body which provides the first technical review of *Internet* standards and is responsible for the day-to-day management of the *Internet Engineering Task Force* (IETF).

Internet Engineering Task Force (IETF) An open international community of network designers, operators, vendors and researchers, who work to coordinate the operation, management and development of the *Internet,* including *protocol* and architectural issues in the short to medium term. The IETF meets regularly and proceedings are made generally available. The IETF Secretariat maintains an index of *Internet-Drafts,* while the *Internet Architecture Board* maintains *RFCs.*

Internet Experiment Note (IEN) A report pertinent to the *Internet.* IENs used to be published in parallel with *RFCs* but this is no longer the case. (See also *Internet-Draft.*)

Internet Explorer *Microsoft's browser* for the *World Wide Web.*

Internet Multicasting Service See *Internet Talk Radio.*

Internet Network Information Center (InterNIC) The joint name for the providers of registration, information and database services to the Internet. Funded by the US National Science Foundation, each service is run by a different company. General Atomics provides information services, AT&T provides directory and database services and Network Solutions, Inc. (NSI) provides registration services. The companies work closely together, as well as in collaboration with other *Network Information Centers* (NICs) in the USA and elsewhere in the world.

Internet number See *Internet address.*

Internet phone A software and hardware solution, which allows long-distance telephone calls to be made via the *Internet*, so that connection is via the *TCP/IP* network, rather than through the usual telephone network. Although the costs are lower, in that the caller pays only local telephone charges, the quality can be much poorer than for standard telephone connections.

Internet Protocol (IP) The *network layer* for the *TCP/IP protocol* suite widely used on *Ethernet* networks. IP is a *connectionless, best-effort packet-switching* protocol, providing packet *routing* through the *datalink* layer.

Internet Registry (IR) The registry of *network* address and *Autonomous System Number* identifiers operated by the *Defense Data Network Network Information Center* on behalf of the *Internet Assigned Numbers Authority*.

Internet Relay Chat (IRC) A facility that allows people to 'talk', i.e., interact directly, with others in real time over the *Internet*. This facility does not allow actual *audio* communication, but see *Internet phone*.

Internet Research Steering Group (IRSG) The governing body of the *Internet Research Task Force*.

Internet Research Task Force (IRTF) The body which considers long-term *Internet* issues from a theoretical point of view. It has Research Groups, similar to *Internet Engineering Task Force* Working Groups, each of which is allocated a different research topic. *Multicast* audio/video conferencing and *Privacy Enhanced Mail* (PEM) are examples of developments which have been initiated in the IRTF.

Internet service provider (ISP) (Also called *access provider*.) A company providing a *point of presence*.

Internet Society (ISOC) A non-profit, professional membership organization concerned with the technical evolution of the *Internet* and with stimulating interest in the scientific and academic communities, industry and the public about the technology, uses and applications of the Internet, as well as promoting the development of new applications for the system.

Internet Talk Radio (Internet Multicasting Service.) A US-based service that broadcasts radio programmes of technical interest over *MBONE*. The best known is probably *Geek of the Week*.

Internetwork Packet eXchange (IPX) Protocol used by *Novell NetWare*. If a *router* has IPX routing, *local area networks* (LANs) can interconnect so that Novell NetWare *clients* and *servers* can communicate.

internetworking The interconnection of two or more *networks*, usually *local area networks* (LANs), using some kind of *router* or *gateway*, so that they appear to be one network.

Internet worm (Or Great worm.) A *worm* perpetrated in 1988 by Robert T Morris, which quickly used up all available processor time on the systems it infected via *email*. It was a significant event in public awareness of the *Internet* and its vulnerability to *hackers*. (See also *Computer Emergency Response Team*.)

InterNIC See *Internet Network Information Center*.

Interpress A *page description language*, developed at *Xerox PARC*, and in many ways the forerunner of *PostScript*.

intranet A network providing similar services to those provided by the *Internet*, but only within an organization, e.g., a *World Wide Web* server on an internal network to provide information within a company. (See also *extranet*.)

inverse video (Also called *reverse video*.) When the image on the screen appears as a 'negative', so that the parts which are conventionally black appear as white and *vice versa*. Inverse video is often used to indicate that something, for example a portion of text, has been selected for copying, moving, deletion, etc.

IP See *Internet Protocol*.

IPA See *International Phonetic Alphabet*. Also used as an abbreviation for Institute of Practitioners in Advertising.

IP address See *Internet address*.

IP-Multicast The *multicast* system operating over the *Internet*. Subsequently called *MBONE*.

IPSS See *International Packet SwitchStream.*

IPX See *Internetwork Packet eXchange.*

IR See *Internet Registry.*

IRC See *Internet Relay Chat.*

IRSG See *Internet Research Steering Group.*

IRTF See *Internet Research Task Force.*

ISBN See *International Standard Book Number.*

ISDN See *integrated services digital network.* (Not to be confused with ISBN, the *International Standard Book Number,* particularly in a publishing context!)

ISDN-2 See *basic rate ISDN* (operating over two channels).

ISDN-30 See *primary rate ISDN,* where 30 channels are available to the user.

I series The series of *ITU-T* recommendations concerning data transmission over *ISDN.*

ISLN See *integrated services local network.*

ISMAP An attribute of the *HTML* tag '<IMG>' (inline image) which specifies that if the image is selected in a *World Wide Web* browser, clicking on a point will generate a request relating to the coordinates of that point. This is often used in maps (as the name might suggest) to provide information about a feature at the coordinates selected.

ISO See *International Organization for Standardization.* Also a prefix to the reference numbers of standards issued by that body. ISO is not actually an acronym for anything, rather a pun on the Greek prefix 'iso-' meaning 'the same'; nonetheless, it is an anagram of the initials of the organization's name. Some relevant ISO standards are included as separate entries below.

ISO 646 The *ISO* standard for seven-bit characters. *ASCII* is the US equivalent, although it differs in a few bracket characters. (See *ISO 8859.*)

ISO 8613 The *ISO* standard defining *Open Document Architecture.*

ISO 8859 (ISO Latin.) An *ISO* standard for eight-bit single-byte coded graphic *character sets* for the major European languages that can be represented using Latin characters. In addition, covers the Greek, Cyrillic, Hebrew and Arabic alphabets. Latin alphabet No. 1 is often used as an extension of and replacement for *ASCII.* *ISO 8879* includes some extra characters used in *SGML.*

ISO 8879 The *ISO* standard defining *SGML.*

ISO 9069 The *ISO Standard Document Interchange Format (SDIF).*

ISO 9241 Part 8 of this *ISO* standard is concerned with representation of colour on computer terminals.

ISO 9660 The *ISO* standard defining a file system for *CD-Roms.* This is equivalent to the *High Sierra* standard.

ISO 9735 (Or *EDIFACT.*) The *ISO* standard for *electronic data interchange* for administration, commerce and transport. First published in 1988, it was amended and reprinted in 1990. It defines *appplication layer* syntax.

ISO 10179 The *ISO* standard for the *Document Style Semantics and Specification Language* (DSSSL).

ISO 10180 The *ISO* standard for the *Standard Page Description Language* (PDSL).

ISO 10646 The *ISO* standard for 32-bit and 16-bit character encoding, which includes *Unicode.* Originally ISO 10646 (32-bit) and Unicode (16-bit) codes were developed separately but, following the failure of the Draft ISO 10646 to be accepted, Unicode was taken within the scope of ISO.

ISO 10744 The *ISO* standard for *HyTime.*

ISO 12083 A revised version of the American Association of Publishers (AAP) *SGML DTD,* covering books and academic journals.

ISO 13818 The *ISO* standard for *MPEG-2 compression.*

ISOC See *Internet Society.*

isochronous A form of data transmission in which the time between two characters is an integral number of bit times, whereas in *asynchronous* transmission, characters may be separated by random-length intervals. Asynchronous data can thus be transmitted over a *synchronous* data link. An isochronous service is used when time-dependent data, such as video or voice, is to be transmitted. *Asynchronous Transfer Mode* (ATM) can provide isochronous service.

ISODE   ISO Development Environment. An implementation of the upper layers of *OSI*.

ISO Latin   See *ISO 8859*.

ISO/OSI model   The *ISO Open Systems Interconnection seven-layer model*, which standardizes levels of services and types of interaction for exchanging data through a communications network. The model separates computer-to-computer communications into seven layers: the *application layer*, *datalink layer*, *network layer*, *physical layer*, *presentation layer*, *session layer* and *transport layer*. Note that *TCP/IP* does not conform to the OSI model.

ISP   See *Internet service provider*.

ISPBX   Integrated services private branch exchange. A telephone switchboard oriented to switching *ISDN* connections both within an organization and from that organization to the outside world.

ISSN   See *International Standard Serial Number*.

iterated function system (IFS)   The *fractal* system, discovered by Michael Barnsley, that is used in *fractal compression* (as marketed by Iterated Systems Ltd). Iterated function systems have been described (by the mathematician Heinz-Otto Peitgen) by comparing them to a multiple-reduction copying machine, which is just like a normal copier except that: there are multiple lens arrangements to create multiple overlapping copies of the original (which is what makes IFS a system); each lens arrangement reduces the size of the original (the contraction aspect); and the copier operates in a feedback loop, with the output of one stage as the input to the next (the iterative aspect). Thus, each image is treated as a combination of many smaller, self-similar images. However, although these principles are widely known, the exact compression algorithm used (and marketed) by Iterated Systems Ltd is a very well kept secret.

ITU   See *International Telecommunications Union*.

ITU-T   See *International Telecommunications Union*.

ivs   See *INRIA Videoconferencing System*.

J

jaggies   The visual effect caused by *aliasing*, so that curves look like a series of steps. (See also *anti-aliasing*.)

JANET   See *Joint Academic NETwork*.

JANET IP Service (JIPS)   Joint Academic NETwork Internet Protocol Service. Note that JANET used the *Coloured Book* protocols before establishing JIPS.

Janus   See *Joint Academic Network Using Satellite*.

Java   An *object-oriented* progamming language, designed for programming the *Internet*. While it is possible to write complete programs in Java, one of its strengths is that *Java applets* can also be written, which can be run within *browsers* such as *Netscape Navigator*, providing additional functionality. In addition, these applets can be linked to specific documents or files so that if, for example, an *MPEG* video is downloaded over the Internet, if appropriate viewing software is not available on the *client system*, an applet will automatically be downloaded so that the video can be viewed. There is also a version of Java, called *JavaScript*, which lacks some of the features but can be included within an *HTML* page. In addition, there is a special *browser* called *HotJava*, but increasingly Java functionality is being included as part of standard browsers, such as Netscape Navigator 3.0 and *Internet Explorer*. (See also *Java beans*.)

Java applets   A form of *Java* program, dedicated to performing a particular task, such as reading a particular type of file, e.g., an *MPEG* video. Applets are not stand-alone *applications* in that they need a Java-compliant application, such as a *World Wide Web browser*, to be running in order to function.

Java beans   A platform-independent *API* that will enable *Java*-based *applets* and objects to interoperate with other *object* technologies such as *OpenDoc*.

JavaScript A version of the *Java* language that can be included directly within an *HTML* page in order, for example, to provide interaction between the user and the *host* system such as validating entries in a *form*. JavaScript lacks some of the functionality of Java, but is thus easier to learn. Using applications such as *LiveWire*, it is possible to produce the equivalent of *CGI-scripts*.

JBIG See *Joint Bi-level Image Experts Group*.

JIPS See *JANET IP Service*.

jitter Small changes in the timing or the phase of a signal transmitted over a *network*, possibly leading to errors or loss of synchronization.

JNT Association The body responsible for the operation of *JANET*, trading under the name *UKERNA*. Formerly the *Joint Network Team*.

Joint Academic NETwork (JANET) The *wide area network* linking UK academic and research institutes. JANET is operated by the JNT Association, trading under the name *UKERNA*. It is an *internet* providing connectivity within the academic community as well as *gateways* to external services, including the *Internet*, of which JANET is a component. The *hub* is a private *X.25 packet-switched* network connecting over 100 sites, at most of which *local area networks* (LANs) are connected. The *Coloured Book* protocols were originally used to support facilities such as *email*, remote terminal access, file transfers and remote batch job submission. (For more recent developments, see *JIPS* and *SuperJANET*.)

Joint Academic Network Using Satellite (Janus) A joint EC-funded research and development project, in which a prototype satellite-based network has been built linking several European academic sites, with courses delivered over the network. The links between sites operate at a bandwidth of around 64 kpbs and the system uses *VSAT*.

Joint Bi-level Image Experts Group (JBIG) A bi-level coding standard, developed by a joint group of *ISO*, *IEC* and *ITU-T* with the same name. Compression is done using a *Q-coder*. JBIG is *lossless* and can be regarded as a combination of two algorithms, the first of which sends or stores multiple representations of images at different resolutions with no extra storage cost, while the second is a very efficient compression algorithm, mainly for use with bi-level images. Compared with *ITU-T Group 4 fax*, JBIG is claimed to be approximately 10–50% better on text and line art and even better on halftones. (For compression of still and moving images, see *JPEG* and *MPEG*.)

Joint Network Team The body responsible for the operation of *JANET* prior to 1994. Now called *UKERNA*.

Joint Photographic Experts Group (JPEG) A standard from the *ISO* and *ITU-T* for coding and *compression* of colour images. Named after the committee (sometimes also called the Joint Picture Encoding Group) that designed the image compression algorithm. JPEG works best on full-colour or *grey-scale* digital images of real world scenes and not so well on non-realistic images, such as cartoons or line drawings, because the technique involves smoothing of the image and loss of detail. JPEG does not handle compression of black-and-white (1-bit-per-pixel) images or moving pictures (although see *moving JPEG*). For these see *JBIG*, *MPEG*.

Joint Picture Encoding Group Another name for the *Joint Photographic Experts Group* (JPEG).

Joint Technical Committee (JTC) A standards body reporting to both *ISO* and *IEC*.

joystick A device, like an aircraft pilot's joystick, consisting of a hand-held device that can be moved in a horizontal plane, the position being transmitted to a computer. Usually used to control games, with one or more push-buttons on the top, whose state can also be read by the computer. Needs a joystick (game control) port. Simple games joysticks are often only capable of moving an object in one of eight different directions.

JPEG See *Joint Photographic Experts Group*.

jpg The usual filename extension for *JPEG* files.

JTC See *Joint Technical Committee*.

jughead An *Internet* search utility which operates within *Gopher*. Similar to *Veronica*, but only searches directory names.

jukebox A way of storing and accessing large numbers of *compact discs*. Used mainly in *document image processing* applications.

Julia set A type of *fractal* image, named after French mathematician Gaston Julia. (See also *Mandelbrot set*.)

Jupiter project A project at *Xerox PARC* based on the development of *Multi-User Dungeon* (MUD) role-playing environments to include a *virtual reality* implementation of the real world, so that participants can communicate about their actual physical environment.

justification The arrangement of text on a page or screen so that it is aligned with either the left or right margin, or with both. Fully justified text has lines of the same length that are perfectly aligned with both the left and the right margins. Both margins are even; full justification is produced by increasing (or sometimes decreasing) the space either between words (wordspacing) or between letters (*letterspacing*) or both. *Hyphenation* is often used in conjunction with full justification, hence the use of the expression H&J. Full justification tends not to be used in electronic publications that are viewed on screen, particularly if the text *wraps* when the window size or the type size is changed.

K

K56 flex A *modem* technology which provides speeds of up to 56 kbps on the *download* side.

kbps Kilobit(s) per second. Transfer rate of 1000 bits per second. (See *bps* and *Mbps*.)

Kerberos An authentication and *key* distribution system, in which authorized users share a secret key with the key distribution centre. This key acts as a master, which effectively gives them access to the system.

Kermit A widely used *public-domain asynchronous file-transfer protocol*, originally developed at Columbia University and made available with-

> AWAY   AWAY

Figure 3 Kerning
An example of unkerned (left) and kerned letters.

out charge. Kermit is available as part of most communications packages and available on most operating systems. The UK centre for Kermit distribution is at the University of Lancaster. Kermit uses intensive encoding and error detection, and hence is fairly slow but very robust. (See also *Xmodem, Ymodem, Zmodem*.)

kerning Adjusting the spacing between two adjacent letters to create a better visual fit, also called aesthetic kerning, which explains the rationale behind the procedure (see Figure 3). Traditionally meant decreasing the amount of space, but has come to mean either increasing or decreasing the space between the letters. Note that this is not the same as *letterspacing*.

key A sequence of characters which is used in *encryption* and *decryption*. (See also *public key, private key*.) Also part of the keyboard.

key escrow encryption The deposit of *encryption* keys in *escrow*. (See also *Clipper*.)

key frame A frame in an animated sequence of frames which was drawn or otherwise constructed directly by the user rather than generated automatically, e.g., by *tweening*.

keyline A line drawn on artwork to show where illustrations or other material should be placed. As documents become more integrated with illustrations included as part of the file, this use is becoming less frequent. However, the concept still survives in software packages which allow display of pages without illustrations, either to reduce transfer time over a communications link or to cut down the refresh time of the screen.

keyword A word which is indexed to improve the speed of *searching*. (Contrast with *free-text searching*.) The term has a special meaning in *SGML* to indicate a property of an *element* or a *marked section*.

77

KI A secret key or algorithm (or formula) embedded within the *SIM* card in a digital *GSM* telephone, employed to validate the user.

killfile A list of subjects or names which a user does not want to appear in the list of messages sent to him or her from a *newsgroup*.

Kilostream A private leased-line 64 kbps service available from *BT*.

Kimball tag A stock-control device used in clothes shops. It consists of a small punched card attached to each item, containing serial number, price, etc. as a pattern of small holes, a barcode or a magnetic strip (and probably as text). The tag (or part of it) is removed at the till and kept as a computer-readable record of the sale. The removable part of the tag often also carries an electronic trigger, so that an alarm is set off if the tag is taken past detectors near the shop door.

kiosk A booth set up in a place where the public can obtain information, such as tourist or banking information. The number of computer multimedia kiosks, where the user can access an *interactive* display to obtain information conventionally provided by a human, is growing rapidly.

kiosk-mode browser A *World Wide Web browser* configured to allow the user access to only a restricted range of documents.

KIS See *Knowbot Information Service*.

kiss-fit Printing on an offset press different colours that touch each other, but using no *traps*. Kiss-fitting is not always suitable for all printing jobs but when it is, the result should be clearer than when traps are used.

knowbot A tool which searches a network for specific information. Also known as a *spider*.

Knowbot Information Service (KIS) A *white pages* 'meta-service' that provides a uniform interface to various white pages services on the *Internet*. With the Knowbot Information Service, a single query can be formed, which will search for white pages information from the *NIC whois service*, the *RIPE* European white pages service and others, and the responses will be displayed in a single, uniform format. KIS can be accessed via *telnet*, via *whois* or via *email*.

Knuth, Donald E The author of *The Art of Computer Programming*, to typeset which he also wrote the T_EX document formatting system and its *font*-design program *Metafont*. T_EX is widely used for formatting mathematical equations.

Kodak Photo CD A format developed by Kodak and *Philips* for the storage of images originated from 35 mm slide or negative film. Originally intended for display, via a television, from a special photo CD player, but now displayable by most graphics display programs.

L

LaborNet A network connecting those concerned about industrial relations. (See *Institute for Global Communications*.)

LAN See *local area network*.

landscape The orientation of a picture, *screen* or page such that its width is greater than its height. Most screens are landscape, while most books, and certainly journals, are *portrait*. This is a limitation on using *Acrobat* technology when reproducing printed pages onscreen, because when a full page is viewed the text is generally unreadable. (See also *aspect ratio*.)

LAN Manager The Microsoft *local area networking* environment.

LAP See *Link Access Protocol*.

LAPB See *Link Access Protocol (Balanced)*.

LAPD See *Link Access Protocol on the D channel*.

LAPM See *Link Access Protocol for Modems*.

laser An acronym of Light Amplification from the Stimulated Emission of Radiation (developed from Maser, where the initial 'M' stands for 'microwave'). Lasers create coherent light, i.e., with a single frequency and phase. This has two effects: the energy is concentrated, so that high-powered lasers can be used for applications such as surgery and welding; and the coherence means that the beam can carry information. The second property is used in *laser-printers*, *fibre-optics* and *holography*.

laser disc An *optical disc* (also known as a *video disc*) that holds both audio and visual images. Generally used to store long recordings of films, plays, opera, etc. Uses *analogue* storage and plays back via a television or monitor. Discs are typically 12 inches in diameter. At one stage, these were expected to be widely used in the education sector. An early example, which carried data as well as audio and video, was the two-disc set that resulted from the BBC's *Domesday Project*.

laserprinter A 'non-impact' printer which works in a similar way to a photocopier, except that the image is put on the photosensitive drum with a *laser* beam controlled by the signal from the host computer, rather than by reflection from an original copy. The electrostatic image area attracts electrically-charged toner particles (magnetized dry ink powder), which are fixed, by heating, on the paper. Print resolution ranges from 300–1800 *dots per inch* (dpi), although 300 and 600 are the most common. *Imagesetters* work on the same principle but because the image is transferred to film or bromide and processed chemically, much higher resolutions (up to several thousand dpi) can be obtained. Print speeds are usually given in pages per minute (or feet per minute for continuous or reel-fed machines), but the output speed normally depends on the complexity of the image. A bank of *LEDs* is sometimes used as an alternative to a laser as the image source. (See *LED printers*.)

latency The time it takes for a *packet* to travel from sender to receiver across a *network* or the period of time that a frame is held by a device on a network before it is forwarded. Latency and *bandwidth* are two of the most significant factors in the performance of a communications channel.

L^AT_EX A document preparation system based on the T_EX typesetting system and developed by Leslie Lamport. L^AT_EX uses commands which relate to the structure of the document, rather than to how it should appear, and thus has similarities with *SGML*. The L^AT_EX formatting software then converts these to native T_EX. L^AT_EX is probably the most widely used version of T_EX, although there are similar systems such as $\mathcal{A}_\mathcal{M}\mathcal{S}$-$T_EX$, developed by the American Mathematical Society, with particular emphasis on mathematical material.

LAWN Local area *wireless network*.

layer An aspect of communications architectures, which are organized using relatively independent protocols, each in a different layer. Each layer is concerned with a different aspect of the communication, so that the lowest layer controls communication between the hardware of different hosts, while the highest is concerned with *application* programs. For each layer, programs at different hosts use *protocols* appropriate to a particular layer to communicate with each other. Each layer uses the layer below it and provides facilities for the layer above; how this is done also forms part of the protocol suite. The use of layers simplifies communications protocols. *TCP/IP* has five layers of protocols; *OSI* has seven.

layer, layering A technique used within *draw* programs for handling *vector* or *object-oriented graphics*. Each object is drawn on its own layer, so that objects can be placed 'in front of' or 'behind' any other object; this arrangement can be changed with the *draw program*. In addition, most draw programs allow objects to be grouped on layers (each object still occupies its own layer within that group layer). This gives great flexibility to the expert user. Image editing programs, such as *Adobe* PhotoShop, also use layering and it is used in other types of program, such as Apple's *HyperCard*, to improve presentation and access to information.

LCD See *liquid-crystal display*.

leaf site On a network or the *Internet*, a machine that merely originates and reads *email* and does not relay traffic. The ratio of the number of leaf sites to *backbone* sites can affect the efficiency of the network.

leased line A private telephone circuit permanently connecting two points. Most *wide area networks* are built out of leased lines. While leased lines can be *analogue* or *digital*, today most are digital. Typically, the *bandwidth* is from 64 kbps upwards. The bandwidths are frequently the same as those of *ISDN*, which can be regarded as an extension of digital leased lines to *dial-up* communications. This equivalence should make it easier for leased lines, forming part of networks, to be integrated with ISDN.

LED   See *light emitting diode*.

LED printer   A printer, similar to a *laserprinter*, which uses a bank of *LEDs* as the image source, rather than a single *laser* beam.

Lempel–Ziv compression   Also known as *substitutional compression*. Two schemes proposed by Jakob Ziv and Abraham Lempel in 1977 and 1978, *LZ77* and *LZ78* (of which *Lempel–Ziv Welch* (LZW) compression is a variant).

Lempel–Ziv Welch compression (LZW)   A file *compression* technique designed in 1984 by Terry Welch, this was originally used with high-performance disk controllers and is the basis of the *Unix* compress command to reduce the size of files for archival or transmission. However, it is now widely used for file compression in application programs, such as *Acrobat*, although that may change as Unisys is claiming that LZW infringes its patent rights (see *Portable Network Graphics* – PNG). LZW is a variant of *LZ78* and relies on the repetition of byte sequences, or strings in the input. A table maps input strings to their associated output codes. Initially the table contains mappings for strings of length one and gradually the string length is increased as the program goes through an iteration loop. The maximum number of entries in the table is usually limited by the number of bits allowed in an output code, so that once this limit is reached, the table is extended no further.

LEO satellite   See *low earth orbiting satellite*.

letterbomb   A piece of *email* containing code that can act rather like a virus, affecting the operation of the recipient's computer, for example locking up the terminal. Often not particularly serious but the potential for serious damage is there, just as with real letter bombs, from which they take their name. (Does not mean quite the same as *mail-bomb*.)

letterspacing   Adding or reducing the space between individual characters, as opposed to between words, in a formatted document. When used correctly, the effect should be pleasing. However, when done automatically in order to reduce the interword spacing in *justification*, the effect can often be the reverse. Although the default of some *DTP* programs, such as *QuarkXPress*, is to use letterspacing, most typographic designers would agree that it should only be used as a last resort in justified text. In *electronic publishing*, letterspacing should only be used as a design tool.

lexical analyser   A tool, designed for use in program compilation, but also useful in text applications for string comparison and conversion. The *Unix* tool Lex is one of the most commonly used.

Lexis/Nexis   An on-line legal, news and business information service, owned by Reed-Elsevier, providing full-text legal information (LEXIS) and news (NEXIS).

LHA   A *shareware DOS* program for compressing and archiving files in a similar way to *PKZIP*. LHA used to be called *LHARC*. Compressed files have extensions lha and lhz. (The program's documentation does not indicate what the abbreviation actually stands for.)

LHARC   The previous name of *LHA*.

lhz   The *filename* extension for a file produced by the *LHA* program.

ligature   A *glyph* (or character) that is a combination of two or more single characters. For example, in many *fonts* when an 'i' follows an 'f', they are printed as a single character 'fi'; a ligature for 'fl' is also fairly common. In the past, particularly when hot metal or cold type were used for typesetting, a whole range of ligatures was used, but their use has become less common as computer typesetting has developed. They are virtually never used in onscreen presentation of text, although they may be seen in *HTML* documents as part of a (designed) text-block transmitted as a graphic.

light emitting diode (LED)   A diode which glows red, green or amber when energized by low voltage. They are commonly employed as a light source in multimode *fibre-optic* systems. In some applications, such as digital watches, they have been replaced by *LCDs* which require less power. They are also used in *LED* printers.

lightness　A measure of relative *brightness*. Used in the *HLS* method of representing colour in computer graphics.

light pen　A device which looks like an ordinary pen, but which can be used to instruct the computer to modify part of a screen image. At its tip the pen has a photoreceptor that emits signals when it receives light from the screen. With an appropriate interface program, the computer is able to calculate the position of the light pen on the basis of a grid stored in memory.

light pipe　A *fibre-optic* cable in contrast to copper wire.

line frequency　See *lines per inch*.

line high　The upper level, i.e the character 1, in *serial communications*. (See *break*.)

line-mode browser　A *World Wide Web* browser program which displays text only. A frequently used line-mode browser is *Lynx*.

line noise　Spurious characters (electrical noise) in a communications link, particularly an *RS-232 serial* connection. Can have many causes, for example poor connections, interference or *crosstalk*, electrical storms, cosmic rays, birds on telephone wires, or telephone wires rubbing against tree branches.

line probing　A feature that will allow a *modem* to identify the capacity and quality of the telephone line and adjust itself for maximum throughput using the highest possible data transmission rate. Line probing is available on some *V.34* modems.

line screen　See *lines per inch*.

lines per inch (lpi)　(Also called line screen and line frequency.) A measure of the *screen* or *resolution* of a *continuous-tone* or *halftone* image. Not to be confused with *dots per inch*, although there is a relationship between them for a particular image and a particular printer (for a more detailed explanation see *halftone*). The number of lines per inch will depend on the model of output device (*laserprinter* or *imagesetter*) and the kind of image involved, as well as the quality of the paper (see *dot gain*). Most personal laserprinters have a default screen ruling of 53 lpi, while *imagesetters* may go up to 300 lpi. Newspapers use screens of 65–85 lpi, while medical images may be output at 300 lpi. In the latter case it is the quality of both the paper and the offset printing (and the skill of the operator) that often determines the final quality of the printed image. The use of *grey scales* provides an equivalent effect on a computer screen.

line turnaround time　In a communications link, the transmission delay between the end of one block of data and the beginning of the next. It is particularly significant in *half-duplex* links. For *RS-232-C* interfaces line turnaround time is the delay between *request-to-send* (RTS) and *clear-to-send* (CTS) signals.

link　(Also called *hotlink*.) In *hypertext* documents, a connection from one document to another (see also *anchor*). The use of links within *HTML* documents can be regarded as perhaps **the** aspect of the *World Wide Web*, in that links can be followed between documents, irrespective of where in the world they are situated. Linking is also used within programs and *applications* (see, for example, *dynamic link library*, *object linking and embedding*, *dynamic data exchange*) in order either to save space by not duplicating data, or to ensure that data is always up to date. Links within hypertext documents may be explicit, i.e., they need to be *clicked* on, or implicit, in that the link is triggered automatically (see *linked images*). In application programs the link is almost always automatic. Links are also used in the *Unix* file system to avoid storing files twice and ensure consistent updating, although the user sees two or more different file names.

Link Access Protocol (LAP)　A protocol specified for the *datalink* layer in the *ITU-T X.25 packet-switched* interface standard. (See also *Link Access Protocol (Balanced)*.)

Link Access Protocol (Balanced) (LAPB)　A balanced version of the *Link Access Protocol*.

Link Access Protocol for Modems (LAPM)　The *automatic repeat request* system used in the *V.42* protocol.

Link Access Protocol on the D channel (LAPD)　An *ISDN datalink layer* protocol.

linkbase A *database* that contains a series of *World Wide Web links* for specific text strings. (See *Webcosm*.)

linked image A *graphic* image that is stored in a different file from the current *hypertext* page, so that it is displayed by selecting a *link*, although the image may also be included automatically, depending on the coding of the hypertext page.

LINX A UK *neutral interconnect*, based at *Pipex's* London *point of presence*.

liquid-crystal display (LCD) The display of characters (e.g., on a calculator) or pictures (e.g., on a pocket television screen) produced by liquid crystals, which are sandwiched between two polarizing filters and grids of transparent electrodes. The two polarizing filters are arranged so that their polarizing planes are at right angles (crossed), so that no light can pass through, except that the liquid crystal molecules rotate the plane of polarization through 90°, so that all the light is transmitted. When a current is applied to a particular crystal by its electrodes, that crystal ceases to rotate and the screen at that point appears dark. LCDs can be made up of either active or passive matrix designs. In active matrix designs, there is a separate transistor for each *pixel* or dot, while in passive matrices there is some sharing. Active matrices produce much brighter displays. Contrast is improved if screens are illuminated by backlighting or edgelighting.

list Often used for *mailing list*.

listserv An automated *mailing list* manager, originally designed for the *BITNET/EARN* network, which processes *email* requests for addition to or deletion from mailing lists, of which there are now thousands, on many different subjects. Some listservs also provide other facilities such as retrieving files from archives.

little-endian The ordering of the components of a hierarchical name in which the *domain name* is specified last (e.g., 'eps-edge.demon.co.uk'). This is now the usual order for *Internet addresses*. (Compare with *big-endian*, where more detailed explanation is given.)

live link Also known as a *hotlink*. (See also *link*.)

live net Any *World Wide Web* server which provides access to live material, probably using video cameras.

LiveWire A visual development environment, developed by *Netscape* and based on the *Java* language.

LLC See *logical link control*.

local area network (LAN) A geographically limited data communications network (typically to a 1 km radius or within a building), which allows resource sharing. A LAN allows computers to have access to common data, programs and peripherals, and it typically consists of PCs with adapter cards, file servers, printers and gateways to other networks. *Ethernet, Token-Ring, FDDI* and *LocalTalk* are examples of standard LANs and data rates up to 100 Mbps are possible. LANs use software to manage the components and the two best known programs are *Novell NetWare* and Microsoft *LAN Manager*, so that *client/server* computing can be supported. (See also *wide area network, metropolitan area network*.)

local bus A *bus*, designed to match the speed of the microprocessor, which extends the central processing unit (CPU) bus in order to speed up data transfer between the CPU, disks, graphics boards and other devices. This benefits *video* applications in particular. There are two common specifications, *VESA* and *Intel's PCI*, although PCI is likely to become the standard, allowing a wider choice of video boards.

local echo A term recently used instead of *half duplex*. The term comes from the need to display (or echo) input at a *terminal* connected to a mainframe computer by a *half-duplex* link.

local loop The telephone circuits between a subscriber's installation and the switching equipment at the local exchange.

local loopback address The special *Internet address*, 127.0.0.1, which is defined by the Internet Protocol for a *host* to send messages to itself.

LocalTalk One of the types of network hardware available in the *AppleTalk* system. PCs can also be connected to a LocalTalk network with the right adapter board.

logical link control (LLC) A protocol specified in *IEEE 802.2* for *datalink* level transmission control. It forms the upper portion of the *OSI* layer 2, the *datalink layer*. The LLC sublayer presents a uniform interface to the user of the datalink service, usually the *network* layer. Below the LLC sublayer is the *medium access control* (MAC) sublayer.

login An alternative term for *log on*, used on *Unix* systems.

log on, logon, logging on The process of connecting a user to a *network* or to a multi-user computer system. In general, although there is no rule, logon is used for networks and *login* for systems.

look-and-feel The general appearance and function of a *user interface* (usually a *graphical user interface* or GUI) including such things as the way *icons* are used, conventions for the meaning of different buttons on a *mouse* and the appearance and operation of *menus*. The first GUI was developed on the *Xerox Star*, but this was not a commercial success, its main look-and-feel concepts being exploited in the Apple *Macintosh*. Subsequently, Apple sued Microsoft claiming that the look-and-feel of Microsoft *Windows* infringed Apple's copyright. The case was mainly decided in Microsoft's favour.

loopback A communications diagnostic procedure, in which the transmitted data stream is looped back to its source, so that it can be compared with the transmitted data.

lossless compression A term describing a data *compression* algorithm in which all the information in a file is retained, allowing it to be recovered perfectly by decompression. Examples of lossless compression are the *Unix* compress and *PKZIP*. (See also *lossy compression*, which is the opposite of lossless.)

lossy compression A term describing a data *compression* algorithm in which the amount of information in the data, as well as the number of bits used to represent that information, is reduced. The lost information is usually assumed to be less important to the quality of the data (usually an *image* or *audio*) because it can be recovered reasonably by interpolation. *MPEG*, *JPEG* and *fractal compression* are examples of lossy compression techniques.

Lotus Notes A group of *workflow application* programs developed by Lotus, but now owned by IBM, which allows organizations to share and coordinate documents and exchange *electronic mail* messages. Notes supports *replication* on multiple *servers* and between the server and the desktop *client*. (See also *Computer Supported Cooperative Work*.)

low earth orbiting satellite (LEO satellite) A polar-orbiting satellite in a low orbit used for communication with hand portable terminals.

lower-case letters Uncapitalized letters, such as those that make up all this sentence (except the first letter). The term is derived from the days of cold type, when the capitals were kept in the top typecase and the small letters in the bottom (or lower) case. Capitals are thus sometimes referred to as *upper-case letters*.

low resolution (Often shortened to low-res.) The opposite of *high resolution*. While some graphics are just low-resolution to begin with, other graphics are created or scanned as complex, high-resolution images (probably for offset printing). However, in order to save disk space and/or to shorten screen display times, low-res versions are produced for use in *page make-up* and placement of the image. Usually the high-resolution version is merged using the *Open PrePress Interface*. (See also *resolution*.)

lpi See *lines per inch*.

lurker Someone who participates in a mailing list or *Usenet Newsgroup*, etc. by reading but not contributing (or *posting*). Although occasionally used in such a way, the term was not meant to be pejorative and, indeed, beginners are encouraged to 'lurk' so as to become familiar with a given community or group.

Lycos A *World Wide Web* index and search engine served by Carnegie Mellon University. It allows users to search on document title and content for a list of keywords. (See also *AltaVista*, *Yahoo*.)

Lynx A *World Wide Web* character-based *line-mode browser* developed at the University of Kansas.

LZ compression   See *Lempel–Ziv compression*.

LZ77 compression   The first algorithm (proposed in 1977) to use the *Lempel–Ziv substitutional compression* schemes. In LZ77 compression, a fixed-size 'sliding window' is moved over the data and when a phrase is encountered that has already been seen, a pair of values is output, giving the position of the phrase in the buffer containing the data that has already been seen and the length of the phrase. There are a number of variants of, and improvements to, the method. All popular archivers, including *lha* and *zip*, are variations on LZ77. (See also *LZ78*, *LZFG*, *Huffman coding*.)

LZ78 compression   A *Lempel–Ziv substitutional compression* scheme which enters phrases in a dictionary and then, when that particular phrase is found again, outputs the dictionary index instead of the phrase. Of the several algorithms based on this principle, which mainly differ in how they manage the dictionary, the best known scheme is the *Lempel–Ziv Welch* (LZW) variant of LZ78.

LZFG compression   A *Lempel–Ziv compression* scheme that includes features of both *LZ*77 and *LZ*78.

LZW compression   See *Lempel–Ziv Welch compression*.

M

MAC   See *medium access control*.

Mac   Common abbreviation for the *Apple Macintosh* computer.

MAC address   The hardware address of a device connected to a *network*. (See *medium access control*.)

MacBinary   A data format used on the *Macintosh*.

MacinTalk   The *speech synthesis* utility on the *Macintosh* that, with appropriate programs, makes things talk. Used in educational packages.

Macintosh (AppleMac or Mac)   A range of personal computers manufactured by Apple Computer, Inc., originally based on the Motorola 68000 microprocessor family and having a proprietary operating system. The Mac was the first commercially successful personal computer with a *graphical user interface* (GUI), although the interface was first used on the *Xerox Star* (see *Macintosh user interface*, *look-and-feel*). The *Finder* is the part of the operating system that simulates the desktop and there is a *multi-tasking* utility called *MultiFinder*. The Macintosh series provides graphics and its own graphics language, called *QuickDraw*, as well as a multimedia utility called *QuickTime* (both of which are now also available on other platforms). In 1994, PowerMacs based on the *PowerPC* microprocessor were launched. The Mac is widely used in the typesetting and design sectors and, while users often have a quasi-religious attachment to the Mac, there is very little today that cannot also be done on *Windows* or *Unix X windows* platforms. The name is based on that of the McIntosh apple, but it had to be spelt 'Macintosh' because 'McIntosh' was already a registered trademark. Apple has always refused to license the Mac operating software for other machines and this has had a two-edged effect, in that it has tended to trap the Mac in a niche market, although admittedly a large one, while, on the other hand, it has ensured that committed users continue to use Macs, even though, in general, they are more expensive than *Dos*-based PCs.

Macintosh user interface   The *Macintosh* included the first commercially successful *graphical user interface* (GUI), although the concept was originally developed at the Xerox Palo Alto Research Center (*Xerox PARC*) and commercially introduced on the *Xerox Star* computer in 1981. It is probably true that the success of the *Mac* can be attributable to the user interface in that it provided the first easy access to computers for those who were not computer experts. In particular, it appealed to designers and typographers as it provided a computer equivalent of the paradigm with which they were familiar. Hence, the wide use of Macs in the typesetting and printing industry, and now in the growing *multimedia* industry, even though GUIs with similar functionality are now available on other platforms. (See also *look-and-feel*.)

macro A combination of commands, used in various kinds of interactive programs, e.g., word-processors, as well as in text formatting or typesetting programs such as T_EX. In an interactive program, a series of commands can be 'recorded' and then can be 'played' to create the same effect, by using either a function key, a menu command or a *button*. Alternatively, macros can be written essentially as small computer programs, including functions and conditional expressions. The more complex macros can take parameters such as a text string or a value for such items as page number, interline spacing or typesize.

Macromedia Director One of the *multimedia* applications development packages from Macromedia. *Authorware* from the same company provides an alternative approach. (See also *Shockwave*.)

magnetic-ink character recognition (MICR) A character recognition system in which special characters printed in magnetic ink are read for rapid input to a computer. Because magnetic-ink characters are difficult to forge, MICR is used extensively in banking for marking and identifying cheques.

magneto-optical A hybrid technology that is used in *compact disc-recordable* (CD-R). Data storage is magnetic. However, the *laser* beam heats the very small area involved before it 'writes', that is, re-orients the relevant magnetic domains. When this area cools, it becomes twice as resistant to change as the equivalent area on a standard magnetic disk. A lower-power laser is used to 'read' the disc. If the area is to be overwritten, then it is again heated by the 'writing' laser.

mail Often used to mean sending a message via *email* to a specific recipient. (Compare with *snailmail*; note difference from *post*.) Also a program running under the Berkeley version of *Unix*. (See also *sendmail*.)

mail-bomb To send, perhaps together with others, a huge number of *email* messages to one person or to a system, aiming to crash the recipient's system. The actual way in which this will happen will vary from system to system. Mail-bombing is rather like 'road rage', in that it is used against someone who has apparently offended against the rules of *netiquette*, but in turn is itself a breech of netiquette, causing inconvenience not only to the target, but also to many other people and systems. (Not quite the same as *letterbomb*.)

mailbox A file, a directory or a message queue on a specific system in which incoming *email* messages are stored for a particular user or for distribution to a *mailing list* or via a *mail server*.

mail bridge A *gateway* that forwards *email* messages between *networks*. (See also *mail gateway*.)

mail exchange record (MX record) A record type used in a *domain name server*, showing which host can handle *email* for a specific *domain*.

mail exploder The part of an *email* system which enables multiple mailing and *mailing lists*. The sender uses a single address and the mail exploder distributes the message to the individual addresses in the list.

mail gateway A *gateway* between two or more *email* systems, transferring and, where necessary translating, messages between them. The translation can sometimes be quite complex and in early mail gateways there were often problems with characters being lost or mistranslated. This was particularly true if non-*ASCII* characters were involved. The use of *MIME* has virtually solved that problem.

mailing list (Or just list.) An *email address*, including many other email addresses, usually of people interested in a particular topic. The mailing list is an *alias*, which is expanded by a *mail exploder* so as to redirect mail to the addresses on the list. This may be automatic or the messages may be *moderated*. The term is also used to refer to the people on the list. Mailing lists predate *Usenet* and remain useful for distribution of information to private groups, e.g., for private information-sharing on topics that would be too specialized for or inappropriate to public *Usenet* groups. Note that requests to subscribe to, or leave, a mailing list should not be sent to the mailing list address, but to a special 'request' address, '-request' being added after name of the list and before the domain name, e.g., 'glossarylist-request@somewhere.com', if the list name is 'glossarylist@somewhere.com'. In this way everyone on the list does not have to see such requests, which go only to the person who maintains the list.

mail path   (Or *source route*.) An *email address* which gives the route of a message, listing the *hostnames* through which it must pass. This is infrequently used on the *Internet*, where the route is determined at each host through which the message passes.

mail reflector   An *email address* that provides a mail forwarding function, either if the recipient has moved (or just changed address) or sometimes to protect the identity of the recipient.

mail server   A program that sends files or information in response to *email* requests. Mail servers were used before *Internet* access was so wide. They are less used today, when information is easily available via the *World Wide Web* or *File Transfer Protocol* (ftp).

Majordomo   A widely used *freeware mailing list* processor that runs under *Unix*.

mall   A set of linked *URLs* on the *World Wide Web*, which give information about commercial products and services for sale that can often be purchased using credit cards or special banking services, such as *First Virtual*, or by using *electronic money*.

MAN   See *metropolitan area network*.

management information base (MIB)   The collection of objects managed, as part of *SNMP*, by an agent or piece of software running in a network component, such as a *router*.

Manchester encoding   A digital encoding technique in which a negative-to-positive voltage transition within a fixed period indicates a binary 0 and a positive-to-negative voltage transition indicates a binary 1.

Mandelbrot set   A mathematical set representing one kind of *fractal* image. It is named after Benoit Mandelbrot, who discovered the fractal principle and this set. Another fractal set is the *Julia set*.

Man–Machine Language (MML)   A language developed by *ITU-T* for telecommunications applications.

Manufacturers Automation Protocol (MAP)   An *applications-layer application* for office automation over *networks*, developed by General Motors on the basis of the *OSI* model based on *token bus*. (See also *TOP*.)

MAP   See *Manufacturers Automation Protocol*.

MAPI   See *Microsoft Mail Application Program Interface*.

marked section   A section of an *SGML* document that is to be treated in a special, usually conditional, manner.

mark sensing   A technique for reading into a computer pencil marks on specially prepared forms. Because the pencil marks contain graphite, which conducts electricity, when the mark sense reader, a series of small metal brushes, touches a mark, an electrical contact is made and thus the mark is detected.

markup   Traditionally, markup was added by editors and interpreted by compositors. However, now that most documents are prepared on computer, markup is a method of indicating either the logical structure of a document or how a page should be laid out. The coding used can be then be interpreted by an appropriate computer program. For example, documents for the *World Wide Web* are marked up using *Hypertext Markup Language* (HTML). While most markup has some kind of structure, *markup languages*, and in particular *Standard Generalized Markup Language* (SGML) have been developed in order to formalize the process. They also allow documents to be run through a *parser* in order to check whether the markup used corresponds to the *Document Type Definition* (DTD). Markup is a useful facility for documents that are used for both conventional print-on-paper publishing and *electronic publishing*, in that the markup codes can be interpreted differently for the two formats. Figure 4 gives an example of markup.

markup language   A language (or *metalanguage*) designed to formalize the *markup* process for text. Markup languages also give facilities for including links to *multimedia* items, such as *graphics*, *audio* and *video*.

marquee   A method of selecting *objects*, usually in a *draw program*, as an alternative to clicking on

```
<MEMO><MEMOHEAD>
<TO>James Smith</TO>
<CC>Admin</CC>
<BCC>Accounts</BCC>
<FROM>David Penfold</FROM>
<DATE>25 May 1997</DATE>
<SUBJECT>EP Glossary</SUBJECT></MEMOHEAD>
<BODY><SALUT>Dear James</SALUT>
<PARA>I am sending the manuscript of my
<EMPH1>glossary</EMPH1> to the publisher next
week. John has commented <quote>It's not
bad!</quote></PARA>
<PARA>It is important that I have your final
approval of the <epmh2>contract</epmh2> </PARA>
<PARA>I also need the following:</PARA>
<LIST>
<LITEM>copies of the artwork;</LITEM>
<LITEM>the cover design;</LITEM>
<LITEM>a quote for printing.</LITEM></LIST>
<PARA>Many thanks</PARA>

<CLOSE>David Penfold</CLOSE></BODY></MEMO>
```

MEMO
To: James Smith
Copy to: Admin
From: David Penfold
Date: 25 May 1997
Subject: EP Glossary

Dear James

I am sending the manuscript of my *glossary* to the publisher next week. John has commented "It's not bad!"

It is important that I have your final approval of the **contract**

I also need the following:

- copies of the artwork;
- the cover design;
- a quote for printing

Many thanks

David Penfold

Figure 4 Markup

A (fictitious) memo marked up to conform to the example given of a *Document Type Definition* together with how it could be printed out. Note that the structure says nothing about the appearance, so that representation of '<emph2>' by bold is a formatting decision (it could perhaps be represented as red on a screen) and the labels 'To:' etc. are also part of the formatting.

specific objects. The *mouse* is held down and moved, forming a rectangle on the screen (indicated in different ways in different programs). Everything that is completely within the rectangle is selected. Care must be taken, however, to ensure that the objects are in the rectangle; graphic objects are often larger than the image onscreen. For example, a quadrant may appear onscreen, even though the object is a complete circle.

MBONE See *Multicast Backbone*.

Mbps Megabit(s) per second. Transfer rate of 1 000 000 bits per second. (See *bps*, *kbps*.)

MCA See *Micro Channel Architecture*.

MCI See *Media Control Interface*.

MCI Mail A large commercial *email* service. Note that this is not related to *Media Control Interface*, but named after the US company, MCI, which operates the service.

MDI See *Multiple Document Interface*.

media The plural of *medium*. The use of media as a singular is to be deprecated.

Media Control Interface (MCI) A standard control interface for multimedia devices and files, used under *Windows*.

media converter A component used in *Ethernets* to link segments, although not part of the *IEEE 802.3* standard, which specifies *repeaters*.

Media Lab at the Massachusetts Institute of Technology One of the leading research organizations concerned with developments in *multimedia* and *communications*. Headed by Nicholas *Negroponte*.

Media Player A *Windows* utility which allows both *audio* and *video* files to be replayed.

medium The means of conveying something; an intermediate. In the topics with which this glossary is concerned, medium means a way of transferring (or sometimes storing) data, often as part of *multimedia applications*. Note that *media* is the plural of medium.

medium access control (MAC) A protocol for controlling access to a specific network. Part of the *IEEE 802* network standards. The lower portion of the *datalink layer*, *OSI layer 2*. Essentially the interface between a computer and a network, determining which unit transmits at any particular time. (See also *MAC address*, *logical link control*.)

Megafloppy A text *compression* technique, developed by Eurofield Systems, Australia and designed to enable the publication of large amounts of data on floppy disk. The technique provides not only compression but also *encryption* in such a way that the files may be transferred to hard disk and accessed without *decompression*, so that the data cannot be copied or, indeed, accessed without a *PIN number*, if so required.

menu A type of *user interface* in which the user is presented with a series of options, from which he or she can select, either with a *mouse* or by entering a text string, often just a number.

menu bar In a *graphical user interface* (GUI), the bar across the top of the *screen* or a *window*, containing the names of *pull-down menus*.

message handling system (MHS) The services and protocols that provide *OSI email*, specified in the *ITU-T X.400* series of recommendations and also defined as the *Message-Oriented Text Interchange Standard* (MOTIS) by *ISO*. It is used by *CompuServe*.

Message-Oriented Text Interchange Standard (MOTIS) The *ISO* version of *MHS*.

message switching A method of transmission in which messages are stored at an intermediate switching centre until a channel is available for them to be transmitted to their final destination. (See also *packet switching*.)

meta An *HTML* tag, defining *metadata*, which is used by many of the *World Wide Web search engines*, either as part of the *indexing* or as part of a *keyword search*.

metadata Structured data which describes types of information. Often used for searching, e.g., using the *Z39.50* protocol, although the data may not actually form part of the viewable document.

Metafont A *font* design and generation package which is a companion to the T_EX typesetting language.

meta-information Information about information, for example how it is structured.

metalanguage A (computer) language in which the logic and statements of another language are discussed and specified. For example, *SGML* is a metalanguage in that it specifies how to do things, rather than what to do.

metropolitan area network (MAN) A network linking users that usually covers an area the size of a city. Often implemented using *optical fibre*. (See also *SMDS, SONET, local area network, wide area network*.)

MHEG See *Multimedia/Hypermedia Information Coding Experts Group*.

MHS See *Message Handling System*.

MHz Megahertz. (See *hertz*.)

MIB See *management information base*.

MICR See *magnetic ink character recognition*.

microbilling A billing technique, gradually being introduced on the *Internet*, which allows small amounts due (*micropayments*, for example for download of an item of information or software) to be accumulated and invoiced together at the end of an agreed period.

Micro Channel Architecture (MCA) (Or just micro channel.) An expansion *bus* used in PCs, now superseded by later technologies, such as *local bus*.

Microcom Networking Protocol (MNP) A series of widely used *modem* protocols, which include *compression* and *error correction*. (See also *V series*.)

Microcosm Software developed at the University of Southampton for automatically inserting cross-references into electronic and *multimedia* documents. The *Open Journal* project is using an extension of this software, now released commercially as *Webcosm*, to develop automatic cross-referencing for *electronic journals*.

microfiche A sheet of film onto which text and images are photographically reduced. Usually 105 × 148 mm, holding 420 A4 sheets. (See also *microfilm, microform*.)

microfilm A roll of film, usually 35 mm, onto which text and images are photographically reduced. *Computer output on microfilm* (COM) is a common form of archival storage, although it is gradually being superseded by *computer output onto laser disc* (COLD) and *document image processing*. (See also *microform*.)

microform Generic name for media onto which text or images are photographically reduced. The main examples are *microfiche* and *microfilm*.

micropayments See *microbilling*.

Microsoft Corporation The world's largest software company. Was first successful in writing PC-DOS (which became *MS-DOS*), the operating system used by PCs, under contract to IBM. Later products include MS *Windows* and *Windows 95*, *Windows NT* and *LAN Manager*, as well as many applications software products.

Microsoft Mail Application Program Interface (MAPI) Microsoft's *email* system for *local area networks* (LANs). (See also *VIM*, which is a rival system.)

Microsoft Windows See *Windows*.

middleware Software that is used between an *application program* and a *network* or between a *client* and a *server* in order to allow applications to have standard *user interfaces* and yet be usable across heterogeneous platforms and networks.

MIDI See *Musical Instrument Digital Interface*.

mid-level network (Also called *regional network*.) The *networks* of the *Internet* that connect the *stub networks* to the *backbone networks*.

Milnet Military Network. Part of the US *Defense Data Network*. Also part of the *Internet*.

MIME See *Multipurpose Internet Mail Extensions*.

mimencode (Originally mmencode.) An improvement on *uuencode* for use in *email*. Uuencode uses some characters that become corrupted across certain *mail gateways* (particularly those converting to and from *EBCDIC*). Uuencode also has a number of variants. Mimencode is more robust.

Minitel The French *viewdata* system provided free by the French telephone system as a way of obtaining directory information. However, Minitel is now widely used to provide information on a range of services.

mirror An *Internet archive site* holding a copy of files from another site, so as to allow users to access them more quickly, as well as reducing the load on the source site. Usually whole directories are mirrored in a structured way, e.g., to provide access in Europe or the UK to a US source. This is different from a *cache* or *proxy server*, which just stores everything which is requested through it, to speed up subsequent access. The term is also used to describe duplication of storage on disk, for example in *RAID* systems.

missile address An alternative term for the *ICBM* address.

mmencode The original name for *mimencode*.

MML See *Man–Machine Language*.

MMX A extra set of instructions built into later (1997) versions of *Intel's Pentium* microprocessors to support operations on multimedia and communications data types. They can handle many common multimedia operations, such as digital signal processing, normally handled by a separate sound card or video card. Intel states that this is not an acronym for MultiMedia eXtension, but an Intel brand name.

MNP See *Microcom Networking Protocol*.

Mobile Station International ISDN Number (MSISDN) The telephone number (0902 XXXXXX) dialled to contact a mobile user.

Mobile Switching Centre (MSC) A telephone exchange for a cellular network.

mod A filename extension for a sampled music file format, which is made up of digitized sound samples (unlike *MIDI* files), arranged in patterns to create a song.

modem An abbreviation for *modulator/demodulator*. A device for converting digital data (typically from a *serial RS-232* port) to and from an *audio analogue* signal that can be transmitted over telephone lines. Modems operate at different *baud* rates, from 300 up to 28 800, and are classified according to the maximum rate at which they can transmit and receive (see *V series*). Some models also support *compression* and *error correction* (see *Microcom Networking Protocol*), as well as features such as auto-dial and auto-answer. The introduction of *digital* communications, in the form of *ISDN* and *asynchronous transfer mode*, as well as increasing communication rates, will mean that modems will no longer be required, although line terminators will still be necessary to handle communications protocols.

moderated The term describing *mailing lists* and *newsgroups* which are edited and managed by a *moderator*.

89

moderator A person or persons editing and managing a *moderated mailing list* or *Usenet newsgroup*. The moderator will read all incoming submissions and decide which ones will be sent out to the mailing list or newsgroup.

modulated Subject to *modulation*.

modulation The modification of the amplitude, frequency or phase of an analogue carrier wave so that information can be transmitted. (See *amplitude modulation*.)

moiré A pattern that can appear in graphic images; a result of the superposition of one regular pattern or *screen* on another, so that interference takes place, causing a periodic variation of intensity. It is similar to the phenomenon of 'beats', which occurs with sound. (See also *aliasing*.)

Mondex An *electronic money* scheme which is being trialed in Swindon, UK. (See also *Cybercash*, *Digicash*, *Ecash*.)

monochrome Literally means one colour, often black on white (although see *bi-level bitmap*), but used for *grey scales*. Used to describe black and white printers and displays, which will usually be white, green or orange on black, or black on white. A grey-scale monitor displays a range of grey values, not just black or white, even though there is still no colour.

monomode fibre A type of optical fibre that has a very fine core, the diameter of which is approximately the wavelength of light. There is very low dispersion of the optical signal and therefore monomode fibres are used for high bandwidths over long distances. (Compare with *multimode fibre*.)

monospaced, monospacing Text characters which all have the same intercharacter spacing, unlike *proportional fonts*. While all fonts can be used monospaced, the visual effect is strange, unless the font has been designed to be monospaced. The most frequently used monospaced font is probably `Courier`, while there are many other such fonts, almost all originally designed for use on mechanical typewriters. The early *OCR* fonts were also monospaced. It is also worth noting that certain fonts (of which Times is probably the best known and most frequently used), although proportional, have all the numerical digits with the same width, so that setting of numerical tables is more straightforward. This will apply in typesetting for both printing and *electronic publishing*, with display on screen.

MOO See *Multi-User Dimension*.

morphing The gradual distortion of one image into another by moving points on the original image to certain corresponding points in the second image. Used in *animation* software. (Compare with *tweening*.)

Mosaic See *World Wide Web browser* or *client* from *NCSA*, which runs on a number of different platforms. One of the most commonly used browsers, but during 1995–96 was gradually superseded by *Netscape Navigator* (developed by the same team) and by *Internet Explorer*, at least on a *Windows* platform.

Motif The standard *graphical user interface* (GUI) for *Unix* systems, based on *X windows*.

Motion Picture Encoding Group Another name for the *Moving Pictures Expert Group* (MPEG).

MOTIS See *Message-Oriented Text Interchange Standard*.

mouse A pointing device, which controls the position of a graphic cursor on screen. It is moved around on the desk (or on a *mouse mat*) and its motion is transmitted to the operating system or application software either mechanically, through a roller ball which causes electrical signals to be generated, or optically, as a result of moving over a grid of lines on a custom mouse mat. A mouse also carries two or more buttons, which can be *clicked* or *double-clicked* on an *icon* or *menu* item to transmit a command. Nonetheless, in some, particularly familiar, applications, keyboard commands are faster. However, if the user is unfamiliar with the commands, then the mouse makes the system more *user-friendly* and allows the use of *drag and drop*. A mouse can also be used in graphics programs to select items (see *marquee*) and for drawing shapes, although *graphics tablets* are probably better for drawing. (See also *graphical user interface*, *WIMP*.)

mouse mat A mat on which a *mouse* can be moved around. For a mechanical mouse, this usually a plastic surface on a foam-rubber backing, while for an optical mouse, the surface is usually a firmer plastic carrying a grid ruled in two dimensions.

moving JPEG A *compression* technique for moving images in which each *frame* is compressed using *JPEG* still compression. Although there is no agreed standard for moving JPEG, there are chips available that are appropriate for television resolutions and frame rates.

Moving Pictures Experts Group (MPEG) (Also called Motion Picture Encoding Group.) An *ISO* standard for coding full-motion video information in a compressed form. Encoding is done off-line while retrieval is performed in real time. (See *MPEG-1*, *MPEG-2*, *MPEG-3*.) MPEG can also be used for audio files (see *audio formats*).

Mozilla An alternative name for *Netscape Navigator*, when it was first designed as a version of *Mosaic*.

MPC See *Multimedia Personal Computer*.

MPEG See *Moving Pictures Experts Group*.

MPEG-1 The first version of the *MPEG format*, which was optimized for *CD-Rom*. It works in a similar way to *JPEG* to compress data within a frame and then uses block-based motion compensated prediction (MCP) to remove data between frames, essentially keeping only information that changes between frames. Audio is also compressed using *sub-band encoding*. MPEG-1 will give quality which is at least as good as VHS video, although the audio quality is not as high.

MPEG-2 An improved version of *MPEG-1* intended for broadcasting compressed video over satellites. Now also includes *HDTV*.

MPEG-3 A development of *MPEG-2* to handle *HDTV* applications. However, after it had been developed, it was later discovered that with some (compatible) fine tuning, MPEG-2 and *MPEG-1* syntax worked satisfactorily for HDTV. Because of this and pressures for standardization, HDTV is now handled under MPEG-2.

mpg The usual filename extension for a file in *MPEG* format.

MSC See *Mobile Switching Centre*.

MS-DOS The *operating system* used on the IBM PC and its clones. Note that *Windows 95* and *Windows NT* run as operating systems themselves, although *MS-DOS* commands can still be accessed in a *window*.

MSISDN See *Mobile Station International ISDN Number*.

MUD See *Multi-User Dimension*.

mu-law A *companding* scheme, based on *sampling*, for *analogue* to *digital* conversion of speech. It is used in *PCM codecs* in the US telephone network.

multicast A form of *broadcast* in which packets are delivered only to specified destinations. Implemented over the *Internet* as *MBONE*.

multicast addressing An addressing scheme used to send *packets* over *Ethernet* to all devices of a certain type or as a *broadcast* to all *nodes*.

multicast backbone (MBONE) A *virtual network* which runs on top of the *Internet* and supports *multicast* and *multimedia* transmission, including *videoconferencing*, shared *whiteboard* and shared editing of documents. The quality is not very good at about 3–5 fps (commercial television is about 10 times that, but this keeps telecommunications data rates low).

multicast IP See *IP-Multicast*.

multidrop A network configuration which has multiple stations, but ensures that only one can transmit at any one time. (See also *multipoint*.)

MultiFinder The *Macintosh* utility which allows *multi-tasking*. It has been incorporated into the *System 7 operating system*.

multimedia Initially a *human–computer interface* term describing interactions with text, graphics, audio and video. In general terms, however, the interactive use of these various media together. This may involve the use of *hypertext* and *generic coding* schemes, such as *SGML* and *HTML*. *Multimedia* became widely available with the development of the *CD-Rom*, but are now being exploited more and more over the World Wide Web, using such facilities as *MBONE* and *MPEG* compression. Within the corporate world, 'multimedia' has a slightly different interpretation, being used to cover such activities as *videoconferencing* and shared *whiteboards*.

Multimedia/Hypermedia Information Coding Experts Group (MHEG) An *ISO* group working on the development of standards for *bit-stream* specifications for *multimedia* and *hypermedia*.

Multimedia Internet Mail Extensions (MIME) See *Multipurpose Internet Mail Extensions*.

Multimedia Personal Computer (MPC) A specification, covering hardware and interoperability, published by the Multimedia PC Marketing Council. In 1997, the MPC2 specification, published in 1993, is still the current version and includes a VGA monitor, 8 Mbytes of random access memory and a *CD-Rom* drive.

multimode fibre Optical fibre with a core that is capable of propagating light signals of more than one wavelength. It has a larger core than *monomode fibre* and is cheaper to manufacture. However, it introduces more *dispersion* and is therefore used for lower bandwidths over shorter distances.

Multiple Document Interface (MDI) Describes applications in *Windows* that allow more than one document (file) to be used at the same time. (See *active document*.)

Multiple Mastering A font technology developed by Adobe Systems for use in conjunction with *Acrobat* and the *portable document format* (pdf). Multiple mastering allows the generation of a substitute font when a pdf document is displayed and the specified font is neither installed on the viewing system nor included as part of the pdf file. This means that any pdf file can be displayed with an Acrobat viewer.

multiple subNyquist sampling encoding (MUSE) A Japanese coding system for *HDTV*.

multiplexer (mux) A device that combines (see *multiplexing*) several signals so that they can be transmitted via a common physical transmission medium. Used in telephone systems, for example. (See also *demultiplexer*.)

multiplexing The combination of a number of signals for transmission over a shared medium, for example a telephone line. The signals are combined at the transmitter by a *multiplexer* and split up again at the receiver by a *demultiplexer*. Common forms of multiplexing are *time division multiplexing* (TDM), *frequency division multiplexing* (FDM), *wavelength division multiplexing* (WDM) and *code division multiplexing* (CDM). If the inputs use the output channel in turn (TDM), then line bandwidth needs only to be the maximum bandwidth of any input. However, if inputs are active simultaneously, then the bandwidth must be at least the total bandwidth of all those active inputs. In the latter case the multiplexer is also known as a *concentrator*.

multiplexor An alternative spelling of *multiplexer*.

multipoint A network configuration in which a communications channel is connected to more than two stations. *Multidrop* operation is used to ensure that only one station transmits at any one time.

Multipurpose Internet Mail Extensions (MIME) An *email* standard that permits the inclusion of non-text files (programs in binary form, image files, and so on) in an email message as attachments. MIME works automatically only if both sending and receiving mail handling programs are MIME-compliant. Uses *mimencode* to encode binary data using a subset of *ASCII*.

multisession When applied to a *WORM CD* or similar device, implies that the CD can be written to on different occasions (i.e., in different sessions), until it is full.

multi-tasking The ability of a computer to work with more than one program at a time without any further action from the user. In fact, the computer uses *time-slicing* to switch between applications, but this happens so fast that users are unaware of it, although all the

N

applications slow down to a greater or lesser extent.

multi-threading   An addition to *multi-tasking* which enables individual actions within an application to run simultaneously, so that it is not necessary to wait for the result of one action before implementing a second. An example might be a *draw program*, where it is unnecessary to wait for the screen to redraw after each change.

Multi-User Dimension (MUD)   (Also called Multi-User Domain and originally Multi-User Dungeon.) A type of multi-player interactive adventure game, accessible via the *Internet* or a *modem*, the name originally being based on 'Dungeons and Dragons'. The game has undergone various developments and modifications since first being launched in 1979. MUDs have also been used as conferencing tools and educational aids. A *MOO* is an *object-oriented* MUD.

Multi-User Domain   See *Multi-User Dimension*.

Multi-User Dungeon   See *Multi-User Dimension*.

MUSE   See *multiple subNyquist sampling encoding*. Also used as an abbreviation for Multi-User Shared Environment, a kind of *MUD*.

Musical Instrument Digital Interface (MIDI)   (Pronounced 'middy'.) A standard covering how computers and musical instruments or synthesizers interact. MIDI covers both the hardware and the protocols for how music is encoded and transferred between different devices, which may be an instrument, synthesizer or computer. A MIDI interface is required and is standard on some *Macintoshes*. It is then possible to input at a standard piano-type keyboard or synthesizer and then edit the music onscreen, each channel being separately editable. The basic unit of information is 'note on/off', together with the pitch and volume, but other information can be added.

mux   See *multiplexer*.

MX record   See *mail exchange record*.

NAK   See *negative acknowledgement*.

Name Registration Scheme (NRS)   A scheme defining the organization, structure and translation of names of network services in the UK academic community.

name resolution   Mapping an Internet name into its corresponding address, for example a *fully qualified domain name* into its *network address*. (See also *Domain Name System*.)

name server   See *Domain Name Server*.

narrowband   The opposite of *broadband*. Generally applied to networks with *bandwidths* less than either 2 Mbps or 34 Mbps. The definition is fuzzy, depending on the user's experience.

narrowcast   (Also described as *personalcast*.) Transmission of information to a defined group of recipients, in contrast to *broadcast*.

NAS   See *Network Application Support*.

NAT   See *network address translator*.

National Center for Supercomputing Applications (NCSA)   The organization where the first version of *Mosaic* was developed.

national characters   An expression used for characters of the Roman alphabet with accents and other diacritical marks that are used in certain written languages, but not in English. They are listed in *ISO 8859*.

National Information Infrastructure (NII)   (Or the *information superhighway*.) The planned integrated communications structure of the USA, based on a nationwide network of (*broadband*) networks, which is intended to give all Americans access to the country's information, communication ,and computing resources. The NII is planned to include all current and future public and private networks, as well as satellite communications and to cover all aspects of information, communication and entertainment.

National Information Services and Systems (NISS)   An information archive service, based at the University of Bath, intended primarily for UK educational institutions. (See also *BIDS*.)

National Institute of Standards and Technology (NIST) US government body that is involved in the development of standards. Formerly the National Bureau of Standards.

National Research and Education Network (NREN) A high-bandwidth network in the USA, devoted to high-performance computing and communications. Similar to *SuperJANET* in the UK.

National Science Foundation (NSF) A US government agency whose purpose is to promote and fund the advancement of science. *NSFNET* is funded by NSF.

National Science Foundation Network (NSFNET) A high-speed hierarchical 'network of networks' in the USA (maximum bandwidth 45 Mbps), funded by the *National Science Foundation*. The NSFNET forms part of the *Internet*.

National Technical Information Service (NTIS) The official resource for US government-sponsored and worldwide scientific, technical, engineering and business-related information.

National Television Standards Committee (NTSC) The body defining the television video signal format used in the USA. NTSC is also used to refer to the format itself (30 fps with 525 lines per frame). The UK equivalent is *PAL*. (See also *SECAM*.)

navigate Generally, to find one's way around. However, often used of *hypertext* systems and, in particular, the *World Wide Web*. A *browser* provides navigation facilities for *hypertext documents* via *links*, which in the World Wide Web are implemented using *HTML* and *HTTP*.

Navigator A program that helps the user to make the most of *CompuServe*. *Netscape Navigator* is a *World Wide Web browser*.

NCSA See *National Center for Supercomputing Applications*.

NDIS See *network device interface specification*.

negative acknowledgement (NAK) A mnemonic for *ASCII* character 21. Sent from a receiving station to a transmitting station, indicating that previous transmission(s) have not been received correctly.

Negroponte, Nicholas Director of the Media Laboratory at Massachusetts Institute of Technology, a founder of *Wired* magazine and author of 'Being Digital'.

Nelson, Ted The originator of the concept of *hypertext* in his 1967 proposal for *Xanadu* and the *Docuverse*.

net A rather loose term, sometimes applied to the *Internet* itself, at others to specific networks. Also used as a prefix to describe people and events related to *Usenet* and the Internet.

netaddress Another name for the *Knowbot Information Service*.

NetBEUI See *NetBIOS Extended User Interface*.

NetBIOS An *applications programming interface* (API) which controls *network* operations on PCs running under MS-DOS. It is a set of network commands issued by an application program and interpreted by a *network operating system*.

NetBIOS Extended User Interface (NetBEUI) The *network transport layer* protocol relating to the *NetBIOS applications programming interface*.

Netcaster See *Netscape Netcaster*.

netCDF See *Network Common Data Form*.

Netfind A *white pages* directory, based on people's names, which will try to find telephone and email information.

netiquette Network etiquette. Mainly refers to the conventions recognized on *Usenet* and in *mailing lists*.

netmask A 32-bit mask that shows how an *Internet address* is divided into *network*, *subnet* and *host* parts.

NetNews A weekly publication that gives news about the *Internet*.

netnews The software used to run *Usenet*, as well as the actual content of Usenet.

Netscape See *Netscape Communications Corporation*, *Netscape Communicator*, *Netscape Navigator*, *Netscape Netcaster*.

Netscape Collabra An information exchange forum that is part of *Netscape Communicator*, intended to be used either publicly or privately.

network architecture

Netscape Communications Corporation Originally Mosaic Communications Corporation, a company set up in 1994 by, among others, Marc Andreessen, who created *NCSA Mosaic*, to market a new version of *Mosaic*, which was called Netscape (also called Mozilla), now *Netscape Navigator*.

Netscape Communicator A suite of software including the latest version of *Netscape Navigator*, as well as *Netscape Netcaster* and *Netscape Collabra*.

Netscape Navigator A *World Wide Web browser* produced by *Netscape Communications Corporation* (now part of *Netscape Communicator*). It evolved from *NCSA Mosaic* and was first made available free on the *Internet* in October 1994. Its functionality is continually being expanded and one feature is the development of *Netscape* plug-ins, which allow other programs, such as *Acrobat*, to be integrated with Netscape Navigator. Thus Netscape Navigator was developed as a *de facto* standard but the growth of *Internet Explorer* has meant that there are now two completely *de facto* standards! There was some concern that Netscape developments would conflict with the proposed developments in *HTML 3.0*, although Netscape has signed up as supporting these proposals. (See also *Java*.)

Netscape Netcaster A *push technology* from *Netscape*, with similarities to *Castanet* and *BackWeb*. Part of *Netscape Communicator*.

Netscape plug-ins Applications which can be integrated with *Netscape Navigator*. These include an *Acrobat* reader, *MPEG* and *JPEG* viewers, and a *QuickTime* viewer.

Net TV The combination of the *Internet* and conventional television on the same hardware. Two approaches are being made: adding a 'set-top computer' to a television and adding TV functionality to a computer. Currently, all US developments rely on using cable TV, but satellite delivery is being developed in Europe. Net TV is generally considered in the context of *push technologies*.

NetWare See *Novell NetWare*.

network A communication or connection system, which allows computers to talk to one another or to other devices. The purpose is to allow access to, and exchange of, data and programs without any physical exchange. Connection may be through cables or via a *modem* or *ISDN*. A network covering a small area or a building is known as a *local area network* (LAN), while there are also *metropolitan area networks* (MANs) and *wide area networks* (WANs). The *Internet* is a network of (wide area) networks. Networks operate using different protocols (*Ethernet*, *Token-Ring*, etc.) and management systems (*Novell NetWare*, *LAN Manager*, *SNMP*, etc.). The *ISO seven-layer model* is an attempt to provide a way of partitioning any computer network into independent modules from the lowest (physical) layer to the highest (application) layer, while *TCP/IP* provides an alternative solution that has become a *de facto* standard; negotiations are going on to bring the two together.

network address Can be considered as the *Internet address* or as part of that address, excluding the address of the *host*. Which bytes of the address are which depends on the *class* of the network: for a class A network, the network address is the first byte of the IP address; for a class B network, the network address is the first two bytes of the IP address; for a class C network, the network address is the first three bytes of the IP address. Also used to describe the *nodes* on a *local area network* (LAN), such as printers.

network address translator (NAT) A hardware device which has been proposed for extending *Internet addresses*.

network application A program, or combination of program and data, that performs a task over a *network*, usually involving more than one computer.

Network Application Support (NAS) *DEC's* approach to integrating applications in a distributed multivendor environment.

network architecture A specification of how a network is to be organized; the hardware and software components which will make it possible to carry out a specific task.

Network Common Data Form (netCDF)
A machine-independent file format for scientific data.

network computer A computer without any local storage, i.e., with no disks, which is designed to be used on a *local area network* (LAN) or connected to a *network* via an *intranet* or even the *Internet*. Because of the lack of storage, network computers are cheaper than standard PCs.

network device interface specification (NDIS) A programming interface for different *network* protocols sharing the same network hardware.

Network extensible Window System (NeWS) A *PostScript*-based windowing environment, invented by James Gosling of Sun Microsystems for *X windows*. It was the first windowing system which allowed PostScript documents to be viewed on screen. (See also *HyperNeWS, OpenWindows*.)

Network File System (NFS) A protocol developed by Sun Microsystems, which makes files on a network appear to a local computer as if they were on its local disk. This protocol is now a *de facto* standard and is widely used. NFS uses the *connectionless user datagram protocol* (*UDP*) in order to make it *stateless*. (See also *PC-NFS*.)

network information center (NIC) An advisory centre for *network* users. May provide telephone and *email* help desk services, as well as network information services based on programs such as Sun Microsystems' *Network Information Service*. Not necessarily the same as a *network operations center*.

Network Information Service (NIS) A *client–server* protocol developed by Sun Microsystems for distributing system configuration data, such as user and host names, between computers on a network. Runs under *Unix*. Originally called *Yellow Pages* but the name was changed because BT (in the UK) has copyright on that name.

network interface card (NIC) The card or board which it is necessary to have in a PC in order to connect to a network, such as *Ethernet* or *Token-Ring*.

network layer The third-lowest layer of the *ISO seven layer model*, which determines the switching and routing of *packets* from the sender to the receiver using the *datalink layer*. It is in turn used by the *transport layer*. IP is a network layer protocol.

network management The set of tasks that are necessary to ensure that a *network* provides the required level of service to its users at a reasonable cost. The *ISO* model defines five categories: fault management; configuration management; security management; performance management; and accounting management. Many network management systems are based on the *Simple Network Management Protocol* (SNMP).

Network News Transfer Protocol (NNTP) A protocol for the distribution, retrieval and posting of *Usenet news* articles over the *Internet*. It is basically a *client–server* system. While NNTP is usually built into a news reader program, it can also be used via *telnet*.

network number Part of the *network address*.

network operating system The system software used to integrate the computers on a *network*. Examples include *Novell NetWare*, Microsoft *LAN Manager* and IBM *Systems Network Architecture* (SNA).

network operations center (NOC) The location at which a *network* or *internet* is managed. This will include the monitoring and resolution of any problems. (Compare with *network information center*.)

Network Time Protocol (NTP) A protocol that synchronizes clocks located on the *Internet*.

network to network interface (NNI) An interface between two *networks* operating the same protocol.

network topology The physical and logical relationship between the elements (*nodes*) of a *network*. Common topologies include a star, bus, ring and tree.

neutral interconnect A *network* infrastructure in which network service providers can freely exchange traffic without any policy restrictions. Examples are the GIX (Global Internet

Exchange) at MAE-East (a Metropolitan Area Ethernet in the Washington area), and the *Ebone* or European backbone and *LINX*, a UK neutral interconnect based at *Pipex's* London point of presence.

NeWS See *Network extensible Window System*.

newsgroup An electronic *Usenet* interest group devoted to a particular topic. Groups can be either *moderated* or unmoderated. Some newsgroups also have parallel *mailing lists* for those without news access, while some moderated groups are distributed as *moderated digests*, with an index.

newsfeed A source from which a regular 'feed' of *Usenet newsgroups* can be obtained.

news-reader A program which makes it straightforward to read *Usenet news* articles. It may run either on the access provider's machine if there is only terminal access, or on the user's machine if there is full *IP* access.

NEWT A *TCP/IP* communication stack for *Windows*, which provides users with direct network access.

Newton The Apple *Personal Digital Assistant*.

NEXIS See *LEXIS/NEXIS*.

NFS See *Network File System*.

NIC See *network information center, network interface card*.

nick A nickname on *Internet Relay Chat* (IRC). It is necessary for every user to 'pick a nick' and while this is sometimes the user's real name, it is often more fanciful.

NII See *National Information Infrastructure*.

Nintendo A Japanese company that produces hardware and software for games.

NIS See *Network Information Service*.

NISS See *National Information Services and Systems*.

NIST See *National Institute of Standards and Technology*.

NLP Network layer protocol, see *network layer*.

NNI See *network to network interface*.

NNTP See *Network News Transfer Protocol*.

NOC See *network operations center*.

node A *host* or device attached to a *network* or, more strictly, a point in a network where communications lines terminate or where a device is connected to the communications lines. Also used to describe a *hypertext* or *HTML* document.

noise Unwanted signals or information which interferes with the required information. This may be literal noise in telecommunications; it may be visual in computer *graphics*, where there are, say, spots on an image; or it may be metaphorical in the sense that a communication contains irrelevant information which obscures the real message.

non-interlaced Not using *interlacing*.

non-return to zero (NRZ) A binary encoding technique in which symbols 1 and 0 are represented by high and low voltages with no return to the zero reference voltage between bits.

non-return to zero inverted (NRZI) A binary encoding technique in which a signal is inverted for 1 and not inverted for 0, so that a voltage change means 1 and no change at the bit boundary means 0. It is also called *transition coding*.

Novell The company that sells *NetWare*, the most widely used operating system software for *local area networks* (LANs). Also sells other software, but has recently (1996) been selling and making acquisitions.

Novell NetWare Operating system for *local area network* from *Novell* running on *Ethernet*. Uses *IPX/SPX*, and *NetBIOS* or *TCP/IP* network protocols. It supports various operating systems, *MS-DOS*, *Windows*, *OS/2*, *Macintosh* and *Unix*.

NREN See *National Research and Education Network*.

NRS See *Name Registration Scheme*.

NRZ See *non-return to zero*.

NRZI See *non-return to zero inverted*.

NSF

NSF See *National Science Foundation*.

NSFNET See *National Science Foundation Network*.

nslookup A *Unix* program for querying an *Internet Domain Name Server* to find the *Internet address* corresponding to a given *host* name or vice versa.

NT See *Windows NT*.

NTIS See *National Technical Information Service*.

NTP See *Network Time Protocol*.

NTSC See *National Television Standards Committee*. Also used to describe the US television format defined by the Committee.

null characters Characters that have no effect on the meaning of a sequence of characters. May be used to pad fields to a required length or to fill in gaps between data blocks. Note that a null character usually has the *ASCII* value 0. (It is not the character zero, which has ASCII value 48.) Note also that the null character does have significance in some programming languages, for example C.

null-modem A special cable that is used to connect the *serial interfaces* of two computers, so that they can exchange data. Essentially it connects pin 2 (transmit) of the *RS-232-C* port of each computer to pin 3 (receive) of the port on the other computer. It also has a male connector at both ends.

O

object A combination of data that has a well-defined, distinct existence. This may be a graphic object, a group of database fields (see *object-oriented database*), a cell in a spreadsheet, a range of cells, or even an entire spreadsheet or a *video clip*. Such objects are handled in *object-oriented programming* and used by such systems and protocols as *object linking and embedding* (OLE). *Draw programs* treat *graphics* as objects, e.g., a line, a circle, a triangle, an irregular shape, etc. (See also *object-oriented design*.)

object graphics See *object-oriented graphics*.

Object Linking and Embedding (OLE) (Pronounced 'olé'.) A distributed *object system* and protocol from Microsoft. A general enhancement to *dynamic data exchange*, which makes it possible not only to include live data from one application, as an object, in another application, but also to edit the data in the original application without leaving the application in which the data has been included. OLE-2 is an improved version of OLE (1) and is a full implementation of object orientation, allowing access to parts of applications without loading the full application associated with the embedded object, so, for example, a spreadsheet's @function engine could be called up from within a word-processor, say to sum a column of numbers. (See also *OpenDoc*.)

object-oriented (OO) To do with *objects*. *Object-oriented graphics* and *object-oriented programming* appear to use the term in slightly different ways but, at a certain level, object-oriented graphics are a particular application of object-oriented programming. Similarly, while the use of objects in *Object Linking and Embedding* (OLE) seems at the *application* level to be transparent to the user, object-oriented programming underlies this.

object-oriented database (OODB) A system offering database management facilities in an *object-oriented programming* environment. Data is stored as *objects* and relationships are defined between objects. *Multimedia* applications can be handled as objects, with the type of multimedia object being part of the object's definition, so that it can be handled correctly (in a similar way to associating specific applications with specific file types).

object-oriented design (OOD) A design method in which a system is modelled as a collection of *objects* and objects are treated as belonging to a *class* within a hierarchy of classes, each class having properties and relationships with other classes, including inheritance, in which properties are 'inherited' from classes further up the hierarchy. Object-oriented design is one aspect of *object-oriented programming*.

object-oriented graphics (Also known as object graphics and *vector graphics*.) Shapes that

98

are represented mathematically, unlike *bitmap graphics*. In a *draw program* each circle, line, rectangle, etc. is a separate *object*, defined by control points of some kind (different kinds of shape have different kinds of control points; see, for example, *Bézier* curves). (See *vector graphics* for more details.) However, because each object has its own properties, once an object has been selected, it can be individually changed in as many ways as it has properties, length, width, orientation, colour, etc. Graphical objects can be selected by *clicking* or by using *marquee*. In addition, objects can be grouped to form composite objects. Objects can also be copied to other documents, using facilities such as *OLE*. *Scalable fonts* (also described as *vector fonts* and *outline fonts*) are also objects, having properties, some of which are defined by the font designer, while others are under the user's control.

object-oriented language A language for *object-oriented programming*. Examples are Smalltalk, C++, Modula-2, SIMULA-67 and now *Java*.

object-oriented programming (OOP) A type of programming which operates on *objects*, or data structures (see *object-oriented design*). Operations that can be performed on particular objects form part of those objects, and will be common to all objects in a particular *class*. This has great advantages in terms of the *user interface* in that, as long as the interface to an object remains consistent, other aspects of the program can be varied as necessary. (See *middleware*.) There are an increasing number of object-oriented languages. The release of *Java* has brought object orientation to the *World Wide Web*.

oblique Slanted, usually used of *type*, or sometimes *graphics*. Note that oblique type, that is, upright type slanted with the computer, is not the same as italic type, i.e., a font that has been designed as italic. However, if a *sans serif type* is used, it may only be the expert who can tell the difference; with serifed faces it should be clear to everyone!

OCLC See *Online Computer Library Center, Inc.*

OCR See *optical character recognition*.

octal A counting system based on 8, widely used in computing, essentially because it is based on powers of two (see *binary system*). The octal digits are 0–7 so that, for example, the decimal number 12 is 14 octal, while octal 10 is equivalent to decimal 8.

octet Eight bits. This term is used in *networking*, rather than *byte*, because some systems have bytes that are not eight bits long.

ODA See *Open Document Architecture* (originally Office Document Architecture).

ODIF See *Open Document Interchange Format*.

ODP See *Open Distributed Processing*.

Office Document Architecture (ODA) The original name for *Open Document Architecture*.

off-line The opposite of *on-line*, so that data cannot be transferred, for example, to a printer or a *network*. Many people read and write *email* messages off-line and then go on-line to send the new messages (see *off-line reader*). Off-line is also used on *Usenet* to mean private, i.e., a private (email) discussion, rather than inclusion in a public *newsgroup*. (See *on-line* for a discussion of hyphenation of these terms.)

off-line reader Software which allows *email* to be read and written off-line (generally to save telephone costs, when users connect to a *point of presence* via a *modem*).

OLE See *Object Linking and Embedding*.

OLE-2 See *Object Linking and Embedding*.

OLTP See *on-line transaction processing*.

OMR See *optical mark reader/optical mark recognition*.

one-way hash function A function that produces a fixed-length hash code from a variable-length message. It is impossible to determine the original message from the hash code. Used in *digital signatures*.

on-line Connected, so that data can be transferred, say, to a printer or a *network*. The opposite of *off-line*. There are different usages concerning hyphenation. Conventional grammatical usage tends to indicate that 'on line' and 'off line' (two words) are used adverbially, e.g., 'a user is on line', while 'on-line' and 'off-line' (with a hyphen) are used adjectivally, e.g., an on-line connection'. However, the use of online (as a single word), and less frequently offline, is becoming very common in both the adverbial and adjectival contexts.

Online Computer Library Center, Inc. (OCLC) A US not-for-profit membership organization offering computer-based services and research to libraries and educational organizations. Provides on-line library services, but has also hosted 'Electronic Journals' on line, over a dial-up link, including the world's first purely electronic journal 'Clinical Trials'. Previously used *Guidon* as its principal viewing software, but now is moving journals to the *World Wide Web*.

online public access catalogue (OPAC) A term used to describe any type of computerized library catalogue. The largest in the UK is that put up by the British Library.

on-line system Originally used to describe any system that allowed user interactivity with the computer. Subsequently used to describe large information providers, such as *DIALOG*, which allow searching and other interactivity. Now refers to almost any system accessed via a *modem* or *network*, more often than not a connection to the *Internet*.

on-line transaction processing (OLTP) The processing of transactions by computers in real time. Used widely in banking and financial institutions.

OO See *object-oriented*.

OOD See *object-oriented design*.

OODB See *object-oriented database*.

OOP See *object-oriented programming*.

OPAC See *online public access catalogue*.

open If applied to a file, either within a programming environment or via a *graphical user interface* (GUI), open means available for manipulation (editing, printing, etc.), as well as for writing to, so that a file must be opened before it is accessible by the user or by software. Open is also used to refer to systems which provide good connectivity. (See also *open systems*, where the term has a special meaning.)

Open Distributed Processing (ODP) A standard describing the extension of the *OSI application layer* communications architecture to the behaviour of the end system in order to make possible distributed multi-vendor systems.

OpenDoc An *object linking* architecture, with similarities to *OLE-2* (with which it is compatible), developed by Component Integration Laboratories (CILabs) and supported by leading vendors, including Apple and IBM. OpenDoc is based on *CORBA*, which OLE-2 is not, and is therefore a more *open* product. It aims to enable embedding of features from different *application* programs into a single working document in the same way as OLE-2, but will work over a wider range of operating systems. Note that, although it is described as an open document architecture, this can be confusing in that OpenDoc is quite different from *ODA* and is not concerned with structured documents in the sense that ODA and *SGML* are.

Open Document Architecture (ODA) (Originally called Office Document Architecture.) *ISO 8613* for describing *structured documents*. It has similarities with *SGML*, but also two main differences: firstly, it does not use simple *ASCII* coding and requires special software (and ideally hardware – only prototype systems have so far been constructed); while, secondly, it provides not only *generic coding* structures based on content, but also a coding system for formatted documents, based on blocks, pages, etc. It can therefore be used to exchange formatted documents, in either revisable or non-revisable forms (see *Open Document Interchange Format*).

Open Document Interchange Format (ODIF) The part of the *ODA* standard concerned with document interchange.

Open Journal Project An *Electronic Libraries* (e-Lib) project concerned with automatic cross-referencing and *hyperlinking electronic journals*. Makes use of *Webcosm* and *Linkboxes*.

Open Software Foundation (OSF) A consortium of computer companies, the aim of which was to develop a *Unix*-based *open systems* standard. Its first operating system release was called OSF/1.

open systems Systems that conform to *Open Systems Interconnect* or *POSIX* standards, almost all based on the *Unix* operating system. However, any system that can communicate with other systems is often described as an open system, particularly by vendors who wish to emphasize the connectivity of their system in contrast to the proprietary systems, such as large mainframe computers, which tied users to a single manufacturer.

Open Systems Interconnect (OSI) (Also called Open Systems Interconnection.) An *ISO* publication (ISO 7498: 1978) defining seven independent layers of communication protocols. Each layer utilizes the services of the layer immediately below it and provides a service to the layer above it, shielding the higher layer from the implementation details of the lower layer. In theory, this means that the layers can be developed independently. The layers, from lowest to highest are the *physical layer*, the *datalink layer*, the *network layer*, the *transport layer*, the *session layer*, the *presentation layer* and the *application layer*. There are various series of non-proprietary protocols and specifications based on OSI, including *ASN.1, BER, CMIP, CMIS, X.400, X.500* and *Z39.50*. (See also *peer-to-peer communication*.)

Open Systems Interconnection (OSI) An alternative term for *Open Systems Interconnect*.

OpenType A *font* specification combining *PostScript Type 1* and *TrueType* technologies, endorsed by all the major font developers. It is intended to remove font compatibility problems.

OpenWindows A *gui* server for Sun Microsystems *workstations*.

operating system The underlying computer software that controls the operation of a computer. Operating systems include *MS-DOS, UNIX, Windows 95, Windows NT, OS/2* and the *Macintosh* operating system.

optical character recognition (OCR) The recognition of printed or written characters by computer. Documents are scanned to produce a digital image (*bitmap*) of the text and then character-recognition software makes use of stored knowledge about the shapes of individual characters to convert the image into a text stream. There are various types of OCR programs, some simply dependent on matching character outlines, while others, based on formal or fuzzy logic or expert systems, utilize information about the characteristics of characters, such as how many cusps there are. OCR using such programs is sometimes referred to as *intelligent character recognition* (ICR). While the accuracy of OCR has improved in recent years, proofreading is still necessary, as even a 0.1% error rate (one character in a thousand) means about two errors in an average printed page!

optical disc A storage medium in which *laser* technology is used to write to and read from the disc. (Note that, because certain standards were spelt thus, the normal convention is to spell optical disc with a final 'c', while magnetic disk is spelt with a final 'k'.) Optical discs can be *analogue* (audio *CDs*) or *digital* (all discs used in computer applications). Types include *CD-Rom, CD-R, laser discs* and *WORM*.

optical fiber See *fibre optic transmission*. 'Fiber' is the US spelling; 'fibre' is otherwise used in this glossary.

optical fibre See *fibre optic transmission*.

optical mark reader (OMR) A scanning device that can read pencil marks on specially designed documents. Can either be optical (similar to *OCR*) or use *mark sensing*.

optical mark recognition (OMR) The use of an *optical mark reader* in *mark sensing*.

Oracle The original name for the UK Independent Television *teletext* service, now, rather confusingly, called 'Teletext'. (Oracle is also the name of one of the world's largest relational database companies.)

O/R address See *originator/recipient address*.

Orange One of the principle providers of mobile communications networks in the UK.

Orange Book The US government's document that characterizes secure computing architectures and defines levels A1 (most secure) through D (least secure).

originator/recipient address (O/R address) A structured address used in *X.400* mail.

ornaments Another term for *dingbats*.

orphan The first line of a paragraph alone at the bottom of a column or page (in printed material). Occasionally used to mean the last line of a paragraph at the top of a page (more commonly described as a *widow* or widow line). Widows and orphans are generally not a problem with *electronic publishing* (onscreen) as the text can easily be scrolled to show subsequent lines (unless a page-based program, such as *Acrobat*, is used).

OS/2 An *operating system*, originally developed jointly by IBM and Microsoft and planned to be a successor to *MS-DOS*. However, once the cooperation between the companies ended, IBM continued to develop OS/2, as OS/2 Warp, while Microsoft extended its development to produce *Windows NT*.

OSF See *Open Software Foundation*.

OSI See *Open Systems Interconnect*.

outline font (Also described as a *vector font* or *scalable font*.) A *font* that is stored in terms of its outline shape rather than as a *bitmap*. Because it is a type of *object-oriented graphic*, an outline font can be scaled to any size and transformed, e.g., by sloping or just using the outline. The most common types of outline fonts are *PostScript* and *TrueType*. In addition, *PCL 5* uses outline fonts to print. Normally, the fonts are stored in association with the printer or software *RIP* and the output bitmaps generated on the fly at the appropriate printer (or screen) *resolution*.

outline graphics Another term for *vector* or *object-oriented graphics*.

overhead In communications, all the information that is transmitted in addition to the user data. This may include control and status information, routing information, error-detection information and any repeated data. The term is also used in other contexts, with a similar meaning.

P

pabx See *private (automatic) branch exchange*.

packet A block, or specified number of bytes, which contains both control information and data. Can be sent by *connectionless* (*packet switching*) or *connection-oriented* communications.

packet assembler/disassembler (PAD) Device (can be hardware or software) for splitting a data stream into discrete *packets* so that it can be transmitted over the specified medium and then the packets recombined at the receiver. Most often used in connection with *X.25* systems.

packet driver Software for *local area networks* (LANs) that divides data into *packets* for transmission over a network. It also reassembles the packets of incoming data so that *application programs* can read the data as a continuous stream, as if arriving at a *serial port*. The use of packet drivers allows multiple *applications* to share the same *network interface* at the *datalink layer*. Different types of packet driver allow applications to make more or less use of network facilities.

Packet InterNet Groper (PING) A program which is used to check whether hosts can be reached. PING sends an *ICMP* echo request and waits for a reply, reporting success or failure, together with various statistics. The term is also used as a verb, so that pinging means running the program and sending the signal. The acronym was probably devised in analogy with the sound produced by ASDIC equipment, when looking for submarines.

packet radio (PR) Communication between computers using amateur (HAM) radio. Can be used for *email* etc. Can be connected through the *Internet* and has a special *domain* in *IP* space. Must be used only by licensed radio amateurs (HAMs).

packet-switched See *packet switching*.

packet switching A data transmission technique in which *packets* (messages or parts of messages) are *routed* between *hosts*, with no previously established communication path. Each packet is individually addressed and will be routed to its destination by the most expedient route, determined by some routing algorithm. The receiving computer reassembles the packets into the correct sequence. Packets travelling between two hosts, even those which are part of a single message, may not follow the same route. Packet switching optimizes *bandwidth* use and reduces *latency*. Packet switching is also called *connectionless*. It is the opposite of *circuit switching* or *connection-oriented communication*. (See also *virtual circuit*, *X.25*.)

packet switch node (PSN) A computer used in a *packet-switched network* to accept, *route* and forward *packets*.

Packet SwitchStream (PSS) BT's *packet-switched* network.

PAD See *packet assembler/disassembler*.

page description language (PDL) A language used to describe, in a device-independent way, the content and layout of a page after formatting. Used to drive *laserprinters* and *imagesetters* and sometimes *screens*. The PDL is interpreted by a *raster image processor*, which converts the language into a *bitmap* for output at the appropriate resolution. The de facto standard is Adobe's *PostScript*, which has been used as the basis for *Standard Page Description Language* (SPDL) and has now been extended as *Supra*, but there are other languages, such as Xerox's *Interpress* (which was probably the first such language) as well as Hewlett-Packard's *Printer Control Language* (PCL). Such programs are usually *object-oriented*. PDLs can also be used for interchange and storage of formatted documents.

page layout program See *desktop publishing (DTP)*.

PageMaker The original *DTP* program; still a leading product. Its main rival is *QuarkXPress*.

page make-up The use of a *page-layout* or *DTP* program to arrange text and pictures on a page.

page-oriented printer See *page printer*.

page printer (Or *page-oriented printer*.) A printer in which the complete image of a page is formed and then printed. Page printers generally use a *page description language*. Virtually all printers used in graphic arts and the printing industry are page printers, including *imagesetters* as well as *laserprinters*. The term was originally developed to distinguish these printers from line printers, such as dot-matrix and daisy-wheel printers. *Inkjet printers* can use either method.

pager (Also called a bleeper.) A small personal radio (receive-only) which is used to alert the person using it. Models are also available to which short messages can be sent.

paint program A software application that provides the ability to create and edit *bitmaps*. Also called *image-editing software*. (Contrast with a *draw program*, used for editing *vector graphics*.)

PAL See *phase alternate/alternating line*.

palette An analogy to the paint palette used by artists, this is a *window* showing the colours available for use in a *paint* or *draw program*. The colours available in the palette will depend on the *screen* resolution (and thus the number of colours) chosen. (See *CMYK*, *RGB*, *colour* and related entries.)

Palo Alto Research Center See *Xerox PARC*.

Panorama A *browser* for *SGML* documents, produced by SoftQuad, Inc., which can be used in conjunction with an *HTML* browser, such as *Netscape Navigator*, to view SGML documents over the *World Wide Web*.

Pantone A colour matching and specification system, in which each colour has a name (and number). Originally, the colours were produced as a book, so that the appropriate colour could be reproduced (printed). However, absolute matching could be guaranteed only if Pantone inks were used and *spot colours* used (rather than *CMYK*). Pantone *palettes* are now available in many *draw* and *paint programs* although, in these cases, any colour selection can only be as accurate as the *colour gamut* of the screen allows. However, many programs will output a *colour separation* for each Pantone colour (using a *page description language*), so that the appropriate ink can be used by a printer. For *electronic publishing*, there will inevitably be some variation in what users see, depending on the hardware they are using and how it is set up. (See *colour* and related entries.)

Pantone Matching System (PMS)   See *Pantone*.

paragraph formatting   The application of a format or style (including such factors as typeface, typestyle, indents, space before and after) to a whole paragraph in a *desktop publishing* system or *word-processor*. To use paragraph formatting, it is usually unnecessary to select the whole paragraph, as long as the cursor position is within the paragraph. (Contrast with *character formatting*, where only the selected characters are affected.)

parallel communication   Data transfer in which each *bit* is transferred along its own line, in contrast to *serial connection*, in which bits are transferred one at a time. Parallel communication is generally used only over short distances, mainly because data integrity is lost over longer distances.

parallel interface   An interface over which *parallel communication* is carried out. Also called a *Centronics interface*.

parallel port   See *parallel communications*. Usually, 'parallel port' describes the physical connection on a computer, most frequently used for connecting printers.

PARC   See *Xerox PARC*.

parity   In general, being either odd or even. In computing and communications, however, parity usually means the number of 1s, as opposed to 0s, in a *byte* or *word*. A redundant parity bit is added to each byte and this is set to make the number of 1 bits in the byte even (for even parity) or odd (for odd parity). Parity bits are a basic form of *error detection*, but will detect only single bit errors because, if an even number of the bits are incorrect, then the parity bit will not show this. Also, unlike more complex *error detection and correction* systems, it is impossible to tell which bit is wrong. (See also *checksum*.)

parity error   An error discovered by checking the *parity*.

parser   An algorithm or program which is used to check the syntactic structure of a file or *structured document*. For example, an *SGML* parser checks that a *document instance* (i.e., a document coded in SGML) corresponds to the specified *Document Type Definition* and will report any errors. SGML parsers are often integrated with editing programs, so that documents can be parsed as they are created or edited.

passive matrix   A design of *liquid crystal display*.

password   A secret (or private) arbitrary string of characters which has to be typed into a computer in order to allow access to a system or a particular program. Normally it is not displayed on the screen, so that it remains private. There are many recommendations about choosing and changing passwords. The main problem is choosing something which is easy to remember and yet difficult for someone else to guess.

paste   To insert text or graphics from the *clipboard* into an open document.

path   The explicitly routed, node-by-node, *Internet address* or the link between two machines. (See also *bang path*.) Path is also used in computer operating systems to specify the order in which directories should be accessed when a program (or executable file) is called.

PBEM   See *play by electronic mail*.

PBM   See *play by electronic mail*.

PBX   See *private (automatic) branch exchange*.

PCI   See *Peripheral Component Interconnect*.

PCL   See *Printer Command Language*.

PCM   See *Pulse Code Modulation*.

PCMCIA   See *Personal Computer Memory Card International Association*.

PCN   See *personal communication network*.

PC/NFS   A version of *NFS* that will allow PCs to connect over an *Ethernet* to a *Unix* system

PCS   (Personal communication services, the US term.) See *personal communication network*.

pcx   A widely used *bitmap graphics* format, originally developed for the program PC Paintbrush by Z-Soft. The filename extension is '.pcx'.

PD See *public domain*.

PDA See *personal digital assistant*.

pdf See *portable document format*.

PDH See *plesiochronous digital hierarchy*.

PDL See *page description language*.

PDS Public domain software. See *public domain*.

PDU See *protocol data unit*.

PeaceNet A *network* concerned with issues of peace and social justice, including human rights, disarmament and international relations. (See *Institute for Global Communications*.)

peer A communications unit (hardware or software) on the same *protocol layer* of a network as another. (See also *peer-to-peer communication*.)

peer-to-peer communication Communication between *peers* using *layered protocols*. Protocol stacks are actually connected only at the physical layer, but it is possible to consider them as linked at higher levels in terms of the services provided by the lower layers. Peer-to-peer communication means connection between corresponding systems in each layer. A useful analogy is two people who are talking to one another: at the physical layer, communication is the result of changes in air-pressure waves generated by one person's larynx and detected by the other person's ear; while the higher layers (on the detection side) will include the conversion of these pressure changes into signals, understanding of language; and, finally, at the top level, understanding of the topics under discussion. Communications between computer systems work in a similar way. (See *OSI seven-layer model*.) The term is also used to describe communication between directly connected *Internet* segments, only one *hop* apart.

peer-to-peer network A group of computers, usually PCs, connected with network cards and cable. Each workstation is as important as its *peers*, acting both as *client* and *server*. With appropriate software, it is possible for each computer to see the disk drives of every computer as a local drive. There is no separate *file server*.

PEIPA See *Pilot European Image Processing Archive*.

PEM See *Privacy Enhanced Mail*.

Pentium A series of chips developed by *Intel*, widely used in PCs, especially those handling *multimedia*.

Peripheral Component Interconnect (PCI) A *local bus* designed by *Intel*. It is more efficient than the *VESA* local bus, running at 33 MHz. It is used on *Pentium*-based computers but is processor-independent.

PERL (Practical Extraction and Report Language.) An interpreted computer language mainly used for processing and converting text and text strings. It is widely used in developing *World Wide Web* tools and applications.

permissions Authorization to read or write a file or to execute a program. Forms an integral part of the *Unix* operating system but, as Unix is the operating system used by most *servers* on the *Internet*, will be encountered by anyone using utilities such as *ftp* and *telnet*.

personalcast See *narrowcast*.

personal communication network (PCN) The communications network based on cellular and fixed telephone networks. (Called PCS, personal communication services, in the USA.)

personal communication services (PCS) The US term for *personal communication network*.

Personal Computer Memory Card International Association (PCMCIA) (Also sometimes 'People Can't Memorize Computer Industry Acronyms'.) A group of manufacturers which developed the cards used for peripherals in (mainly) portable/notebook computers. These cards are described as PCMCIA cards and include memory circuits, modems, network adapters and even disk drives.

personal digital assistant (PDA) A small hand-held computer. Many, including the Apple *Newton*, will now take hand-writing input. The original idea was that eventually PDAs will become multi-functional, acting as telephones, faxes and remote terminals to other systems, as well as providing local services, such as a diary, scheduler, etc. *BT* has already produced a prototype which straps to the wrist.

personal identification device (PID) A device, such as a magnetic card, which carries machine readable identification, so as to provide authorization for access to a computer system. PIDs are often used in conjunction with PIN numbers in, for example, *automatic teller machines*. (See also *smartcard*.)

personal identification number (PIN) A *password* which is used for access, either physical via a digital door lock, or to a computer system. Often used in conjunction with a *PID*.

personal information manager (PIM) Software that includes a diary, address book, etc., as well as various other programs, which may include small databases and basic spreadsheets (for expenses). May well be used on a *personal digital assistant* and potentially can be extended to include personal communications.

PGP See *Pretty Good Privacy*.

phase alternate/alternating line (PAL) The television standard used in most European countries. France, which uses *SECAM*, is the principal exception. (See also *NTSC*.)

phase modulation An alternative term for *phase shift keying*.

phase shift keying (PSK) A *modulation* technique used to transmit digital information. The phase angle of the carrier wave is changed to represent the values of different bits (or groups of bits).

PHIGS (Programmers Hierarchical Interactive Graphics System.) A three-dimensional *graphics* standard including language-independent functions for *applications* that produce computer-generated images on either *raster* or *vector-graphic* output devices.

Philips Dutch electronics company. Has had great influence, with *Sony*, on the development and standardization of the *CD*. In particular, developed *compact disc interactive* (CD-i) and, jointly with Kodak, the *Kodak Photo CD*.

PhoneNet A networking system connecting devices that are *AppleTalk*-compatible. It uses ordinary telephone cabling.

Phong shading A method of shading or *rendering* used in *animation*. It is similar to Gouraud surface shading but instead of the colour being linearly interpolated between normals to adjacent polygons, the normals themselves are interpolated, so that there is one normal per *pixel* in the rendering window, from which the colour shades are calculated. The results are similar to Gouraud shading, except that any reflections on the surface of an object are sharper. Phong shading also allows detailed editing of the rendering.

Photo CD See *Kodak Photo CD*.

photo retouching The modification of (usually *scanned*) *bitmap* images, using *image-editing* or *paint programs*.

photonics The optical equivalent of electronics, i.e., transmission of information using photons rather than electrons, or light instead of electricity. Often used as an equivalent for *fibre optics*.

Photoshop An image manipulation (*paint*) program from *Adobe*. Probably the most widely used such program in the graphic arts industry.

physical addressing The *Ethernet* low-level addressing scheme. Uses a 48-bit address in a single *packet*. (See also *Internet address*.)

physical layer The lowest layer in the *OSI seven-layer model*. It is concerned with the electrical and mechanical connections and *MAC*. It is used by the *datalink layer*. Typical physical layer protocols are *CSMA/CD* and *token ring*.

pica A typographical unit of measurement. Each pica is divided into 12 points. Although originally 6 picas equalled 0.996 of an inch, in the development of *PostScript* the point has been standardized, so that there are 72 points per inch (thus on a screen with 72 *pixels per inch*, one pixel equals one point). Although most *desktop publishing*, *word-processor* and *graphics* programs allow size specification in inches or centimetres, typographic units are almost always another option. Typesize is always specified in points. Pica was also used for typewriters with 10 characters per inch, as opposed to 'elite', which had 12 characters per inch. Pica and elite are sometimes used to describe typefaces, but really refer to pitch. (See also *font size*.)

PICS See *Platform for Internet Content Selection*.

PICT A *graphic file format* used on the Apple Macintosh. The format uses *QuickDraw* to display images onscreen. PICT is not *PostScript*-compatible and the incompatibilities can lead to unpredictable results.

Picture Quality Scale (PQS) A system in which image quality is rated on the basis of image features that are perceived by the human eye, rather than on the *signal-to-noise ratio*, in which quality is assessed *pixel* by pixel.

PID See *personal identification device*.

PII See *Publisher Item Identifier*.

Pilot European Image Processing Archive (PEIPA) An archive at the University of Essex, UK devoted to *image processing, computer vision* and *computer graphics*. It includes software, images (such as weather satellite pictures) and reference material. The archive is funded by the British Machine Vision Association.

PIM See *personal information manager*.

PIN See *personal identification number, positive intrinsic negative*.

Pine (Program for Internet News & Email.) A menu-driven program, running under *Unix*, for reading, editing, sending, and managing electronic messages.

PING See *Packet InterNet Groper*.

ping An alternative name for (and the pronunciation of) the *Portable Network Graphics* (PNG) format.

Pink operating system An *object-oriented operating system* being developed jointly by IBM and Apple. Now officially called *Taligent*.

pipelining Breaking information up into *packets* which traverse networks successively. This leads to fewer network delays.

Pipex A UK *Internet* provider to other commercial companies and public-sector organizations. Services include a commercial *internetworking* service and a *backbone* with multiple international links. Pipex uses re-sellers connected to its backbone to provide services to end-users.

pixel An abbreviation for 'picture element' (or 'picture cell'). The smallest resolvable rectangular area that can be displayed onscreen or stored in memory. In a monochrome image the pixel may be just black or white but, if *grey scales* are used, then each pixel will have its own brightness, from 0 for black to the maximum value (255 for an eight-bit pixel) for white. On a colour monitor, each pixel is made up of a triple of red, green and blue phosphors (see *RGB*) and each is controlled by a number of bits (see *8-bit colour, 24-bit colour*). This will affect the *palette* and will be related to the *screen resolution*. (Compare *voxel*.)

pixmap (A contraction of 'pixel map'.) A three-dimensional array of bits that corresponds to a two-dimensional array of *pixels*, so that properties or attributes can be associated with specific pixels. Can be thought of as a stack of N *bitmaps*. Is used in *X windows* and *QuickDraw GX*. Improves handling of *icon* images and *animation*. A pixmap can be used only on the screen on which it was created.

PKUNZIP A program for decompressing files compressed with *PKZIP*.

pkzip Probably the most widely used file *compression* and archiving utility on PCs. Also used for transferring files over the Internet. It uses a variation on the *sliding window compression* algorithm. (See also *PKUNZIP, gzip*.) There is also a related Windows version, *WinZip*.

plain ASCII Means just the real *ASCII* characters including none of the *extended ASCII* characters. (See *flat ASCII*.)

plaintext A message before *encryption* or after *decryption*, in its readable form, rather than its encrypted form. (Compare with *ciphertext*.)

platform A rather loose term, which means a combination of a particular computer and *operating system*.

Platform for Internet Content Selection (PICS) An infrastructure for associating labels (*metadata*) with *Internet* content. Originally designed to help parents and teachers control what children access on the Internet, it can also be used to cover other aspects, including privacy and *intellectual property* rights.

play by electronic mail (PBEM, PBM) A kind of game in which the players use *email* to communicate. A natural extension of 'play by mail' games in which the players use *snailmail*.

Playstation A games console produced by *Sony*.

plesiochronous Nearly synchronized. A term describing a communication system where transmitted signals have the same nominal digital rate, described as bit-synchronous, but are synchronized on different clocks of comparable accuracy and stability. Signals can be regarded as plesiochronous if significant events occur at nominally the same rate, with any variation in rate constrained within specified limits.

plesiochronous digital hierarchy (PDH) A transmission system for voice and data communication using *plesiochronous* synchronization. PDH is the conventional *multiplexing* technology for networks, including *ISDN*, but is gradually being replaced by *SONET* and other SDH (*synchronous digital hierarchy*) schemes.

Plexus A *World Wide Web server*.

plug-in A term describing *applications* associated with *Netscape Navigator* (although the term is now used more widely). Plug-ins are rather like *applets*, in that they enable certain types of file, e.g., *QuickDraw* movies, to be accessed from within Netscape Navigator.

PMS See *Pantone Matching System*.

PNG See *Portable Network Graphics, ping*.

POC See *point of contact*.

POE See *PowerOpen Environment*.

point (*noun*) A typographical unit of measure, one-twelfth of a pica. (See *pica* for more details.)

point (*verb*) To locate a *pointing device* (usually the *cursor*, controlled by a *mouse*) on a screen item, such as a word, menu or icon, in a *graphical user interface* (GUI). (See *point-and-click*.)

point-and-click To *point* at something on the screen and then *click* a *mouse* button. This is a common way of selecting an item, such as an *icon*, a *menu* item or a word in a *graphical user interface* (GUI). However, it is a somewhat generic, not to say ambiguous, term, in that sometimes it means point-and-click (once), sometimes it means point and double-click, while occasionally it really means point and then hold the mouse button down. (See *drag and drop*.)

PointCast A free service, based on *push technology* and providing personalized delivery of public information, such as news, weather, sport, etc. Displays the information in a *screen saver*. A later rival service is *HeadLiner*. (See also *BackWeb, Castanet, Netscape Netcaster*.)

pointer (See *pointing device*.) Also, within certain computer programming languages, pointers are used to describe the location of data. (See also *hash table*.)

pointing device A device used to control the movement of a pointer or cursor on the screen, usually in a *graphical user interface* (GUI). The *mouse* is the most common pointing device, but *trackballs, joysticks, graphics tablets* and *light pens* are others which are used in particular applications and situations. Pointing devices always carry at least one button, which allows the user to *point-and-click*.

point of contact (POC) An individual who is associated with a particular *Internet* entity (*network, domain, ASN*, etc.).

point of presence (PoP) A site, run by an *Internet service provider*, which users can access via *modem* or *ISDN* connections. Such a site will usually have banks of modems and other telecommunications, together with access to an *Internet backbone*. PoPs may be geographically distributed to improve access and keep telephone costs down. *Virtual PoPs* may also be accessible through third parties.

point of sale (POS) The place in a shop (or other business operation) where a sale is transacted, e.g., a supermarket checkout. (See *point-of-sale terminal, EFTPOS, electronic funds transfer*.)

point-of-sale terminal (POS terminal) A computer terminal (often part of the checkout equipment – or cash register) used in shops to input and output data at the *point of sale*. At a POS terminal, information about items sold is input, often using a *barcode* or *Kimball tag*. Details of price etc. are then retrieved from a central computer and a fully itemized receipt is printed. The transaction may also provide input to a stock-control system and be used for aspects of market research. In addition, it may be possible for *electronic funds transfer* to be carried out from the POS terminal. (See *EftpOS*.)

point-to-point A circuit connecting two *nodes* directly.

Point-to-Point Protocol (PPP) The protocol which provides the *Internet* standard method for transmitting *IP packets* over *serial point-to-point* links. PPP was designed to be an improvement on *SLIP*, operating both over *asynchronous* connections and bit-oriented *synchronous* systems.

Polite Agent A patented agent that is part of *BackWeb* and monitors on-line activity.

polling Checking every so often to see if an operation needs to be carried out, for example if there is email to be transferred from a server. The term is sometimes also used to include actually carrying out the operation itself.

POP See *Post Office Protocol*.

PoP See *point of presence*.

POP3 Version 3 of the *Post Office Protocol*. Email software often provides this as an alternative to *SMTP*.

pop-up menu A *menu* that is brought to the screen by clicking on a word or *icon*, which can be anywhere on the screen, or even in some applications just by *clicking* the right *mouse* button.

port A socket or 'input/output connector' to which a cable is connected, (usually) on the back of hardware, such as computers, monitors and peripheral devices. There are many different kinds of ports, e.g., *parallel ports*, *serial ports* and *SCSI ports*, as well as *video*, *audio* and *MIDI* ports. In fact, there will potentially be a port for every kind of connection protocol. Port is also used to describe the logical channel in a communications system and *TCP* and *UDP transport layer* protocols use port numbers on *Ethernet* and the *Internet* to demultiplex messages. Each *application program* has a unique port number

which is associated with it so that, for example, by default *finger* uses port 79 and *telnet* port 23, while *HTTP* uses port 80. Port, used as a verb, means rewriting software so that it will run on a different operating system or platform.

portable document Any document — for instance, in *pdf format*, *SGML* or *HTML* — which can be transferred between systems.

portable document format (pdf) The format used by *Adobe Acrobat* files. Note that *pdf* files are not the only *portable documents*.

Portable Network Graphics (PNG) A new (1995) graphics format for compressed, *lossless* bitmapped image files. Introduced to replace *GIF*, partly because of GIF's shortcomings, but also because Unisys is claiming copyright to *LZW* compression, which is the basis of GIF.

Portable Pixmap (PPM) A colour *image file format*. (See *graphic file format*.)

portrait The orientation of a picture, *screen* or page, such that its height is greater than its width. Most books, and certainly journals, are *portrait*. (See also *landscape*, *aspect ratio*.)

POS See *point of sale*.

positive intrinsic negative (PIN) A type of detector used in *fibre-optic* data links.

POSIX An acronym loosely based on 'portable operating system interface for computing environments', the 'X' indicating the association with *Unix*. A set of *IEEE* standards that describe how applications can be written so that they can run unchanged on different systems. This was one approach to making interfaces to operating systems vendor-independent. Unix was the basis of POSIX but subsequently other vendors have changed their (proprietary) operating systems to become POSIX-compliant, which means that they provide an *open systems* interface and are able to communicate with all other POSIX-compliant systems. *Open Systems Interconnect* (OSI) is a related approach to solving the same problem.

post To send an *email* message, usually to a *mailing list* or a *newsgroup*. (Contrast with *mail*, which is generally used to mean sending a message to specific recipients.)

posterization A technique in which the number of colours or *grey levels* in a *bitmap image* is reduced, with the effect that there is no longer a continuous variation in the shades. *Paint (image editing) programs* often have this as an editing option.

postmaster Both the person who supervises electronic mail at a particular site on the *Internet* and a special *email* address set up to which any messages regarding the email service at that site, e.g., problems or queries, should be sent. This allows messages to be *aliased* to the person who is acting as postmaster (not necessarily the same person all the time).

Post Office Protocol (POP) A protocol designed to allow single-user hosts to access mail from a server, either over a *network* or a *modem* link. There are three versions: POP, POP2 and POP3, and the latter two are not backwards compatible. These versions were developed to make the protocol available to a wider range of hosts. POP3 is often used as an alternative to *SMTP*.

PostScript The *object-oriented page description language* created by *Adobe Systems* (based on earlier work at *Xerox PARC*; see *Interpress*), which has become the *de facto* standard and the basis for the *Standard Page Description Language*. PostScript is both *device* independent and *resolution* independent, in that PostScript files can be output on any device equipped with a PostScript *raster image processor* and such output will be at the resolution for that device. While PostScript is mainly used for printing, there is a version called *Display PostScript* which allows documents to be printed to the screen, although it is used on few computer systems. (See also *NeWS*.) Adobe has subsequently developed *PostScript Level 2*, as well as *Acrobat* and *portable document format* (pdf), based on PostScript, and recently (1996) a new format called *Supra*, which will effectively provide much of the functionality of PostScript within a pdf-like environment. (See also *Printer Control Language*, *TrueType*, *Encapsulated PostScript* (EPS).)

PostScript clone A *raster image processor* (hardware or software) that will interpret *PostScript*, but is not using the true *Adobe* PostScript interpreter. These processors are also described as PostScript compatible. Such interpreters, e.g., *GhostScript*, may either be available as *public domain* software or — even if they are commercial products, such as *Hyphen* — they may be cheaper (partly because there is no royalty payment to Adobe) or provide features not available in PostScript itself.

PostScript fonts See *outline fonts*, which form part of the *PostScript* language. It was in PostScript that such fonts were first widely used. There are two types of font, *Type 1* and *Type 3*. Type 1 fonts use *hinting* and Adobe's proprietary format, while for Type 3 fonts there is no hinting and the format is publicly available. Type 1 fonts can be interpreted by *Adobe Type Manager* (ATM) for display onscreen, while Type 3 cannot. Similar font technologies are *TrueType* and *QuickDraw GX*. A new font specification, *OpenType*, has recently been developed with the aim of removing font compatibility problems. (See also *Supra*.)

PostScript Level 2 An improved version of *PostScript*. Features include: better handling of colour *halftone* screening and colour matching; compression for large files; and more facilities for handling Japanese Kanji and other Asian-language fonts. Not all PostScript printers will handle Level 2 and many users will not require most of the features. (See also *Supra*.)

PostScript Level 3 An even further improved version of *PostScript*, intended to provide enhanced image technology, faster page processing, closer integration with the *World Wide Web* and 'PlanetReady' printing to handle local language needs in different parts of the world.

post, telephone and telegraph administration (PTT) A provider of a public telecommunications service, e.g., British Telecom or Mercury in the UK and the Bell operating companies in the USA. May also be involved with setting national standards and policy on telecommunications issues.

POTS Plain old telephone system. See *public switched telephone network*.

Power Macintosh See Apple Computer's *Macintosh*, based on the *PowerPC* chip. A significant difference from earlier Macintoshes is that, although it is designed to be used with Macintosh operating system, *System 7.5*, other operating systems can also be used. (See also *PowerOpen Environment*.)

PowerOpen Environment (POE) A definition containing *API* and *ABI* specifications based on the architecture of the *PowerPC* processor. It is similar to *POSIX*, but goes further as it includes *binary* compatibility.

PowerPC A *RISC* microprocessor jointly designed by Motorola, IBM and Apple Computer. Used in the *Power Macintosh* and various IBM models.

PPM See *Portable Pixmap*.

PPP See *Point-to-Point Protocol*.

PQS See *Picture Quality Scale*.

PR See *packet radio*.

Premiere Desktop *video* editing software from Adobe.

presentation graphics A program which can be used for slide presentations. Such presentations can now usually incorporate a range of *multimedia* features and can be presented electronically.

presentation layer The second-highest layer (layer 6) in the *ISO seven-layer model*. This layer is concerned with aspects such as text *compression* (*encryption*) and code or format conversion. Provides service to the *application layer* and accesses the features of the *session layer*.

Presentation Manager The *graphical user interface* (GUI) in IBM's *OS/2 operating system*.

Prestel *Viewdata* service provided by *BT*, in which information is presented on a television screen but accessed via the telephone network.

Pretty Good Privacy (PGP) A high-security *RSA*-based *public-key encryption* application for secure *email* communication, providing privacy and authentication. (See also *Privacy Enhanced Mail* (PEM).)

PRI See *ISDN primary rate interface*. (See also *basic rate ISDN* (BRI).)

primary rate interface (PRI) A type of *ISDN* connection, which in North America and Japan consists of 24 × 64 kbps channels (B – 'bearer' – channels) for speech or data, plus a 16 kbps channel (D – 'delta'– channel) used for signalling and control purposes, based on the *T-1* interface. Elsewhere, PRI usually has 30 B channels and 1 D channel, and is based on the *E-1* interface. PRI is typically used for commercial connections.

primary rate ISDN See *primary rate interface*.

PRIMIS A service set up by publisher McGraw-Hill as a form of *document delivery*, such that academics could make up customized textbooks from parts of books published by McGraw-Hill and collaborating publishers.

Printer Command Language (PCL) A *page description language* developed by Hewlett-Packard for its LaserJet and DeskJet printers. Early versions simply included a string of instructions, indicating what to put where and, for example, were unable to handle *scalable fonts*, needing *bitmap fonts* for each size specified. The latest version, PCL Level 5, which first appeared in the LaserJet III, has many of the features of *PostScript*. Generally, PCL printers require less memory than PostScript printers and are therefore cheaper.

print server A *server* (or computer) that handles the printer access and buffering for a *network*.

Privacy Enhanced Mail (PEM) *Internet email* which provides privacy, authentication and message integrity using various combinations of *DES* and *RSA encryption* methods. (See also *Pretty Good Privacy* (PGP), *RIPEM*.)

private (automatic) branch exchange (PABX/PBX) A switching telephone exchange located within an organization to connect users both internally and to the public telephone network.

private key See *public-key encryption*.

private line Another term for a *dedicated circuit* or line.

process colour(s) The four colours *CMYK*, used in printing and the *colour separation* process.

Procomm A PC-based communications program widely used for accessing *bulletin boards*. There are various versions for both DOS and Windows.

Prodigy An on-line service developed in the USA by IBM and Sears (an advertising company). Provides electronic mail and information, although files cannot be downloaded, as well as shopping and travel arrangements. Includes commercials. However, is also now acting as a host for *World Wide Web* pages, which can be accessed (and downloaded) in the usual way.

Project Gutenberg A collection of electronic texts at the University of Illinois at Urbana-Champaign, USA, available for wide distribution over the *Internet*. The first text on-line was the Declaration of Independence and it is hoped to have 10 000 texts by the year 2001.

promiscuous mode A communications mode in which all *packets* are accepted, irrespective of their actual destination addresses.

propagation delay The time taken for a signal to travel from one end of a transmission channel to the other. Within optical fibres, signals travel at the speed of light, while the propagation speed in electrical cables is half to three-quarters of that. (Compare with *latency*.)

proportional fonts See *proportional spacing*.

proportional spacing Spacing letters in text so that each takes up its own width, rather than all taking the same width (see *monospaced fonts*). Thus 'm' and 'w' take up a comparatively wide space and 'i' a narrow one. Virtually all material is now set in proportionally spaced fonts, whether for printing or display on the screen. (See also *hyphenation, justification*.) In one sense, monospaced fonts can be seen as a transient development, forced on users by the limitations of the mechanical typewriter; handwriting is, after all, proportionally spaced.

Prospero A distributed file system containing virtual files on a central *host*, each one representing an *Internet* resource. For example, a file may represent a telnet session to a particular host or a file which is available using ftp, together with the information needed to obtain that file. Prospero can thus be used to integrate Internet information services, including *Gopher, WAIS, Archie*, and the *World Wide Web*.

protocol In general, an agreed set of rules on how something should be carried out. In communications and networks, these govern areas such as data format, timing, sequencing, access and error control and syntax of messages. Different layers of the *OSI seven-layer model* use different protocols.

protocol converter A program or hardware device to translate between different *protocols* concerned with the same function.

protocol data unit (PDU) A *packet* of data which is passed across a *network* at a specific layer of the *OSI seven layer model* using a specific *protocol*.

protocol stack A set of *protocols* which work together on a layered model to provide a set of communications functions, so that each *layer* uses the protocols of the layer below it to provide a service to the layer above. The *OSI seven-layer model* provides a standard framework within which such a protocol stack can be defined.

proximity search A *searching* technique in which, for example, one is able to search for the ocurrence of a group of characters within, say, 20 words of another group or groups.

proxy Using one *Internet address* name to mean another. This is usually done by a *host* answering *Address Resolution Protocol* (ARP) requests intended for another host and rerouting *packets* to the actual destination. A *listserv* is a kind of proxy.

proxy gateway See *proxy server*.

proxy server A server which controls indirect access to an *Internet server*, so that external systems, excluded for security reasons by a *firewall* can communicate (also described as a *proxy gateway*). The term is also used, particularly on the *World Wide Web*, to describe a server that holds a *cache* of files or documents, in order that they can be accessed more quickly or easily. Any documents requested which it does not hold, it will obtain from the remote server and save a copy so that when the user next requests that document, it will be available more quickly.

PS, ps Both an abbreviation for *PostScript* and the file extension which is often used for PostScript files.

quadrature amplitude modulation (QAM)

PSDN See *public switched data network*.

PSK See *phase shift keying*.

PSN See *packet switch node*.

PSS See *Packet SwitchStream*.

PSTN See *public switched telephone network*.

PTT See *post, telephone and telegraph administration*.

public carrier A provider of a public telecommunications service. (See *PTT*.)

public domain (PD) If *intellectual property* (books, computer programs, images, etc.) is in the public domain, it is available to anyone without charge. Most commonly, this applies to public domain software, which is usually software developed on behalf of the US government and which by law has to be available in this way. It is important to distinguish such software from *shareware*, which is not free, or at least free only for evaluation.

public key See *public-key encryption*.

public-key cryptography See *public-key encryption*.

public-key encryption (Or public-key cryptography.) An *encryption* scheme in which each user has a pair of keys, called the public key (which can be generally known) and the *private key* (that is, of course, kept secret). A message is encrypted using the public key of the person to whom the message is to be sent; this can then be decrypted only using the recipient's private key. This means that secret information never has to be transmitted over publicly accessible networks or other communications media, as only the public key is ever communicated. Public-key cryptography is used both for encryption and for authentication, often of *digital signatures*. RSA is probably the best known and most widely used public-key encryption system.

public switched data network (PSDN) Usually a digital network (and of a higher *bandwidth* than the *PSTN*), particularly suitable for data communications. Generally operated by a *PTT*.

public switched telephone network (PSTN) A public telephone network or the collection of them around the world, operated by *PTTs*. Sometimes called *POTS* in contrast to *PSDN*.

Publisher Item Identifier (PII) An extension of the *ISBN* and *ISSN* system, introduced by a group of leading US academic (scientific) journal publishers so as to provide a way of identifying individual items, such as articles, within both books and journals. It also provides a unified identification system for books and journals.

pull-down menu A *menu* which is brought to the screen by clicking on a word or *icon* in a *menu* bar.

pulse code modulation (PCM) A method by which an *analogue* signal is represented as *digital* data. The analogue data is sampled at regular intervals (a fixed frequency), and the sampled values converted into binary codes for transmission using a digital link.

push technology The *download* of information by information providers, either over the *Internet* or using *broadcast* techniques, on the basis of information profiles supplied by users, in contrast to the pull technology of the *World Wide Web*, in which information is downloaded by users when they specify a *URL*. Examples of push technologies are *Castanet*, *Pointcast*, *BackWeb*, *Headliner* and *Netscape Netcaster*. (See also *NetTV*.)

Q

QAM See *quadrature amplitude modulation*.

Q-coder The coding scheme, patented by IBM, which is used in *JBIG* compression. Bi-level *pixels* are coded as symbols depending on the probability of occurrence of these symbols in different contexts. Has similarities with *Huffman coding*. The less probable a symbol, the more bits will be assigned to it. The Q-coder can also assign one output code bit to more than one input symbol, which the Huffman coder cannot.

quadrature amplitude modulation (QAM) A form of transmission in which *digital* data is

113

encoded in an *analogue* signal by a combination of *amplitude modulation* and *phase modulation*. This is used when the modem bandwidth is 9600 bps or higher.

quadtone The use of four (possibly *Pantone*) colours in combination to produce a particular effect in printing. May be used to produce a finer *grey-scale* effect. (See also *duotone*.)

QuarkImmedia *Multimedia* authoring and viewing tool which is based on *QuarkXPress*.

QuarkXPress Probably the leading *DTP* or *page layout* program, at least in the graphic arts industry. Originally written for the *Macintosh*, but now also runs under Microsoft *Windows*.

QuickDraw The *object-based* graphics display system used by the Apple *Macintosh*. QuickDraw controls how text and images are drawn on the screen. (See also *PICT images*.) QuickDraw can also be used to control printers and, although text will be indistinguishable from that on a *PostScript* printer if *Adobe Type Manager* or *TrueType* is used, images may be of lower quality.

QuickDraw GX An *imaging model* that works alongside *QuickDraw* but controls the Mac's video and print output directly. It consists of three parts: graphics, typography and printing. The graphics part is *object-oriented* and provides full control over graphic objects, including colour, while the printing module ensures that the colours are reproduced accurately. The typography provides a *font* technology, *TrueType GX*, which has the greatest functionality of any font technology so far, but requires applications able to take advantage of this functionality. In other cases the fonts act as standard *TrueType* fonts.

QuickTime A general *multimedia*-handling utility developed by Apple, initially for the *Macintosh*, but now also available for *Windows*. QuickTime makes it possible to display 'movies' and animated sequences with synchronized high-quality sound. It operates as a software extension (or *plug-in*), so that multimedia can be embedded in other documents. QuickTime includes its own *video compression* technology.

R

RACE (Research into Advanced Communication Technologies in Europe.) A European Commission R&D programme.

radio frequency (rf) Frequencies (of electromagnetic radiation) above about 300 Hz, at which electromagnetic waves can be transmitted.

ragged Text layout that is not justified. Most text on screen is ragged right, i.e., the left-hand margin is aligned while the right-hand margin is not. Ragged left and ragged centre (ragged on both margins) are also used in books, but only usually as a design feature.

RAID (Redundant arrays of inexpensive/independent disks.) An approach to storing large amounts of data in a secure fashion. RAID is increasingly used in *multimedia* installations, running either under *Unix* or on a *network* with the *NetWare* network operating system.

Rainbow Document Type Definition An *SGML Document Type Definition* (DTD) that specifies a document in terms of its appearance, in some respects similarly to *HTML*. Descriptions of documents in terms of this DTD are used as an intermediate stage in converting *word-processor* documents to SGML.

rainbow series A series of technical manuals, each of which has a different coloured cover. Originally used to describe the US government's security series, e.g., the *Orange Book*, the *PostScript* 'Cookbooks' (*Red Book*, *Green Book*, *Blue Book*, *White Book*) have also been described in this way, so what is meant depends on the applications with which the user is familiar.

RARE See *Réseaux Associés pour la Recherche Européenne*.

RARP See *Reverse Address Resolution Protocol*.

raster The horizontal pattern of lines on a video display or television that makes up the picture. Each line is made up of a series of dots or *pixels*. Also used generally (as the equivalent of *bitmap*) to describe a similar pattern, as in *raster graphics* and *raster fonts*.

raster font See *bitmap font*.

raster graphics The same as *bitmap graphics*, in which an image is made up of an orthogonal array of *bits* (or *pixels*). (Compare with *vector graphics*.)

raster image processor (RIP) Either a program or a piece of hardware that converts a file in a *page description language*, usually *PostScript* and possibly containing *vector graphics*, to a *raster* or *bitmap* image for output on a *page printer* or *imagesetter* or on screen. The *RIP* will create a bitmap at the correct resolution for the output device, so that the page description file can be *resolution* independent. *Adobe Type Manager* rasterizes PostScript fonts so that they can be displayed or printed on non-PostScript devices.

rate adaptation Can either refer to conversion in a *terminal adaptor* between the data rate at a *V.24* serial interface (with a probable maximum of 28 800 bps) and the 64 kbps of *ISDN*, or mean conversion between the European (64 kbps) and the North American (56 kbps) versions of ISDN. Which is meant will depend on the context.

ray tracing A method of creating realistic images, in which the paths taken by rays of light are traced, from an observer's eye, through a point in the image plane to an object. Each object can then be considered as a collection of differently shaped surfaces, each with properties such as colour, reflectance, transmittance and texture.

rcp (Remote copy.) A *Unix* utility for copying files over *Ethernet*. Similar to *ftp*.

Realaudio A program, implemented as a client/server architecture, for playing *audio* over the *Internet*. Sound is compressed into Realaudio files by an encoder which is part of the Realaudio server. The client, a Web *browser plug-in* or add-on (and the latest browsers have the facility built in) decompresses the stream of data sent from the server, which is then output using the sound facilities of the computer. A 28.8 kbps *modem* is required for music-quality sound.

Red Book A term used to describe books in various different reference series. These include *The PostScript Language Reference Manual* (one of the *PostScript* 'Cookbooks') and the 1984 standards issued by the *ITU-T* eighth plenary assembly, including the *X.400 email* specification, the Group 1 through 4 *fax* standards, the *I series* recommendations for *ISDN* and the *V series* recommendations. Superseded by the 1988 *Blue Book*.

Red Sage A joint project between the University of California, San Francisco, *AT&T* Bell Laboratories and a number of publishers of biomedical journals. Provides on-line access to scanned images of biomedical journals via the *RightPages* server software developed by AT&T Bell Laboratories.

redundancy Inclusion of duplicate information. This is often used as a check, particularly in transferring information between systems, so that an additional check digit or bit is included. (See also *validation*.)

reference concrete syntax The syntax, i.e., the delimiters, notation, etc., that is defined in the *SGML* standard. In other words, this is the form of coding that the standard recommends, although it can be changed in the *SGML declaration*.

regional network See *mid-level network*.

registration The alignment of the different colours in the printing of coloured material; see *CMYK*. Registration marks are printed for alignment purposes outside the area of the finished publication. Most *DTP* and *page layout* programs have inclusion of registration marks as an option on their print menus.

relational database A type of *database* in which entries are structured in defined fields, usually of a fixed length. By using tables which relate to one another by having a field in common, most information need only be stored once. Thus, for example, a database may include a table containing spare parts and another containing customer details. Ordering a part will entail referencing both these tables. Relational databases are increasing in their flexibility but are still not appropriate for applications including large amounts of unstructured text. *Text databases* are more appropriate for this, particularly if they are *SGML* compatible. The most widely used relational databases used on *open systems* include Oracle, Informix and Ingres. (See also *object-oriented database*.)

reliable communication Communication in which there is a guarantee (i.e., a check) that messages will reach their destinations both complete and in the correct order. This is done by including a *checksum* or *cyclic redundancy check* as part of each message or *packet*, so that, if the check fails, indicating that the message is incomplete or corrupt, the sender is notified. *Transmission Control Protocol* (TCP) is the reliable *protocol* used on both *Ethernet* and the *Internet*.

remote A *terminal* or *host* that is connected over a *WAN* and/or via a *modem* and a telephone line.

remote login Connecting to and using a remote computer, via a *protocol* over a computer network, as though locally attached. (See also *rlogin, telnet*.)

remote procedure call (RPC) A *protocol* used in *client-server* computing, in which a program (the client) sends a message, together with specific arguments, to a remote system (the server) requesting it to execute a designated procedure, using the arguments supplied, and return the result to the client. Because there are many incompatible RPC *protocols, middleware* has been developed to convert the protocols and thus allow more general communication.

render, rendering The process of applying colour, shading and shadows to a computer-generated image, on the basis of a mathematical model, to make it appear realistic. *Ray-tracing* is a common method. (See also *Gouraud shading, Phong shading*.)

repeater Equipment used to allow transmission over long distances, in which signals are amplified, retimed or reconstructed before retransmission. Also used in *Ethernets* to connect segments. (See also *media converter*.)

Replay A *video* system used on Acorn computers. Uses *compressed* images with real-time decompression.

replication A function of *Lotus Notes* in which document databases can be distributed across networks. Can use various *protocols* including *X.25* and *TCP/IP*. Replication is also used more generally to mean duplication, e.g., as in 'illegal software replication'.

Request For Comments (RFC) The series of numbered *Internet* information documents (begun in 1969), including standards (all Internet standards are recorded in RFCs, but most RFCs are not standards). Unlike the formal development of *ITU-T* and *ANSI* standards, RFCs are developed on the basis of proposals put forward by the Internet research and development community (hence the name).

request to send (RTS) Signal sent in a communications system before a message can be sent. Before transmission can take place *CTS* (clear to send) must be received.

Réseaux Associés pour la Recherche Européenne (RARE) An association of national and international European research networks.

Réseaux IP Européens (RIPE) A collaboration between European networks to provide *Internet* services using *TCP/IP*.

resolution The number of dots per unit length which can be reproduced on a screen or printer and therefore the number of dots per unit length in an image and thus how sharp and clear an image looks, although this will also be affected by the number of *grey levels* or the number of *colours* used. A common screen resolution for colour monitors is 75 dpi (dots per inch), but it is often higher if handling colour is a specific requirement of the monitor. Laser printers typically have resolutions between 300 and 1800 dpi, while image setters can have resolutions of up to 3000 lines per inch. See the discussion under *halftone* of the relationship between *dots per inch* input and *lines per inch* output.

resolver The *TCP/IP* software that formats requests sent to the *domain name server* for *hostname*-to-*Internet* address conversion. (See also *address resolution*.)

Reverse Address Resolution Protocol (RARP) A protocol that provides the reverse function of *ARP*, mapping a hardware address (*MAC address*) to an *Internet* address.

reverse video Another term for *inverse video*.

Revisable Form Text (RFT) See *Document Content Architecture/Revisable Form Text*. Note that RFT and *RTF* are not the same.

rf See *radio frequency*.

RFC See *Request For Comments*.

RFT See *Revisable Form Text*.

RGB (Red, green, blue.) The (additive) colour system used in televisions and computer monitors. In a cathode ray tube display, signals from three different electron guns (each carrying a different colour signal) activate the appropriately coloured phosphor coating on the screen, creating a colour image; *liquid-crystal displays* work similarly but use a different technology. Compare this with the (subtractive) *CMYK* system. Note that the two systems do not always give the same colour for an equivalent image. (See *colour space, colour gamut*.)

rib site An intermediate *Internet* site (analogous to a *backbone* site) with on-demand high-speed link between a backbone site and *leaf sites* (which, if the analogy were followed strictly, should be called 'finger' or 'toe' sites!)

Rich Text Format (RTF) An ASCII format for word-processing and related files, developed by Microsoft for exchange of files between systems. It should be noted that, over the years, Microsoft has modified the format, so that care needs to be taken with its use. It provides a step towards *structured documents* and *SGML* in that styles are explicitly coded and can be separated from their typographic representation. It is sometimes used as an intermediate step in converting *word-processor* documents to SGML. (See also *Rainbow Document Type Definition* and *RFT*, which is not the same as RTF.)

RightPages A *server* and *browser* for scanned images, developed by *AT&T* Bell Laboratories and used in the *Red Sage* and *SuperJournal* projects.

ring A network topology in which a loop (or closed path) is formed, so that each node is connected to two adjacent nodes (like an electrical ring main). (See also *token ring*.)

RIP See *raster image processor*, *Routing Information Protocol*.

RIPE See *Réseaux IP Européens*.

RIPEM (Riordan's Internet Privacy Enhanced Mail.) An implementation of *Privacy Enhanced Mail* (PEM).

RISC (Reduced instruction set computer.) A type of computer processor architecture. The instructions are to the processor from the *operating system* and do not affect *applications*, except in that they are intended to increase processing speed.

RJ-11 An American-style telephone connector. May be found on the back of US-manufactured *modems*.

RJ-45 A telephone cable connector for an *ISDN* line.

RLE See *run-length encoding*.

rlogin (Remote login.) A *Unix* utility which allows a user to log in to a remote computer via the *Internet*. (See also *telnet*.)

Rockwell Protocol Interface (RPI) A *modem* interface in which data *compression* and *error correction* are provided as software, rather than as part of the hardware. Maximum speed is 14 400 bits per second.

ROMP (Regionally organized modem pool.) The service providing *virtual points of presence*.

root See *root directory*.

root directory The top directory in an (inverted) *tree-and-branch filing system*. It contains all the other directories. *Unix* systems use this system, which it is important to understand if utilities such as *ftp* and *telnet* are to be used over the *Internet*. *MS-DOS* also uses this system, although the root directory is always the disk drive descriptor, e.g., C:\.

rot13 (Rotate alphabet 13 places.) A simple *encryption* routine in which each English letter is replaced with the one 13 places forward or back along the alphabet. Used in *Usenet* news reading and posting programs to hide items which may offend. rot13 is self-inverse, in that the same program can be used to *encrypt* and *decrypt*.

round-trip time (RTT) The time taken to send a packet to a particular *host* and receive it back, giving a measure of the current network delay. Can be obtained with *ping*.

route   Either a noun or a verb. As a noun, it is the path taken over a *network* from source to destination. As a verb, it describes the actions taken by a *router* (or in *routing*).

router   A device which allows connection between dissimilar networks (such as *Ethernet* and *Token-Ring*), although a common protocol is required. A router will calculate the shortest route for each destination, based on *network layer* information and routing tables. (See also *bridge*, *gateway*, *Exterior Gateway Protocol*, *Interior Gateway Protocol*, *brouter*.)

routing   The process, carried out by a *router*, of selecting a suitable path through a network. (See also *Exterior Gateway Protocol*, *Interior Gateway Protocol*.)

routing domain   A set of *routers* that exchange routing information within an *administrative domain*.

Routing Information Protocol (RIP)   A protocol which uses distance vector *routing*, that is, the number of *hops* required to the destination. This does not, however, always give the fastest route because it does not take account of the *bandwidth* of the connections.

RPC   See *remote procedure call*.

RPI   See *Rockwell Protocol Interface*.

RS-232   A standard type of computer interface used to connect *serial* devices, equivalent to *ITU-T V.24* and *V.28*. It is used for *modems* and other peripheral devices. Also described as a *serial interface*. (Compare with *parallel interface*.) The 'RS' stands for Recognized Standard (of the US Electronics Industry Association – EIA). The interface is also described as RS-232-C, the C indicating that this is the third version of RS-232, which is that commonly used. (See also *Data Communication Equipment*, *Data Terminal Equipment*.) RS-232 specifies the physical connections of the interface, while *RS-423* specifies the electrical signals.

RS-422   A data transfer protocol developed by the US Electronic Industries Association (EIA), providing a higher data transfer rate than the *RS-232* protocol, as well as improved immunity to electrical interference. It is part of *RS-449*, which is equivalent to *ITU-T V.35*. RS-422 is used by the Apple *Macintosh*.

RS-423   A specification for the electrical signals on a *serial* (*RS-232* or *RS-422*) line. Together with *RS-422*, forms *RS-449*.

RS-449   A physical interface standard specified by the US Electronic Industries Association (EIA), for interconnection of *DTE* and *DCE* using *rs-422*/*rs-423* signals, equivalent to *ITU-T V.35*.

rs-485   An enhanced version of standard *RS-422*, permitting up to 32 stations to be attached to a common *bus*.

RSA encryption   A *public-key encryption* and *authentication* system (the acronym is based on the initials of the authors, R Rivest, A Shamir and L Adleman). It is based on the product of two large prime numbers and the difficulty of factoring these. While the system has been broken, the amount of computing power and the time required underlined the security of the approach. (See also *DSS*.)

RTF   See *Rich Text Format*.

RTS   See *request to send*.

RTT   See *round-trip time*.

run-around   The flow of text around a, usually irregularly shaped, graphic. The ability to do this is a feature of a *page layout* program. Note that it is not a feature of electronic documents, such as those coded with *HTML* (because they are dynamic), although page-based electronic documents, such as *Acrobat* files, will include such a feature.

run-length encoding (RLE)   A *compression* algorithm which replaces sequences of repeated characters (or groups of characters) with a single character and the length of the run. It is mainly used for storing *bitmaps*, since it encodes the points at which there is a change from black to white, on to off, 0 to 1, and the distance since the last switch (in the opposite direction). *Huffman coding* works in a similar fashion, but is more complex.

S

SAA See *systems application architecture*.

SAID See *Security Association ID*.

sampling A technique used in converting signals from *analogue* to *digital*, in which the values of an analogue signal are measured at fixed time intervals and the measured values converted to digital values. To reproduce the analogue signal a *digital to analogue converter* is used. Sampling is used in making digital *audio* recordings.

sanserif type See *sans serif type*. Either spelling is correct.

sans serif type (*Sanserif* is an alternative spelling.) A category of type in which there are no *serifs* (for example, this text). Sans serif type tends to be used for display and for headings but less often for text. There is some argument as to which is better for use in *electronic publishing*, i.e., in onscreen applications, but the balance is probably the same as for paper publications: more formal documents use serif typefaces, while less formal documents are more likely to use sans serif faces.

SAR See *segmentation and reassembly*.

SATAN See *Security Administrator Tool for Analysing Networks*.

satellite communications The use of, usually geosynchronous, satellites to reflect digital communications signals back to earth. Satellites are required because, at the frequencies used, there must be a direct line of sight between the source and the receiver and, for obvious reasons, this is not generally possible at ground level, quite apart from the effects of the earth's curvature.

saturation In *colour measurement* (see *HSV*) the measure of how much colour ('colourfulness' is the term used by experts) is present at a particular *brightness*.

scalable font A *font* that can be used at any size and any resolution, on a screen or in output from a *laserprinter* or *imagesetter*. Scalable fonts are *outline fonts*.

scanner A device that is used to produce a *bitmap* image of a document, essentially by reflecting light from it and recording the reflected image with an array of sensors. Scanners can be *monochrome, grey scale* or colour. If what is scanned is text, then the image can be passed to *OCR* software for conversion into characters. Bitmapped images can also be converted to vector images using *tracing programs*. There are various types of scanners ranging from hand-held scanners, through flat-bed scanners and video scanners (which use a video/digital camera), to drum scanners, which are used to produce high-resolution images for printing. *Facsimile* transmission is also based on scanning. (See the discussion under *halftone* concerning the relationship between *dots per inch* input and *lines per inch* output.) The term is also used to describe a *lexical analyser*.

SCPC See *single channel per carrier*.

screen The display device on which computer input (and some output) is viewed. (See also *shield*.) The term is also used in the traditional graphic arts industry to describe the *halftone* pattern overlaid on a continuous tone photograph in order that it can be reproduced. The term is less used in the electronic reproduction of photographs, because the same effect is achieved by scanning at a particular *resolution* and number of *grey scales*.

screen capture, screen dump Copying the image on the computer screen (or part thereof) to a file or a printer. Often used in manuals etc. and books about computer applications to illustrate what the screen looks like (see Figure 5).

screen font A font that is designed specifically for viewing on screen. In principle, with *Adobe Type Manager* and *TrueType*, any font can be used in this way but, in practice, certain fonts (often *bitmap* fonts) are used to present screen information (e.g., menus, file names, screen labels) at a constant size in *guis*. However, *electronic publishing* applications, such as the *World Wide Web*, in general use *scalable fonts*.

screen saver An application which, when a computer, although switched on, is not used for a predetermined period, either blanks the screen or replaces whatever was on the screen with a moving image. This both avoids any

script

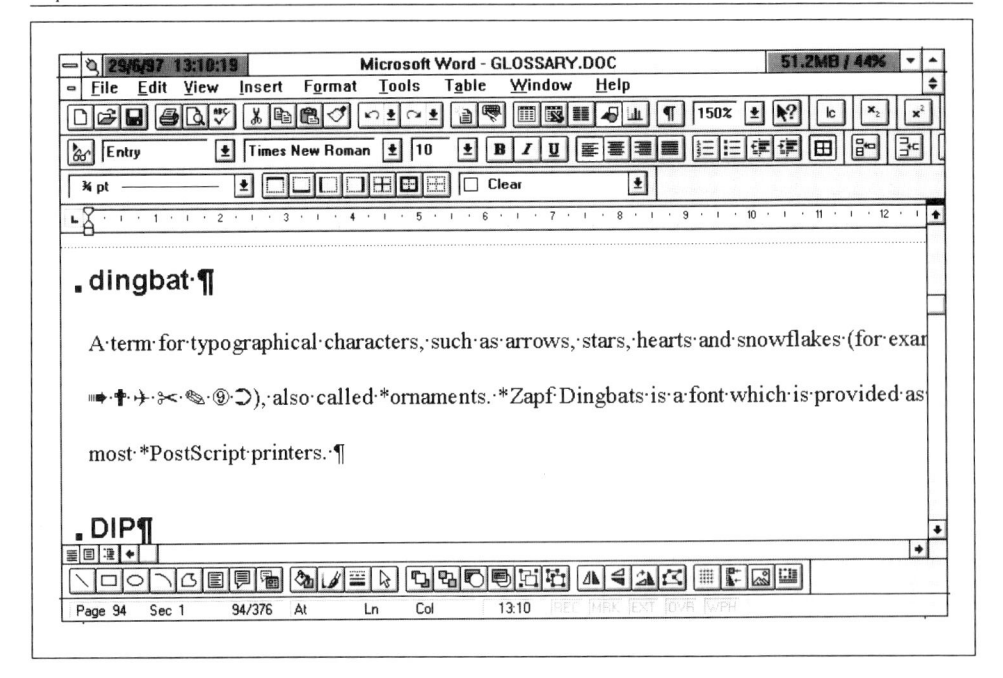

Figure 5 Screen dump

burn-in effects and protects what was on the screen from casual oversight. *Clicking* a *mouse* button or pressing a key restores the original image. There are a wide variety of screen savers, some of which are even games. Indeed, the production of screen savers is a whole genre of *electronic publishing* in itself.

script A series of commands that can be executed as a single unit. For example, a DOS batch file is a kind of script. *Unix* includes whole programming languages of this kind described as 'shellscripts', which can include parameters and variables. Similarly *CGI-scripts* are used to create dynamic *HTML* applications, while *JavaScript* is a version of *Java* that can be used within HTML documents.

scroll, scrolling Upwards, downwards or sideways smooth motion of data across a screen, as if a window were being dragged across the data. In a *GUI* environment, it is usually activated with the *mouse*, although in other environments it may be activated by holding down the 'arrow' keys on the keyboard.

SCSI (Small computer system interface.) (Pronounced 'scuzzy'.) An eight-bit *parallel interface* used by the Apple *Macintosh* and the PC for connecting peripheral devices, such as disk and CD-Rom drives, printers, and tape drives. SCSI can support high data transfer rates (up to 4 Mbytes per second). *SCSI-2* and *SCSI-3* are later versions with wider data buses, supporting even higher transfer rates.

SCSI-2 A version of the *SCSI* interface specification, including 'Fast SCSI' mode (up to 10 Mbytes per second) and 'Wide SCSI' (16 bit, up to 20 Mbytes per second, or occasionally 32-bit, up to 40 Mbytes per second). Another major enhancement has been the definition of command sets for different device classes. SCSI-2 also allows a wider range of peripherals to be connected. While *SCSI-3* is being developed, an intermediate version, Ultra-SCSI, has been proposed, which has twice the speed of SCSI-2.

SCSI-3 An interface standard under discussion to provide faster data transfer and increased functionality than *SCSI-2*. Because of the problems of *parallel communication* at higher transfer rates and longer distances, SCSI-3 will use *serial interfacing* with clock information included in the data stream to avoid signal delay problems.

To provide backward compatibility, SCSI-3 will still allow the use of parallel communication. To provide this flexibility, SCSI-3 will consist of layered protocol definitions, similar to those used in networking.

SCSI chain Several *SCSI devices* linked together with SCSI cables. This is necessary because there is usually only one SCSI port on the back of the computer, so devices must be linked one to another in a chain, with the first and last devices terminated.

SCSI device Any device, such as a scanner, CD-Rom drive or external hard disk, that is connected to the computer by a *SCSI* port.

SDH See *synchronous digital hierarchy*.

SDIF See *Standard Document Interchange Format*.

sdlc See *Synchronous Data Link Control*.

SEA See *self-extracting archive*.

search engine Software which makes it possible to search files and/or *databases* for specific terms. The two principal approaches are *Boolean* search and *free-text* search, which usually involves using *indexing*. The more *structured* the data/files, the more precisely a search can be defined, depending on the functionality of the search engine. Search engines used on the *World Wide Web* include *AltaVista* and *Yahoo*; another popular search engine is *Topic*, which forms part of the *Acrobat* suite.

searching Trying to locate required character strings or words. Examples are *keyword* searching and *free-text* searching. (See also *proximity searching*.)

SECAM (Sequential Colour and Memory or Système Electronique Couleur avec Mémoire.) A television coding standard used in Europe (mainly France and some Eastern European countries). (See also *PAL*, *NTSC*.)

secret key cryptography *Encryption* when both sender and recipient usually have the same key. (See *symmetric key cryptography*.) The opposite of *public-key cryptography*.

secure HTTP (S-HTTP) An extension of *HTTP*, providing independently applicable security services for transaction confidentiality, authenticity/integrity and non-repudiability of origin. The protocol will allow, for example, credit card transactions, over the *Internet*. (See also *HyperText Transmission Protocol (Secure)*.)

secure sockets layer (SSL) A *protocol*, originated by *Netscape Communications Corporation*, in order to provide secure communications on the *Internet*. It is used by *HTTPS* and as a layer below *HTTP*, *SMTP*, *NNTP*, *ftp*, *Gopher* and *telnet*, but above *TCP/IP*.

Security Administrator Tool for Analysing Networks (SATAN) A tool for gathering information about remote systems, especially security aspects, via a *network*. The results can be stored in a database and viewed with an *HTML* browser such as *Mosaic* or *Netscape*.

Security Association ID (SAID) A 32-bit field which will be added to *packet* headers in the proposed *Internet Protocol* Version 6 in order to provide *encryption* and *authentication*.

security firewall See *firewall*.

SEGA One of the leading manufacturers of video games.

segmentation The division of a *packet* of information into shorter packets for transmission over a communications system.

segmentation and reassembly (SAR) A sublayer of the *ATM* adaptation layer which is concerned with segmenting the *application layer* information into ATM cells of the correct length for transmission and reassembling them on receipt.

Seiko RC-4000 An information-storage wristwatch containing a *serial interface*, so as to allow information to be transferred without the need for input using very small keys.

self-extracting archive (SEA) An *archive* format originally used on the Apple *Macintosh*, in which *double-clicking* on a file *icon* would extract the contents. However, the term is now also applied to executable files which run under MS-DOS, frequently used as a way of downloading software over the *Internet*. Running the SEA file once it has been received unpacks and often expands the files contained within it.

SENDIT See *Systems Engineering for Network Debugging, Integration and Test*.

sendmail A *Unix email* system.

sequence, sequencer Software (although sequencers can also be stand-alone) used to control the input of music and sounds — either from a piano-type keyboard or other instrument connected through a *MIDI* interface or on screen using a computer keyboard — the editing of those sounds, and output of the sounds, again via a MIDI interface.

Sequenced Packet Xchange (SPX) A guaranteed delivery protocol used by *NetWare*.

serial communication Data transfer in which one bit is transferred at a time, in contrast to *parallel communication*, in which a number of bits are transferred concurrently. Serial communication has various advantages over parallel communication, essentially the result of all bits being transferred along a single connecting wire (although other wires are still required for control). (See also *serial device, serial interface, RS-232*.)

serial device A peripheral device that is connected to a computer through a *serial interface*. Modems are probably the most commonly used serial devices, although a *mouse* and other devices can be connected in this way. Keyboards are also examples of serial devices.

serial interface An interface through which data is transmitted one bit at a time, unlike a *parallel interface*. Also described as an *RS-232* interface.

serial line Wires, or a telephone line, connecting two *serial ports*. (See *RS-232, RS-422*.)

Serial Line Internet Protocol (SLIP) A version of the *Internet Protocol* (IP) which is used over a *serial line*. *Point-to-Point Protocol* (PPP) was designed as an improvement upon SLIP.

Serial Line IP (SLIP) See *Serial Line Internet Protocol*.

serial port Another term for a *serial interface*, although often used to refer to the physical connection on a computer. (See, in contrast, *parallel port*.)

serif The terminal stroke at the end of a line making up part of a character. Thus the characters in serif typefaces (such as the one used for this glossary) carry serifs, while characters in *sans serif* (or sanserif) typefaces do not (see example under *sans serif*).

server A computer which either holds information accessed by other computers over a *network*, e.g., a *file server* or *database server*, or provides a service, e.g., a *print server*, a dedicated computer which carries out the printing processes for all computers on a network, reducing the load on the other machines. The *Internet* is based on a network of servers. Also a program providing a service to a *client program*. (See *client-server*.)

service provider See *Internet Service Provider*.

server side include A *World Wide Web* server feature, which makes it possible for information to be included in *HTML* documents when they are called up by a browser. This works by replacing HTML tags in one file by the contents of another file, essentially using *macros*.

session A period of connection to a *server*, e.g., via the *Internet* or *World Wide Web*.

session layer The third-highest layer (sometimes referred to as layer 3 and sometimes as layer 5) of the *osi seven-layer model*. It uses the *transport layer* to establish a connection between processes on different hosts and handles the security and creation of a *session*. It is used by the *presentation layer*.

seven-layer model See *Open Systems Interconnect*.

Seybold The *Seybold Reports* were originally produced by John Seybold to cover technical developments in the publishing industry. Subsequently, they have developed to cover *desktop publishing* and, in 1996, *Internet* publishing. In addition, a series of conferences is held each year to report on developments; they are now organized by John's son, Jonathan.

SGML See *Standard Generalized Markup Language*.

SGML declaration The first part of an *SGML* document, which defines the syntax used in the document, i.e., the coding structure,

delimiters, the character set, etc., with changes from the *reference concrete syntax*. Note that, although logically this is the first part of any document, preceding the *Document Type Definition*, the SGML declaration may well be part of the SGML *application* software and therefore not visible to the user.

sgmls A *public domain SGML parser* developed by James Clarke.

shareware Software that may be obtained and tested for free, usually for a limited time period. It is often distributed through *Internet* file transfers or on floppy disk. After the trial period is complete, users are asked to pay a registration fee to the author or distributor of the package. Payment of the fee often brings additional facilities or documentation.

shield (Or screen.) The *grounded* (or earthed) conducting material that surrounds the transmission medium, for example the central conductor of a *coaxial cable*. Its purpose is to stop interference from other electromagnetic radiation and noise.

Shockwave A delivery platform from Macromedia for creating and packaging multimedia for the *World Wide Web*.

short message service (SMS) A service which allows messages of up to 160 characters to be received and displayed on a *GSM* telephone, even when the telephone is being used for speech.

s-HTTP See *secure HTTP*.

sideband The upper and lower frequency bands around a *carrier frequency* that are produced when a signal is *modulated*.

signal element The smallest unit of a signalling code.

signal-to-noise ratio (s/n ratio, SNR) The ratio of useful information ('signal') to useless 'noise'. Originally used in electronics and communications and measured in decibels. However, now often used as well to describe communication in a more general sense, particularly on the *Internet* referring to *Usenet* newsgroups, where the term is a measure of the quality of the information *posted*.

signature The few lines of information added at the end an *email* message or *news posting*, giving information about the sender. (See also *digital signature*.) Signature is also used to mean the section of a book, printed as a single sheet. The *imposition* laydown ensures that the pages are in the correct sequence when the sheet is folded.

SIM See *subscriber identity module*.

SIM card serial number (SSN, SIM serial number) The 19-digit number used to identify a *SIM* card.

SimCity A simulation game from Maxis Software, in which the player designs, builds and runs his or her own city. SimCity 2000 is an upgraded version. The game also has applications in system dynamics studies.

Simple Mail Transfer Protocol (SMTP) A *protocol* used to transfer *email* between computers, either over *Ethernet* or over the *Internet*.

Simple Network Management Protocol (SNMP) A *protocol* used for managing interconnected *IP networks*. It is used on the *Internet*. Version 2 (SNMP v2) is a revision of SNMP with improvements in performance and security.

simplex Communication in one direction without any provision for transmission in the reverse direction. (See also *duplex, half duplex*.)

single-attached An *FDDI* interface where a device is connected to only one of the FDDI *token-passing* rings. This kind of connection is usually used for a *host* computer. (See, in contrast, *dual-attached*.)

single channel per carrier (SCPC) A multiple access communications technique in which each signal is allocated a specific carrier, instead of a number of signals being *multiplexed* onto a single carrier, as in *FDMA*.

single ended An electrical connection, such as a *coaxial cable*, where one wire carries the signal and another wire or a *shield* is *grounded* (earthed). This is in contrast to a *differential line*.

single image random dot stereogram (SIRDS) A *stereographic* picture (or *stereogram*) made up of differently coloured dots. When the picture is viewed correctly (and acquiring the *single-sideband transmission (ssb)*

correct technique may be difficult), it appears to be three-dimensional.

single-sideband transmission (SSB) A transmission in which only one *sideband* is transmitted, while both the frequency of the *carrier signal* and the other sideband are suppressed in order to minimize the bandwidth needed.

SIRDS See *single image random dot stereogram*.

sitename See *hostname*.

SkipJack An *encryption* algorithm that encrypts 64-bit blocks of data with an 80-bit key. It was created by the US National Security Agency and is used in the *Clipper* chip.

sliding window compression An approach used in *compression* techniques, such as *LZW*, where in effect a window is moved over the data and the program analyses the content and position of strings within that window before sliding the window to the next block of data. How much the window moves depends on the structure of the strings.

SLIP See *Serial Line Internet Protocol*.

slotted ALOHA See *ALOHA*.

smartcard A plastic card (similar to a credit card) with an embedded microprocessor and memory for storing information. It can store, for example, personal data, identification and bank account details, to enable it to be used as a credit or debit card. Other uses include hotel door 'keys', passports and medical records. Electronic money can also be stored on such a card (see *Mondex*). (See also *personal identification device*, *personal identification number*.)

SMDS See *Switched Multimegabit Data Service*.

smiley See *emoticon*.

s-mime (Secure *MIME*.) A specification for secure *email* in MIME format. Includes *authentication* (using *digital signatures*) and *privacy* (using *encryption*).

SMS See *short message service*.

SMTP See *Simple Mail Transfer Protocol*.

SNA See *System Network Architecture*.

snailmail A somewhat pejorative way of describing the traditional postal service as compared with *email*. Originated in the USA, but now used internationally.

snd When used as a file extension or as part of a filename, indicates that the file is a sound file. (See also *sound resource, audio formats*.)

sneaker net A perhaps ironic term describing the transfer of data between computers by taking a removable medium, such as floppy disk or magnetic tape, and walking (wearing 'sneakers') from one machine to the other. It is probably worth noting that, in spite of the irony, the bandwidth in real time for such a transfer may be very high, i.e., it can be the quickest method!

sniffer A network monitoring tool used to capture data *packets* and, by decoding them, show the *protocol data*.

SNMP See *Simple Network Management Protocol*.

SNR See *signal-to-noise ratio*.

S/N ratio See *signal-to-noise ratio*.

Society for Worldwide Interbank Financial Telecommunications (SWIFT) A *value added network* used by banks throughout the world.

socket The interface between an operating system, such as *Unix* or *Windows*, and *network* communication facilities. It can either be bi-directional (*stream-oriented*) or *datagram* (destination-addressed messages with fixed length). The socket provides a communications end-point (in analogy with an electrical socket) and a file descriptor with which to access that socket. Each socket has an associated socket address that is made up of a *port* number and a network address. (See also *Windows sockets*.)

socks A security package that makes it possible for *host* behind a *firewall* to access resources outside the firewall while maintaining the security requirements. Replacements are provided with features such as *sockets*, so as to allow programs such as *finger*, *ftp*, *telnet*, *Gopher* and *World Wide Web browsers* to be used in the normal way.

soft carriage return A carriage return that is inserted by the software as a line *wraps*, i.e., not the end of paragraph (*hard carriage return*) that is inserted by the user.

soft font   See *downloadable font*.

softmodem   The provision of *modem* software in such a way that it is loaded into the computer's memory when a system is booted, so that modem facilities are provided transparently to the user.

software flow control   An alternative term for *software handshaking*.

software handshaking   (Or software flow control.) A technique for regulating the flow of data across an interface using software programs. (See *handshaking, hardware handshaking*.)

SONET   See *Synchronous Optical NETwork*.

SONET ring   An architecture used for *SONET* in metropolitan areas, which makes it possible for the network to continue functioning if a network component fails.

Sony   A Japanese electronics company, which originated the Walkman and subsequently the Data Discman. Also had great influence, with *Philips*, on the development and standardization of the *CD* and manufactures the popular *Gameboy* console.

sound   See *audio*.

SoundBlaster   The most widely used make of *sound cards* for the PC. Has become the *de facto* standard. *VOiCe* is a related *audio format*.

sound board   See *sound card*.

sound card   A plug-in board (also called a sound board), usually for a PC, which provides output of high-quality stereo sound, controlled by *application* software. An essential if *multimedia* is to be used and standard on most new PCs. The *de facto* standard is the *SoundBlaster* card.

sound resource   A file which, when accessed with appropriate software in the presence of a *sound card*, will produce audio signals.

source quench   A control message within the *Internet Protocol* (IP) that requests a *host* to transmit more slowly over a particular connection in order to avoid congestion.

source route   An *email address*, determined at the source of a message, which specifies as a series of *hostnames* the route a message should take. A *bang path* is the most usual kind. However, it is now more usual for the route to be determined at each stage.

space segment   Part of a satellite communications system, including the satellite and the space transmission links.

spamming   Sending messages to a large number of *newsgroups* irrespective of relevance to the subject of those newsgroups. The intention is often to advertise, but the intent may also be malicious or just mischievous. Spamming usually gives rise to *flames*, which increases the *traffic* even more.

spanning tree algorithm   An *IEEE 802* standard which will provide distributed *routing* over multiple *LANs*. It is still under consideration.

SPDL   See *Standard Page Description Language*.

speech recognition   (Or voice recognition, voice input.) A technique in which spoken words are interpreted by a computer system. Most systems must be 'trained' by the user giving the interpretation of a series of representative words, and may need training for each individual using the system. Usually it is necessary for words to be spoken in a rather unnatural, detached manner although recent software has been developed to recognize more natural patterns of speech, as well as to analyse strings of words and interpret the context, distinguishing, for example, between 'no' and 'know'. Speech recognition is particularly useful in ideographic languages such as Chinese.

speech synthesis   (Or voice output.) The generation from a textual or phonetic description of a waveform which sounds like human speech. The generation of numbers, e.g., associated with an onscreen calculator, is quite common. Speech synthesis is also used in *voicemail* systems.

spider   A program that automatically explores the *World Wide Web*. It finds one document and then recursively retrieves the documents referenced in it. May be used to find specific information or to create an index. Also called a *crawler* or web crawler. Can also be regarded as an *intelligent agent*.

spoofing   A technique used to reduce *wide area network* overhead. *Packets* sent for management purposes are answered by *bridges* or *routers*, rather than by the remote *LAN*, fooling (spoofing) the local device into thinking that a remote LAN is still connected, whether it is or not, thus reducing the traffic on the *WAN*, because no packet is ever sent out. Current LAN protocols are not able to handle spoofing well but, because *bandwidths* are generally greater than on WANs, the facility is not so necessary.

spot colour   Colour that is usually specified in a document as a particular, often *Pantone*, colour, say for text or graphical features. This is in contrast to *process colour*.

spread spectrum   Another term for *code division multiple access*.

sprite   A small *bitmap* image, which can be defined, by progam, in terms of its shape, colours and other graphic characteristics. Sprites are then manipulated, singly or together, as part of screen displays or games.

SPX   See *Sequenced Packet Xchange*.

SQL   (Often pronounced as 'sequel'.) See *Structured Query Language*.

SSB   See *single-sideband transmission*.

SSL   See *secure sockets layer*.

SSN   See *SIM card serial number*.

Stacker   A hard-disk *compression* utility, now owned by Microsoft.

Standard Document Interchange Format (SDIF)   ISO 9069, a standard for exchanging *SGML* documents.

Standard Generalized Markup Language (SGML)   A generic *markup language*, defined by *ISO 8879*: 1986, for representing documents in terms of their hierarchical structure. SGML is a language and not a coding system, so that for each application a *Document Type Definition* (DTD) is defined in which the hierarchy of the class of documents is described in terms of the coding to be used. SGML describes structure and not appearance (although there are facilities for including appearance-related information if required). A DTD, as well as describing the hierarchical structure, can also include references to external entities, such as *graphics, video, audio* and computer programs. SGML can therefore be used, not only to code structured documents for multiple use, but also as the basis of *multimedia* applications, the code being interpreted by *browsers* such as *Dynatext* and *Panorama*. HTML is based on an SGML DTD and *World Wide Web* browsers are only able to interpret the HTML DTD. Note, however, that *cascading style sheets* now provide appearance-related functions not specified in the HTML DTD. An SGML document actually consists of three parts: the *SGML declaration*, the DTD and the *document instance* (what the user thinks of as the document), but in many SGML *applications* it is only the document instance that is seen by the user.

Standard Page Description Language (SPDL)   The *ISO* standard (ISO 10180) for *page description languages*, based very closely on *PostScript*.

start bit   The bit which signals the start of a block of data in *asynchronous* communications. (See also *stop bit*.)

start-stop transmission   An alternative name for *asynchronous* transmission. Data blocks are preceded by a *start bit* and followed by a *stop bit* (or bits).

start-tag   The tag which indicates the end of an *element* in *SGML* or *HTML*. For example, this entry could be represented as '<entry>start-tag</entry>', where '<entry>' is the start-tag. Although this syntax is that usually used, it can be modified in the *SGML declaration*, if so required. (See also *end-tag*.)

stateless server   A *server* in which each request is treated independently, without reference to any previous request. There is no need for storage to be allocated to keep information about any request and, if a transaction fails, it is up to the client to repeat the request. However, this will usually mean that more information has to be included in each request and this has two effects: increasing the amount of information in the request and requiring the server to interpret it each time it is received, both slowing down end-to-end response. The *World Wide Web* server is stateless, in contrast to an *ftp* server, which exchanges information with the client before the file is transmitted.

static IP address   An *IP address* that is permanently allocated to a user. (Compare with *dynamic IP address*.)

station   *Data terminal equipment* on a *datalink* or *network*.

STD 1   The *Internet Architecture Board* official list of *Internet* standards, each of which is given an STD number, so that, for example, STD 2 is the document listing the current Internet *assigned numbers*, STD 9 is the STD defining *File Transfer Protocol* (ftp), and STD 15 the STD defining the *Simple Network Management Protocol*. (STD is not an acronym, but an elision of 'standard'.)

stepped index   A type of optical fibre in which the core has a different refractive index to that of the cladding, with a sharp change in refractive index at the boundary between them. It is usually used for transmission at high speed over long distances.

stereogram   A two-dimensional image, e.g., *SIRDS*, which appears three-dimensional when viewed correctly. It is also used more generally to describe a *stereographic* diagram, which is of two types. In the first there are two slightly offset images of different colours (usually green and red); when these are viewed with special 'glasses' in which one 'lens' is green and the other red, the two images are combined in the brain to produce a three-dimensional image. Early three-dimensional cinema used this technique and it can, in principle, be used in any *multimedia* presentation. It has the advantage over SIRDS that no special adjustment of the eyes is required. The other type of stereographic diagram uses two images, set at the interocular distance (about 6 cm) apart. Again special viewers can be used, although some people are able to achieve the three-dimensional effect without the use of a viewer.

stereographic   Viewing two-dimensional objects (pictures, drawings) so that they appear to be three-dimensional. (See also *stereogram, single image random dot stereogram (SIRDS)*.)

stop bit   The bit (or bits) which signals the end of a block of data in *asynchronous* communications. (See also *start bit*.)

store-and-forward   A method of transmitting messages over a *network*, in which a complete message is received before it is passed on to the next node, and within which a message may be stored at an intermediate mode until conditions are more appropriate for transfer. *UUCP* is an example of such a method. (See also *hops*.)

streaming   Playing *audio* or *video* in real time as it is downloaded (usually over the *World Wide Web*), rather than storing the file and playing it when download is complete. There are *plug-ins* to *Netscape Navigator* that decompress and play the data as it is transferred, although in newer versions of this and other browsers, streaming audio and video will be part of the functionality of the browser. For streaming to operate effectively, it is necessary to have a connection with a high *bandwidth*, as well as a computer that has enough power to carry out *decompression* in real time. (See also *Realaudio*.)

stream-oriented   See *connection-oriented*.

structured document   A document that is coded in such a way as to indicate its structure, rather than its formatting, so that, for example, there will usually be no concept of page, although sections and perhaps chapters may be coded since they are structural elements. While a word-processor document can be a structured document, use of a *parser*, together with a standard such as *SGML*, will guarantee that the structure of the document is as defined in the *DTD*. Structured documents are important in the context of *electronic publishing* because parsing provides a 'proofreading' facility, conventional checking of material often being impractical because of either the size or complexity (or both) of the files in a *multimedia* application.

Structured Query Language (SQL)   (Often pronounced 'sequel'.) A language designed for searching for information within *relational databases*, usually within a *client-server* architecture, and retrieving the information in a structured form. SQL commands can also be used to add to or change the information in a database.

127

SQL has a structure which is similar to natural language (English), which is intended to make it easy for non-specialists to use; however, the syntax must be adhered to, so it is not easy for a novice to use. Alternatively, it can be embedded in other languages. SQL is both an *ISO* and an *ANSI* standard, although it is under revision. SQL-3 is expected to be published as an ISO standard in 1998.

stub network A *network* which carries *packets* between a *backbone* and local *hosts*.

stuffed Compressed with the compression utility *StuffIt*, although the term is also used to describe a file compressed by other means. (See also *zip*.)

StuffIt A file *compression* utility for the *Macintosh*, developed by Aladdin Systems, Inc. Also used for *archiving*. (See *stuffed*.)

stx Start of text. A control character within a *packet* or message designating the end of the *header* and the start of the text of the message.

style Typographically, whether text is bold, italic, reversed or underlined. The term is also used to describe a set of formatting characteristics, such as typeface, typesize, interline spacing (leading), indents, *hyphenation* and *justification* parameters and even language, that can be applied to a paragraph and saved under a defined name. Almost all *word-processors* and *desktop publishing* systems (*page layout* programs) allow the use of styles. These can be combined into *style sheets* or *templates*. The principle is now being extended to *HTML* authoring tools.

style sheet A combination of *styles* or formatting (also called a *template*) which is appropriate for a particular type of document. Thus, there will be different style sheets for letters, invoices, reports etc. The principle is now also applied in *HTML* under the name *cascading style sheets*.

sub-band encoding An *audio compression* technique in which the signal is split into frequency bands. Parts of the signal which are not detectable by the ear are then removed and the signal encoded using variable *bit* rates, so that more bits per sample are used in the middle frequency range. Sub-band encoding is used in *MPEG-1*.

subnet Part of a *network* that shares a *network address* with other portions of the network and can be identified by a *subnet address* or *number*. A subnet has the same relationship to a network as a network does to an *internet*.

subnet address The *subnet* portion of an *IP address*. (See *address mask*.)

subnet mask See *address mask*.

subnet number See *subnet address*.

subscriber identity module (SIM) A *smart-card* which a user needs in order to use the *GSM* digital network.

substitutional compression An alternative description of *Lempel–Ziv compression*, in that an occurrence of a particular phrase or group of bytes in a block of data is substituted by a reference to a previous occurrence of that phrase.

subtractive colour The colour seen when white light is reflected from a coloured object. Subtractive colour is used in printing (see *CMYK*). Screen displays use *additive colour*.

SuperATM A version of *Adobe Type Manager* in which *Multiple Mastering* technology is enabled. (See also *pdf*, *Acrobat*.)

superhighway See *information superhighway*.

SuperJANET A broadband expansion of *JANET*, started in 1989. Partly uses *PDH*, which is to be replaced with *SDH*, and a high-speed switched data service (*SMDS*) which now (1997) links most UK higher education sites. The PDH/SDH component will be used for the development and deployment of an ATM (*asynchronous transfer mode*) network. By combining up to four 34 Mbps ATM channels, bandwidths of up to 132 Mbps will be possible for applications such as video transfer. (See *MBONE*.)

SuperJournal project One of the demonstrator projects, run in 1993, to give an indication of the potential of the *SuperJANET* network. Provided one of the first examples of *electronic journals*, including full-colour illustrations, running over a network. SuperJournal 2 is an *e-Lib* project.

super source quench A special packet within the *Internet Protocol* (IP) which is designed to stop an *Internet* host transmitting. It is rather like a *source quench*, except that it is a redirect control packet, which looks as though it comes from a local router, instructing the host to send all packets to its own *local loopback address*. Thus, no packets will be transmitted. A *breath-of-life* packet can be used to restart transmission.

Supra An extension of Adobe *PostScript* to provide the functionality required for high-resolution *imagesetters*.

surfing (Or 'surfing the Internet', 'surfing the Web'.) Use of *World Wide Web browsers* to move around *URLs*, following cross-references. The analogy with surfing arose because of the apparent ease of moving around the Web.

SWIFT See *Society for Worldwide Interbank Financial Telecommunications*.

Switched Multimegabit Data Service (SMDS) A *connectionless* transport protocol developed by Bellcore and based on *DQDB* for use in *metropolitan area networks* in the USA. CBDS, developed in Europe, is almost identical. The data format has the same length and structure as that used for *asynchronous transfer mode* (ATM), providing an easy upgrade path to ATM.

symbol A waveform produced by a *modulator* or *modem* that may be uniquely identified by a *demodulator* or a second modem. As a symbol may be generated from several bits, the symbol rate (or *baud rate*) may not be the same as the *bit rate* for a transmission. The term is also used in typesetting and *desktop publishing* to describe a non-alphabetical or mathematical character, which usually does not form part of the *ASCII* character set.

symmetric key cryptography A *cryptography* system where both parties have the same *encryption key*, as in *secret key cryptography*. The opposite of *public-key cryptography*.

synchronous Occurring either with a regular time relationship or in a predictable sequence. The reverse of *asynchronous*.

Synchronous Data Link Control (SDLC) An IBM protocol similar to *ISO HDLC*.

synchronous digital hierarchy (SDH) An international (European) digital telecommunications network hierarchy with standard data rates based on multiples of the bit rate 51.84 Mbps (called STS-1). STS-3 (155 Mbps) is the lowest bit rate expected to carry ATM (*asynchronous transfer mode*) *traffic* and this is also called STM-1 (Synchronous Transport Module — Level 1). The highest rate is 2488 Mbps (STS-12). SDH specifies the data structure and how *packets* are transported synchronously across *fibre-optic* transmission links. The US equivalent is the *Synchronous Optical Network* (SONET). SDH and SONET are gradually replacing *plesiochronous digital hierarchy* (PDH) as they have additional facilities for automatic management and *routing*, offering increased flexibility and performance.

synchronous key encryption Data *encryption* using two interlocking keys, which is the basis of *public-key encryption*. It is not possible to determine one key from the other. (See also *Pretty Good Privacy* (PGP).)

Synchronous Optical NETwork (SONET) The North American version of *SDH*.

synchronous transmission A communications technique in which uninterrupted data blocks are transmitted at a fixed rate, the transmitting and receiving devices being synchronized. While each block is preceded by special synchronization bits, no *start* and *stop bits* are used.

synthesizer An electronic device that makes musical notes or other sounds. It may be a chip on the *sound card* that can create sound in response to digitized instructions. With a *MIDI* interface, a computer can control one or more synthesizers.

SyQuest disk The brand name for a removable hard disk drive and cartridge hard disk with a high storage capacity. The term is often also used to describe removable disks from other manufacturers. These devices first became popular when it was necessary to transfer large colour *PostScript* or *bitmap* files for printing. With the development of *multimedia*, they have become even more widely used.

System 7 The 1991 version of the *Macintosh operating system*, which provided much greater functionality than the previous operating system, including *multi-tasking*.

System Network Architecture (SNA) A proprietary communication architecture, or protocol, developed by IBM for mainframes and initially based upon *sdlc*. SNA was incorporated in many IBM hardware and software implementations. It performs a similar task to the *TCP/IP* and *OSI* protocols.

Systems Application Architecture (SAA) An IBM architecture for *client-server* computing.

Systems Engineering for Network Debugging, Integration and Test (SENDIT) A two-year project funded by the European Commission and intended to produce software tools for distributed applications running on networks of microcontrollers.

System X A modular, computer-controlled, digital switching system used in telephone systems.

T

T-1 A *digital leased-line* communications service available in the USA, used for *ISDN* at 1.544 Mbps. It is equivalent to the European *E-1* service.

T-3 A *digital carrier* facility used to transmit a DS-3 (see *data service levels*) signal at 44.736 Mbps. (See also *ISDN*.) It is equivalent to the European *E-3* service.

TA See *terminal adaptor*.

tablet See *graphics tablet*.

TAC See *terminal access controller*.

tag The coding which starts (*start-tag*) or ends (*end-tag*) an *SGML* or *HTML* element.

tagged image file format (tiff) A *graphic file format* used for *bitmap* images. Tiff files can be black and white, *grey scale* or in colour.

Taligent An *object-oriented operating system* being developed jointly by IBM and Apple. Formerly called *Pink*.

talk Communication over a *network* or the *Internet* in real time. (See *Internet Relay Chat*.)

Tandem A *network* configuration in which *point-to-point* circuits are linked together.

TAPI See *Telephone Application Program Interface*.

targa A *graphic file format* used for *bitmap images*, often used as the format for output from *ray-tracing programs*.

TCL See *Tool Command Language*.

TCP See *Transmission Control Protocol*.

TCP/IP See *Transmission Control Protocol/Internet Protocol*.

TDM See *time-division multiplexing*.

tdma See *time-division multiple access.*

technical/office protocol (TOP) An *applications-layer application* for office automation over *networks* developed by Boeing on the basis of the *OSI* model based on *Ethernet*. (See also *MAP*.)

TEI See *terminal endpoint identifier*, *Text Encoding Initiative*.

telecommunications Communication via telephone systems. Telecommunications today range from simple voice communication over the telephone to complex systems involving computers, *fax* machines, *modems* and related equipment.

telecommuting (Or *teleworking*.) Working at home and communicating with colleagues and others over *telecommunications* systems, instead of physically commuting to work (see also *computer supported cooperative work*). Usually implies being employed by a company, rather than working freelance, although the distinction is not clear. Has advantages and disadvantages for both employers and employees: employers have reduced overheads but less control, while employees are subject to fewer interruptions but may feel disadvantaged by the lack of social contact.

teleconferencing Either *audioconferencing* or *videoconferencing*. (See also *audiographic teleconferencing*.)

telegraphy Transmission of data, predating *telephony*, using bipolar DC current signalling. Output was on teleprinters.

telematics The combined use of *telecommunications* and computing. The word comes from the French 'télématique', which means relating to telecommunications. The term is widely used in the European Union.

Telephone Application Program Interface (TAPI) A *Windows 95* application program interface that enables hardware-independent access to telephone based communication. (See also *CTI*.)

telephony See *telecommunications*. Involving voice transmission, as opposed to *telegraphy*.

telepresence The experience which the user of *multimedia* applications, such as virtual reality, undergoes so, although not physically in the virtual world, the user feels psychologically that he or she is, for example, travelling at very high speed.

teleprocessing Using *telecommunications* to carry out data processing on a remote basis.

telepublishing Another term for *electronic publishing*. Applied specifically to the *Individual Electronic Newspaper* project.

Telescript An *object-oriented* programming language, developed by US company General Magic and designed specifically for handling communications. The intention is to make communications programming simpler and provide cross-platform, network-independent messaging, in much the same way as *PostScript* did for formatted files.

teletex An international text exchange service, which is 40 times faster than *telex*. It is subject to the *ITU-T* series recommendations and was intended to replace telex. However, as *email* provides the same functionality, together with additional services, all from the user's own computer, it has never been widely used. Note that teletex is not *teletext*.

teletext A broadcast system, in which information is displayed on a television screen. The information can be of any type, although any graphics are only schematic, and is organized in a page format. The user has access to an index and is able to select a specific page by keying its number on the television remote control. The system then finds that page and displays it. If the information requires more than one screen, then these are automatically shown in rotation, although individual screens can be 'frozen'. Teletext is a form of *videotex* (but not of *teletex*); amongst the first implementations were the BBC Ceefax service and the UK Independent Television Oracle service, although the latter, rather confusingly, is now called by the brand name 'Teletext'. It can be argued that teletext was the first real *electronic publishing* medium although, because it is a one-way system, with no path for the user to talk back to the data provider, it can perhaps be more strictly described as a *document delivery* system. (See also *viewdata*.)

television receive only (TVRO) A satellite dish and receiver combination to receive television from a satellite. The more powerful the satellite, the smaller (and therefore cheaper) the dish needs to be. Similarly, for more powerful signals, the receiver needs to have less complex (and thus again cheaper) decoding circuitry.

teleworking See *telecommuting*.

telex (Teletypewriter exchange service.) An *analogue* service based on teleprinters. Now virtually superseded by *teletex*, *fax* and, most recently, *email*.

telnet The standard *Internet* protocol that allows users of one *host* to log into a *remote* host so that they are seen as normal terminal users of that host. Essentially provides the same facilities as directly dialling in to a remote host, but over the Internet, and thus avoiding telephone charges – or at least reducing them to the cost of a local call to the nearest *point of presence*. (See also *tn3270*.)

template A standard document that can be used as the basis of a class of documents, so that, for example, in a *word-processor*, a template for a letter can include the letter heading, including graphics, and any other standard information, such as the date, which can be generated automatically from the system date. Templates are now widely used in many applications and in most cases any document can be saved as a template. A similar term is *style sheet*.

TERM A program that runs under *Unix* and allows users dial-up access to the *Internet* without using *SLIP* or *PPP*.

terminal   A device, usually a keyboard and screen, that is connected to a computer or network, on which data may be input or displayed, but has no processing power of its own. Also described as *dte*.

terminal access controller (TAC)   A device that connects *terminals* to the *Internet*, usually via *modems*.

terminal adaptor (TA)   Equipment used to connect terminal equipment with *RS-232* ports to *ISDN basic rate interface*. TAs replace the *modems* used on *analogue* lines and, as far as the user is concerned, effectively perform the same task, connecting to a telephone line.

terminal emulation   Connecting a computer to another computer using a *terminal emulator*.

terminal emulator   A program that makes it possible for a computer (often a PC) to act as a terminal to another system, often a mainframe or *Unix* system (although see *X-windows emulation*). The commonest type of terminal emulated is the *VT 100*. Note that it is not important how the physical connection is made and this can be via *telnet*, by dial-up or even as a direct or *network* connection.

terminal endpoint identifier (TEI)   (Or terminal equipment identifier.) The identifier used for specific items of communications equipment, e.g., telephone, fax machine, modem, in an *ISDN* installation.

terminal equipment identifier   See *terminal endpoint identifier*.

terminal server   A device that allows many *terminals* (*serial lines*) to be connected to a *local area network* (LAN) through a single network connection.

termination   Adding a *terminator* to a series of *SCSI* devices.

terminator   The device which must be added at the beginning and end of a *SCSI* chain.

TEX   (Pronounced 'tek' — Greek tau, epsilon, chi.) A *public domain* document formatting and typesetting language developed by Donald Knuth, originally for setting Volume IV of his *The Art of Computer Programming*, as he had become dissatisfied with the quality of the setting in Volumes I to III. The language uses *macros* and has a number of different implementations, such as L^AT_EX, which incorporates macros that describe document styles and has become a standard for setting technical material. This is partly because it provides facilities for setting equations and mathematical material, but also because the mathematical syntax is described in the language of the mathematician or computer scientist (rather than that of the compositor — hence the reluctance of conventional typesetters to use it). In addition, T_EX input is entirely in *ASCII*, so that is easy to transmit by *email*. It is also used as a screen formatter for equations by such *browsers* as *Dynatext* and also by organizations such as the American Mathematical Society for distributing academic journals electronically. Note, however, that T_EX is not *WYSIWYG*, although in some implementations screen preview of pages is possible. (See also *Metafont*.)

text   Essentially the (human-readable) letters and spaces which make up a document or a transmission over a communication system. These will usually be coded as *ASCII* (or perhaps *EBCDIC*) and the term generally excludes any formatting information or control codes, whether given in ASCII or not. Sometimes, however, used to mean an ASCII representation of a file (see *flat ASCII*). In either sense, it means that a text file can be edited using a *text editor*, rather than needing a program such as a *word-processor* that understands the coding system used. In communications terms, this also means that such files can be transmitted over *email* systems without needing to be *MIME* encoded and without any danger of modification at mail *gateways*.

text database   A database for handling large amounts of, often unstructured, text. These were originally designed to handle newspaper archives and utilize *tags*, together with specially designed software for indexing, searching and extraction. Recently, some of these databases have been made available in *SGML*-compatible versions. Well-known examples include BRS Search, Status and Basis Plus.

text editor   An editing program used, most frequently by programmers, to edit *text* or *ASCII* files. Unlike *word-processors*, text editors provide no control over formatting except indirectly when, for example, T$_E$X files are edited and these include (ASCII-coded) formatting information that is subsequently interpreted by the T$_E$X program.

Text Encoding Initiative (TEI) An initiative designed to make possible the exchange of electronic texts for academic research purposes, rather than for publishing. *SGML* coding is used and a TEI *DTD* has been published. In spite of its academic emphasis, there is much in the TEI work which is relevant to *electronic publishing* in general.

texture A descriptor for the graphic properties of a surface in terms of smoothness/coarseness and regularity. Approaches used to define texture are statistical, structural and spectral. Statistical and spectral techniques are based on the distribution of *grey levels* over the surface (described in the two different ways), while in the structural approach textures are considered as composed of simple texture elements ('texels'; see for comparison *pixels*).

tftp See *Trivial File Transfer Protocol*.

thick Ethernet A colloquial name for the original *yellow cable Ethernet* standard, *10Base5*.

thin Ethernet See *cheapernet*.

thinnet See *cheapernet*.

thread See *topic thread*.

thumbnail A reduced-size version of an image or a document page. While the term originated in graphic design, it is now widely used in *electronic publishing* and *multimedia* applications, often interchangeably for *icon*. It is probably on the *World Wide Web* that thumbnails are now most widely used, so that a small image (with consequent small file size) can be downloaded and displayed. The user is then able to decide whether the full-size image is required and *clicking* on the thumbnail will cause either the larger image or a related *HTML* file to be transferred to the user's system, for opening in his or her *browser*, for interpretation by other software or just for storage. The use of thumbnails also allows a range of images to be displayed on a single screen, a facility that is useful in such applications as electronic catalogues or where images need to be compared.

tiff See *tagged image file format*.

tile, tiling The arrangement of *windows* in a *graphical user interface* (GUI) so that they abut rather than overlap (or *cascade*).

time-division multiple access (tdma) See *time-division multiplexing*.

time-division multiplexing (tdm) (Or time-division multiple access.) A type of *multiplexing* in which data from several users is transmitted onto a single channel in series, each user having its own time slot. Used in both satellite communication and long-distance telephone systems.

time-out The use of a timer to limit the period of a program's operation. Often used in communications, so that if there is no transmission over a communications link during a specified time, then the link is broken.

time-slicing The technique used by computers to switch between concurrent *applications* and programs. Effectively a time slot is allocated to each process and the computer switches between them. On a powerful computer, the user appears to have access all the time. *Time-division multiplexing* uses a similar approach. (See also *multi-tasking*.)

time to live (TTL) A field in the header of the *Internet* protocol that indicates how many more *hops* a *packet* may make before it is discarded or returned to the sender.

title bar In a *graphical user interface* (GUI), the bar across the top of the *screen* or a *window*, containing the names of the *application* and sometimes also of the file being used.

tn3270 A program used to connect a local computer to a remote IBM mainframe *host* which, because it uses a proprietary *operating system*, does not understand *telnet*. The program emulates an IBM 3270-type terminal.

token passing A procedure used in *token bus* and *token ring networks*.

token bus A topology used in *local area networks* (LANs). In order that there are no 'collisions' or priority conflicts on the network, a special control frame (the token) must be received by a station before it is allowed to transmit on the *bus*. Once that station has transmitted its messages, it passes the token to the next station on the bus, which is then allowed to transmit. Most commonly used as specified by the *IEEE 802.4* token bus standard.

Token-Ring The IBM implementation of the *token ring* network topology.

token ring A topology used in *local area networks* (LANs). Stations are connected in a closed ring and a special control frame (the token) is passed around the *ring*. In order that there are no 'collisions' or priority conflicts on the network, a token must be received by a station before it is allowed to transmit on the ring. Once that station has transmitted its messages, it passes the token to the next station on the ring, which is then allowed to transmit. Most commonly used as specified by the *IEEE 802.5* token *ring* standard. *Token-Ring* (with capital letters and a hyphen) is an IBM implementation of the protocol.

TokenTalk Software that makes it possible for Apple *Macintoshes* to connect to a *Token-Ring* network.

toolbar An area of a *window*, usually at the top or bottom, carrying *buttons* for commonly used commands.

Tool Command Language (TCL) A programming language, similar to *perl*, that is used in developing *World Wide Web* tools and applications.

TOP See *technical/office protocol*.

Topic (Verity Topic.) A *search engine* both used as part of large *Web* sites and quite widely integrated into other applications, such as *Acrobat*.

topic thread A series of postings, for example to *Usenet* or *CompuServe*, on a single topic, or more correctly connected by reference header information. If a user 'follows a thread', he or she will access a series of Usenet postings connected in this way. Most newsreaders give the option of following *threads* automatically.

topology The mathematical study of interconnections. A *network topology* shows the stations or *hosts* on the network and how they are connected. Within a communications protocol, the *network layer* must be aware of the network topology in order to be able to *route packets* correctly.

TOPS See *transcendental operating system*.

touch screen An input mechanism in which a user can communicate with the computer by touching a particular location on the screen with his or her finger. Touch screens are most widely used in applications where the users are unfamiliar with computers, e.g., in public information systems. Generally, other pointing devices, such as the *mouse* or *joystick*, are more common. The point at which the screen is touched is detected either using a sensitive membrane or as a result of light beams being interrupted.

touch-tone The method employed in telephony throughout the USA to communicate the keys pressed when dialling. (See *dual tone multi frequency* (DTMF).)

tracing programs See *autotracing*.

trackball An input device that performs the same function as a *mouse*, but remains stationary, the rotation within its mounting controlling the cursor position. Trackballs are generally used in portable or laptop computers and form an integral part of the keyboard in most cases.

traffic In general, transmissions over the *Internet*, but usually used to indicate the number of transmissions at any one time.

transceiver A communications device that is capable of both transmission and reception. More specifically, the physical device that connects a *host* interface, for example an *Ethernet* controller, to a *local area network* (LAN). (See also *CSMA/CD*.)

transcendental operating system (TOPS) A *local area network* (LAN) that provides *peer-to-peer* file transfer and is used to connect PCs and *Macintoshes* in such a way that files appear on a user's system in a form compatible with that system.

transducer A device that converts sound, temperature, pressure, light or other physical signal to or from an electronic signal.

transient Short-duration *noise* or the perturbation of a signal or power supply for a short period.

transition coding An alternative term for *Non-Return to Zero Inverted*.

transit network A *network* that carries *traffic* between other networks; it may also carry traffic for its own *hosts*. Almost by definition it must be connected to at least two other networks. (See also *backbone*, *stub*.)

Transmission Control Protocol (TCP) The *transport layer protocol* used on the *Internet*, as well as on many *Ethernet* networks. TCP is generally used as *TCP/IP* (TCP over *IP*). TCP provides *flow control*, *multiplexing* and *connection-oriented* communication for *full-duplex*, process-to-process connections. (Contrast with the *User Datagram Protocol*.)

Transmission Control Protocol/Internet Protocol (TCP/IP) (*Transmission Control Protocol* over *Internet Protocol*.) The set of *network* protocols generally used on *Unix* systems and on the *Internet*, as well as on many *Ethernet* systems. It was developed mainly by the US Department of Defense and includes both *network layer* and *transport layer* protocols. The term is often used to include *telnet*, *ftp* and *UDP*. Note that TCP/IP is a *de facto* standard and not directly compatible with the *OSI* model (although discussions are frequently held to try to integrate the two approaches).

transparency See *data transparency*.

transponder A device, mainly used in telecommunications, that receives a signal, amplifies it and then retransmits it, possibly at a different frequency. Transponders are widely used in satellite communications.

Transport Control Protocol/Internet Protocol See *Transmission Control Protocol/Internet Protocol*.

transport layer The middle (fourth) layer in the *ISO seven-layer model*. Also called the host–host layer, it uses the *network layer* to provide reliable end-to-end message transport including message sequencing, *flow control* and *multiplexing*, so that messages sent from one *host* to another arrive both uncorrupted and in the right order. The most widely used implementation is *Transmission Control Protocol*.

trap, trapping The overlap between two colours used in printing to ensure that there is no white appearing between them as a result of paper movement or poor registration. Gives a slightly less clear impression than *kiss-fit*, but allows for variation in printing conditions.

trap-door function A mathematical or programming function that is easy to compute, but whose inverse is very difficult to compute. Widely used in *cryptography*, particularly in *public-key* cryptography.

tree A *topology* based on the branches of a tree converging at a trunk or *root*. The concept is used, inverted, in *tree-and-branch filing systems*. Tree topologies are also widely used in *broadband* networks so that there is only one route between any two stations.

tree-and-branch filing system A filing system in which all files are stored within directories, in analogy with a(n) (inverted) *tree* structure or like folders in a filing cabinet. Each directory may in turn be stored within another directory. The *root* directory contains all the other directories and corresponds to the filing cabinet.

Trinitron A cathode ray tube manufactured by *Sony* that produces an especially bright, sharp picture without distortion.

triple DES A form of *encryption* which uses the *DES* cipher three times.

Triple-X (XXX) An abbreviation for the combination of *X.3*, *X.28* and *X.29* protocol standards documents defining the operation of a *PAD*, particularly in *X.25* networks.

tritone The use of three (possibly *Pantone*) colours in combination to produce a particular effect in printing. May be used (with cyan, yellow and magenta hues) to produce a finer *grey-scale* effect. (See also *duotone*.)

Trivial File Transfer Protocol (tftp) A simple *file transfer protocol* that is used for *downloading* bootcode (code which will restart the *operating system*) to diskless workstations.

TrueImage A *page description language* and *imaging model* developed by Microsoft for printers, similar to *PostScript*. (See also *TrueType*.)

135

TrueType A *font* system, developed by Apple as a rival to *PostScript* and subsequently supplied as part of Microsoft Windows 3.1. TrueType fonts are *scalable* (or *outline*) fonts and incorporate *hinting*. TrueType is also used to refer to the software that converts the TrueType font for rendering onscreen or on a printer. (See also *Type-1 fonts*, *Type-3 fonts* and *Adobe Type Manager*.) A new font specification, *OpenType*, has recently been developed with the aim of removing font compatibility problems.

TrueType GX A version of *TrueType fonts* that is used in *QuickDraw GX*.

Trumpet A *news reader* for Microsoft *Windows*, using the *WinSock* library.

trunk A high-capacity communications circuit that carries many channels. (See *tree*.)

T series The series of *ITU* recommendations governing *teletex*.

TTL See *time to live*. It is also used in electronics to mean transistor–transistor logic.

TUBA An *Internet addressing* proposed scheme which will allow longer address names and therefore more addresses, to be used. This is necessary because the Internet is growing so fast that the existing supply of *IP* numbers will be exhausted before long.

TULIP (The University LIcensing Program.) A program set up by the publisher Elsevier at a number of US universities, providing electronic access to journals in materials science and engineering.

tuning Within *font* technology, means to improve the appearance of a font onscreen and in printed documents.

turnaround document A document produced by a computer that is subsequently used as input after additional data has been added. Such documents are usually a type of form or card, which is printed in a typeface readable by OCR, with a standard grid suitable for OMR. Once the form or card, for example a survey form or some kind of meter reading, has been completed, then a universal document reader, capable of handling both OCR and OMR, is used to input the data.

turnaround time The time taken to reverse the direction of transmission in a *half-duplex* communication.

TVRO See *television receive only*.

TWAIN (Technology without an important name.) An interface that makes it possible for image data to be input from external sources such as *scanners* without the user having to leave the current software application. Can be used under Microsoft *Windows* and on the *Macintosh*.

tweening An interpolation technique used in *animation*, in which a program generates extra frames between the *key frames* created by the user. This gives smoother animation without the user having to draw every frame. Tweening uses mathematical formulae to generate the coordinates of important elements at a series of discrete times. (See also *morphing*.)

twin-axial cable A shielded *coaxial cable* with two conductors within the outer *shield*.

twisted pair A cable in which pairs of conductors are twisted together in order that *crosstalk* from nearby wiring and other noise is randomized. (See also *unshielded twisted pair*.)

two-binary, one-quaternary (2B1Q) The encoding for *basic rate ISDN*.

two-wire circuit A circuit used to connect a telephone subscriber to the local exchange, usually consisting of a *twisted pair*.

Type 1 font A *PostScript outline font* having the highest typographic quality, mainly because Type 1 fonts incorporate *hinting*. For some years, as Adobe kept the Type 1 specification a secret, other font developers could generally only develop *Type 3 fonts*. Now, however, the specification is publicly available and therefore almost all fonts created are Type 1. As well as the outline specification, Type 1 fonts also include a screen, *bitmapped*, font, although the development of *Adobe Type Manager* now means that the outlines can be directly rendered for viewing onscreen. (See also *TrueType fonts*.) A new font specification, *OpenType*, has recently been developed with the aim of removing font compatibility problems.

Type 2 font Type 2 font technology was developed by Adobe Systems, but subsequently abandoned before release. Thus there are no Type 2 fonts.

Type 3 font A *PostScript font* developed, probably by a type vendor other than Adobe, before Adobe made the *Type 1* specification publicly available; almost all these have now been converted to Type 1. Although Type 3 fonts can be more ornate, incorporating grey shades, variable stroke widths or graduated fills, they have a number of disadvantages. These are principally that they cannot incorporate *hinting* (and thus do not print well at smaller sizes), they have larger file sizes and they cannot be rendered by *Adobe Type Manager*.

type face A set of characters of a particular design. Text fonts will almost always include the *ASCII* character set, but symbol fonts may include a wide range of characters. Today the term 'face' tends to be used interchangeably with *font*, although historically they both had different meanings, there being several typefaces, e.g., bold, italic, etc., within a font. (See also *Unicode*.)

typewriter font A term for a *font* which derives from those used on typewriters. Such fonts are usually *monospaced* and are often used for representing extracts from computer programs, in which there is an advantage (in terms of clarity of interpretation) in each character having the same width.

U

UART See *universal asynchronous receiver/transmitter*.

UDP See *User Datagram Protocol*.

uhf See *ultra high frequency*.

UK Education and Research Network Association (UKERNA) The body responsible for *JANET* and *SuperJANET*. Formerly the *Joint Network Team*.

UKERNA See *UK Education and Research Network Association*.

ultra high frequency (UHF) The band in the electromagnetic spectrum between about 300 MHz and 3 GHz that is used for television transmission and voice communication.

Ultra-SCSI See *SCSI-2*.

Unicode A 16-bit character-encoding system that is intended to include all characters in all languages (including Chinese and similar languages). It forms part of *ISO 10646* and is backwards compatible with *ASCII* (7-bit encoding). Instead of the 128 characters which can be encoded with ASCII, 65 000 can be encoded with Unicode. *QuickDraw GX* is one of the first applications to take advantage of the standard, but it is gradually expected to become the standard approach, so that the current incompatibilities between coding schemes for non-ASCII characters become a thing of the past.

uniform resource characteristic (URC) (Formerly called uniform resource citation.) A method of encoding *Internet* resources, including types of *URI*. The method is based on *SGML* and includes approaches to searching that bear some similarity to *SQL*.

uniform resource citation Former name for *uniform resource characteristic*.

uniform resource identifier (URI) (Formerly called universal resource identifier.) A general way of addressing resources on the *Web*, including *uniform resource locators* (URLs) and *uniform resource numbers* (URNs). (See also *URC*.)

uniform resource locator (URL) (Formerly called universal resource locator.) A way of specifying an *Internet* resource, such as a file, a *World Wide Web* site or a *newsgroup*. URLs are used in *HTML* documents to specify the target of a *hyperlink*. An example URL is 'http://www.telegraph.co.uk/' and the part before the first colon specifies the protocol to be used, which may be *ftp*, *telnet*, *Gopher*, etc., rather than *http* (http being perhaps the most common). Note also that http may be substituted by the word 'file', in which case a target or resource on the local *host*, i.e., your system, is identified. The part of the URL after the colon is interpreted differently depending on the protocol. Normally, a hostname (or a *port*) will follow the double slash. Other information can follow the single slash and this may be a directory and file structure or, for example, a query.

uniform resource name (URN) (Formerly called universal resource number.) A proposed way of describing *Internet* resources that is based on content, rather than the location (see *uniform resource locator* – URL). The URN concept is being developed because the URLs change (for various reasons, e.g., because documents are moved around within directory structures or the *host* changes). The syntax will be similar to that of URLs and URNs will require a registry, so that the actual location of a document can be accessed directly. Initially called uniform resource number.

uniform resource number Former name for *uniform resource name*.

universal asynchronous receiver/transmitter (UART) An integrated circuit used within a computer system to handle *serial* communication. Essentially the UART converts the internal *parallel* signals, used on the computer's internal *bus*, to a serial data stream, sent to a serial port. (See also *USART*.)

universal resource identifier Former name for *uniform resource identifier*.

universal resource locator Former name for *uniform resource locator*.

universal synchronous/asynchronous receiver-transmitter (USART) An integrated circuit used in a computer to convert data to a *serial* form for *synchronous* or *asynchronous* transmission. (See also *UART*.)

Unix (Pronounced 'you-nix'.) A multi-user *operating system*, developed at *AT&T* Bell Laboratories in the 1960s and 1970s and now written in the C programming language, with which it has a close relationship. Unix is the basis upon which *open systems* were developed and is also the operating system used by most of the large *hosts* on the *Internet*. Note that the name is sometimes written all in capitals, UNIX, but it is not an acronym (unlike, for example, BASIC). The operating system, unlike MS-DOS, is case-sensitive, which can lead to problems for new users of Internet processes, such as *ftp*, where host file names need to be specified. The other way in which it differs from MS-DOS is that the directory structure uses a forward slash (/) as a separator, rather than the backslash (\) used in DOS. Most of the commonly used Internet programs were developed on the Unix system.

Unix to Unix Communication Protocol see *Unix to Unix Copy Program*

Unix to Unix Copy Program (UUCP) A protocol used for communication between *Unix* systems, now also developed for other *operating systems*, but increasingly replaced by protocols such as *SMTP* and *NNTP*. UUCP is also used to describe the international network of hosts which communicate using the UUCP protocol, and is also known as *Unix to Unix Communication Protocol* (See *UUCPNET*.)

unshielded twisted pair (UTP) A form of cabling used for *local area networks* (LANs), rather than *coaxial cable*. Also used for telephone connection in the USA. (See also *twisted pair*; the lack of a *shield* is possible because of the effects of twisting.)

unstuff To decompress a file that has been *stuffed*.

unzip To decompress a file that has been *zipped*. (See also *PKUNZIP*.)

uplink The link (or sometimes the earth station) which conveys signals to a *geosynchronous satellite*. The opposite of *downlink*.

upload To transfer files over a communications link or a *network*, usually from a smaller system to a larger *host*. This may, for example, be a *bulletin board*. The opposite of *download*, although see comment under download concerning the interchangeability of the two terms.

upper-case letters Capitalized letters, such as the first letter of this sentence. The term is derived from the days of cold type, when the capitals were kept in the top (upper) typecase and the small letters in the bottom (or *lower*) case.

URC See *uniform resource characteristic*.

URI See *uniform resource identifier*.

URL See *uniform resource locator*.

URN See *uniform resource name*.

usart See *universal synchronous/asynchronous receiver-transmitter*.

Usenet (Pronounced 'use-net'; a contraction of 'Users' Network'.) A distributed *bulletin board* system, based on *Unix* systems, which contains a very large number of *newsgroups* on virtually every subject there is. It is not synonymous with the *Internet* but there is a large overlap and most people today probably use the Internet to access Usenet. (See also *Network News Transfer Protocol* (NNTP).)

Usenet news See *Usenet*.

User Datagram Protocol (UDP) An *Internet* protocol similar to *TCP* and layered on top of IP, used for sending *packets* of information between applications. However, UDP is *connectionless* and does not guarantee delivery. Thus, error processing and retransmission must be handled by the application.

user-friendly A term, perhaps obvious in meaning but difficult to define, used to describe systems, software and *user interfaces* which are easy to interact with, needing little or no prior training or documentation for the user.

user interface The way in which a user interacts with a program or system. *Graphical user interfaces* (GUIs) are increasingly becoming the norm, although *command interfaces* are still used. Both of these may also include *menu*-driven interfaces. (See also *HCI*.)

UTP See *unshielded twisted pair*.

UUCP See *Unix to Unix Copy Program*.

UUCPNET The international *store-and-forward* network made up of all the interconnected *Unix* machines in the world, together with some machines running *UUCP*-type software on other *operating systems*. If a machine is on UUCPNET, it can be reached by giving the *bang path*.

uudecode A program (originally written for *Unix*, to be used with *UUCP*, but now widely used on other systems) to convert *ASCII* text produced by *uuencode* back to a *binary* file.

uuencode A program (originally written for *Unix*, to be used with *UUCP*, but now widely used on other systems) to convert *binary* files into a special *ASCII* format that can then be transmitted by *email* (which is only able to handle ASCII characters). The file is converted back using *uudecode*. (See also *SMTP*, *MIME*.)

UUPC *UUCP* for *MS-DOS* and Microsoft *Windows*.

V

V.21 The *ITU-T protocol* for a basic 300 bps *modem*.

V.22 The *ITU-T modem protocol* allowing data rates of 1200 bps.

V.22 bis The *ITU-T modem protocol* allowing data rates of 2400 bps. Bis means the second version, rather than twice the speed.

V.23 The *ITU-T modem protocol* allowing *half-duplex* (unidirectional) data transmission at 1200 bps. This was used for *Prestel*.

V.24 The *ITU-T* standard defining *serial* interchange circuits between *DTE* and *DCE* (and not related to *modems*, except that the frequencies recommended were chosen so as not to interfere with the control tones used in telephone systems). Together with *V.28*, this is equivalent to *RS-232-C*.

V.25 The *ITU-T* standard concerned with *auto-answer modems*.

V.28 The *ITU-T* standard that defines the electrical signal characteristics of *serial* interchange circuits. Together with *V.24*, this is equivalent to *RS-232-C*.

V.32 The *ITU-T modem protocol* allowing data rates of 4800 or 9600 bps.

V.32 bis The *ITU-T modem protocol* allowing data rates of up to 14.4 kbps. Bis means the second version, rather than twice the speed.

V.32 terbo This is not an *ITU-T protocol*, but a proposal from a group of *modem* manufacturers for a 19.2 kbps modem. It has been overtaken by the development of *V.34* modems. Originally called *V.32ter* (i.e., the third version of *V.32*), but renamed (and mis-spelt) because of a misunderstanding.

V.34 The *ITU-T modem protocol* allowing data rates of up to 28.8 kbps and also allowing the sending of *fax*. *K56 flex*, however, can give up to 56 kbps on the *download* side. (See also *V.FC*, *V.fast*.)

V.35 The *ITU-T* standard for data transmission at 48 kbps over *serial* connections. It is the equivalent of *RS-422/RS-449*.

V.42 The *ITU-T* standard *protocol* for *error correction* between *modems*. (See *MNP*.)

V.42 bis The *ITU-T* standard for data *compression* for *modems*. An extension of *V.42*. Compression ratios of up to 4:1 can be obtained. Bis means the second version, rather than twice the speed.

vactor (Virtual actor.) A character in *animations*, controlled by a human actor, who provides the voice and uses a *data glove* to provide movement.

validation Checking data to ensure that it is valid, which may mean that it is complete, accurate or reasonable. Validation may be carried out in a number of ways, including comparison with a mask, calculation of a *checksum* or *parity* checking.

value In *colour measurement* an alternative term for *brightness*.

value added network (van) A network which offers users more than just data transmission. This can include anything from a simple *email* storage service up to a range of commercial services.

van See *value added network*.

VDT See *video display terminal*.

VDU See *visual display unit*.

vector font Another name for an *outline font*.

vector graphics Another name for *object-oriented graphics*. The term arises because graphics are defined in terms of vectors, or geometric formulae, rather than as *bitmaps*.

Vendor Independent Messaging (VIM) An *email* system for *local area networks* (LANs), developed by a group of companies headed by Lotus as a competitor to Microsoft's *MAPI*.

Ventura A *desktop publishing* program, originally developed at *Xerox PARC*, but now owned by Corel. Ventura was the first DTP program to use *styles* or *tags* in any systematic way, preceding in practice the wide implementation, if not the development, of *SGML*.

Verity Topic See *Topic*.

Veronica A keyword search service that allows the user to search all *Gopher* sites for *menu* items (files and directories).

Vertigo A media player technology developed by Adobe, to work with *Bravo* and *Java*.

very high frequency (VHF) The band in the electromagnetic spectrum between about 30–300 MHz, that is used for television transmission, FM radio broadcasting and voice communication.

very small aperture terminal (VSAT) A kind of *groundstation* used for communications with communications satellites.

VESA local bus A *local bus* defined by the Video Electronics Standards Association (VESA — a US industry body) for use originally in PCs. Now rivalled by *PCI*.

VF See *voice frequency*.

V.fast A 28.8 kbps *modem protocol* proposed by some manufacturers before *V.34* had been approved. Some V.34 modems will handle the V.fast protocol. (See also *V.FC*.)

V.FC A 28.8 kbps *modem protocol* developed by modem manufacturing companies *Hayes* and *Rockwell* before *V.34* had been approved. While V.FC is not compatible with V.34, V.34 modems manufactured by Hayes and Rockwell will also support V.FC. (See also *V.fast*.)

vhf See *very high frequency*.

video Moving images, conventionally considered in terms of television images and usually in a recorded form, but now extended to include moving-image files of all types and live images capable of being stored on computer systems and transmitted over networks. Common formats include *QuickTime*, *MPEG* and *avi*. The term is also used to describe an individual video tape or film. (See also *video on demand*, *full-motion video*.)

video accelerator A *video board* designed to speed up what happens on the computer *screen*. Depending on the application, it may either improve motion on the screen or cause the screen to remap faster.

video adapter Another term for a *video board*.

video board (Or video adapter, video card.) The circuit board which controls the *screen* display on a computer. The term predates the use of *video* to describe moving pictures (as seen on a video recorder). Examples in the PC world are VGA (video graphics adapter) and CGA (colour graphics adapter), which provide different levels of functionality. Modern, high-specification machines may use proprietary video boards to provide additional functionality, such as power saving.

video capture board (or card) A circuit board that acts as an *analogue-to-digital converter*, so that analogue signals (usually video or single frames) can be saved to file. This is not the same as a *video board*.

video card Another term for a *video board*.

video CD *Compact discs* that comply with the *White Book* standard. They require a drive which is eXtended Architecture (XA) compatible. (See *compact disc eXtended Architecture*.)

video compression The *compression* of sequences of images. Algorithms for video compression take advantage of there usually being only small changes from one frame to the next, so that the first frame is recorded using similar techniques to those for still images (see JPEG, for example) and then only the differences between frames are recorded. (See *MPEG*, *H.261*.)

videoconferencing A meeting between two or more groups of people in different places, who can both see and hear one another using *video* and *audio* links. *Video compression* is often used but, because of *bandwidth* limitations, images are quite often disjointed and may sometimes break up. (See also *virtual meeting*.)

video disc A 12-inch digital disc which looks rather like a long-playing (vinyl) record and can store full-motion video, audio and data. Video discs have been used both for entertainment (e.g., complete operas) and for interactive learning applications, but are being superseded by various types of *CD*. They are likely to be made completely obsolete by *DVD*.

video display terminal (VDT) A type of *terminal* that consists of a keyboard and a *screen*. (See also *visual display unit*.)

video on demand (VoD) A projected system in which viewers can request a particular video (film), either over *cable* or over *ISDN*, at any time and it will be downloaded for (one-time) viewing.

videophone A telephone by which users can communicate both visually and audially.

video RAM See *video random access memory*.

video random access memory (VRAM) (Or video RAM.) Fast memory chips used for storing the image(s) to be displayed on a computer *screen*.

videotex A communication system that uses television sets or low-cost terminals to provide information from a central database. There are two types: *teletext*, which is one-way and essentially non-interactive, and *viewdata*, which is interactive via a telephone line. While teletext is fairly successful in the UK, *Prestel*, the BT viewdata service, is used only in specialist applications, for example by travel agents. In France, however, the *Minitel* system is widely used. It is probably fair to say that the *World Wide Web* provides most of the functionality of videotex, but with a much better user interface. Note that, confusingly, teletext is a form of videotex, but *teletex* is something different.

viewdata A form of *videotex* used for displaying information interactively on a television or computer screen. Within the UK, *Prestel* is the best-known implementation, while in France, *Minitel* is widely used.

viewer An application that allows a particular format of file to be viewed, e.g., a *JPEG* viewer. It is also another term for a *World Wide Web* browser.

VIM See *Vendor Independent Messaging*.

virtual channel An individual connection within a *virtual path*.

virtual circuit A connection in a network that appears to the user to be an end-to-end circuit or physical connection, while it is actually a dynamically variable network connection.

virtual corporation A corporation or company that has no physical existence, usually being a collaboration between people or companies that are geographically separated and conduct their business using electronic communications, such as *email*, *videoconferencing*, etc.

virtual document A document which is generated in response to a request, for example by a *CGI-script*, but otherwise does not exist.

virtual LAN A *local area network* (LAN) which appears to be a single LAN but is actually connected via a dynamically variable connection.

virtual meeting A service in which users can observe and, if they wish, take part in multiparty *videoconferencing*.

virtual network See *virtual LAN*.

virtual path The location of a file or directory on a particular *host*, as seen by a remote user accessing it via, for example, the *World Wide Web*. Within the *URL*, the virtual path appears as '. . . /~name/. . .', where '~name' is replaced with the real path, which is configured by the local administrator. The effect of this is to restrict access from external users to specific parts of the local network, as well as providing for private *home pages*.

virtual point of presence (VPoP) (Or virtual PoP.) A telephone number which is accessed by an *Internet user*, from which the call is relayed, via a *ROMP*, to a bank of *modems* at the access provider's actual *point of presence*. This service is usually operated as a separate service by someone other than the service provider. In this way users have to pay only for local calls.

virtual PoP See *virtual point of presence*.

virtual reality (VR) A form of computer simulation that uses three-dimensional *graphics* and *video*, together with such devices as the *data glove* and a helmet with independent television screens for each eye, to allow the user to interact with the simulation. Indeed, the user will feel that he or she is actually part of the artificial environment. (See *telepresence*.) Versions of virtual reality have been used in aircraft and other simulators for a long time, but now virtual reality is being used in design applications, as well as in the entertainment industry, while there are obvious educational opportunities. While virtual reality over the *Internet* is possible in theory (see *Virtual Reality Modelling Language* — VRML), in practice it is limited by the *bandwidth* available.

Virtual Reality Markup Language Another expansion of *VRML*. See *Virtual Reality Modelling Language*.

Virtual Reality Modelling Language (VRML) A specification for the design and implementation of a *platform*-independent language for *virtual reality* scene description so that three-dimensional environments (or *cyberspace*) can be implemented over the *World Wide Web*. Also called *Virtual Reality Markup Language*, because of its relationship with *SGML*.

virtual telecommunications access method (VTAM) A data communications access method that is used with IBM's *Systems Network Architecture* (SNA).

virus A program, usually written anonymously with malicious or mischievous intent, which attaches itself to executable program files so that when these are transferred from computer to computer (on disk or via the *Internet*), it spreads (like a biological virus). A virus is usually triggered by a particular stimulus, which may be running the program to which it is attached or just the system date reaching, for example, 'Friday the 13th'. A *worm* is a specific kind of virus. (See also *Internet worm*.)

vision system A computer system for interpreting signals from a video camera. Used in robot systems to increase their functionality.

visitor location register (VLR) A database of information in the *MSC* containing information about visiting (roaming) mobile telephones from other networks.

visual display unit (VDU) The unit of a computer system containing a *screen*; usually part of a *video display terminal*.

visualization Producing a visual or graphical representation of numerical data. Representations can be anything from a simple graph to a complex three-dimensional surface with colours representing different kinds of data. Visualization is used increasingly in *executive information systems* so as to provide managers with an easily and quickly understood interpretation of trends and related data.

VLR See *visitor location register*.

voc The file extension for the *VOiCe* audio format.

VoD See *video on demand*.

Vodaphone One of the principle providers of mobile communications networks in the UK.

VOiCe An *audio* file format developed for the *SoundBlaster* card. The file extension is '.voc'.

voice activation (Or speech recognition, voice recognition, voice input.) Giving commands to a computer by speaking rather than by using the keyboard or *mouse*. Although frequently featured in science fiction, it is now a reality.

voice band See *voice frequency*.

voice frequency (VF) *Analogue* signals that are within the frequency range used to transmit speech (between 200 Hz and 3.5 kHz), i.e., the range of the human voice.

voice input An alternative name for *speech recognition* or *voice activation*.

voice mail An electronic mailbox system in which spoken messages from telephone callers are recorded. Outgoing messages are often generated electronically using *speech synthesis*.

voice modem A *modem* that can handle voice (and usually *fax*) communications as well as data communications. (See also *fax modem*.)

voice output An alternative name for *speech synthesis*.

voice recognition An alternative name for *speech recognition*, *voice activation* or *voice input*.

voxel In analogy with *pixel*, the smallest identifiable part of a three-dimensional space, identified by the cartesian coordinates of either its centre or one of its corners. The term is used in three-dimensional modelling.

VPoP See *virtual point of presence*.

VR See *virtual reality*.

VRAM See *video random access memory*.

VRML See *Virtual Reality Modelling Language*.

VSAT See *very small aperture terminal*.

V series The *ITU-T* series of recommendations for data transmission over telephone. They are usually used in connection with *modems*, for which they define operating speeds (*bandwidths* in *bps*) and other features, such as error correction. The commonly used recommendations are listed as separate entries. Note that *ISDN* is covered by the I series. (See also *H series*, *T series*, *X series*.)

VT 100 A *DEC video terminal* produced in the 1980s. However, the command set which was associated with it has become a *de facto* standard in communications, so that almost every communications program offers VT 100 compatibility or emulation.

VTAM See *virtual telecommunications access method*.

W

W3 An abbreviation (occasionally) used for the *World Wide Web*. Also a World Wide Web *browser* designed to work with the *Unix* editor Emacs.

W3C See *World Wide Web Consortium*.

W3 Consortium See *World Wide Web Consortium*.

WAIS See *wide area information server*.

WAN See *wide area network*.

WAV See *Windows Waveform*.

wavelength division multiplexing A *multiplexing* technique used in *fibre-optic* communications. An optical multiplexer is used to combine light of different wavelengths into a single wavelength for transmission. A demultiplexer is used to separate the signals.

WEB A self-documenting programming language developed by Donald *Knuth* and used in writing T_EX.

Web An alternative way (usually, but not always, with a capital 'W') of describing the *World Wide Web*. A web of information, more generally refers to any *hypertext* system.

Web browser See *browser*.

webcrawler See *spider*.

Webcosm A development of *Microcosm* for *World Wide Web* documents so that users are able to set up *linkbases* which, for each specific text string, contain a link to one or more *URLs*. This can then be overlaid on a *Web page* to add user-controlled links. Different linkbases can be overlaid on the same page to reflect the different interests and levels of experience of the user(s).

Web master The person responsible for maintaining and administering a *Web site*.

Web page A *World Wide Web* page, i.e., an *HTML* document.

Web server A program that serves file and data to *Web browsers*. (See *client-server*.)

Web site The related set of *Web pages* operated by a single organization or individual, usually identified by a single *IP* number (with the first part of the *URL* the same, e.g., 'http://www.pira.co.uk') and accessed through a *Web server*.

welcome page Another term for a *World Wide Web home page*.

well connected A description of a *host* or a computer installation, indicating that it has good *email* and *Usenet* links.

whiteboard See *electronic whiteboard, audiographic teleconferencing*.

White Book The fourth book in Adobe's *PostScript* series, giving the specification for *Type 1 fonts*. The earlier volumes are *Red Book*, *Green Book* and *Blue Book*. Also a *CD-Rom* standard, which in 1994 replaced the Green Book and covers what are described as *video CDs*. (The term is also used to refer to Kernighan and Ritchie's standard book on the C programming language.)

white pages A directory service in which individuals can be found by name (like the telephone directory). The *Internet* supports several such *databases*. (See also *finger*, *Knowbot*, *Netfind*, *whois*, *X.500*.)

whois An *Internet* directory service for looking up names of people on a remote *host*. The service originated at the *DDN NIC*, but other hosts use different approaches, such as *finger*. (See also *white pages*.)

wide area information server (WAIS) A distributed information retrieval system available over the *Internet*, which can retrieve text or *multimedia* documents. Input is in natural language and uses indexed searching so as to provide fast retrieval. It also includes a 'relevance feedback' mechanism so that the results obtained in each search have an effect on subsequent searches. WAIS uses *Z39.50* protocols.

wide area network (WAN) A *network* that covers areas larger than those serviced by a *local area network* (LAN). This usually means that *serial communications* are used, either via telephone lines (usually a *leased line*) or by satellite. An example is *SuperJANET*. (See also *metropolitan area network*.) The *Internet* can either be regarded as **the** WAN or as a network of WANs.

wideband A communications bandwidth higher than *voice band*, but how much higher is undefined. (See also *broadband*.) A wideband amplifier is one which will handle a wide range of frequencies.

Wide SCSI A variant of the *SCSI-2* interface that uses a 16-bit bus (and therefore not compatible with SCSI-1).

widow The last line of a paragraph, printed at the top of a page, although sometimes this is described as an *orphan* and a widow is defined as the first line of a paragraph at the bottom of a page. In either case, good typographic design means avoiding them. As noted under *orphan*, however, this is not really a problem in *electronic publishing*.

WIMP *Window, icons, menus* and *pointing devices* (or sometimes *pull-down menus*). A way of describing the *graphical user interface* (GUI), originally invented at *Xerox PARC* for the *Xerox*

Star and first widely used on the Apple *Macintosh*, but now almost universally used, for example in Microsoft *Windows* and *X windows*. The term was originally developed by *hackers*, essentially as a term of contempt for those who needed an easy, *user-friendly interface*.

window A rectangular area on a computer *screen*, in which a particular application or document, a list of the files on a disk or some other specific collection of information can be viewed. A window usually forms part of a *graphical user interface* (GUI) and is a component of *WIMP*. It is possible to have a number of windows open on the screen at any one time, so that the user can switch between them or *cut* and *paste* between them. The window in which the user is actually working is called the active window, but switching to another window usually just means *clicking* in that window, if it is visible. If the required window is not visible (and it is possible to have windows hidden by others), then there are keyboard shortcuts which allow switching. In addition, not only is it possible for operations started in one window to continue in the background when that window is no longer the active window (see *multitasking*), but windows can also be minimized, that is reduced to an *icon*. *Double-clicking* on the icon maximizes the window (brings it back to its previous size) and makes it active. Common systems using windows are Microsoft *Windows*, the Apple *Macintosh*, *X windows*. (See also *NeWS*.) In the communications context a window is a flow control mechanism controlling the number of *frames* or *packets* that may be transmitted before an acknowledgement is needed from the receiver.

window manager The software which controls *windows*, i.e., their positioning, sizing, etc.

Windows (With a capital 'W' and a final 's'.) The *graphical user interface* (GUI), or *window*, software developed by Microsoft for the PC. It has been developed over a period of about 10 years, through the original version, Windows and 2 and Windows 3 (together with the enhanced Windows for WorkGroups), so that the current version is now *Windows 95*. There is also a multi-user version, *Windows NT*. Windows versions up to Windows 3.1 were 16-bit and ran using the underlying *MS-DOS operating system*, although the later versions effectively took over the operation of the computer, including the peripherals, such as printers. Windows 95 and Windows NT are 32-bit operating systems in their own right, although DOS applications can still be run in a *window*. Note that as Windows has developed, so has the minimum specification for the hardware required, so that current versions will not run on older machines. *TrueType* was introduced as part of Windows 3.0.

Windows 95 The successor to Microsoft *Windows* 3.1. A 32-bit *graphical user interface* (GUI) and an *operating system* in its own right. While it requires a fairly high minimum hardware specification, because it is 32-bit it provides increased functionality. Windows 95 has now been enhanced to Windows 97.

Windows 97 An updated version of *Windows 95*.

Windows BitMap A *bitmap graphics* format for Microsoft *Windows* applications. Any Windows application that can handle bitmaps can read such a file. The file extension is '.bmp'.

Windows Metafile Format An *object-oriented graphics* format for Microsoft *Windows* applications. Any Windows application that can handle object-oriented graphics can read such a file. The file extension is '.wmf'.

Windows NT ('NT' stands for 'New Technology'.) A 32-bit *operating system* developed by Microsoft, after its split with IBM, on the basis of previous development work on *OS/2*. NT is a complete multi-user, *multi-tasking operating system*, which was aimed at the corporate network market and seen as a competitor to *Unix*. The *user interface* was very similar to that of Windows 3.1, although the latest version is closely related to *Windows 95*. It is not limited to running on the *Intel* chip range and some large installations have used the DEC alpha chip.

Windows sockets (Winsock) A *socket* system developed for *Windows* systems, providing both a standard *API* and a standard *ABI*.

Windows Waveform (WAV) A sound format developed by *Microsoft* and used principally in Microsoft *Windows*. The file extension is '.wav'.

Winsock See *Windows sockets*.

WinZip An implementation of *PKZIP* for Microsoft *Windows*. (See also *zip*.)

Wired A US magazine concerned with the 'digital revolution' (see *Negroponte*). There is also, not surprisingly, a *World Wide Web* version (http://www.wired.com). A UK edition was started but was not a commercial success.

wireless Usually used to describe *networks* that are connected, not by wires, cables or optical fibres, but by radio communication (in much the same way as radio broadcasting was once commonly described as the 'wireless').

wmf See *Windows Metafile Format*.

word-processor An editing and formatting program with which documents, including graphics, can be input, edited, formatted and printed. (Contrast with *text editor*.) Most word-processors now run as *graphical user interface* (GUI) applications and the distinction between high-end word-processors and low-end *page make-up* programs is very hazy. The two most common word-processors are Microsoft Word and WordPerfect.

word wrap The facility, which exists in *word-processors* (and a few *text editors*), in which at the end of a line a word is automatically taken to the next line, rather than split arbitrarily at the specified line length. If *hyphenation* is specified, the word will be broken at an appropriate (or sometimes inappropriate) hyphen, rather than being transferred as a whole. Word wrap is also used in *electronic publishing* applications, in *browsers*, both for *HTML* (e.g., *Netscape Navigator*, *Internet Explorer* or *Mosaic* for the *World Wide Web*) and for *SGML* (e.g., *Dynatext* and *Panorama*), so that when the type size or the *window* size is changed, the text wraps to fit the window. Unlike page-based applications, such as *Acrobat*, this means that the text is always visible without horizontal scrolling being necessary.

workflow The control of documents moving around an organization. (See also *Lotus Notes*, *computer supported cooperative work*.)

workgroup computing Groups of people working together over a network to coordinate and organize their activities. (See *groupware*.)

workstation A terminal, usually with its own processing power, often running *X windows* and connected to a *Unix* system. The term is also used more generally to mean any *intelligent* terminal connected to a network. More popularly, the term is used to mean a special desk on which a computer is used.

World Wide Web (WWW, W3) A *hypertext*-based system for accessing information over the *Internet*. WWW was originally developed at *CERN* by a team led by Tim *Berners-Lee*, in order to provide easy access to high-energy physics information. Files are coded using *HTML* and users view the information with a browser, such as *Netscape Navigator* or *Internet Explorer*. First publicly released in late 1991, since when it has become one of the most important methods of information transfer in the world, with a growth rate that has turned the Internet from a tool used by academics and researchers to a medium of popular communication. (See also *Docuverse*, *URL*, *HTTP*.)

World Wide Web Consortium (W3 Consortium, W3C) An organization based at the Massachusetts Institute of Technology (MIT) originally created to develop common standards for the evolution of the *World Wide Web*. The director of the Consortium is Tim *Berners-Lee* and there are more than 120 organizations involved. The consortium, jointly with *INRIA*, reached an agreement in March 1996 with leading vendors to develop interoperability standards for *HTML* features such as *multimedia* objects, style sheets, forms, scripting, tables, high-quality printing, and improved access for the visually impaired.

World Wide Web Worm (WWWW) An automatic indexing tool for the *World Wide Web*.

WORM See *Write Once Read Many times*.

worm A piece of programming code that propagates itself over a network, replicating itself as it goes. It is a kind of computer *virus*. The term is generally used in a negative fashion, since the notorious *Internet worm* in 1988, which incidentally was not intended maliciously, being a bug in some software that was intended to investigate the size of the *Internet*. However, this is not always the case. (See also *World Wide Web Worm*.)

wormhole routing A form of message passing in which parts of the message are transmitted independently, unlike *store-and-forward* routing, where the whole message must be received by a node before the message can be forwarded to the next node. It reduces the *latency* and the storage requirements at each node.

wrap See *word wrap*.

Write Once Read Many times (WORM) An *optical disc*, similar to *CD-Rom*. WORM discs are generally used for archiving and in *document image processing* systems. (See also *COLD*.)

WWW See *World Wide Web*.

WWWW See *World Wide Web Worm*.

WYSIWYG Acronym for 'What You See Is What You Get' and pronounced 'Whizzy Wig'. Originally used to describe *page make-up* in early *desktop publishing systems*, when what appeared on the screen was a direct representation of what would be printed. In time, it was realized that the representation was not completely faithful, so that other acronyms, such as WYSIMOLWYG (What You See Is More or Less What You Get) and WYSIAWYG (What You See Is Almost What You Get) have been suggested. However, WYSIWYG is the only one which has really become part of the language and 'quasi-WYSIWYG' is probably an easier way of describing the real situation than the more obscure acronyms.

X

X.3 The *ITU-T* standard that specifies the basic functions and user-selectable capabilities of a *packet assembler/disassembler* (PAD). Together with *X.28* and *X.29*, X.3 specifies the functions, interfaces and control procedures for a PAD that give start-stop-mode terminals access to a *packet-switched* public data network.

X.25 The *ITU-T* recommendation that specifies the interface between *data terminal equipment* (DTE) and *data communications equipment* (DCE) in a *packet-switched* network. X.25 defines the standard *physical layer*, *datalink layer* and *network layers*, and is used in packet-switching networks all over the world.

X.28 The *ITU-T* standard specifying how to control a *PAD* from *DTE* on a public network. (See also *X.3*.)

X.29 The *ITU-T* standard, specifying procedures for the exchange of control information and user data between remote *packet-mode DTE* and a *PAD*. (See also *X.3*.)

X.75 The *ITU-T* standard that specifies the *protocols* for communication between two *packet-switched* data networks in different countries.

X.400 series The *ITU-T* standard for electronic mail (*email*) systems. Such services have been implemented by *PTTs* in a number of countries and are normally connected to the *Internet*. X.400 addresses are rather different from *IP* addresses and tend to be very long. One problem with X.400 for large organizations is that the directory is normally public, which may not always be desirable.

X.500 The set of *ITU-T* standards that are concerned with electronic directory services such as *Knowbot*, *white pages*, and *whois*.

XA See *CD-Rom XA*.

Xanadu The first proposal, by Ted *Nelson*, for a *hypertext* system. It was in this context that the term 'hypertext' was proposed. Although Nelson continues to work on this project and the *Docuverse*, it is arguable that the *World Wide Web* has brought it about already.

X bitmap The format for *bitmaps* in the *X window* system. This is one of only two formats (the other is *GIF*) in which inline images can appear in an *HTML* document. The file extension is '.xbm'.

xbm See *X bitmap*.

X client An application process in an *X window* system, which calls upon an *X server* to gain access to a window.

Xeikon One of the leading *digital presses*.

Xerox Palo Alto Research Center (Xerox PARC) Where many of the initial developments were made that led to products which have had a significant effect on computer-assisted and *electronic publishing*. These include: the *Xerox Star*, which had the first icon-based *graphical user interface* (GUI), together with the *mouse*; *Interpress*, a forerunner of *PostScript*; Xerox *Ventura*, one of the first *desktop publishing* programs; the *laserprinter*. In addition, the *local area network* (LAN) and the *object-oriented programming language*, Smalltalk, were pioneered at Xerox PARC. It was unfortunate that in almost every case, Xerox failed to exploit these developments commercially and this was done by other companies, often formed by ex-members of the PARC staff.

Xerox PARC See *Xerox Palo Alto Research Center*.

Xerox Star The computer which had the first *graphical user interface* (GUI), developed at *Xerox PARC* but never really exploited. Most of the know-how which went into the Star was exploited in the Apple *Macintosh*.

x-height The height of the lowercase letter 'x' in a particular *typeface* or *font*; 'x' is used because it the only letter that effectively has a clearly defined flat top. The x-height determines the apparent size of the font, while the relationship between the x-height and the *cap height* (the height of the capital letters) is a characteristic of a typeface and can affect its readability. Figure 6 shows several different typefaces, which appear to be different, although they are all the same type size. Thus a typographic designer needs to take the differences into account when choosing a typeface. This applies in *electronic publishing* applications just as much as in conventional print on paper.

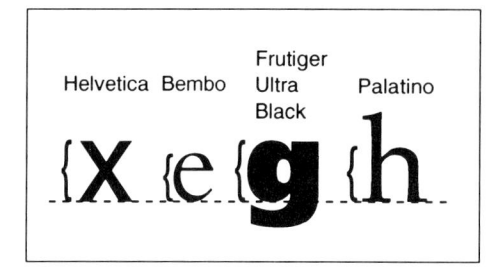

Helvetica Bembo | Frutiger Ultra Black | Palatino

{X {e {**g** {h

Figure 6 x-height

Examples of type in different types faces, showing the variations in x-height

XML See *eXtensible Markup Language*.

Xmodem An *asynchronous file-transfer* system *protocol* used over *modems*, which works by transferring blocks of data and then waiting for acknowledgement. This makes the transfer slow but accurate. *Ymodem* and *Zmodem* are enhanced versions of Xmodem which work at higher transmission rates. Another widely used *File Transfer Protocol* is *Kermit*. Over the *Internet*, *ftp* is the most commonly used protocol.

Xmodem-1K A version of *Xmodem* that uses 1 kbyte *packets*.

x-on/x-off The flow control procedure generally used in communications. An X-on character starts data flow and an X-off character stops it. Note that 'X-on' is equivalent to keying 'control-q' while 'X-off' is equivalent to 'control-s'.

X protocol A standard *protocol* used by *clients* (applications) and *servers* in the *X window* system for exchanging requests for window operations.

XRN A newsreader program running under *X windows*. (See *Usenet news*.)

X series The series of *ITU-T* recommendations governing data transmission over public data networks. The most widely applied are listed individually. Note that this series does not include the *X.400* or *X.500* series.

X server Software which produces an *X window* display. Can run on an *X terminal*, a *Macintosh* or a PC running *Windows*.

X terminal An *intelligent* terminal or *workstation* which operates as an *X server* on a *network*, usually *Ethernet*.

X windows A windowing system based on *TCP/IP* networking and originally developed at MIT, widely used on *Unix* systems. May run on a dedicated *X terminal* or some other system, e.g., a *Macintosh* or a PC under *Windows*, running an *X server*. The process uses a *client-server X protocol*. The *X client*, an application program, issues a request to the X-server, which generates the *bitmapped* display. *Motif*, now the standard *graphical user interface* (GUI) for *Unix* systems, is based on X windows. Note that in this case it is the screen/keyboard which is acting as the server (of the display), while the X clients run on the main file server system. This can lead to some confusion.

X window BitMap graphic A *bitmap graphic file format* for *X windows*. The file extension is '.xbm'.

XXX See *Triple-X*.

Y

Yahoo A hierarchical index of the *World Wide Web*. Allows searches in specific subject areas. Other widely used search utilities are *AltaVista* and *Lycos*, but there are a large number of search engines available.

Yellow Book A *CD-Rom* format, compliant with *ISO 9660*. Discs in this format can be played on most drives and are suitable for most *multimedia applications* for PCs. The term 'Yellow Book' is also used to describe a printed version (1991) of the 'Jargon File', a glossary/dictionary of accumulated *hacker* terminology, which is available on the *World Wide Web*. The on-line file is thus much more up to date than the book.

yellow cable The cabling defined in the original *thick Ethernet* specification.

Ymodem An *asynchronous file transfer protocol*, which is an enhancement of *Xmodem*. It provides a greater block size and allows batches of files to be transferred, while Xmodem allows only transfer of single files. (See *communications*.) *Ymodem-g* is a non-stop version, i.e., not batch, which is much faster but if there is an error, the transfer will abort. (See also *Zmodem*.)

Ymodem-g See *Ymodem*, *Zmodem*.

Y-NET An experimental *X.400* service for European research.

Ytalk A multi-user *Chat* program, running under *X windows*, that supports multiple connections.

Z

Z39.50 An *ANSI* standard for information retrieval. It is a *network protocol*, working on a *client-server* basis, giving a set of rules governing the formats and also providing a query syntax. It is intended to be *user-friendly*, so that the user does not need to be aware of the communication between the computers, in much the same way as with tools such as *WAIS*, but it has the advantage that it is session-oriented so that criteria and the results of previous searches can be reused. There is now, however, a *gateway* to the *World Wide Web*. Z39.50 is mainly used by librarians and information scientists.

Zapf Dingbats A typeface designed by Hermann Zapf, which includes common *dingbats*. It is usually provided as one of the standard fonts with a *PostScript laserprinter*.

ZDNet (Formerly called *Ziffnet*.) An electronic information service provided by Ziff-Davis, the publisher of computer magazines, giving access to electronic versions of these magazines, as well as much other information. There is a complementary *CompuServe* version, which also provides a software archive.

Ziffnet (Formerly the name of *ZDNet*.) An information service associated with the *Wall Street Journal*.

zip A file format widely used for data *compression*, for example in transferring programs and other large files on floppy disk or over the *Internet*. The files used to compress and decompress are *PKZIP* and *PKUNZIP*. There is also now a *Windows* version, WinZip. Note that PKZIP is *shareware* and not *public domain* software, although the supplier, PKWare, provides run-time licences for PKUNZIP.

Zmac The former name of the *World Wide Web* site of the Ziff-Davis *Macintosh* magazines. Now part of *ZDNet*.

Zmodem A *File Transfer Protocol* that is a development of *Xmodem* and *Ymodem*, but which includes error checking and crash recovery, so that if a transfer is interrupted, it can be continued later, rather than completely repeated. The transfer rate is similar to that of *Ymodem-g* as it runs continuously, rather than in batch mode.

zoom In analogy with a photographic lens, to make what appears in a screen *window* (in a *graphical user interface*) larger (zoom in) so that a smaller area is seen, or smaller (zoom out), so that a larger area is seen. Depending on the *application*, either the magnification may be selected from a menu or, for zooming in, the *cursor* changes (usually to a magnifying glass) and the area to be zoomed in on is *marquee* selected. If zooming in is performed by the latter method, zooming out is usually achieved by *clicking* an *icon* which has the effect of undoing the last zoom in (marquee selection itself cannot be used because the desired area of viewing is larger than what can currently be seen on the screen).